MW00785930

African Christianity

African Christianity

An African Story

Edited by
Ogbu U. Kalu

Africa World Press, Inc.

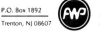

P.O. Box 1892
Trenton, NJ 08607

P.O. Box 48
Asmara, ERITREA

Africa World Press, Inc.

P.O. Box 1892
Trenton, NJ 08607

P.O. Box 48
Asmara, ERITREA

First Printing 2007

Book design: Saverance Publishing Services
Cover design: Ashraful Haque
Cover photo: St. George Church in Lalibela. There are eleven churches in Lalibela cut from single stone formations.

Library of Congress Cataloging-in-Publication Data

African Christianity : an African story / edited by Ogbu U. Kalu. -- 1st Africa World Press ed.

p. cm.
Includes bibliographical references and index.
ISBN 1-59221-580-7 (hardcover) -- ISBN 1-59221-581-5 (pbk.)
1. Christianity--Africa. 2. Africa--Church history. I. Kalu, Ogbu.

BR1360.A525 2007
276--dc22

2007014939

For Andrew F. Walls and Brian Stanley

Many have bemoaned the collapse of Christian scholarship in Africa, you both have done something about it.

Table of Contents

Preface xi

PART ONE: THE INSERTION OF THE GOSPEL

Chapter One
Introduction: The Shape and Flow of African Church Historiography 3
Ogbu U. Kalu

Chapter Two
African Christianity: an Overview 23
Ogbu U. Kalu

Chapter Three
Early Christianity in North Africa 41
Kenneth Sawyer & Youhana Youssef

Chapter Four
Christianity in Sudan and Ethiopia 67
William B. Anderson & Ogbu U. Kalu

Chapter Five
Islamic Challenges in African Christianity 103
Akintunde E. Akinade

Chapter Six
African Chaplains in Seventeenth Century West Africa 123
David N.A. Kpobi

Chapter Seven
Iberians and African Clergy in Southern Africa 151
Paul H. Gundani

PART TWO: MISSIONARY PRESENCE AND AFRICAN AGENCY

Chapter Eight
Back to Africa: White Abolitionists and Black Missionaries 167
Jehu Hanciles

Chapter Nine
The Missionary Factor in African Christianity, 1884-1914 191
Chukwudi A. Njoku

Chapter Ten
Ethiopianism in African Christianity 227
Ogbu U. Kalu

Chapter Eleven
Bakuzufu: Revival Movements and Indigenous Appropriation in African Christianity 245
Graham Duncan & Ogbu U. Kalu

Chapter Twelve
Zionists, Aladura and Roho: African Instituted Churches 271
Afe Adogame & Lazio Jafta

Part Three: New Dimensions of African Christian Initiatives

Chapter Thirteen
African Christianity: From the World Wars to Decolonization 291
Ogbu U. Kalu

Chapter Fourteen
Mainline Churches in the Public Space, 1975-2000 315
J.W. Hofmeyr

Chapter Fifteen
"Born of Water and the Spirit": Pentecostal/Charismatic Christianity in Africa 339
J. Kwabena Asamoah-Gyadu

Chapter Sixteen
Gender and Power in African Christianity: African Instituted Churches and Pentecostal Churches 359
Philomena Njeri Mwaura

Chapter Seventeen
A New Way of Facilitating Leadership: Lessons from African Women Theologians 389
Nyambura J. Njoroge

Chapter Eighteen
Half a Century of African Christian Theologies: Elements of the Emerging Agenda for the Twenty-First Century 409
Tinyiko Sam Maluleke

Chapter Nineteen
African Christian Communities in Diaspora 431
Afe Adogame

Chapter Twenty
Christianity and the African Cultural Heritage 451
J.N.K. Mugambi

Select Reading List 475

Index 501

Preface

In the last five years of the twentieth century, five books have appeared on Christianity in Africa written by Adrian Hastings, 1994, John Baur, 1994, Elizabeth Isichei, 1995, Mark Shaw, 1996, and Bengt Sundkler in co-operation with Christopher Steed, 2000. Admittedly, some were long-standing projects that took either a decade or more to write but it became glaring towards the end of the millennium that a general text on African Christianity was required. Each text has met with various degrees of success with students. Adrian Hastings's book starts from 1950 because he had covered the period from 1950-1975 in a previous monograph that served as a sequel to the Jos (Nigeria) Conference on *Christianity in Post-Independence Africa*. Adrian's work is very readable and his Africanist periodization is intriguing. Isichei's book is useful for postgraduate students but appears to throw too many facts at unprepared undergraduate students especially in the Western world. Sundkler's is laced with so many "small stories" that its size and cost intimidate. There is no doubt about its usefulness as a resource and reservoir of information. Shaw's is rather marred by the extreme application of the Kingdom of God motif but the maps are very helpful.

The effort in this book is ideologically-driven: it seeks to argue that an identifiable African Christianity exists. It also seeks to build up a group of African church historians who will tell the story as an African story by intentionally privileging the patterns of African agency without neglecting the roles of various missionary bodies. We believe that if we do not tell our story, other people will tell us our story. The effort is to identify the major themes or story lines in African Christianity and comment on them in such a manner as to elicit new research approaches before a fuller multi-volume text could emerge. To that extent, this work is a signal of a process. When a solid band of African church historians is mobilized, the goal is to tell a longer story of how the rain of the gospel met African communities living in diverse regions of a large continent. Perhaps this is a task for another generation that will prayerfully have more success than my generation in co-operating to tell our story. Since we are conscious of the fact that we are telling our story to non-African audiences, the book starts with an overview that many students could use to map the paths bristling with details. We also invite the readers to think about the meaning of church history and how to do church history in an African context. It is only by reflecting on the larger issues that church history could be a mode of accountability among the people of God.

This work owes its inspiration to the distant past when Enrique Dussel tried to persuade Africans to join in writing the history of the *Church in the Third World.* In 1977, he spoke so eloquently in Accra. As if to demonstrate leadership by example, he mobilized Latin American church historiography through an association called CEHILA. African efforts have failed in spite of the 1986 Nairobi seminar made possible by Dr. Masamba ma Mpolo (from DRCongo and serving the World Council of Churches, Geneva) and Dr N. Abeng (from Cameroon), who was serving the Roman Catholic organization, Missio at Aachen, Germany. The endeavor has taken so long that younger church historians have emerged. The task will be passed on to them with greater hope of success. The doyen, Andrew F. Walls, has encouraged this endeavor through his writings, teaching, mentoring, deep insights, and friendship. He has reared more African scholars than any one single person and interpreted Africa to the West with a strong influential voice. Every year, he teaches at Akroffi-Christaller Center in the belief that if Africans built academic ashrams, they would overcome the desolation caused by the collapse of economies, legitimacy crises, and the decimation of educational infrastructure and resources. Similarly, Lamin Sanneh's muscular scholarship has shaped the contours of interpretation and influenced the study of Christianity and Islam in Africa. His turns of phrase and inimitable prose allure and are often quoted. Similarly, Kwame Bediako's scholarship has been combined with more "hands-on", intentional, and dedicated nurturing of African Christian leadership through the ATF program and conferences. He is deeply involved with the grain of African church life and reflection. He has been an inspiring churchman and scholar in this generation. Brian Stanley used the opportunity generated by the Currents in World Christianity program (1998-2001) to promote African Christian scholarship. His own scholarship covers Africa from a wider vista. But the task of deliberately building a band of scholars to work together and redeem a scorched environment is a different kind of academic engagement. Many young African scholars openly and unabashedly acknowledge their indebtedness to Brian Stanley. He is always sympathetic and helpful. I am only a mouthpiece of what I have seen and heard!

Two individuals have made this project possible by working behind the scene: Linda Hofmeyr hosted the many meetings of the core group with grace and generosity and deserves our gratitude. Petrus Maritz brought the zeal he employed in organizing the Pretoria Conference of Currents in World Christianity to the job of proof-texting and production of this book within the Perspective series in the University of Pretoria. More amazing is that he combined it with writing his own doctoral dissertation on Professor Marais,an intriguing ecumenist and critic of a church that deployed theology to underpin apartheid. Professor Marais was a maligned scholar, a churchman and a very humble, genial person whom God granted the grace to live beyond the apartheid system, and to receive the apology from his detractors. There is a rich story still waiting to be told in the future about the lives of black and white Africans who have served Christ with all they have. This book opens the possibility that African scholars will co-operate to tell the story of where the rain of the gospel met our ancestors, its thick showers on us, and the torrents that will meet our future generations as the gospel deluges Africa.

Ogbu U. Kalu

Part One

THE INSERTION OF THE GOSPEL

Chapter One

Introduction: The Shape and Flow of African Church Historiography

Ogbu U. Kalu

I. CHRISTIAN ROOTS IN AFRICAN PRIMAL RELIGION

Darkness has hit Africa at noon. As Henri Marou would say, the historian is a "missionary dispatched to the past to strike a hyphen between the past and the present." The Igbo people have a proverb that says that a man who does not know where the rain met him is unlikely to know where he is going. There is no brand of African scholarship that can be done in our times without a concern to explore the dilemma and seek a solution for our continent's condition. This is what Eduardo Hooanert calls, "re-animating the memory of Christian communities so that it defines their social consciousness."[1] History could be a certain type of memory that evokes liberative power; not mere knowledge of the past but one that is commitment. It should lead people to the truth of their condition in a scientific manner, not violated by cant or propaganda.

Therefore, in every enterprise, the historian must ask afresh, why do I write, for whom and for what purpose? Commentators have characterized Africa as a laboratory in which new dimensions of Christianity are being explored amidst life-threatening conditions and among ancient peoples and cultures. The soil has the same texture as Jesus walked on; so, his message pulsates with vivid reality in technicolor. The responses of Africans must have serious import for World Christianity. Significant in this regard are the shifts in contemporary church historiography designed to interpret the events more clearly and to enable the church in Africa to critique her faithfulness in witness. Some say that Christianity in Africa is like a river that is broad but shallow. Internal criticism (*metanoia*) is of the essence of the Christian race because sanctification is a process but it must be acknowledged that some of the criticisms are rooted in an old racist bias that equally calls for repentance. This chapter shall focus on only four key concerns in modern African church historiography. First, the continuity of African primal religion in African Christianity; second, a strong theological and Christocentric understanding of the church and its story; third, a shift from missionary and nationalist genre to ecumenical historiography; and fourth, the emergence of a theology of political engagement which postures the life and ministry of the church as mission-to-culture or "baptizing the nations". The memory of the people of God could become a tool for engaging the public space.

It is important to start African church history from African primal religion and culture because both the church and her enemies, namely, the politicians and other religious forms derive their character, and source their idiom from the interior of African worldview. For instance, the dominant political culture is often a deliberate attempt to weave the modern state into traditional ethics of power; however, often done in a manner to vitiate the salient aspects of the traditional. The dominant theory of obligation is rooted in traditional values. This is why rulers in Africa act as chiefs and wield symbols such as the fly whisk, the leopard skin and the "big man's" walking stick. The effort is a form of villagization, the transfer of patriarchal ethics from the village to the town and to the modern state, a deliberate manipulation of public space in the quest for legitimacy. African rulers deliberately create two publics so as to escape the accountability that the modern state demands. Other religious forms, in their symbols, invented histories, goals and demands on the state, radicate themselves in primal culture.

This means that we should explore how African Christianity is essentially rooted in primal religion whose cults are manipulated to sustain the contest for the dwindling resources of the modern states. It is rooted within the strand that explores the endurance of primal religion in the forms of Christian allegiance. Some brands of African Christianity have shown a creative response to the deep-level challenges of our environment by applying the spiritual resources of biblical theology that the missionaries muted. Working within African maps of the universe, they have shown how the biblical promises could serve as tools of hope. They have exploited the elasticity in African worldview, its capacity to make room, within its inherited body of traditions for new realities, which though seemingly from outside, come in to fulfill aspirations within the tradition. Kwame Bediako says that this is what Paul did with Jewish tradition in the letter to the Hebrews, providing a conceptual scheme for interpreting African Christianity.[2]

Bediako has stepped on a creeping plant that is entangled with much of African church historiography, namely, the specific identity, or the "Africanness" of our Christianity within the African worldview. During the Edinburgh-Yale seminar in 1992, Andrew Walls, a doyen of African Church History, observed that in the history of religions:[3]

> African Christianity appears in two capacities: first, as a new period in the history of African religion, continuing the story begun in the primal or traditional religions; and the second, as a new period in the history of Christianity, in which the tradition is being expressed

> in intellectual, social and religious milieus which it has not previously entered.

He compares this to the relationship between early Christianity and the religion of old Israel. Thus, in doing modern church history, the concerns, agenda, and the responses of people to the gospel can best be interpreted through the reordering of worldview and the introduction of new symbols and sources.[4]

Professor Walls could easily have pulled together a dozen or varieties of the argument from existing literature even though the proponents were pursuing other interests. For instance, right from the beginning of the nineteenth century missionary enterprise, a certain consistent and encrusted paradigm in African historiography emerged accusing missionaries of failing to weave their message into the primal worldview. It portrayed missionaries as "imperialists at prayer". E.A. Ayandele castigates them as "pathfinders for colonial boots" and A.E. Afigbo, in *Ropes of Sand,* intones that "it was not one of the aims of the colonialists to preserve the cultural identity of subject peoples. In fact, the opposite was the case."[5] John Ngugi in his novel, *The River Between*, paints Christianity as a dysfunctional, iconoclastic force that disrupted communities and robbed people of their self-identity. From here, it was a short step to ridicule indigenous collaborators. Joyce Cary in *Mister Johnson* calls them "Black Englishmen", and the film version is indeed a painful career of a schizophrenic buffoon who was used and dropped by those whose magic circle he sought in an illusionary quest. Wole Soyinka, the Nobel laureate, caricatures them as interpreters who watched white men from the periphery and endeavored to mimic what they saw in their home communities. The chorus of the historians and novelists hark to a strain heard among the "Ethiopian" nationalists of the nineteenth century who felt that missionary Christianity was struggling too vigorously to install a pre-packaged hardware of Enlightenment agenda that would destroy the indigenous African religion and culture.

It consisted of a dualistic mind-set, scientific racism and the verdicts of armchair theorists who disengaged the dreamy origins of primitive religion from Christianity. It was decorated with ethnocentrism and hubris. The nationalists saw their task as calling for an indigenized alternative. They had heard the priests of many shrines announcing godly whispers of new covenants and warning that people should eat with prospective visitors with long spoons. Indigenization was a call for continuity in change, rooting Christianity in the soil of Africa. Kofi Awoonor, in his poem, *Easter Dawn* sang of the discomfiture which the guardians of the ancestral calabash feared:[6]

> The gods are crying, my father's gods are crying for a burial ... for a final ritual ... but they that should build the fallen shrines have joined the dawn marchers singing their way towards Gethsemane ... the gods cried, shedding clayey tears on calico, the drink offering had dried up in the harmattan and the fetish priest is dressing up for the Easter Service.

Of course, the missionary enterprise was not that successful but white power and cultural iconoclasm constituted an enduring theme in church historiography. Cross-cultural mission as civilization project created a bad press for the gospel and may have emasculated the full impact. This fact stands at the backdrop of African charismatic agency and response to missionary Christianity.

A variation of the diatribe on the collusion between the commissar, trader and missionary focused on the jaundiced perception of African traditional religion. E.B. Idowu[7] catalogued the inappropriate terms used in western literatures of various genres to the extent that a reviewer accused him of quarrelling with dead men. But Idowu was a child of the cultural renaissance that came at the heels of political nationalism and raised the question about the role of primal religion and culture in Christian living. Perhaps, this is because culture stands at the gates, market squares and gable ends of each community. As a new religion comes, the tensile strength of the culture of the people may determine the prospects. The relationship between religion and ecology is extensive and ecology could be geographical, human and cultural. Idowu was concerned that the purveyors of change paid scant and unstudied attention to primal spirituality, declaring it to be mumbo-jumbo. This attitude made Christianity a foreign religion or as D.I. Nwoga dubbed it, *Supreme God as a Stranger*.[8]

Some apologists rose in defense to argue that Africans had the knowledge of God before the missionaries came. They utilized the Greek concept, *spermatikos logos* precisely because they were educated in missionary schools. Okot p'bitek cried foul against the hellenization African primal religion. But John Mbiti ignored the red flag and prospected with the concept of *praeparatio evangelica*, arguing that:[9]

> We can add nothing to the Gospel, for this is an eternal gift of God; but Christianity is always a beggar seeking food and drink, cover and shelter from the cultures it encounters in its never-ending journeys and wanderings.

The incarnational nature of the gospel provided African theologians with much food for thought through many years because culture loomed large in the enterprise. Soon, Roman Catholic theologians shifted the terminology to inculturation arguing that the discussion should go beyond the initial insertion of the gospel into cultures and deal with making the gospel "a principle that animates, directs and unifies the culture; transforming it and remaking it so as to bring about a new creation."[10] Even in biblical studies, scholars such as Kwesi Dickson, the out-going moderator of the Methodist Church in Ghana, sought to establish the kindred spirit between the Old Testament world and the African.[11] The elements of continuity not only served to restore the bashed image of the African but pointed to evangelical models. The most thorough and extant work is Kwame Bediako's *Theology and Identity: The impact of Culture upon Christian Thought in the Second Century and Modern Africa*. He essentially urges a shift from a paradigm that conceives Christianity and African primal religion as the correlation of two entities thought to be independent.

It would appear so in the Christianity written by intellectuals. But living faith, in real-life situations and in field experience, operates differently. In the very process of indigenous assimilation, the decoders weave a new pattern following the lines of congruence, making their religious experience an organic, unified one. This is reciprocity that enables us to study the fate of the gospel in a community from the perspective of the receiver—the decoders of the message. Attention should therefore, turn of from the mode of *transmission* towards the mode of *assimilation* or *appropriation*. However, the fact that many Africans bore the brunt of evangelization meant that, quite often, the pursuit of elements of continuity was an ongoing task. In *Christianity in Africa*, Bediako sets out to show the prospects and adequacy of the faith for the realities of African life: to root it by claiming for it a past in the spiritual harvest of African pre-Christian religious heritage.[12]

Lamin Sanneh's seminal contribution explores the irony that the missionaries were forced by the logic or exigencies of the mission field to realize the debilitating effect of iconoclasm and turn to translating the message. Translation of de-stigmatized indigenous languages and cultures as proper vehicles for conveying the gospel, opened the innards of cultures, preserved them from extinction and became an instrument of uplifting many people.[13] Whenever the name of God was rendered in an indigenous tongue, the Almighty was brought into the centre of the people's lives and woven into their pre-Christian past. Translation was a potent evangelical tool. Thus, the pursuit of the strands of continuity has always been a response to the exigencies of the field, of power encounter, a realization that certain kinds of iconoclasm can be self-defeating even as an evangelical tool. It was more than these, because, translation introduced new aspects to African Christianity by buttressing certain elements in African religious experience which the Enlightenment had forced missionaries to abandon. For instance, Africans saw that there is biblical support for revelatory phenomena such as dreams and visions and prophetic utterances. They discovered the possibilities of new modes of church polity; the ethics in Leviticus underpinned their precarious vision of the universe. Christianity may have introduced the figure of Jesus obtrusively but the enlargement of the God component of their cosmology came to their aid. Translation raised the issue of discontinuity by providing exits that will be pursued later.

These factors became clearer in the implosion of the spirituality of African indigenous churches: their re-constructive, pneumatic challenge to mainline churches tapped the vibrancy of primal African spirituality, substituted black for white power in church matters and incorporated ingredients of African culture in polity, liturgy, ethics and doctrine. The literature has burgeoned to the point of romanticization in spite of the fact that some of these are not Christian. As Andrew Walls would say:[14]

> The effectiveness of Christian faith, or of any particular manifestation of it, is accordingly open to the test whether it gives access to power and prosperity for protection against natural or spiritual

enemies, purposes to which much traditional practice was directed, and satisfactorily enforces familial and social unity.

It was the career of Archbishop Emannuel Milingo (Lusaka, Zambia) that brought this pursuit of spiritual continuity into the ambits of the Roman Catholic Church in Africa. It touched off a furor characterized by the writings of Aylward Shorter. Happily, scholars such as Adrian Hastings and M.L. Daneel rose to interpret Milingo with more nuance.[15] The pursuit of continuity, not only raised the discussion on exorcism or deliverance but introduced another conceptual scheme, namely, the covenantal idea in African church history and theology. This postures the relationships between Africans and their gods as binding covenants; rituals and festivals become re-energizing sacred moments. This explains why the spirits that guard the gates of communities have remained unconquered, creating a dilemma and calling for a revisit to inculturation theology.[16]

Covenants can only be reversed by recognizing their existence, potent reality, character and appropriate rituals of disengagement. They are legally binding and may not be simply wished away without due processes. The net effect of all these has been a new method of studying African Traditional Religion, no longer as fossilized or exotic religion but as a living faith to be taken seriously. It contains both elements that proffer abundant life as well as those which threaten life. This is what Laurenti Magesa has argued recently in his, *African Religion: The Moral Foundations of Abundant Life*.[17]

Christianization process must take cognizance of the element of continuity in the religious lives of Africans instead of banding everything under the umbrage of syncretism. Undoubtedly a dirty epithet, the word began life in the search for an appropriate quality of the mix—the enduring problem of Christ and Culture.[18] Africa is currently boiling with much religious ferment. In summary, these dozen strands have informed the theology, character and witness of African Christianity. They give a peculiar flavor as she seeks to share the gospel with power amidst the pulsating problems of the ecosystem. Modern African church historiography is buttressed in the efforts by African Christians of various hues, scholars, novelists and political nationalists to interpret the gospel from their meaning system. Admittedly, some of these efforts arose from antagonism and others from an anti-structural intention to install a different but more kerygmatic Christianity than missionaries envisaged.

II. WHAT IS CHURCH HISTORY?

The Theological Context

The type of church history which one writes is determined by the person's definition of the *church*. For instance, *edha* in Hebrew and *kuriakon* in Greek refer frequently to the assemblage of people.It emphasizes the notion of the church as an institution. But *qahal* and *ekklesia* move beyond the institutional perception to focus attention on those people who have assembled. It is people-sensitive. The Greek word *ekklesia* speaks of people who have been called out of the world into the kingdom. The world, *kosmos* has three meanings including the world order, worldly goods,(endowments and riches), and pleasures or allurements (*kosmetikos*) which seduce people away from God. Thus, behind the classical idea of *kosmos* as an orderly arrangement, is the recognition of a mind behind the system, a world system that was established after the fall by a *kosmokrator*, a world ruler described as the prince of this world who operates in rebellion. Friendship with him breeds enmity with Christ. The church, therefore, is a special people of God, a pilgrim people with a mission. Mark 3:13-15 spells out why they are called: (i) to be companions of Christ; (ii) to hear and preach the good news which will be (iii) confirmed with signs and wonders as the Christians confront the forces of darkness. These dark forces could be poverty, corrupt ethics of power, false religiosity, social injustice, or environmental degradation. The church's task is to bring the gospel to bear on all the things which concern the well-being of the human person and to carry a spiritual warfare against forces which deface people. This theological roots of Christian social engagement must be clearly stated because those who go to war without clear commitment fail. It also informs how to do church history in an African context where these dark forces dance in broad daylight. The image of the church is as a band of people who represent the kingdom of God in human communities, who are the sign and foretaste of the kingdom in the character of their presence, by what they say and do. The church is a band of people engaged in a spiritual warfare against the world system.

The Bible images the church as the mustard seed which is sensitive, fragile, and vulnerable to the challenges from strong forces. But it has a divine mission with assured victory. Vertically, the fragile seed will shoot out branches symbolizing the quantitative indices of growth. The historian measures the story of the church by first computing the numbers of parishes, priests/pastors, the baptized, and the communicants. Horizontally, the roots of the mustard seed will spread being nurtured by the soil of the community, that is, their cultures, values, allegiances, and all the things that constitute the identities of the communities.In the symbiotic relationship, the soil will nurture the roots and the roots will transform the soil. As the roots of the church spread, they will affirm and challenge the "soil of communities": the primal worldview, core values, and allegiances.

Church history is, therefore, a different genre of history with a distinctive goal, a theological mooring, and a deep concern for people. Institutions remain important organizational vessels for order but they are made for the people. The church historian's goal is to tell the story of how laughter is being banished in Africa by predatory politicians and how thw church has responded to these "possessed" agents of a *kosmokrator* with the festival of a new life in Christ. To achieve this would require (a) a clarification of the nature of the enterprise and an ecumenical posture which rejects crass forms of vested confessional interests. At issue are deep questions of fundamental intellectual clarity and methodological identity. What are the values, presuppositions and basic orientations that have consciously, or unconsciously shaped the prevalent methods and theories in the study of church history? It is both a question of the nature and method of the discipline.

Recently, the history of religion has gone through in-house criticism with one side struggling to discount the supernatural dimensions of life and to concentrate on the natural and real. If one were to discount religious experience and concentrate on religious expression would that constitute an accurate history of a lived faith? Others would pool all canons in one basket and give them equal rating by employing a scientific inquiry that would avoid concern for the quality of what people believe. This "hermeneutics of suspicion" could serve the study of comparative religions but would be unhealthy for Christian history. The dominance of social sciences that originated, and still maintain the atheistic roots has become a problem for church history. There is a crisis of identity in the discipline that cannot be ignored.

Let us begin with clarifying the meaning of church history. The question is complex, partly because of the differing understandings of what history is. History could be understood as the record of the past: both the distant and the contemporary past. In ancient times this view produced chronology or the recording of events against time frames when the events occurred. It was soon recognized that facts are not necessarily history. A story must be told. Literary historians such as Trevelyan insisted that the story must be told in a fascinating, entertaining, and educative manner. In the nineteenth century, German idealists formulated the idea of history as a scientific reconstruction of what happened (Lat. *res gestae*), a task performed with intense archival research. This perspective was flawed not only because it assumed that all historical facts existed in written records but because it pretended that all historical facts could be accessible to the practitioner. Much to the contrary, historical facts are fragmentary. They can be likened to the story of Humpty-Dumpty who sat on a wall, had a great fall, and broke into pieces. All the kings men could not put Humpty-Dumpty together again because some pieces were irretrievably lost. Each built his own version of Humpty Dumpty. The historian, as a detective, works from fragments to reconstruct the past for the benefit of the present and future. Even Ranke could not follow his own precept, and instead became the most vigorous propagandist for the Prussian monarchy.

Two elements dominate the writing of history: the historian who is performing the task and his interpretation. Thus, E.H. Carr in his book *What is History?*[19] admonishes readers to know about authors' backgrounds. As Rudolf Bultmann asserted at the close of his Gifford Lectures:[20]

> Always in your present lies the meaning in history and you cannot see it as a spectator, but only in your responsible decisions.

All histories are written from an interpretative perspective. Some have, therefore, drawn a distinction between history representing the idealist posture and history as a more realistic acceptance of the practitioner's subjective involvement. Does this make historical writings relative? Not necessarily. There are rules of evidence by which the validity and quantity of data can be judged exegetically. Exposed biases can be accepted and critically tested by moral standards. Moral judgment in history is a problem to the extent that making such a judgment is not invalid. Trevor-Roper could dub a Stuart Bishop, Montaigne, a canary-eating, honey-sucking prelate. Ayandele could study missionary enterprises in modern Nigeria only in terms of their impact on traditional societies, and portray them as pathfinders for imperialists. History can from this perspective be an ideology used for various purposes to legitimize, govern, dominate, oppress, liberate, or predict the trends of the future.

In his inaugural lecture, "History and Society", B. Olatunji Oloruntimehin emphasized the ideological and purposeful use of history in African societies. History was used to relate the past to the present and future in all aspects of life. History was not just a record and interpretation of the past but was lived and felt. The griots among the Mande or the *arokin* among the Oyo Yoruba had a very ideological perception of history. History was a means of transmitting and preserving culture, an instrument for organizing and interpreting collective and individual experiences so as to provide understanding of the present and a guide for the future. It was a means of providing political education and leadership elites. History served as a means of promoting understanding and respect for the institutions and practices of the community. The court historians combined oratory with historical expertise and would have won the applause of a Trevelyan.[21] But their goals determined their bias.

The question of bias becomes much clearer when we deal with different branches of history, for instance, church history. The adjective constricts as much as it creates complications.

The first complication relates to the many images of the church. There are over ninety-six images in the New Testament covering a wide range of metaphors drawn from the physical structure of the human body, from the mineral world, the animal world, the vegetable world, and the world of nature. Beyond the Biblical images are the myriad denominations. The ecclesiological map looks like the shell of a tortoise! The earthly manifestation of the church is a gathered community that affirms Christ in their center.Denominations are mere local assemblies.

A third problem arises from the particularistic, unique claims of Christianity. Does the pursuit of faith imperatives clash with the need for the objective, irenic, scientific practice of history? Montgomery[22] argues that the way the term history is used betrays the fact that the Christian faith imposes a certain perspective on interpreting history. It imposes a certain underlying meaning which forces theological perception of historical events. Its time frame, for instance, links the "here-and-now" period to the "not-yet" period and thereby subjects the former to the latter. It subjects our understanding of the past to the ultimate reason for creation as well as the future of creation. It is in this undergirding conceptual scheme where the difference between church history and other genres of history can be found. Church history interprets facts from an understanding of what God was doing in Jesus Christ in each peculiar environment or ecosystem.

Tom McIntire has, therefore, avoided the term church history for Christian history. He argues that the Christian understanding of history has existed for a long time and:[23]

> radically transformed the conception of history and historical reality which prevailed in the Greek and Roman worlds. The writings and Christian perspectives of Sextus Julius Africanus, Eusebius of Caesaria, Orosius, and Augustine provided alternatives to classical pagan views of Polybius, Plutarch and Livy.

He demonstrates how the legacy and contributions of Christian historiography are within the central concepts of historical time or periodisation, the concept of history as a process, historical universality, historical contextuality, human-beings as the makers and creators of history, and the coherence and meaningfulness of historical reality. He argues that the notion of church history as the study of churches was a nineteenth century phenomenon paralleling the

> schism between Christianity and the predominant patterns of Western culture. Christianity increasingly came to be associated primarily with churches while most of the rest of culture came to be regarded as essentially secular and properly unaffected by Christian motives.[24]

Christian historiography is a means of showing the unique Christian perception of reality.[25] It

> refers not simply to history written by Christians, nor to historical studies of the church and theology, but to a historiography which itself examines the histories of peoples, societal structures and institutions, ideas, things, mores, and patterns of life, according to the sort of insights and values provided by a Christian view of man, society, norms, history, the world, and the whole of created reality. Christian historiography involved self-conscious reflection on foundational things in order that the vocation of Christian histories may more readily be transformed by the motivation of the Gospel and that the product of their labors may carry implicitly the marks of the Gospel.

McIntire's viewpoint is a good take-off point and critique of a number of conceptual schemes or goals in church historiography: the first is the institutional approach. This view assumes that church history begins when missionary X arrives in a community, sets up shop, and builds up a congregation or a church. From that point, church history reconstructs the vertical and horizontal growths of the institution, the pattern of responses, and the impact of the change-agent on the community.

A number of problems arise from the institutional understanding of church history. It reinforces the notion of church history as an extension of salvation history (German: *heilsgeschichte*). The church is portrayed as the custodian of saving grace. This is a short step from the exclusivist clause: "*extra ecclesiam nulla salus est*" (there is no salvation outside the church). The church is idealized, and a dichotomy is created between the institution and the people. The idealized entity now serves as the spiritual ally of the sword-wielding state. Church history may even derail into civilization history. Thus, the pioneering enterprise of 1841 to the Niger River in West Africa was dubbed a "Civilizing Mission of 1841." Fowell Buxton's book *African Slave Trade and Its Remedy* urges this close relationship in the quest for Glory, Gold and God.

A worse effect of the institutional approach is its support for denominationalism. Many contemporary parish histories are forms of denominational propaganda. They make it difficult for Africans to see themselves as Africans instead of products of warring confessional groups in Europe. Official histories that must win an official nod before publication are the least likely to be critical and inspiring to Africans.

Rather, the institutional approach to church history imprints the image of God as a stranger to the Africans' world. The argument is that the gospel cannot be indigenous to Africa in the true meaning of the word because the arrival of the missionaries could be dated. So, the gospel is imported. During the nationalist struggle for political independence, the nationalists, caricatured the church in Africa as the hand-maid of disruptive foreign agents. This position has been strengthened by the exposure of the sad history of church's co-operation with oppressive colonial regimes. We must recall Livingstone's assertion that "Already Africa is God's. God did not wait for me to bring Him. I found Him in every village."[26]

Finally, the institutional approach to church history diverges from the Biblical images of the church. The biblical images pay more attention to a people who have discovered something precious and are joyfully sharing, proclaiming, and publishing the good news. They are the people of God, the body of Christ, a band of pilgrims, a leavening yeast, salt of the earth, and a light on the hill. These images purvey openness, dynamism, uncloistered and unsequestered existence, uncluttered with pomp and hierarchy. Indeed, they suggest a non-institutional, critical, prophetic voice. The church's *raison d'être* is to bring salvation to the poor. Within this perspective, church history is about the understanding of God's activity among the poor and their responses to the presence of the Kingdom in their midst. It is a people's history of their perception of God's saving grace in the midst of their struggles for survival. But the church is not for the materially poor only. It may be as difficult to win over a rich man as it is to pass a camel through the eye of a needle, but it is clear that the exercise of power affects both the wielder and the victim, that the church has a great responsibility for the salvation of the rich. The definition of the term poor (Gk. *ptokhois*, Heb. *hanavim*) must include the poor in spirit who may nonetheless be rich in material things or in power. The church is the whole people of God and church history is the story of the past and present life journey of the whole people, the powerful as well as the marginalized.

Very close to the institutional approach is a genre dubbed *missionary historiography*.[27] This refers to histories of missions written by missionaries and their protégés. These accounts are usually suffused with missionary ideology, based on missionary sources—archival and personal recollections—and designed to tell the story of how a particular missionary or a group crossed the culture barriers with the gospel. They detail the labors of nurturing the message and the level of success. The ulterior motives might be to preserve and record the missionary enterprises, boost morale and material support, provide entertainment, or build up the ego of the author. The motivation may be informed by evolutionary ideologies and carry such hidden racial agenda as the Manifest Destiny laid on the whites to save the benighted pagans and lower races of humanity. Missionary ideology tended to share the scientific racism of the nineteenth century. Thus, missionary historiography is often hagiographic, triumphalist, and disdainful of indigenous non-European cultures. As Peter Foster put it, a premium was put upon distortion and degradation of receiving cultures.[28]

There are at least seven categories of missionary historiography mostly distinguished by who wrote and why:

- Histories of missions written by someone who is still serving;
- Recollections of a past officer either autobiographical or about a whole period;
- Histories of an individual or a mission written by a non-participant e.g. Livingstone on Slessor, Jordan on Shanahan, Kendall on Charles New;
- General histories of missions e.g. by Lautorette, Stephen Neill, Adolf Harnack, C. P. Groves, Morehouse, Roland Oliver, Max Warren;
- Official histories especially of denominations e.g. Eugene Stock, Hewitt Gordon, Bartel on Ghana Methodism;
- Historical accounts by the protégés of missionaries or "literature of tutelage";
- Scholarly works which are unaware of the undergirding missionary ideology.[29]

This last category may appear to have some critical approach but in fact often told the story of missions with the focus on the institution, the missionary, or denomination. These could be written by whites as well as Africans. They are the staple diet of bad church history curricula in seminaries.

The propagandist value of the first category seems obvious. Some missionaries took the cue from government officials who were encouraged to write. Works under the second category are usually full of anecdotes that demean the "natives." As examples are some works written by missionaries in southeastern Nigeria: *The River Highway* by the Scottish Presbyterian J.A.T. Beattie, or *Pilgrim with a Limp* by the Apostolic Church Welshman Idris Vaughan, or *Ibo*

Opening by the indomitable Primitive Methodist, William Dodds. Hagiography predominates in missionary historiography. Recent works expose the trend; for example critical contemporary biographies from eastern Africa: Murray Steele's biography of Arthur Shelley Cripps, or John Weller's on Alston May, the Bishop of Northern Rhodesia.[30]

The broad sweep, scholarship, and even commitment in works by nationalist historians may have blinded the unsuspecting reader to the genre of nationalist historiography that sets out to counter the missionary image of Africa and Africans. Recently, it has become fashionable to point out that missionary historiography ignored the roles of the African agents. A number of church historians have, therefore, set out to fill the gaps: Ajayi, Ayandele, Isichei (Nigeria), Jenkins and Odamtten (Ghana), Temu and Nthamburi (Kenya), Tuma and Waliggo (Uganda), Ranger, Byzavaire, Maxwell (central Africa) and many others. Concern for unsung "native agents" and cultural revivalism are predominant motifs in nationalist historiography.

Within this genre there is a minor debate on the categorization of "native agents". Some would exclude the West Indians and African Americans who pioneered the spread of Christianity in Sierra Leone and Liberia. They themselves subscribed to the battle cry that "Africa must be evangelized by Africans" and made immense contributions, as Jean Herskovitz has shown in *A Preface Modern Nigeria*, Okon Uya in the study of the career of Alexander Crummel, and Lamin Sanneh in *Abolitionists Abroad*. A broad cross-section of native agents includes:

i. Noble patrons, men of local prominence who on their own initiative invited and patronized missionaries.
ii. Interpreters and wards that influenced expansion.
iii. Converts, including traders, migrant workers, acting in groups or individually to use their social powers in aid of missions.
iv. Catechists, evangelists, church elders and school teachers, who bore the brunt of running new parishes; poorly-paid and poorly-trained, they constituted an important cog in the wheel.
v. Congregations that pioneered expansion through evangelical crusades to neighboring areas and paid for the upkeep of ministers.
vi. Local communities that built and maintained church and school infrastructures.
vii. Charismatic, prophet figures that quickened the pace of Christianization in their brief careers.

The irony in nationalist historiography is that while condemning missionaries and showing that Africans were the real agents who spread Christianity, the authors fail to show that the Africans internalized western models, and served as the interpreters to their communities. These agents domesticated western culture in the hinterlands. Many of these agents would have worn Frantz Fanon's label, "Black Skin White Mask" with much pride.

The concern of the book and this chapter focuses on the African scholars who should have benefited from the changing vistas of historiography. Many betray a lack of concern with methodology in either secular history or church history. Thus, with eyes closely fixed on archival sources, they pose non-relevant, non-creative questions and fail to relate the history of the church to the secular political, economic and social realities of the day. It is as if church history operated in a closed plane with no underlying meaning and lesson.

Indeed, novelists and sociologists have made more contributions than historians in redressing the sad situations. The Heinemann-based African Writers Series has a number of novels which have focused on the religious change agent in the encounter between Europeans and Africans: for instance,Achebe's *Things Fall Apart* (1958), and *Arrow of God* (1964), Mongo Beti's *Poor Christ of Bomba*, Ngugi's *The River Between* (1965), Munonye's *The Only Son* (1966), Nzekwu's *Blade Among the Boys* (1962), and Echewa's *The Lands Lord* (1976). The novelists wove the activity of the church into the fabric of the life of the community. As Father Higler in *The Land's Lord* reflects:[31]

> Before he came here he used to think of hauling them (i.e. converts) in net-fulls. But the forces held them back, the soil, their gods, and jujus, rampaging devils. He could fish only with a line here, not a net. And the line often tangled in the weeds ... The new church, conceived in the highest hopes, hopes so heavy they seemed to weigh down the walls and forever keep them near the ground.

In the novels by Achebe, Beti, Echewa, and Ngugi wa Thiong'o failure bred reflection and the willingness to dialogue with the cultural contexts. Unburdened by concerns of periodization, footnotes, and drudgery of facts, novelists wade into the heart of the matter with intriguing insight.

> African Christian scholarship has been dominated by Western sociologists and anthropologists such as Beidelman, Peel, Horton, Jon Miller, Ranger, van Dijk, Meyer, Maxwell, ter Haar and their protégés. At one level, they provide very insightful analyses. As Beidelman's social theory of mission and his *Colonial Evangelism* demonstrates, the importance of sociological method and insights in painting a fuller, critical history of missions cannot be overemphasized.[32] Admittedly, historians have always been suspicious of sociological models. Thus, Lamin Sanneh, explained his new venture into a history of *West African Christianity* with a strident plea:[33]

The second reason for a fresh initiative lies with the nature of the subject. Christianity in Africa has had more than its share of the attention of Western writers, including throngs of social scientists and their disciples. It is as if in our concern to describe the sunlight we concentrated on the shadows, using that derivative relationship as the justification for a reductionist approach. This book, by contrast, is concerned with the straight religious aspect of Christianity.

To a certain extent Lamin Sanneh is correct. The Norwegian Jarle Simensen once applied transactional analysis in social theory to the study of the Norwegian missionary enterprise to Zululand, South Africa, 1850-1906. At the end, he admitted:[34]

> Our approach to the question of religious change has been a partial one. We have concentrated on its *outward manifestations* in the form of change of religious adherence, registered in the growth of station society and Christian congregations. Without discarding purely religious motives we have tried to define the role played by African material and political needs and the missionary offer in this respect.

He recognized that sociological methods that concentrate on the secular effects of missions, that is, both in the social, economic and political field, often fail to deal with the internal or purely religious dimensions. They focus on religious expression because the method cannot adequately handle religious experience. Functionalism has bred a strong interpretative model that fails to take people's religious longings seriously. Thus, we are told that those who flock to Pentecostal movements are questing for modernity as if these churches are better purveyors of modernity than secular institutions such as finance houses and other vestiges of Western structures.

In the African world, however, the religious is inextricably intertwined with the political, economic, ecological and other social forces. Indeed, history has been compared to a jade who renews her vigor by marrying new spouses. For instance, the philosophy of history became fashionable when historians endeavored to avoid the stigma of sloppiness by strengthening their conceptual framework. Similarly, the quantitative analysis of social scientists that Laslett make famous with his book *The World We Have Lost* opened new vistas in the study of past societies. The methods of social science will continue to enhance the historian's understanding of man in society.

There must be a balanced concern with the inward level of the religious as well as the outward level of political and economic interests, because religious expression as opposed to religious experience operates within cultural forms. Thus, the gods of forest dwellers emerge from the dank forest while the gods of riverine communities visit from the depths of the sea. Following from this is a second aspect, namely, that the explanation for religious change must consider both the purely religious factors as well as the ecological, political, cultural and economic factors. The reactions of African communities to Christianity were influenced by a host of these factors. The key questions in African church history are why and how Africans abandoned the gods of their fathers for Christianity? The answer cannot come from only looking at the "straight religious aspect of Christianity."

To state the central premise: the organizational structure does not constitute the total character of the church, even though it is undeniable that the church operates as an institutional organization. Thus, church history is more than the history of the institutional structure. It is the story of the pilgrim people of God and their experiences of God's redeeming grace in the midst of their existence in various cultural and ecological milieus.

The role of those engaged in cross-cultural mission in spreading the gospel and message of salvation is equally undeniable. The historian must reconstruct the profiles of the home bases of missionary groups. However, the idealization of missionary agents and structures distorts the history of the church. Ronald Allen in 1913 queried this model, and in recent years McGravran, Wagner and their colleagues in The School of World Mission, Fuller Theological Seminary, Pasadena, California, have proposed a wider understanding of both the types and the strategies of evangelization.

Indeed, studies on the role of the Holy Spirit in evangelization process and church dynamics further rebel against contemporary missionary historiography. Finally, the perspective given by the renaissance of African historiography turns the institutional and missionary historiographies on their heads. The story begins among African communities that had viable structures for existence. It then delineates the permeation of Christian influence into the values and structures of the communities, attentive to the varieties of the reactions, however ambiguous, of the communities to the Christian change agent. Doing church history from this perspective could become a liberating enterprise for Africans. Attention shifts from the process of insertion to the process of appropriation.

III. THE ECUMENICAL PERSPECTIVE:

Story-Telling and Mobilizing against Poverty and Oppression

The perspective suggested here is to pursue a scientific study of history with a theological bias and goal. One concept that describes the goal most aptly is ecumenism, from the Greek word, *oikumene*. It is a geographical term referring to the whole inhabited earth. In its theological usage, it refers to God's creation, lordship and ruler-ship over the whole inhabited world and human history. The root is in the Pentateuch tradition, especially in the Genesis myth of creation. The implication is that human history consists of the out working of divine and continued revelation of God in human life, human situations and nature. Church history is, therefore, the story of God's presence in human communities and the responses to divine love in time perspective. It is a new understanding of what God has done in Jesus Christ, who invites us to a new and wider vision, learning, commitment and action.

A certain problem arises: the universal idea involved in the concept has often been challenged by constricting, particularist views. In the Genesis saga, the story details the history of a single people, Israel. But it soon escapes this narrow bound with the concept of a new Israel, an assertion of God's love for the whole world, Jews and Gentiles, and an affirmation of the mandate to corporately express the Christian hope for the fullness of life.The implications are immense.

First, ecumenism calls for a wider understanding of the church. The unity of all Christian peoples challenges the African to contribute to the task of stewardship and mission. Church history is, therefore, not the story of the role of white missionaries in cross-cultural mission. Missionary incursion into a living African context must be put in its proper perspective. The church is not the denominations "transplanted" from Europe to Africa. African church history is the study of the past and present experiences of the people with the gospel, both during and at the end of the missionary period. As K.O. Dike intoned, "African history must be the history of African people and not merely the history of the invaders."[35]

Second, the study of church history must eschew elitism. Every period, every aspect of culture, every community, every class of people is an ingredient in a holistic approach to history. This approach precludes insular, non-comparative, nationalist historiographies which lack universal perspective.[36]

Third, since Christ came for the poor, Enrique Dussel, therefore, argues that "the task of the historian is to trace out the history of the gospel in relation to the poor and oppressed." Thus, events must be "viewed from below", and ecumenical church history can be a perspective on the world as seen by the suffering, the poor, and the marginalized.

Fourth, an ecumenical approach calls for a dialogical methodology. It rejects the easy condemnation of non-Christian religions and spiritual traditions. African church historiography starts with African religions and material cultures not simply as an introductory background but because God has created those communities in His own image. This approach recognizes the resilience of the force of African religiosity among Christians. It demands that the Christian engage the interior of the indigenous worldview and reclaim it for Christ. This is not merely breaking from the past.It recognizes that Christ is within each culture and judges all cultures.

The ecumenical perspective in church history, therefore, reconstructs from the grassroots the experiences of men and women in a community and the meaning of Christ in their midst. It assumes that as the spirit of God broods over the whole inhabited earth human beings would increasingly recognize the divine presence and their lives would be changed in the encounter. In spite of particularistic claims, Christianity should not become a dysfunctional *River Between* as the African novelist Ngugi characterized it.

Beyond the hortatory and ideological dimensions, is the argument proffered by T.O. Ranger on the need to understand the inner history of African traditional religiosity as a means of assessing the encounter with Christianity. He saw four aspects: first, conversion to Christianity was possible because of the general openness of African religions to new myths, rites, symbols and techniques. Thus, in the second place, responses to missionaries varied because what was needed from them in terms of myth, ritual, symbol and technique varied. Third, in the conflict of religious ideas between rulers and the ruled, intruders and indigenes, each party sought the advantage of alliance with the missionaries. Fourth, the functional and structural differences between the various types of African traditional religions produced different responses to missionary Christianity. Ranger uses the changing concepts of God amidst the enlargement of scale, the powerful rituals of eradication and cleansing, and the usability of Christian symbols and themes as illustrations. This viewpoint carries further Robin Horton's urging for a historical approach to the study of African religion in an effort to explain why Africans abandoned the gods of their fathers.[37] Horton urges for an understanding of then changes that occur in a community's indigenous worldview when confronted by the gospel.

Finally, an ecumenical approach should make the writing of history a process of liberating, self-discovery for the individual as well as the community. In the midst of legitimacy crises and the poverty unleashed by predatory states on the masses, only an ecumenical mobilization of countervailing forces will suffice. In contemporary African churches, the capacity to respond adequately to the social violence, poverty, and legitimacy crises in the public space has been vitiated by the trauma of growth. Christianity has grown so rapidly that the resources have been challenged: modes of ministerial formation, the maze of theologies, the competition from other religions, and the rise of ethnicity are only a few of the indices of trauma. The church historian has a difficult job in understudying the large numbers of churches and their activities. Meanwhile, fraudsters as wolves in sheep's clothing have entered the field and the energy of the churches have like molten lava flowed out into the western world as Africans escape from the collapsed economies. It is both an exciting and a challenging period to attempt to tell the story of African Christianity.

Notes

1. E. HOORNAERT, *The Memory of the Christian People* (Maryknoll, NY: Orbis Books, 1989), 9.
2. Kwame BEDIAKO, *Christianity in Africa* (Maryknoll Orbis Books, 1995).
3. A.F. WALLS & C. FYFE, *Christianity in Africa in the 1990's* (Edinburgh: Centre for African Studies, University of Edinburgh, 1996), 1.
4. *Ibid.*, 6.
5. A.E. AFIGBO, *Ropes of Sand* (Lagos: Oxford University Press, 1981), 384; E.A. AYANDELE, *The Missionary Impact on Modern Nigeria 1842–1914, A Political Analysis* (London: Longmans, 1966).
6. In Ullier BEIER, *Modern Poetry from Africa* (London: Penguin Books, 1979).
7. E.B. IDOWU, *African Traditional Religion: A Definition* (London: SPCK, 1973).
8. D.I. NWOGA, *Supreme God as a Stranger in Igbo Religious Thought* (Ekwereazu in Imo State, Nigeria: Hawk Press, 1984).
9. J.S. MBITI, "Christianity and Traditional Religions in Africa", in *International Rev. of Missions*, 59, 236, 1970: 430-441.
10. Aylward SHORTER, *Toward a Theology of Inculturation* (Maryknoll: Orbis Books, 1988), 11.
11. Kwesi DICKSON, *Theology in Africa,* (Maryknoll: Orbis Books, 1984), 146.

12. Kwame BEDIAKO, *Theology and Identity* (Oxford: Regnum Press, 1992); Bediako, *Christianity in Africa*, 76.
13. Lamin SANNEH, *Translating the Message* (Maryknoll: Orbis Books, 1989).
14. A.F. WALLS, *Christianity in Africa in the 1990s*, 5.
15. A. SHORTER, *Jesus and the Witch Doctor* (Maryknoll: Orbis Books, 1995); A. HASTINGS, *African Catholicism: Essays in Discovery*, (London: SCM Press, 1989); M.L. DANEEL, "Exorcism as a Means of Combating Wizardry", in *Missionalia*, 18, 1 1990: 220-247.
16. O.U. KALU, "The Dilemma of Grassroot Inculturation of the Gospel, in *Jnl. of Religion in Africa*, 25, 1995, 48-72.
17. L. MAGESA, *African Religion: The Moral Foundations of Abundant Life* (Maryknoll: Orbis Books, 1997).
18. O.U. KALU, "Gospel, Culture and Mission: Revisiting an Enduring Problem", in *Skrif en Kerk*, 19, 2, 1998: 283-300.
19. E.H. CARR, *What is History*? (London: Penguin Books, 1964).
20. Cited in John W. MONTGOMERY, *Where is History Going? A Christian Response to Secular Philosophies of History* (Minneapolis: Bethany Fellowship Inc., 1970 ed.), 199.
21. B.O. OLORUNTIMEHIN, "History and Society", in *Inaugural Lecture Series*, 18 (Ile-Ife: University of Ife, 1976).
22. MONTGOMERY, *Where is History Going?*, 187.
23. C.T. MCINTIRE, *The Ongoing Task of Christian Historiography* (Toronto: Institute of Christian Studies, 1974), 7.
24. Ibid., 12.
25. Ibid., 6.
26. Cf. Hoger B. HANSEN, *Mission, Church and State in a Colonial Setting: Uganda, 1890-1925* (London: Heinemann, 1984). The dichotomy and its effect has been tackled by a research group in France led by Jean Delumeau in the series entitled, *History as Lived by the Christian People*. Their inspiration comes from the *Annals* tradition founded by March Bloch and Lucien Febvre. See, Francesco CHIOVARO, "History as Lived by the Christian People" in L. VISCHER (ed), *Church History in an Ecumenical Perspective,* Papers and Reports of an International Ecumenical Consultation, Basle, 12-17 October 1981.
27. See, O.U. KALU, "Over a Century of Christian Presence in Africa: A Historical Perspective", in *Bulletin de Theologie Africaine,* 1, 1 (January-June, 1979), 112-126; See also ch. 1 of Robert W. STRAYER, *The Making of Mission Communities in East Africa* (London: Heinemann, 1978).
28. P.D. CURTIN, "Scientific Racism and British Theory of Empire", in *Journ. of the Hist. Soc. of Nigeria, (JHSN)*, 2,1, 1969, 40-51; Peter FOSTER, "Missionaries and Anthropology: the case of the Scots of Northern Malawi", in *Journ. of Rel. in Africa*, 16, 2, 1986, 102.
29. Vestiges of Missionary Mentality are as persistent as colonial mentality. See, Thomas O'TOOLE, "The Persistence of Colonial Thinking in African Historiography" in *UFAHAMU* (California), 7,2, 1977, 43-52; P. TURNER, "The Wisdom of the Fathers and the Gospel of Christ", in *JRA,* 4, 1, 1971, 45-68.
30. (i) These are discussed in O.U. KALU, *Embattled Gods, Chrisitianization of Igboland, 1841-1991* (Trenton: World Press, 1996), ch. 1; (ii) They are discussed in

Part II of T.O. Ranger & John Weller (eds), *Themes in the Christian History of Central Africa* (London: Heinemann, 1975).

31. Echewa, T. Obinkaram, *The Land's Lord* (New York: Laurence Hill & Co, 1976), 84.
32. O.U. Kalu, *The History of Christianity in West Africa* (London: Longman, 1980), pp. 6-7; See, Ph. D. Thesis of my student, S.C. Chuta, "Africans in the Christianization of Southern Igboland, 1875-1952" (University of Nigeria, Nsukka, 1986).
33. Lamin Sanneh, *West African Christianity* (Maryknoll: Orbis Books, 1983), p. XI.
34. Jarle Simensen, "Religious Change as Transaction: The Norwegian Mission to Zululand, South Africa, 1850-1906", in *Journ. Of Religion in Africa,* 16,2, 1986, 82-100.
35. Cited in A.E. Afigbo, *K.O. Dike and the African Historical Renaissance* (Owerri: RADA Publ. Co., 1986).
36. For a critique of nationalist historiography in Africa, see, A. Temu & B. Swai, *Historians and Africanist History: A Critique* (London: Zed Press, 1981).
37. R. Horton, "African Conversion", in *Africa,* 41,2, 1971, 87-108. See also *Africa,* 45,3, 1975, 219-235; *Africa,* 45,4, 1975, 373-399; T.O. Ranger & B. Ogot (eds), *The Historical Study of African Religion* (London, 1972), Ranger & Weller, *Themes in the Christian History.* For a summary discussion on the literature on religious change in Africa, see, O.U. Kalu, "Gods in Retreat: Models of Religious Change in Africa", in *Nigerian Journal of Humanities*, 1,1, 1977, 42-53.

Chapter Two

African Christianity: An Overview

Ogbu U. Kalu

INTRODUCTION

Since the conversion of Emperor Constantine, the story of Christianity has increasingly appeared to be the story of a western religion. Appearances can be deceptive precisely because there are communities in Africa that could claim an involvement in the Jesus movement from its inception till today. When Christianity abandoned its Palestinian roots, its new home in the Graeco-Roman world included North Africa (Maghrib), which was the breadbasket of Rome, and shared extensive commercial and cultural relations with Palestine and the Levant. Before the story of Judich, the treasurer to Candace (Queen Mother) of the Nubian kingdom of Meroe, who met Philip en-route from a pilgrimage to Rome, geographical contiguity had made it possible for the infant Jesus to take refuge in Africa. The Coptic Orthodox church celebrates this event annually. Later, Christianity shifted its center of gravity yet again into barbarian Europe where every effort was made to domesticate and repackage it in western imagery. Recently, commentators have observed another shift from the northern hemisphere into the south. David Barrett's annual statistics in his *World Encyclopedia* (1982, 2000) reads as follows:

Year	World Pop.	Christian	Christian	Non-West	West
1900	1,620m	558m	34%	14%	86%
1950	2,510m	856m	34%	36%	64%
1970	3,696m	1,236m	34%	44%	56%
1990	5,266m	1,747m	33%	56%	44%
2000	6,055m	2,000m	32%	60%	40%

He shows that the number of Christians in Africa grew from 8.75 million in 1900 to 117 million in 1970 to 335.1 million by mid-2000, and projects a figure of 360 million for mid-2003 and 600.5 million for 2005.[1] Thus by 1999 most Christians in the world lived in Latin America, Africa and Asia in that order; that out of 1.87 billion Christians in the world, 1.11 billion are non-white. Africa looms large again. Out of 210.6 million Evangelicals, Africa tops the list with 69.5 million; out of 423.7 million Pentecostals/Charismatic Christians in the world, 126 million live in Africa.

Given the growth rate, these figures are much larger now. There are more Anglicans in Nigeria (with a Christian population of 49 million) than in England and Europe put together. The significance of Africa's role in the formation of Christianity was remembered in 1971 when the All African Council of Churches convened an emergency session to reflect on an indigenous confession of faith in Alexandria, because the Alexandrian School was prominent in the task of consolidating Christian theology and identity amidst the constraints of Roman imperial culture. When the doctrines, polity, liturgy and ethics of Christianity were still being formulated, African voices were powerful. Alexandria and Antioch constituted the dominant and competing schools in Christian apologetics. St. Augustine and Tertullian were not Italians! The Islamic scourge in the seventh century gradually dismantled certain aspects of African Christianity as it retreated into Coptic villages as a symbol of nationalism and as it struggled in Nubia (till the fifteenth century) and in Ethiopia to witness amidst the harassments by various Muslim dynasties. Ken Sawyer and Youhana Youssef argue strongly that this story is a part of Africa's history just as Akin Akinade urges that Islam is also important in Africa's religious journey and must not be perceived as hostile religions dividing the communities.

In the fifteenth century, Europe abandoned the crusades and initiated a more creative response to Islamic economic, cultural and political challenges. In this attempt to use sea routes to circumvent the Muslims, new efforts were made to evangelize Africa but both the slave trade and colonization combined to stunt the vigor of evangelization. Christian presence in Africa retreated into the *feitoras*, trading forts, of various European nations until the large-scale missionary enterprise commencing in the nineteenth century created a resurgence into the hinterlands of the communities that lived south of the Sahara Desert. This enterprise laid the roots of the numerical explosion and maturity of the modern period. The poignancy of this is buttressed by the fact that at the World Missionary Conference, Edinburgh, 1910, no African was present; Asia including Japan occupied more of the interest of the conferees. Significantly, contemporary Africa is the laboratory of Christianity in the twenty-first century. Its story could be told in four sequences.

I. THE FIRST TIME: EARLY CHRISTIANITY IN NORTH AFRICA

There is little certainty about the date of entry of Christianity into Egypt and much of the regions to the west such as Cyrenia, Numidia, Africa and Mauretania. The story of the Pentecost event indicates clearly that people from this region were present at the crucial launching of the church; they were both diasporic Jews and non-Jewish proselytes. Indeed, the Coptic Orthodox Church claims that both Thomas and Mark were in Egypt during the persecution of the Jesus movement; that Thomas moved from here to India and that Mark was the first of the over 100 *abunas* of the church. The pattern of vertical expansion of Christianity indicates that there was an insignificant Christian presence in Egypt in about 239AD, and that from 274AD the percentage of Christians in the population grew at a significant rate, more than the percentage growth rate for the rest of the Graeco-Roman world.

A number of reasons have been adduced: the first relates to the political and social forces that shaped the movement, especially the shift of the class structure of membership as upper class women joined and provided facilities for the predominantly lower class votaries. Equally crucial was the conversion of some Jews; their social and commercial prominence protected the fledging movement in its early days because Judaism was the only non-Roman *licita religio* in the sprawling empire. The measures of suppression and repression against the new religion ironically benefited the new subversive religion; the intermittent persecutions, such as the Decian, Severian, Valerian and especially the long-drawn Diocletian, strengthened rather than weakened the confessors, and as they escaped the onslaught they spread their belief. From this perspective, those debates about purity and against *traditores* betrays the degree of commitment by ordinary believers who served as everyday evangelists. Committed agency was the core of Christian survival and martyrdom became a means of witnessing. The power of the message of Christianity was important but the indigenous worldview was equally crucial as traditional Egyptian religion contained much that resonated with the new: notions of salvation, eschatology, ethics and liturgy could find parallels in the Osiri-Horus myth; so did the intellectual environment that comprised gnostic thought forms—preserved in papyrus manufactured in ancient Egypt. Alexandria was the intellectual capital of the Mediterranean and paraded Egyptian contributions in writing, philosophy, art and architecture. The catechetical school in Alexandria under famous leaders such as Pantaneus, Origen and Dionysius used both allegorization and creative syncretism, known as "spoiling the Egyptians" to interpret the Christian faith to a less educated populace and for the consolidation of the new religion amidst competing prescriptions about the way to heaven.

In this fluid period of the Jesus movement, theological debates were rife about the nature of God, Jesus and the character of the Holy Spirit. It was often argued whether Jesus was truly human or only appeared to be so; had one nature; two natures (human and divine); or two natures in one person; whether the Holy Spirit issued *from the Father* or *from the Father and the Son*; and how both were related to God. Such theological issues have not been resolved until this day. Whoever had the power to uphold their views, would declare the opponents as heretics. The canon did not have clear boundaries as many manuscripts circulated with the semblance of authenticity. These same manuscripts are fuelling the denial of the speech of God and repudiation of canonicity in Western Christian traditions such as in contemporary feminism and the Jesus Seminar. Power politics in the church became the tradition partly because Constantine's conversion that removed persecution thrust Christianity into the center of the public space and created more opportunities for ecclesiastic politics, debates and conciliarist posture that was bereft of consensus. The councils held at Nicaea and Chalcedon created more warring parties. Constantine's conversion may have weakened the tensile strength of the Jesus movement. Yet the period yielded many doctrinal confessions that have stood the test of time and brought Africa into the center of World Christianity.

For some, the indigenization of the message was achieved through the vernacular translations of the Bible into Coptic languages such as Sahidic (Upper Nile), Boharic (Nile Delta) and Bashmuric (Middle Nile). The use of the Coptic language in the liturgy and Bible domesticated the message and aided personal witnessing, which was the most powerful form of evangelism in this period. Evidence of deep religious consciousness was betrayed by the proliferation of Christian art especially the distinctly embellished genre of icons. Indeed, the indigenous culture was reshaped as evident in the funerary artifacts found in a tomb excavated at Antinoe in Upper Egypt; however, mummification persisted as indigenous religion proved resilient. Another lasting contribution of this region was the eremitic tradition as hermits of various types and numbers built their retreats in the deserts and mountains. The Pachomian regulation was adopted by many hermitages in due course. These enclaves contributed in nurturing Christian spirituality, sense of mission, and served as havens for the persecuted or for those who got tired of the virulent politics of the day. In later years, as the gilded Christianity in metropolitan Alexandria was emasculated, monasteries would prove to be the surviving centers of the Jesus movement. It should be stressed that Christianity in Egypt flourished amidst resilient ancient mystery religions that would later enjoy a renaissance.

At some point in time, the movement flowed west and exhibited a character typical of those who are far from urban centers and its flaunt of learning and scholarship. Two types of Christianity developed in Africa and Numidia: one was the ascetic tradition typified by the Donatists. They mixed Christianity with nationalism and saw the Romans, whether clerics or merchants in agricultural goods, as exploiters. By this time, this region had replaced Egypt as the granary of Italy. A particular group, the Circumcellion, became pirates who terrorized the upper classes. The socio-economic and class dimensions were as important as the insistence that those who did not stand faithful during the persecutions had no business in leadership roles in the church; after all, translation ensured that the lower classes understood the Scriptures. Similarly, the conflict between

Gospel and culture troubled the Montanists who emphasized the pneumatic tradition in Christian life and despised the tango with Roman idolatrous culture in the philosophical theology of the Alexandrian school. Yelling that they had Jesus and did not need the schools, they rejected the "spoiling of the Egyptians", a method that sought to express the fundamentals of Christian faith in the idiom of Rome's imperial religion. The vitality of this Christian movement breathed through the ardent apologetics in Tertullian's *Ad Uxorem* as well as his treatise on baptism. As fishes they lived in the water of the new birth. They enlarged the space for women and challenged the patriarchal tradition of the period. Needless to add, many of these issues dominate contemporary theology on the continent.

The tendency has been to argue that the virulent debates, arid philosophy and the lack of a vibrant evangelism among the indigenous Berber, Tuareg and Kworaraffa people embedded a weak Christianity that could not survive the fiery test of Islamic onslaught. The story is more complicated. Christianity in Africa was only gradually becoming African Christianity. The Maghrib passed through many foreign rules; each left its imprint on the language, racial composition and sense of community. As the Roman Empire declined, Byzantine rule was riddled with heavy taxation, doctrinal controversies, competing claims between Rome and Constantinople over supremacy, before the period of rule under the Vandals privileged Arianism and more financial burden. The re-conquest of Africa by the Byzantines was carrion-comfort relief and naturally the populace mistook the arrival of Islam as a welcome. Quite important is the fact that the early Muslim dynasties did not try to wipe out Christianity. Their victory over the Christian territories was so rapid and extensive that they lacked the human resources for governance and needed Christian bishops of all doctrinal persuasions to serve as civil officials. The early Caliphs themselves were not secure; assassinations boiled their political pots; and they were still close to the tolerant teaching of the prophet towards "the people of the book". Christianity enjoyed growth until the period of the fourth Caliph when new leadership and new political conditions compelled an intensified the program of Arabization.

William B. Anderson, who worked for many years in Sudan, has contributed an aspect of the research on Sudanese Christianity that he did with Wheeler and Werner. The cultural flows between Egypt and its southern neighbor included the spread of the gospel. South of the first cataract was the region that Egyptians called the Kush Kingdom, a reference that included both Nubia and Abyssinia or Ethiopia. It covered the region between Egypt and central Africa and its mineral resources and commercial potentials allured the Egyptians. The relationship remained rife with ambiguities as the warlike Blemmyes (the ancestors of the Beja people) constantly raided the Egyptian towns around Thebes; yet the Nubians pilgrimaged to the cultic center at Philae. Egypt occupied parts of Nubia at certain points in time; for instance, in retaliation against Nubian attacks they sacked the ancient Kush capital of Napata and Nubians retreated to the second cataract and founded the rich kingdom of Meroe, whose court is referred to in the pages of the Bible. This fact and other archeological evidence shows that Christianity had moved down to this region before Empress Theodora of Byzantium subverted her husband by dispatching a Monophysite priest, Julianos in 543AD.

First, vast commercial and cultural contacts introduced Christianity to the Kush; second, Judich's story suggests familiarity with the Septuagint within a few years after the resurrection; third, archeological evidence shows that a church existed at Farah in the fourth century; fourth, Jewish communities at Elephantine and the evangelistic bishops of Philae must have introduced the Hebrew Bible and Christianity into Nubia; and fifth, many who escaped from the various persecutions took their Christianity down the Nile. Julian's enterprise in the sixth century reflects on the new political context when the Nobadian rulers who benefited from dismantling the Meroe kingdom, sought political alliance with Emperor Justinian. The fall of Meroe was brought about through a combination of raids by the king of Ethiopia and the incursion of Kush communities from the interior into the Nile basin. Both Julianos and Longinus, who came later, actually evangelized the Nobadian court and initiated the spread of the gospel further down the Nile to the Alowa though the other Nubian community, Makuria had a Melkite (pro-Chalcedonian) version of the gospel.

The spread of Christianity gradually moved from the courts as churches took over the temples of indigenous gods; Episcopal sees with cathedrals were built in Faras, Ibrim, Sai, Dongola and other places. Egyptian influence continued to hold sway as the Patriarch of Alexandria supplied the leadership and personnel with monks from Egypt, Syria and a muscular corps of indigenes. Eremitic tradition planted the gospel into the soil such that Christianity in Nubia survived Islamic onslaught until the fifteenth century. The unification of the northern kingdoms of Nobades and Makuria after the seventh century meant that the whole of Nubia acted in concert as a Christian kingdom. But state-driven Christianity tends to privilege an institutional character and archeology does not leave much evidence of the level of the conversion of the people or the appropriation of the charismatic resources of the gospel for everyday life.

Further down the fourth cataract, Ethiopian (Abyssinian) Christianity has survived from the early period to the present. Ogbu Kalu tells the story from two perspectives: the insider and outsider versions of the history. Court influence was equally the key to the survival. The reference, Ethiopia, only became the designation for the entire region when the translators of the Septuagint in 300BC mistakenly translated the Hebrew "Kush" into Greek *Aithiopia,* a word that the Greek used for any country south of their known world, and derived from their word for "black face", *aithiops*. Inscriptions confirm that King Ezana converted as a child and imaged himself as a Constantine whose victories over the straw houses of the Nobia and the stone-built cities of the Kush came from God. Two young Syrian Monophysites, who were captured on the Red Sea port of Adulis, became creative evangelists in the Aksum court located a hundred miles inland. They were brought to the court when it was under a regency. Frumentius not only reared the young king but was enthroned as the first bishop. This stamped the power of the state on the character of the church as various kings sustained the church: Digna-Jan in the ninth century, Dilna'od in the tenth, and Amda-Siyan who restructured the church extensively in the fourteenth century. Yohannes IV (1872-1889) and Menelik II (1889-1913) left indelible imprints on the modern face of Ethiopian Orthodox Church. The kings built many churches and monasteries while Egypt supplied the *abuna*.

The Nine saints or *Sadaqan* (Syrian Monophysite exiles) not only extended rural evangelization, but established monasteries that became important in rooting the gospel and an identifiable spirituality. Soon rival abbots of monastic houses, standing on the precedence of their foundations, turned church politics around the tripod of king, *abuna* and abbots. When the power of Aksum declined and the center of Ethiopia shifted south from the Tigre, the story remains one of inculturation of the gospel within the vernacular: retention of Jewish traditions of the early church; liturgical innovations that utilized ingredients of traditional culture; and virulent debates on Sabbath observation and other finer points of theology. Ethiopian contributions to Christian art, architecture, music, literacy and liturgy have remained enduring. The Ethiopian church, with its large number of aesthetic crosses, remained in splendid isolation and served as an ingredient of the national culture, until Europe rediscovered it in the fifteenth century in the quest for the mythical kingdom of Prester John. This contact saved it from the jihadist attacks of the imam, Ahmed Gran (the left-handed), but it exposed it to disruptive foreign influences especially efforts to annex it to Rome. A combination of soft state and foreign influences created more internal debates that weakened the church by the nineteenth century.

The story of Islam and Ethiopia is a long one, because just as Jesus was sheltered in Egypt so also was the prophet Mohammed in Ethiopia, when the king refused to repatriate him in spite of all blandishment from his enemies in Mecca. He instructed a tolerance that his followers reneged. The survival of Christianity once again was linked to the recovery of the state due to two able monarchs, Yohannes IV and Menelik II, who dealt with the problem of foreign influence, held off the Mahdists from Sudan (1899), defeated Italian colonial endeavor in 1896, and recovered the impetus from the Muslims who had gained high political positions as supporters of Gran. Yohannes revitalized the church through four Coptic bishops and evangelized the Galla who had clung tenaciously to traditional religion through the years. Menelik established the structures of modern Ethiopia which was inherited and developed by Emperor Haile Selassie. This story will be important for reconstructing the anti-structural agency of those dubbed as "Ethiopians" in the nineteenth century.

II. THE SECOND CHANCE: IBERIAN CATHOLICISM

Two scholars, David Kpobi and Paul Gundani deal with the extensive Iberian presence started when a new style of European response to the challenges of Islam was signaled by the recapture of Ceuta in 1415. Imaged as a crusade, its immense significance included the recovery and retention of the source of grain supply from Muslims' clutch; the information about the extent of Arab trans-Saharan commerce in salt and gold that extended into western and central Sudan or the Senegalese Futa Jallon region. Psychologically, it released a daring temper and maritime exploits. Prince Henry's nautical school at Sagres experimented with sails, keels, compasses and astrolabes. The Portuguese could dare sail the Atlantic in the quest for a sea route to the source of the spices, encircle, circumvent and cut into the Arab trans-Saharan gold trade from the south. Couched in Christian idiom, they sought to reconnect with the empire of Prester John and convert the heathens. In the combined motives for gold, glory and God, the Christian motif fitted into the rhetoric of the period while the commercial drive remained privileged. Papal bulls offered the *padroado* rights to the Portuguese monarch to appoint clerical orders for evangelization and to fend off competing European interests.

Iberian Catholic presence in Africa from the sixteenth through to the eighteenth centuries was characterized by certain facts: Portugal was a small country and did not possess the manpower to control and evangelize the large territory that was "discovered" between the years 1460 and 1520, and stretched from Cape Blanco to Sumatra and Java. They chose to stay on the islands and coastal regions of their shoe-string empire. Iberian Catholicism was a social ornament, a religion of ceremonies and outward show; thus in the islands and a few areas where they established Christian presence on the mainland, adherence supplanted strong spiritual commitment. Court-alliance used religion as an instrument of diplomatic and commercial relationship. A missionary impact that insisted upon transplantation of European models remained fleeting, superficial and ill-conceived. In the islands of Cape Verde and Sao Thome, the Portuguese built prototypes of Lisbon and established churches and cathedrals that also formed the pastors for interior ministry. In the Gold Coast of the Atlantic Ocean and at Kilwa in the Indian Ocean, they built their first forts, but the only serious evangelization was among the *mestizo* children of the traders. The incursion into the Kingdoms of Benin and Warri soon failed as the Portuguese found more pepper in India. The enduring presence only occurred in the Kongo-Soyo kingdoms until the eighteenth century. Here they priested some indigenes, especially the children of Portuguese traders and gentlemen and some of the servants of white priests, but the force of the ministry weakened with the changing pattern of trade, internal politics and the disbanding of the Jesuits.

Celebrated cases, such as the conversion of the *Monomotapa* of Mashonaland, central Africa, soon faded in disasters, while the Iberian presence in *Estado da India* or East African coast was riddled with competition against Indians and Arabs. The thirteen ethnic groups of Madagascar warred relentlessly against the Portuguese while the Arabs of Oman re-conquered the northern sector of the eastern coast. Finally, other European countries challenged them for a share of the lucrative trade, which then turned primarily into slave trading. Iberian hegemony collapsed; broken statues in certain parts of Africa betrayed the missionary exploits of yesteryears. In the Gold Coast, a syncretistic religion that uses crosses and candles is aptly named *Nana Antoni*, perhaps in faded memory of St Anthony. By the end of the eighteenth century, twenty-one forts dotted the coast of West Africa; some had chaplains and many did not. These were poorly paid in compromising trade goods. The Dutch and Danish experiments that employed indigenous chaplains equally failed. The fleeting encounter with Christian presence in South Saharan Africa after the debacle on the Maghrib collapsed as the gospel bearers concentrated on enslaving prospective converts.

III. RESILIENT VISION: ABOLITIONISM AND EVANGELICAL REVIVAL

In the twilight of the eighteenth century, two forces combined to regenerate the evangelization of south Saharan Africa: abolitionism and evangelical revival. Spiritual awakenings occurred in many nations from the mid-eighteenth century into the nineteenth century. Its register included an emphasis on the Bible, the cross-event, conversion experience and a pro-active expression of one's faith. Their connection with abolitionism was through the social activist component of evangelicalism that proposed to stop slave trade by involving the chiefs who controlled the supply side. Through the establishment of legitimate trade, a new administrative structure secured, with agreements and the use of Christianity as a civilizing agent, an enabling environment. This was established for combating slave traders. A network of philanthropists and religious groups prosecuted the abolitionist agitation across the Atlantic Ocean. As Jehu Hanciles argues, the crucial dimension in the story is the role of African Americans, including liberated slaves, Africans in diaspora such as Cuguano and Equiano (who wrote vividly about their experiences), and entrepreneurs such as Paul Cuffee, who spent his resources in creating a commercial enterprise between Africa, Britain and America. Motives varied: religion; politics; commerce; rational humanism; and local exigencies.

In England, the Committee of the Black Poor complained about the increasing social and financial problem caused by the number of poor liberated slaves. In America, an educated African American elite became concerned over the welfare of the race and drew up plans for equipping the young with education and skills for survival. Meanwhile, those slaves who took the dangerous option to desert their masters and fight on behalf of the British forces in the War of Revolution complained about their excruciating conditions. They had perceived the revolutionary war as an opportunity for their liberation; absorbed the liberal constitutional ideology and struggled against odds in Nova Scotia and the West Indies to create a space for the practice of their ideals. Anglican patriots had emigrated out of America with their racism intact. Indeed, the next century would witness many rebellions in the West Indies over liberation from slavery. The liberated slaves also created a link between abolitionism and mission by weaving the intriguing link between de Tocqueville's liberal philosophy and Henry Alline's New Life Evangelicalism; between Enlightenment ideas and Christianity. They shared the same ideals of individual enterprise, personal responsibility, equality before the law, and freedom to practice one's religion, as the Republicans against whom they fought.

As Jehu Hanciles shows, when the British philanthropists chose Sierra Leone as a haven for liberated slaves in 1787, the experiment nearly foundered because of the attacks from local chiefs and the lack of adequate provisions for the new settlers. At this point, the Nova Scotians and West Indian maroons were dispatched to Sierra Leone. From their own perspective, they went out on mission to Sierra Leone in 1792, before any British missionary society was founded and with a clear vision to build a new society under the mandate of the gospel, and one that avoided the indigenous chiefs who had been compromised through the slave trade. Indeed, they advocated a separation of church and state so as to de-link the missionary enterprise of redeeming Africa through religion from the patronage of the Governors of trading companies. They set the cultural tone of industry and religion that nurtured thousands of recaptives in Sierra Leone between 1807 and 1864. These freed slaves became agents of missionary enterprise throughout the West Coast. The liberated slaves who returned to Yoruba land served variously as educators, interpreters, counselors to indigenous communities, negotiators with the new change agents, preachers, traders and leaders of public opinion in many West African communities. Adjai Crowther, who was made a bishop in 1864, signified their achievement. Furthermore, the Colonization Society recruited enough African Americans to found Liberia in 1822 and from this period until 1920s, African Americans were a significant factor in the missionary enterprise in Africa. Specifically, their Methodist and Baptist spirituality created a form of appropriation of the gospel that endured.

But other crucial factors determined the patterns of Christian presence in nineteenth century Africa. The resurgence of the missionary enterprise enlarged in the scale of number of missionary bodies, individuals, theologies, motives and vocations, and modes of funding and training. In spite of wide acceptance by denominations, the significance was its popular appeal as all classes of society in various countries voluntarily sustained the enterprise. By mid-century, the faith movements encouraged individuals to foray into mission fields without institutional support. Many women used the opportunity. Biblical roots and the general optimism of the century set the tone, perhaps to the chagrin of Western Europeans who had started missions in the eighteenth century before England and America became engaged. Education, translation of the Scriptures into indigenous languages and charitable institutions such as medical/health care delivery and artisan workshops domesticated the message and equally changed the character of Christian presence. These bred loyalists.

Evangelicalism accomplished certain functions in the resurgence: it reconciled the developed consciousness of individual responsibility to the Christian faith; by developing a close fellowship of believers, it served as antidote to atomistic individualism; and its distinction of nominal/formal Christians from real Christianity yielded a corps of committed personnel that could be mobilized and deployed into mission. Through its network, an organization emerged that could recruit, train, fund and network with global centers. Logistics, access to indigenous people and organization changed the face of Christianity. The bands of evangelicals of various hues were able to extend the campaign for a life of holiness from the boundaries of the individual to family and society; radical discipleship and personal decision meant responding to a call to save the heathens. As America warmed to foreign missions, it brought enormous energy, optimism and vigor and human resources. It was felt that the development of technology and the strength of North Atlantic powers created a viable environment for missions; that there was civil and religious liberty at home and that popery was diminishing. Other racial theories, such as chosen people, covenant, burden, responsibility, civilization, manifest destiny, and other Rudyard Kipling ideas, came later and linked missions to the imperial idea. It is important to understand the development of these ideas as well as their impact on the character of Christianity in Africa. Emphasis changed through time and each phase compelled different rationalizations.

The Roman Catholics revamped their organization and fund raising strategies for missions such that the rivalry with Protestants influenced the pace and direction of the spread of the gospel. However, these changes coincided with new geopolitical factors. Competing forms of European nationalism changed the character of the contact with Africa from informal commercial relations into formal colonial hegemony by mid-nineteenth century. The Berlin Conference of 1884/5 partitioned Africa and insisted on formal occupation. It introduced a new spirit that overawed indigenous institutions and sought to transplant European institutions and cultures. Collusion with the civilizing project diminished the spiritual vigor of missionary presence and turned it into cultural and power encounters. This explains the predominant strategy of enclavement in the missionary presence in southern Africa. Holy Ghost Fathers, at Bagamoyo, off the coast of Zanzibar, turned their plantation into a lucrative exploitation of young people. The white settler communities in East Africa established a tight control of ministry that spurned the cultural genius of the people. Quite typical was the change in the attitude towards the Bombay Africans, who had been repatriated from Bombay where they had acquired education and whose resources sustained the CMS activities in Mombasa as the mission moved further inland. Their enormous contributions were spurned in a welter of hostile antagonism. The Catholic missionary presence in the Congo colluded with the brutality of Leopold, until the international outcry of 1908 forced him to sell the colony to Belgium. The abusive Portuguese presence in Angola, Mozambique, Guinea Bissau and Cape Verde Islands would later elicit anti-clerical and Marxist response after the forced decolonization.

Indeed, the dominant aspect of the story became the forms of African Christian initiatives, hidden scripts and resistance to the system of control that sought to make the agent legible. In one place after another, indigenous prophetic figures inspired a charismatic response to the gospel and through their efforts Christianity grew. "Native" agency became the instrument of growth. Some Africans gave voice to the indigenous feeling against Western cultural iconoclasm and control of decision-making in the colonial churches. Using the promise in the Psalms that Ethiopia shall raise its hands to God, "Ethiopianism" became a movement of cultural and religious protest. As a form of cultural appreciation, it indulged in social and historical excavation, a recovery and recontextualization of black traditions of emancipation hidden from consciousness of black people by colonial hegemony. In its religious guise, it breathed with hope that Africans would bear the burden to evangelize and build an autonomous church devoid of denominations and shirk European control of the church. They wove a network of educated Africans across West Africa to evangelize, inculturate, and create African Christianity. Typical of their ideology was *Ethiopia Unbound* by the Gold Coast lawyer, Casely Hayford and *The Return of the Exiles* by Wilmot Blyden of Liberia. Mojola Agbebi and others changed their English names, wore African clothes and decided to exit from the colonial religious establishment by founding African churches without foreign aid. Products of missionary enclaves in southern and central Africa did the same.

In southern Africa, the movement gained strength by its alliance with the American African Methodist Episcopal Church and its black ideology. Its leaders used the ideology to reintegrate their dispersed communities. Meanwhile, a strong charismatic religious force emerged. As racism divided whites and blacks in the Pentecostal impulse that came from Zion City, Indiana, the latter claimed the Zion and Apostolic rubrics and integrated symbols from indigenous religions to reformat the polity, liturgy and ethics of Western Christianity. Through mine workers, the movement percolated through the region. Between 1913 and 1990, the number of African Indigenous Churches in South Africa grew from 30 to more than 6,000. By the late 1920s, and in the midst of the second wave of the influenza that came with the First World War, visions and dreams and prayer led some to tap the pneumatic resources of the gospel, emphasize healing and use of African symbolism, musical instruments and leadership. The space for women enlarged as it did with the Montanists of the early years. African Indigenous/ Initiated Churches (AICs), differently referred to as *Zionists* in southern Africa, *Aladura* in West Africa and *Roho* in East Africa, changed the face of Christianity in the twentieth century in Africa. Graham Duncan and Ogbu Kalu image the varied forms of revivalism that characterized the period as patterns of indigenous appropriation of the gospel message. But specifically, the AICs are paid closer attention by Afe Adogame and Lizio Jafta, because these churches constitute an important African contribution to world Christianity.

However, a number of AICs separated from the classical forms and mutated into the genres that had tenuous roots with the original impulse; for instance, in

Nigeria, the Zionist type, Cherubim and Seraphim, split into 51 groups between 1925 and 1975. Other genres emerged such as the *vitalistic* (who in the quest for miraculous power resort to occult resources as in the Sixth and Seventh Book of Moses), and *nativistic* healing homes that clothe indigenous religion with a veneer of Christian symbolism. The fastest growing groups among them are the *messianic* forms in which the leader claims to be one or the other of the Trinity. These have shifted from the centrality of the Bible. Sabbatharian forms emerged that did not confess that Jesus is Lord. Some have incautiously romanticized the AICs because they wish to be inclusive and non-judgmental. This is a dilemma that church history must face and a call must be made. H.W. Turner, who pioneered this field, pointed to the need for a typology, however difficult, imprecise or lacking in political correctness. An eye to typology aids analysis as the movement has widened beyond the pale of Christianity. Some *revivalist* groups are nationalistic apologists who feel that Africa knew and worshipped God; they repackage indigenous religion with Christian format such as statements of belief, Christian architecture and the resonance between the Bible stories and African religions. One group calls itself, *Godianism*, another, *Orunmila* and yet another, *Afrikania*.

The story of Christianity in Africa has always been linked to the Muslim factor. Islam benefited from colonialism and expanded south of the Sahara, not just because of jihads that led to state formations but because Europe shifted from an idea that Islam was a form of superstition to the acceptance that since it acknowledged one God, it was superior to African religions. Bosworth Smith provided the arsenal that combined evolutionary theory with observations in India to argue that it was a religion suited for primitive races; that a religion that prohibited the use of alcohol was best for the 'natives'. For other political reasons enshrined in the Indirect Rule strategy, the official policy protected Islam that used improved modes of communication to trade and spread. The battle with Christian "Soudan" parties merely modified protectionist structures to "one, one emirate". The power of Islam has continued to challenge Christianity even when the state adopts a secular ideology because Islam perceives the state as an instrument for promoting religion. Thus, Moslems grab the center of power in every state. Akintunde Akinade explores these challenges.

The significant aspects of the nineteenth century are that—as missionaries sowed the seed of the gospel—Africans appropriated it from a primal, charismatic worldview and read the translated Scriptures from that hermeneutic. Indigenous agency subverted control through voice and exit; recovered the pneumatic resources of the Gospel and challenged missionary Christianity to be fully biblical. This set the stage for the decolonization process that followed the world wars. New forces such as the implosion of the state challenged the heritage of African Christianity; the collapse of the dictatorial states and attendant poverty probed the tensile strength of the church's stewardship. Inexplicably, charismatic and Pentecostal spirituality resurfaced to provide the energy for growth and sustainability in the midst of untoward circumstances.

IV. NEW DIMENSIONS IN AFRICAN CHRISTIANITY: POWER, POVERTY AND PRAYER

Ogbu Kalu examines the vast changes that occurred in African Christianity between the world wars and that catalyzed decolonization. Between the First World War and the emergence of political independence, several denominations sought to consolidate their enterprises just as many religious entrepreneurs hatched various "Christianities" out of a vibrant religious culture. The two world wars and economic depression created so much disquiet that the pace of revivalism and religious innovation increased. Wade Harris, for instance, trekked across Liberia, Ivory Coast to the Gold Coast, preaching and healing. His ministry benefited the mainline churches and inspired charismatic movements. In the Congo, Simon Kimbangu prophesied that the global disorder signaled that God was changing the baton from whites to blacks. His imprisonment did not deter the growth of his movement. In the 1930s the Balokole Movement spread from Rwanda through the Congo into Uganda, Kenya, Tanganyika and into the Sudan. It urged repentance, holiness ethics and a closer relationship to Jesus.

Examples could be multiplied to show that, just as the wars increased African confidence and shifted the vision of cultural nationalists to the quest for political independence, so were the efforts of missionaries to consolidate denominationalism confronted by intensified, subversive, indigenous initiatives. Missionary response to nationalism was informed by a number of factors—including individual predilection, the negative racial image of Africans, some liberal support, and regional variations as those in the settler communities—and responded with fright and built bulwarks with apartheid laws. As the wind of change gusted more brutally, it became clear that the missions had weak roots: few indigenous clergy; a dependency ideology; undeveloped theology; poor infrastructure; and above all, little confidence in their votaries. From the 1950s, the Roman Catholics led in the hurried attempt to train indigenous priests. Missions conceived opportunities to waltz with nationalists because the educated elites were products of various missions and their control of power could aid their denominations in the virulent rivalry for turf. This strategy implicated Christianity in the politics of Independence.

Matters went awry when the elite grabbed the politics of modernization, mobilized the states into dictatorial one-party structures, castigated missionaries for under-developing Africa, promoted neo-Marxist rejection of dependency syndrome, and seized the instruments of missionary propaganda such as schools, hospitals and social welfare agencies. J.W. Hofmeyr analyses the impact of the implosion of the state that challenged the churches. But the failure of the states produced the rash of military coups and regimes, abuse of Human Rights and economic collapse. Poverty ravaged many African countries. Militarization of the society intensified inter-ethnic conflicts and civil wars. The religion of displaced people in refugee camps is a key aspect of contemporary African Christianity. Natural disasters such as drought in the Horn of Africa worsened matters. A part of the problem could be traced to weak leadership; a part to external forces that used the continent as fodder in the Cold War; patronized dictators exploited the mineral resources and manipulated huge debts that have burdened and crippled many nations permanently. Meanwhile, the structure of the countries changed dramatically, as each country became more pluralistic in comparison to the beginning of the century. In many countries, Islamic rulers dominated and Christianity fought for space in the public square. A good example of the new dispensation is the Christian Association of Nigeria, which was formed in 1975 and brought many forms of embattled Christianity together to explore new models of presence that could serve as balm of Gilead in the untoward circumstances. As civil society was decimated, Christianity remained as the survivor. This explains why, at the end of the Cold War and the renaissance of Western interest in democratic structure, Christian leaders were chosen in one country after another to serve as presidents of consultative assemblies that sought to renew hope and banish the pessimism that imaged African problems as incurable.

A number of factors explain the survival of Christianity: the first, as Sam Maluleke shows, is that the development of African Christian theologies from the mid 1970s enabled a critique of inherited traditions and theologies. In southern Africa, the emphasis shifted from cultural theologizing to black consciousness; this sustained a black revolution against apartheid in South Africa, Namibia and Zimbabwe. The second is the rise of youthful charismatism and Pentecostalism. Kwaben Asamoah-Gydau provides a readable historical understanding of this subject matter, which has attracted a wild number and versions of sociological analyses. One commentator observed that in one country after another, young puritans emerged as if from the wormwoods in urban settings from 1970 onwards. With a message of repentance and holiness ethics, secondary school and university students transformed dowdy organizations such as Scripture Union and Students Christian Movement into emotionally expressive charismatic movements. Mainline churches struck back with disciplinary rebuttals that forced them out into organizations that changed the face of Christianity. The classic Pentecostal and Holiness groups that had entered Africa between 1906 and the 1940s suddenly came alive during the 1970s, benefiting from the youthful revivals. Women featured prominently in these organizations and churches were compelled to create a space for charismatism or otherwise lose their members to new-fangled Pentecostalism.

This form of Christianity has changed shape in every decade, absorbing American prosperity preaching in the 1980s and reverting to holiness and intercessory traditions in the 1990s. Pentecostal-charismatic influence is generating rapid growth in Africa. Reasons include the cultural "fit", because they bring the resources of the Gospel as answers to questions raised within the primal worldviews. Healing and deliverance feature prominently. As an instrumentalist response, they provide coping mechanisms in the midst of economic collapse. The religious dimension is the inexplicable power of the Holy Spirit in Africa that has set the missionary message to work. The movement has flowed from urban centers into rural Africa.

Nyambura Njoroge and Philomena Mwaura explore a third feature of the times, namely, the rise of Christian feminist theology challenging the churches to become less patriarchal. Through many publications and programs, churches are compelled to ordain women and increase their participation in decision-making processes. Two challenges stare visibly, whether the churches will mobilize their resources and use the new opportunities to combat poverty in pluralistic environments and what the resurgence of Christianity in Africa could contribute to world Christianity. A fourth feature has two prongs: the explosion of African Christianity in the Western World; as well as the emergence of charlatans in the religious landscape. Afe Adogame has done much research on the African churches that are proliferating in Europe. The largest Pentecostal Church in Kiev, Russia was founded by Sunday Adelaja. In America, the Nigerian-based Redeemed Christian Church of God and the Ghanaian-based Church of the Pentecost are highly visible. African churches have woven linkages with both western and southern Asia. Quite interesting is the social relevance of charismatic religiosity: many people boldly use biblical names for their businesses, and political leaders declare themselves to be born again. Charismatic and evangelical bodies are founding crèches, Bible schools and universities and regaining a Christian hold on the family through education. Beyond quantitative growth there is much evidence of the deepening of the Gospel in the lives of people who would have been lost to secularism. Contemporary Africa looks like a replay of early Christianity in the Maghrib.

Notes

1. Barrett, D.B., Kurian, G.T. & Johnson, T.M. (eds), *World Christian Encyclopedia: A Comparative Survey of Churches and Religions in the Modern World* (New York: Oxford University Press, 2001), 25.

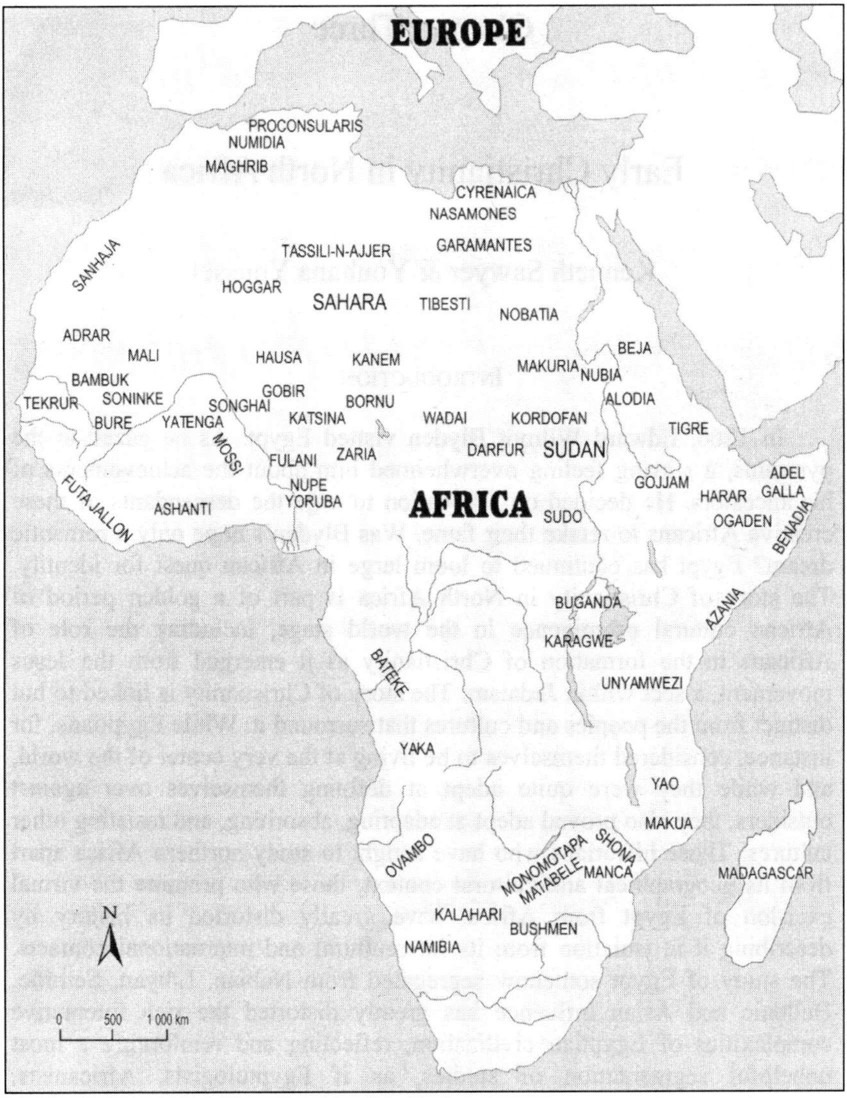

Map 1: The Early Africa

Chapter Three

Early Christianity in North Africa

Kenneth Sawyer & Youhana Youssef

INTRODUCTION

In 1866, Edward Wilmot Blyden visited Egypt. As he gazed at the pyramids, he was by the achievements of his ancestors. He decided on a vocation to urge the descendants of these creative Africans to retake their fame. Was Blyden's hope only a romantic dream? Egypt has continued to loom large in African quest for identity. The story of Christianity in North Africa is part of a golden period of African cultural prominence in the world stage, including the role of Africans in the formation of Christianity as it emerged from the Jesus movement, a sect within Judaism. The story of Christianity is linked to but distinct from the peoples and cultures that surround it. While Egyptians, for instance, considered themselves to be living at the very center of the world, and while they were quite adept at defining themselves over against outsiders, they also proved adept at adapting, absorbing, and resisting other cultures. Those historians who have sought to study northern Africa apart from its geographical and cultural context, especially those who promote the virtual excision of Egypt from Africa, have greatly distorted its history by describing it in isolation from its intercultural and international contacts. The study of Egypt somehow segregated from Nubian, Libyan, Semitic, Hellenic and Asian influence has greatly distorted the rich interactive complexities of Egyptian civilization, reflecting and reinforcing a most unhelpful segmentation of studies, as if Egyptologists, Africanists, Classicists and Semiticists were incapable of a shared subject or a common perspective. A simple test remains useful: look at the map to answer whether Egypt or any part of northern Africa could be recognized as part of Africa. Once this question is answered responsibly, then the distinctiveness and internal dynamics of its cultures and histories can be more readily recognized against a broader African and Mediterranean backdrop. The history of the Maghrib *is* African history. The current controversies regarding various forms of Afrocentrism have helped challenge its undue separation from broader African and Mediterranean themes, and have prompted review and revision of interpretative categories rooted in nineteenth century prejudices.[1] Many Westerners find it difficult to believe that the early church fathers were Africans. It is easier for some to regard Augustine as an Italian! The central task remains to be sufficiently attentive to the particularities of Maghrib cultures without abstracting the region from its context. This chapter is itself a contribution offered to this ongoing discussion.

The rhythms and particularities of Nile culture are well known: a thin ribbon of fertile land unencumbered by forest or animal predators; the stability of protective deserts to the east and west, and forbidding river cataracts to the south. With regular flooding, and the introduction of effective irrigation techniques, Egypt became the breadbasket to the ancient world through migration, trade, and conquest. The allures of Egypt led to a series of interventions by regional and "world" powers, each seeking to secure the wealth and products of Nilotic culture and agriculture. For example, in the Third Intermediate Period (1069-664BC), Egypt was ruled by Libyans, Assyrians, Kushites and Nubians. Likewise, 664-332BC were years of struggle against Persian control in successive periods of independence and subjugation, yet in these years Egypt extended military and commercial presence well beyond historic borders, throughout the Mediterranean world, including armed interventions into Judah, and as far east as the Euphrates River. Throughout these centuries, military action and trade brought the world to Egypt. Most importantly for the subject of this chapter, colonies of Greeks and of Jews are found in Egypt from these years forward, as evidenced in the works of Herodotus. From the sixth century BC, Jews were found in the south of Egypt in service to Persian interests, and by the time of Alexander's triumphs in Egypt in the last third of the fourth century BC, Jews were living along the Nile, with growing settlements subsequent in Lower Egypt. While the stories of Joseph, Moses, and the Exodus substantially predate the focus of this chapter, the Jewish presence in Egypt is crucial to discussions of the history of Christianity in Egypt, since the identity of Egyptian Christianity would be formed in engagement with the fullness of Egyptian culture.

The conquests of Alexander of Macedon clearly began a new and important phase in Egyptian history, especially in cultural relations. Alexander's complete mastery of Egypt was shown by his welcome there—he was hailed as liberator of Egypt from Persian domination, and was named Pharaoh in November of 332BC. Alexander set in place governance structures characteristically attentive to local cultural traditions, while privileging Greek traditions like the gymnasium and the athletic games. The Greeks neither suppressed nor encouraged traditional Egyptian religious and cultural forms, thus co-opting opposition without provoking a reactive rejection. While some Egyptians sought to maintain a clear distance from Greek forms, others found the lure of Hellenism irresistible. Hellenism thus facilitated a hybridity among Egyptians, Greeks, and Jews, especially in the increasingly cosmopolitan cities of the lower Nile. With the death of Alexander, his general Ptolemy established control of Egypt, and gave the name to the ruling dynasty that reigned until its end with the death of Cleopatra VII. Three hundred years of Ptolemaic Egypt saw a slow but clear decline toward the status of Roman client state, with Rome blending its interests with the pliant Ptolemies against the Syrian Seleucids. Crucial signs of this process are shown in Rome forbidding Antiochus III to advance into Egypt in 205BC, or the justly famous scene of 168BC, described by Polybius, when Gaius Popillius Laenas presented to the invading Antiochus IV a decree of the Roman Senate instructing him to abandon his Egypt campaign and release his prisoner (Ptolemy VI). When Antiochus IV delayed answering, the Roman legate drew a circle around the Seluecid king, telling him to answer before stepping out of the circle.

The ability of the Romans to intervene effectively in Egypt marked the lengths to which they would go to protect their grain interests. During the second and first centuries BC, Roman political and commercial presence increased dramatically in Egypt, with Egypt developing its share in the broader Greco-Roman cultural and trade world under the protection of Roman arms. Roman intervention in the dynastic disputes of the Ptolemies, whether by Sulla, or Pompey, or Gabinius, anticipated a time of direct Roman rule. The end of the House of Ptolemy was tied to civil war in both Egypt and in Rome. Ptolemy Auletes' death in 51BC brought two of his children to reign: daughter Cleopatra VII and son Ptolemy XII. Julius Caesar's alliance with Cleopatra brought a temporary peace to Egypt, and took Cleopatra to Rome in 46BC. The death of Caesar sent Cleopatra back to Egypt and into alliance with Antony. After a dozen years of intrigue, Antony and Cleopatra were defeated by Octavian at the Battle of Actium in 31BC, with their suicides following in 30BC. Thus began under Octavian Augustus centuries of direct Roman rule in Egypt. Though the Egyptian traditions would continue, seeking to accommodate and incorporate new realities and rulers by listing and depicting the new Roman rulers as Pharaoh in various temples, the Roman reign showed a casual disregard for the claims of Egyptian traditions.[2]

These matters are significant for this chapter for several reasons: Rome came in power to rule Egypt with a different spirit and intent than the earlier Greeks. The Egyptian engagement with Hellenism did not end with the last Ptolemy, but rather continued through the next centuries as an essential component of Egyptian cultural and religious life, now joined with the new realities as a Roman province. The blending of traditional Egyptian, Greek, Jewish, and Roman culture became a characteristic of Egyptian urban culture, especially in Alexandria and its cultural orbit, with each now contesting distinct privileges under a Roman regime uninterested in political accommodation or cultural assimilation. The Romans imposed a set of governance codes with severe biases against the native Egyptians, with lesser but still quite onerous burdens for Greeks and Jews. Rome conducted official business in Latin and Greek, excluding the Egyptian Demotic. The Romans were interested in Egypt only insofar as preventing a break in the grain supply or in pre-empting political intrigue.

Though some emperors (Domitian, Trajan, and others) showed interest in traditional Egypt, even importing Egyptian religious iconography and practice to Rome and elsewhere in the empire, the overall pattern showed the Romans to be preoccupied by challenges on other borders and other regions, and thus often inattentive masters who were content with the often brutal exploitation of Egypt and its peoples. Rome considered Egypt a province best suited for the placement of legions and the raising of tax revenues.

After Rome, Alexandria was the great second city of the Empire, and under Rome, Egypt was sufficiently secure as to be strategically marginal among the provinces of Rome, while the steady decline of agricultural productivity under Roman management rendered Egypt increasingly marginal economically and sociologically. The severe Roman military response to the Jewish rebellions of the 60s, AD, and again from 112 to 117AD, were but steps toward the temporary eclipse of Egyptian Judaism. The oppressive burdens of Roman taxation prompted revolt by some and disengagement by many in Egypt, while the slow atrophy of traditional Egyptian religion was shown through displacement by a variety of challengers, especially Christianity, leading eventually to the expression of Christian identity in the formation of a national Church that blended monastic with episcopal aspects, rural with urban cohorts, and overall compliance with a strong narrative of faithful and costly dissent.

I. CHRISTIAN ORIGINS IN EGYPT

Current debates regarding the origins of Christianity in Egypt have several foci: the references to Egypt and the Cyrene in the New Testament; the absence of accepted archeological and textual evidence prior to the later second century; the complex identity of Jewish Christianity in the first and second centuries; the place of literacy in the formation of Christian identity in Egypt; the nature of "orthodoxy" and "heresy" in the early churches of Egypt; and the relative importance of the gnostic traditions in explaining the diversity of voices in early Egyptian Christianity.

While Egypt, Egyptians, and other Africans are mentioned in the New Testament, specific details of the introduction of Christianity into Egypt remain a textured interweaving of mysteries and myths often more compelling for believers than historians. While respectful of the place of honor given to later narratives and gospels purporting to tell of first-century conversions and miracles in Egypt, we must recognize a sizable evidentiary gap between the New Testament documents and the time of Alexandria's Bishop Demetrius and teacher Pantaenus towards the end of the second century AD. The various second century documents purporting to tell of first century events remain valuable reflections of later Christian interests, and they do not prevent abiding with several reasonable conjectures, given the connections of Egypt with the broader Hellenistic and Roman world, the documented pattern of evangelism within diasporic Judaism, the range of Biblical and extra Biblical references, the significance of the Biblical literary expression in the formation of Christian identity, and the subsequent appearance of Christian communities throughout Egypt.

1. Biblical Texts

Among those listed in Acts 2.10 are those from "Egypt and the parts of Libya belonging to Cyrene," though no names are mentioned and no details are given. The flow of faithful Jews throughout the diaspora provides one likely route of diffusion of information regarding the work of John the Baptist, the life and work of Jesus, and the events from Passover to Pentecost. Given the prevalent use of Greek within the Jewish communities of Egypt, especially Alexandria, some consider likely a rapid spread of the news from Palestine. Acts 18.24 refers to "a Jew named Apollos, a native of Alexandria ... instructed in the Way of the Lord...." Though later texts speak of Apollos having received his teaching in his native land, commentators note it remains unclear when and what forms of the Gospel were brought to Egypt. If Apollos taught in Ephesus and Corinth what he had learned in Alexandria, then Apollos had learned of Jesus, but knew only of the baptism associated with John. Some view Apollos as indicative of the diversity of early Christianity, possibly even in Egypt itself. If Apollos was presenting accurately the Christianity he knew in Egypt, then we must note the significance of differences shown in the continuing conversations with Aquila and Priscilla (Acts 18), and Paul's rebaptisms of some who had been taught by Apollos (Acts 19). Beyond the Book of Acts, some have cited 1 Peter 5.13 as referring to a Egyptian Babylon near contemporary Cairo, linking Peter with Mark to an Egyptian location, but this reading does not enjoy scholarly acceptance.

The Gospel of Matthew tells of the flight into Egypt (2.13 ff), with Joseph, Mary and Jesus remaining there until the death of Herod. The significance of this narrative, its use of dreams and angels, and the strong parallels with the infancy of Moses are part of the larger theological purposes of the author. No details are included in this narrative regarding events in Egypt, though in the second and subsequent centuries, a host of non-canonical works sought to provide rich and abundant detail without historical referent or evidence. These apocryphal sources, like the *Arabic Infancy Gospel*, or the *Gospel of Pseudo-Matthew*, purport to tell stories of the passage of the Holy Family through many sites in Egypt, of miracles performed by Jesus and of miraculous responses to Jesus by Egyptians. These apocryphal works are yet without historical foundation.

2. Tradition and Traditions

Beyond the apocryphal stories regarding the Holy Family in Egypt, Christian tradition associates Mark with Egypt. A late second century fragment from Clement refers to Mark as the founder of churches in Egypt, and the fourth century historian Eusebius reports the accepted traditions regarding Mark:[3]

> And they say that this Mark was the first that was sent to Egypt and that he proclaimed the Gospel which he had written, and first established churches in Alexandria.

Other sources repeat this Markan connection, but historians have been unable to move from report to endorsing or discrediting this connection. Scholars agree that Christianity may have appeared in Egypt as early as the middle decades of the first century, but no one can write with confidence of its characteristics or content.[4] Continuing investigation of extra-canonical, tradition, and papyri offer hope of providing greater detail regarding Christianity in the first and early second centuries. Pending other evidence, are the patterns observed in Luke-Acts applicable to Egypt? Assessments of the Book of Acts recognize a distinction between theological and historical components of that work. While the theological mandate of the text claims all the world, whether in "whole world" lists (Acts 2) or in universal mandates (evangelism *into all the world*), the focus of the Book of Acts is oriented to the work of Peter, then of Paul, ever toward Rome and the expected consummation of Paul's journeys there. Given these purposes, the spread of the gospel towards Rome is privileged in Acts, while the spread of the gospel elsewhere, carried by others, is marginal and incidental. As we have seen the response to Apollos, and note the place of those other evangelists mentioned in Acts 11, scholars ask whether the Palestinian pattern of evangelism should be assumed as *the* pattern of Christian implantation and expansion in Egypt, or whether we should assume multiple points of Christian contact with Egypt, along the Red Sea, overland routes, and in the Delta, and multiple forms of Christianity carried by individuals and groups—whether Jewish or Gentile. Some look to Arabian sources of evangelism into Egypt, suggesting Paul's three year desert sojourn was spent in preaching and organizing for evangelism throughout those regions, with possible contact with Egyptians. Others look to the rich matrix of Egyptian Judaism as the best model to explain the movement of the Gospel through Egypt.

II. JUDAISM AND CHRISTIANITY IN EGYPT

By the first century of the Common Era (AD), Alexandria held perhaps as many as a half million in population, with about one-fifth Jews. Egyptian Jews relied on the Greek translation of the Hebrew Scriptures (the Septuagint) and were less directly linked than Palestinian Jews to Jerusalem Temple activities. Hellenic openness to lay-oriented temple culture contrasted with the formal clericalism of traditional Egyptian temple religion, having more in common with the dynamics of diasporic synagogue life. Platonic speculative traditions sometimes mingled with Persian and Egyptian counterparts, and found adherents among Jews and pagans in Egypt. This emergent religious diversity influenced but did not displace the inherited forms of religion, as some continued the traditional Egyptian temple religion, others overtly imitated Greek traditions, some (for example, the Therapeutae) pursued ascetic ways, and yet more developed varieties of syncretic perspectives blending Hermeticism with Hebrew wisdom, ever seeking some adapted combinative rapport between/among worldviews.

The learned Alexandrian Jew Philo (c.20BC-c.50AD) did best what many attempted: the reconciliation of Judaism and Greek philosophy, and the explanation of the Biblical mysteries to the broader world. Some find in Philo aspects of what would later become an Alexandrian Christian interpretive tradition. Scholars attentive to sociological contexts note the downward mobility and general social dislocation of Jews in Egypt under the Romans, contributing to a receptivity to Christianity. The rich diversity of Egyptian Judaism, with its biblical base, its political contests and its openness to speculative philosophical traditions, is compatible with a view of an encounter with and adaptation of the Jesus movement in the first century AD, whether in its literate forms among the cultural elite, in its esoteric forms, or as a movement of popular assent among illiterate Egyptians whose use of the "sacred name" may suggest an oral, rather than textual, proliferation of the Gospel.

1. Gnosticism

These issues are significant because of the continuing discussions regarding the form and content of teaching in the early church. While second and third century authors like Irenaeus taught that true teaching had always *preceded* heresy, this view is unhelpful in assessing the sheer diversity of groups and views found in the early church prior to the emergence of ecclesial authority associated with the bishops of Alexandria. Discerning a line dividing "orthodoxy" from "heresy" is a very difficult task before the last third of the second century, when bishops like Irenaeus and Alexandria's Demetrius spoke on behalf of the apostolic traditions and interpretations.[5] While acknowledging the emergence of this line of "orthodox" ecclesial teaching, we must also recognize the prominence in the second century of other contemporary forms of Egyptian Christianity, especially speculative, ascetic, apocalyptic, and "gnostic" forms, well into the third century. Difficulties abound in assessing the place of the various forms of gnosticism found in Egypt, but several gnostic "schools" or groups attracted followers. Derived from the Greek word "gnosis," and rooted in widely eclectic sources, gnosticism is associated with many religious traditions, is part of the Pauline polemic found in the New Testament canon, but found more broadly in a rich array of non-canonical sources.[6]

While the forms of Christian gnosticism were as varied as its adherents, all were rooted in a central dualism that questioned the goodness of material creation and the redemption of the material realm. This dualism viewed material existence as an unfortunate reality or mistake; that humanity had fallen from a spiritual realm into an existence of bondage to the material realm; that humanity could escape and return to the spiritual realm by receiving a secret, esoteric knowledge; and that the true interpretation of human identity and destiny was hidden from everyone except the gnostics. Most gnostic groups rejected outright the Hebrew scriptures as too earthy, too fleshly, and rejected or radically revised/reinterpreted texts associated with Jesus, eliminating the infancy narratives, the suggestion of bodily suffering or bodily resurrection of Jesus, and the folly of honoring "the body" of flesh, since the flesh was unworthy of redemption. These views are rooted in a series of dualisms between God and the subordinate deity or Demiurge who or by whom the created order came into being; between the good spiritual realm and the evil material realm; and between the spiritual people who have the saving knowledge (gnosis) and all those who either did not or *could not* receive that knowledge. While some gnostic groups are reported to have indulged the flesh in libertine ways, most pursued some form of asceticism. Some groups repudiated marriage and procreation as inappropriate in the realm of the spirit, while the Valentinians held marriage in very high regard.

The opponents of gnosticism like Irenaeus and Hippolytus preserved much of what was known of gnostic groups until recent discoveries of ancient texts. The *Gospel of the Egyptians*, and the *Gospel of the Hebrews*, indicate aspects of gnostic Egyptian Christianity, linked with better known texts like the *Epistle of Barnabas*, with its sharp critique of aspects of Judaism. Current scholars speak of thinkers like Basilides (ca. 120AD) and Valentinus (ca. 150AD) as persons who appropriated and "Christianized" aspects of various gnostic traditions, blending Biblical, esoteric, and individual experience that affirmed the salvific role of Jesus, but as a gnostic redeemer, one who was less the revelation than the *revealer* of knowledge. For gnostic Christians, Paul, the Apostles and Mary were more interesting because Jesus revealed himself to them and revealed to them a secret message, rather than that they constituted a coherent tradition or line of doctrine or succession. The presentation of this cosmic and spiritual redemption rendered history less important than cosmology, as shown in the *Apocryphon of John*, or in the schemes of reincarnation found in Basilides and others.

Discussions of the relationship of gnostic groups within Christianity are among the liveliest in the current academic world, with the debates shifting decade by decade. Some stress the openness of gnostic groups to continuing revelation, others the prominence of apocalyptic perspectives, while others note the prominent roles played by women within the gnostic groups as prophets and teachers and leaders, with the *Gospel of Thomas*, and the *Gospel of Mary* presenting challenges to male apostolic authority. Is this diverse literature evidence of simultaneous strains of Gentile Christianity and Jewish Christianity in Egypt during the second century? With the continuing discussion of the various theological categories of creation and redemption, all note the central mandate to recognize gnostic voices as constituent parts of the early church. The discovery of a collection of Coptic texts, including gnostic materials, at Nag Hammadi in 1945, only reinforced the mandate to incorporate gnostic views in the emerging portrait of Egyptian Christianity.

While these fourth-century gnostic texts tell nothing of first and early second century life, they testify to the continuing competition among gnostic groups and between the gnostics and the orthodox ecclesial church, centered in Alexandria and connected with others throughout Egypt and the emerging Christian world. As the investigation and discussion of the gnostic texts continues, the portrait of Egyptian Christianity has necessarily broadened to include these important gnostic sources, slowly reconstructing a very diverse religious culture in the second-century. Clearly, various forms of Christianity coexisted and competed before and after the formation of distinctions and divisions into "orthodoxy" and "heresy", and may indicate themes that run through the first centuries of Egyptian Christianity. This competition is shown in the denunciations of the Gnostics by Catholic polemicists, and in later gnostic critiques of the ecclesiastical Catholic leadership in Alexandria. For example, the gnostic *Apocalypse of Peter* refers to those called "deacons" and "bishops" as debased and deceived "dry canals."[7] While the Great Church drew lines by which gnostic perspectives were to be evaluated and, if need be, excluded, we must continue to listen for gnostic (and later Manichean) voices and debates in the early church, whether among the heretics espousing reincarnation, or among the orthodox teachers in Clement's use of gnosis, or in the capacious cosmology of Origen.

III. THIRD AND FOURTH CENTURY EGYPTIAN CHRISTIANITY

1. Catholic Ecclesial Leadership in Alexandria

By the last decades of the second century, the church in Alexandria was led by those who had joined the line of theological perspective and episcopal leadership seen elsewhere around the Mediterranean; shown in the power of a community of bishops in conversation with one another and with increasing control over their local population. With Demetrius, bishop from 189-231AD and his successors, Alexandrian Christianity took up a prominent role in broadly Catholic Christianity, extending its reach southward along the Nile, and extending its influence in the larger church as a center of learning and leadership.

The significance of these developments must neither be underestimated nor overestimated: under Demetrius and his successors, Egyptian bishops joined the community of bishops; suffered along with the other churches in periods of persecution; began to influence the rest of the church through the appointment of Alexandrians to other bishoprics; followed a line of development away from gnostic and apocalyptic sources and traditions; and developed a distinctive line of biblical and theological interpretation that favored allegory and began with the language of the inherent unity of the Godhead. At the same time, competing voices continually challenged the Alexandrian leadership with its Greek orientation. Until the break with Catholic Christianity, following the fifth-century Council of Chalcedon of 451AD, Alexandria was the complex but formidable power of Catholic Christianity, competing with Rome, then also with Constantinople—in forming theological opinion, fomenting political opposition, and fostering Christian identity throughout the church. The Alexandrian traditions in speculative and Biblical theology took on a decidedly orthodox hue under the leadership of a series of bishops and teachers of the Great Church. The voice and identity of Christianity in Egypt retained ascetic, speculative, and apocalyptic components, adapted to orthodox purposes. As African Christianity took form within the larger Roman world, distinctive voices of leadership and dissent could be heard across the Mahgrib.

2. The Catechetical School and its Prominent Teachers

While those preparing for baptism were certainly trained by the Christian teachers in Alexandria in specific programs of instruction, the "Catechetical School of Alexandria" is a term applied more broadly than referring to one place or one specific curriculum; it is more an interpretive tradition, an idea and a series of influential teachers in positive relation with Catholic Christianity. The series of teachers distinct from the ecclesiastical leadership of the city, indicates a creative distinction between clergy and laity, with interests and perspectives (and constituencies?) overlapping but not identical. Given the likely lengthy preparation for baptism among the Catholic Christians, and with the philosophical traditions of Alexandria and other cosmopolitan cities (as in Justin Martyr's "school" in Rome), a school (or schools) for catechumens and auditors emerged in the second half of the second century. Pantaneus was associated with the teaching tradition from about the year 180AD. Detail of the life of Pantaneus is scant, but intriguing. He was called the "Sicilian Bee" by Clement, trained in Stoic philosophy, had traveled and perhaps preached as far as India, and some believe him a possible author of the apologetic work *Letter to Diognetus*. While he may have left written works, none are known to have survived. He taught in Alexandria until his death in 200AD.

A slightly younger contemporary, Clement (Titus Flavius Clemens Alexandrinus, ca. 150-215AD), taught in Alexandria during the same years, leaving an important group of writings that blends speculative and Biblical traditions. Clement was not ordained until rather late in his life, after he had left Alexandria for Palestine. His writings show a deep engagement with the contemplative life, and a profound commitment to the exposition of the relation between theology and philosophy. He condemned Valentinian and Basilidian forms of gnosticism as exceeding the Biblical warrants, while he retained the term *gnostic*, properly used, to describe the Christian seeking knowledge of God in service of the people of God. For Clement, philosophy necessarily testified to the same truths as revealed theology, since all truth is one. In critiquing pagans and gnostics, Clement proclaimed the gospel as the fulfillment of philosophy and serious speculation, available to all, but known by comparatively few. Like Justin Martyr and Irenaeus, Clement made use of *logos theology* to commend Christ to the broadest cultural audience.

Clement's views stand in sharp contrast with his contemporary based in Carthage, the Latin Christian Tertullian (c.155-c.225AD), who considered philosophy, poetry and literature so well known and quoted by Clement, to be anathema to believers. When Tertullian asked, "What has Athens [philosophy] to do with Jerusalem [theology]?" he answered, "Nothing!"—whereas Clement answered emphatically, "Everything!" While Clement disapproved of excessive speculation or excessive self-denial, he considered all in life was a gift to be used by a freed humanity in praise of a loving God. Clement suggested that high social standing (including riches) was not (necessarily) an impediment to Christian calling. He encouraged the permeation of the Christian movement into the higher echelons of society. As we will note later in this chapter, interesting similarities appear between later Coptic Christianity and the Latin Christianity of Tertullian, Cyprian, and some of the Donatists, linking the types of Christianity in North Africa across the Maghrib.

Clement is best known for three works, each properly considered an admixture of apologetics and letters of instruction for those seeking wisdom: *The Exhortation to the Greeks* (the *Protreptikos*); *The Teacher* (the *Paidagogos*); and the *Miscellanies* (the *Stromateis*). These works are not systematic treatises, they cover a great many topics, seeking above all to provide adequate evidence that literature, philosophy, mythology and poetry all point to the truths revealed in the scriptures. His *Who is the Rich Man to be Saved* sought to teach the pursuit of a moral and contemplative life without a hairshirt. Clement's sifting of the Greco-Roman-Egyptian cultural heritage would be in service of a larger evangelization of the empire, which, for succeeding generations, would know nothing of the sources Clement quoted.

Origen (185-253 AD) came to prominence in Alexandria at a very tender age. His love for the Scriptures, his mastery of the text and his exuberant proclamation of God's loving good news, set him as one of the greatest teachers of the Christian tradition, though not recognized among the "doctors" of the early Church because of some doctrinal shortcomings of his Christology and his decidedly neo-Platonic perspective. Nevertheless, his influence, so great in the century following his death, continues down to our own era. The vastness of his learning renders him a great wonder and an ornament of the Church. It is understood that several personal scribes were provided him just to keep up with his literary production. His father, Leonides, died in the Severan persecution of 203AD and he was supported and promoted by a patroness who recognized his promise.[8] Following Clement's departure, Origen was appointed leader of the "catechetical school" in his native Alexandria at the age of eighteen. He continued to learn from the best teachers of his time, including the neo-Platonist Ammonius Saccas, under whom the great Plotinus (205-270AD) himself would study. Origen also steeped himself in the Hebrew text and its traditions, in service to his apologetics with contemporary Jews. His *Hexapla*, a remarkable accomplishment, gathered and collated the text of the Old Testament in six variants. His *On First Principles*, completed before 220AD, presents a cosmic apologetic, seeking to present to a Platonic world a compatible reading of the Gospel. For Origen, the loving plan of God promises nothing less than the restoration,and redemption of all things (even Satan), even if through the means of a seemingly limitless series of incarnations. Crafting a language to describe the relation of the Son to the Father, Origen makes use of emmanationist images and a hierarchy of Divinity, subordinating the Son to the Father, and the Spirit to the Son.[9]

Origen was dazzled by the rich gift of the Scriptures and was shocked by what he considered crude and crassly material interpretations that demeaned the glory and defamed the character of God. To those portions of the Scripture for which a literal reading would offend an understanding of the character and ways of God, he pressed the literal text toward its various levels of true meanings, appropriate to a Platonic three-fold division of existence into body (the literal/historical meaning), soul (the moral meaning), and spirit. When explaining the spiritual meaning of the Parable of the Good Samaritan, Origen writes:[10]

> ... the man *who went down* is Adam; *Jerusalem* means Paradise; *Jericho*, the world; the *robbers*, the enemy powers; the *Priest* stands for the Law; the *Levite* for the Prophets; the *Samaritan* for Christ. The *wounds* stand for our disobedience; the *beast,* the body of the Lord. The common house, that is the *inn*, which receives all who wish to enter it, is interpreted as the Church. Furthermore, the *two denarii* are understood to mean the Father and the Son; the *innkeeper*, the Head of the Church, to whom the plan of redemption and its means have been entrusted. And concerning that which the Samaritan promises at his return, this was a figure of the Second Coming of the Saviour.

Origen was steeped in the Scriptures, committed to the message of the Gospel entrusted to the Church, and disciplined by a practiced asceticism joined to a skilled philosophical perspective. As he moved from Alexandria to Caesarea, his influence grew throughout the Greek speaking eastern Church. In addition to his commentaries, letters of exhortation, and disputations, Origen wrote apologetic works, including the *Against Celsus* (ca. 248), less a response to the work by Celsus—*The True Doctrine*—of seventy years earlier, than a summary of the struggle between Christianity and the classical traditions, written now by a man of equal intellectual and cultural facility as his earlier opponent, Celsus. Origen's work shows the resources and stature now belonging to Christianity, and the enhanced social standing of Christians in the middle of the third century. No longer the tiny minority voice of the "Greek Apologists" of the second century, addressing the majority Greco-Roman world claiming more than it knew, now Christianity was an increasingly powerful voice contesting control of the empire itself, with much at stake in considering power, resistance, and martyrdom. Though a broadening cultural, social, and theological chasm was opening between the Latin speaking western churches and the Greek speaking churches of the east (including Egypt), "Christianity," in all its various forms, was being attacked in new ways in waves of persecutions during the third century.

3. Martyrs

Neither scholarship nor ignorance protected Christians from persecution for being members of the still officially illegal cult. Origen lost his father in the Severan persecution, Clement also fled Alexandria in those years, and Origen himself perished from injuries suffered under the Valerian persecution. The advance of Christianity within the Roman Empire depended upon the support, or at least the inattention, of local and regional authorities. Peter Brown has written of the "equipoise" of paganism and Christianity in the late second and into the third century, with a defacto toleration of Christianity punctuated by periods of intense and extensive persecution.[11] The nature of persecution within the Roman Empire changed from being sporadic and inter-personal during the first and second centuries, to forming a systematic aspect of state policy, meeting the expectations of the emperors Septimus Severus, Maximin, Decius, Valerian, with a final struggle in the "Great Persecution" under Diocletian. By the middle of the third century, authorities accepted *libellum pacis*, a document by which individuals bought their peace by swearing that they had met the requirements of the law. Many, including Christians, obtained these *libelli* through fraud in an effort to avoid the increasingly demanding imperial cult. Church discipline broke down. In Carthage bishop Cyprian declared that Christians trampled each other to obtain *libelli.* Both Decian and Valerian persecutions confiscated books, buildings, and belongings of Christians, and began a round up of higher clergy, then moved along a broadening line of terror and intimidation against common lay Christians unwilling to bow before the increasingly imperious imperium. The reach of the Severan persecution indicates that by 200AD Christianity had spread throughout Egyptian society, along the Nile, and in each of the four main urban centers, and across the linguistic divide into the Latin speaking western territories. In Egypt, the Coptic Church begins its calendar from the time of these martyrs, recognizing that a true cost of discipleship is measured in suffering.

4. Monasticism

The ascetic impulse ran deep throughout the ancient world. The emergence of monasticism in Egypt must be seen as part of a larger process of identity and spirituality as Christianity gained prominence in the Mediterranean world, so that Egyptian monasticism is connected with Syrian and Asian forms of asceticism, and is also linked with similar forms of resistance and renunciation in other parts of North Africa. Nevertheless, the Egyptian context had its own particular dynamics as ascetic forms of Christianity were reinforced by two opposing processes: social dislocation *and* social advancement. The social crises of the third century, in which the agricultural and economic decline of Egypt was intensified by Roman oppression, encouraged strategies of resistance throughout Egyptian society. Disengagement *from* the world followed disenchantment *with* the world. In the same years, however, some Christians took increasingly prominent positions and cultural advancement throughout Egypt and the Roman world.[12]

The rise of a Christianity less interested in eschatology, more attentive to the opportunities of evangelism and faithfulness with the removal of the stigma of illegality and the threat of persecution, provoked a reaction moved more by the absolute demands of the Gospel than by the prospect of preferment and advancement. It is a measure of the skill of the bishops of Alexandria that they were able to forge alliances within the monastic traditions, many of which were distinctly non-ecclesial or explicitly anti-ecclesial in outlook and organization. It is a measure of the inevitable tension of individual piety and institutional policy that sent thousands into desolate places to seek God. The ascetic impulse reached rich and poor alike, and ranged from elite to popular forms. In spite of its popular social foundation, the stories of the saints of the desert would be unknown had they not been mediated by the ecclesial elite of bishops and teachers in translations and distributed throughout the Christian world.

The story of the unordained, unlettered, unsophisticated Antony (c.251-356AD) came to speak to generations of Egyptian Christians and all those who yearned for holiness. It is important to note that virtually all we know about Antony is told by Athanasius, a bishop centered in the bumptious ecclesial culture of Alexandria and the broader Catholic traditions. His *Life of Antony* reflects on and formed spiritual expectations of the era. Antony was raised in comfort by Christian parents, was left an orphan in his teens, and was unable to spiritualize the message of Matthew 19.21 when he heard it being preached. After attending to the needs of a younger sister, placing her with a group of pious women, he sold his possessions and devoted himself to a life of spiritual disciple and an escalating series of disengagements with society, eventually seeking to live alone in desolate places, pursuing the life of the spirit along the Nile south of Memphis at Pispir, then later near the Red Sea. While his piety was individual and non-ecclesial, many sought him out, and countless others were prompted by the same impulse to seek spiritual truth apart from common towns, family, or Church.

Numbers are impossible to establish, but in Antony's lifetime the model of the holy man or holy woman spread, with women and men forging new arrangements, new communities, new families devoted to new forms of holiness. Antony's eremite (hermit) existence was one pattern of what would become the monastic way. Communal monasticism is associated with Pachomius (c. 290-346AD) called Coenobitic (from *koinos bios*). After his conversion and baptism, Pachomius learned of the ascetic tradition from an older holy man, Palamon, and by 320AD he had begun to organize communities regimented in accordance to his own earlier years in army service. While Antony prized solitude as preparation for the struggle of the soul with the forces of the Devil, Pachomius saw unregulated life as liable to fraud, self-delusion, and dissipation.

The monastic traditions made room for visions, angelic visitations, and a lively apocalyptic expectation. The Pachomian community at Tabenese, in the Thebaid, founded no later than 329AD, provided the pattern for women and men organized (in separate communities) according to his "Rule" or instructions, to seek God and to serve and monitor one another in that search. Small cottage industry and lives were ordered according to the needs of holiness, creating "a city in the desert" of regimented lives, with regular access to priests, the sacraments, and the discipline of the Church.

Many fled from towns to the desert, or lived for a season away from family and friends, or sequestered themselves within family compounds, or gathered in unregistered and unregulated communities, seeking holiness. Families and friends and pilgrims came to see and supply these communities and individuals, and soon the stories of the holy men and holy women circulated in oral, then written form, and pilgrims came from Rome, Spain, Asia Minor, and Syria.[13] Antony and others were be enlisted in the theological disputes of their times, and quickly the monastic communities themselves became powers to reckon with in the many complex theological debates that divided Egyptian Christians. The hermit Macarius (d. ca. 405AD), an imitator of Antony, and the shadowy figure Macarius the Egyptian (c.300-390AD), a disciple of Antony, were forced into exile during periods of theological dispute. By the beginning of the fourth century, monastic groups were under the influence but not the control of bishops.

For example, the schism associated with Melitius, the bishop of Lycopolis, centered on disagreements regarding those who had lapsed during the Diocletian persecution. Bishop Peter of Alexandria faced a rebellion, as Melitius disputed Peter's rulings, and ordained those with whom he agreed. When comparing Pachomian monastic communities with those associated with Melitius, the Melitian communities were run along more hierarchical lines, with less range of freedom for local leadership or members. Similarly, the fifth-century communities associated with Shenoute (d. ca. 450) were strictly run organizations, with vertically integrated leadership and discipline. In light of the mixed group of material found at Nag Hammadi, scholars continue to ponder the probable contacts between gnostic and orthodox monastic communities, and the probable use of some gnostic materials within some orthodox monastic communities.

These main components of Egyptian Christianity formed and reformed over the centuries: leadership under a series of powerful bishops; the broader and broadening influence of the Alexandrian "school" of theology and biblical interpretation; the image of the martyrs; the voluntary martyrdom of those pursuing holiness through monastic spirituality; the remarkable leaders of monastic communities; the ongoing competition between the monastic and episcopal forms of Christianity; and the fractious debates within and among these groups. While the leaders of the Church moved and lived in the Greek world, some bishops, most monastic communities, and nearly all the rural faithful from the third century onward, used Coptic—the language of the people, the language of the countryside, disdained in the corridors of power, but sustained among the powerless. The four dialects of Coptic, Bohairic, Sahidic, Akhmimic, and Fayumic, all enjoyed early translations of the New Testament, and a great wealth of papyri generated in service of the Church. The study of these Coptic papyri continues to re-frame the received portrait of Egyptian Christianity, especially in its monastic forms.

5. From the Council of Nicaea to Chalcedon

The conversion of Constantine brought great changes to the legal and social status of Christians within the Roman Empire, but since Christianity had spread widely throughout Egypt during the third century, the coming of Constantine was less significant for Egyptian Christians than the passing of Diocletian and the end of state-sponsored persecution. Of greater consequence were Constantine's efforts to achieve religious unity in the Empire by direct intervention in local disputes. The doctrinal differences within Christianity prompted Constantine to seek unity through uniformity, and rendered Christian theology a central aspect of imperial policy throughout the empire. Constantine's attempt to resolve the Donatist conflict proved a failure, while his intervention in Egypt provided its own challenges. The First Ecumenical Council was convened at Nicaea in 325 by Constantine to address a cluster of Egyptian controversies. At issue were matters of theology, discipline and authority, and practice. All the components of the Egyptian Church were to be found in these controversies, but all of Christianity had a stake in the outcome of the conflicts. The Council of Nicaea showed new realities for Christianity in the Constantinian world: the empire would be deeply involved in ecclesial affairs, though the doctrinal substance of that involvement could shift with each emperor and his preferences. The significance of the Council of Nicaea is found both in doctrinal formulation and institutional formation, since the unity of the empire was predicated on doctrinal uniformity, bringing together "church" and "state." For our purposes we will note the central role of some of the Alexandrians in debates related to the doctrine, method, and language of the Trinity and Christology and how the response to the debates determined the character of African Christianity.[14]

Arius (c.250-336AD) was a presbyter serving a working class section of Alexandria in the opening decades of the fourth century. He had ties to the schismatic Melitians, and he was an effective preacher quite capable of popularizing his message. His preaching presented a sharply subordinationist Christology, probably reflective of his own training by Lucian of Antioch (d. 312AD). For Arius, Christ was worthy of great honor, but only as the first born of all creation, for "there was when he was not." According to Arius, Christ was, by his nature as a creature (however that nature was defined) distinct from God the Father by essence, status, and being. No later than 320AD, Bishop Alexander of Alexandria condemned the teachings of Arius, and sought to stop Arius from appealing to allies in Palestine and beyond. Efforts to still the controversy failed in local councils and much correspondence, and the Emperor himself intervened by sending his trusted theological advisor Hosius of Cordova. Hosius secured the condemnation of Arius at a local council in 324, and prepared for the broader council at Nicaea in 325, convened and controlled by the Emperor. The argument of the Nicaean Creed, that Jesus is *homoousios*—of the same substance—with the Father, defined basic structure and language of Trinitarian formulations of Christian orthodoxy. The specific wording of this Trinitarian formulation was debated for a half-century and finally secured at the Council of

Constantinople in 381. The Nicaean Creed found its most able and persistent defender in Athanasius of Alexandria (c.296-c.373AD), Alexander's successor after 328AD. No one individual is more closely associated with the advocacy of the Nicene position than Athanasius, though his success was based on his efforts to strengthen links between the Alexandrian Church and the Coptic monastic leaders.

Less known than his older ally, Athanasius, or his own younger students, Didymus the Blind (c.313-398AD) stood in the broadly Origenist tradition, combining a practiced asceticism with a rich knowledge of the Scriptures. While Athanasius was thoroughly immersed in the politics of the day, Didymus was a scholar who shunned the public fights. His defense of Origen would much later bring about his own condemnation at Constantinople in 553AD, but his reputation was secured through his advocacy of Nicene orthodoxy, and his work as teacher to Gregory of Nazianzus, Rufinus, and even Jerome. In addition to his Biblical commentaries, his treatise *On the Holy Spirit* disputed with the "Macedonians", who denied the divinity of the Holy Spirit, consistent with their Arian denial of the divinity of Christ. His treatise *On the Trinity* joined with the powerful essays of the Cappadocians leading up to the triumph and subsequent defense of Nicaean orthodoxy at the Council of Constantinople in 381. Didymus also contributed to the terminology of the Christology debates, in his critique of all those who suggested that Christ's human soul was somehow displaced by the divine *logos*. Didymus wrote against Arians and Manichaeans, but in later generations his arguments were applied to the anti-Arian Apollinarius of Antioch, a defender of traditionally Alexandrian perspectives. It is part of the remarkable character of Athanasius that he was able to be effective in so complex a field of competing interests and perspectives. His alliance with Didymus, his successful interpretation (co-optation?) of Antony, and his efforts to secure the support of the monastic communities, all testify to his abilities in Egypt, apart from his better known efforts among the Latin and Greek Christians beyond Egypt.

The eventual triumph of Nicaean Orthodoxy secured a general formula specifically excluding an Arian reading, but prompted the discussion regarding the relation of divinity and humanity in the person of Christ. As Frances Young writes:[15]

> The problems of Christology were a direct result of the Arian controversy and its outcome at Nicaea. Two different ways of meeting the Arian position produced two different Christological traditions which came into conflict. The tensions between these two types of Christology have left a continuing mark on subsequent church history, for Monophysite and Nestorian churches survive in the Middle East to this day, and in the West, Chalcedon has proved less a solution than the classic definition of a problem which constantly demands further elucidation.

The Alexandrian Church was deeply involved in the politics and theology of the Christology debates, with political/personal grudges blending with theological concerns, as Alexandrians viewed Rome a rival and Constantinople a threat. Doctrinal formulation and character defamation often proved a useful combination. For Alexandrians, several issues rankled. The third canon of the Council of Constantinople (381AD) elevated Constantinople as "second in honor to Rome." This was seen as both an insult and a provocation, with redress most often sought in the defeat of Alexandria's rival cities and their supporters. Thus, in addition to differences in theology, the advancement even of qualified men from other sees, was deemed harmful to Alexandrian interests, and the leadership of the great Church of Alexandria often joined in campaigns to remove or defame challengers.

The leadership of the Church in Alexandria sometimes made use of threats of force and violence. For instance, Patriarch Theophilus fomented the mobs that sacked the pagan temple, the Alexandrian Serapeum, in 391AD, and encouraged pagan priests to flee Alexandria. Monks were encouraged to take pagan temples throughout Egypt, converting them to Christian use.[16] Theophilus also gathered the voices that undermined John Chrysostom (c.347-407AD), and drove him from Constantinople. Similarly, his nephew Cyril managed the campaign against Nestorius, enlisted the support of Shanoute and the monastic communities of Egypt, and ensured that Nestorius was deposed. Cyril led the Alexandrian Church from 412AD until his death in 444AD. An agile theologian and politician, he showed himself as astute in character defamation as in doctrinal formulation. In addition to his alliance with the sometimes violent visionary Shanoute, mobs in Alexandria did his bidding, or acted without his censure, as when in 415 a mob seized Hypatia, the foremost pagan philosopher of the era, and tore her to pieces.

Cyril was successful politically and astute theologically, and he triumphed in forming alliances by which Nestorius was deposed, but the triumph of Alexandria in the Latin and Greek speaking Catholic Church was temporary. Cyril's prominence masked deepening divisions within the Egyptian Church that would destroy Cyril's less agile successor, Dioscurus (Patriarch from 444-454AD), and would lead to a break with the Catholic Church over the Chalcedonian formula. The emergence of a nationalist Coptic Church, distinct from and defensive toward the broader Catholic Church, is a testimony to the distance of the Coptic Egyptian Church from the Greek-oriented Catholic leadership in Alexandria, echoed along the length of the Nile, and across the northern coast of Africa. Though the intention of the Council of Chalcedon was to secure a formula sufficiently encompassing to unite the various factions in the Christology debates, Chalcedon instead resulted in a fragmenting of the Catholic Church into three main traditions: the Monophysite churches of Egypt, Ethiopia, and Syria including the Jacobites; the Nestorian churches centered in Persia; and the Chalcedonian churches associated with Catholicism and Eastern Orthodoxy. Both the Monophysite and Nestorian traditions rejected

Chalcedon, but for opposing Christological reasons. Though some supporters of Chalcedon were found in Alexandria and among a few Pachomian monastic communities, the greater majority of the Egyptian Church could not accept the Chalcedonian Christological formulation, and remained opposed to those of the "Melchite" (imperial) group who accepted Chalcedon and cooperated with Rome or Constantinople. These divisions spread with the Gospel through North African communities. In 457AD rival bishops sought control of Alexandria, one Monophysite, the other Melchite. When imperial soldiers arrested the Monophysite leader, an angry crowd found the unfortunate Melchite, Proterius, and killed him. The death of Proterius signaled a growing crisis in the imposition of imperial command and control in Egypt in the aftermath of Chalcedon. As the Roman governance of the Empire unraveled, and the eastern (Byzantine) governance endured civil war and Persian attacks, North Africans felt the impact of the disintegration of the empire. As in other parts of the empire, the Christian Church remained when the empire faltered, but often with internal divisions. In Egypt the resilient Church was Coptic in character, theology, art, and culture. Like other forms of African Christianity, the Coptic Church found its identity in worship and cultural resilience and resistance, whether under Persian, Byzantine, or Muslim domination. Chalcedon marked a significant break with the broader history of Catholic Christianity, but as the Coptic tradition predates Chalcedon, so Coptic Church history incorporates all that came before it, and shares some characteristics with other components of African Christianity.

6. From Carthage to Cyrene: Christianity in the Roman Province

Much space has been devoted to Egyptian Christianity because less is known about the origins of the Jesus movement as it moved west of Egypt, the Roman Province of Africa. This is as much a problem of sources (artifacts and texts) as of lenses and interpretation. The less the fragments of evidence the less the possibility of reconstructing what happened before the last decades of the second century. The region was rich in agriculture and had been occupied by a variety of power adventurers such as the Punics before the Romans. Thus, many languages and racial groups lived there with the indigenous people whom the Arabs deprecated with the name, Berbers or barbarians. Grain merchants and other ex-service men, who had been granted land in the colony, inhabited the cities such as Carthage. However, there is evidence of Christian presence by the second century because persecutions drew attention to some people who suffered martyrdom in 180AD. The story of Perpetua and Felicitas, whose bravery in facing the lions in 203AD inspired many, indicates that the church was growing in this region among the indigenous population, encompassing lower and upper classes. The narrative of the martyrdom of Perpetua and Felicitas lays emphasis on the continuing work of the Holy Spirit, the role of visions and prophecy, indicating a likely Montanist connection. By the turn of the third century, AD, Tertullian spoke in a mature Latin voice for so young a tradition. His treatises contrasted the stark mandate of the Church with the blandishments of Roman society and culture. His *Apology* contended ably with the historic opponents of Christianity. His *Prescription Against Heretics* drew lines within the Christian community. His *Letter to His Wife* describes a real marriage enlivened by an ascetic ideal. His many treatises against the complacent society of his day sound a note of disdain in favor of the beauty of holiness. By the middle of the third century, the Bishop of Carthage, Cyprian (c.200-258AD), spoke confidently to Rome and the wider ecclesial world on matters ranging from the sacraments to pastoral responses on persecution to the foundations of ecclesiology. Cyprian was but one of hundreds of North African bishops mentioned in various documents; for instance over ninety bishops attended a synod at Carthage in 240AD. Perhaps the Church grew more in the urban than rural areas, as should be expected, especially as the gospel was not translated into indigenous languages and Latin was the prominent language of liturgy and theological debate.

Martyrdom was a source of great strength and firm identity for the North African Church, with Tertullian famously saying, "The blood of the martyrs is the seed of the Church." But with each wave of persecution, an internal debate would start about the fate of those who compromised, whether through partial compliance or occasional conformity. Some called all such people *traditores* who should lose their membership in the Church; others differentiated between those whose who feigned compliance to imperial worship by signing the little book of peace and those who actually handed over books or church property to the officials. A further distinction drew a boundary over church officials and lay people and argued that any bishop or priest who compromised had forfeited the integrity to lead the Church or to offer the sacraments. These were very practical matters to the Christians of the third century. While Tertullian urged rigor in the face of persecution, spoke with disdain of the empire and the Roman control, and joined the sectarian Montanists in the last third of his life, he himself apparently did not die as a martyr. Cyprian crafted a pastoral response to the lapsed, making ways for the lapsed to rejoin the Church, yet he himself died as a martyr in the persecutions of 258AD. The conflict, gathered under the name of "Donatism," continued to express these tensions regarding the nature of the Church and the norms of behavior. Rooted in a disputed episcopal election, the deeper tensions of North African Christianity bloomed in a rancorous division of the Church into the "rigorous" Donatists and the Catholics. Behind the divisions were competing ecclesiologies, biblical hermeneutics, and social doctrines. The Catholics urged an inclusive view of the Church as a mixed assembly, excluding only the unrepentant and scandalous, while the Donatists advanced a vision of the Church as a gathered community of those whose lives reflected a holiness not found in the broader society.[17] The difficulties of the Donatist position were quickly revealed in various schisms and scandals, and the inability to formulate and maintain a standard of purity sufficiently demanding and rigorous, yet attainable within the community of the faithful.

Though Augustine (d. 430AD) was perhaps the greatest gift of African Christianity to the larger church, he is often abstracted from his African context. Born into a home divided between a Christian mother and a pagan father, he was raised to chase after the blandishments of Roman preferment and promotion. His *Confessions*, written in 395AD after his elevation as bishop, tell his story through an overtly theological lens, of his ambition, of his loves, of his sorrows, of his years among the Manichaeans, of his repeated conversions from inferior loves to something much greater than himself or his preferences. Through his later conflicts with the Manichaeans, with the Donatists, with Pelagius and his disciples, and in reflecting on the meanings of the sacking of Rome, Augustine crafted the terms of arguments that would reverberate down to our own time.[18] Augustine was drawn into the Donatist conflict upon his return to Africa from his years in Italy, and he confronted the intolerance of the Donatists with an increasingly intolerant policy of his own. Though pursuing the Donatists in the interests of a more inclusive Church, the contradictions of Augustine's increasingly coercive policies were not lost on the Donatists. Augustine accused the Donatists of a lack of charity in their refusal to join with their Catholic brothers and sisters, but came to employ an uncharitable strategy of enclosure and opposition when the Donatists proved resistant to his invitations.

The remarkable growth of Christianity within the Roman Empire may cloak the tensions between the "normative Christianity" associated with Constantine, and the various competitors to the imperial forms of Christianity favored by the Emperors. The Church in Africa reflected these tensions, even in the period of great prominence of Alexandrian bishops from the last decades of the second century down to Chalcedon in 451AD. Through these prominent Alexandrians, but also through others in the Latin western regions, the southern Nubian areas, and in Ethiopia, the Church struggled to define its identity in relation to and in dissent from the imperial models. The varieties of rigorism extended throughout the Maghrib: asceticism, monasticism, Montanism, Donatism, divided by Christology, ecclesiology, and pneumatology, but united by an uneasiness with power and preferment, suggesting that the faithful may have more pressing callings than to provide comfort to those who rule the kingdoms of this world.

CONCLUSION

Scholars accept a general population figure for Egypt in the year 600AD of approximately three million persons, a decline from the peak of five million under the Romans.[19] The once cosmopolitan and connected larger world of affairs had yielded in Egypt to the rural, the agricultural and the local. Likewise the pagan had yielded to the Christian, with the leader of the Coptic Church in Alexandria in alliance with the Coptic monasteries and Nile communities. Egypt continued to contribute grain to Constantinople, even in the years of the Phocan rebellion, down to a dozen years of disruption by Persian control of Egypt from 617AD until 629AD. Byzantine Heraclius regained control of

Egypt in 629AD, but the costs of disruption and dislocation showed in the privatization of many formerly public civic tasks. As in other portions around the Mediterranean, Church authorities took on tasks once carried out by local governments.

What was happening to the churches in these years? Egypt continued to attract Christian pilgrims, Egyptians continued to travel to other parts of the Christian world, and Alexandria authorized the leadership of the Church of Ethiopia. It is useful to note the transition of governments, included more negotiation than military engagement, with the Persians and the Byzantines concerned more with events in Mesopotamia than the unfolding drama in Arabia under the Prophet and the Caliphate. A conflict between the Coptic Patriarch, Benjamin, and a rival, Cyrus, divided the Church on the eve of the Muslim advance into Egypt. Both factions sought some delay through negotiation with the forces of Amr ibn al-As, the Muslim invader. The eventual Muslim capture of Egypt still raises many questions regarding strategies of resistance. The successful advance of Muslim forces in Palestine and Syria made it seem inevitable that Egypt would be next. After initial successes in 640AD, Muslim advances slowed, but after the death of Heraclius in 641, the leadership of Byzantium fell to a regency government, resulting in confusion in military plans. It is clear that the fall of Egypt to Islam was due neither to complicity nor capitulation, but rather to a complexity of factors involving leadership, exhaustion, and an entirely mistaken hope that Arab control might, like a tide, recede as readily as it had surged into Egypt. Throughout these centuries the Coptic Church has remained, honored by its special service to the Holy Family, rooted in the earliest days of the gospel in Egypt, rightfully proud of its contributions to Church doctrine from Nicaea to Chalcedon, encouraged by the faithfulness of its early martyrs, and steadfast in its witness into our own time, a new age of martyrs.

However, there remain debates about the fate of Christianity in North Africa after the Islamic insurgence. Some have argued that Islam won an easy victory because of its disciplined army comprised of good horsemen, imbued with a muscular religious belief that they were engaged in a victory for Allah. The discipline was maintained even after victory because, in these years before the emergence of Damascus as a command center, the Muslim forces usually quarantined themselves outside the city walls to avoid mixing with infidels and to remain highly mobile. The expansion of Arab Islam, and the range and speed of the conquest of former Christian states was staggering. How best to explain this rapid expansion and conquest? Some explanations focus on the occupied peoples: the oppressive taxation by the Byzantines had created a deep resentment among its client states, and a receptivity to Islam. Similarly, the contests between Persia and Byzantium were at the expense of the Egyptians. Moreover, the effort of Islamic forces was less the engagement of cultures than the expansion of territories. Muslim victories were consolidated by the three options given to captured peoples: to surrender and pay a tribute; to convert to Islam; or face a continued jihadist attack. While the category of *dhimma* evolved over time, the strategies of Christian (and Jewish) survival emerged much faster. Nubia successfully resisted the forces of Islam, thanks to the archers of Dongola, leading to a negotiated treaty, the *Baqt*, which protected Christian Nubia for several centuries.[20]

African resistance was already evident in Carthage, elsewhere among the Donatists, shown in the raids by the Circumcellions on the agricultural merchant elite in urban areas, who exploited the Maghrib as the bread basket of Europe, bred a resistance in Libya, Tunisia and Algeria. It is alleged that Carthage fell easily because an African commander preferred the Arab incursion to the rule by the Byzantine or Romans, while Alexandria held up for three months because a Greek commanded the defense. But Berber nationalism was equally uncomfortable with Roman, Byzantine, or Arab rule. A striking feature of North African Christianity is a prominent strain of hostility toward institutions and imperial governance.[21] The storied prophetess, Cuhna (Damia al-Kahena) Queen of the Aures from the hill country near Tunis, illustrates this point. Regardless of its historical accuracy, African memory gloried in her bravery shown in her victory against an initial Arab attack on Carthage. When the Arabs regrouped, she applied a scorch-earth policy to deny them the wealth of Africa; she lost the war but refused to convert to Islam. As long as the Moslems did not insist on forced conversion, their expeditions could be interpreted as liberation.

These realities challenge the simplistic verdict that Christianity in North Africa sat lightly and was easily overawed because it lacked roots among the indigenous Tuaregs and Kwororaffa; lacking a vernacular Bible; mired in arid doctrinal disputes and consequently, vulnerable. A defense has been canvassed in the introduction to this book. A first step is to establish timelines and distinctive strategies among distinct groups, freed from an uncritical acceptance of special pleadings of Islamic or Christian narratives. One danger is to read later coherence back into the first half-century of the Islamic expansion. Another danger is to read later rationalizations back into the first half-century of Christian resistance. It is also important to note changes in strategies: the Islamic forces did not immediately lash out against Christians. As soon as the Coptic Christians adopted a neutral stance and did not oppose them, the Arabs conciliated by even recalling the Patriarch, Benjamin. Similarly, the strategies useful in conquering territories yielded to strategies of governance. Because Arab conquerors did not have the manpower to govern the large territories, they used bishops as advisers, ambassadors, governors and tax collectors. Naturally less concerned with doctrinal differences among Jacobites, Melchites, Copts, and Nestorians, they pursued pragmatic co-operation, with restrictions against Christian public proselytism, marriage boundaries and other burdens increasing through time, providing increasing incentives to conversion, and increasing costs to resistance.

Contemporary students must resist the temptation to oversimplify the first century of Islam. A concern for periodisation is important because of early Islamic sensitivity to the Prophet's toleration of the "People of the Book" than later Caliphs. The process of migration, Arabization and new trading patterns took time to emerge. By the end of the first Muslim century, Arabs were found throughout northern Africa, and new caravan trade routes were challenging the ancient river commerce system along the Nile. Internal squabbles among the Moslems had consolidated different regimes and lineages that governed different parts of the new Islamic Empire. Thus, the Ummayyad who consolidated their rule over North Africa by 661AD were more tolerant towards Christians than the Abbassids who overthrew the Ummayyad in 750AD. Similarly, the Fatimids, who were themselves North Africans and not Arab Moslems, showed greater toleration than their successor the Mamlukes from the 990s. Besides, the Bible was translated into a number of Coptic dialects and the rural Copts deployed Christianity as a cultural signifier. However, there is no gainsaying the gradual decline of Christian presence in the Maghrib.

If one were to combine the data from Rodney Stark and Phillip Jenkins, a certain statistical image would read as follows:[22]

Year	**% of Christians in Empire**	**% of Christians in Egypt**
239	1.4	0
274	4.2	2.4
278	5.0	10.5
280	5.4	13.5
313	16.2	18.0
315	14.4	18.0

Clearly, Africa was an important center of early Christianity and remained so much longer than the four-volume study on the planting of Christianity in Africa by C.P. Groves would lead us to believe.[23] By 500AD, argues Jenkins, there were about 8 million Christians in North Africa, this declined to 5 million by 1000, 2.5 million by 1200 and 1.5 million by 1500. The argument is that Christianity grew at certain points in time under Islamic rule and that the decline accelerated during and after the Crusades. Nonetheless, Christian presence down the Nile continued to be important till the fifteenth century in Nubia and much later in Ethiopia. This is the subject of the next chapter.

Notes

1. As shown by the lengthy bibliographies by and in response to Martin BERNAL, *Black Athena* (New Brunswick, New Jersey: Rutgers University Press, 1987). See also Stephen HOWE, *Afrocentrism: Mythical Pasts and Imagined Homes* (New York: Verso, 1998).
2. See Robert K. RITTER, "Egypt under Roman rule: the legacy of Ancient Egypt," in Carl F. PETRY (ed), *The Cambridge History of Egypt* (vol. I, New York: Cambridge University Press, 1998), 1-15.

3. Eusebius, *Church History* II.16.1.
4. See Birger A. PEARSON & James E. GOEHRING (eds), *The Roots of Egyptian Christianity* (Philadelphia: Fortress Press, 1986).
5. See W. BAUER, *Orthodoxy and Heresy in Earliest Christianity* (R. KRAFT & G. KRODEL eds, Philadelphia: Fortress Press, 1971 [1934]). See also H.E.W. TURNER, *The Pattern of Christian Truth: A Study in the Relations Between Orthodoxy & Heresy in the Early Church* (London: Mowbray, 1954).
6. See K. KING, *What is Gnosticism?* (Cambridge, Massachusetts: Belknap Press of Harvard University, 2003). See also B. PEARSON, *Gnosticism, Judaism, and Egyptian Christianity* (Minneapolis: Fortress, 1990).
7. See C.W. GRIGGS, *Early Egyptian Christianity from its Origins to 451 CE* (New York: E.J. Brill, 1990), ch.4.
8. See Eusebius. *Ecclesiastical History*, Book VI.
9. See Joseph Wilson TRIGG, *Origen* (Atlanta: John Knox Press, 1983).
10. Origen, *Homily* 34.
11. Peter BROWN, *The Making of Late Antiquity* (Cambridge, Massachusetts: Harvard University Press, 1978).
12. See J. GOEHRING, *Ascetics, Society, and the Desert: Studies in Early Egyptian Monasticism* (Harrisburg, Pennsylvania: Trinity Press International, 1999).
13. See Benedicta WARD, *The Sayings of the Desert Fathers* (London: A.R. Mowbray: Kalamazoo, Michigan: Cistercian Publications, 1975). See also P. MILLER, *Biography in Late Antiquity: A Quest for the Holy Man* (Berkeley: University of California Press, 1983).
14. See Frances YOUNG, *From Nicaea to Chalcedon* (Philadelphia: Fortress Press, 1983).
15. YOUNG, *From Nicaea to Chalcedon*, p. 178.
16. RITNER, "Egypt under Roman rule", p. 29.
17. See W.H.C. FREND, *Martyrdom and Persecution in the Early Church: a Study of a Conflict from the Maccabees to Donatus* (Oxford: Blackwell, 1965). See also Peter BROWN, *Augustine of Hippo* (Berkeley: University of California Press, 1967), 212-225.
18. See BROWN, *Augustine of Hippo*.
19. Walter E. KAEGI, "Egypt on the eve of the Muslim conquest," in Carl F. PETRY (ed.), *The Cambridge History of Egypt* (vol. I, New York: Cambridge University Press, 1998) 34-40.
20. See Roland WERNER, William ANDERSON & Andrew WHEELER, *Day of Devastation, Day of Contentment: The History of the Sudanese Church across 2000 Years* (Nairobi: Paulines Publications Africa, 2000) 40-45.
21. See W.H.C. FREND, *The Donatist Church* (Oxford: Clarendon Press, 1952), 102-105. See also Maureen A. TILLEY, *The Bible in Christian North Africa: The Donatist World* (Minneapolis: Fortress, 1997).
22. Rodney STARK, *The Rise of Christianity* (Princeton: Princeton University Press, 1996); Phillip JENKINS, *The Next Christendom* (New York: Oxford University Press, 2000).
23. Charles P. GROVES. *The Planting of Christianity in Africa* (4 vols, London: Lutterworth Press, 1948-1958).

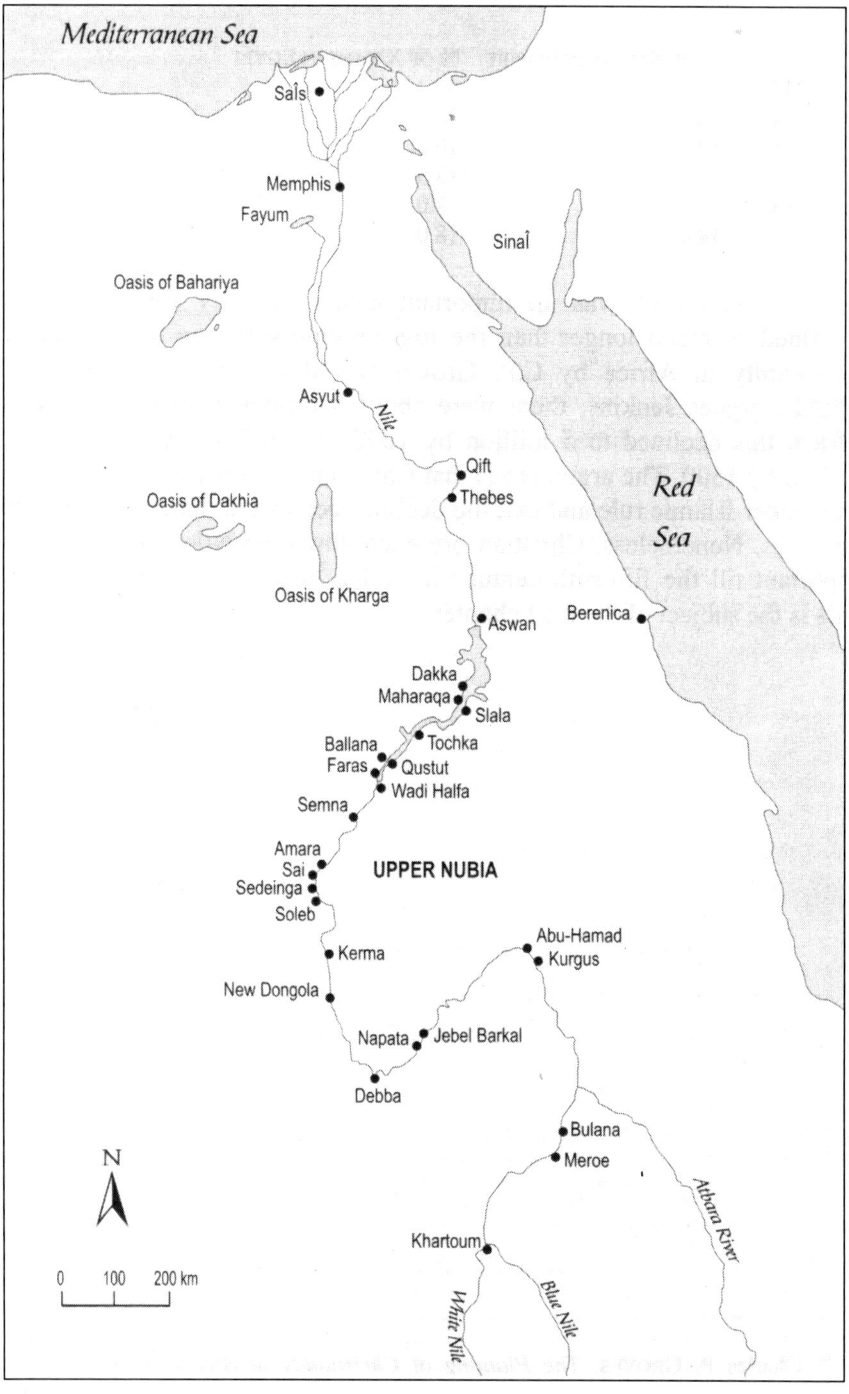

Map 2: Early Christianity in Egypt

Chapter Four

Christianity in Sudan and Ethiopia

William B. Anderson & Ogbu U. Kalu

"Ah, land of rustling wings, beyond the rivers of Kush."

(Isaiah 18:1)

Sudan is a biblical land. It is not at the center, like the Holy Land—or even a major player like Egypt, Syria and Babylon. It is not part of the central geography: the fertile crescent or the Mediterranean world. Yet it is not outside like Japan or the Americas. Kush is found in our Bibles 48 times. It begins early: Kush is one of the sons of Ham.[1]

Kush is a clear *geographical* place, its northern boundary very distinct. Ezekiel talks of the whole of Egypt "from Migdol (in the north) to Syene (i.e. Aswan), *as far as the border of Kush*."[2] For at Aswan, the fertile Nile valley, which south of the Delta is 16 miles wide, narrows drastically, as the rocky hills crowd to the edge of the river, forming the Nile's first cataract. It is the heart of the Sahara desert, with the world's longest river winding through it. Kush is all the land south of the first cataract—Aswan. Kush is also racial. At Aswan, the Black or Brown, the Negroid people began. Kush meant the *black race.* The Nile was the most accessible road to reach that race. Beginning with Egypt's first dynasty, Egypt sought gold and slaves there. Kushites were noted as warriors. And finally, Egypt's 25th dynasty was Kushite: Napata in Nubia conquered and ruled Egypt, and appeared in the prophecies of Isaiah.[3] For that reason, the Greek translation of the Old Testament used "Ethiopia" for "Kush", and "Ethiopian" for "Kushite". *Ethiopian* in Greek meant literally a black person. Almost every modern reader assumes it is the ancient version of the modern nation of Ethiopia. In the Bible an Ethiopian is a black person—or from Nubia.

The arenas of the Bible were: the *holy land;* the *fertile crescent;* and the *Mediterranean world.* Kush belongs to the *outside arenas.* The Old Testament projected a break-out from the arenas of Israel and the ancient world. The Ideal

King envisioned by Psalm 72 "will rule ... to the ends of the earth." "Distant shores" as well as "Sheba and Seba" will be the King's domain. Jesus took this up. He told his disciples that they were his witnesses "in Jerusalem, all Judea and Samaria, and *to the ends of the earth.*" The *ends of the earth were crucial*: they proved the truth of the Good News itself, that the Great King had truly come. The Kingdom was for everyone, anyone who simply believes. So Acts 10 tells how Peter was led to preach to a Roman centurion, and that story directs the church throughout the remainder of the book of Acts.[4] Yet, as a matter of fact, the first Gentile baptized appeared before Acts 10, in Acts 8:26-40, the story of Philip unfolding the Good News to a black man—and when he believed, Philip baptized him.[5] He was the first believer from outside the Bible world—and its arenas. He was an official for a queen-mother, from Meroe, along the Nile in northern Sudan. Here Sudan moved out of the edges into the center of the biblical story: the Gospel to "the ends of the earth", Act One. The story of Cornelius the centurion was really Act Two of the same biblical drama. And then it continued—even until now.

I. "KUSH WILL SUBMIT HERSELF TO GOD"

Many people naturally assume that the conversion and baptism of the Treasurer of Candace (Acts 8:26 ff) was the beginning of the history of the Nubian Church. History rarely goes in such neat straight lines. The Treasurer was an official of the Meroitic Empire. Its center was at Meroe, south of where the Atbara River joins the Nile. It is between the fifth and sixth cataracts, just north of Khartoum. This empire lasted a thousand years, but it dissolved by 300AD, and disappeared. We do not yet know how to decipher its language. There are no Christian remains from that period.

The land immediately south of Aswan—Lower Nubia[6]—between the first and second cataract, went through great changes as well. From the time of Moses to the time of baby Jesus, Lower Nubia became empty of people. They only began to return in the first century AD, when the *saqia*[7] was introduced. This was very important. Agricultural land was scarce in Lower Nubia, since it was a rough, rocky country. Strips of land were not very large, and were often high above the river. The *saqia* made it possible to water fields more than 25 feet above the Nile. As the Meroitic Empire broke up, Nuba peoples from western Sudan moved in. Eventually, they formed three kingdoms, stretching from Aswan to south of modern-day Khartoum. These were called *Nuba*,[8] *Maqurra*,[9] and *Alwa*:[10] all independent of each other, all independent of Egypt and the Byzantine Empire. An animal also had revolutionized transportation: the introduction of the camel, just before the Christian era. This made travel in the desert much easier. As a result, most travel did not follow the Nile, but cut through the desert to miss the great bend in the Nile between cataract 1 and Abu Hamid (between cataract 4 and 5).

1. Beginnings of Nubian Christianity

At first, there was a seeping of Christianity into Nubia. Mark is credited with founding the Church of Alexandria. The Christian message went out to villages in the Delta, and spread to Upper Egypt. Its wide growth caused consternation to the Roman rulers, and in 250AD, and then again in 297, great persecutions fell on Christians in Egypt—as well as throughout the Roman Empire. Probably some of the persecuted found refuge in the quiet, less populated parts of Nuba. Others probably came: some hermits looked for God in the desert, and perhaps some of them wandered into Nuba. There is no record of them. However, the people changed. In the early fifth century, the Christian Byzantine (Roman) rulers of Egypt decided to stop worship of the goddess Isis[11] in the temple of Philae, on a little island near Aswan. The Nubans were furious. Isis was a favorite goddess in Nuba. They often marched with her image through the country blessing the crops. They violently demanded the temple remain, and even forced the Byzantines to make a "Treaty of Philae" which gave Nubans the right to process with the Isis image at any time.

One hundred years later, about 540AD, Byzantine Emperor Justinian came to Egypt. He wanted to strengthen Christianity, and to extend Christianity to peoples on and beyond the Empire's borders. He ordered Philae converted to a Christian cathedral. This time Isis had no defenders. Very soon after, missionaries came to the land. Their message was readily accepted by king and people.

There also was as early as mid-fifth century, a Christian church in the capital of Nuba, Faras. It was in the humbler part of town. This probably helped in the rather dramatic turning of the kingdom to Christianity. Probably early hermits, and monks, or maybe traders settled in Faras. They had their worship, and quietly spread the faith to some Nubans.

2. The Mission to Nubia and Conversion of the Kingdom

Another story unfolded as well. In the sixth century, missionaries were sent to Nuba, Maqurra and Alwa, and those kingdoms all accepted the Christian faith.

The first with a vision for Nubia[12] was Theodore, Patriarch of Alexandria. He was in exile in Constantinople. While on his death-bed, he called the Deacon Julian, and commissioned him to be a missionary to Nubia. The Patriarch and Julian were both Egyptians. They were in Constantinople in exile because they were Monophysites, opposed to the Orthodox definition of who Jesus Christ was. One hundred years before, in 451, a church council met at Chalcedon. It declared that Jesus should be understood as having two natures—that of man and of God—joined together perfectly in one person. Other opinions were condemned. There was an extensive movement which disliked this definition. They were called Monophysites (believing that Christ had only one nature) or Jacobites (named for the Syrian bishop who was an outstanding leader of the movement). Most Egyptians (called Copts) were Monophysites. They opposed anything coming from Constantinople, the imperial capital. And their favorite

Bishop, Cyril of Alexandria, had taught that Jesus had two natures, that of God and man, but these two were joined by the Incarnation. So he said, "after the Incarnation, there is one nature of God-incarnate." "One nature of God-incarnate" became the watch-word for Egypt. Justinian revived the Byzantine Empire greatly, and did all he could to promote and defend the Orthodox Christian faith. But, Justinian married Theodora, an Egyptian Copt, friend of Julian and Patriarch Theodore.

Julian spoke of his calling, of his commissioning by the dying Patriarch, and of the spiritual need of Nubia, lost in idolatry. She equipped Julian to go to Nubia, but Justinian, hearing about it, sent an orthodox mission. He ordered the governor of Thebaid (Upper—i.e. southern Egypt) to prepare stores and camels for the mission. Theodora wrote to the same governor, ordering him to see to it that the mission of Julian reach Nubia first. If not, she threatened, she would have his head cut off. The governor complied. He delayed Justinian's Orthodox mission, saying the gifts and camels were not yet collected. When Julian arrived, the governor arranged for them to "steal" the camels and baggage, and went with them on the mission to Nubia. The governor had some more explaining to do to the Orthodox mission, but at least he saved his head.

Julian went to the king of Nuba, and found him very receptive to Christianity. The new religion was embraced, and the king of Nuba was baptized with his household and nobility. Then, in that hot country, Julian found a cool cave where there was water. There he instructed and baptized people in great numbers. He also carefully instructed the Nuba king not to accept the mission from the king (the Orthodox mission). The Christian message spread quickly. When Julian left Nuba in 545, after just over two years' ministry, he turned the work over to Bishop Theodore. Theodore was the first Bishop of the cathedral, made by converting the temple of Isis in Philae. He was a tireless missionary, and appointed a number of priests to lead in Nuba's conversion. The missionary usually started by coming to a new town or village, and planting a cross there. Then he started instruction, and baptism. As in Egypt before, and as at Philae, they often converted idol temples into churches. When the people accepted the new message, the pictures and hieroglyphic texts were plastered over, and idols destroyed. Christian pictures were painted: Christ, the angels, the apostles, etc. The temple of Dendur was one of the first Nubian temples so changed. An inscription which was left there reads:[13]

> By the will of God and the command of the King, Eirpanome... zealous in the word of God, and by our receiving the cross from the hand of Theodore, bishop of Philae, that I, Abraham, the humblest priest, should place the cross on the day of the founding of this church.

That church was founded in January 559, 16 years after Julian arrived. The king Eirpanome may have been the king converted through Julian's mission—or he may have been his son or grandson. But whoever he was, the work, started by

Julian and other missionaries from Egypt and directed by Bishop Theodore, prospered.

3. The Mission of Longinus

There seems to have been some concern about the new church and mission. Another Jacobite Patriarch of Alexandria, Theodosius, on the day of his death in 566, commissioned a fellow Jacobite Patriarch, Paul of Antioch, to consecrate a new missionary for Nuba—Longinus. They believed they had an opportunity: the emperor Justinian died the year before, in 565. They hoped his successor, Justin II, would be more liberal. He turned out to be much less tolerant. Longinus had been representing the Jacobites to the Emperor in Constantinople, so was well-known. Justin immediately threw him in prison. He could not easily escape either, for Longinus was bald—and every time he tried to leave the capital, he was recognized and arrested. Finally in 569 or 570, he disguised himself with a wig, and slipped past security during a heavy storm. He reached Nuba, and set up the organization of the church, and established the worship. Liturgy was in Greek—as it was for all the Eastern churches of the Empire. The Nuba king testified that Longinus helped them truly understand and follow their new Christian faith.

4. Spread to Maqurra and Alwa

As usual, each Nubian state had problems with its neighbors. One of the first instructions Julian gave the king of Nuba was: "Do not accept the mission from the king." So when Justinian's mission, the *Melkite*[14] mission, came to Nuba, the king rejected them. The mission soon learned that the Nubian kingdom just to the south—Maqurra—would welcome them. Evidently, they took up the opportunity. Maqurra was a much larger kingdom, centered on Dongola, reaching to the Atbara river or beyond.

The southernmost Nubian kingdom, Alwa, learned of the ministries of Longinus—and asked for him to come. The Melkite mission tried to extend from Maqurra—but Alwa refused. Alwa and Nuba were friends: Maqurra was a rival to both. That posed a problem for Longinus. He prepared to go, but Maqurra—much the larger kingdom—prepared to block him, and even warned him that they were endangering their lives if they even tried. Longinus and the Nuba took the long way around, going far east through the country of the Beja. Seventeen camels died, and the party barely made it. Longinus reached Soba, the capital, near present-day Khartoum. The missionary party was welcomed as heroes. Longinus found Soba a great city. It included among its people some who were already Christians, although their understanding of Christianity was quite faulty. They believed that Christ, because he was the Spirit of God, never suffered pain on the cross, or anywhere. Julian helped turn them to the Apostolic faith—that Jesus indeed "suffered under Pontius Pilate, was crucified, died...." He instructed the king of Alwa, and that Nubian kingdom also turned to the Christian faith. Soon Longinus called in two more bishops from Egypt to help with the newly-converted people.

5. What Did the Conversion of the Nubian Kingdoms Accomplish?

The change looks outwardly to have been superficial. It started with the king, and then to the people in a very short time. How much did it touch the common man's life? We cannot be entirely sure. But it certainly had a dramatic effect on the faith and hope of the people. Already, we have noted that when Justinian turned the Temple of Isis into a cathedral around 540—before the official conversion of Nubia—there was no complaint from the people. Already among the people there was an extraordinary readiness to change, to leave idolatry. In another dramatic way, the people changed: in their attitudes toward death. Before the sixth century, Nubians buried people with wealth and goods: food, water, clothing and weapons. They often mummified the bodies. After Julian and Longinus, they buried their dead without anything: no food, water or weapons, and wrapped only in a cloth. No more mummies, either. Each Christian was buried in an East-West position, on the back, with the head on the western side. This was because Christ would return to summons believers from the eastern sky, and would raise up each person to greet Him face-to-face.

Even the kings and royal families made the same change. For 2,500 years in the past, the major public work of a king was building his personal tomb and monuments. For the great kings it was a pyramid: Nubia has more pyramids that Egypt! After Julian and Longinus no tombs were built. No pyramids either. Kings were buried wrapped in a cloth, without clothing, weapons, food or drink for the after-life. No slaves or others were killed to accompany them. The king was no longer divine. Jesus was the last King who was both God and man. Now decisions and treaties were no longer done by the divine genius of the god-king, but by the king under God's leadership and protection. Man had taken a step forward towards making his own decisions. The king was no longer the religion of the realm. Many of the old kings' temples were remote and difficult to access. The Christian faith made God available to all, and a church was built in all the towns and villages of Nubia.[15]

Other great changes came. Of the four written ancient languages of that corner of the world—Coptic, Ge'ez (Old Ethiopic), Nubian and Meroitic—three of them were written in languages created by or influenced by Christianity. Only the Meroitic language was an exception: it used an old Egyptian Demotic script, and it has never been deciphered. A new spirit was born. Reading and writing in Greek, Coptic and later "Old Nubian" became more common. Christians often visited Philae, the first Nubian cathedral. Several left graffiti, saying in effect "I came here". One graffiti has these scrawled words: "The Cross has won, it always wins!"[16] The Christian revolution was a fact, a sweeping one indeed.

II. CHRISTIANITY AND THE STATE

Nubia had extended periods as a victim in its early history. Egypt, from the first dynasty, went to it for gold and slaves. It mined beautiful stone for its graystone monuments. Black slaves were usually household servants of the rich and great, or more often the soldiers of the Pharaoh. Then the Egyptian Empire faded.

Egypt broke into warring factions—Nubia was enticed into that confusion, and took over for a hundred years. The 25th dynasty was a Nubian dynasty. Nubia (with its capital then at Napata) became a regional super-power, even threatening Palestine for a short time. That is why Isaiah 18-20 talks about Kush (Ethiopia), but that Kush was actually Nubia-Egypt. Nubia soon retreated to Napata.

The center was moved further south to Meroe, and a strong long-lasting empire of a thousand years was built there. The Meroitic Empire traded African elephants—used as war-elephants—with the Ptolemaic Greek rulers of Egypt just before the Christian era. The Romans mined some gold, but gave up mining and occupying parts of Lower Nubia. Instead it made Nubia the guardian of the southern edge of the empire, at the first cataract. Soon after Nubia's conversion to Christianity, it changed its role: it became a recognized power for many centuries.

1. Egypt in Trouble

Christian Egypt had a special relationship with Nubia. The missionaries first sent there—Julian, Longinus and Bishop Theodore—all were Egyptians; all were Jacobites; all had trouble with the Empire. Longinus developed the structure of the Nubian church. It was ruled by bishops, and bishops came only from the monasteries of Egypt. They were chosen and consecrated only by the Patriarch of Alexandria. These Patriarchs were constantly under the suspicion of the Empire, even exiled from Egypt. The three Nubian kingdoms had no restrictions. They were independent.

Then the Byzantine Empire began to rock. In the year 618, the Sassanids of Persia took much of Syria-Palestine and the whole of Egypt. They may have reached a little into Nuba. Sassanids believed in the God of Fire: so they torched a large number of churches in Egypt, and the most holy cathedral, the Church of the Holy Sepulcher in Jerusalem. After a few years, the Byzantines recovered and drove out the Persians. But it was a much-weakened, much-shaken Byzantine Empire.

In 638 the Arab conquest of Egypt started. The Byzantine forces had little stomach for the fight. Many Coptic Christians saw Arabs as possible liberators, and some Copts gave the invaders crucial help. In a surprisingly short time of 3 years, Cairo and Alexandria fell. The Arabs offered Christians conversion to Islam, or payment of *jizya,* the special head tax on all "people of the book". *Jizya* was at first no more oppressive than the huge Byzantine taxes. Greeks and Nubians living in conquered Egypt were given the option: "submit to Islam, or leave Egypt." Coptic Christians believed the Arabs, like the Sassanids, would not remain. That was a serious misperception. The Arabs, under Islam, were on a *jihad,* a holy obligation to conquer the world and bring it to Allah. That *jihad* lasted a hundred years, from 632 to 732. These warriors of God found nothing which could stop them, until they reached the center of France 100 years later; nothing, except Nubia.

2. Invasion of Nubia, and the *Baqt*

Nubia appeared to be three small, weak states, nothing like the great armies of the Byzantines they had defeated in Damascus, Jerusalem and Alexandria. In 642 an army crossed the desert to the capital of Maqurra, Dongola. Unlike Egypt, Dongola fought fiercely, and the invaders withdrew. Ten years later, a more determined effort was made. This time, parts of Dongola were destroyed, but the Maqurrans defended the inner walls of the city. They were so accurate and deadly with the bow they were dubbed "pupil-smiters". They were reputed to hit anyone with an arrow in the eye!

With the battle stalemated, the Arabs drew up an agreement with the Nubians. It was called the *Baqt*—from the Greek word "pakton". Like a pact, it was a non-aggression and trade agreement. Egypt wanted yearly from Nubia 300 slaves,[17] plus many African goods: frank-incense; ivory; and performing baboons. Egypt paid for this with wheat, lentils, horses, cloth and other Egyptian goods. The place for the exchange was *al Qasr,* five miles south of Aswan. Both parties agreed to not attack the other. One important regulation was that Arabs were not allowed to buy land or settle in Nubia, but could travel for purposes of trade. Nubians could similarly travel through Muslim territory, but not settle there.

3. The Great New Christian Champion

The impact of all this was profound: Nubia emerged as a great power, a mighty Christian Empire reaching into the heart of Africa. It had inflicted the only serious set-back to the Islamic *jihad,* until the defeat at Tours, France, much later in 732. Nubia declared itself the champion of all Christians, Jacobite and Melkite, in the new Islamic empire. It was defender particularly of the Egyptian Church, and several times it forcefully intervened. The Arab invasion was probably a shock for Christian Nubia as well. Islam appeared as a highly dangerous opponent and rival. Soon after the *Baqt* treaty, at about 700AD, Nuba and Maqurra united peacefully, with Dongola the capital city.

The new united kingdom made its first mark on Egypt under King Kyriakos (c.747-797) The Arab government in Egypt fell into chaos for several years. Around 745, the Sultan demanded a huge payment from the Coptic Patriarch, Michael I, to meet his debts. The Patriarch could not raise the money, so he was imprisoned. Kyriakos invaded Egypt, picking up Coptic support along the way. The Sultan would not budge; so Kyriakos besieged Cairo. The Sultan finally gave in, freeing the Patriarch. The incident made an indelible impression on the Egyptian Church. They had a powerful friend in the South. One glowing Egyptian said of Kyriakos, that he was "the Great King upon whom the crown had come down from heaven."[18]

4. Unification—the New Constantine

At a certain stage, close to 700AD, Nuba and Maqurra formed a united kingdom. The move appears to have been peaceful. The king lived in Dongola, the capital. The much less-populated Nuba, between 1st and 2nd cataracts were under a sub-ruler, given the Byzantine title of Eparch, and headquartered at Faras. The king, who led the unification, was Merkurios, whom enthusiastic outsiders dubbed "the New Constantine". Although Dongola (Maqurra) had become Christian through Melkite missionaries, and the smaller Nuba was Jacobite (Monophysite), there appeared to be no quarrel. The theological differences meant very little to Nubians when their political rivalry was over-ruled by the threat of a great danger from warring Islam.

Traditions die hard. The Meroitic official (or "Ethiopian eunuch") of Acts 8 was said to be "the treasurer of the Candace, queen of the Ethiopians". (Acts 8:27—NRSV) The title was Kandaka. It was that of the Queen-Mother of Meroe.[19] Meroe passed on the kingship through the son of the king's sister, and often the Kandaka ruled as regent while her son matured. Often the Kandaka had some authority, and always much honor. Although the Meroitic Empire expired by 300AD, the tradition of the Kandaka remained alive. Nubian inheritance was through the son of the sister of the dead king—usually.

III. PIETY AND POWER: CHRISTIANITY AND ISLAM

Zacharias was the son of Merkurios, the "new Constantine". He showed the combination of Christian piety along with kingly power which was the hallmark of the Nubian church. The church in Nubia was closely associated with the Patriarch of Alexandria, and the whole Coptic Church. It depended totally on the Patriarch for bishops, and without bishops the Church could really not function. For a long time priests and monks were sent from Egypt. The Egyptian church functioned independently of the government. This was because it was under Islam, but was just as true when it resisted the Byzantine power and the imposition of Melkites. Not so for the Nubian church. The king, from the first acceptance of the missionary message to the end, had a key, important church role. Zacharias resigned early from the throne to give himself to the "Word of God and the salvation of his soul."[20] Zacharias was also concerned with the salvation of the kingdom, for he was the king-maker, even while in the monastery, for four successive kings. The first three are easy to forget. The fourth was a king of stature—Kyriakos. His invasion of Egypt, and the rescue of the Patriarch from prison, marked him as an outstanding king, and raised the reputation of Nubia in Coptic Egypt.

1. George I Visits Baghdad

Almost a hundred years after Kyriakos, the Arab empire fell into more than a decade of chaos, particularly in Egypt. Then, in 833, Ibrahim al Mutasim took over and stabilized power, and demanded from Nubia 14 back years of *Baqt* to be paid, at once. The Patriarch sent a letter accompanying the Caliph's demands. He advised the Nubian king to pay. The king, Zacharias II, met with all his counselors, discussing what response to make. The amount demanded was clearly impossible. One set of advice was to make a deal with the Caliph.

The other was: "Go to war". George, Zacharias' bright young son pushed for war. Zacharias II mulled over the case, then made a bold decision. He decided to send his young son, George—Kirki in Nubian—to Baghdad to confer with the Caliph. George was only 20 years old. Zacharias first had him crowned, to send him as the crown prince, the highest possible emissary. So, an incredible event unfolded.

George set off with a large caravan heading north into Egypt. George was seated on a horse, holding in his hand a scepter and a golden cross. In front of him was a retainer, carrying a large golden cross. This solemn and large procession containing many servants and officers went through Upper Egypt to Cairo. This was astonishing to the Christian population of Egypt, which at that time was quite big. Christian processions were banned: the display of the cross was offensive to Muslims. But this was the powerful crowned king of the Christian kingdom of Nubia! In Cairo he first met with the Patriarch, and then with the Sultan. Honors were showered on him: he received a daily allowance of 30 dinar, and was given many camels to carry his gifts to the Caliph. His passage through Syria was awe-inspiring: the great black Christian king ruling to the ends of the earth. Before he reached Baghdad, he contacted Patriarch Dionysios, the senior Jacobite churchman from Antioch, asking if he could visit. The Patriarch was delighted at the news. Dionysios could not meet with George in Antioch, but promised to meet with him in Baghdad.

When he finally reached Baghdad, the visiting king hit a snag. Accusations were made that George was not a genuine king. In fact, his father Zacharia II had a real problem of legitimacy, but not George. Nevertheless, it took a full six months to confirm George's status. In the meantime, the Patriarch of Antioch came, and the two met. George, although a young man of between 20 and 21 years, impressed the Patriarch with his knowledge and devotion to the Christian faith. He could even distinguish the Monophysite doctrine of Christ's one nature, from the Orthodox Chalcedonians.

When confirmation of George's status reached Baghdad, he met with the Sultan.

(1) The first problem—the 14-year *Baqt* debt—the Sultan cancelled it, said it must be forgiven. He even straightened out the terms of the treaty, saying that the exchange should take place every three years rather than annually.
(2) The Sultan immediately released a number of Nubian prisoners into the control of King George.
(3) However, other requests he refused. George had ordered the withdrawal of the Muslim Egyptian garrison from al Qasr near Aswan—this the Sultan could not accept. According to the *Baqt* treaty, no Arab/Muslim was to buy land or live in Nubia. Many had bought land and settled in Lower Nubia. George insisted that any purchase of land was illegal, since purchases had to be made through the king according to the *Baqt* treaty. The Sultan insisted that these purchases were made in good faith on both sides, and could not be cancelled.

The visit of George to Baghdad had wide repercussions for Nubia, and for the Christians in the Middle East. It was an extraordinary sight for Muslims. As Werner states it, a Christian prince met with the supreme Muslim potentate "not as a defeated foe ... but as the head of an independent Kingdom."[21] The story of this fabled visit was repeated many times in accounts of both Christian and Muslim chroniclers. It added greatly to the fame of Nubia as a powerful and proud people, who were of a clear, definite Christian faith, which they actively defended.

George's return was triumphant. He probably stopped in Jerusalem, and received a piece of the "true cross"—although this cannot be confirmed. Patriarch Joseph of Alexandria heaped on him gifts and honors. He asked from the Patriarch, and received, a portable wooden altar for his worship. When he returned to Dongola, the kingdom celebrated by erecting a grand new church. George insisted that it be cruciform: a rather square building, with the worship area in the form of a cross. This was a style George had observed widely in Syria-Palestine—and later it became the predominant new style for Nubia. This great new church was called "*Isoun Kisee*"—"Church of Jesus", and became the Church most often used to crown new kings. George I went on to rule for a very long time.

2. George II

George II came in the line of George I, but reigned a hundred years after. He was on the throne in the middle of the tenth century, when a great change took place in Egypt. In 969, Egypt fell under the rule of the Fatimids. The Fatimids were a line of Shi'ite rulers who had reigned over a North African empire for many years. Although they besieged Egypt and held her for 200 years, they made no dent in the staunchly Sunni Islam of Egypt. The Fatimids, with one exception, were tolerant towards Christianity, and friendly with Nubia. Jawhar was the first Sultan, and he despatched Selim al Aswani to Dongola to learn more about Egypt's Nubian neighbors. Selim wrote an excellent account of his visits to Nubia and Alwa, and about his findings in those mysterious kingdoms.

Selim gave George II a letter from Jawhar, which was a presentation of the truths of Islam, and the errors of the Christian faith. The Nubian King was urged to embrace Islam. George called a great consultation of the dignitaries of the kingdom—church and state—for both were inextricably entwined in the kingdom. After careful discussion, George called in Selim, and refuted all Jawhar's arguments in favor of Islam as the true religion, demonstrating hereby that Christianity was the real faith. He then invited Selim himself to become a Christian. In state matters their discussions were fruitful. Selim stayed many months, and asked permission when *Eid al Adha* (the great Festival of Sacrifice) rolled around if he could be permitted to celebrate. George gave his assent, but told him he must celebrate outside the city. Some of George's councilors criticized him for being so liberal. However, the act shows that the Christianity of Nubia was strong, but not intolerant.

In one way George II served the wider church. Ethiopia was a sister church, linked also to Egypt. Like Nubia, all its bishops were consecrated by the Patriarch of Alexandria. Early in the century, Patriarch Kosmas (901-903AD) had consecrated an Archbishop for Ethiopia. The Ethiopian king rejected the man appointed. Instead, he elevated an Egyptian monk, already serving in Ethiopia. The monk had forged papers, indicating that he had been consecrated by the Patriarch. Kosmas immediately put the whole kingdom under the ban. For decades, no new priests were ordained, no new bishops consecrated. After 60 years, the emperor was faced with growing rebellions, so he sent an appeal to the sister Christian kingdom, Nubia. George II then wrote a strong appeal to Patriarch Philotheos (AD 979-1003) asking him to take action. The Patriarch did: he went to Wadi Natrun, the foremost convent of Egypt, and consecrated a monk to be the new Archbishop in Ethiopia.[22]

King Solomon, who came to the throne in Dongola around 1079, abdicated and went to a monastery in Lower Nubia. He was a deeply devout man, but the Egyptian commander at Aswan remembered how a former monarch-monastic Zacharia had been king-maker of four rulers. Taking no chances, he sent troops to arrest Solomon and bring him to Cairo, where the former king devoted himself to prayer and fasting in an Egyptian monastery.

There were dangers lurking among the friendly Fatimids. Al Hakim, who inherited the throne in 1096 (as a boy aged 11) was mentally disturbed and very unbalanced. He launched several persecutions against Christians in Egypt and Palestine, destroyed thousands of churches—including the Church of the Holy Sepulcher in Jerusalem. This earned him the nickname from Copts of "Nero" for his persecutions against the Christians. Al Hakim was somewhat liberal towards Nubians, allowing them to pass through Egypt and Palestine to go on pilgrimages.

Nubians were much favored in Egypt, particularly as soldiers, especially in the Fatimid period. Black soldiers from Nubia had been sought for a long time. Shishak the Egyptian Pharaoh (long before Christ), used them in his assault on Judah.[23] Sultans in the Muslim era liked them. Mercenary troops were more reliable, less likely than the locals to be involved in plots. During the Fatimid era, the Nubians were not only numerous in the army, but they became a large community in Cairo, up to 50,000. All or virtually all of them were Muslim. However, they were caught up in racial clashes, especially with the "Turkish" or white troops from the northern regions of Islam. Under Al Mustansir (died 1094), who was half-Nubian himself, Nubians were favored, but also massacred and driven out of Cairo, by a serious uprising. Nevertheless, they returned, and after some decades had reached 50,000 again.[24]

IV. FAITH AND LIFE OF THE NUBIAN CHURCH

There is much we do not know about Nubian faith and worship. The sources are incidental: the pictures they left behind; the ruined churches; and some documents. This gives us a few glimpses of what certain leading people believed and did. How the common believers were taught, and what they really believed is only partly known. Yet we can reconstruct some of it, and form a fuller picture of what that faith and life was like. At the beginning, it is important to say that it differed much from the earlier religion. Early Nubian religion was based strongly around the king, his court, and the nobility. It was devoted much to the glorifying of the king as an example of divinity. For the Nubians, there was a church in every village. It became a part of their every-day life.

1. Pictures and What They Say

Faras was the capital of Lower Nubia, all of it covered with drifted sand. Under the threat of flooding by the Aswan High Dam in the 1960s, a Polish team of archaeologists was given the job of excavating the site. They selected the highest mound. After much luckless digging they feared they had made an unlucky choice. Just then they came upon a wall and unearthed the brilliant picture of the three men in the fiery furnace, saved from death by the Archangel Michael.[25] The Poles had discovered Faras' cathedral, long deserted and buried in sand.

Pictures played a fundamental role: for teaching Christian truth and for worship. Two types of pictures are found most widely: pictures of the Nativity, the birth of Jesus Christ; and pictures of the three men saved inside the fiery furnace. The Nativity pictures were commonly found on the northern walls of churches, the women's entrance, but visible for most worshipers on their left. It spoke of one fundamental truth of the Christian faith, the Incarnation: "The Word (of God) became flesh, and made his dwelling among us."[26] A picture of the three men in the fiery furnace was usually found on the southern wall of the church, the men's entrance. It could be visible to worshipers on their right. This spoke of another foundational truth of Christian faith, Salvation: "Christ Jesus came into the world to save sinners."[27] Had these verses been written on the walls, hardly a soul could have read them. The common people, almost all without exception illiterate, were taught through pictures. This was a translation of the Savior's ways, who taught his disciples in parables, which were picture-language.

Other pictures and representations were part of the believers' worship. The Church was always built so that the altar where the Eucharist was celebrated was on the eastern side. This had a particular meaning: Christ would return again after His sign—the cross in the sky—appeared in the East. The altar was under an apse, an archway. At the top of the apse was a picture of Christ on his throne in glory. Worship was directed to the reigning Christ in heaven. Underneath him was a picture of Mary on a throne, with the twelve apostles: six on her right, and six on her left. Then below was a picture of birds. This was teaching that, when we look above the world, there are the apostles and Virgin Mary leading us to Jesus, the King. He is the supreme object of worship. There were many other themes as well. The Trinity was taught in pictures. One picture showed three likenesses of Jesus side by side in heaven. This is the Trinity, with each Person being alike. Another showed three crosses on earth—then clouds—and then above them three crosses in heaven. This declares that the God who is three-in-one in heaven also appears and rescues man on earth, as Father, Son and Holy Spirit.

2. Languages of the Church

Three languages were used in the Nubian church. Greek was the language of liturgy: prayers; songs and chants; and Scripture recitation. This was the language used throughout the Eastern Church. Coptic was the language of communication with the mother-church, the patriarchate of Alexandria. Nubian languages were increasingly used as time went on. They were used to recite Psalms or prayers. The priest would recite the first line in Greek, the congregation would repeat that line in Old Nubian (or Old Dongolawi); or the priest and congregation alternated, the priest reciting in Greek the first line, and the congregation reply the next line in their own language.

At first, the Scriptures were only in Greek, but as time went by, translations were made. In hardly anything did the Nubian church divert from the practice of the Church in Egypt. However, it did develop its own lectionary, a set of Scripture readings which appears not to have been copied from any lectionary in Egypt or the East. This is unusual. The spirit of Nubian Christianity was not at all to develop along its own lines, to be innovative. Rather, it was out-and-out Orthodox, not diverting from the traditional Christian faith as it could discern it. It copied Coptic and Syrian styles of holy art, and adopted the cruciform Church building from models in Syria and Palestine, introduced first by George I.

There was also a translation of the Scriptures into the "Old Nubian" language. No complete Bible or even book has been discovered, but fragments have. These make it clear that there was extensive translation. We have translations from seven Old Testament, and fifteen New Testament books, including the four gospels. Many of these were probably translations of the lectionary, but translations were probably made of some complete gospels, if not of the entire New Testament.

3. Sacraments and Activities

Nubians followed the traditions of the Coptic Church in Egypt. The sacrament of Eucharist was celebrated with loaves of leavened bread. This was to celebrate a living, resurrected Jesus Christ, and was a break from the Jewish tradition of unleavened bread for Passover. Like all Orthodox, they insisted that the Bread and Wine were indeed Christ's body and blood. Nubia like the Copts in Egypt was somewhat distinct in the mode of the sacrament of baptism: it was by total immersion, even for babies. Churches had on their south-eastern corner a baptistry, dug large enough in the ground to take two adults, and deep enough for immersions. At first many baptisms were of adults.[28]

Many activities the Church developed were distinctive to the life of Nubia itself. On special feast and celebration days, Christians loved to make pilgrimages. Many trekked to famous monasteries. Others went to caves or hovels belonging to a pious and powerful hermit. Church centers, such as Faras, Qasr

Ibrim, Dongola—and many others—became sites for pilgrimages. The great pilgrimage through the centuries was a trip to the Holy Land, especially to the Church of the Holy Sepulcher in Jerusalem. In later years, the Nubian Church made a chapel deep under that Church staffed by Nubian monks, who sang songs day and night.

4. Jesus, the Glorious Cross—Center of Faith

There can be no doubt that the center of faith in the Nubian church was Jesus Christ. Their Jesus, as seen in writings, hymns and pictures had a number of sides.

He is the bringer of the Gospel, the Good News; King of kings; Great healer; Incarnate God; and Second Person of the Trinity.[29] Even something of the distinct teaching of the Jacobites was commonly shown by Nubian Christians. When they made the sign of the cross, it was done with only one finger. This indicated that after the Incarnation, Jesus had one nature only, the nature of the God-man. How much the common believer understood this is impossible to know now. His suffering on the cross hardly appears in the Nubian piety which has survived to us today.

All in a sense are summed up in the fascination of Nubians with the Cross. The cross was the omnipresent symbol of their faith. For a time, young babies were branded on their foreheads with the sign of the cross. George I carried a golden cross all the way to Baghdad and back. He began the tradition of the cruciform church, which became the model for Nubia after the nineth century. The cross for them meant Jesus—as indeed the first cruciform Church in Dongola was called *Isoun kisee*—"the church of Jesus".

Devotion to the cross centered on "the Glorious Cross". This is a square cross, festooned from arm to arm, anchored in the soil, but sprouting up with live shoots.[30] The tradition of it is much wider than Nubia: it was deep in Eastern Christianity. The background story goes like this. Between Jesus' resurrection and ascension, Peter asks why the sign of Jesus' glorious return is the light cross in the eastern sky. Jesus replies, "The cross, once a symbol of defeat and shame, now is the sign of indestructible glory." Then follows the hymn of the Glorious Cross, in what is known as the *Stauros Text*.[31]

Several striking elements are found in it. The "Glorious Cross" has some similarities to how the cross has been described over the centuries, and even now. The cross is called "the forgiveness of sinners" and "the hope of the forlorn". And the beautiful last line: "The cross is life-giving, on account of God, who hung upon it in the flesh, because he conquered for us, who need peace." But clearly the Glorious Cross represents much more: it is primarily the resurrected, reigning and coming Christ. It is the living Christ who heals. As Nubians in the past paraded the goddess Isis through their lands for fertility, now the Cross brings the "watering of seeds". The Glorious Cross brings hope to people with nothing—the slave, the poor, the forlorn. The "glorious cross" was a representation of the glory and power of Jesus Christ: it stood for Him in a unique way.

5. Saints and Angels

Saints appear frequently on the walls of cathedrals, and must have occupied a large place in believers' lives and devotions. Some were monks and hermits. Others were famous Christians of all sorts. St. George was a warrior, and to a warrior nation he could be very popular—as a number of kings took his name. Another warrior, St. Menas, was not remembered for his military exploits. The story was told that a woman in the Delta (northern Egypt) was barren. Because of a prayer addressed to St. Menas, she conceived. As a result the woman believed. This story was told again and again in Nubia—and seemed to be popular, for it dealt with the problem of barrenness—and of faith.[32]

Biblical saints were most addressed in people's prayers. And of these all, the saint on most people's consciousness was the Virgin Mary. It is striking how large the Virgin Mary is. Some historians feel that as she was a "continuation of the goddess Isis" in Egypt, she was very similar to the Kandaka among the Nubians. There are not only the scenes of the birth of Christ, with a large Virgin Mary, and a rather small Joseph. There are the many pictures of her standing behind or with a bishop, a queen, a king or princesses, as their protection.

There was a particular fascination with archangels. These could be diversions as well. Nubians had a great passion for the bizarre. Angels and archangels, their names and their functions were one of their obsessions. The angel in the fiery furnace with Shadrach, Meshach and Abednego is named: he is Michael. Other spiritual beings as well: especially the "four living creatures" which appear first in Ezekiel 1:5 ff. Each creature has four faces, four wings, and four hands under the wings. They fly in a square. After appearing all through Ezekiel 1, they re-appear in Revelation 4:6 ff., before the throne of God. These held endless fascination for the common man. Magic and wonderful tales grew increasingly important in the later centuries of Nubian Christianity.

6. The Organization of the Church

Nubian Christianity, like that of Ethiopia, depended on the priest. He was the one who brought Christ to the table at Eucharist. And he had to be ordained by a bishop. Priests came from the people: they were expected to marry; to have children; to farm or do something to support themselves. The bishops had to be consecrated from a different source: the monastery. They were selected and consecrated by the Patriarch, the Jacobite Bishop of Alexandria. At first, all bishops were Egyptians. However, in later years, a number of Nubian bishops were consecrated.

The monasteries were therefore a key institution. At least 30 monasteries have been located in Nubia; perhaps there were many more. However, exactly what they did is not so clear. Some seem to have contained mostly or entirely Egyptian monks. The very fact that some Nubian kings became monks indicates that this was considered a true godly calling. Nevertheless, very little is known about these monasteries, their ministry, their contributions. In near-by Ethiopia, monasteries were a key instrument in Christianizing newly-conquered, and even unconquered peoples.

It is clear that Nubian Christianity spread. The Nuba people came from the West—from the area today labeled Kordofan. There is evidence that Christianity also went West—to Kordofan and to DarFur. Who took it, or how it went is not known. When the Catholics first reached the Nuba Mountains at Dilling, they found the people had a tradition of monotheism, and still practiced baptism. There may have been attempts to reach the Beja in the Eastern Red Sea hills. Nubians were frequently fighting the Beja—that would certainly have inhibited good relations. How far they moved south is pure speculation. Arab travelers in Dongola and especially at Soba found people who practiced traditional African religion. These great centers were reputed to be reaching out in influence to the ends of Africa, but whether or not they took their faith there is unknown.

Finally, the role of the king was crucial in Nubia. It is extraordinary that Nubia and Ethiopia, the two churches in Africa started and nurtured by Alexandria, were dominated by strong lines of Christian kings. Beginning from the decision to accept Christianity as the national faith, kings in Nubia were key actors. When Zacharias II faced the demands of 14 years' payment of *Baqt*, he called all his advisors, church and state. When George I traveled to Baghdad, he represented church and state. In Baghdad he visited both a Patriarch and a Caliph. When George II was challenged to "embrace Islam" by Selim al Aswani, he called all his advisors, church and administration, to formulate an answer. Vantini[33] mentions three vital roles of the Nubian king. First, he was patron, the protector, of the Orthodox faith. Its well-being and defense were tied up with his well-being. One great example is George II's desire to bring a settlement to the estranged Ethiopian Church. Second, the church was his protector. There are paintings of the king or members of the royal family under the protection of Mary, and of Christ-Emmanuel. And third, he was the builder or initiator of new church buildings, such as *Isoun kisee,* the Church of Jesus, initiated by George I in Dongola.

There was always the danger that the King could "use" the church for his purposes—and vice-versa. No doubt it happened, probably many times. But also there is the memory of a Zacharia resigning from kingship to become a monk; there is King Solomon who also did the same, and lived and died a very humble pious man. Nubians set up their own chapel at the Church of the Holy Sepulcher in Jerusalem, alongside Jacobite brothers like Egypt and Ethiopia. But there was nothing very different, African or Nubian, about the Church. They recited the same Apostles' Creed as did other churches. As Werner remarks:[34]

> Because the Nubians as Christians adhered to all the central beliefs and teaching of the Christian Church there was no specific 'Nubian' faith as if they had invented a new kind of Christianity. The Nubians were Christians in the full sense of the word.

It had some very clear characteristics, but anyone looking for an "*authentic* early African" Christianity of a distinct nature, should not look at Nubia. Ethiopia was more like that, and anyhow the Ethiopian church has left far more documents detailing its history.

V. NUBIA'S CHURCHES COLLAPSE

Nubia, the powerful giant, can be compared with Samson the judge and warrior. He seemed to have had limitless power against his enemies. Then his wife cut his hair, the hair that could not by covenant be cut. He woke up: nothing had changed. But, for the first time, his strength was gone. In as sudden a way, Nubian Christianity, the Nubian Kingdom, the powerful champion of Egypt's Christians, woke up to find that everything had changed, its power was gone.

1. Changes in Palestine and Egypt

Egyptian rulers loved Nubian soldiers. They were not involved in plots and politics like the "Turks" from the north. They were the favorites of the Fatimids. But the large Nubian community was a problem. They had already been driven out once when Mustansir was Sultan. Nubians slowly returned—but still they were resented by the people of Egypt, especially the people of Cairo—and the rest of the non-Nubian army.

Then, into Palestine came the Crusaders: European Christians who were determined to liberate the Holy Land from the infidels (i.e. Muslims). They stormed into Jerusalem in 1099, took it, and set up their rule in Palestine. At first, the Arab Muslims did not stir. Their empire was too broken up and dysfunctional. Trouble came first in Cairo. The "Turks" (or white northern mercenaries) turned against the Nubians, the darlings of the Fatimids. It was a desperate fight, but the people joined with the rebels to drive out the Nubians; and a new commander, Salah ad Din,[35] came to power. Nubia rushed to the defense of their Fatimid allies, and invaded Egypt—but were driven back. Then Salah ad Din sent his brother into Nubia. He wanted to see if his own rebel army could retreat there in case they were defeated in Palestine, or pushed out by the Egyptians. The campaign was relatively simple. Faras Cathedral was partly destroyed. But the country was so poor, so lacking in food, Salah ad Din was advised not to think of retreating there. He went on to capture Jerusalem from the Crusaders, and to drive them out of Palestine, and set up the Ayyubid dynasty in Egypt. Now Nubia was in a fix: it had lost its friends the Fatimids in Cairo, and Egypt was wary and suspicious of them. The Muslim world feared the powerful Nubians would join with the Crusaders from Europe to drive Islam out of Egypt.

2. Nubia Falls into Disarray—Egypt Intervenes

In spite of fears, Egypt and Nubia remained stable, the early doubts went away. Then in 1260, the Ayyubids were driven from Egypt, and that land fell under the rule of the *Mamlukes*—a military caste. The first Sultan was Baybars. He did not want to test Nubia's power—its reputation was that of a great African nation. The *Baqt* remained in force and stabilized relations between Egypt and Nubia. So the *Baqt* was all Baybars demanded.

Then, out of the blue, in 1272, King David I of Nubia suddenly sacked the Egyptian Red Sea port of Aidhab. Three years later, David II sacked Aswan. Baybars sent in his army, captured and executed the "Lord of the Mountain", the Eparch of Lower Nubia. Suddenly, the rules changed. Plotters and pretenders to the Nubian throne went to Cairo for help for the first time, and Cairo listened, and acted. There followed a numbing array of coups and counter-coups as the kingdom descended into complete disarray.[36] Shekanda, with a claim to the throne, went to Baybars for help. Baybars was interested. He gathered an army, went in, besieged and took Dongola. There were no "pupil-smiting" archers, in fact no archers at all. The Nubian army was a shadow of the army which had turned aside the Arab invasion 600 years before. Part of Dongola and the great Church of Jesus was destroyed, but Shekanda was crowned king in another church, and put on the throne, in 1276. He took the throne, putting himself under the Mamluke sovereignty. Nubians were ordered to become Muslims, or pay the *jizya*. So a Nubian claimant opened the door for the Mamlukes, the first Nubian king to invite in a Muslim power. This was also the first time Egypt seriously involved itself in the governance of Nubia. This proved to be the effective end of the large Christian Nubian kingdom.

Shekanda invited some even more fateful guests from Egypt. He was the first to bring in Arab bedouin. These were coming in great numbers from Arabia to Egypt. Egyptians were farmers, and could not tolerate sharing their land with nomadic tribesmen and their goats. So Egypt happily forwarded them to Nubia. Beginning with Shekanda, the chaos in the Nubian Kingdom made it impossible to limit or control these nomads.

In 1315, Abdallah Barshambo became the first clearly-Muslim king of Nubia. In 1317, he turned a room in the Palace into a mosque, the first for Dongola. Nubia was now becoming Islamic at the top, but the population remained Christian. However, the Arab bedouin intermarried with the Nubians. Through Nubian matrilineal inheritance Arabs gained land, and even the kingship. The Arabs, though, were split into clans, and they fragmented the kingdom. The chaos was such that by 1365 Egypt was no longer interested in Nubia. Dongola city was ruined: Egyptians turned it over to the Arabs. The ancient Christian kingdom of Nubia was gone, at least from Dongola to the Atbara River. For a time, it was a kingdom, or fragments of a kingdom, with a Muslim king, and a Christian population. However, the king had always been a key player in the Nubian church. Christians either mixed with the Arabs and were absorbed into Islam—or moved north to the smaller kingdom of Dotawo. Christianity slowly died in what was the old Kingdom of Maqurra, from Dongola to the Atbara River.

3. The Christian Kingdom Continues—at Dotawo

The Christian kingdom of Nubia did not actually die out with Shekanda and Abdallah Barshambo. The royal line was reconstituted at Daw, further down the Nile. This centered on Lower Nubia, the old Nuba Kingdom, from south of the second cataract until the first at Aswan. The Christian kingdom remained with a line of Christian kings far into the fifteenth century. Even after it disappeared as a kingdom, Christianity remained as a relic in certain villages until the eighteenth, maybe the nineteenth century.

4. Alwa

Alwa was the southern Nubian kingdom. Several travelers visited it, including Selim al Aswani. He and Ibn Hawqal—both of them Arab visitors of the tenth century, mentioned that Alwa was larger than Nubia, it had a larger population, it had connections and trade with the outside world to the East and to the West. Its army was also larger. However, we know much more about Nubia than Alwa.[37] Alwa not only had irrigation farming, but also large inland farms growing *dhurra* (Arabic name for sorghum) and other crops from rain. They had large herds as well. One archaeological fact has confirmed the conversion of Alwa. By the seventh century, the people of Alwa no longer mummified the dead, nor did they bury them with clothes, food or weapons. As in Nubia, graves were all situated East-West in expectation of the resurrection.

Selim al Aswani said the people of Alwa were mixed: Nuba—from the West—and Beja—from the East. Even in the tenth century, Alwa had a Muslim community in Soba, the capital city near today's Khartoum. They controlled the White and Blue Nile, including a large part of what is now the Gezira. The Nile River there fits Isaiah's description of Kush—"Land of rustling wings", with birds and wild animals.

Alwa seems to have extended its Christianity to the West—to parts of the Nuba Mountains and Darfur. But it could not stop powerful enemies. Its rule extended east as far as today's Ethiopia. The Funj Empire began to grow and prosper there. Arab nomads caused the downfall of Soba. The Abdullab Arabs had settled in the northern regions of Alwa, from the Atbara River to near Khartoum. They grew in power, and then in about 1500, they took Soba. Probably not long after that, the Abdullab Arabs—and Soba—were added to the growing Funj Empire. The Christian kingdom ceased to exist.

This was not the last word. In 1520, a delegation from Alwa visited the Ethiopian court. There they found a delegation from Europe: Alvarez and his party had been sent by Portugal to report on the fabled "Kingdom of Prester John".[38] The people of Alwa said they were Christians, but they needed priests, for their priests had died out, and they had no bishop. Ethiopians gave them a discouraging reply. Ethiopia was living through a very tense time. Militant Islam was on the move, and active, and trying to isolate them. They complained they found it difficult to receive their bishops from the Patriarch of Alexandria. The Christians of Egypt were experiencing great difficulties—for the rule of the

Mamlukes was a harsh rule for the Copts ... Alwa's cry was unheard. This was the last call for help.

5. Evaluating the Collapse of Christianity

(1) External Circumstances

Most of those circumstances came to the Nubian churches unexpectedly, unintentionally. They could not have been anticipated or avoided. These circumstances are particularly:

a) The involvement and interference of the Mamluke Egyptian government in affairs in Nubia (which of course was instigated by Nubian claimants to the throne);

b) The Crusades made the times more tense, and probably pushed Egypt into a higher degree of interference;

c) Allowing Arab nomadic tribes to enter was the undoing of Nubia and Alwa. They spread Islam, but the great damage they caused was to break up Nubia completely;

d) Isolation. Nubia was isolated. It could not find help when it needed it. In fact, at the time of the fall of Alwa, the Egyptian Church was experiencing perhaps its most difficult testing time;

e) The imposition of *jizya* after conquest by Egypt was an incentive to conversion to Islam.

(2) Internal Weaknesses of the Nubian Church, of Nubian Christianity

The strengths of the Nubian Church became its weakness in the end. The church was powerful, effective, and had a strong organization. But that same church could not adjust significantly to a radical change. Every detail of its Christianity was sacred, too sacred—so it was untouchable and unchangeable. The church did not function without bishops or priests or king. No one dared to innovate: that would be interfering in the ways of God.

The contrast may be seen in 1964. All missionaries, Catholic and Protestant, were swept out of South Sudan, Blue Nile and Nuba Mountains. Some expelled missionaries gloomily said or thought that the church was "condemned to death". Although many churches were paralyzed for a time, Sudanese leadership emerged. There was a spirit of innovation—and the church grew powerfully.

6. New Ambassadors to the "Land of Rustling Wings"[39]

Nubia and its failing church dropped off the Christian world's radar screen. Alvarez and his delegation from Portugal told about the appeal of Alwa. Ethiopia, Egypt and even Portugal could not or did not respond. Catholics sent missionaries who passed through Nubia on their way to Ethiopia, and an Ethiopian monk went down the Nile. They all noticed a fading Christianity—but nothing was ever done to help.

Much later, in the nineteenth century, Egypt conquered northern Sudan, and gradually moved up the White Nile to Lake Albert (in today's Uganda). A priest in Malta read about Sudan, and heard the unnoticed cries of the exploited and enslaved, especially in the Nuba Mountains.[40] So, missionary societies were started. In contrast to the missions of Julian and Longinus, missionaries could no longer muster the support or opposition of the emperor, but had to organize their support from ordinary Christians. The first missions of the nineteenth century were all Roman Catholic. And in contrast to Julian and Longinus, they did not always go first to the king, but to the ordinary people, and worked much with freed slaves. They hoped to defeat slavery, and plant the Church—and made heroic efforts to do so. Indeed, they produced a great missionary hero, Bishop Daniele Comboni, who gave his life to Sudan, and died in Khartoum in 1881.

Again, though, a new epoch ensued. A holy man, Muhammad Ahmad, in the same year as Comboni's death, was proclaimed "Mahdi". His call was for Sudan to rid itself of the "godless Turk", and to bring to the world the righteous rule of God. During 1885 in Berlin, while the colonial powers were regularizing Europe's scramble for Africa, the Mahdi stormed into Khartoum. Egyptian rule ended, and General Gordon, Khartoum's defender and British hero, died in its defense. No open practice of Christianity was allowed.

However, by 1898, Britain and Egypt moved back into the Sudan. They were eager to renew the empire, and to permit Christianity—but not to allow in missionaries. In the end, the new Sudan Government permitted missions as long as they focused on the non-Muslim southern Sudan. The messengers of Christ returned to that land, sailing up the White Nile. The flocks of birds whirring reminded them of the punishments and promises found in Isaiah 18. Their message was the same message brought by Julian, Longinus and Bishop Theodore. But, in contrast, it was directed not so much to kings, but to the people—as perhaps the first monks and refugees from persecution had done in Nubia long before Julian. The missionaries studied the languages of Sudan, they started education, they started medical services and a few hospitals. They even tried to evangelize Muslims in northern Sudan, with limited success.

The Sudanese demanded their independence, and in 1956, they took over from the British. The ones who took over government power were northern Sudanese. They were Arab by culture, Muslim by religion. Their program for unity was the Arabic language: English and the local languages had predominated in the South. Underneath, though, there was anger that the British had sown a "foreign religion" in their land, stopping the march of Islam into Africa. That anger fell on the missionaries, and on the few Sudanese Christian leaders. An Arabization and Islamization program, begun in 1958, pushed southern Sudan into active revolt. The missionaries were blamed, and in February 1964, all missionaries in southern Sudan, southern Blue Nile and the Nuba mountains were ordered out of the country. Pessimistic missionaries declared that the fledgling church in Sudan had been "condemned to death". In some places it seemed so. In Doro, in southern Blue Nile, there were only about seven Christians. Missionaries predicted the church would collapse when they left—and it did. But, when they returned to visit Doro 11 years later, in 1975, they found

40 churches had sprung up. These had even re-ignited the failed church at Doro mission. Churches grew in many areas, particularly in places where there had never been any Christianity before.

The "Anyanya War" of 1963-1972 came to an end with a political settlement. Peace lasted only 11 years. Peace brought new opportunities for development. Exploration discovered oil, and that oil was found mostly in southern Sudan. Oil is a corruption of development, and a developer of corruption. Leaders began to plot the overthrow of the peace plan that ended the Anyanya war. Islamists demanded that Sudan become Islamic; and political plotters contrived to cut up the country in order to grab control of the oil. Sudan was declared an Islamic state, ruled by *shari'ah*. Rebellion, already bubbling, boiled over. War has been devastating. What the politicians did not gain by politics, they have worked to gain by violence. More than 4 million people were uprooted, with more than a million seeking shelter in northern Sudan, and hundreds of thousands fled as refugees. There have been attempts to annihilate the Southerners, mostly by devastating raids and manipulating famine relief. Perhaps two million, perhaps more, have perished.

Christianity has flourished and grown even amid the devastation. Christians have believed the days of Isaiah 18 are here. One Dinka prophet, Paul Kon, went naked for three years, preaching repentance to his people, as Isaiah had done when proclaiming judgment to Judah in Isaiah 20.[41] They have felt the terrible punishments of famine and war—declaring these to be what God had willed to punish Kush. Also, in hoping that the day would come when the people of Kush could become the people of God, bringing their gifts to Mount Zion. In 1999, the Episcopal Church in Sudan celebrated its centenary.

VI. ETHIOPIAN CHRISTIANITY: "HEAR O ETHIOPIANS, THE LORD OUR GOD, THE LORD IS ONE."

Further up at the source of the Nile, beyond the divide of the White and Blue Nile lies Abyssinia that inherited the name for the entire region, Ethiopia. Their relationship with their northern Nubian neighbors was often fraught with hostility. Inscriptions brag about the defeat of Meroites and it is said the constant raids from the south broke the back of the kingdom of Meroe. Here the story of the Ethiopian Orthodox Church claims an existence that spans the roots and branches of the Jesus movement harking earlier than the birth of Jesus and thereafter. To symbolize this long pedigree, their priests start every worship act by first proclaiming an adapted version of Jewish *shema* of Deuteronomy 6:4. Rulers would do so before issuing any public decrees or modifications to the law. There are in fact two voices in the story of Christianity in this region, sometimes converging and at other times betraying a gulf of ideological biases.[42]

The history books provide the basis of the introductory overview that is like the voice of the outsider. We must listen to the insider, the Ethiopian Orthodox Church. Their story embeds their journey into the Egyptian experience. Thus, the sojourn of the infant Jesus is a shared heritage as the party allegedly crossed the Sinai peninsula by the northern caravan route from Gaza to Raphia to present-day al-Arish; then to al-Farama (Pelusium). Equally shared was the ministry of Mark, the first Patriarch of Alexandria whose parents were from Cyrenaica. His charismatic ministry ended when he dared to build a huge church building in the suburban part of Alexandria called Baucalis. The enraged mob of unbelievers attacked him while celebrating the Easter mass, but he had written the gospel known by his name. The Ethiopian church laid claim to a long history that was not surrogate. Though other historians may place Queen Sheba in Yemen, the Orthodox Church's account claims that she resided in Axum, a great city built by a grandson of Ham named *Aksumawi*.

Planting the feet firmly in two ancient documents, *Kebra Negast (the glory of the kings)* and *Fetha Negast (the law of the kings)*, it claims that the queen was Medaka whose grand parents reigned from 1076-1026BC. Of great beauty and endowed with an inquisitive mind, she was attracted to King Solomon through the stories of a merchant prince, Prince Tamrin who was supplying Solomon with some of the materials for constructing the temple. He organized the trip to visit King Solomon and the six month's stay included long conversations and other forms of learning. The salacious part of the *Kebra Negast* (sections 29-32) is about Solomon's wise trickery or old-fashioned seduction that resulted in her pregnancy and the ring that she took back with her. Later, her son, *Ebria Hakim, the son of the wise one*, visited the father. Solomon recognized his image and ring as proofs of paternity, but failed to persuade the young man to stay and inherit the throne instead of the foolish Rehoboam. He commanded the princes of Dan, Levi and Gad with Azariah, the son of Zadok (the priest), to go back to Ethiopia with Hakim. More trickery followed as Azariah made a dummy ark and replaced it with the stolen real ark that he took to Ethiopia. Hakim came to the throne with the royal name of Menelik I and proceeded to establish a Judaistic religion.

This explains the heavy dosage of Old Testament aspects of Ethiopian Orthodox spirituality. Matters did not end there: when Christ was born, the claim is that the three magi were all Ethiopians. This disputes the other reconstructions that claim that one was the king of Afghanistan, the other the king of Persia, and the third the king of Ethiopia. As if the fuse has not been blown, the story continues that the Ethiopian eunuch was really from Ethiopia not Nubia, even if the *Kandace, Queen Mother*, sounds like Meroitic language. He was Djan Darada, baptized in 34CE and died in 55CE and the queen was Qarsemot, the fourth Axumite queen. The treasurer's conversion and extensive preaching installed Christianity in the kingdom.

But there is the fact that the conversion of the court was known to have commenced in the third century, when the young people Frumentius and Sidrakos Adesius were captured at the Red Sea port of Adulis (Assab in Saba?). These Syrians arrived there unaware of the controversy between the Ethiopians and foreign traders from Egypt and South Arabia. The reigning couple, King Ala-Amida and Queen Sofya (294-325AD), engaged them as servants in the court.

According to this story line, it was king Ala-Amida who sent a delegation to Rome to congratulate Constantine on his victories. At the king's death the queen appointed Frumentius the teacher of her sons, Abaraha and Asbeha. They later succeeded jointly to the throne as Ezana and Shaizana, and declared Christianity to be the official religion of the state; installed the statues of saints, decorated worship places with icons and dedicated the Church of St. Mary of Zion as the location for the ark. The task was to blend the inheritance from the Levites and the missionary achievements of the famous eunuch into a Christianity that was typically Ethiopian. The rest of the intriguing story centers on the illustrious career of Frumentius, who was sent to Nicaea in Bithynia when the Council was still in session over the claims by the Lybyan, Arius. From there, he traveled to Egypt, where he was detained and re-trained in the Alexandrian School before ordination as *Abba Selama*, the Archbishop of Ethiopia, in 330CE. This wove Ethiopia into the heritage of the Alexandrian School that was the most prominent place of learning in the early church and served as conservatory of the Monophysite tradition. More: as Abba Selama returned to Axum in 334CE, he brought back ancient manuscripts such as the Greek Old and New Testament, Apostolic Canons, Apostolic Traditions, Didascalia, the Didache and books by the doyens of the school, Pantaneus, Clement, the much-maligned Origen, Dionysius, Didymus (who headed the school during the student days of Frumentius), Alexander and Athanasius. This would have been like a drop of water in a bucket compared to the resources he used in his studies, or the number of volumes that survived in King Ptolemy II's (283-246BC) smaller library in Alexandria after Julius Caesar behaved like a Vandal, and destroyed the larger of the two libraries that housed over half a million volumes and was one of the wonders of the world.

In this insider perspective, the crucial position of the royal family in the church is moored with the *Fetha Negast*, which provides that the legal position in the church would be based on their loyalty to the canons and discipline of the church. The power in the church was, therefore, rooted in the combined interactions between the *abuna*, king and monastic heads. Monasticism became significant in the fifth century after the "Tsad-kan" (just), or Tesseaton Kiddussan (nine saints) arrived. These were Monophysites who escaped from the imperial harassment that followed the Council at Nicaea.[43] They evangelized the hinterland, translated ancient manuscripts into Ge'ez, Amharic, Tegreniya, Gallina and other indigenous languages, established the eremitic tradition and domesticated Christian values in Ethiopia beyond the courts. For instance, Abba Aregawi went to Debra Damo, confronted the worship of the python and established a monastery and schools just as Gerima went to Mettera near Senafe, Afese, and compromised the worship of fertility gods at Yeha. As they dispersed, so did learning and the inculcation of matured and informed Christianity. The significance is not usually manifest until one looks behind the history of Ethiopia.[44] Certain groups from across the Red Sea had come in large numbers into Ethiopia, overawing the indigenous people and establishing at Yeha, Matara and Asmara in present Eritrea, building temples, palace compounds, covered markets that displayed circles and crescents that signified their gods, Mahrem and Almuqah. Admittedly, Ethiopians migrated into South Arabia and founded communities, but the point is that these diverse communities were being molded in this period into a national entity through Christianity. Moreover, the new Christian communities came into conflict with Jewish communities that had established since the exilic period. The Sedaqan also mentored the future leaders of the church, such as the most beloved St Ayared, who was educated at the school established beside St Mary of Zion, Axum where the ark rested. His composition of music and hymns dominate Ethiopian liturgy whether it was the *kum-zema* or the *zemane* whose melody swings back and forth like a pendulum or the chanted *meregde* or hand-clapping *tsfat*, the entire range was like a doctrinal commentary.

Oral tradition has it that the decline of Axum started in the ninth century under Anbessa Waddem when the Felasha queen, Yodit, who was not from the Solomonic line but may have descended from Queen Sheba's handmaid, essayed to rout Christianity and install Judaism. She initiated the Zagwe line that ruled from the tenth to the thirteenth century. About the same time, Muslims successfully took over Ethiopian communities of South Arabia. Ethiopia lost intimate contact with Egypt and could not secure the appointment of an *abuna* because of Fatimid rulers who used this ploy to ensure that the people in the south did not unilaterally declare themselves as independent from paying tributes in gold, salt and frankincense. The story line of the internal history is that this was the period when the Solomonic line was destroyed as the new Zagwe rulers moved the capital from Axum in Tegray southwards to Wollo. The spirituality survived through its concentration on sacramental liturgical worship, ascetic life, daily calendar of fasting and feasting, use of icons and illustrated handwritten copies of the Old and New Testaments.

Since the Solomonic lineage is the core of the internal story line, Brahan Selassie could declare with glee:[45]

> ... in 1270 Atse Yekuno Amlak became Emperor and restored the Solomonic line to power. He held these cords of power until 1285. During his time as Emperor, the province of Shoa became the center of the nation, and the population underwent a renewal of its political, social, legal, educational and religious institutions.

He put one third of his kingdom in the custody of the monastery at Debra Libanos. This brought to prominence the career of St Tekla Haimanot (1215-1313) whose evangelistic campaigns and itineration refreshed Christianity throughout the nation. He had studied in the great monasteries, Debra Estifanos and Debra Damo, and mastered the lives of Egyptian saints; he could ride rough shod of intra-mural conflicts and appeal to the masses with a show of sterling credentials of orthodoxy. There is a painting of this saint which depicts him as praying so long standing on one leg that the other dropped off. To help keep him standing, he had spear points placed on all four sides so that if he became drowsy and fell, the spears would awaken him.[46] He made the monastic life attractive as some sought an access to his mystical powers, others pursued the education by monasteries, some of the devotees escaped from their evil past while the allure to power through the endowed cloisters remained strong. Monasteries themselves enfolded a wide variety of personalities, including healers, prophets, seers, scribes and scholars, confessors, fathers and mothers, icon painters, musicians, vestment makers, carpenters and masons, chefs and bakers, weavers, farmers, and those who lived in solitude for five days a week and would re-emerge on Saturdays and Sundays. Motivations therefore varied.

Seven significant themes serve as a guide through the rich tapestry of the presence of the gospel in Ethiopia and the people's responses. These include the relationship between the church and the state, especially the significant roles of various monarchs in determining the expansion of the faith; the level of popular participation and how the gospel challenged the cultural soil of Ethiopia; theological development as could be perceived in some of the doctrinal debates about two-day Sabbath; patterns of spirituality and fashioning of liturgical tradition, especially achieved by the distinguished lives of monastic figures; the challenge from Islam; the disastrous attempt to integrate Ethiopian Christianity into the Papacy; and the resurgence of Ethiopian Christianity in the twentieth century after some dark days.[47]

As indicated, the fortunes of the church were always tied to the fortunes of the throne and bound with legal cords. Thus, the crown practically funded the clergy, founded most of the monastic houses and supported them by donating revenues from parts of the kingdom or the payments from Egypt for using the waters of the Blue Nile. Emperors provided diplomatic cover in the negotiations for the *abuna* from Egypt and promoted the struggle to have indigenous archbishops. Text-books mention some of the great kings but there was an unusual king who left indelible imprints. Emperor Lali-bella (1185-1225) was born in 1140 at Roha in the Lasta region (northern Ethiopia) and it was said that mysterious signs appeared around him at birth. A thick cloud of bees engulfed the child and the mother had a revelation that he would be a great king and accordingly named him, *the bees know that the child will be a great king*! In his youth he sojourned in Jerusalem for twenty-five years, visiting shrines, living an ascetic life. Reputable seers visited this mystic. When he ascended the throne, he commissioned eleven churches to be carved out of the rock based on a vision he had. Masons and icon painters were sourced from Nubia, Egypt and all over the country. He named the buildings after a liturgical formula: *Alem (Savior of the world), Geneta Mariam (the paradise of Mary), Beit Masqul (house of the cross), Beit Dengel (house of the Virgin), Beit Kiddus Mikael (house of the archangel Michael), Beit Golgotha*. The beauty of the architecture has amazed generations. The Muslim invader, Ahmad Gran, was stunned in disbelief while the Jesuit missionary, Francisco Alvarez who visited Ethiopia between 1520 and 1527, feared that readers may not believe his descriptions of these churches in the *Narrative of the Portuguese Embassy to Abyssinia*. After the completion of the churches, he secured archbishops from Egypt, retired from the throne and went back into solitary life of silent prayers in the wilderness.

Kings expanded the church, as when Emperor Kaleb invaded Zafar and Najram in 525BC, in revenge for the massacre of Christians in that region. He established Ethiopian churches in South Arabia and gave the Ethiopian monarchs the reputation of being great warriors and defenders of the faith in Africa. But sometimes, a king would derail and face the rebuke of the clergy as when Emperor Amde Zion (1314-1344) became sexually promiscuous. Abba Anorewos, from one the prominent monastic houses confronted him; the king had him whipped in public and persecuted many houses until he was stunned by an incredible fire outbreak that consumed his palace; he repented and became one the most generous patrons of the church. Kings posed as arbiters in matters of doctrine, convoked debates on doctrinal matters and threw their weight on one side or the other. For instance, Emperor Zera Yacob (1434-1368) intervened in the debate on two-days Sabbath, which ranged some indigenous heads of monastic houses against the Egyptian archbishops; but the king insisted upon two days to remember the period that Christ spent in the grave and the resurrection day. He summoned the Council of Mitmaq in 1450.

Zera Yacob, *the seed of Jacob,* was unusual in the broad range of his reformation of the church: he must have understood that the character of Christianity in his domain was centered on the court and the monasteries and that the rural dwellers resorted to magicians and sorcerers for solutions to urgent life problems. The challenge was to move beyond a religion of ceremonies and redolent liturgy; a religion that served as a cultural signifier. Indeed, the monastic leaders would occasionally lash out at the prosperous merchants and courtiers who engaged in slave trade in Nubia and Adal and yet lavishly endowed monasteries as if to bribe God. The Emperor strove to ensure that the masses would exchange the covenants with deities such as *Dasek, Dial, Guidale, Tafant, Dino, Maku-uawze* for the Christ; he demanded that Christians wear arm and head bands with Biblical affirmations; he revised the church calendars and promoted pilgrimages to the Holy Land. It should be recalled that the calendar has many Jewish features but is related to the Julian as used in the Egyptian Orthodox Church. It starts from September and each year is sacred to one of the four evangelists. Luke usually gets the leap year and nearly every day is named after a saint. Jesus was born 55501 years after creation.

Above all, he increased Ethiopian contact with Europe and sent a mission to the Council in Florence, 1432-1445. It is said that when the Ethiopian delegation was on its way, Pope Eugenia IV moved the meetings to Rome so as to give them an appropriate reception. The hidden agenda was the effort to unite the Byzantine, Armenian and Ethiopian Orthodox Churches with the papacy to shore up his reputation and mobilize against Muslims. The resistance of Ethiopia continued for many more years as the contact initiated the intrigues by Rome to rein the land of *Qevs,* as the Ethiopians called themselves, into the papal ambit.[48] But the exposure attracted a beehive of explorers, ambassadors, soldiers and Roman Catholic missionaries to the kingdom. After a long period of splendid isolation, Zera Yacob opened the Pandora's box.

The pressure from Rome and Portugal dovetailed into the series of Muslim attacks that had intensified since the 12th century. Various rulers spent enormous military resources to ward off Muslims, who gradually consolidated around the coast and forced the capital to be relocated a number of times. Perhaps, Emir Almad ibn Ibrahim, who was nicknamed, Ahmed Gran, because he was left-handed, conducted one of the most devastating raids in the period between 1527 and 1578. By 1539, he had destroyed many churches, palaces and libraries; and carted away national heirlooms. In desperation, Emperor Lebna Dengel pleaded for Portuguese intervention which came in October 1542 and rescued Ethiopia. The price was to subject the monarch, under pressure from a Jesuit mission, to accept papal authority. Forged documents, blandishments and military attacks were pressed into service until it boomeranged as the people suspected that their emperor had succumbed and rose up in arms to defend the faith of their fathers. Rumors circulated among the nobility and monastic houses that Emperor Za-Dengel had yielded to the pressures by Pero Pais who arrived in 1603 and made it clear that his mission was to reform Ethiopian spirituality and ensure submission to Rome. Za Selassie led the rebellion that killed the emperor. Matters did not end there as his successor, Emperor Susenyos was badgered by Pais, who died in 1622. Alfonso Mendes took over the task when he became, not only the new papal envoy, but was brazenly consecrated Patriarch of Ethiopia by Pope Urban VIII. He forced the emperor to swear a formal oath of allegiance to the pope. The cultural history of Ethiopia was electrified as revolt after revolt broke out, and civil wars went on without any hope of ending. The Emperor's loyal followers, including his son, began to argue with him to break with Rome; his army began to murmur against having to fight fellow Ethiopians. By 1630, the emperor was forced to back down and restore the pristine Ethiopian Christianity.

The civil war may have damaged the fabric of the society more than was apparent because Ethiopia lost its peace throughout the eighteenth and early nineteenth centuries as rival princes and theological factions tore the seams apart. One disastrous debate was over the nature of Christ. It should be explained again that the Ethiopian Church held that Christ had two natures before incarnation, but only one after the union; the humanity being absorbed by in the divinity. In the new debate, one side held a conception that was nicknamed, *Karra Haimanot* meaning, *"the belief of the knife as it cuts off the third birth"*. This was maintained against those who believed that Christ had three births from God the father, at conception and at baptism from the Holy Spirit. Worse, Ethiopia could not secure an archbishop from Egypt from 1803 to 1816. The story of Christian presence at the beginning of the nineteenth century was a gloomy tale. It was as if a desolate wind scorched the efforts of yesteryears. In the Horn of Africa, the decline had been steady with the incursion of Islam from the seventh century. However, the varied policies of different Islamic regimes preserved signs of life among the rural Egyptian Copts, permitted Nubia to remain Christian till the fifteenth century and left Ethiopian Christianity in a splendid isolation with an image of a muscular church with the character of pristine first century Christianity, monastic spirituality, creative music, fine architecture and fascinating art. However, by the end of the eighteenth century, Ethiopian Christianity was in a traumatized state. Henry Salt painted a sorry picture in *Voyages and Travels* (1809):[49]

> The nation, with its religion, is fast verging on ruin; the Galla and Mussulman tribes around are daily becoming more powerful; there is reason to fear that, in a short time, the very name of Christianity may be lost among them.

The state structure had grown soft, its boundaries dwindled and internecine theological debates on the Sabbath and Nature of Christ created virulent divisions between the court, the leading monastic houses and the *abuna*. Its ancient liturgy in Ge'ez became less intelligible to Amharic speakers and less inspiring; learning declined as the infrastructure decayed. Indeed, hundreds of churches were destroyed or abandoned amidst violent strife. Henry Salt referred to the fact that non-Christian Galla communities and Muslims had settled over large areas that were once Christian. This is the period known as *zemane mesafint, the era of the princes.* This backdrop gave much significance to the regenerating careers of Emperor Tewodros (1855-1868) and Emperor Yohannes IV (1872-1889). But this was also a period when a number of foreign interest groups, Jewish, Protestant and Roman Catholic had discovered Ethiopia. Quite intriguing is the first group of Germans employed by the British-based Church Missionary Society into Tigre, Gondar and Shoa from 1830. Their goal was ostensibly to purify Ethiopian Christianity rather than to open new mission stations. They deployed evangelical doctrines as the litmus tests on such practices as praying to Mary, and saints, venerating images, kissing the cross, keeping fasts and cherishing monasteries. All these would indubitably contest Protestant perceptions and evoke hostile response from the indigenous folk. The missionaries invited the imperial powers of Britain and France to soften the unyielding ground with violence around 1842. Equally intriguing is that the Roman Catholic Lazarists who came later, appeared to be more culturally sensitive and equipped to operate in such cross-cultural contexts, and used the ordination of indigenous priests to gain influence before the contemporary Abuna Salama saw through the insidious project and attacked it with as much violence as he could muster to preserve Ethiopian identity.

The man who initiated the regeneration of Ethiopia, Kassa Hailu was born in Qwara, brought up by an uncle, trained in monastic education but soon joined a band of bandits, became a mighty warrior and one of the princes who held a part of the land. His victories over other warlords gave him the crown and he took the royal name of Tewodros, *King of Kings*. He has intrigued historians because of his sheer energy and activities. First, he was the one who tried to consolidate the Solomonic pretences of the crown by designing the titles and acting it out; he choreographed it from the conflation of myth and history that always played at the background of Ethiopia's story. He was perhaps driven to this by the enormous energy spent by various missionary groups in propping the Falasha whose Jewish origins were much clearer. Second, he attempted to unify the nation by military conquest. His persistent success impressed upon him that the divine hand was strong on him and that he was special. Third, he reformed the church by insisting on monogamy and down-sizing the number of the clergy so as to enforce stricter discipline. Fourth, he had a deep social conscience and sensitivity towards the masses. His populist agricultural reform included land redistribution that evoked the opposition of the monastic houses, the biggest land-owners. As other rulers, he intervened in doctrinal disputes and ruled against three births and, commissioned the translation of the Bible into Ahmaric because Ge'ez was becoming incomprehensible to many.

It was his foreign policy that brought his death as the French and the British tried unsuccessfully to trick him. He arrested and imprisoned the British representatives and when diplomacy failed, he lost in battle but proudly killed himself, a king to the end. The ruler of Tigre had become the prominent prince and was crowned in 1872 at Aksum as Yohannes IV, *King of Zion of Ethiopia*. The flamboyant title was not lost on many observers as he built on the tradition of Tewodros. He ruled until 1889. The same problems followed him to the grave, namely, unification of the nation, doctrinal uniformity, a viable foreign policy and an adequate response to Islamic insurgence. Military engagement that required a reliance on foreign technological support eased the first problem; the Council of Borumeda tackled the second; an ingenious division of the state into four Coptic bishoprics was equally helpful and even enhanced the Christianization process among the Galla. It was the Madhist revolt that snuffed off his illustrious career. Menelik II completed most of the ambition of Yohannes. The defeat of the Italian imperial greed at Adwa in March 1896 inspired black imagination all over the world and made Abyssinia, the hub of Ethiopia, a name that Western writers meant for the whole region inhabited by the sons of Kush. Adrian Hastings puts it aptly:[50]

> the years after Adwa were for Ethiopia years of exceptional peace. The authority of Menelik was almost unchallenged, the feudal independence of the great provinces was quietly diminished. His rule was far more a revival of the traditional royal system, the combination of a network of great lords, a loyal army, and the church" ... and yet more.

Notes

1. Genesis 10:6.
2. Ezekiel 29:10.
3. See Isaiah 18-20.
4. See Acts 11:1-18 for the first Jerusalem Church Council. Also Acts 15:7-11, again refers to Acts 10.

5. *Ethiopian* meant simply a Black man. It did not mean a man from modern-day Ethiopia, but was the Greek word used to translate the Hebrew for a *Kushite.*
6. Note: "Lower Nubia" means northern Nubia, just south of the first cataract. *Nubia* is used in the text to designate the people from Aswan to Khartoum—and for their land. But the particular people of Lower Nubia, in Christian history, I will call the *Nuba*, and their land *Nuba*, the Arabic name. In Arabic, there is actually no distinction between Nubia and Nuba.
7. Ox-driven water-wheel (Arabic).
8. Greek name—Nobatia.
9. Greek name—Makuria.
10. Greek name—Alodia.
11. Isis was an extremely popular Egyptian goddess. She had restored the god-king Osiris back to life— and he became the god of resurrection. So Christians replaced Osiris with Christ, and Isis with the Virgin Mary. The Nuba needed Isis for the fertility of their fields.
12. Here "Nubia" means any and all of the Nubian Kingdoms in general: Nuba, Maqurra and Alwa, see note 5.
13. R. Werner, W. Anderson & A. Wheeler, *Day of Devastation, Day of Contentment: The History of the Sudanese Church Across 2000 Years* (Nairobi: Paulines Publications Africa, 2000), 32.
14. The Orthodox were dubbed "Melkite"—which meant "the king's party" by the Jacobites. All considered and called themselves Orthodox, so the Jacobite Monophysites were named Orthodox.
15. W. Adams, *Nubia, Corridor to Africa* (Princeton: Princeton University Press, 1977), 535-538, 441.
16. Werner, *Day of Devastation*, p. 39.
17. It was not entirely clear if the exchange was yearly or not. Different accounts say the agreement was to give 300 or 360, or even 400 slaves.
18. Werner, *Day of Devastation*, p. 48.
19. The modern African nation, Ethiopia, only took on that name in the twentieth century. Traditionally it has been known as Abyssinia (Arabic, *al Habash*) Unfortunately, the NRSV has not cleared up this confusion even though it explains that "the Candace" was not a name but a title.
20. See Werner, *Day of Devastation*, p. 47. Note: this whole history was written by John the Deacon, Coptic secretary to the Patriarch Michael I (744-768), see footnote p. 46.
21. Werner, *Day of Devastation*, p. 52.
22. In the Orthodox churches, bishops are chosen only from the monasteries.
23. See II Chronicles 12:3.
24. G. Vantini, *Christianity in the Sudan* (Bologna: EMI Publishers, 1981), 119-131.
25. The story is found in Daniel 3. Faras Cathedral had many paintings on the walls. The original paintings had been covered with a layer of plaster, then another painting made on top. The archaeologists were able to separate multiple layers, and angels were important. The angel in the fiery furnace with Shadrach, Meshach and Abednego is named: he is Michael, found in 150 pictures on various walls of the

church. The picture of the three men in the fiery furnace (and others) is found in WERNER, *Day of Devastation*, in section of pictures between pp. 64 & 65. A picture of the cathedral under excavation is found on pp 70-71.

26. John 1:14, NIV.
27. I Timothy 1:15.
28. WERNER, *Day of Devastation*, pp. 85-86. *Pictures of baptistry*, p. 87.
29. John 14,9 NIV.
30. WERNER, *Day of Devastation,* in the middle of the colored picture section between pp. 64-65.
31. *Stauros* is the Greek word for Cross. Nubians called it *staurosil,* from the Greek.
32. WERNER, *Day of Devastation*, p 74.
33. Rev. Giovanni Vantini is a missionary and one of the longest students of Nubian Christianity.
34. WERNER, *Day of Devastation*, p. 78.
35. In English, his name is usually spelled *Saladin.* He was actually Kurdish.
36. In 1275, Shekanda pulled Baybars and Egypt into Nubia, sacked Dongola, captured and executed David. Shenamun took over—but was pushed out two times by intervention from Cairo. Budemma was installed by Cairo—but was caught and executed by Shenamun. Shenamun ruled until death, Kudanbes was the last Christian King. In 1315 Egypt deposed him.
37. The reasons are: Alwa did not connect with Egypt, except for the Church which was related to Egypt as the Nubian church was. Alwa was in a rainy zone. As a result, documents and mud buildings did not last—and none have come to us by archaeology. The archaeology of Nubia flourished because of the High Dam at Aswan: over a short period great teams tried to save what they could.
38. Europeans believed there was a great Christian Empire in the East, under the rule of "Prester John"—which meant "Priest John". Christians in Europe hoped to link up with him and together overthrow Islam. When Ethiopia was discovered, it was labeled that fabled kingdom.
39. For a very detailed record of Christianity in Sudan, see WERNER, *Day of Devastation,* pp. 121-667.
40. The Nuba Mountains are called that because many people who use Nuba languages live there. Since it is mountainous, it has received many other peoples as well, who run there to escape extermination. In Arabic, both Nuba Mountains and Nubia (along the Nile) are called *Nuba.*
41. Isaiah 20:2, "The Lord said, 'take off the sackcloth from your body and the sandals from your feet,' and he did so, going around stripped and barefoot." NIV. For story of Paul Kon, see, WERNER, *Day of Devastation*, pp. 545-546.
42. The insider view is represented by Brahana SELASSIE, *Towards a Fuller Vision* (Leicestershire: Upfront Publishing, 2003).
43. They were: Abba Aregawi; Abba Gerima; Abba Likanos; Abba Pantalewon from Constantinople; Abba Gubba from Cilicia; Abba Afese from Asia Minor; Abba Tsehma from Antioch; Abba Alef from Caesarea and Abba Yemata from Cooz.
44. Laszlo TORK, *The Kingdom of Kush* (Leiden: E.J. Brill, 1997).
45. SELASSIE, *Towards a Fuller Vision,* p. 176.
46. Ephraim ISAAC, *The Ethiopian Church* (Boston: Henry N. Sawyer Co., 1967), 24.

47. See, Taddesse TAMRAT, *Church and State in Ethiopia, 1270-1527* (Oxford: Clarendon, 1972).
48. J.E. HARRIS (ed.), *William Leo Hansberry: African History Notes, vol. II: Africa and Africans as Seen by the Classical Writers* (Washington: Howard University Press, 1981), 9.
49. Cit. in HASTINGS, *The Church in Africa,* p. 224.
50. HASTINGS, *The Church in Africa*, 238.

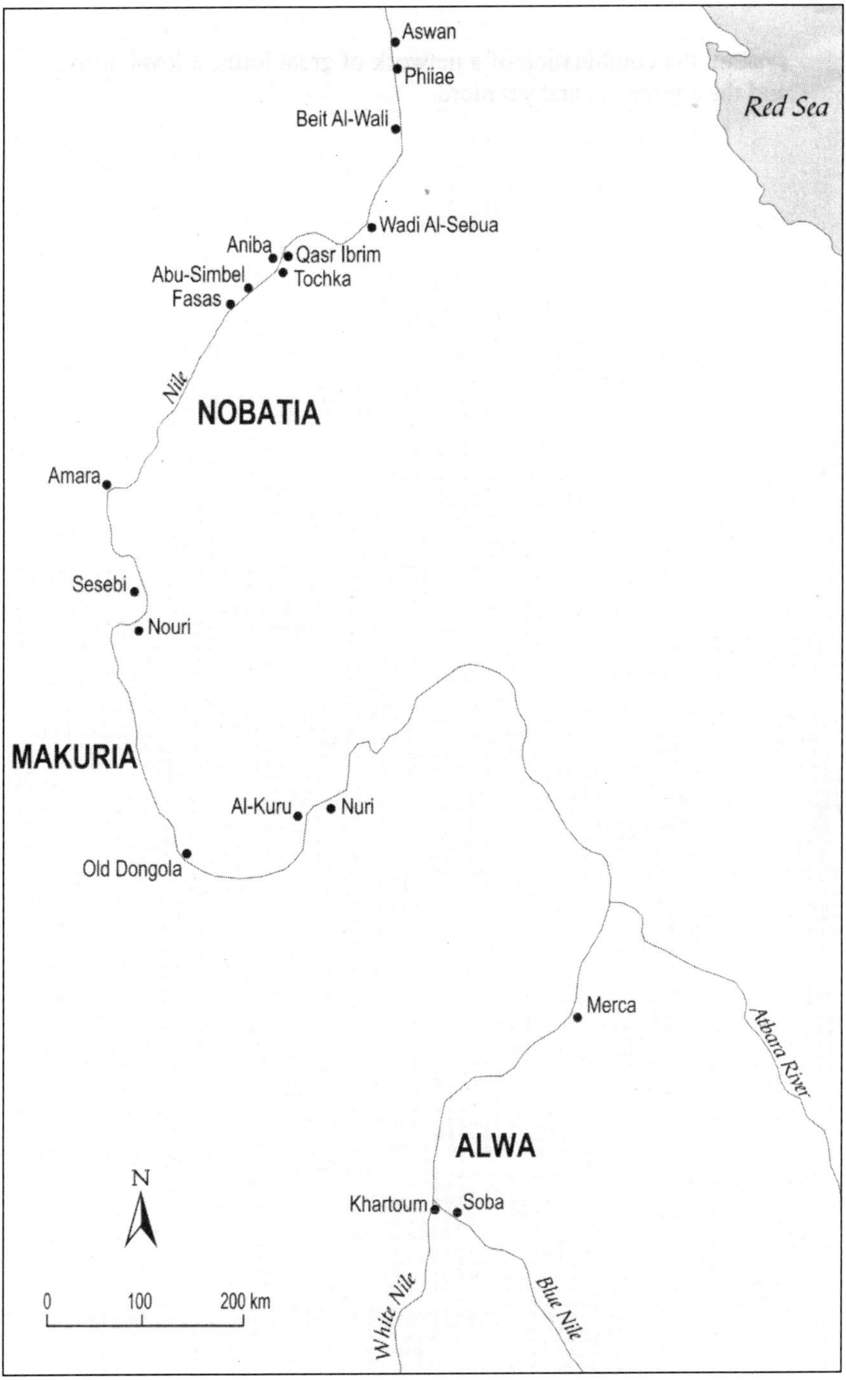

Map 3: Early Christianity in Nubia

Chapter Five

Islamic Challenges in African Christianity

Akintunde E. Akinade

INTRODUCTION

The legacy of Christian-Muslim encounter in Africa is well established and thoroughly documented.[1] The interaction between the two Abrahamic faiths has gone through several historical incarnations. It has taken the shape of dialogue, open exchanges, vitriolic conflicts, and violence. It is a history sated with meaningful engagements and baffling ambiguities. This chapter examines several case studies and historical landmarks that will enable students to understand the dynamics and the dynamism of the Christian-Muslim encounter in Africa. I will analyze the various patterns of Islamization in Africa and the variety of ways Christians have responded to the Islamic challenge in Africa. In addition, this work will offer some heuristic devices for comprehending both historical and contemporary issues that relate to the interaction of the two religions on the African continent; a continent known to Arab geographers and historians as *Bilad al-Sudan* (land of the black people). These vignettes from different nations will provide insights into the various ways that Christians and Muslims relate to one another within the African context. Phillip Jenkins has correctly declared that one of crucial challenges of Christianity in the twenty-first century is how to relate to Islam, especially as the latter is the fastest growing religion in the world today. According to Jenkins, "Christian-Muslim conflict may in fact prove one of the closest analogies between the Christian world that was and the one coming into being."[2] This realization is crucial to contemporary Africa. In fact, the continent provides a veritable laboratory for analyzing a host of emerging themes relevant to relations between the two faiths.

I. THE GENESIS OF THE ENCOUNTER AND THE NORTH AFRICAN EXPERIENCE

Africa has a long connection with Islam. When the early followers of the Prophet Muhammad were facing persecution in Mecca, he advised many of them to seek refuge across the Red Sea in Axum (which is in modern day Ethiopia). In the Muslim tradition, this remarkable event is known as the first *hijrah*, or migration. Iman Buhari reported in his *Sahih Buhari* that these Muslim refugees later went back to Arabia after Muhammad had won the peninsula over to Islam. Islamic legends call those who returned to Medina the "people of the ship".

Islam would quickly return to Africa. In 639, just seven years after Muhammad's death, an Arab army invaded Egypt. The rapidity of the Islamic advance across northern Africa was breathtaking and sensational. In fact, within two generations, an Arab hegemony extended across the entire Maghrib to the Atlantic Ocean. The assistance of several important people, most notably Cyprus, the Melkite Patriarch of Alexandria, and a Byzantine governor who surrendered the fortress of Alexandria, greatly contributed to the success of the Arab conquest. For their part, the Arabs recognized the heretofore-persecuted Monophysite church, and the Copts received the *dhimmi*, or religious protection, accorded to the "people of the book" (*Ahl al-Kitab*) in return for paying poll tax. The Arabs not only valued the Copts as taxpayers but as civil servants. There was even a stern order that prevented their conversion to Islam.

In northern Africa, Arab Muslims met a moribund and internally divided Christianity, which collapsed like a house of cards. While Christians constituted a majority in Egypt until the tenth century, their relative number declined as a result of incessant waves of Arab immigration. Intense persecution under the Mamluks from the mid-thirteenth to the early-sixteenth century further undermined Egyptian Christianity. Likewise, in the tenth century, most Egyptian Christians spoke Coptic, but by the end of the twelfth century, most had adopted Arabic and Christian literature was translated into Arabic. The fact that Arabic was the language of administration and commerce further contributed to the Arabization of Egypt. The same changes occurred all across Muslim-occupied North Africa.[3]

The Arab conquest led to state formation and the organization of North African society into Muslim communities. Tunisia in the eighth century, Morocco in the eleventh, and Algeria in the sixteenth acquired territorial autonomy. The conquests also resulted in the institutionalization of Islam for all and sundry. Starting in the eighth century, the Maliki School of jurisprudence became entrenched throughout North Africa, and remained the basis of law, education, and government until the nineteenth century. From about the twelfth century, Sufism too became a way of life for multitudes of people, especially in the outlying areas. Sufis became the leaders in rural communities in Algeria, Morocco, and Tunisia.

II. RELIGIOUS TRANSMISSION AND APPROPRIATION IN AFRICA

The spread of Christianity and Islam in Africa has continued to generate interesting insights that relate to the character of each faith. As already has been seen, both confessions have a long and a distinguished history in Africa. The two religions have engendered passionate piety and yet have maintained their unique character and form. The origin and metamorphosis of both religions in Africa lend considerable credence to the role local agency and indigenous appropriation plays in religious transmission. As Lamin Sanneh has argued, it is important to:[4]

> Assess the respective impact of Christianity and Islam through the eyes of African religions, and in so doing release these two missionary faiths from the fixed, motionless time-frame in which they have been frozen and submit them to the animated surge of history where nothing stands still.

This is a significant affirmation. It is imperative to see both Christianity and Islam as African religions. Indeed, Africans have stamped their indelible prints on the two religions, and they rightly continue to claim both religions as their own. Religious chronology is important, but this must not blind us to the different ways in which African people have appropriated and re-interpreted these two religions. It is through the second process that African creativity and genius can come to the fore.

The Ghanaian Pan-Africanist, Kwame Nkrumah, captured this idea well when he declared:[5]

> Our society is not the ancient society but a new society broadened by Euro-Christian and Islamic influences. So, a new ideology is necessary, an ideology that can be stated in a philosophical definition, but which is at the same time an ideology which does not abandon Africa's original and human principles ... an ideology whose aims will be to contain the African experience of the Islamic and Euro-Christian presence as well as the experience of African traditional society.

Nkrumah's statement underscores the central place of religion for Africans. He saw African society as deeply entrenched in African traditional religion and further broadened by Islam and Christianity. Nkrumah asserted that Islamic civilization and Christianity are both part of the historical experience of pre-colonial Africa. They constitute significant changes that have left indelible prints in the minds and psyches of Africans. He strongly believed that African people needed successfully to appropriate values and ideas from the outside world, but then creatively add an authentic African dimension to create a new worldview.

Nkrumah's optimistic vision largely rests on the attitudes that the followers of the two Abrahamic religions in Africa have towards each other. Traditional African religion has proven to be receptive towards Islam and Christianity (indeed, more so than they have been of it). Such a hospitable African milieu has provided the soil for both religions to flourish and even develop a commanding presence in parts of the continent. The cross and the crescent thus have found a permanent place within Africa's wide landscape. The character of Islam and Christianity in Africa is different from other manifestations of these religions around the world because each has been reinterpreted through the idioms and precepts of African culture and worldview. Africans have embraced both religions and put their own unique stamp and affirmation on them. This perspective is very useful for understanding the distinctive African contribution to interfaith discourse.

III. ISLAMIC MOVEMENTS IN AFRICA: SEVERAL REGIONAL EXAMPLES

From the seventh to the twelfth century, Arab warriors and merchants introduced Islam to many areas in Africa. The expansion of Islam involved different agents and catalysts. In North Africa, nomadic Arabs introduced the faith. In West Africa, the religion spread by peaceful negotiations among merchants and missionaries. In some situations, the spread of Islam depended upon its adoption by the ruling elite; in others, urban groups found it attractive. Occasionally, political and economic benefits enhanced its appeal, and sometimes spirituality and culture were the main attraction. In the Saharan and Sudanic regions of Africa, Arab and Berber traders and settlers introduced Islam. Along the East African coast, the religion was propagated by Arab and Persian settlers, while in West Africa, missionaries, Arab Dyula traders and teachers helped spread the faith. In Sudanic Africa, colonies of Muslim traders cooperated with the governing élites, and encouraged the rulers of the African states of Ghana, Mali, Songhay, Kanem-Borno, and Dogomba to convert to Islam.

Conversion to Islam became the veritable avenue to consolidate political power, guarantee commercial patronage, and mobilize spiritual powers in favor of the politically influential. Just like in North Africa, adherence to Islam provided for the legitimization of states as well as for alliances among diverse group and the organization of commercial ventures. Within Muslim states, an *ulama*, or group of religious authorities, arose. In essence, Islam became the religion of the political and commercial elite. In West Africa, Arab traders encouraged these governing classes to convert to Islam. In East Africa, Arab merchants gained political leadership of small states. In Somalia and Ethiopia, Arab leaders assimilated into local lineages and gained control of many tribal coalitions and groups. In East African societies, Arab settlers and merchants inter-married with local peoples and became dominant elite of the coastal Swahili societies.

Muslim communities gradually emerged with the integration of peoples and the formation of new cultural identities. In the Sudan, the spread of Arabic and contacts with northern Africa helped to establish Islam among the masses. By the eighteenth and nineteenth centuries in West Africa, the consolidation of Muslim trading networks connected by lineage, trade, and Sufi brotherhoods had reached a crescendo and this enabled Muslims to wield tremendous political influence and power. Throughout Africa, the spread of Islam led not only to the creation of new communities but also to the re-configuration of existing communities and empires based on Islamic models.

The literature on conversion to Islam in Africa is very extensive. Scholars have proffered many theories to explain the massive conversion of Africans to the faith. Thus, Lamin Sanneh contends that the success of Islam as a missionary religion lies in the perpetuation of the sacred Arabic text. The fundamental missionary institution of Islam is the Qur'anic school. There, young people learn by committing to memory passages in Arabic from the sacred text. Memorization becomes the avenue for Islamic expansion in Sub-Saharan Africa. Muslims describe Arabic as a revealed language, and it is, of course, the medium of the Qur'an.

The unparalleled eloquence of the Qur'an has a venerable status in Islam. The famous African missionary, Dr. Edward Blyden, eloquently wrote about the importance of the Qur'an to African Islam in 1875, when he affirmed that for Africans,[6]

> The Koran is, in its measure, an important educator. It exerts ... a wonderful influence. It has furnished to the adherents of its teaching in Africa a ground of union which has contributed vastly to their progress. Hauseas, Foulahs, Mandingoes, Soosoos, Akus (Creaoles of Yoruba extraction) can all read the same books and mingle in worship together, and there is to all one common authority and one ultimate umpirage. They are united by a common religious sentiment, by a reverence and esteem. And even where the ideas are not fully understood, the words seem to possess for them a nameless beauty and music, a subtle and indefinable charm, incomprehensible to those acquainted only with European languages. It is easy for those not acquainted with the language in which the Koran was written, and therefore, judging altogether as outsiders, to indulge in depreciating its merits. Such critics lose sight of the fact that the Koran is a poetical composition, and a poetical composition of the earliest ... kind, and that therefore its ideas and the language in which they are conveyed cannot well be separated.

The sacred language of Arabic became the canon of orthodoxy. It was also the basis of religious reform within Islamic communities in Africa. It propelled religious developments and brought African Muslims closer to their faith. Muslims were not discouraged from learning other languages, but these tongues were inconsequential in the Islamic dispensation. African Muslims learned Arabic by rote, and this played a remarkable role in the missionary expansion of Islam.

IV. OTHER ATTRACTIONS TO ISLAM

There were several reasons why Africans accepted Islam.[7] There is no gainsaying the fact that Islam gave some benefits to new converts. Many Sub-Saharan

African rulers used the religion to establish diplomatic connections with North Africa, to secure positive economic connections and to win new associates. As a Muslim may not enslave another Muslim, personal conversion was a reliable way of protecting oneself against being captured and sold into slavery. Such was the case especially along East African trade routes. On another level, Islam allowed converts to continue with some old practices. For instance, converts could still marry more than one wife. Consequently, conversion to Islam did not entail substantial changes in day-to-day religious practices because Islamic practices often existed side by side with indigenous religious beliefs.

At an institutional level, Islam introduced new ideas into African societies. The arrival of Muslim clerics into an African society often signaled the establishment of *madrasseh*, or Qur'anic schools. Such institutions arose to paramountcy in many African societies. In most cases, they co-existed with indigenous centers of learning. Another important contribution of the Islamization process in Africa was the introduction of *tariqa*s, or Sufi brotherhoods (the mystical tradition in Islam). Nehemia Levtzion has noted, however, that these brotherhoods became significant in the West Sudan only in the eighteenth and nineteenth centuries. In addition, the introduction of the Sufi brotherhoods engendered Islamic jihads in Africa south of the Sahara. Led by people such as Uthman Dan Fodio, Maba Jahu, Sati Mati, Foday Kaba, Shaikh Muhammad, Abdille Hassan, and Muhammad Ahmad ibn Abdallah, these movements fuelled the flame of religious fervor among their followers. Some of the advocates of jihad felt that they have been given divine responsibility to purge Islam of corruption and heretical innovations.

In the western Sudan, Islamic cities such as Timbuktu, Gao, Katsina, and Kano emerged and became significant commercial and religious centers. These urban sites attracted many Muslim immigrants, including scholars, scientists, and lawyers. This was the genesis of a Muslim intellectual élite in West Africa. Islam placed considerable emphasis on the training of clerics, as well as scholars, lawyers, doctors, and administrators. Missionaries were active as early as the tenth century in the city of Gao, and by the eleventh century, there were many active missionaries throughout the western Sudan. Islamic schools emerged during the fourteenth century in the empire of Mali and, by the end of fifteenth century, there were *madrasseh* in Songhay. At the close of the sixteenth century, Timbuktu had about 180 Qur'anic schools and thousands of students who came from all over the Sudan and Sahel regions.[8]

Islam also offered a new worldview. In many instances, it was helpful that there was what Peter Clarke has called a "significant equivalence" between Islamic and African conceptions of crucial issues relating to ethics and society. The belief systems further shared perspectives concerning the explanation of natural and sacred events. For example, Humphrey Fisher has revealed that there is a strong affinity between Islam and African traditional religion in the interpretation of dreams and visions. Fisher contends that the "dream may have been an avenue for the acceptance of new ideas or objects, or even of religious beliefs, being thus in itself a channel of conversion."[9]

On the political front, the introduction of Islam promoted centralization and the creation of a large, administrative organization. As a politico-religious system, Islam provided a generally accepted norm for legitimate authority for African societies. Moreover, in the western Sudanese states, political leaders used the services of Islamic scholars as secretaries, jurists, and advisers. Sudanese rulers such as Askiya Mohammed of Songhay, Mansa Musa of Mali, and Idris Aloma of Borno, employed Islamic scholars as political consultants and counsels. One such renowned scholar, Muhammad al-Maghili, wrote *The Obligations of the Princes*, which discusses the nature of Islamic government and provides an important code of conduct for Muslim rulers.

V. JIHAD, REFORM, AND RENEWAL IN ISLAM

No survey of Islam in Africa is complete without an examination of the movements that have endeavored to reform the faith and return it to its pristine position during the seventh century. Several factors fueled the embers and led to the religious revitalization in African Islam. These included the perceived need to safeguard the oneness of God, the maltreatment of believers, and the religious compromises that some Muslims accepted. The dominant impetus for the reformers of Islam was the distinct religious stamp created in the African milieu. Such zealots believed that they followed a divine injunction to purify Islam of alien practices, unbelief, polytheism, and corruption.

The term jihad is often interpreted as holy war, the word is derived from a word root meaning "to strive" or "to make an effort" on behalf or for the sake of something. The word jihad is usually followed by the Arabic expression *fi sabil illah*, meaning "in the path of God". The concept has many manifestations: the jihad of the sword (*jihad bi-al-sayf*); the jihad of the tongue, preaching jihad (*jihad al-qawl*); or the jihad of the heart, jihad against one's sinful propensities (*jihad bi al-nafs*). The last form of jihad is exalted with the mystical Sufi tradition. The Sunni tradition of jihad is enshrined in bifurcation of the world into *Dar al-Islam*, the House of Islam, in which the teachings of Allah prevailed, and *Dar al-Harb*, the House of war, the domain of infidels.[10]

The earliest jihads occurred in Mauritania and the Senegambia region in the late-seventeenth and eighteenth centuries. The jihad in Mauritania originated as part of the resistance of Berbers to the hegemony of the Arab Banu Ma'qil. Their spokesperson, Nasir al-Din, condemned the rulers for their religious laxity and oppression. He proclaimed the end of time and the coming of the Madhi, or the rightly guided one, and demanded that his followers conform to the teachings of the Qur'an. In Senegambia, jihad began with the efforts of Muslims to overthrow local rulers and establish autonomous states. Elsewhere, in central Sudan, Jibril b. 'Umar encouraged Muslims to establish an Islamic society based on the life of the Prophet Muhammad and his early successors. 'Umar taught the doctrine of "double jihad", which entailed the internal jihad, or struggle against all evil inclinations, and which preceded the external jihad, or war against infidels and corrupt Muslim governments.

Mervyn Hiskett's magnum opus, *The Sword of Truth* gives a compelling analysis of the legacy of Uthman Dan Fodio's jihad movement against the Hausa in nineteenth-century northern Nigeria. Building on the pioneering work of Murray Last, Hiskett presents the jihad tradition as a reform movement orchestrated around bringing about an authentic Islam that is bereft of innovation and corruption. Dan Fodio (1754-1817), the creator of the nineteenth-century caliphate of Sokoto, was the scion of a family renowned for intellectual accomplishments and piety.[11] He was well conversant with the writings of other reformers, especially those of al-Maghili, a Tunisian jurist. Concerning his own *modus operandi*, Dan Fodio declared:[12]

> To make war upon the king who is an apostate, and who has abandoned the religion of Islam for the religion of the heathendom is obligatory by assent, and that to make war against the king who is an apostate—who has not abandoned the religion of Islam as far as the profession of it is concerned, but who mingles the observances of Islam with the observances of heathendom, like the kings of Hausaland for the most—is also obligatory by assent, and that to take government from him is obligatory by assent.

Uthman Dan Fodio's revitalization movement can be traced back to 1794 when he had a dream in which he was given "the sword of Islam" to defend his people and society. Between 1804 and 1808, the jihad of Dan Fodio defeated most of the rulers of the Hausa states and founded a new capital at Sokoto in 1809. Concurrent revolts throughout Hausaland involving pockets of Fulani, Tuareg, and Hausa populations culminated in the establishment of the largest political community in West Africa since the fall of the Songhay Empire in 1591. The Sokoto Caliphate exercised political hegemony over a wide region comprising an area of 180,000 square miles. Eventually, fifteen loosely confederated emirates arose with each emir affirming the religio-political leadership of Dan Fodio as the "commander of the faithful".

The tradition of reform and revival that Dan Fodio proclaimed was deeply entrenched in African Islam. Already in the fifteenth century, al-Maghili had condemned the corrupt and un-Islamic practices of West African Muslim élites. He denounced unjust taxation, the seizure of personal properties, and "venal" clerics who served rulers without any knowledge of Arabic or Islam. Al-Maghili advocated the implementation of *shar'ia*, or Muslim law, by serious Muslim leaders, and introduced into West African Islam the concept of the *mujahid*, or fighter in the path of God.

Dan Fodio's plan for reform was to restore the lost purity and prestige of Islam and to establish a renewed mode of Islamic piety. He did not support the idea that Muslims should live in *bilad al-harb*, or the territory of non-Muslims, because of what he considered the socio-religious decadence of Hausa society.

After the creation of Sokoto, Dan Fodio advanced an ambitious agenda for reform declaring:[13]

> Most of the people are ignorant of the Sharia, and it is obligatory that there should be, in every mosque and quarter in the town, a faqih [general knowledge] teaching of the people their religion. So also is it, in every village, obligatory on every faqih who has completed his fard'ayn [collective duty binding on Muslims] and has devoted himself to the fard kifaya [individual obligation without collective implication], that he should go out to the people neighboring on his town in order to teach them their religion and the obligatory parts of their Shar' [religious code]. If one person does this, sin falls off the remaining people: otherwise all of them will carry the sin together. As for the learned person, the sin will be because of his neglecting to go out [and preach]. But as for the ignorant, it will be because of his shortcomings in avoiding knowledge.

Uthman Dan Fodio's legacy is impressive. He succeeded in uniting the peoples of Hausaland and many of the surrounding areas into a single unit. He established a high standard of literacy, publication, thought, and action that was unparalleled in the history of Islam in northern Nigeria. Dan Fodio's jihad also provided a new impetus for Islamic learning and literacy because Dan Fodio, his brother Abdullah, and his son Mohammed Bello were Islamic scholars as well as political leaders. Their scholarly endeavors arose out of the need to provide a rational explanation and justification for jihad and its concomitant political re-alignments. Through their efforts, Islamic intellectualism spread beyond the borders of the Fulani Muslim territories in northern Nigeria to different parts of West Africa. Arabic eventually became the official language of commerce, literacy, and correspondence. Arabic schools were established to promote Islamic religion and education. Finally, the Sokoto jihad provided the inspiration for other reformers in West Africa, especially the jihads of Seku Ahmadu and that of al-Hajj 'Umar. To this very day, the Sokoto Caliphate continues to have a strong religio-cultural influence in Nigeria.

Mervyn Hiskett originally contended that the jihadist model is very attractive to African Muslims "whether the Muslims involved came to Islam as a result of nineteenth century reformist ardor or were drawn in less spectacularly by slower influences during the colonial period."[14] While there is a kernel of truth in this assertion, one must be weary of the triumphant ideology that is inherent in such perspective. Hiskett's romantic view of jihad glosses over the perspective of those who suffered the anguish of the sword. Hiskett himself corrected this one-sided perspective in the second edition of *Sword of the Truth*. Thus, he wrote:

> The non-Muslim, "pagan" point of view has been left largely untold. The brutality and intolerance of all "jihad of the sword", and especially that of the nineteenth-century western Sudan, has been veiled by an assumption of moral righteousness, based on the Muslim

> claim of divine revelation and a written law, that leaves no place for an approach from the point of view of the victims. The stark intransigence of this stance has not diminished over the generations.[15]

There undoubtedly remains a need for a critical review of our understanding of the jihad movements in Africa. This revision will take religious ideals and vision into consideration. At the same time, the inglorious consequences of the jihad cannot be ignored. This approach is a *sine qua non* in a religiously pluralistic context as Africa. As one scholar has pointed out:[16]

> Not only as concrete examples of shifting perceptions of Islam in the region, but also as indicating the likely consequences of modern Islamism because of the similarities in the orientation and objectives of the two phenomena. Like the previous jihad, modern Islamism is not only committed to an exclusive, legalistic, intolerant and militant conception of Islam as sharia, but also actively seeks to transform the state and society to bring them into conformity with that model.

Resurgent Islam takes many shapes and forms. One is a persistent call for return to the *shari'a* as the legal code for civil and criminal matters. This controversy has created a great brouhaha in contemporary Nigeria. The *shari'a* issue became particularly volatile with the announcement on October 22, 1999 of the adoption of Muslim law in Zamfara state by its governor, Ahmed Sani Yerima. Since Nigeria's population is roughly divided between Christians and Muslims, many pundits feared that the imposition of *shari'a* would further polarize the country. Yet, several states in northern Nigeria have also followed the example in Zamfara, and have adopted Muslim law.[17] Recent events in Nigeria have shown that one has to take a more critical look at Peter Clarke's assertion:[18]

> Many Christians who see the contemporary revitalization of Islam in Nigeria as a threat and are not entirely confident it can be contained, are, however, inclined to exaggerate both its impact and the radicalism of its demands. Many of these demands are neither new nor radical in themselves. What is new . . . is the context in which the demands are made and the means used to obtain these demands.

Indeed, sectarian conflicts in Nigeria have reached alarming proportions. More than a thousand people died in the northern city of Kaduna in 2000 when Christians and Muslims clashed over plans to introduce *shari'a* in Kaduna state.[19] A frustrated President Obasanjo declared that the riots were the worst outbreak of mayhem in Nigeria since the civil war of the 1960s. Moreover, the strife in Kaduna triggered revenge killings of Muslims in southeastern Nigeria. A cycle of violence has developed since President Obasanjo came to power. In a more recent and widely publicized episode, more than two hundred people perished in clashes between Christians and Muslims in November 2002. These disturbances ultimately forced the relocation of the Miss World beauty pageant from Nigeria to London.

The *shari'a* issue has generated tremendous tension between Christians and Muslims in Nigeria. Christian minorities in the north and the Christian Association of Nigeria (CAN) vehemently oppose the implementation of Muslim law in Nigeria. They continue to argue that the 1999 constitution makes such a move illegal. On the other hand, Muslim leaders continue to claim that since the constitution guarantees freedom of religion, they have the legal right to implement *shari'a*. It is important to note that not all Muslims support the implementation of Muslim law in Nigeria. For example, Sheik Ibrahim El-Zakzaky on September 21, 1999 declared that establishing *shari'a* at the present time "might end up creating an instrument of oppression and exploitation in the hands of the leadership, particularly when they lack commitment and discipline."[20]

Wole Soyinka, the Nigerian Noble Laureate, has likewise remarked that there is no religious basis for such theocratic madness, and says that the call for imposing *shari'a* is motivated mainly by politics. His remarks echo the dominant feeling of southern Christians that northern Muslim elite, finding themselves out of political favor, have decided to create religio-political problems for the government of Olusegun Obasanjo, who is a Christian from the south. In the words of Adebayo Williams:[21]

> Once it became obvious that Obasanjo would marginally tinker with the status quo to ensure some measure of authority and legitimacy for his own minimalist agenda, the northern power mafia opted for the sharia gambit and thereby severely undermined the authority and legitimacy of the state.

The issue of the constitutionality of implementing *shari'a* continues to rage in Nigeria. Nigeria, like most African countries, is still wrestling with the herculean task of creating a national consciousness among different ethnic groups that are divided by history, language, and religion. There are many dimensions to this issue. *Shari'a* has been locally appropriated in various societies under different circumstances over the centuries. Any attempt to restore it to its original form, or any other time for that matter, is to distort its inherent flexibility. As Sajida Sultana Alvi has rightly declared:[22]

> Change is actually the essence of Islam—a very dominant and central feature. If you rob Islam of that dynamism and that capacity for change, then it becomes static. That is why there are so many difficulties in the minds of Muslims all over the world. They are trying to cope with the demands of modernity and looking for solutions within the scriptures.

VI. THE IMPACT OF ISLAMIC ORGANIZATIONS

The Islamic challenge and agenda in Africa have been engineered and facilitated by numerous Islamic organizations and associations. These organizations have provided an avenue to promote the agenda of the Islamic ummah. These organizations have been particularly active in Nigeria, Africa's most populous nation. Archibishop Tessier from Algiers once described this country as the greatest Islamo-Christian nation in the world. Nigeria, with an almost equal percentage of Christians and Muslims living side by side provides an excellent resource for understanding the role and impact of Islamic organizations. A preeminent Islamic organization in the country is the Jama'atu Nasril Islam. Ahmadu Bello, the late Sardauna of Sokoto, and Premier of the northern region established this body in January 1962. Its primary objective was to organize Muslim efforts in Nigeria. During the time of Ahmadu Bello, this Islamic organization was very active in building mosques, organizing conversion campaigns, and publishing newsletters. In contemporary Nigeria, this Islamic body stills commands considerable power and influence. The Nigerian Muslim Brother led by Ibrahim Zakzaky of Zaria is another organization that has been very prominent in Nigeria. Inspired by the thought of Sayyid Qutb and Hassan al-Banna of Egypt, the Nigerian Muslim Brothers have advocated for an Islamic state and the implementation of *shari'a* in Nigeria. They reject the Nigerian constitution and all other judicial institutions in the country.

The Supreme Council of Nigeria was established in 1973 to "cater for the interest of Islam throughout the federation, to serve as a channel of contact with the government of Nigeria on Islamic affairs, where necessary, and to serve as the only channel of contact on Islamic matters."[23] The organization has been very outspoken on the questions of *shari'a*, and religion and state.

Christians in Nigeria have responded to these organizations by forming an ecumenical body that can serve as a forum for Christians to table their complaints and present their own story. The Christian Association of Nigeria (CAN) was formed in 1976 as an ecumenical body of Protestants, Catholics, and African Independent Churches. Enwerem sees the formation as an amalgamation of distinct southern and northern strands. Its closest forerunner was the Northern Christian Association established in 1964 at the time of Sarduanna's Islamization policies. With the rising tide of Islamization, there was a need to have a permanent Christian organization to arrest this phenomenon. Since the 1980s, the violence between Christians and Muslims in Nigeria has escalated to an alarming proportion.[24] CAN's strategy has inevitably shifted from diplomacy to militancy. The body's political objectives moved to continue the assurance of Nigeria's secular status, and the procurement of resources for the Christian constituencies within the nation. In contemporary Nigeria, CAN has been very outspoken against the implementation of *shari'a* in some northern states. CAN continues to maintain that the implementation of *shari'a* to cover both civil and criminal matters is a blatant rejection of Nigeria's secular status. The body has issued many public statements against any overt or surreptitious moves to make Nigeria an Islamic state. CAN claims that although the *shari'a* legal system has always existed in Nigeria, the Constitution only recognizes the customary and personal aspects of the Islamic legal system. *Shari'a* can offer useful guidelines on such issues as marriage, divorce, or the execution of personal will; *shari'a* cannot be enforced in criminal matters especially in a religiously pluralistic society like Nigeria.

The Islamic Brotherhood (Al-Ikhwan Al-Muslimun) continues to have considerable influence in many countries in Africa. This reform movement was established in 1928 in Egypt by Hassan al-Banna. The Muslim Brotherhood embodied the revolutionary ideas of Al-Afghani, the revivalist jurisprudence of Muhammad Abduh, and the reformist vision of Rashid Rida. In response to the comatose state of the ummah over the past two centuries, al-Banna articulated the reasons for this decline in ways that added more depth and intellectual edge to the contributions of the pioneers of reform. He attributed the decline of the ummah to a number of factors including colonialism and an uncritical imitation of the West. In Egypt, the Brotherhood cooperated with other Islamic youth movements to reform education and fight poverty and ignorance. It campaigned for the establishment of an Islamic government based on the recommendations of the *ulama* (Islamic clerics) and the full application of the *shari'a*. The Brotherhood emerged out of al-Banna's passionate concern about the negative consequences of a Western secular form of modernization upon Islamic life and values and the inability of the government to tackle pervasive socio-economic inequalities in Egyptian society. In being consistent with other Islamic revivalist (*tajdid*) movements, al-Banna attributed societal problems to its rejection of the Islamic ideals as found in early Islam—during the time of the Prophet Muhammad and its followers. Therefore, he called for a return to Islamic sources—the Qur'an and the Sunnah (examples and practices) of the Prophet. He underscored the political dimension of Islam and the urgent need for a proper state based on Islamic law and belief. For the Muslim Brotherhood and its allies, Islam presented the most authentic blueprint for a complete modern society and was the best ideological and political alternative to Communism. In less than twenty years of its establishment, al-Banna's movement gained popularity and credibility unparalleled in the religio-political history of Egypt. By then, he had followers all over North Africa. The movement is still the most influential movement in modern times. Many Muslims in Egypt, northern Nigeria, Sudan, Algeria, and Tunisia find spiritual succor and intellectual satisfaction in this organization. Many of the groups that are labeled by the West as fundamentalists[25] belong to this group.

VII. OTHER EASTERN AND SOUTHERN AFRICAN EXAMPLES

This section examines Christian-Muslim encounters in two African countries—Uganda and South Africa. Uganda with a population of over 23 million people is ostensibly a Christian country with 85 percent of the population being Christian and 11 percent Muslim. The remaining four percent follow other religions including African Traditional Religion. The bond of kinship has created positive relationships between Christians and Muslims in Uganda. It is common to see one single family that could be composed of people from different religious traditions. This is a condition that is very analogous to the experience of many countries in West Africa. In Uganda, this situation has contributed to the healthy relationship between Christians and Muslims, especially in the rural areas. Christians and Muslims have been able to team up to fight oppressive governments from 1980 to 1986, when the National Resistance Movement came to power under the leadership of Yoweri Museveni, the current President of Uganda. Uganda is a secular and a multi-religious state. The government has continued to promote a situation in which religious freedom would flourish. The government has also allowed many Muslim organizations from the Muslim world to establish branches in the country in order to contribute to the country's socio-economic development. These Muslim organizations eventually provided the basis for the rise of militant Islam. The members of the Tabligh organization have had many violent confrontations with Christians. This organization gets considerable encouragement and inspiration from the radical message of Hassan Turabi from the Sudan. In spite of isolated cases of open confrontations and mutual suspicion on many political issues, Christian-Muslim relations in Uganda is very cordial. President Museveni continues to counsel the people of Uganda:[26]

> The common enemy for both Christians and Muslims is neither Christianity nor Islam but those few corrupt Ugandans who embezzle public funds meant for the improvement of the country's infrastructure.

The South African religious context presents another fascinating paradigm in Christian-Muslim relations. The 1993 South African census states that the total number of Muslims is half a million, of whom 2.5 percent are Africans, 49.8 percent Coloureds, 47 percent Indians, and 7 percent Whites. This number will increase in the twenty-first century. Islam came to South Africa in two stages. The first (1652-1807) was led by Dutch colonialists. The second phase (1860-1914) was organized by British colonialists from India. Since the nineteenth century, South African Muslims have established movements and organizations to fight discrimination, injustice, and unjust governmental policies. In the 1970s and 1980s, South African Muslims were inspired by literature from the Middle East and Indian subcontinent, especially the writings of the Egyptian Sayyid Qutb, the Iranian Ali Shariati and the Pakistani Mawlana Abu al-Ala Mawdudi. The Durban-based Muslim Youth Movement of South Africa (MYMSA), which was established in 1970, has been essential in propagating Islamic values and teachings in South Africa. The MYMSA has given birth to other organizations such as the Islamic Medical Association, South African National Zakat Fund, Women's Islamic Movement, Muslim Students Association, and South African Association of Muslim Social Scientists.

Christians and Muslims in South Africa have co-operated on the political front. They have come together to fight obnoxious apartheid policies and proclamations. In a lecture delivered by Nelson Mandela in Oxford in July 1998, he praised the immense contribution of South African Muslims to the struggle against apartheid. He also applauded the Islamic contribution to the creation of an equal and just society. The South African context provides a good lesson in Christian-Muslim solidarity against injustice and oppression.

VIII. THE LEGACY OF *PROCMURA* IN AFRICA

This section of the chapter will focus on the movement that has boldly responded to the Islamic challenge in Africa. With independence, a new understanding of Islam became imperative for Christians in sub-Saharan Africa. In 1959, this need was realized with the creation of the Islam in Africa Project or the Project for Christian-Muslim Relations in Africa Project (PROCMURA) as it came to be known in 1985. The Late Babs Mala, a professor of Islamic Studies at the University of Ibadan, suggested this name. The project was initiated in order for African Christians to understand Islam and ultimately create avenues and resources for Christian-Muslim dialogue. The program affirmed the importance of Islam in Africa and seeks to develop the need for churches to educate their members about their responsibilities toward their Muslim neighbors. The primary purpose of the project was:[27]

> To keep before the churches in Africa their responsibility for understanding Islam and the Muslims of their region in view of the churches' task of interpreting faithfully in the Muslim world the Gospel of Jesus Christ and to effect the research and education necessary for this."

This initiative was fueled by an optimistic fervor. The optimism was not a naïve one, rather it was engendered by a new sense of Christian responsibility in Africa. In a statement drafted by the Christian Council of Nigeria in 1962 entitled *Christian Responsibility in an Independent Nigeria*, Nigerian Christians affirmed:[28]

> Closely related to the need for more Christian love in our approach is the need for evangelists among Muslims who have a thorough understanding of the Koran. We are critical of those who reject Christianity, as do the Muslims, without any real attempt to grasp the full significance of the Biblical message. Can we expect to have more success with the Muslim if we are ignorant of the social, political and spiritual teachings of the Koran and how these are interpreted today? Can we expect to have success if we are unwilling to become involved in face-to-face encounter in which Christian and Muslim share the most intimate concerns about their religion? Dialogue between Christian and Muslim is of little avail if we are not willing on our part to re-read and 'rethink' the Bible and re-examine our own theological presuppositions.

Under the leadership of PROCMURA, area committees were established in Ghana, Sierra Leone, Benin, Nigeria, Cameroon, Ethiopia, Kenya, and Malawi. PROCMURA has organized many consultations and conferences in many countries. It has created the forum that has enabled Christians and Muslims to come together to discuss many issues that are germane to Christian-Muslim understanding and engagement in Africa. The project has been particularly helpful in encouraging Africans to tap into the legacy of dialogue of life that is very pervasive in many African nations. Within the dialogue of life, Christians and Muslims relate to one another without any theological impediments. In this context, African traditional ethos of hospitality and tolerance radiates in a compelling way. In the post independence era, PROCMURA tapped into Africa's legacy of hospitality and tolerance to deepen inter-religious awareness in both Francophone and Anglophone countries in Africa.

CONCLUSION

The way forward in Christian-Muslim relations in Africa is to develop the capacity for dialogue that can mobilize Christians and Muslims to see beyond the manipulations of the nation-state and the vicious agenda of some self-proclaimed religious demagogues. Both Christianity and Islam contain value systems that can contribute to meaningful inter-religious dialogue within a pluralistic nation like Africa. Dialogue is not the elimination of religious particularities; rather, it is living together with the full recognition of the best in both religious traditions. This form of dialogue is not an abstract construct. It must be deeply rooted in the social, political, economic, and cultural realities of specific societies. This makes the theme of contextualization very relevant to any discourse in Christian-Muslim relations. Dialogue can only be meaningful when the whole range of the human experience, context, and circumstances are taken into consideration. One of the primary objectives of dialogue is the common search for a workable paradigm of society and cooperation in building a human community that safeguards religious freedom and respects differences and particularities.

Notes

1. See Andrew Walls, "African as the Theatre of Christian Engagement with Islam in the Nineteenth Century", in *Journal of Religion in Africa,* 1999, 29,2, 155-74; Lamin Sanneh, *Piety and Power: Muslims and Christians in West Africa* (Maryknoll, NY: Orbis Books, 1996); J. Haafkens, *Islam and Christianity in Africa* (Nairobi: Procmura, 1992); Lissi Rasmussen, *Christian-Muslim Relations in Africa: The Cases of Northern Nigeria and Tanzania Compared* (London & New York: British Academic Press, 1993); and Noel Q. King, *Christian and Muslim in Africa* (New York: Harper & Row Publishers, 1971).
2. Philip Jenkins, "A New Christendom" in *The Chronicle Review*, Section 2, March 29, 2002, B.10.
3. See Sulayman S. Nyang, *Islam, Christianity, and African Identity* (Vermont: Amana, 1984) for an excellent discussion on the twin processes of Arabization and Islamization in Africa. Lamin Sanneh has however cautioned that Sudan is the only black African country where these two processes worked effectively. He affirms that in the rest of the continent, one can only speak of the use of the sacred Arabic language as the most visible sign of Islamization.

4. Lamin SANNEH, *West African Christianity: The Religious Impact* (Maryknoll, NY: Orbis Book, 1983), xvi.
5. Kwame NKRUMAH, *Conscientism* (London: Heinemann, 1964), 93-94.
6. Quoted in Lamin SANNEH, "Translatability in Islam and in Christianity in Africa: A Thematic Approach", in Thomas D. BLAKELY, Walter E.A. VAN BECK & Dennis L THOMSON (eds), *Religion in Africa* (London: John Curry Ltd., 1994), 25.
7. On conversion to Islam in Africa, see the two articles H.J. FISHER, "Conversion Reconsidered: Some Historical Aspects of Religious Conversion in Black Africa," in *Africa*, 1973, 43, 2, 27-40; and ID, "The Juggernaut's Apologia: Conversion to Islam in Black Africa," in *Africa*, 1985, 55,2, 153-70. N. LEVTZION (ed.). *Conversion to Islam* (New York and London: Holmes & Meier, 1979), is also an important study.
8. S.I. CISSOKO, "The Songhay from the 12th to the 16th Century", in D.T. NIANE (ed.), *Africa from the Twelfth to the Sixteenth Century* (London: Heinemann, 1984), 209.
9. Quoted in Peter B. CLARKE *West African and Islam* (London: Edward Arnold Publishers, 1982), 260.
10. For a comprehensive discussion on the jihad and reform movements in Islam see J. KELSAY & J.J. TURNER, *Just War and Jihad: Historical and Theoretical Perspectives on War and Peace in Western and Islamic Traditions* (New York: Greenwood Press, 1991); and N. LEVTZION & J.O. VOLL (eds), *Eighteenth-Century Renewal and Reform in Islam* (New York: Syracuse University, 1987).
11. See S.U. BALOGUN, "Arabic Intellectualism in West Africa: The Role of the Sokoto Caliphate", in *Journal Institute of Muslim Minority Affairs*, July 1985, 6, 2, 394-411.
12. Thomas HODGKIN, *Nigerian Perspectives: An Historical Anthology* (London: Oxford University Press, 1975), 247-248.
13. Quoted in SANNEH, "Translatability in Islam", 33-34.
14. Quoted in John Alembillah AZUMAH, *The Legacy of Arab-Islam in Africa: A Quest for Inter-Religious Dialogue* (Oxford: One World, 2001), 11-12.
15. Ibid.
16. A.A. AN-NA'IM, "Islam and Human Rights in Sahelian Africa", in David WESTERLUND and E.E. ROSANDER (eds), *African Islam and Islam in Africa: Encounters between Sufis and Islamists* (London: Hurst, 1997), 83.
17. The other states are Sokoto, Gombe, Kebbi, Niger, Katsina, Jigawa, Kano, Yobe, Borno, Bauchi, and Kaduna.
18. Peter CLARKE, "Islamic Reform in Contemporary Nigeria: Methods and Aims", in *Third World Quarterly*, 1988, 10, 2, 535.
19. It is important to add here that in spite of the internecine Christian-Muslim conflicts in countries like Nigeria and the Sudan, Africa has a long legacy of peaceful co-existence between Christians and Muslims. Yorubaland in southwestern Nigeria and the Gambia are two compelling examples in this regard. Lamin Sanneh writes that "the Gambia is probably the first and only Muslim country in the world that has observed as national holidays Christian feasts such as Good Friday and the Feast of the Assumption of the Blessed Virgin.", in SANNEH, *Piety and Power*, 150. For a good discussion on the Yoruba example see David LAITIN, *Hegemony and Culture: Politics and Religious Change Among the Yoruba* (Chicago: University of Chicago

Press, 1986); Peter McKenzie, *Inter-religious Encounters in West Africa: Samuel Ajayi Crowther's Attitude to African Traditional Religions and Islam* (Leicester: Leicester University Bookshop, 1976); and J.D.Y. Peel, *Religious Encounter and the Making of the Yoruba* (Indiana: Indiana University Press, 2003).

20. Quoted in Jonathan T. Reynolds, "Nigeria and Shari'a: Religion and Politics in a West African Nation", in Meghan Appel O'Meara (ed.), *History Behind the Headlines: The Origins of Conflicts Worldwide* Vol. 2 (Farmington Hill, MI: Gale Group, 2001), 217.
21. Adebayo Williams, "Transition Without Transformation", http://nigeriaworld.com, July 8, 2001, p. 4.
22. Quoted in Mary Pat Fisher, *Living Religions* (Upper Saddle River, NJ: Prentice Hall, 1999), 387.
23. Joseph Kenny, "Sharia and Christianity in Nigeria: Islam and a 'Secular' State", in *Journal of Religion in Africa*, 1996, 26, 4, 345.
24. See Toyin Falola, *Violence in Nigeria: The Crisis of Religious Politics and Secular Ideologies* (Rochester, NY: University of Rochester Press, 1998), for a discussion on the legacy of inter-religious conflicts in Nigeria.
25. It should be noted that Muslims believe that the term fundamentalism has a pejorative connotation. They strongly believe that it connotes ignorance and narrow-mindedness, and therefore do not believe it is appropriate to apply the term to genuine Islamic revival movements. Scholars like Frederick Denny, Bernard Lewis, Seyyed Hossein Nasr, and Riffat Hassan have objected to the application of the term to Muslims because of its Christian provenance. John Esposito, who, recognizing the problem with the term speaks of 'Islamic revivalism and Islamic activism.' See John Esposito, *The Islamic Threat: Myth or Reality?* (New York and Oxford: Oxford University Press, 1992) 7-8.
26. Solomon Mugyenzi, "Seeking Understanding in Uganda" in *Transformation* 2000, 17, 1, 42.
27. Johann Haafkens, "The Direction of Christian-Muslim Relations in Sub-Saharan Africa", in Yvonne Yazbeck Haddad *et. al.* (eds), *Christian-Muslim Encounters* (Gainesville: University of Florida Press, 1995), 306.
28. J. Haafkens, "PROCUMURA and the Churches in Africa," *Project for Christian-Muslim Relations in Africa,* May/June 1994, 3, 3, 8.

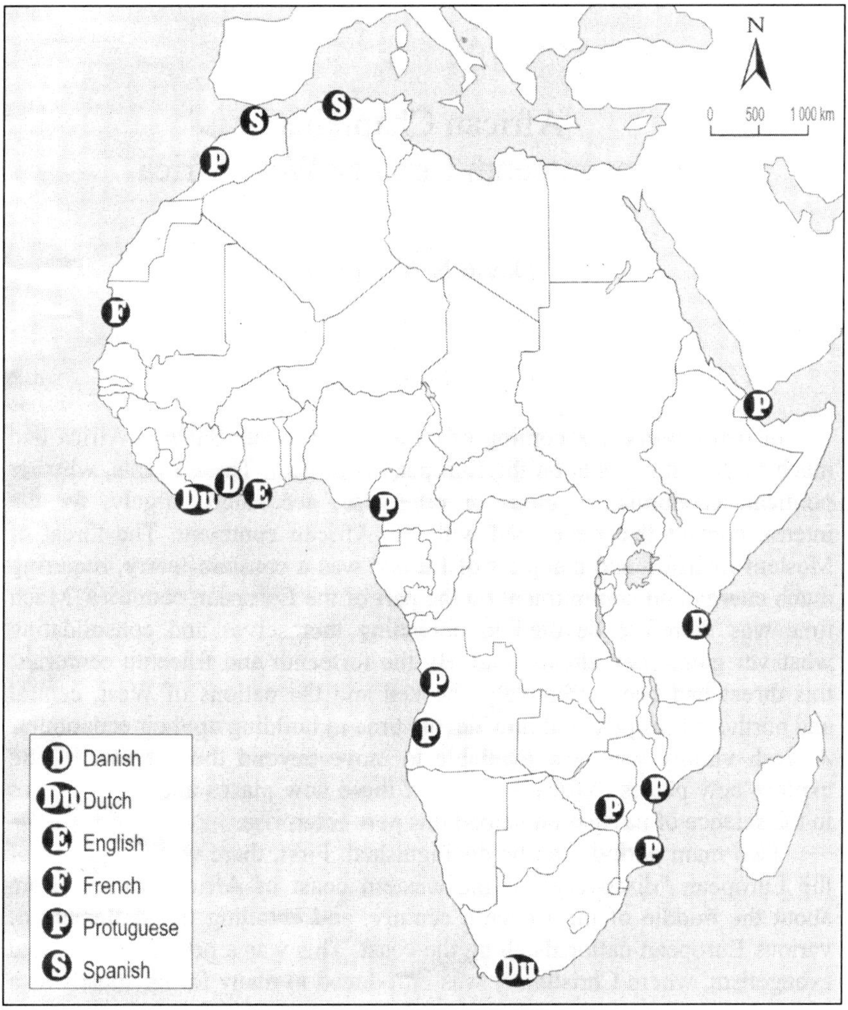

Map 4: European Discovery of Africa between the 1400's and the 1700's

Chapter Six

African Chaplains in Seventeenth Century West Africa

David N.A. Kpobi

INTRODUCTION

In many ways, the coming of Christianity to sub-Saharan Africa had much to do with events on the European continent. These events, whether political, economic, religious or otherwise, accounted, largely, for the intense contact that developed with the African continent. The threat of Moslem invasion and conquest of Europe was a constant worry, requiring much energy and commitment on the part of the European countries. Much time was therefore devoted to defending themselves and consolidating whatever gains they already had. By the forteenth and fifteenth centuries, this threat had been effectively checked and the nations of West, central and northern Europe could now devote time to building up their economies. A fresh vitality was now available to move beyond their territories and explore new places. Africa was one of these new places and the advances in the science of navigation helped this new enterprise.

Two main periods can be distinguished. First, there was the period of the European "discovery" of the western coast of Africa, starting from about the middle of the fifteenth century, and entailing the settlement of various European nationals along the coast. This was a period of trade and evangelism, where Christianity was introduced in many forms, mostly as a "sterilized European institution, safely quarantined in hygienic enclaves along the coast whence it occasionally timidly emerged to make local contact."[1] During this period the church was no more than an appendage to the commercial enterprise and therefore had very little attraction for the African population. Under such conditions, Christianity was not sustainable in spite of the few converts, which even included chiefs and community leaders. The second period can be dated to starting from the middle of the eighteenth century, when some isolated attempts were made at evangelization alongside the slave trade. This again was an unfruitful period as far as mission was concerned, although, as we shall come to see, the ground was being prepared for greater success. The real beginning of success became visible only in the following century when mission organizations, from Europe (and later from the USA), with the collaboration of many Africans helped root Christianity in the African soil. Various historians with varying emphases have captured the many stories of these exciting periods and it is not our intention to provide the details here.[2] Needless to say, the African perspective on these stories has been obscured for many years because not many Africans have been writing about them. The situation has been changing in the last 30 to 40 years and we are now hearing and reading from more and more Africans who are telling their own story. This of course does not mean that we now possess the full and accurate story of the African past, for whilst history still remains a narration of past events, the interpretation of these events will continue to vary as long as it is done by humans like us.

I. THE IBERIAN FACTOR

Africa remained a continent of mystery and intrigue for Europe for many centuries. Since North Africa used to be a strong Christian territory until the seventh and eighth centuries, many Europeans did not consider it to belong to Africa. It suited their prejudices to consider Africa as beginning at the Sahara Desert. The European imagination was fired by the impression that the vast Sahara stretch, including the area beyond, was the domain of wild human beings who were in the grips of the devil and were subject to every kind of brutish behavior. Ignorance and superstition fueled many frightful and often unfounded stories about the continent, so the very thought of penetrating it would not be entertained. There was, for example, a story of Satan standing guard, ready to destroy anyone who would venture beyond the known frontiers. This fear was, however, mitigated by the story of an ancient Christian kingdom ruled by a Prester John, somewhere in the midst of the wild, which European travelers were eager to find and be acquainted with.

Following the disappearance of Christianity from North Africa, only pockets of Christians remained in places like Egypt, Algeria, Morocco and Tunisia. The Church, however, did not give up trying to restore its fortunes in these places. The Crusades organized by the Church in the tenth, eleventh and twealth centuries, had as one of its primary aims the recapturing of holy places and re-establishing Christian presence in North Africa. The Roman Catholic Orders, the Franciscans and the Dominicans, were the first to make such attempts at evangelizing Moslem territory. St. Francis of Assisi (founder of the Franciscan Order) is known to have visited Egypt in 1219 during the 4th Crusade. However, after three centuries of crusading the Church had very little to show for its efforts. Hope did not die completely, as the Portuguese took up the leadership in exploration and conquest, thereby awakening a new spirit in the Church and in Europe generally. It is for this reason—for opening up this part of the world— that it is impossible to overlook the Iberian connection when writing the history of Christianity in sub-Saharan Africa.

Portugal, a strongly Catholic country, eventually made the first inroads into West Africa as part of the growing navigational adventurism of the time. The Portuguese nation had been a sea faring nation for many years and in the forteenth and fifteenth centuries spearheaded the exploration of the sea routes to many parts of the world. They had previously been quite active fighting against Moslems in and around Morocco and occasionally carried off a few captives to Lisbon as slaves.[3] These adventures formed only part of a special European desire to find a sea route to India. India was believed to be an exotic land, a worthy destination for any traveler or trader. The spirit of adventurism was also fired by the notion that as a nation, Portugal had been chosen by God to hold the Moslem forces at bay, by not only preventing their advance into Europe, but also keeping them from spreading Islam in Africa. Luis de Camoes (1524/1525-1580), a prominent Portuguese poet, wrote that Portugal had been "sent by God to strike terror into Moslem hearts and to win vast new regions of the world for the faith."[4] The whole enterprise was directed from the royal quarters and was supported by all those who mattered, including no less an institution than the Vatican.

1. Henry the Navigator

One man was the moving spirit behind the explorations. Without his keen leadership and direction, the course of the history of West Africa would have been very different. Prince Henry, the son of the Portuguese king, John I, was born in 1394 and grew to become an accomplished patriot and statesman. At the age of 21, he played an important role in the fight against Moslems when he helped capture the island of Ceuta from their hands. In the ensuing years, he acquired the name Henry the Navigator, because he directed a number of expeditions down the western coast of Africa to obtain information about the area and beyond. He had heard about the trans-Sahara trade in gold and was eager to benefit from it; and also use the opportunity to advance the cause of the church. The motives of Henry were varied, ranging from commercial and scientific to military and evangelistic. According to Azurara, the respected chronicler of the time, four main motives can be distinguished.

First, as a navigator, Henry was interested in reaching further beyond Cape Bojador, which was then the southernmost limit reached by his sailors. Europeans were eagerly trying to find a sea route to India and Henry was participating actively in this search. Secondly, Henry was trying to improve the commercial interests of Portugal by discovering new trade commodities. Thirdly, he sought through his expeditions to assess the real strength of the Moslem rulers in Africa, whom he considered enemies that had to be vanquished. Fourthly, he hoped to find any of the isolated Christian kingdoms believed to exist in Africa—particularly that of Prester John—who would then become his allies against the Moslems. This way he might be able to advance the cause of the church.[5]

The success stories of these explorations are often recounted as if they were smooth operations without any hitches. The truth is that it took more than twenty years before any meaningful achievement could be recorded. Between 1421 and 1445 Prince Henry organized ten such expeditions.[6] The crossing of Cape Bojador was delayed for almost twelve years, due to fear of the nature of the sea currents beyond, as well as the prevailing stories that the region was the domain of Satan. In 1434, however, Prince Henry's men ventured beyond Cape Bojador and found vast stretches of inhabited coastal land. They established trading links with the inhabitants, and proceeded further, crossing the River Senegal by 1445. By the time Prince Henry died in 1460, Portuguese traders had settled on the Cape Verde Islands, crossed the River Gambia and the Rio Grande, and were moving on down south. Within two years after his death, a further 600 miles of coastland had been explored. It was now only a matter of time before they reached the coasts of Sierra Leone and Cabo Mensurado (present day location of Monrovia) in 1465, and continued on to Elmina, Benin, Sao Tome, Principe and Fernando Po to complete the Portuguese discovery of the Guinea Coast. By the end of the century, the Congo as well as the southernmost parts of the continent had all been sighted. There is no doubt that Portugal was the first European nation to reach the west coast of Africa. Other claims to the contrary about earlier arrivals are now largely disregarded by historians as unreliable or even forgeries.[7]

This notable achievement made Portugal most important on the West African coast. The king of Portugal was proud to assume the additional title of "Lord of Guinea", and was careful to stamp his authority on every territory discovered. With Portuguese presence stretching all along the coast, the region became more or less a "mini Portugal". This was given further credence when, in the Treaty of Tordesilas (1494), Pope Alexander VI divided the newly discovered world between Portugal and Spain, giving the former exclusive rights over all newly discovered African territory.

2. Iberian Catholic Mission

The Portuguese discovery of the Guinea coast is important for our study of Christianity in Africa, because, as we have noted, there was a strong missionary motive behind these explorations. Portugal at least professed a Christian motive, even if it were only one of many other motives and although this motive would eventually be obscured. It is, however, significant for the first contacts between West Africa and the Christian Gospel.

The originator of the expeditions, Prince Henry, was a devout Catholic, who had been honored with the title "Grand Master of the Order of the Knights of Christ".[8] He championed the fight against the Moslems as a means of preventing them besieging Africa before the Christians arrived. He therefore made it a policy that all Portuguese ships would have priests on board, who would use every opportunity to preach the Gospel wherever they went. The king of Portugal also stressed Portugal's Christian duty in the explorations. He was known to have said that the possibility of "getting even one soul to the faith by baptism out-weighed all inconveniences."[9] The Catholic Church saw this as a new opportunity to re-establish Christian presence in Africa. The Pope immediately granted Letters of Indulgence to the traders along the coast, urging them to act "for the destruction and confusion of the Moors and the enemies of Christ, and the exaltation of the Catholic faith."[10] With the experience of the Canary Islands, where Franciscan monks had labored since the beginning of the fifteenth century, the Christian mission continued alongside the commercial activities. By the following century, the Bishopric of Madeira was overseeing the mission work in Cape Verde, Sao Tome and the Azores. In 1462, Pope Pius appointed Alfonso of Bolano, a Portuguese Franciscan, as "missionary prefect" of the Guinea coast. Alfonso had already been involved in missionary work in the Canary Islands, and his appointment was an indication of the Catholic Church's desire to establish a Christian presence on the West coast.

It was no wonder therefore that the first Christian celebrations on the coast were all undertaken by the Portuguese. A Catholic priest in the Gold Coast has recorded one such celebration as a celebration of the first mass. This was in 1482, when the Portuguese sailors, after they landed in Elmina, gathered under a big tree, set up an altar and performed what they believed would be the foundation of a great church. Even if this act hardly led to the establishment of a church, it was a declaration of intent by these first sailors. In the ensuing years, the Catholic religious orders took over the mission work. These were the Jesuits, Dominicans, Franciscans, Augustinians and Capuchins. They appear to have achieved some initial success, especially in the Gold Coast, but also in other parts of the continent. Nigeria had been touched by Catholic missions, which reached the islands of Sao Tome and Principe. Through their trading activities, the Portuguese made contact with the king of Benin and eventually convinced him to allow some of his sub-chiefs to be baptized in 1516. This was however only cosmetic, for soon after the death of the king Christianity vanished from the kingdom. Augustinian monks were also working in Warri, where the king allowed his son to be baptized and sent to Lisbon for training as a priest. When the son returned, he could not be both king and priest and had to choose. By 1650, some conversions took place in both Warri and Benin, but a breakdown in trade relations always meant a breakdown in mission, and this affected the Nigerian mission significantly. Catholic missionaries were also reported to have passed through Borno in northern Nigeria in the 1680s, but to have made no impact due to the strong presence of Islam. Another attempt, in 1710 to Katsina, also failed to produce results. In nearby Cameroon, missionary attempts were marred by Spanish-Portuguese rivalry and thus no results were produced at all. Similar stories could be told of other parts of the continent, especially of the western and southern coasts; although conversions that took place do not appear to have lasted for long. Records indicate that the work of the religious orders was hardly ever sustained after the monks had left for one reason or another. Yet, even the considerably limited success of the Catholic Church in the evangelization of the Africans, would not have been achieved without these orders. They were ready to send priests whose primary task was to convert Africans to Catholicism. They succeeded was because they were largely separated from the trading establishments based in the castles. This was in contrast to the attempts made by ship chaplains, who displayed little evangelistic zeal, and whose association with the commercial companies created a barrier between them and the African people.

In 1622, after more than a century of attempts and with very little recorded success, Pope Gregory XV established the "Sacred Congregation for the Propagation of the Faith" (*Sacra congregatio de propaganda fide*), known as the *Propaganda Fide*. This was an attempt to bring all Catholic mission work under the direction of one central authority; but it was, more importantly, another desperate attempt to maintain a Catholic mission presence in Africa. The Portuguese influence was waning fast, and so also their missionary activities.

In the second half of the seventeenth century, French Capuchin monks also championed a few missionary enterprises on the West coast with little success. The *Societe des missions etrangeres*, founded during 1663 in Paris, played an active role in these attempts.

Iberian Catholicism, therefore, maintained a presence in West Africa for well over two centuries, but by the end of the seventeenth century, the mission was, for all practical purposes, over. It was almost two centuries later that a revival of mission was attempted and more enduring success stories could be recounted.

3. Impact of Iberian Catholicism

Did the Iberian Catholic mission make any impact on the African population? This is a question that must be answered with a little bit of caution since the impact could be considered from various perspectives. That the mission made an impact is a fact that cannot be denied, since a number of Catholic adherents could always be distinguished on the coast. For example, about one hundred years after the Dutch had expelled the Portuguese Catholics from the Gold Coast, Roman Catholics could still be counted among the population of Elmina.[11] However, considering the length of time during which Iberian Catholicism held sway over West Africa, it is a sad commentary that the impact was neither greater nor more enduring. Various factors contributed to this state of affairs, chiefly the domination of trade with its corrupting influence. But of equal importance was the reaction of the African population to the Catholic Gospel. African culture and religion appear to have shown much resilience, making the transmission of the Gospel message rather difficult. The African chiefs, who were often the missionaries' first contact, often had mixed motives for converting to Christianity. In the socially and religiously integrated African society, the conversion of the chief was bound to upset the delicate balance between the living and the dead as well as negatively influence social norms and taboos. Often the chief and his elders were unable to accept the conditions set for conversion by the missionaries. As Lamin Sanneh puts it, "the intrusion of Christianity into royal courts and palace circles threatened the position of the traditional religions whose keepers would be anxious to try to prevent their further erosion...."[12] There is the example of Behemoi, the chief of the Wolof, who, in seeking a military alliance with the Portuguese was asked to submit to baptism. He refused, because he was aware that his people were not in favor of Christianity and his conversion would further jeopardize the loyalty of his troops.[13] Again, the practice of mass baptism by Catholic missionaries could be cited as a reason for the low impact of Iberian Catholicism, since the supposed converts easily lapsed into their former religion without much persuasion.

However, one of the interesting aspects of Iberian Catholicism was the influence it had on the local religion in Elmina. The Catholic heritage, whilst retaining some of its original characteristics, also lent itself to some rather unusual adaptations. There are two interesting remnants of the religion in and around Elmina existing to this day. When the Dutch attacked Elmina in 1637, the local people are said to have fought on the side of the Portuguese, and when it became clear that Elmina would fall to the Dutch, "the African Catholics of Elmina hid away missals, vestments, candlesticks, statues and sacred vessels."[14] These articles were no doubt kept in the homes of the Catholic faithful, but with the passage of time, they must have lost their meaning and appeal to younger generations, who had no use for them. The statue of St. Anthony of Padua found its way into a local shrine in Elmina and became a central object of worship, to the extent that the name of the shrine became known as the *Ntona* Shrine (an obvious corruption of saint's name).[15]

Another group of devotees, later known as Santa Mariafo (literally, the Santa Maria people), kept the statue of the virgin Mary as an object of worship. A statue of St Francis of Assisi, which was said to have turned black on arrival in Elmina (a supposed indication of the saint identifying himself with Africans), has not survived. Many people in and around Elmina were said to have invoked the saint's name for many years.

4. Further European Missionary Presence

It is not to be assumed that only Portugal was responsible for mission in Africa at this time. The rest of Europe was by no means inactive while these Portuguese explorations were taking place. Other European nations joined the trade on the West coast, establishing their presence in many ways. Europe, at this time, was not the industrialized and largely prosperous place that we know today. There was much poverty and hardship, and subsistence depended very much on trade. Many of the European nations were therefore waiting eagerly for favorable conditions in order to launch their own expeditions in search of "greener pastures". Spain, for example, was already a world power and was like Portugal involved in new explorations, but there was much rivalry between the two nations—so much so that it often threatened to break out in open war. The drawing of a line on the map by the Pope was not enough to deter others from venturing into areas previously claimed by the Catholic Church.

By the middle of the sixteenth century, the English trader, William Hawkins of Plymouth (father of the famous sailor Sir John Hawkins), had arrived on the coast. He traded alongside the Portuguese who did not consider him a threat. In the years following 1500, other English traders joined him gradually, establishing a foothold on the coast and eventually securing a trade charter from Queen Elizabeth. The formation of the *Company of Adventurers of London Trading into Africa* in 1618 and their building of two forts on the coast[16] confirmed their desired permanent presence.

The other European nation of significance to arrive on the Guinea Coast was the Netherlands, which was then steadily building its maritime expertise. The Dutch nation had always detested the hegemony of Spain and Portugal, which had the tacit support of the Pope, and they were therefore always seeking ways of exerting themselves. This desire was given impetus by the outbreak of the Protestant Reformation of the sixteenth century, so that the Dutch combined their struggle for freedom from Spain with a struggle for freedom from the Pope. Dutch sailors began to flout the Spanish and Papal embargo on ships sailing into their areas and joined the growing number of *interlopers*.[17] By 1581, the Dutch Republic had been declared, and defiance of Spain had become widespread. By 1593 the first Dutch sailors had settled on the Guinea coast. Barent Ericzoon, who was the first Dutchman to form a company to trade on the Guinea Coast, was believed to have been one these first arrivals.[18] Like the English, they soon realized the need to build a fort as both a trading post and a defense against attacks. The first Dutch fort was therefore constructed at Moree near Elmina and later fortified and named Fort Nassau. In the ensuing years the Dutch presence would become more pronounced. The Dutch eventually succeeded in capturing the Portuguese castle at Elmina in 1637, making them the most powerful nation on the coast for many years.

The success of England and Holland in establishing a foothold on the West coast eventually opened the way for other European countries. Before long, the French were also forcing their way into the region. They initially attempted to join the trade in Elmina, but were repelled by the Portuguese. They then moved on to Accra, but were again chased out by the Portuguese. Other unsuccessful attempts were made at Assini, Komenda, Anomabu and Dahomey, so that for many years the French had no permanent base on the coast.[19] The arrival of the Swedes was more dramatic. Debrunner narrates how a Swedish ship arrived and took away land from the English in 1652 at Cape Coast and started building a fort.[20] The Swedes went ahead and maintained a governor for a few years before selling the property to the Danes. They, however, continued to fight other nations and acquired much property in the process, although, in the end not much of it remained. It was the Dutch takeover of Fort Carolusburg at Takoradi in 1663 that effectively ended the period of the Swedes on the coast.

Much more enduring was the Danish presence, which started in the seventeenth century. The Danes initially had to battle the Swedes, their traditional enemies, and they could only establish themselves after the Swedes had eventually been overpowered by the Dutch. They built a small fort, Frederiksborg at Takoradi, which remained their main base until they acquired the Christiansborg Castle at Osu in 1683, and turned this into their headquarters.[21] From this point on, they maintained a strong presence and became one of the most formidable competitors in the coastal trade.

Most of these European nations also attempted some mission work, facing the same problems as the Portuguese and achieving sporadic success and failure. Before long, trade had assumed worrying proportions. The commodities for trade gradually shifted from gold, spices and other such commodities to slaves. The resultant impact on mission was overwhelming.

5. Iberian Christianity and the Slave Trade

One of the greatest drawbacks to mission work on the African continent was the incidence of the slave trade, which started on a small scale and grew to become one of the most dehumanizing and offensive practices in world history. The concept of slavery is, however, much broader than the Slave Trade of the seventeenth, eighteenth and nineteenth centuries. The impact of slavery on mission in Africa is very much related to its social and historical developments; since slavery has existed and been practiced for ages in many societies.[22]

In Africa, as in feudal Europe, slavery was a normal part of the social system, although the practice differed considerably. The type of slavery practiced in Africa in ancient times is often referred to as "limited slavery", which means that it was not a permanent condition. The practice of slavery in Africa, however, began to change with the growing interaction with people from other parts of the world. The first experience occurred with the arrival of Arab Moslem traders from the Mediterranean in the eleventh century, who started purchasing slaves and taking them away to their countries. This was a new phenomenon for Africa because the slaves so purchased were taken away to a far away land to become slaves for the rest of their lives. Some of these slaves were sent beyond Arab lands to Turkey, Spain and Portugal. Therefore, by the fifteenth century when the Portuguese found themselves in Africa, they were already familiar with African slaves and the use to which they could be put. It is no wonder then that it did not take long for the Catholic Portuguese to get involved in the purchase and shipment of African slaves.[23] Historians refer to this trade in humans as the old World Atlantic Slave Trade, since a new form of the trade (the Atlantic slave Trade) developed later. It was the Spanish discovery of the Americas in 1492 that gave impetus for the new development in the slave trade. The Atlantic slave trade spanned a period of almost four centuries and introduced so much carnage and devastation on the continent that the effects are still present with us today.[24]

Christian mission in such circumstances was most difficult, if not impossible. However, it is important to note that the Portuguese Catholics who came to West Africa were not always opposed to the practice of slavery. In spite of their presence, the first slaves were bought and sent to Lisbon as early as 1442, and after that contingents of slaves were dispatched every year. By the time of the death of Prince Henry (1460), an estimated 700 slaves were being exported to Portugal annually.[25] Also important for our study is the fact that slavery was sanctioned by the Vatican as a legitimate means of acquiring servants and labor. Moreover, the slave trade was believed to afford the Africans an opportunity to accept Christ and save their souls. As the practice degenerated, in 1525 King John III of Portugal tried to prohibit the slave trade with very limited success.

II. THE CHAPLAINCY FACTOR

In the study of the whole period of the slave trade, one question that is raised constantly and forces itself onto the stage is: Where was the church in Europe when this obnoxious practice was taking place? What happened to the spirit of evangelism that existed in the early years? The answer is not difficult to find. The church in Europe still existed, and Europe remained largely Christian, but the church was co-opted. It lost its voice and eventually its conscience and therefore did not only look on as the trade in human beings went on, but even participated, both overtly and covertly. Few church people saw any correlation between the practice of slavery and their faith. Occasionally, there were debates in some European countries on the subject of slavery and the Christian faith, in which various philosophical, theological and legal arguments were advanced, but these had little or no impact on the practice.[26]

The chaplaincy institution, which was maintained by many of the European slave trading nations, was the only sign that Christian mission still had a little breath left. Chaplaincy was first introduced to the West African coast by the Portuguese in the fifteenth century. It was a policy of the Portuguese to place a priest on board all their ships, whose primary task was to keep spiritual oversight over the sailors. They preached, prayed for the sick and said requiem mass for the dead. It was also part of their responsibility to make contact with the local Africans and bring the Gospel to them, a task which was only rarely fulfilled. The shipping companies were obliged to bear the full cost of their upkeep for the duration of the voyages as well as the time spent on shore. There are a few recorded instances of Portuguese chaplains making converts on the West Coast, sometimes even converting whole households. These, however, were never on any regular scale and the conversions often fizzled out after a few years.[27]

This system of chaplaincy was adopted by all the other European nations that traded on the African coast. The chaplains became the principal representatives of the European churches even during the period of the slave trade, struggling against many odds and having to do their job in very unfavorable conditions. It was often difficult to find clergymen willing to take up the post because, among other things, sea voyages in those days were risky undertakings, and lasted for months at a time. Owing to the unpopularity of the position, some of the chaplains were no more than mere adventurers who made no impact at all. One Dutch writer describes the early chaplains sent to the Guinea coast as "recruited from among shoe-makers and peat-carriers, bakers and shearers ... and woefully incompetent for their job."[28] The situation appears to have improved a little bit after castles and forts were constructed and chaplains could be stationed at particular locations for a specific number of years. The latter crop of chaplains especially in the eighteenth century, were better trained and more suited to the job of evangelism. Some of them made impressive strides in evangelization, making converts from among the African population and sometimes giving Christian leadership training to some of the Africans.

In the Gold Coast, the names of a few chaplains stand out clearly, because of the impact they made on the process of mission work. The Danes maintained an almost unbroken succession of chaplains at the Christiansborg Castle well into the nineteenth century until that Castle was sold to the British. One such chaplain, the Rev. Elias Svane, took his preaching to the local people and succeeded in sending two African boys, Christian Protten and Frederick Pederson Svane (who adopted the name of his benefactor) to Copenhagen to be trained as ministers of the Gospel in 1726. They came back as missionaries and did some intermittent work in and around Christiansborg for many years.[29]

The English had a similar record. Chaplaincy played an important role in their settlements all across the West and South Coast. The crown colony of Senegambia always had a chaplain attached to its administration. In addition to their functions of conducting services for the British colonists, they were also charged to "induce" the local population to embrace the Protestant faith.[30] In spite of much rivalry with the French, this system was sustained for a number of years until mission stations were established in Bathurst and other places along the river Gambia. In the Gold Coast, the outstanding name was that of the Rev Thomas Thompson, who was sent, at his own request, to be a missionary of the SPG at Cape Coast. Thompson had some experience working with Africans when he served as missionary in the United States and spent time evangelizing the slaves in New Jersey. In Cape Coast, his primary responsibility was to evangelize the African population, but he also became chaplain to the inhabitants of the Cape Coast Castle. He worked there from 1751 to 1756, until his failing health compelled him to return to England. He, however, encouraged three African boys to go to England and be trained as missionaries. Although two of the boys died in England, the third, Philip Quaicoo, graduated in theology and was ordained a minister of the Anglican Church. Philip Quaicoo returned to Cape Coast and served as priest, chaplain and school master for many years.[31]

The Charter establishing the Dutch West India Company in 1621 had an explicit clause requiring the company to make the spread of the Reformed Christian religion one of its principal objectives, and it was the chaplain (also known as *ziekentrooster* or "comforter of the sick") who was charged with this responsibility. The company maintained a steady succession of chaplains for many years. Here the position of the chaplain was often the third most important position in the administrative setup after the Director-General and the Superintendent.[32] Later however, it became more and more difficult to find ministers willing to take up the position, leading to a situation of intermittent absence of chaplains. By far the most well known Dutch chaplain was the Rev.

Jacobus Capitein, an ex slave who was trained and ordained in Holland by the Netherlands Reformed Church.[33]

Almost all the chaplains, irrespective of which country or denomination they came from appear to have faced some general problems. Apart from the unfavorable climatic conditions that they had to endure, they were more often than not left alone to grapple with their social and economic problems. It was the period of the slave trade, and one wonders how these chaplains were expected to do any meaningful mission among people who were regarded as nothing more than commodities for sale. The professions of commitment to evangelism by the home churches appear to have been no more than half hearted precepts to satisfy their consciences. No wonder that particularly during the period of intense slave trading, there was not much commitment on the part of the home churches that sent them. In many instances, they were left without the necessary logistical support to accomplish their tasks. Moreover the trading companies that employed the chaplains had no real interest in mission work and therefore could not be much bothered. Added to this was the general situation of degeneracy among the Europeans on the coast. The majority of workers in the slave industry were not interested in religion or the church. Immorality, concubinage and loose living were rampant and the chaplain had a hard task ministering to persons who were not good examples of Christian living. It is, however, clear that some of the chaplains themselves had characters that created problems for the work. There are records of some of them abandoning their work and getting involved in trading or doing other things unbecoming of a minister of the Gospel.[34]

III. NOTABLE AFRICAN CHAPLAINS

Chaplaincy as we have noted, was devoted primarily to the spiritual care of the Europeans who worked on the coast, and eventually extended to cover the mulattoes. In spite of various statements to the contrary, the evangelization of the African population was always of secondary importance. Things, however, started to change as more and more mulattoes and Africans became educated and proved capable of handling the job of the chaplain. By the third decade of the eighteenth century, a number of Africans could be counted among the ranks of the chaplains on the West African coast. Most of them were connected in one way or another with the forts and castles on the Gold Coast and only occasionally reaching into Togo, Ivory Coast and beyond. Our information on these chaplains is gleaned from various sources including diaries, which some of them kept. The Danes particularly encouraged their chaplains to write their daily experiences down and to share with their successors. The writings of three Danish chaplains have been preserved and have become an important reference for the periods of their service. These were the Reverends Wilhem Johann Mueller, Johan Rask and H.C. Monrad. These gentlemen appear to have been interested in African affairs generally, and therefore tried to describe what they understood of the African way of life regarding politics, economic activities and religion.[35]

Information on the few African chaplains was also preserved in reports, diaries and other documents of the places they served. It appears that the novelty of a member of the African race rising to such a position must have generated much interest in their life and work. Owing to the varying circumstances under which these chaplains served, it is impossible to treat their stories in a uniform manner as regards detail or narration. This section therefore does not intend to give full detailed accounts of the lives and times of these chaplains. Only specific, important detail is mentioned.

1. Jacobus Elisa Johannes Capitein (1717-1747)

The date of birth of Capitein cannot be established with any certainty. Neither he nor his guardians knew when he was born because of the circumstances of his birth. We may, however, use the records of the Academic Senate of the University of Leiden where he studied to establish that he was born in the year 1717.[36]

Capitein had been captured and sold as a slave to Captain Arnold Steenhart at the age of seven or eight years, but instead of being shipped with the others, his master decided to keep him as a slave at Shama. When Steenhart was leaving the Gold Coast, he gave the little boy to his friend Jacobus van Goch, a chief commissary stationed at Shama, who gave him the Dutch name Capitein (which means "captain"), because he had been given as a gift by a ship captain. Van Goch left the shores of Elmina on 14th April 1728, taking along the child slave Capitein, and arrived in Middleburg in the Netherlands three months later. Since slavery was then not permitted in the Netherlands, Capitein became a free person, but as a child, was still dependent on Van Goch, who became his adopted father. Van Goch took him to The Hague, his hometown, where Capitein started school at the age of 13 or 14 years. He also attended catechism classes under the Rev. Johan Philip Manger, who prepared him for baptism in July 1735. He was then 18 years old. It was at his baptism that he received his three other names, namely, Jacobus, after his adopted father Van Goch; Elisa, after Van Goch's sister, Elizabeth and Johannes, after Van Goch's niece, Anna Mulder.

Capitein's education was financed by Van Goch as well as other persons, mostly church people in The Hague, who saw in him a great potential for mission work in Africa. He completed the first stages of his schooling in 1737, having written a treatise, *De Vocatione Ethnicorum* (The Calling of the Heathen) in which he argued in support of mission work among the African population. He was immediately admitted to the University of Leiden to follow a course in theology, enjoying full scholarship from the Hallet Foundation. The four-year course also included lectures in Philosophy, Greek, Hebrew, History and Oratory. When he graduated in 1742, he was adjudged the best student of his class. His thesis, produced in Latin, was entitled, *Dissertatio Politica-Theologica de servitude, Libertate Christianae non contraria* (Politico-Theological Dissertation on Slavery as not being Contrary to Christian Liberty). The topic of the dissertation was as controversial as it was explosive. The topic of slavery was a contentious issue in the Netherlands, with varying positions and hardly any agreement. The entry of Capitein into the debate was quite intriguing, if for nothing at all, for the fact that he, being a former slave, was arguing in favor of the continuation of slavery. He became an instant hero in the Netherlands and his dissertation was immediately published and widely distributed. A Dutch translation was completed within a matter of months and portraits of Capitein were sold alongside the book. "What many thought privately, but few dared to say publicly, had now been said, and not only in public but also in print. Moreover, it had been said by a most unlikely person—a freed slave!"[37]

It has been said that Capitein's defense of slavery was orchestrated by his benefactors, who used him to legitimize their support for the institution of slavery. This charge may not be completely denied because there were many interested parties in the life of Capitein. Apart from the Dutch Reformed Church, which must have considered the dissertation an appeasement of the Christian conscience in tolerating the slave trade, the West India Company (WIC) must have pulled the strings from behind the scenes. The WIC was the institution that stood to reap the single largest benefit from the defense of slavery, since it then provided a justification, and indeed a Christian one, for their slave trading activities. Yet we may not completely absolve Capitein from his responsibility for what he wrote. Even if he succumbed to pressure from his benefactors, he must have believed at least the core message of the dissertation, namely that slavery and Christian freedom were compatible.

Capitein was ordained on 7 May 1742 by the Presbytery (Classis) of Amsterdam as a minister of the Dutch Reformed Church, becoming the first African to receive Protestant ordination in a European church.[38] He was immediately appointed school master and chaplain by the WIC and designated to Elmina in the Gold Coast. He undertook a preaching tour of the Netherlands which took him to the Pieterskerk in Leiden, the Kloosterkerk in The Hague and the Ouderkerk aan den Amstel before his departure for Elmina in the same year.

a. Work in Elmina

Capitein was 25 years old when he was ordained and had spent fifteen years in the Netherlands. His anxiety to see Elmina again was therefore great. He arrived to a warm welcome from the Dutch governor of the Castle, De Petersen on 8 October 1742 and immediately set out to organize his mission work. He tried to relate to the Europeans in the castle as well as to the Africans in Elmina town, and therefore had to relearn Fanti, his mother tongue. He experienced so much hostility from the Europeans that he was easily discouraged in his pastoral work with them. They obviously could not accept an African as their spiritual leader, and they could not tolerate his attack on their moral ineptitude. His work among the Africans, however, proved much more interesting and fruitful although that too was not sustained. He established a school for both mulatto and African children and within six to seven months, the number of children in the school had reached 45. He even went to the elders of the Elmina town to convince them to send their children to the school, and conceived the idea of sending the brilliant ones among them to Holland for further training.[39]

Apart from his work in education, Capitein also did much in promoting the writing of the local Fanti language. Within one year of his arrival in Elmina, he was able to produce a Fanti translation, from Dutch, of three important documents: the Lord's Prayer; the Ten Commandments; and the Twelve Articles of Faith. This was the first successful attempt by any chaplain to use the local language in teaching and learning. Capitein's work in Elmina made such impact that the Asantehene, Nana Opoku Ware I sent twelve boys and two girls to study at the school. The original intention of the Asantehene was to have the fourteen children educated in Holland, but this plan did not realize, and they were made to stay in Capitein's school.

b. The Frustrating End

Although he made a great impact in a short time, Capitein's successful beginning did not last long. The expected growth and progress of the work did not come easily, and although he persevered, he eventually sank under the weight of the frustration. His first frustration had to do with his intention to marry an African girl from Elmina as a means of integrating into the African society. In his view, this marriage would prove to the Africans that "although I differ from them in manner of life and in religion, they are nevertheless not despised by me...." This plan, however, failed because the church authorities in Amsterdam opposed it accusing him of impropriety in wanting to marry an unbaptized girl. They rather arranged and sent Antonia Ginderdros to Elmina to become his wife. However, the greatest hindrance and source of frustration to Capitein was the apathy of his superiors in Amsterdam, both of the WIC and the church. When his school work ran into difficulties, because of the death of two of the teachers and the lack of teaching materials, he wrote a number of letters to his superiors for the situation to be rectified, but very little response was received, causing his enthusiasm to decline gradually. He again complained many times in his letters about the appalling immoral lives of the Europeans on the coast as well as their disregard of his leadership, but no remedy appeared to be coming from Amsterdam.

Gradually, Capitein's situation became untenable. He offered to resign but continued to stay on hoping for an improvement in his situation. When this did not happen, he involved himself in trading, but failed so miserably that he accumulated much debt, which became an embarrassment to himself and the church. By 1746, Capitein was a completely frustrated person who could not see any good prospects ahead. He died on 1 February 1747, aged about 30 years, having labored in Elmina for five years. The cause of his death has never been established, resulting in a number of speculations, including suicide or possibly murder. These speculations, however, have no basis whatsoever. His period of service was quite short but his impact on education and evangelism among the

Africans was far reaching. It is a pity that the life of such a significant person of African descent has remained obscured for a long time.

2. Philip Quaicoo (1741-1816)

Philip Quaicoo[40] was born on 13th March 1741 at Cape Coast. He was the son of Obirempong Kodwo Egyir who was a wealthy middleman[41] in the slave trading business at Cape Coast. He was also a local magistrate employed by the governor to help settle cases between natives and was a well known person among both the Europeans and the Africans. The name of his mother is unknown.

Philip's father enrolled him in the Castle School then run by the SPG missionary and Royal Africa Company chaplain, Rev. Thomas Thompson. Owing to his strong views on the use of Africans for mission work among their own people, Rev. Thompson convinced Philip's father to send him for training in England to become a minister. The father readily agreed to the suggestion hoping that it would open up a bright future for his son.[42] Thompson selected two further boys from the school, William Cudjo and Thomas Cobbers. The three set sail together with Rev. Thompson from Cape Coast and arrived in Islington in 1756. They were immediately admitted into the elementary school in Islington where they spent four years under the tutelage of first Mr Hickman and then Rev. John Moore. At the end of this period of study, and based on their brilliant performance, they were recommended for admission to university education, but both William Cudjo and Thomas Cobbers died before this could materialize. William is said to have had a mental breakdown and Thomas gave in to tuberculosis and small pox. Philip therefore continued alone for another four years, studying Theology, Philosophy and History.

On completion of his studies, Philip Quaicoo was ordained as a deacon of the Anglican Church on 25 March 1765 by the Bishop of Exeter at the Chapel Royal in St James. About two months later, on 1 May 1765, he was ordained as priest in the same chapel by the Bishop of London. This ordination made Philip the first African to receive holy orders in the Anglican Church. The ceremony of ordination was witnessed by the bishops of Canterbury, Winchester and Lincoln. A few days before his ordination, Philip married Miss Catherine Blunt of Holborn. The wedding ceremony was officiated by his mentor the Rev Moore. He was immediately appointed a "missionary, schoolmaster and clergyman to the negroes on the Gold Coast", as well as a chaplain to the Company of Merchants at Cape Coast.

a. Work in Cape Coast

After ten years away from his native home, Philip Quaicoo, together with his wife, arrived back in Cape Coast on 8 February 1766, and was accommodated in the Castle. He immediately revived the school for Africans and mulatto children where he himself had been a pupil. The school appears to have flourished for a number of years, attracting even some European children. The Royal Africa Company was so impressed with Philip's performance that they opened other schools in the areas where they were operating along the coast, and convinced Philip Quaicoo to recruit teachers for them. Soon he was overseeing schools in Anomabo, Winneba, Komenda, Dixcove, Sekondi and Tamtumquerry. He also undertook an evangelistic tour of these coastal towns and succeeded in introducing Christianity to portions of the communities. During 1772 he even extended his tours to Accra, where he stayed for four months and started a school before leaving. He was in Axim in 1779 for a similar exercise. In 1787, together with a group of friends, Philip Quaicoo became a founding member of the Torridzonian Society, which was devoted to the advancement of the African and mulatto populations. This society became the first indigenous organization to devote special attention to physically handicapped children. The society attracted some of the most prominent citizens of Cape Coast at the time, and Governor William Fielde (1789-1791) was so impressed with their work that he attended some of their meetings and supported them financially.

b. Hindrances and Difficulties

Philip Quaicoo's work at Cape Coast encountered many difficulties. As early as 1774, he was known to have said that he was tired of being there. He undertook a number of trips outside Cape Coast just to get away from the frustrations at home. One of the greatest drawbacks of Philip Quaicoo's ministry was his inability to speak his native Fanti language. His ten year stay in England had wiped out his knowledge of Fanti completely, such, that on his return to Cape Coast, he spoke to his people through an interpreter. This was surprising since he was about 15 years old when he left the Gold Coast and could have retained much of the Fanti during his sojourn in England. F.L. Bartels suggests that his English mentors must have persuaded him to abandon Fanti in favor of English, since the English believed that "the English tongue was the heaven sent medium of religion and civilization."[43] No doubt, this created a barrier between him and his people. The presence of his English wife did not help matters either. The local people were not sure how to relate to this black Englishman and his white wife.

He also encountered the hostility of the Europeans to whom he was supposed to be a spiritual guide. This was also the experience of his compatriot, Capitein in Elmina. One incident is recorded where some Europeans in the castle flatly refused to attend services officiated by Rev Quaicoo, because they did not want to "hear any Blackman whatever". The moral lives of the Europeans were also so appalling that ministering to them was a difficult task. Some were even known to have demanded gifts from him before agreeing to attend church.

Philip Quaicoo's work was also plagued by the unstable conditions on the coast. There were constant conflicts with the Dutch in Elmina and the Danes based at Christiansborg, which made the spread of the gospel and the establishment of schools difficult. He was expected to show allegiance to the English even when he thought that their actions were wrong. For example, in 1791 when the Anomabo fort was attacked, Quaicoo was ordered by the governor to take up arms in its defense. His refusal to do so cost him his salary for four months, leading to a hold up in his educational and evangelistic work. His salary was restored after he made an appeal to the Royal Africa Company. In his frustration, he tried his hand at trading to make ends meet, but he withdrew quickly after his employers complained that he was neglecting his work. They accused him of deviating "from the intentions of the Society (SPG) and his proper line of duty by paying more attention to the purposes of trade than of religion."[44] To add to his woes, his house was burgled in 1785 while he was away on holiday in England.

The ministry of Philip Quaicoo spanned a period of fifty long years, but the impact was not commensurate with the length of time. By the time of his death in 1816, he himself felt that he had achieved very little. Some people also pointed to his inability to convert his own father to Christianity as a failure. Yet it would be wrong to write off his achievements with such ease. His initial success in education produced many educated Africans, which in turn produced the bulk of Christians who later became instrumental in the spread of the Gospel on the coast. Some of the products of his school in Cape Coast were known to have been instrumental in encouraging the Wesleyan Methodist Missionary Society to begin work on the Gold Coast. Philip Quaicoo's marriage to Catherine produced two daughters and a son.

3. Christian Jacob Protten (1715-1769)

One of the least known missionary endeavors in the Gold Coast is the work done by the Moravians. This group, founded by Count Nicolaus Ludwig von Zinzendorf, was also known as the United Brethren (*Unitas Fratrum*) or the Herrnhutters. They were products of the Pietist movement, which flourished in Europe in the eighteenth century. Ignoring the systematic mission theories of the time, the Moravians emphasized personal conversion and piety and reached out beyond Europe into Africa and the Caribbean. One of the first missionaries to undertake this work was Christian Protten from the Gold Coast.

Christian Jacob Protten was the son of a Danish merchant based at the Christiansborg castle and an African mother from Christiansborg (Osu). Born in 1715, he attended the mulatto school run by the Danish chaplain, Rev. Elias Svane. The Rev. Svane found in the young boy a willingness to learn and work for the church. He therefore arranged to have him sent to Denmark for training as a teacher and theologian. Protten, together with another mulatto boy, Frederik Pedersen, accompanied the Rev. Svane to Copenhagen, where he followed a series of courses ending with a theological course at the University. He was introduced to the Danish king, Frederik IV, who agreed to pay for his education and general upkeep. King Frederik was a patron of the missionary movement and was eager to see the Christian religion preached in Africa. After eight years of study, Protten visited Herrnhut, the headquarters of the Moravians, where he spent a further two years.[45] He was then commissioned by the Moravian movement, along with Henry Huckoff, as missionary to Africa. They were to be based at the Elmina Castle and were commended to the Dutch governor there.

a. Work in the Gold Coast

Protten and Huckoff arrived in Elmina in 1737, but before they could start any meaningful work, Huckoff died. Protten appears to have had many misunderstandings with the governor at Elmina, which even resulted in his being imprisoned on an island for a number of weeks. With his efforts at starting a school thwarted, Protten decided to move to Christiansborg, hoping to make some impact there. But he was struck down with malaria and could do very little. In 1741, Zinzendorf decided that Protten should take a holiday in Europe to recuperate. After only two years, he requested to be sent to the Island of St Thomas as missionary. There also he faced one problem after another, and returned to Europe after only a year and half. He married a mulatto, Rebecca Freundlich, the widow of a Moravian missionary, in 1746, and traveled with her back to Christiansborg. He stayed at the Castle for many years trying his hands at various mission projects until he was finally appointed "catechist and assistant schoolmaster" in 1756.[46] He held on to this position until 1761, when an accident resulted in the death of one of his pupils.[47] He was arrested, charged with murder and kept in the castle prison for a while. The Moravians, however, managed to secure his release and he was sent to Copenhagen to be punished. He was pardoned by the Danish king and sent back to Christiansborg in 1764, where he served as chaplain and teacher for the next five years. During this period he stayed intermittently at Ningo, where the Danes had a fort, and did some evangelistic work there. He is also known to have ventured into preaching at La and Teshie.

In spite of his topsy-turvy career as a missionary, Protten did achieve quite a bit for the Christian mission on the Gold Coast. Protten was one of the first missionaries to try and reduce the Ga language into writing, producing a translation of the Shorter Catechism and the Lord's Prayer and some parables.[48] He also produced a Ga Grammar book for use in his school. This was a remarkable initiative, especially since he lost the use of his mother tongue, Ga, during his stay in Denmark. It must have taken real commitment and dedication to achieve this. His attempts encouraged others like Governor Wrisberg and Governor Schoening to study the Ga language and translate other important Christian documents.[49]

Both Groves and Bartels mention that Protten is also known to have tried his hand at the Fanti language, with Groves claiming further that he produced a Fanti grammar book.[50] This book, however, cannot be traced anywhere. A Ga-Fante-Danish Catechism, which he claimed to have written and printed in Denmark and which he was bringing to use in the Gold Coast, was destroyed when the whole consignment fell into the sea as he disembarked at Christiansborg in 1765.[51]

Christian Protten died in 1769. His entire mission work was fraught with much frustration arising partly from his own natural disposition and partly from circumstances beyond his control. He appears to have been a rather difficult and uncompromising character, who was angered by the apparent indifference of his countrymen to the Gospel. He is known to have insisted on a complete break with "African heathen practices", and to have preached fiery sermons against alcohol use and polygamy. It is, however, wrong to conclude, as the Moravians did, that he "accomplished absolutely nothing for the Lord."[52] There was no doubt about his commitment to evangelism and education for the Africans, and as many times as he failed, he was always willing to begin again. Protten certainly deserves a place in the history of mission and evangelism on the Gold Coast.

4. Frederick Pedersen Svane

Frederick Pedersen Svane has the honor of being the first African missionary sent to the Gold Coast, and yet information on him is rather scanty and inconsistent in many parts. Although his date of birth is not recorded, he was a contemporary of Protten and was perhaps a few years older. Like Protten, his mother was a Ga from Osu and his father a Danish merchant. In 1726, he was taken, together with Protten, to Denmark by the Rev. Elias Svane where he was baptized in the Garrison Church in Copenhagen.

After years of elementary education, he was admitted to the University of Copenhagen to study Theology. Svane's period of study in Copenhagen was a time of conflict between the Pietists and the orthodox theologians in Denmark and other parts of Europe. Svane, however, opted for the Pietists, resulting in his expulsion from the hall of residence of the university and the withdrawal of his scholarship. He found sympathy and support in Count Von Plessen, a committed Pietist, who proved to be a worthy benefactor for many years. Svane is known to have eventually also denounced what he called the "unscientific and unhealthy sentimentality" of the Pietists.[53] He graduated in 1735 in Philosophy and Arts and was ordained for mission work. He then married a Danish woman, with whom he traveled back to Christiansborg that same year to work as chaplain and teacher.

a. Work in Christiansborg

Svane worked in the Castle for ten years running the school for mulatto children. His attempts to increase the number of African children in the school were discouraged by the governor, and his appeal to his benefactors in Denmark did not yield anything positive, since the Von Plessens themselves were mainly committed to supporting mission work among the Europeans and mulattoes. His work among the castle staff was full of frustration and conflict. He appears to have faced many financial difficulties and his wife was compelled to do laundry services for the castle staff to supplement her husband's income. The wife was once nearly raped by one of the castle workers, and therefore offered to go back to Denmark in 1738. Svane had wanted to join her, but was prevented from leaving his post by the governor. He therefore stayed without his wife for about eight years before finally resigning in 1746 and returning to Denmark.[54] It is not clear whether he lived with another woman after the departure of his wife, but he was accused by the governor of being involved with other women.[55] During his years of loneliness, he tried his hand at the slave trade and made some money, and even built a stone house in Osu. The governor was unhappy with his involvement in private trade whilst still being employed by the Castle. His house was therefore pulled down and he was imprisoned for seven months (November 1742 to June 1743).

Svane retained most of his native Ga language and used it for teaching, but he was unable to transmit important terms of the Christian faith into Ga. He claimed that the Ga language was incapable of being developed to contain certain terms.[56] This assertion was disproved by the Basel missionaries, who succeeded in promoting the use of Ga for all aspects of teaching and learning in the next century.

In Frederick Pedersen Svane, we have another attempt by an African to bring the Gospel to their own people. Although there is not much to recount concerning his achievement, he nevertheless was an important factor in the Protestant Mission in West Africa in the eighteenth century.

5. Anton Wilhem Amo

Amo was not a chaplain or missionary in the same sense as the other Africans we have been considering in this section. He, however, deserves to be mentioned because he was a product of the same circumstances that produced the others. He never became ordained, but made an impact as one of the most celebrated African intellectuals of the eighteenth century.

As with many other Africans of the time, Amo's date of birth is not known with any certainty. It is believed that he was born in 1703, in or around Axim in western Gold Coast. He was probably of Aowin or Wassa ethnic extraction. In 1707, when he was about seven years old, he was taken to Amsterdam, apparently with the knowledge of his parents. This is most likely because when he returned home almost fifty years later, he was still able to locate his father and sister. After a short stay in Amsterdam, he was taken to Brunswick, Germany, where he was adopted by the Duke of Brunswick-Wolfenbuttel and put in the care of the Duke's son, Wilhem Augustus. He became a favorite of the royal household and many of the royals shared in his upbringing.

Amo appears to have received a Christian upbringing in the Protestant environment of the Brunswick court, which subscribed to the Augsburg Confession. He was baptized on 29 July 1708 in the chapel of the Saltzthal Castle and given the names of his benefactors (Anton Ulrich and Wilhem Augustus). His family name, Amo, was retained for a reason that is not known. The probability was that his parents were expecting him to return after his education and would expect him to still use his African name. When he was 18 years old (1721) he was confirmed.

He enrolled at the University of Halle on 9th June 1727 after probably following earlier study at the Brunswick State University (University of Helmstedt). At Halle he studied Philosophy and Jurisprudence, all his fees being paid by the Duke. His period of study coincided with the controversy between Pietism and Rationalism, represented by August Herman Francke and Christian Frederick

Wolff respectively. In spite of his upbringing and environment, Amo appears to have chosen the side of the Rationalists and to have maintained that position.[57]

a. Academic Work

Amo became one of the greatest scholars of his time, excelling in every way. He defended his thesis entitled, "*De jure maurorum in Europa*", in November 1729. He dealt with the legal aspects of slavery, investigating "to what extent the freedom or servitude of the Moors in Europe who had been purchased by the Christians was in conformity with the usual laws."[58] His conclusion was that the Roman law, on which European law was based, did not permit the purchase and enslavement of Africans by Europeans. This thesis, which unfortunately cannot be traced, earned him a degree in law.[59] He then moved on to the University of Wittenberg, where in the following year, 1730, he was awarded the Magister of Philosophy and Liberal Arts. The award emphasized the great achievement of Amo and added that he had "acquired the respect and affection of all his university teachers, and by his extraordinary honesty, diligence and erudition, had easily excelled all his classmates." Here he defended a dissertation entitled, "*Inaugural philosophical dissertation on the apathy of the human mind or the absence of feeling and the faculty of feeling in the mind, and the presence of them in our organic living body*". This degree was converted to a Doctor of Philosophy degree a few years later.

b. Amo as Lecturer

With his achievements, Amo was appointed as lecturer at the University of Wittenberg, where he lectured in Philosophy and Logic. Between 1734 and 1737 he worked on his magnum opus, a treatise on logic, covering more than two hundred pages, and published in Halle in 1738. He then moved on to the University of Jena where he lectured from 1739 to 1740, and achieved fame as a philosopher in addition to his lectures in Psychology and Para-psychology.[60] In 1740, he was appointed a councilor at the court of the King of Prussia in Berlin. One of his closest associates and confidants during his days of teaching was the Chancellor of the University of Halle, Prof. Johann Pieter von Ludwig (1668-1743). They were so close that the death of his friend in 1743 affected Amo's whole outlook on life. He lost interest in his work at the University, and in 1753 he opted to return to the Gold Coast.

Amo returned to Axim after having spent about four and half decades in Europe. His father and one sister were still alive when he returned, and he reunited with them. He was revered by the local population as "a man who knew the future", because of his knowledge in astrology and astronomy. Amo is however said to have preferred to live alone and therefore moved to settle in the Dutch fort (Sebastian) at Shama, where he remained a virtual recluse till his death in 1756.

Unlike the other Africans mentioned in this section, Amo was not closely associated with the church or with mission work. We have nevertheless included him because he was also a product of European Christianity. Although he was baptized and brought up as a Christian, his inclinations appear to have been towards a more African spirituality. As Debrunner points out, the kind of Christianity he experienced in Germany could not challenge him or "fulfill his deepest African aspirations toward the wholeness of life."[61] The Pietism of Halle was too utopian and narrow for his liking. Amo was fundamentally interested in the spiritual values espoused by the African tradition and his aim was to achieve a synthesis of "the African personality, highest scholarship and whole-hearted Christianity." Back in his native Axim, the environment he left behind had changed so much that it proved no better for the spiritual enlightenment that he sought. A life of meditation and asceticism was perhaps his only refuge.

CONCLUSION

Our brief survey of mission work in West Africa has revealed some worthy insights that need to be captured in our ongoing efforts to tell the African story of African Christianity. In the first place, it is clear that for the most part, Africans encountered the Gospel with seriousness and goodwill. In the whole history of mission in the period we have been dealing with, the Africans rarely showed hostility to the Gospel as long as it was presented with respect and consideration for their own beliefs and practices. Contrary to the picture of intolerance that is sometimes presented of Africans, it is clear that in most cases Africans were willing to "try" the new religion of Christianity. Again, the slave trade has been shown to be one of the greatest drawbacks to mission work. By and large, this trade reduced the seriousness with which Africans were willing to consider Christianity. Although some Africans participated in the trade, Africans were no doubt the victims, and the sheer brutality of the trade was enough to dilute the Christian message of love. Finally, this survey has revealed the enormous contribution of gallant men of African descent in the work of evangelization in West Africa. Apart from the five outstanding characters we have mentioned, there were hundreds of other unsung African heroes who were active players in the mission field. Their stories are yet to be told. The story of African Christianity is still unfolding.

Notes

1. Lamin SANNEH, *West African Christianity: The Religious Impact* (Mary Knoll: Orbis Books, 1983), 20.
2. Some of the most useful references have been listed in the Bibliography.
3. Basil DAVIDSON, *Africa in History: themes and outlines* (London, Weidenfeld & Nicolson, 1991), 198-204.
4. See Luis DE CAMOES, *The Lusiads*, Canto 1, 40. Quoted in H. DEBRUNNER, *A History of Christianity in Ghana* (Accra: Waterville Publishing House, 1967).
5. See C.P. GROVES, *The Planting of Christianity in Africa* (London: Lutterworth Press, 1948-1958), 119.
6. S. NEILL, *A History of Christian Missions* (2nd Edition, New York: Penguin, 1986), 117-119.

7. See, for example, a claim by French sailors to have reached the coast in 1382: D. Kemp, *Nine Years at the Gold Coast* (London: Macmillan & Co. Ltd, 1898), 11.
8. K.S. Latourette, *A History of the Expansion of Christianity*, Vol. III, *Three Centuries of Advance A.D. 1500 – A.D. 1800* (New York: Harper & Brothers, 1939), 241.
9. Debrunner, *A History of Christianity*, 17.
10. Groves, *The Planting of Christianity*, 121.
11. See D.N.A. Kpobi, *Mission in Chains* (Zoetermeer: Boekencentrum, 1993), 135.
12. Sanneh, *West African Christianity*, 28.
13. See Groves, *The Planting of Christianity in Africa*, 126.
14. Debrunner, *A History of Christianity*, 33.
15. Some historians also believe that the statue was not incorporated into an already existing shrine but that the shrine originated around the statue, which was said to have been used by the Portuguese in miraculously healing a mentally sick person many years back. See Debrunner, *A History of Christianity*, 33; R.M. Wiltgen, *Gold Coast Mission History 1471-1880* (Techny: Divine Word Publication, 1956), 43-46.
16. The first fort was built at Cormantine in the Gold Coast and the other in the Gambia.
17. *Interlopers* were merchant ships that were not flying the flag of any of the Spanish accredited chartered companies. Such ships were often attacked and either made to return or seized.
18. J.M. Postma, *The Dutch in the Atlantic Slave Trade 1600-1815* (Cambridge: Cambridge University Press, 1990), 17.
19. Debrunner, *A History of Christianity*, 28, 42.
20. Debrunner, *A History of Christianity*, 42-43.
21. A detailed history of the forts and castles can be found in Albert van Dantzig, *Forts and Castles of Ghana* (Accra: Sedco Publishing Ltd, 1980).
22. The subject of slavery as an institution has been studied by many writers, and there is abundant literature to be consulted. So also is the subject of the Slave Trade. See Bibliography.
23. See Basil Davidson, *The African Slave Trade: Precolonial History, 1450-1850* (Boston: Little Brown, 1961), 33.
24. For a description of the conditions under which slaves were kept prior to shipment, refer to Postma, *The Dutch in the Atlantic Slave Trade*, 227-234. See also Kpobi, *Mission in Chains*, 161-162 and Sanneh, *West African Christianity*, 25-26.
25. Davidson, *The African slave trade*, 33.
26. Kpobi, *Mission in Chains*, 100-103.
27. Sanneh, *West African Christianity*, 22-25.
28. Quoted from Kpobi, *Mission in Chains*, 135.
29. Debrunner, *A History of Christianity*, 61.
30. Groves, *The Planting of Christianity*, 153 & 186.
31. Debrunner, *A History of Christianity*, 65.
32. Groves, *The Planting of Christianity in Africa*, 151; Kpobi, *Mission in Chains*, 36.

33. For a comprehensive account of the life and work of Capitein, see KPOBI, *Mission in Chains.*
34. WILTGEN, *Gold Coast Mission History*, 18. See also KPOBI, *Mission in Chains.*
35. See H. DEBRUNNER, *Notable Danish Chaplains on the Gold Coast* (1956), 13-39.
36. The Roll Book actually states that when Capitein was admitted to the University on 22nd June 1737, he had obtained the age of twenty years. See KPOBI, *Mission in Chains*, 52.
37. KPOBI, *Mission in Chains*, 66.
38. Note that the Catholic Church had ordained Don Henrique, a prince of the Congo as early as 1518. See NEILL, *A History of Christian Missions*, 118.
39. *Brieven en Papieren van Guinea aan de Vergadering der Thienen* (WIC inv. No.113), 140.
40. The spelling of this name varies considerably in the different documents that contain information about him. It is variably spelt Quaque, Kwaikoo, and Quarcoo.
41. These agents of the castle were known as "caboceers".
42. Thomas Thompson mentions a (another?) son of Caboceer Kodwo, Frederick, who was also sent to England before Philip. It is not clear whether this was a brother of Philip or the child of another caboceer with the same name. It is also not known what happened to Frederick. See Thomas THOMPSON, *An account of two missionary voyages* (London: SPG, 1758), 35.
43. F.L. BARTELS, "Philip Quaque", in *Transactions of the Historical Society of Ghana*, vol. I, part 5, p.167.
44. GROVES, *The Planting of Christianity in Africa*, 176.
45. Gustav WARNECK, *A History of Protestant Missions* (tr. George ROBSON, New York: Revell, 1906), 59. See also Harris MOBLEY, *The Ghanaian's Image of the Missionary: An Analysis of the Published Critiques of Christian Missionaries by Ghanaians 1897-1965* (Leiden: Brill, 1970), 18-19.
46. I.S. EPHSON, *Gallery of Gold Coast Celebrities 1632-1958* (Accra: Ilen Publications Ltd, 1969), 21.
47. Protten was said to have been cleaning his gun when it accidentally went off and killed the boy.
48. DEBRUNNER, *A History of Christianity*, p.92.
49. Wrisberg translated the Sermon on the Mount and parts of Luther's Catechism whilst Schoening translated the Ten Commandments, the Apostle's Creed and the Lord's Prayer.
50. GROVES, *The Planting of Christianity in Africa*, 173. See also F.L BARTELS, *The Roots of Ghana Methodism* (Cambridge: Cambridge University Press, 1965), 22.
51. DEBRUNNER, *A History of Christianity*, p.72.
52. WILTGEN, *Gold Coast Mission History*.
53. DEBRUNNER, *A History of Christianity*, p.74.
54. DEBRUNNER, *A History of Christianity*, p.68.
55. DEBRUNNER, *A History of Christianity*, p.68.
56. DEBRUNNER, *A History of Christianity*, p.70.
57. Norbert Lochner, *Anton Wilhem Amo*, 1959, p.169-179.
58. op. cit., p.172

59. Only a summary of this thesis is produced in Gottfried Ludwig, *Universal History*.
60. Amo probably left Wittenberg under pressure from the Pietists who had the upper hand there and would not countenance Amo's Wolffian rationalism.
61. H. Debrunner, *A History of Christianity*, 82.

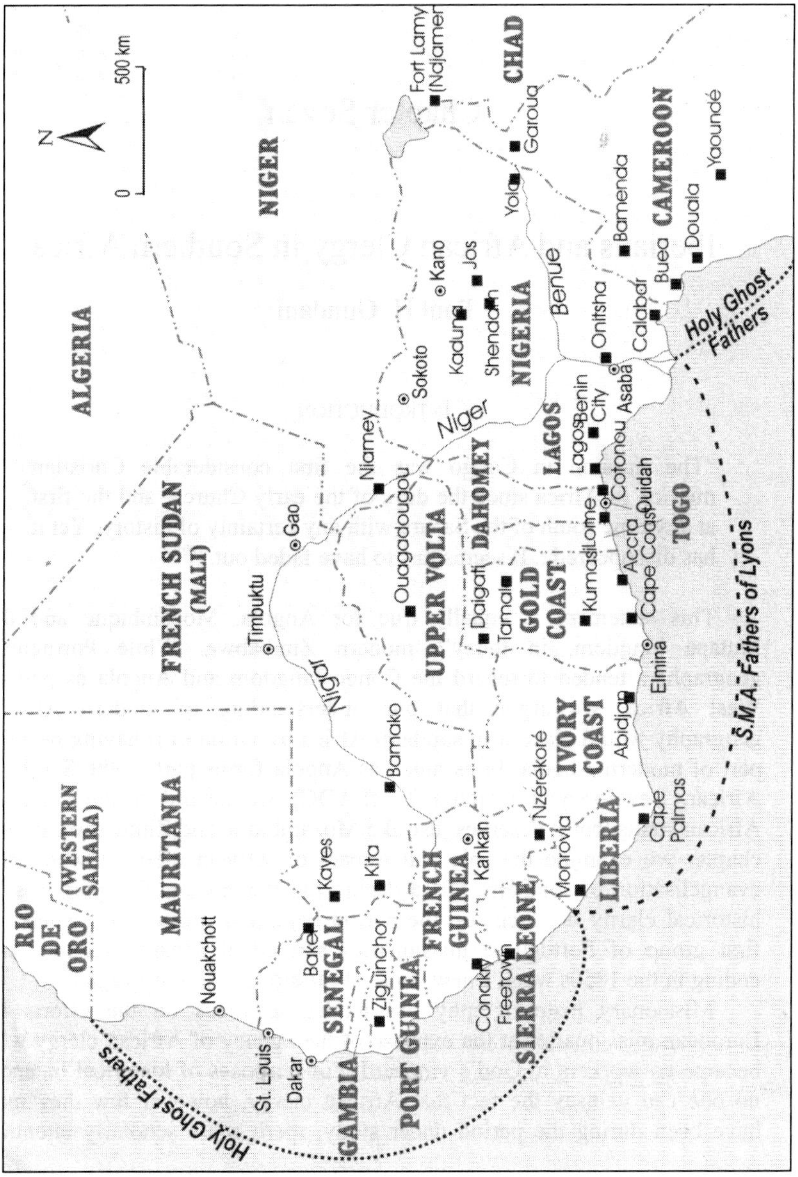

Map 5: Early Roman Catholic Missions in West Africa

Chapter Seven

Iberians and African Clergy in Southern Africa

Paul H. Gundani

INTRODUCTION

> *The mission in Congo was the first considerable Christian mission in Africa since the days of the early Church, and the first at any time south of the Sahara with any certainty of history. Yet it has disappeared... It seems just to have faded out.*[a]

This statement is equally true for Angola, Mozambique and the Mutapa kingdom, in today's modern Zimbabwe. While Portuguese geographers tended to regard the Congo kingdom and Angola as part of West Africa, we argue that our understanding of modern African geography would place it in southern Africa by virtue of it having become part of modern Angola. In as much as Angola forms part of the Southern African Development Community (SADC) we accord it the southern African status that it deserves just like Mozambique and Zimbabwe. In this chapter we examine the role and impact of African clergy towards the evangelisation of southern Africa during the Iberian era. For purposes of historical clarity we focus on the period beginning from 1491, when the first group of Portuguese missionaries arrived at Mbanza Kongo, and ending in the 1850s when a new wave of missionary activity began.

Missionary historiography has tended to focus on the efforts by European missionaries at the expense of the agency of African clergy who became co-workers in God's vineyard. For purposes of historical balance, no one can gainsay the fact that African clergy, however few they may have been during the period under study, merit more scholarly attention than they have received hitherto. There are problems, however, that we encounter, when we deal with this historical period. The first one has to do with the sources at the disposal of the historian.

As Sigbert Axelson observes, "Practically all historical research on sub-Saharan Africa is seriously hampered by the lack of original sources."[2] The records that are available, however, are generally provided by non-African sources, that is, by European and Arab visitors to the sub-continent, who came as explorers, conquerors and missionaries. As such, sources are laden with ideological biases and prejudices that were common during the times of the writers.

I. FACTORS BEHIND THE SHORTAGE OF MISSIONARIES IN SOUTHERN AFRICA

According to Eric Axelson, some of the key factors that explain the limited impact of Christianity in southern Africa include the vitality of traditional culture and the shortage of clergy.[3] The latter, was in itself a symptom of many factors that we consider below. Firstly, it is important to understand that the jurisdiction granted to the Portuguese government through the *padroado* was too vast and beyond the capacity of its human resources. It covered lands extending from Brazil to the Far East. Little wonder that the vocations in Portugal alone could not be adequate to supply missionaries to the new world. Secondly, the shortage of clergy was also linked to the Portuguese tendency to avoid the interior, which was associated with disease, insecurity and an inclement weather. Sao Salvador, the old Mbanza Kongo, was notorious for its high mortality for missionaries. It should be understood that the causes and cures of tropical diseases were not understood before the nineteenth and twentieth centuries. This situation deterred Portuguese clergy and caused the bishop and the small contingent of missionaries under him to relocate to Angola. Thirdly, the mission to Africa was very poorly conceived both by the Portuguese state and by Rome. By virtue of the *padroado*, the Portuguese state insisted on recruiting only Portuguese citizens for mission in the areas under its jurisdiction. In spite of the changes brought about by Rome in 1622, when all foreign missions were theoretically put under the jurisdiction of the *Propaganda Fide*, the Council for the Propagation of Faith in the Vatican, the Portuguese state continued to put restrictions on the recruitment and travel of non-Portuguese missionaries who wanted to work in Africa. Although Iberian Catholicism survived for as long as it did before fading away due to the support of the Portuguese government, the support was not enough to ensure continuity because of the shortage of missionary vocations. As A. Hastings avers, "the shortage of priests was acute almost from the beginning."[4]

II. POLICY AND POLITICS : THE DEVELOPMENT OF AN AFRICAN CLERGY

In an attempt to improve the shortage of priests, especially for the Kongo kingdom, the Portuguese government approved of the idea of training native priests by the early sixteenth century. This explains why many relatives of the king were sent for education and training at seminaries and universities such as Coimbra in Portugal. The positive attitude of the state regarding the training of an African was supported by Rome in 1518 when a papal Brief was promulgated, "authorizing the royal chaplain at Lisbon to ordain "Ethiopians, Indians and Africans, who might reach the moral and educational standards required for the priesthood."[5] The authorities in Lisbon pursued the idea of developing a native clergy in Angola after the conquest, occupation and pacification of the Angolan coastal regions in 1575. Such policies were not necessarily followed by Church authorities.

Invariably, missionary authorities in Africa scorned and scoffed at the policies from Lisbon and Rome. For instance, Bishop Francisco de Vilanova (1590-1602) reversed a policy to send African students to Coimbra in Portugal. He argued that it was "a waste of money to educate mulattoes and Negroes for the priesthood. In his view, it was better to send out to West Africa poor white clergy, who had no benefices or livings in Portugal, and to educate white orphan boys for the priesthood at the seminary in Coimbra."[6] The Jesuits in Angola adopted their own policy on the development of an African clergy. They opted for the training of an African clergy in Africa arguing that it would be cheaper for the crown and more convenient for the trainees. Hence they set up a college at Sao Salvador that functioned from 1625 to 1669. They also established a college at Luanda which functioned for a longer time than the one at Sao Salvador. Both were, however, dependent on the endowments of a wealthy ex-slave trader, Gasper Alvares, who joined the order as a lay brother after a shattering sexual experience.[7] The African clergy trained at these colleges were, however, to lower ranks of priesthood, and therefore did not become members of the order.

The situation in Mozambique and Mutapa kingdom was worse off than that in the Kongo and Angola. Although authorities in Lisbon suggested in 1694 and again in 1761 that efforts should be made to develop an indigenous clergy, for over three centuries, not a single clergyman was ordained in the two countries. Efforts to have a seminary set up were resisted by both state and church authorities in Mozambique. It was only in 1875 that a seminary was opened on the Mozambique Island, but was closed two years later for lack of students.[8] Only a few Africans from the Mutapa kingdom "were ordained at Goa or in Portugal in the sixteenth, seventeenth and eighteenth centuries, but they worked in Portuguese India and did not return to the land of their birth."[9] As a result, the Mutapa kingdom and Mozambique were ministered by a small group of white Jesuit and Dominican priests, supported by either mestizos or more commonly, Goanese secular clergy. As Philippe Denis rightly observes, the Dominican friars, who dominated the whole period under study in the Mutapa kingdom and in Mozambique, were not inclined to accept indigenous clergy too hastily.[10] Overall, the irony, however, was that, "in many places and for long periods the formation of a responsible native clergy was opposed by those missionaries who should have been in favour of it...."[11]

In the process of training an indigenous clergy, the missionaries invariably favoured and promoted members of royal blood. While this was generally practised in the whole region, one finds it particularly true of the Kongo and Mutapa kingdoms.

III. CASE STUDIES OF AFRICAN CLERGY IN SOUTHERN AFRICA

1. The Kongo Kingdom

The coronation of Afonso Nzinga as king of Kongo in 1506 ushered a new era in the planting of Christianity in the kingdom. Afonso persistently made pleas for more priests and teachers from Portugal with an idea of making his kingdom a leading African Christian state. His plans were to make Mbanza Kongo an episcopal see. Apart from having Portuguese missionaries, he also developed a clear plan for the indigenisation of the Church. He wanted to see "sons of the soil" evangelizing their own people. According to Sigbert Axelson, such a vision could only be understood as "an attempt ... to create a national and rather independent church administration, headed by Congolese...."[12] In an attempt to accomplish this vision, King Afonso made many attempts to develop a Congolese priesthood. He even tried to set up a college at Sao Salvador to educate and prepare Congolese priests. He was not successful, however, mainly because he "lacked a group of permanently committed and competent priests to run it."[13]

After failing to set up a college in the Kongo, Afonso decided to send out a number of young men to Lisbon to be educated and ordained. This effort was also in the main a failure due to a number of reasons. Firstly, the concept of celibacy was not easy to accept considering the world view and culture from which the students came. Secondly, when the students went to Portugal, they found themselves attracted to alternative careers. In most cases, they remained in Portugal after completing their courses. Thirdly, a good number of the students suffered from ill-heath which interfered with their studies. Hence, they returned home before completing their studies. Learning in Latin compounded to the problems that Congolese students encountered while they were in Portugal. All in all, however, whilst a steady trickle of noble Congolese youth were trained at St. John the Evangelist, popularly known as Santo Eloi, in Portugal, only a small number went back to the Kongo.

Later in 1624, Jesuits opened a seminary in Sao Salvador, where a number of black and mestizo Congolese were ordained. Unfortunately, by this time Christianity in the Kongo was already on the decline. According to James Duffy, "By 1615 most traces of Christian life had disappeared...."[14] From the Kongo kingdom, two clerics stand out, for detailed narration as case studies. They are bishop Henrique Nzinga and Fr Manuel Roboredo.

a. Bishop Henrique Nzinga (c1495?-1530)

Henrique Nzinga was son to King Afonso Nzinga. Henrique was the most famous of those priests who were trained in Portugal. This is mainly because he was the first and last African bishop in the Kongo kingdom. He was a veritable symbol of his father's commitment to see an indigenous church grow in the Kongo kingdom.

The date of birth of Henrique is not known with certainty. However, from his life story one can deduce that he was born about 1496/7. Afonso sent Henrique to Portugal to be educated and trained for priesthood in 1508. Since King Afonso was himself fluent in Portuguese and committed to the technical development of his kingdom, it is highly probable that he contracted teachers to teach Henrique from a tender age. That he could send Henrique to Portugal when he was just about twelve may be evidence that he had prepared him for advanced studies. Henrique lived and studied theology under the canons of St. John the Evangelist in Lisbon.

In 1518 Henrique was ordained to priesthood. Because of his fluency in Latin, he became a member of the embassy for the Kongo kingdom in Rome. According to Hastings, Henrique "apparently studied well and made an excellent impression so that the King of Portugal proposed that he be made a bishop."[15] There is evidence to the effect that King Manuel's suggestion to Pope Leo X caused much controversy in Rome.[16] The controversy had a racist dimension to it as the question centred on whether it was acceptable or not to have a "Negro" appointed bishop. Many considered this possibility out of the ordinary. There was another question hanging in the balance though, which had to do with Henrique's age. In Roman Catholicism, the canonical age for one to be bishop is 25. Apparently, Fr Henrique Nzinga was below that age. This issue is reflected in the communications between King Manuel I of Portugal and the Pope. Ultimately, however, the Pope agreed to appoint him as titular bishop of Utica, and Vicar Apostolic of the Kongo, but was only consecrated in 1521 when it was assumed that he had attained the age of twenty-five. According to James Duffy, bishop Henrique was auxiliary to the bishop of Madeira and received instructions through Sao Tome.[17]

Henrique returned home in the Kongo soon after his consecration in 1521. Little is known about the kind of work that he did back home, and how he worked with Portuguese missionaries there. From 1526 he was continually ill, and later died in 1530. In Boxer's view, Bishop Henrique had "become too acclimatized during his long stay in Portugal, since he complained in 1526 that he had been unwell ever since his return to Africa and would like to return to Portugal."[18]

Ostensibly, Bishop Henrique Nzinga's contribution to and impact on Christianity in Kongo was negligible. Perhaps James Duffy evaluation of his work best summarizes his role in the evangelisation of Kongo when he says, "... His role in the evangelization of his people was insignificant. Constrained by his father from leaving the capital, he was a witness to the laxity and selfishness of the white clergy, whose scorn he suffered ... He died a useless product of Afonso's vanity and two nations' aborted hopes."[19]

It should be noted, however, that during the episcopacy of Henrique, King Afonso persistently sent various young nephews and cousins for training in Portugal. His hope was that possibly "two or three would likewise be consecrated bishops, as the Kongo was too vast for one prelate to supervise adequately."[20]

b. Fr Manuel Roboredo (1665†)

Emmanuel Roboredo was a Mestizo cousin of kings Garcia and Antonio I. He was one of the priests who were educated in the Jesuit seminary at Sao Salvador. He was ordained in 1637 as a secular priest. He became canon of the cathedral of Sao Salvador and confessor of King Antonio I. His ministry in Sao Salvador was of exceptional influence.

In 1653, Fr Roboredo joined the order of Capuchins, an Italian order that joined the mission in the Kongo kingdom during the seventeenth century. He had played a critical role in welcoming the order to Sao Salvador in 1645. Since then he had served them as an interpreter. He also instructed the capuchin in the local languages. Fr Roboredo was proficient in many African and European languages.[21] Upon joining the order he adopted the name Francisco de Sao Salvador. This was the practice in the Roman Catholic Church for hundreds of years up to the Second Vatican Council (1962-1965). His confreres, however, called him Francesco Conghese.

Fr Roboredo was a skilful teacher and catechist, and was instrumental in the transformation of the religious climate in Sao Salvador of the 1650s. As a result he became one of the most popular confessors in Sao Salvador. His success generated jealousy from his colleagues. Fortunately, the Jesuits, with whom he had worked so well, came to his defence.

In the 1660s Fr Roboredo became royal chaplain and adviser of king Antonio I. The latter ranks high on the list of kings who wanted to see Kongo become independent of Portuguese influence. His attempts to stake the interests of the Kongo against Portugal sparked a war that resulted in defeat at the hands of his enemies. Fr Roboredo was, however, being drawn into the war against the king in 1665/6. Although Antonio I did not take advice from him, Fr Roboredo remained faithful to the king. He paid the price of loyalty as he died at the side of Antonio on the battlefield. The battle of Ambuila was the defining moment in the history of relations between the Kongo kingdom and Portugal.

Fr Manuel Roboredo clearly deserves much merit for his sterling contribution to his country and to the church in the Kongo. His commitment and service to his people was of rare quality. Surely, as S. Axelson avers, Fr Roboredo "deserves much merit amidst all the European missionaries, who usually attract greater interest in the history of the Church than their Congolese brothers."[22]

2. The Mutapa Kingdom

In the Mutapa kingdom there were two dominant religious orders, the Jesuits and Dominican friars. Nothing much developed in the kingdom by way of developing an African clergy. Thus the presence of the Jesuits and Dominicans, since 1560 and 1610 respectively, did not leave a mark in the kingdom. Although Dominicans established churches at Portugese *feiras* (markets) such as Masapa, Dambarare, Ruhanje, Bukutu and a few other places during the seventeenth century,[23] "there is nothing to suggest the growth of what could possibly be called a Church beyond small groups of Portuguese traders and settlers, their mestizo children, and the slaves that obeyed them."[24] In terms of the development of an African clergy, those who became priests were trained in Goa. Evidence suggests that those who trained to become priests came from the royal family. It seems that there were three Mutapa princes who became Dominican friars. They include Diogo and Philippe, the sons of Pedro Mhande Mavhura, who reigned briefly in the 1690s, and Miguel Kapararidze. The two brothers "preferred a marginalised life in a foreign land to a return home...."[25] The most celebrated of the Shona friars is Miguel Kapararidze.

a. Miguel Kapararidze (c.1515-1670)

Little is known about Miguel's Shona name. We do know, however, that he was the eldest son of Nyambo Domingos Kapararidze, who was emperor of the Mutapa Empire from c1624 to 1629 and from c1631 to 1632. Documents by Portuguese writers and by the Dominicans do not say. It is also difficult to calculate the age and date of his birth because the Shona society was then non-literate. Miguel was a young boy when his father was defeated by Mhande Mavhura in May 1629. The Portuguese took him prisoner, possibly in an attempt to groom him for the Mutapa throne. He was handed over to the Governor of Mozambique, who, in turn, entrusted him to the viceroy of India. The latter gave him the name Miguel. Later Miguel was taken to Goa where he was to be educated by the Dominicans.

It is not clear how many years Miguel spent in the Dominican convent at Goa. However, in 1630 the Vicar General of the Dominican order sent him to Portugal where he was placed in another Dominican institution. It was here that he was baptized. After three years in Portugal, he received a Dominican habit and a Dominican name, Miguel da Presentacao. Following this, Miguel was recommended to Cardinal Barberini, the prefect of the Congregation for the Propagation of Faith by the collector of Portugal, Lorenzo Tramallo. Scholars are of the opinion that Miguel traveled to Rome possibly because of the intervention of the Portuguese royal administration. Denis argues that this "black African Dominican friar of the eastern parts", was accepted into the Dominican order at barely 15 years. The reason for this, he argues, could have been his royal status on which Portugal wanted to capitalize. Just as in the case of Henrique Nzinga, the Portuguese administration always saw political gain in interacting with Miguel. Thus, it is perfectly understandable why Miguel was officially the protégé of the King of Portugal throughout his stay in Portugal.[26] It was not only the Portuguese Administration that saw gain in Miguel, Mudenge argues that the Dominicans also tried to use him "to promote the interests of their order at Rome and Lisbon."[27] After ordination, he was sent back to the priory of Basaim in India.

The ageing of Mutapa Mavhura created an opportunity for the Portuguese king to express his opinion on the successor. In 1560, the king of Portugal suggested that Miguel should return to the kingdom in order to be crowned emperor. Miguel turned down the offer arguing that he preferred to stay in

India.[28] Up to the time of his death in 1670 Miguel stayed in the Santa Barbara priory in Goa. He taught theology, and later became Vicar of Santa Barbara parish. "In 1670 the master general of the Dominican Order, Thomas Rocaberti, awarded him the title of Master in Theology."[29]

There is evidence that Fr Miguel was a victim of racism in Goa. To substantiate this point Mudenge suggests that:

> It appears that in 1664 one Fr Miguel da Presentacao, vicar of the parish of the convent of Santa Barbara, was a member of the group of rebel revolutionary priests who demanded far-reaching changes at the Convent of Santa Barbara, including the temporary closure of the Convent and dismissal of students.[30]

This story is confirmed by Denis who refers to an internal conflict which caused Miguel to act in common cause with a group of twenty-three religious who requested the temporary closure of the priory.[31]

That racism existed in the Dominican priory at Goa is confirmed by Miguel's contemporary, Fr Antonio Ardizone Spinola, an Italian Theatine priest, who knew him well in the 1640s. He wrote, "Although he is a model priest, leading a very exemplary life, saying mass daily, yet not even the habit which he wears secures him any consideration there, just because he has a black face. If I had not seen it, I would not have believed it."[32]

Like many African clergy who were trained in Portugal or Goa, Fr Miguel never went back to the Mutapa kingdom to serve his people. This was not because he was not given a chance: he was accorded one but he turned it down. Although he may not have wanted to be the leader of the Mutapa Empire, possibly because he felt that he was not prepared, he could have taken the chance to go back home to minister to his people. About him Adrian Hastings says: "He at least moved fully into Christian History, but he had also moved quite out of Zimbabwean history."[33] It is not true, however that Fr Miguel moved out of Zimbabwean history if one considers the way he is celebrated by Mudenge, who portrays him as an icon of Zimbabwean intellectual prowess and a doyen of academic excellence. In an attempt to re-insert him in Zimbabwean historiography, Mudenge wants him to be understood as a model Zimbabwean who went abroad and became known for his industriousness and academic leadership. The exaggeration that he makes of the award of the Master of Theology is meant to put across this sole point. It is only Mudenge who make the claim that the Master of Theology that he was awarded is "equivalent to today's doctorate in divinity."[34] He claims that

> Dom Miguel, priest, prince, professor, heir to the imperial throne of the Mutapas and the first to receive a doctorate degree in any field of study, died in Goa at the Convent of Santa Barbara sometime after 1670.[35]

However,it is not only Mudenge who writes about him appreciatively. P. Denis, a Dominican brother and church historian says that the Dominicans "had cause for rejoicing" because of Miguel's "extra-ordinary career."[36]

3. Mozambique

From the sixteenth century right up to the nineteenth century Portugese missionaries in Mozambique made minimal contact with the interior. Substantial contact with the black African population was only made in isolated areas lying behind the coastline from Sofala to Quelimane during the sixteenth and seventeenth centuries. For the rest, argues Hastings, Portuguese missionaries were dealing with a coastal people, Arab or Swahili.[37] Dominican and Jesuit missionaries dominated the Mozambican mission field. The Dominican order established their first permanent house on the island of Mozambique in 1577.[38] Their last Portuguese friar died in 1837. Their work in the Zambezi region was at best erratic and unfruitful. Similarly, the Jesuits, who had been to Mozambique since 1559, had several stations along the Zambezi. After a long but unrewarding stay in the area, they finally conceded that their work among the Bantu was not successful.[39] In such a mission field it would be too much to expect a thriving program for the development of an African clergy. The best that the Jesuits did was to establish a seminary at Sena for children of Portuguese and the sons of chiefs. Nothing much was yielded for the latter group. There is, however, one native cleric that we will profile in this section. He is Fr Luiz de Esprito Santo.

a. Luiz de Espirito Santo

Mudenge calls Fr Luiz de Esprito Santo, "a native of Mozambique."[40] This may be read as implying that he was a black priest. Eric Axelson seems to confirm this thinking by the suggestion that Fr Espirito Santo was "probably a scion of the royal house."[41] By this one would assume that he was a member of the royal house of one of the Mozambican chieftaincies. He should have been one of the few African priests of Mozambique sent by the Dominican order to train in either Portugal or Goa.

According to Denis,[42] Fr Espirito Santo was well versed with the customs of his people and contributed significantly to the Dominican order. He was trusted by the Portuguese Administration. He could well have been a chaplain of Portuguese soldiers on their military forays. This may explain the way he died in the Mutapa kingdom, where he was a captive of Emperor Kapararidze. In the 1620s he became deeply entangled in the politics of succession within the Mutapa kingdom. In a tussle for power between Mhande Mavhura and Nyambo Kapararidze, Fr Espirito Santo naturally favoured Mavhura, the Portuguese lackey. He thus helped in the defeat of Kapararidze in 1628.[43] His friendship with Mavhura resulted in him winning the Mutapa to Christianity. He christened Mhande Mavhura Dom Filippe. Fr Espirito Santo, had "hope of great consequences" out of his relationship with Mavhura.[44] He apparently read too much from the victory of Mavhura over Kapararidze. Mudenge says that:

> Fr Luiz thought that the victory of the anti-Kapararidze alliance was achieved in part through the intercession of our Lady of the Rosary. With this victory, the Mavhura forces entered the Zimbabwe where a victory mass was celebrated and a little church, dedicated to Our Lady of the Rosary was built.[45]

In 1631 Kapararidze began a counter-offensive, which restored his power, albeit for a short period of time. Fr Luiz de Espirito Santo was captured in one of the bloodiest military encounters between Mavhura and his Portuguese supporters and Kapararidze with his Moslem supporters. In a rather comical scene before he departed this world, Fr Luiz was asked to do Kapararidze homage, instead he "made a long harangue declaring his loyalty to Mavhura, the Portuguese crown and Jesus Christ, the 'King of Kings'."[46]

Furthermore:

> He likened Kapararidze with Lucifer and threatened him with hell-fire, 'the horrible lake' where he would burn 'for all eternity as miserable fuel to the inextinguishable fire! Return,' cried the good friar, 'return to reason, now that God counsels thee by my voice, and bend thy knee before the True Lord, rather than expect me to bend to thee.' Tired of what must have sounded as the rantings of a crazy but politically dangerous friar, Kapararidze ordered him put to death. He was tied to a tree-trunk and killed with assegais.[47]

We know almost nothing about his work of evangelisation inside Mozambique. Thus it is difficult to evaluate what exactly Denis means when he says that Fr Luiz Espirito Santo contributed significantly to the work of the Dominicans. It is also incomprehensible (not unfortunate) that fellow Dominicans like Fr Catharina saw him as a "martyr". As Mudenge rightly argues, "... it would appear more likely that the good friar went to face his Creator to answer some serious charges about his role in the spilling of so much innocent blood in those wars."[48]

4. Angola

Portuguese interest in Angola was first manifested in 1519. In 1526, the paramount of the Ngola people was converted.[49] By 1570, the Portuguese began the conquest of Angola. They finally established an European-controlled port in Luanda. Immediately thereafter, the Jesuits relocated to Luanda.[50] In spite of the long period that missionaries spent in Angola there was little to show for it after nearly three hundred years of toil. Hastings' evaluation sounds apt when he says:

> The history of the Church in Angola is depressingly lifeless, even though with time it became relatively considerable in size, because it remained so emphatically a colonial religion, present as part of a foreign establishment without almost any of the signs of indigenous vitality one can detect in the Kongo.[51]

Clearly, to think that such a mode of Christianity would produce a vibrant African clergy would be to expect too much. However, there were a few African priests who were trained at the seminary in Sao Tome. This seminary was a victim of regular temporary closures, because of lack of vocations and due to poor management. The persistent efforts to establish and maintain an indigenous clergy were mainly unsuccessful. For this reason, we will only give a brief history of one African priest from Angola.

a. Francisco das Necessitades

Little is known about Fr Francisco except the passing references that one comes across from missionary sources. There are no details as to where he was trained. However, he is one of the few African priests who remained in Angola in the 1840s, when white missionaries left Angola. In a period of 18 months that he visited the northern part of Angola, he is said to have baptized 100 000 people.[52]

IV. OVERALL EVALUATION ON THE ESTABLISHMENT OF AN AFRICAN CLERGY IN SOUTHERN AFRICA

Boxer makes an appropriate comment on the development of an indigenous clergy during the Portuguese era when he says,

> However desirable the development of an indigenous clergy may have been in theory, in practice such a clergy took a long time to develop in most countries outside Europe, and in some regions it never existed to any significant degree until very recent years.[53]

This was definitely true for southern Africa, and there are many reasons for that. Firstly, in most cases there was poor co-ordination between Portugal and the missionary administration in Africa and in Goa. Secondly, white members of religious orders resisted efforts to train an African clergy. This explains some of the cases of racism to which we have referred. Thirdly, poor planning and lack of resources accounted for the poor results. Fourthly, there was no clear-cut policy on the purpose of training an African clergy. Many who were trained in Portugal and Goa decided to work there and never returned to Africa to serve their people. This happened more often with the Dominican order than others. Fifthly, we should accept the point that there were limited vocations in southern Africa, due to the fact that Christianity there was very thinly spread. A corollary to this situation was the practice by most missionaries to resort to royal families as the constituency for recruiting an African clergy. Unfortunately, even this strategy failed to work out.

CONCLUSION

In spite of the difficulties faced by Iberian missionaries during the era under study, it is worth noting that the contribution of a few African clergy to African Christianity needs re-telling. Although sources are scant, and the Portuguese names conceal the identity of most African clergy that were trained, surely, it is worth while to learn about these few Africans who committed themselves to serving the Christian God, whether they managed to return to Africa or not. These few characters, that we managed to say something about, and many more whose knowledge we lack, are part of the complex history of African Christianity.

Notes

1. C.P. Groves, *The Planting of Christianity in Africa* (London: Lutterworth Press, 1948-1958), 130.
2. S. Axelson, *Culture Confrontation in the Lower Congo. From the Old Congo Kingdom to the Congo Independent State with special reference tot the Swedish Missionaries in the 1880's and 1890's* (Uppsala: Gunmessons, 1970), 18.
3. Axelson, *Culture Confrontation in the Lower Congo*, 73.
4. A. Hastings, *The Church in Africa: 1450- 1950* (Oxford: Clarendon Press, 1994), 82.
5. C.R. Boxer, *The Church Militant and Iberian Expansion: 1440-1770* (Baltimore: Johns Hopkins University Press, 1978), 4.
6. Boxer, *The Church Militant*, 6.
7. Boxer, *The Church Militant*, 9.
8. Boxer, *The Church Militant*, 10
9. Boxer, *The Church Militant*, 10.
10. P. Denis, *The Dominican Friars in Southern Africa A Social History (1577-1990)* (Leiden; Boston, MA: Brill Academic Publishers, 1998), 25.
11. Boxer *The Church Militant*, 2.
12. Axelson, *Culture Confrontation in the Lower Congo*, 68.
13. Hastings, *The Church in Africa: 1450- 1950*, 90.
14. J. Duffy, *Portuguese Africa* (Cambridge MA: Harvard University Press, 1959), 22.
15. Hastings, *The Church in Africa: 1450- 1950*, 83.
16. Axelson, *Culture Confrontation in the Lower Congo*, 64.
17. Duffy, *Portuguese Africa*, 18.
18. Boxer, *The Church Militant*, 4.
19. Duffy, *Portuguese Africa*, 18.
20. Boxer, *The Church Militant*, 4.
21. Axelson, *Culture Confrontation in the Lower Congo*, 122.
22. Axelson, *Culture Confrontation in the Lower Congo*, 121.
23. S.I.G. Mudenge, *A Political History of Munhumutapa c1400-1902* (Harare: Zimbabwe Publishing House, 1988), 227.
24. Hastings, *The Church in Africa: 1450-* 1950, 121.
25. E. Isichei, *A History of Christianity in Africa: From antiquity to the present* (London: SPCK, 1995), 69.
26. Denis, *The Dominican Friars*, 32.
27. Mudenge, *A Political History of Munhumutapa*, 259.
28. Denis, *The Dominican Friars*, 33.
29. Denis, *The Dominican Friars*, 33.
30. Mudenge, *A Political History of Munhumutapa*, 260-261.
31. Denis, *The Dominican Friars*, 33.
32. Boxer, *The Church Militant*, 11.
33. Hastings, *The Church in Africa: 1450- 1950*, 121.
34. Mudenge, *A Political History of Munhumutapa*, 260.

35. MUDENGE, *A Political History of Munhumutapa*, 261.
36. DENIS, *The Dominican Friars*, 31.
37. HASTINGS, *The Church in Africa: 1450- 1950*, 26.
38. DENIS, *The Dominican Friars*, ix.
39. GROVES, *The Planting of Christianity in Africa*, 165.
40. MUDENGE, *A Political History of Munhumutapa*, 255.
41. ISICHEI, *A History of Christianity in Africa*, 71.
42. Cf. DENIS, *The Dominican Friars*, 26.
43. DENIS, *The Dominican Friars*, 26.
44. MUDENGE, *A Political History of Munhumutapa*, 225.
45. MUDENGE, *A Political History of Munhumutapa*, 257.
46. MUDENGE, *A Political History of Munhumutapa*, 261.
47. MUDENGE, *A Political History of Munhumutapa*, 261-262.
48. MUDENGE, *A Political History of Munhumutapa*, 261-262.
49. DUFFY, *Portuguese Africa*, 51.
50. HASTINGS, *The Church in Africa: 1450- 1950*, 85.
51. HASTINGS, *The Church in Africa: 1450- 1950*, 119.
52. AXELSON, *Culture Confrontation in the Lower Congo*, 158.
53. BOXER, *The Church Militant*, 2.

Part Two

MISSIONARY PRESENCE AND AFRICAN AGENCY

Chapter Eight

Back to Africa: White Abolitionists and Black Missionaries

Jehu Hanciles

Africa, thou ebon country, how we long to see thee free!
E'er shall we, for thy redemption work and pray, till thou shalt be
Free from every degradation, that has cursed thy sunny land....[1]

History is replete with bittersweet ironies. But few of these compare, in poignancy or magnitude, to the association between the Atlantic slave trade and the subsequent expansion of Christianity on the African continent. As with so many epochal turning points in history, people movements provided the seedplot. In this case, the massive transatlantic transfers of population (African and European; voluntary and involuntary) enmeshed the fate of three continents and generated unprecedented levels of cultural interaction. It also unleashed powerful ideological movements that drew much of their energy from the "back to Africa" policy originally adopted by the British government and white abolitionists, and also espoused by Americans. This chapter focuses on the "back to Africa" movements from Britain and America and evaluates their significance both for the expansion of Christianity in Africa and the development of an African Christianity.

Accounts of the European-African encounter (from the fifteenth to early twentieth centuries) typically depict European initiatives and actions as dominant or decisive and, inevitably, enforce a portrayal of the African or black element as passive, dependent, and exploited. This approach is strongly Eurocentric and has the potential effect of reducing the histories and legacies of the African component to mere episodes in a much wider drama detailing the exploits and accomplishments of Western agents. It is also overly simplistic. As John Thornton has shown in connection with the early period of the encounter, Africans "controlled the nature of their interactions with Europe" in military and political relations, and were "active participants in the Atlantic world, both in African trade with Europe (including the slave trade) and as slaves in the New World."[2]

The same could be said of the African encounter with Christianity—even in the New World context of slavery and white domination. To affirm this is not to devalue the hugely significant Western missionary movement, nor to minimize the impact of white dominance. But when the narrative reconstruction of a people's past is held captive to the imagination of the dominant group the historical record becomes distorted, even if, in Richard Evans's insightful comment, "we all pull out of the seamless web of past events a tiny selection which we then present in our historical account."[3]

I. THE BRITISH DIMENSION

By the eighteenth century England had emerged as the first modern industrial nation. The attendant transformation effected spectacular changes in English society and politics; but the nation's rising prosperity accentuated egregious class divisions and forcibly exposed a pervasive religious decline.[4] Contemporary accounts passionately denounced the prevailing religious malaise, with the strongest criticisms directed at the Established (Anglican) Church to which the majority of English subjects belonged.[5] Wrote William Wilberforce (1759-1833), a member of the Established Church and renowned politician: "Religion also has declined: God is forgotten; his providence is exploded ... Improving in almost every branch of knowledge, we have become less and less acquainted with Christianity."[6] William Carey (1761-1834), a "dissenter" and cobbler by profession was equally forthright: "In respect to those who bear the Christian name, a very great degree of ignorance and immorality abounds amongst them."[7]

While the disparateness of their social and religious background arguably strengthens the testimony of these two men, it could be argued that the evangelical convictions they shared accounts for an unflattering view of society. But such saturnine assessments were not restricted to evangelicals. Rev Sydney Smith (1771-1845), no friend of evangelicals and renowned for his acerbic wit, was equally critical of the state of religion. "In England ... (except among ladies in the middle class of life)," he wrote, "there is no religion at all," and the clergy "have no more influence over the people at large than the Cheesemongers of England."[8]

It is necessary to point out that what critics deplored was a palpable lack of earnestness in matters of religion or, as Wilberforce would have it, the prevalence of professed (as opposed to real) Christianity. That England or Britain was essentially Christian was not at issue. The prevailing conception of Christian faith and allegiance was denoted by Christendom, a construct in which Christianity was defined in territorial or tribal terms and the church perceived as coterminous with the entire society. The offices and officials of the church were the object of more specific condemnations—anticlericalism was widespread—but charges about the erosion of Christian knowledge and values implicated the whole of society.

Specifically for this reason, the prospects for change seemed all the more daunting. Yet the pervasive sense of religious dissatisfaction probably meant that innumerable souls were ripe for a new religious experience. Change came in spectacular fashion, in the form of one of the most celebrated revivals in history: the eighteenth century evangelical revival.

A meaningful consideration of this revival is outside the scope of this chapter, and only the briefest of comments can be made. The eighteenth century evangelical revival generated extensive spiritual fervor and transformed Christian life throughout Britain. In its wake emerged religious ideas and philanthropic movements which "altered the whole course of English history."[9] It was also, it has to be said, an international phenomenon. Simultaneous with the outbreak in Britain, a wave of revivals swept through most of the American colonies in the period 1734-1735 and 1740-1742. Collectively designated "the Great Awakening", these events marked the beginning of popular evangelicalism in America. These revivals on both sides of the Atlantic are typically presented in scholarly accounts as wholly isolated, geographically contained, movements. More recently, however, an emphasis on their resemblance and remarkable simultaneity has produced arguments in favor of treating them as expressions of one phenomenon, the shared experience of a transatlantic community.[10] The best approach perhaps requires distinguishing between the similarities of expression and the peculiarities of experience they entailed.

Particularly significant is the fact that in Britain there was an immediate and vital connection between the evangelical revival, the antislavery campaign, and the modern missionary movement. Like all revivals, the eighteenth century phenomenon was spontaneous and unpredictable, and hugely shaped by contextual factors or agents. Even within Britain the revival was not an entirely homogenous movement in all its aspects. The British historian David Bebbington has identified four distinctive strands: namely, Evangelicals within the Church of England, Methodism, Calvinistic Methodism, and Dissenters or Nonconformists.[11] Only the first of these groups commands our attention here because its leading members formed the vanguard of the abolition movement.

Evangelicals within the Church of England were largely a group of ordained clergy and their associates. They were distinguishable from "Methodists" primarily by their relationship to the Church of England and their acceptance of the traditions of Anglicanism. There was also a social distinction: evangelicals were largely associated with the upper and upper-middle classes while Methodism drew its following mainly from the lower and lower-middle classes. Emerging perhaps by the late 1730s, the former spread through the formation of clerical societies and clubs.[12] In a context where the placement and removal of clergy was in the hands of lay aristocrats, who "were rarely sympathetic to the cause of the gospel,"[13] sustained evangelical influence within the churches was severely hampered. Effective evangelical clergy could be removed at will by unsympathetic patrons. This difficulty was minimized in two ways. First, leading evangelicals used their wealth to purchase livings to which evangelical clergy were appointed. Second, the movement eventually secured significant following in the universities and thereby exerted a profound influence on the "breeding grounds of the [Anglican] ministry."[14]

This (Anglican) evangelical movement became identified with two main centers: Cambridge and Clapham (a suburb of West London). Cambridge was considered its intellectual centre, while Clapham emerged as the movement's spiritual and executive nucleus and became the focal point of the most prominent and influential evangelicals of the day.[15] Under the leadership of William Wilberforce, the "Clapham Sect", as this group was known,[16] came to share a unique identity and exert an influence on the society of their day that was out of all proportion to their numbers.[17] Among their numerous undertakings were various educational schemes (including the Sunday School movement), the establishment of the British and Foreign Bible Society, the Church Missionary Society, the African Institution, the Sierra Leone Trading Society, the Society for Bettering the Condition and Improving the Comforts of the Poor, and a multitude of unorganized personal charities.

Activism was, and remains, a hallmark of evangelicalism. Like other movements associated with the evangelical revival, the energy and zeal exhibited by the Clapham Sect was a function of the movement's doctrinal stress on the salvation of the individual with its attendant focus on the human condition. The fusion of religious fervor and humanitarian endeavor became the driving force behind the Clapham Sect's most outstanding achievement, the abolition of the slave trade.[18]

II. THE ABOLITION MOVEMENT IN BRITAIN

It somehow seems fitting that Britain, the chief slave-trading nation for more than two centuries (prior to the 1780s) produced the most able abolitionists. At the same time, the fact that the slave trade was by then considered "inseparably associated with the commerce and welfare, and even the national security" of Britain meant that opposition to its abolition was powerful and entrenched. By the 1790s, the trade was estimated to annually employ over 5,500 sailors, more than 160 ships, and (in the West India trade alone) generate over £6, 000,000 in exports and imports.[19] Not only had the large accumulation of profits become "a major factor in the accumulation of English and French capital" the trade itself made "a large, and at certain points probably decisive, contribution to the whole process of industrialization."[20] Even the more humanitarian minded reconciled themselves to its horrors and inhumanity "on the grounds of its sheer necessity."[21]

The members of the Clapham Sect were by no means the first to oppose or tackle the issue of slavery and seek its abolition. Many voices in the eighteenth century had already been raised against this nefarious traffic, noticeably among Quakers. But the Clapham brotherhood embarked on the antislavery campaign with unprecedented militancy. Their determination to tackle the slave trade on a national level and elicit government action was clearly signaled in Wilberforce's first speech to Parliament on the issue (in 1789):

> When we consider the vastness of the continent of Africa; when we reflect how all other countries have for some centuries past been advancing in happiness and civilization; when we think how in this same period all improvement in Africa has been defeated by her intercourse with Britain; when we reflect that it is we ourselves that have degraded them to that wretched brutishness and barbarity which we now plead as the justification for our guilt ... What a mortification must we feel at having so long neglected to think of our guilt, or to attempt any reparations!
>
> A society has been established for the abolition of this trade, in which dissenters, Quakers, churchmen ... have all united ... Let not parliament be the only body that is insensible to the principles of national justice. Let us make reparation to Africa....[22]

The first major victory in the abolitionist cause came with the Somerset Case. James Somerset, a runaway slave boy, was brought up for trial before Lord Chief Justice Mansfield (in February 1772) mainly through the prodigious efforts of Granville Sharpe, the oldest of the Clapham group. Self-taught, eccentric, and tenacious in his commitment to seemingly impossible causes, Sharp has been described as "the father of the Abolitionist movement".[23] He personally conducted two years of exhaustive research to strengthen Somerset's defense and financed the effort. In the end the five lawyers employed in the case were so moved by its merits and Sharp's selfless commitment that they declined to accept compensation for their services.[24] In a momentous legal verdict, Lord Mansfield declared (on 22nd June 1772) that slavery was against the law of the land.

This judgment automatically made all slaves within the British Isles free, but it did nothing to stop the slave trade. The abolitionists now focused efforts on getting the British Parliament to pass an anti-slavery bill. To this end they constituted an Abolition Committee in 1787.[25] This committee was short lived; but under Wilberforce's dedicated leadership, the parliamentary campaign never faltered—indeed, four more members of the growing Clapham circle won parliamentary seats over the next two decades. But strenuous opposition from powerful vested interests turned this effort into a long and arduous struggle. It quickly became obvious that winning public opinion was imperative. To this end, the abolitionists embarked on a massive propaganda campaign throughout the country that included numerous petitions, extensive pamphleteering, public meetings, and boycotts.[26] Increasingly also, they propagated the view that Africa held great potential, both as a source of raw material and new markets, which could only be realized with the abolition of the slave trade.

The argument that legitimate commerce should replace the slave trade was reinforced by the personal researches of the indefatigable Thomas Clarkson[27] and became a central plank in the abolition argument. It gained increasing support with the passing of years, winning powerful allies among manufacturers. White abolitionists made much of this economic argument, but among the first to advance it was an ex-African slave, Olandah Equiano (or Gustavus Vassa), an Ibo from Nigeria. In 1789, Equiano published his autobiographical *The Interesting Narrative of the Life of Olaudah Equiano, or Gustavus Vassa, the African in His Own Words*, in which he contended with no little passion:

> [Africa] lays open an endless field of commerce to the British manufactures and merchant adventurer. The manufacturing interest and the general interests are synonymous. The abolition of slavery would be in reality an universal good.
>
> Tortures, murder, and every other imaginable barbarity and iniquity, are practiced upon the poor slaves with impunity. I hope the slave trade will be abolished. I pray it may be an event at hand. The great body of manufacturers, uniting in the cause, will considerably facilitate and expedite it; and, as I have already stated, it is most substantially their interest and advantage, and as such the nation's at large ... In a short time one sentiment alone will prevail, from motives of interest as well as justice and humanity. Europe contains one hundred and twenty millions of inhabitants. Query—How many millions doth Africa contain? Supposing the Africans, collectively and individually, to expend 51. a head in raiment and furniture yearly when civilized, &c. an immensity beyond the reach of imagination!
>
> This I conceive to be a theory founded upon facts, and therefore an infallible one. If the blacks were permitted to remain in their own country, they would double themselves every fifteen years. In proportion to such increase will be the demand for manufactures. Cotton and indigo grow spontaneously in most parts of Africa; a consideration this of no small consequence to the manufacturing towns of Great Britain. It opens a most immense, glorious, and happy prospect—the clothing, &c. of a continent ten thousand miles in circumference, and immensely rich in productions of every denomination in return for manufactures.[28]

Equiano's intimate knowledge of the slavery experience and passionate belief in Africa's potential made him a powerful antislavery figure. Unfortunately, despite the immense interest which his book attracted, this irrepressible African abolitionist remained a marginalized figure in the anti-slavery movement.[29] But the economic argument was strong; so strong, in fact, that some have argued that the abolition of slavery occurred when it did, not so much because the nation's conscience had been aroused by moral arguments, but because the trade itself had become economically expedient.[30]

But, ultimately, neither economic expediency nor the much celebrated humanitarian effort is in and of itself sufficient to explain the abolition of the slave trade—the trade, after all, persisted for decades after legal proscription and in the face of military blockades. A variety of complex impulses all contributed to the ultimate outcome. Among other things, opportune changes in Britain's political leadership, a growing acceptance among plantation owners that "breeding" was just as effective as "buying", the spread of enlightenment values, and the religious transformations associated with the evangelical revival, all played a role. For their part the abolitionists were convinced that their cause would only succeed if it first of all triumphed in the court of public opinion. Declared Wilberforce, "I rely on the religion of the people of this country—because the people of England are religious and moral, loving justice and hating iniquity."[31]

Overstated perhaps, but such convictions mattered. As already mentioned, the abolitionists' chief weapon was propaganda. They perfected the art of soft protest and pioneered mass media techniques: they "pamphleteered, lobbied, pressured, stumped the country in speaking campaigns ... They engineered debates, promoted commissions of inquiry, drew up 'bodies of evidence' ... [and] tapped the gathering tide of humanitarian liberalism that flowed through those years."[32] Not for the first (or last) time an entire nation was aroused by the actions of a few men and women of ability and uncommon fervor, championing a cause whose time had come.

The British parliament faced increasing pressure from the public to take action. In March 1807, with the passing of a bill entitled "The Slave Trade Abolition Act" in the House of Lords, the abolitionist cause gained a landmark victory. It had taken nineteen years of parliamentary struggle. America and Denmark also abolished the slave trade. But the battle was far from finished. Further actions were required to secure full international agreement—Spain, France, Holland and Portugal had yet to be won over.[33]

Over the next thirty years Britain induced other European nations to cooperate with her in the prohibition of the trade; but there was an even greater battle yet to be won: the elimination of slavery itself. Knowledge of the brutality and dehumanization that characterized slavery was now widespread; but the degradation of the African and the deep contempt for African humanity that this "monster iniquity" fostered in European minds presented innumerable mental and psychological impediments in the way of emancipation. By now, however, the antislavery movement boosted a broad front. Evangelical churchmen, Methodists, Quakers, and regular dissenters, all brought their influence to bear on the campaign, and the government was inundated with petitions.[34]

In the early 1820s, leadership of the parliamentary campaign passed from Wilberforce to the youthful Thomas Fowell Buxton.[35] Progress was slow and fitful; but the extraordinary assiduousness of the abolitionists eventually paid off. On July 25, 1833, the Emancipation Act guaranteed the emancipation of all slaves in British dominions. Four days later, Wilberforce, the Agamemnon of the abolitionist cause, breathed his last. Slavery was not immediately abolished (in America emancipation came much later), but the death knell of the institution had been sounded.

III. BACK TO AFRICA: THE SIERRA LEONE SETTLEMENT

Lord Mansfield's ruling in the Somerset case signaled the freedom of thousands of African slaves living in Britain at the time. Added to this number were former American slaves, the so-called "black loyalists", who had served under the British flag in the American War of Independence and made their way to England after the peace of 1783. Many more had escaped from their masters in the West Indies and elsewhere to seek a haven of freedom in England. Estimates put the overall number of blacks in England between ten and twenty thousand by the end of the eighteenth century.[36]

The influx of such a large number of blacks in and around the streets of London created a grave social problem. Unemployed, homeless and destitute, they caused an alarming increase in the number of beggars and vagabonds and were dubbed "the Black Poor" by the press. Their presence unnerved the white population unaccustomed to such huge numbers of blacks; and deep racial prejudices fueled exaggerated fears. Echoing popular sentiment, *The London Chronicle* (in March, 1773, a year after the Somerset Case) expressed the hope that:

> Parliament will provide such remedies as may be adequate to the occasion, by expelling Blacks now here ... prohibiting the introduction of them in this kingdom for the future, and save the natural beauty of Britons from the Morisco tint.[37]

In keeping with such sentiments the predominant response was to explore every avenue of evacuation. In 1786, a group of philanthropists and other concerned citizens, including Granville Sharpe, formed the "Committee for Relieving the Black Poor" to spearhead relief efforts. When Henry Smeathman, an "amateur botanist", presented a plan for the repatriation of these blacks to Sierra Leone on the West African coast, the committee immediately seized the idea.[38] The British government, alive to the possibility of ridding itself of an awkward problem, also agreed to finance the scheme. The new settlement was billed as a "Province of Freedom". Smeathman died, in July 1786, before it became clear that his knowledge of Africa was as defective as his motives were suspect. On April 8, 1787, after two abortive attempts, 411 passengers sailed from Plymouth. The blacks on board were mainly ex-soldiers adventurous enough to make the journey. Along with them were a handful of Europeans (officials or craftsmen and their families) and seventy London prostitutes.[39] The scheme ended in disaster. Within three months, disease and death had taken the lives of a third of the group. By March 1788, only 130 of the original number were left. In 1789, King Jimmy, a neighboring Temne chief, attacked the settlement (which had been named "Granville Town") and completely destroyed it.

Sharpe and the other philanthropists remained undaunted. They were convinced that with the right type of colonialists or settlers and the establishment of legitimate commerce a settlement could be successfully established in Sierra Leone. To this end they formed the Sierra Leone Company (in 1791) which was empowered by an act of parliament to govern the settlement. The directors of the Company included Sharpe, Wilberforce, and Henry Thornton (a London Banker). There was only one problem: the settlement the Company was set up to govern was populated only by a tiny remnant. Rendered cautious by previous failure, the directors of the Company were reluctant to send out more blacks, while the high mortality rate among white colonists made them an impractical alternative.

This predicament ended when Thomas Peters, a freed slave, arrived in London, in 1791, to plead the cause of black settlers in Nova Scotia. Lured by promises of freedom and economic opportunities, these "black loyalists" had fought on the British side in the Revolutionary War.[40] Shipped off to Nova Scotia after the war their lot had become desperate. Peters was in London to express their grievances and present a petition for emigration. The timing could not have been more propitious. Plans were soon under way to transport the Nova Scotian blacks to Sierra Leone. Eventually, in January 1792, 1190 blacks set sail from Nova Scotia in five vessels. The new settlers renamed the settlement "Freetown".

The entire community of Nova Scotian blacks were baptized Christians and they landed in Sierra Leone complete with their own churches and preachers. Their religious fervor and bibliocentric lifestyle was palpably manifest. Their arrival was of epochal significance. It marked the establishment of the first black church in modern Africa[41] and arguably signified the beginning of the "modern" missionary movement.[42] In effect, the story of modern African Christianity began not with white missionary agency but as the initiative of ex-African slaves. As the rest of this chapter will show, this black missionary element grew stronger and exerted a profound influence on the nature and spread of Christianity in nineteenth century Africa.

In 1800, the Nova Scotian settlers were joined by another group of ex-African slaves. These Maroons, as they were called, numbered some five hundred and fifty and hailed from Jamaica. Fiercely warlike, they had been granted their freedom by the colonial government only to resume fighting much later.[43] Briefly deported to Nova Scotia, where they found conditions harshly inhospitable, their clamor for redress led to repatriation to the Sierra Leone settlement.

By now, the Sierra Leone Company and other evangelical promoters were fired by a vision of the settlement as a Christian centre, a strategic foothold for commercial undertakings (to counter the slave trade) as well as a springboard for the spread of Western civilization and Christianity in Africa. But visions of a "Christian nation"—a veritable Christendom—proved illusory, even after 1808 (the year in which the Sierra Leone Company, under threat of insolvency, ceded its administration to the British Crown). The Nova Scotian settlers, dissenters all, were revivalistic in their practice of religion and thus more attentive to the designs of heavenly powers than earthly authority. Indeed, they were conditioned by long experience to be deeply suspicious of white authority; and their penchant for rebelliousness and political agitation squelched any hope of a politically directed religious structure.[44]

As a Crown colony, Sierra Leone became the focus of yet another abolition scheme which saw the blockade of the West African coast by the British squadron and the recapture of thousands of African slaves, who were now relocated in Freetown and villages established around it for the purpose. Included among these "recaptives" (or Liberated Africans) were many Muslims who resisted conversion to the Christian faith while enjoying the full benefits of colonial rule and the same protection accorded to British citizens.[45] Additionally, the earliest European missionaries sent to Sierra Leone insisted on individual confession and conversion (a corollary of their evangelical convictions), and resolutely resisted an approach whereby baptism was a mere formality that signified civil status and ecclesiastical identity.[46] In short, the reproduction of Christendom was subverted by its chief representatives (the missionaries) and the dynamics of colonial expansion.[47]

Sierra Leone was destined to be a Christian experiment of a different sort. The recaptives, who numbered 18,000 by 1825 (an estimated 67,000 by 1840), became the dominant element in the life and future of the colony. Freed from the clutches of villainous traffickers they became captive audiences for Nova Scotian evangelists and European agents of missionary societies (predominantly the Church Missionary Society [CMS], formed in 1799 by members of the Clapham Sect). Their conversion to Christianity in vast numbers represents one of the most spectacular achievements in modern mission history and "the first mass movement to Christianity in modern Africa." These developments augured well for an experiment aimed at making the settlement "the beacon of light to Africa [and] the springboard of missionary enterprise."

The ill-fated 1841 Niger Expedition (inspired by the ideas of T. Fowell Buxton) emphatically underlined the notion that African agency was indispensable for the Christianization of Africa.[48] No other missionary society was more resolute in translating this belief into policy than the CMS. Under the leadership of Henry Venn (from 1841 to 1872), whose father (John Venn) had been a leading member of the Clapham group, the Society strengthened its commitment to training African clergy and adopted the "three-selfs" strategy aimed at the development of self-supporting, self-propagating, and self-governing churches. First implemented in the colonial context of Sierra Leone and later in the CMS Yoruba Mission, Venn's vision for African church autonomy had profound implications for the development of the African Church.[49]

In Sierra Leone, colonial domination and European control of the churches created significant roadblocks to Venn's strategy; but the opening of the Niger mission allowed a motivated African missionary force to test-drive Venn's ideas. Most significantly, Venn's revolutionary ideas launched the career of Bishop Samuel Adjai Crowther (1807-1891), arguably the most celebrated African Christian of the nineteenth century. Headed by Crowther and staffed almost entirely by Sierra Leonean Christians (recaptives evangelized in earlier decades), the Niger Mission was a bold experiment in African leadership and initiative that witnessed one of the most remarkable periods of Christian expansion on the African continent in nineteenth century.[50]

If the stratagems championed by white abolitionists and missionary thinkers like Henry Venn provided the framework for an emerging African Christianity, African agents, particularly ex-slaves remained a driving force. In the first half of the nineteenth century, black Christians from the West Indies joined Christianized recaptives, Nova Scotians, and the small group of African American missionaries in the missionary effort. The West Indian presence in Sierra Leone dated back to the establishment of a West Indian regiment in 1819; but immigration and a brief burst of missionary activity significantly increased the number of West Indians in West Africa. The most well known among them was Thomas Birch Freeman (1809-1890), the son of a West Indian father and an English mother, who arrived in Ghana (in 1838) as a missionary of the Wesleyan Missionary Society. Freeman's long and distinguished career as a pioneer missionary has earned him historical recognition as the "father of Ghanaian Methodism".[51]

Like their African American counterparts, West Indian Christians brought with them strong race consciousness and a propensity for political activism. It is noteworthy that Freeman had a brief stint in government service on the Gold Coast. In Sierra Leone, West Indian agitation and outspokenness on white dominance contributed to an incipient nationalism that drew much inspiration from Venn's experiment in ecclesiastical self-government to stimulate the emergence of movements like "Ethiopianism" that extolled African instincts and initiatives.

Over the next three-quarters of a century, Sierra Leone would play a pivotal role in the expansion of Christianity in the region. Between 1840 and 1900, it provided over 60% of Anglican "native clergy" in West Africa. By mid nineteenth century, Sierra Leone Christians already formed the vanguard of a huge missionary movement, carrying back the message of the Gospel and the attendant benefits of education to the various lands throughout West Africa (and beyond) from which they or their ancestors had been uprooted as slaves.[52]

Clearly then, the African (or black) element played a central role in the establishment of Christianity in Africa in the modern period. But transatlantic connections are critical to the story; and for that an assessment of the American dimension is necessary.

IV. THE AMERICAN EXPERIENCE

The first batch of African slaves arrived in the North American colonies in 1619. By the time of the Great Awakenings (in the 1730s), the system of slavery was solidly entrenched in American society, and the church was an active agent in enforcing it. Protest against the institution came only from a small band of Quakers and German Mennonites. The American Revolution of the 1770s heightened hopes for freedom; hopes which for many thousands of blacks were linked to British victory. For these the outcome was not as expected, but the "fever of liberty" was abroad.[53]

Rev. Dr. Samuel Hopkins (1721-1803), one of Jonathan Edwards' closest friends and most influential disciples, led calls for the abolition of slavery and propagated a scheme whereby Christian blacks could be repatriated to Africa to build new lives and lead in the evangelization of the continent. Little came of this idea at the time, but it would be revived by blacks themselves several decades later. In 1775, the Quakers—the most prominent and persistent anti-slavery group—organized the first abolition society in Philadelphia. Two years later slavery was abolished in Vermont (albeit a state with a negligible slave population). From a variety of motives other states, north and south, enacted legislation which curtailed the trade or fostered emancipation.[54] But the anti-slavery movement fell far short of its ideals; by 1790, more than nine-tenths of the black population remained in bondage.

Meanwhile, the Great Awakenings provided the first systematic attempts at evangelizing blacks[55]—though it is noteworthy that Jonathan Edwards (1703-1758) and George Whitfield (1714-1770), the revivals' towering figures, kept slaves. The system was so well established, in fact, that the widespread conversion of slaves and their incorporation into the church left the system itself intact—though new voices would be raised condemning it.[56] But with some 700,000 slaves and 59,000 free blacks (by 1790), America had one of the largest communities of Africans anywhere in the world outside Africa. Christianization of such a large group was bound to have enduring consequences.

In the New World, the emergent black Christianity was limited to four main forms:[57] segregated worship within white churches, separate worship supervised by a white pastor, secret meetings, and, much later, independent churches. By most accounts, blacks understood the evangelical message very differently from whites.[58] Conditioned by the experience of slavery and oppression, their response to the gospel message fused religion and freedom in a manner that was patently subversive.[59] Gayraud Wilmore argues that they "used Christianity not so much as it was delivered to them by racist white churches, but ... to reinforce an enculturated religious orientation and to produce an indigenous faith that emphasized dignity, freedom, and human welfare."[60] In the final analysis, black Christianity served African ends while satisfying European requirements. Noll describes it as "a singular blend of African, European, and American elements, which made for both continuity and discontinuity with the white churches."[61] What mattered was that the emergent faith was shaped by African concerns and spirituality.

For blacks, neither conversion to Christianity nor emancipation from slavery (in 1865) delivered legal equality, economic progress, or educational opportunity. Systemic oppression and the indignity of segregation remained corollaries of blackness. Still, the admixture of biblical faith and black religiosity fostered a new identity consciousness and stimulated religious protest that triggered the emergence of independent African denominations in the north. Perhaps the most significant of these was the African Methodist Episcopal Church (AME), established in 1814 under the leadership of Richard Allen (1760-1831), its first bishop.[62] From origins in Philadelphia the independent black church movement gathered pace in what Wilmore terms "a widening circle of rebelliousness".[63] Numerous black congregations of Methodists, Baptists, and Presbyterians emerged and merged to formed denominations or associations. By 1890, over thirty percent of blacks was enrolled in one or the other of the three largest African denominations—the National Baptist Convention, the African Methodist Episcopal, and the African Methodist Episcopal Zion.[64]

Among black Christians, the struggle for freedom and the longing for racial dignity drew on a deep-seated African spirituality as well as the new biblical faith. In particular, Psalm 68:31—which declares, "Princes shall come out of Egypt; Ethiopian [symbolic of Africa] shall stretch forth her hands unto God"—exerted a profound influence on the black Christian consciousness. Widely interpreted throughout the nineteenth century as epitomizing the divine will for black redemption and elevation, this verse became the focus of the deepest spiritual aspirations and self-understanding of black Christians. Most important, it spawned "Ethiopianism",[65] an ideology (and movement) which denoted strong affirmation of the African heritage (cultural, spiritual, and historical—including a glorification of the ancient African churches), a rejection of white domination, and a conviction that Africans must take the lead in the Christianization of the African continent. Put another way, Ethiopianism embodied race consciousness, religious protest, and a redemptive vision.[66] In America as well as Africa it came to signify "black nationalism".

The conviction that black Christians (the descendants of ex-African slaves) were God's chosen instruments for the redemption of Africans generated a new missionary impulse. Black Christians were inspired "to win Africa not only for Africans, but for Christ, by mass emigrations from the West and by forging bonds of friendship and collaboration between Africans and African-Americans".[67] Missionary emigration was greatly bolstered, in the short term, by the establishment of a Christian settlement in Sierra Leone using ex-African slaves. Further impetus was provided by the publicity surrounding on-going explorations of the African interior and the fever of interest in the evangelization of Africa among white missionary societies. Incidentally, the latter also spotlighted the promise of Psalm 68:31 as part of their mobilization campaign.

Thus, "back to Africa" movements emerged in Britain and America, independent of each other but with common stimuli and objectives. Both blended colonization, abolition and commercial opportunism with the central aim of Christianization. As in Britain, white support for black emigration was motivated by tacit rejection of racial equality and forebodings about the emergence of a "mongrel" nation.[68] The steady escalation in the numbers of free blacks also triggered fears, accentuated by various "uprisings", about the safety of their former oppressors. Here, even more than in Britain, freed African slaves were considered an acute social problem solvable by repatriation to Africa. The American colonization movement was the fruit of such sentiments. For its proponents, the mass repatriation of blacks to Africa must accompany emancipation as a necessary safety-valve. Furthermore, it was in Africa's best interest.

Thus, their widely propagated colonization scheme called for the "civilizing and Christianizing Africa through the instrumentality of emigrants from the United States."[69] This movement culminated in the formation of the American Colonization Society (ACS) in 1816 and the founding of Liberia (in 1821) as a home for free blacks.

The colonization scheme was strongly condemned by abolitionists (in America and Britain) who feared that it detracted from both the antislavery struggle and the reform of American society.[70] Noting the enthusiastic support which southern slaveholders gave to the movement, most black leaders publicly opposed emigration, even when it was linked to missionary enterprise. They pointed to the contributions that blacks had made to American prosperity and insisted that blacks had every right to stay and work for a better future. Others ventured that evangelizing blacks, even whites, in America was a priority and even more pressing task for black churches.[71] Not until the late 1870s, when disillusionment about the creation of a racially equal society had set in, did black emigration grow substantially.[72] Even then, many who had motivation did not have the means.

V. BACK TO AFRICA: AMERICAN IDEALS

The ideal of missionary emigration never lived up to even modest expectations. But in the long run a vital avenue of interaction was opened between American blacks and African Christians that would have important consequences for the development of Christianity on the continent. Among the first to act on this new missionary impulse was Paul Cuffee, an ex-slave, Quaker, and wealthy ship-owner. In 1815, Cuffee financed the emigration of nine families and thirty-eight other persons whom he brought over on one of his ships to Sierra Leone. Cuffee's example was conspicuous in its singularity. Blacks of independent means with genuine interest in missions were thin on the ground. Ultimately, the black missionary movement was severely curtailed in the first half of the nineteenth century by a number of factors: among these were opposition from blacks critical of emigration, a preoccupation among newly formed black churches with expansion into the South (or home missions), and lack of financial resources.[73]

Blacks with a strong sense of missionary calling had perforce to work through white institutions, which by happy coincidence were strongly predisposed to sending black missionaries. Reasons for this included the high mortality among white missionaries in tropical Africa, the paucity of white volunteers, and the relatively lower costs of supporting blacks.[74] Walter Williams reports that "before 1880 almost all black evangelists working among indigenous Africans were supported by white churches."[75] The majority labored in either Sierra Leone or Liberia. Among the most successful were Joseph and Mary Gomer, who, under the auspices of the United Brethren, served among the Mende people on the Island of Sherbro (south of the Sierra Leone peninsular) from 1871 to 1892.[76] Both Alexander Crummell and Edward W. Blyden, two of the most influential black leaders of the period, were also sponsored by white denominations. Outside West Africa, the name of William Sheppard stands out. Sheppard labored in the Congo among the Kuba people as a missionary of the Southern Presbyterian Society for two decades. His pioneering spirit, evangelistic efforts, campaign on behalf of the Africans against colonial atrocities, and somewhat colorful life has prompted fascinating comparisons with the famed Scottish missionary-explorer, David Livingstone.[77]

Amidst strong criticisms of the colonization movement, notwithstanding, a few notable blacks also availed themselves of the resources of the ACS to finance individual missionary efforts. Included among these were Lott Cary, a black Baptist minister, who inspired a strong missionary interest among Baptists and briefly became acting governor of the Liberia colony (1828), and Daniel Coker, a founding member of the AME Church, who emigrated to Liberia (1820) and extended his ministry to Sierra Leone.

By the 1880s, however, the number of black missionaries sent by white denominations or mission boards had begun to decline sharply. Medical advances enabling whites to survive in a tropical climate, increasing racial conflicts between blacks and white missionaries or colonialists, and the presence of a large pool of trained African converts were among the factors which contributed to this development. As it happened, the final decades of the nineteenth century also witnessed heightened missionary interest among black churches, which by now had a huge membership base to draw on. Moreover, emancipation in the wake of the Civil War ended slavery for thousands of blacks and revived the emigration movement. By the end of the century the three largest black denominations had overtaken white institutions in their support of missionary work in Africa.[78]

But blacks who went out as "missionaries" from black denominations were heavily concentrated in the "Europeanized areas of the continent": primarily Liberia, Sierra Leone and South Africa.[79] In Liberia, where well over half were located, these "missionaries" (with few exceptions like John Seys)[80] labored mainly among other black American settlers and made little effort to convert the surrounding indigenous tribes. Mission by migration (or long term settlement) no doubt engendered complacency. Williams also suggests that for black churches an African mission "replicated their expansion into the American south"—an effort aimed at "attracting previously converted blacks who were dissatisfied with racism in white churches."[81] But the fact remains that, with few exceptions like William Sheppard, black emigrants and missionaries invariably saw themselves as representatives of Western civilization and shared the extremely negative views of African cultures prevalent among their white counterparts. In their thinking, Africans needed to be rescued from the deep darkness of heathenism by the imposition of Western civilization as much as their souls needed to be redeemed by conversion to Christianity. Racial identification did not translate into cultural affinity or produce an alternate missionary vision.[82]

Everywhere on the continent, such attitudes of condescension and disparagement weakened the desire for sustained interaction with indigenous Africans and undermined effective evangelistic efforts. In the case of Liberia, the myriad internal problems besetting the colony, not to mention the hostility of the indigenes who felt cheated of their land, further reduced the possibility of effective mission. And, unlike Sierra Leone where the black settlers were quickly outnumbered by African recaptives, the Liberian settler community outnumbered recaptives and were able to perpetuate a separate society modeled on American ideals. In time, however, strong voices were raised in defense of indigenous Africans and African culture; none stronger than that of Edward W. Blyden (1832-1912), the most accomplished African nationalist of his day and a masterful advocate of Ethiopianism.[83]

Wilmore argues, not unreasonably, that unqualified comparisons between black and white missionary attitudes can produce distorted conclusions.[84] Black Christians, he insists, tried, with meager resources and inadequate training, to accomplish abroad "what they could scarcely do for themselves at home." Moreover, motivated by racial pride and respect, they were committed to the advancement of Africans in a way unmatched by their white counterparts for whom Africa was one field among many and often not a primary focus. This argument points to a significant paradox at the heart of the black missionary movement: namely that while it did exhibit the negative attitudes and ethnocentrism typically associated with white missionary enterprise, it also presented African Christians in the colonial context with a potent ideological framework for religious protest and resistance to white domination, notably with the spread of Ethiopianism from the New World to Africa.

Ethiopianism is covered in greater detail in the next chapters; so only the briefest comment is necessary here. With the earliest manifestation occurring in the Sierra Leone colony (by the 1860s),[85] Ethiopian movements emerged in different parts of sub-Saharan Africa in the late nineteenth century, invariably deriving impetus from, and taking the form of rebellion against white missionary control. As a movement of protest, Ethiopianism evoked responses that ranged from the quiescent to the radical; and it did not always translate into ecclesiastical independency, at least in so far as some of its most articulate proponents remained within the mission established denominations. Ultimately, the varieties of Ethiopianism mediated a focus on racial equality, cultural identity and religious independence, and provided an outlet for the frustrated aspirations of African Christians in a colonial context.

The fact remains that, in so far as abolitionism paved the way for colonialism, Africans were freed from one form of slavery, only to be shackled by another more subtle and enduring form in which the structures of dominance were equally reinforced by racial and cultural ideologies. Western missionaries, to a large extent, were conscious or unconscious agents of this latter process. But the variety of responses subordinated under Ethiopianism surely exposes any attempt to depict the black element as a useful but ultimately expendable element in the solvency of Western imperial domination. As the most potent African Christian reaction, Ethiopianism epitomized anti-slavery, sowed the seeds of African nationalism, and enshrined alternative visions of African Christianity that found full expression in African independent church movements.

In the divine providence the abolition movement stimulated one of the most compelling missionary movements in history. Critical to that story is the black element, so much overlooked or marginalized in popular accounts. The European dimension was hugely significant, but black missionaries, predominantly ex-African slaves, were key agents in the establishment and spread of Christianity in the African context. In truth, the "back to Africa" movements rested in mixed motives and never quite fulfilled expectations—the number of African Americans who went to Africa as missionaries, estimated at just over 115 in 1900, was exceedingly small.[86] But numerical evaluation is an inadequate tool for measuring intangibles like ideological influence and transfer of consciousness. Due in no small measure to the transatlantic connection and interlocking histories forged in the African slave trade, the emergent African Christianity incorporated elements of religious protest which subverted European missionary control mechanisms and allowed distinctive expressions of the faith to flourish in time. Crucially, white abolitionists were among the first to recognize that African initiatives and African empowerment were indispensable for the fulfillment of the Scriptural promise that "Ethiopia shall stretch forth her hands unto God."

Notes

1. Extract from "A Hymn of Sympathy and Prayer for Africa", written by Alexander P. CAMPHOR (an African American) in 1894. For reference details, see Walter L. WILLIAMS, *Black Americans and the Evangelization of Africa 1877-1900* (Madison: University of Wisconsin Press, 1982), 179f.
2. John THORNTON, *Africa and Africans in the Making of the Atlantic World, 1400-1680* (New York: Cambridge University Press, 1992), 6f., 44. See Basil DAVIDSON, *The African Slave Trade* (New York: Back Bay Books, 1980 [1961]), 27-29, for a similar assessment.
3. Richard J. EVANS, *In Defense of History* (New York: N.W. Norton & Company, 1999), 122.
4. Among other things the Toleration Act of 1689 deprived the Church of England of its power to compel church attendance, with the result that church attendance dwindled considerably. See John WALSH, "'Methodism' and the Origins of English-Speaking Evangelicalism", in M. NOLL, D.W. BEBBINGTON & G.A. RAWLYK (eds), *Evangelicalism: Comparative Studies of Popular Protestantism in North America, the British Isles, and Beyond, 1700-1990* (New York: Oxford University Press, 1994), 19-37, 25).
5. Cf. L.E. ELLIOT-BINNS, *The Early Evangelicals: A Religious and Social Study* (London: Lutherworth Press, 1953), 117.

6. William WILBERFORCE, *A Practical View Of The Prevailing Religious System of Professed Christians in the Higher and Middle Classes in this Country contrasted with Real Christianity* (London: 1797), p. 362.
7. William CAREY, *An Enquiry into the Obligation of Christians to use Means for the Conversion of the Heathen*, (London: 1792), p. 65. He adds, "Papists ... are in general ignorant of divine things, and very vicious. Nor do the bulk of the Church of England much exceed them, either in knowledge or holiness; and many errors, and much looseness of conduct, are to be found amongst dissenters of all denominations."
8. Letter to Mrs Beach, dated 15 July 1798, in S. SMITH, *Letters of Sydney Smith*, vol. I (London: Longmans, 1850), p. 21. Significantly, Smith maintains that the "Scotch", in contrast to the English are very much in earnest in their religion.
9. E.M. HOWSE, *Saints in Politics: The 'Clapham Sect' and the Growth of Freedom* (London: George Allen & Unwin Ltd., 1971 [1953]), p. 7.
10. See WALSH, "Methodism" 19-37.
11. David BEBBINGTON, *Evangelicalism in Modern Britain: A History from the 1730s to the 1980s* (New York: Routledge, 2000 [1989]), 27-34.
12. Tindal A. HART, *Clergy and Society, 1600-1800* (London, 1968), 94-95. It must be noted that expansion through small groups was a peculiar feature of the eighteenth century Evangelical Revival.
13. BEBBINGTON, *Evangelicalism,* 31f.
14. HART, *Clergy,* 95.
15. HOWSE, *Saints,* 17f.
16. This designation is misleading since they were hardly a "sect" and some of their members never lived at Clapham. Prominent members of the group included Henry Thornton, a politician and banker; William Wilberforce, a politician; James Stephen, a young Scottish lawyer; Zachary Macaulay, formerly an overseer of a Jamaican estate (later Governor of the newly founded Sierra Leone colony; Edward Elliot, brother-in-law of Pitt; John Shore (later Lord Teignmouth), who became Governor-general of India; Charles Grant, Director of the East Indian Company; John Venn, Rector of Clapham; Granville Sharp, a Government clerk; Hannah More, a philanthropist and writer; Thomas Babington, "a man of high character and evangelical piety"; Isaac Milner, Dean of Carlisle and Provost of Queen's College, Cambridge; and Charles Simeon, Vicar of Holy Trinity Church, Cambridge.
17. According to HOWSE, *Saints*, 173, the Clapham Sect and the people associated with them never numbered more than twenty or thirty.
18. For a treatment, see HOWSE, *Saints, 173*; also J. WALVIN, "The Rise of British Popular Sentiment for Abolition, 1787-1832", in C. BOLT & S. DRESCHER (eds), *Anti-Slavery, Religion, and Reform: Essays in Memory of Roger Anstey* (London: Wm. Dawson & Sons, 1980), 149-162, 149; also, R. ANSTEY, *The Atlantic Slave Trade and British Abolition 1760-1810* (London: Macmillan Press, 1975), pp. 189-192.
19. HOWSE, *Saints*, p. 29.
20. DAVIDSON, *The African Slave Trade*, 83.
21. Eric WILLIAMS, *Capitalism and Slavery* (London: Andre Deutsch, 1964), 39, explains that prior to 1783 "all classes in English society presented a united front

with regard to the slave trade. The monarchy, the government, the Church, public opinion in general supported the slave trade. There were few protests, and those were ineffective."

22. Cited in HOWSE, *Saints*, 35-36.
23. R. COUPLAND, *The British Anti-Slavery Movement* (London: Frank Cass, 1964), p. 75; for more on Granville Sharp, see Prince HOARE, *Memoirs of Granville Sharp* (London: Henry Colburn & Co., 1820).
24. HOARE, *Memoirs*, 83, 91.
25. HOWSE, *Saints*, 11.
26. Lady KNUTSFORD, *The Life and Letters of Zachary Macaulay* (London: Edward Arnold, 1900), 17-18. cf. HOWSE, *Saints*, 40-41.
27. For more on Clarkson's monumental contribution to the abolitionist cause see J. POPE-HENNESSY, *Sins of the Fathers: A Study of the Atlantic Slave Traders 1441-1807* (London: Weiden & Nicholson, 1967), ch. 14; R. COUPLAND, *The British Anti-Slavery Movement* (London: Frank Cass & Co., 1964).
28. Olaudah EQUIANO, *The Interesting Narrative of the Life of Olaudah Equiano, or Gustavus Vassa, the African*, vol. II (London, 1789), 249-254. For a more recent edition of this book, see O. EQUIANO, *The Life of Olaudah Equiano, or Gustavus Vassa, the African* (New York: Dove Publications, 1999), 178-179.
29. Cf. Lamin SANNEH, *Abolitionists Abroad: American Blacks and the Making of the Modern West Africa* (Cambridge, MA: Harvard University Press, 2001), 24-31.
30. See WILLIAMS, *Capitalism and Slavery*; also, DAVIDSON, *The African Slave Trade*, 76-92. For counter-arguments, see H. TEMPERLEY, "Anti-Slavery as a Form of Cultural Imperialism", in C. BOLT & S. DRESCHER (eds), *Anti-Slavery, Religion, and Reform: Essays in Memory of Roger Anstey* (London: Wm. Dawson & Sons, 1980), 335-350; Seymour DRESCHER, *Econocide: British Slavery in the Era of Abolition* (Pittsburg, PA: University of Pittsburg Press, 1977).
31. Cited in HOWSE, *Saints*, 153.
32. DAVIDSON, *The African Slave Trade*, 87.
33. In particular, Portuguese involvement in the trade was as extensive as ever.
34. In June 1814, reports HOWSE, *Saints*,144, "nearly eight hundred petitions bearing nearly one million signatures"—almost one-tenth of the entire population of the country—was sent to the House of Commons.
35. HOWSE, *Saints*, 152f. T.F. BUXTON'S, *The African Slave Trade and Its Remedy* (London: Dawsons of Pall Mall, 1968 [1839]), became one of the most influential abolitionist treatises. Ill-fated, but ultimately historically significant, the 1841 Niger Expedition was inspired by Buxton's conviction that the British government, commercial companies and missionary societies (using African agency) must work together if the slave trade was to be terminated and Africa regenerated.
36. Estimates of the slaves manumitted in England as a result of the Mansfield judgment vary from 14,000 to 30,000.
37. Cited in Mavis C. CAMPBELL, *Back to Africa, George Ross & the Maroons: From Nova Scotia to Sierra Leone* (Trenton, NJ: Africa World Press, 1993), iii.
38. Smeathman extolled the commercial advantages of such a venture to the committee and painted a picture of "a land of immense fertility, where the soil need only be scratched with a hoe to yield grain in abundance, where livestock propagated themselves with a rapidity unknown in a cold climate, where a hut provided ade-

quate shelter at all seasons"—cf. C. FYFE, *A Short History of Sierra Leone* (London: Oxford University Press, 1962), 15.

39. Fyfe, *A Short History of Sierra Leone*, 17.
40. Cf. SANNEH, *Abolitionists*, 50-53.
41. A.F. WALLS, "A Christian Experiment: The Early Sierra Leone Colony", in C.J. COMING, *The Mission of the Church and the Propagation of the Faith,* Studies in Church History 6 (London: Cambridge University Press, 1970), 107-129, 107f. Also, SANNEH, *Abolitionists*, 62. P.E.H. Hair also affirms that "Freetown is by far the oldest Christian community" in tropical Africa—cf. P.E.H. HAIR, "Freetown Christianity and Africa", in *Sierra Leone Bulletin of Religion*, 6 (December 1964), 13-21, 14 & 16f.
42. Cf. SANNEH, *Abolitionists*, 62. It certainly predates the founding of the missionary societies associated with the evangelical revival.
43. Cf. CAMPBELL, *Baçk to Africa*, 1; FYFE, *A Short History of Sierra Leone*, 79-81.
44. P.E.H. Hair, describes their agitation as "the beginning of African political nationalism"—see P.E.H. HAIR, "Africanism: the Freetown Contribution", in *The Journal of African Studies*, 5, (December 1967), 521-539, 526.
45. Andrew Walls' observation that "by the end of the nineteenth century...Queen Victoria had become the world's leading Islamic ruler" is telling—cf. A. WALLS, *The Cross-Cultural Process in Christian History* (New York: Orbis Books, 2002), 219.
46. On this issue, SANNEH, *Abolitionists*, 113-122, provides a superb treatment of the early confrontation between Governor Charles MacCarthy (whose loyalty to the Crown belied his Roman Catholic heritage) and the enterprising Rev. William A. B. Johnson, a German missionary.
47. For more on this thesis, see WALLS, *The Cross-Cultural Process*, 194-214.
48. See BUXTON, *The African Slave Trade*, and James Frederick SCHÖN & Samuel CROWTHER, *Journals of the Rev. James Frederick Schön and Mr. Samuel Crowther: who, with the sanction of Her Majesty's Government, accompanied the expedition up the Niger in 1841 on behalf of the Church Missionary Society* (London: Frank Cass & Co. Ltd, 1970 [1842]).
49. For a detailed treatment, see J.J. HANCILES, *Euthanasia of a Mission: African Church Autonomy in a Colonial context* (Connecticut, CT: Praeger Publishers, 2002).
50. For more on this see J.F.A. AJAYI, *Christian Missions in Nigeria, 1841-1891: The Making of a New Elite* (Evanston: Northwestern University Press, 1969); A.F. WALLS, "The Legacy of Samuel Ajayi Crowther", in *International Bulletin of Missionary Research* (January 1992), 15-21, 19; J.J. HANCILES, "Bishop and Archdeacon Crowther: Inter-Generational Challenge and Opportunity in the Building of an African Church", in *Studia Historiae Ecclesiasticae* 28, 2 (December 2002), 170-196.
51. Cf. HASTINGS, *The Church in Africa*, 179.
52. For a treatment, see J.H. KOPYTOFF, *A Preface to Modern Nigeria: The Sierra Leoneans in the Yoruba, 1830-1890* (Madison: University of Wisconsin Press, 1965). The Freetown contribution was not confined to missionary activity either: for most of the nineteenth century, from the 1840s, it "provided most of the African clerks,

teachers..., merchants, and professional men in Western Africa from the Senegal to the Congo". Cf. HAIR, "Africanism", 531.

53. Cf. Gayraud WILMORE, *Black Religion and Black Radicalism: An Interpretation of the Religious History of African Americans* (New York: Orbis Books, 1998 [1973]), 104.
54. Cf. SANNEH, *Abolitionists*, 31-41.
55. Cf. THORNTON, *Africa and Africans*, ch. 9. The fact that many African slaves had some knowledge of Christianity before embarkation, "as a result of missionary endeavours and the proselytization of Christian merchants and other settlers", arguably augmented this process—cf. THORNTON, *Africa and Africans*, 254. See also, WILMORE, *Black Religion*, ch. 2.
56. Cf. Mark NOLL, *A History of Christianity in the United States and Canada* (Grand Rapids, MI: Wm. B. Eerdmans, 1992), 109.
57. See Emmanuel L. MCCALL, "Black Christianity in America", in R. Pierce BEAVER (ed.), *American Missions in Bicentennial Perspective* (Pasadena, CA: William Carey Library, 1977), 249-274; also, WILMORE, *Black Religion*, ch. 2.
58. Cf. Milton SERNETT, "Black Religion and the Question of Evangelical Identity", in D.W. DAYTON & R.K. JOHNSTON (eds), *The Variety of American Evangelicalism* (Downers Grove, IL: InterVarsity Press, 1991), 135-147, 139.
59. Cf. SANNEH, *Abolitionists*, 59-63.
60. WILMORE, *Black Religion*, 25. For a similar evaluation, see SERNETT, "Black Religion".
61. NOLL, *A History of Christianity*, 199.
62. For details of this story, see WILMORE, *Black Religion*, 103-117; also, J. Mutero CHIRENJE, *Ethiopianism and Afro-Americans in South Africa, 1883-1916* (London: Louisiana State University Press, 1987), 3.
63. WILMORE, *Black Religion*, 108.
64. WILLIAMS, *Black Americans*, 32.
65. The term "Ethiopianism" signified black Africa (or Africa south of Egypt, the sense in which it was first used by the Greeks).
66. For more on "Ethiopianism", see G. SHEPPERSON, "Ethiopianism: Past and Present", in C.G. BAËTA (ed.), *Christianity in Tropical Africa* (London: Oxford University Press, 1968), 249-264; Albert J. RABOTEAU, "'Ethiopian shall soon Stretch out her Hands': Black Destiny in Nineteenth Century America", lecture at Arizona State University (January 27, 1983); WILMORE, *Black Religion*, chs 5 & 6; HANCILES, *Euthanasia of a Mission*, ch. 8; Ogbu KALU, "Ethiopianism and the Roots of Modern African Christianity", in Brian STANLEY, *et. al.* (eds), *Cambridge History of Christianity,* vol. 8 (London: Cambridge University Press), forthcoming.
67. WILMORE, *Black Religion*, 126.
68. Cf. CAMPBELL, *Back to Africa*, if.
69. Cf. SANNEH, *Abolitionists*, 192-203; also Joseph R. COAN, "Redemption of Africa: The Vital Impulse of Black American Overseas Missionaries", in *The Journal of the Interdenominational Theological Center*, I, 2 (Spring, 1974), 27-37, 28.
70. Cf. SANNEH, *Abolitionists*, 194, 219f.

71. Cf. David KILLINGRAY, "The Black Atlantic Missionary Movement and Africa, 1780s-1920s", in *Journal of Religion in Africa*, 33, 1 (February 2003), 3-31, 8.
72. Cf. WILLIAMS, *Black Americans*, 126f.
73. Cf. WILLIAMS, *Black Americans*, 35-40; also, RABOTEAU "Ethiopian shall soon Stretch out her Hands", 10.
74. WILLIAMS, *Black Americans*, ch. 1.
75. WILLIAMS, *Black Americans*, 9.
76. On the success and significance of the Gomers' missionary endeavors, see WILLIAMS, *Black Americans*, 16; also Ogbu KALU, "Black Missionaries and White Abolitionists: The Careers of Joseph and Mary Gomer in the Good Hope Mission, Sherbro, Sierra Leone, 1871-1894", in *Neue Zitschrift Für Missionwifsenschaft* (June, 2003), 161-174.
77. See William E. PHIPPS, *William Sheppard: Congo's African American Livingstone* (Louisville, KY: Presbyterian Publishing, 2002).
78. WILLIAMS, *Black Americans*, 44. Between 1880 and 1900 the A.M.E. alone had at least sixty missionaries in Africa— WILLIAMS, *Black Americans*, 58.
79. WILLIAMS, *Black Americans*, 89.
80. John Seys, a clergyman of West Indian origin, took over the AME mission in 1834 and promoted evangelization of the indigenous peoples. By his enforced return to American in 1841, he and his fellow workers succeeded in converting several chiefs and church membership had increased to an estimated 1,000 members (from 204 when he arrived)—cf. Peter B. CLARKE, *West Africa and Christianity* (London: Edward Arnold, 1986), 39.
81. WILLIAMS, *Black Americans*, 63, 175.
82. CLARKE, *West Africa and Christianity*, 40, suggests, in fact, that viewing Christianity as a badge of their higher status, many settlers were opposed to the idea of incorporating the indigenous population into their communities.
83. On Blyden see, among others, H.R. LYNCH, *Edward Wilmot Blyden: Pan-Negro Patriot, 1832-1912* (London: Oxford University Press, 1967); M.Y. FRENKEL, *Edward Blyden and African Nationalism* (Moscow: Institute of Academy and Science, 1978); E. HOLDEN, *Blyden of Liberia* (New York: Vantage Press, 1966). On Blyden's influence on Americo-Liberian attitudes, see WILLIAMS, *Black Americans*, 167-169.
84. Gayraud WILMORE, "Black Americans in Mission: Setting the Record Straight", in *International Bulletin of Missionary Research*, (July 1986), 98-102.
85. Cf. Hanciles, *Euthanasia of a Mission*), 147-195.
86. Cf. Killingray, "The Black Atlantic Missionary Movement", 22.

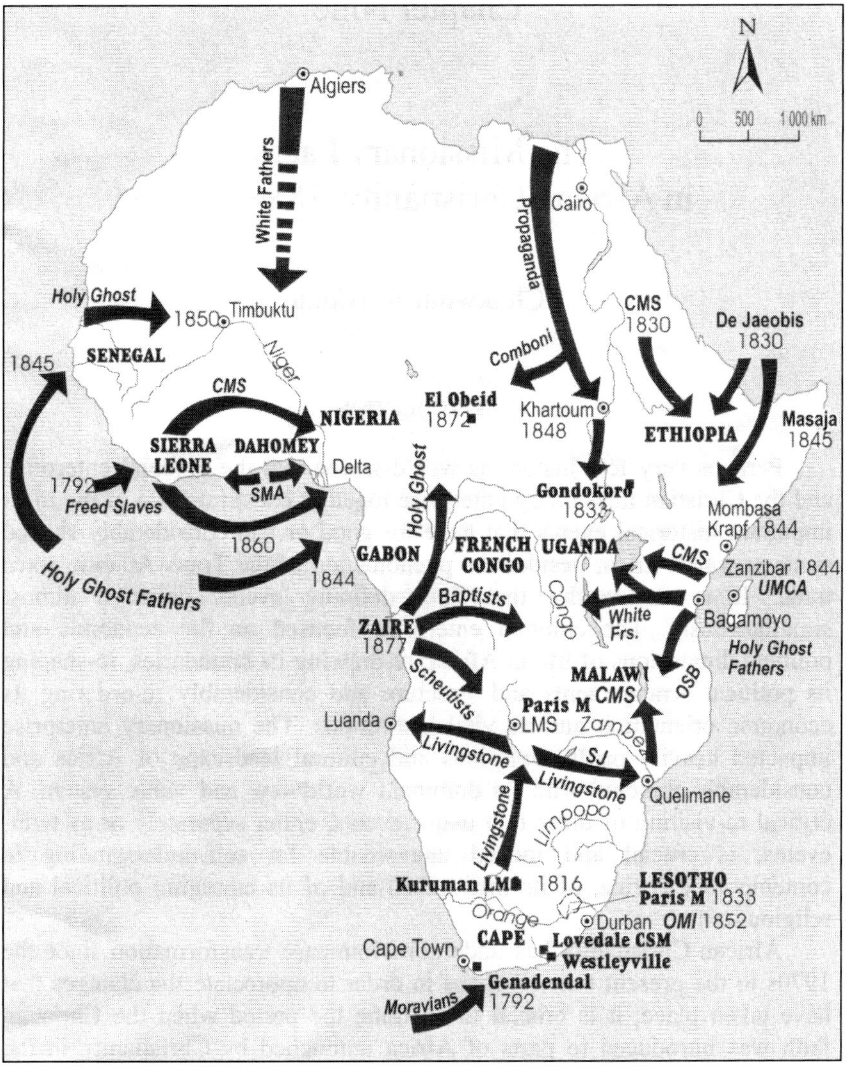

Map 6: The Gospel into the heart of Africa (1790-1890)

Chapter Nine

The Missionary Factor in African Christianity, 1884-1914[1]

Chukwudi A. Njoku

INTRODUCTION

Perhaps very few historians will disagree that the colonial enterprise and the Christian missionary enterprise together constitute two of the most important historical events that have for good or bad considerably shaped contemporary Africa, besides the phenomenon of the Trans-Atlantic slave trade. It is noteworthy that both defining events occurred almost simultaneously. The colonial enterprise focused on the economic and political dimensions of life in Africa, re-drawing its boundaries, re-shaping its political arrangements and structure and considerably re-ordering its economic orientation and its vital institutions. The missionary enterprise impacted heavily on the religious and cultural landscape of Africa and considerably tinkered with its dominant worldview and value system. A critical re-visiting of these two major events, either separately or as twin-events, is crucial and indeed unavoidable for self-understanding in contemporary Africa, of its institutions and of its emerging political and religious culture.

African Christianity has undergone immense transformation since the 1970s to the present time. Perhaps in order to appreciate the changes that have taken place, it is crucial to examine the period when the Christian faith was introduced to parts of Africa untouched by Christianity in the nineteenthand twentieth centuries, with a view to understanding the why, the how and the context of that foundational introduction. The major external agents for the introduction of Christianity to Africa were European missionaries. As we shall later make clear, African agents and circumstantial logic played an active and pivotal role in this process.

This chapter critically examines the missionary factor in African Christianity during the colonial era, between 1884/5 and 1970. We attempt to lay bare the circumstances of the missionaries who came to Africa and the varied approaches they adopted in their work of evangelization. This chapter also examines the mingling of the evangelization project with the colonial project with a view to highlighting the impact of the colonial enterprise on the missionary enterprise in Africa. Finally, we hope to briefly appraise the work they did, the methods they employed and the lasting contributions they made to both the religious and cultural landscape of Africa. Our style is unavoidably thematic rather than detailed, aiming to highlight in a representative manner the key issues that arise in the missionary factor in African Christianity during the period under review.[2] While some of the themes taken up here relate to certain trends in the South African missionary context, the peculiarities of the Christian mission in South Africa, particularly its apartheid entanglements, demand special attention and are largely left out in our present consideration. We have also deliberately left out of the present work the African response to the missionary enterprise, itself a rich area of discourse.

I. PERIODISATION

Of course both the European colonial powers and the missionaries of various hues and colors were already present in parts of Africa before 1884/5.[3] However, as is perhaps well known the Berlin Conference of 1884/5 played a pivotal role in formalizing and structuring the colonial enterprise in Africa. It was at that conference that European powers, hell bent on getting a piece of the huge cake that was Africa, held talks to declare for themselves "spheres of influence" and authority and put some civility and "legitimacy" into the scramble for Africa.[4] Like the World Missionary Conference that was to follow about two decades later (Edinburgh 1910), the Berlin Conference was geared towards saving the European powers the unnecessary shame, damage and wastefulness that would arise from waging wars with one another in order to acquire and consolidate colonies in Africa.

By giving clear form and order to the scramble for Africa, the Berlin Conference indirectly paved the way for stability and order in the missionary enterprise. While the scramble for "conversion-territory" by the missionaries lasted throughout their stay in Africa, the controlling and moderating presence of the colonial powers prevented this recurring religious scramble from becoming unduly disruptive and even explosive. It is also interesting to note that the formal end of the colonial enterprise marked the beginning of the end of the foreign missionary presence in most of Africa. The gaining back of political independence seems to have triggered and sustained the hand over of the reigns of control of the churches to indigenous successors. In broad terms, the period between 1884/5 and 1970, when most of Africa had gained their political independence, was one of intense missionary evangelization and witnessed an enormous flow of foreign missionaries into Africa. It was also a period that left its marks on the nature and character of the Christianity that eventually flourished in Africa.[5]

As a prelude to our analysis, we first examine the general background to the Christian missionary enterprise in Africa as well as the background of the missionaries themselves. This general survey is aimed at providing the broader scope in which the missionaries did their work. The reasons why they came, where they came from, what kind of education they had as preparation for the mission, all entered into affecting the defining choices they made on the grounds in the mission.

II. INSERTION OF THE GOSPEL

The discoveries in navigational technology in the fifth century were momentous for Europe.[6] It enormously extended their hands and legs to reach far distant shores that hitherto lay only in the fertile imagination of some visionaries, dreamers, poets and scientific thinkers. It enabled them to put to test the numerous claims of legends about treasures that lay in far distant lands.[7] With regard to Africa, however, that singular event had an ominous ring to it, for it would clear the way for three centuries long subjection to the obnoxious Trans-Atlantic slave trade. The high seas that lay between Europe and Africa would be kept busy day and night, with ships crossing and criss-crossing one another on the way to or returning from Africa laden with human cargo.

There is an intimate tie between the formal end of the Trans-Atlantic slave trade and the beginning of the Christian missionary enterprise in Africa. In their decades long campaigns to end slavery, the abolitionists, which included ex-slaves, argued for mercy and compassion and reminded Europe and America of their Christian culture and the moral demands of that culture with respect to the other, particularly the enslaved other.[8] A number of abolitionists suggested that rather than trade in human beings, Europe would profit more in trading in commodities with Africa.[9] With the formal end of slave trade therefore, some Christian groups felt an obligation to pass on their Christian faith to Africa.

However, this obligation was construed and seen as a kind of remedy for the slave trade and as a civilizing mission.[10] It was not exactly *mea culpa.* Some of the ex-slaves, possibly as a way of reconciling with their African homelands, also volunteered to be agents of the propagation of the Christian message and values to Africa.[11] In any case they were recruited into the mission by the European ministers and missions principally because they were seen as better suited to the vagaries of the tropical climate, and therefore considerably immune to the Land where the mosquito reigned supreme and played a critical role in dissuading Europeans from settling. This was especially the case in the West Coast of Africa.[12]

In some ways therefore the end of the slave trade overshadowed the nineteenth century Christian missionary enterprise in Africa and colored its motivation, as a reconciling mission as well as a "civilizing" mission. The greater emphasis, as far as European missionaries were concerned, was on the civilizing thrust of the mission. The reconciling mission and the need to share what they saw as "liberating faith" with their kith and kin in Africa were propelling the black missionaries more. They were there to re-claim and re-build their homeland and to restore its dignity tainted by the slave trade.[13]

III. THEOLOGICAL BACKGROUND TO THE MISSIONARY ENTERPRISE

The most important theological backdrop to the nineteenth and twentieth centuries' missionary enterprise was the reformation event. Even though the actual event seemed to be in the dim past, its effects, its echoes, the religious structures and cleavages it unleashed were abroad and seeking firmer consolidation. The fragmentation of the one church by the reformation events had continued unabated along national lines, along cultural lines, and along linguistic lines. The reformation gave various groups that resented the authority of Rome the opportunity to seek their freedom and hoist their own religious flags. By questioning the authority of Rome so deeply and courageously, the reformation also unleashed a secularizing strain into Christendom, creating several interpretations of the Bible, a profusion of doctrinal positions, a variety of liturgical forms and practices and a growing church literature that spoke from varied perspectives. A multiplicity of languages came into the liturgical and theological arena, signaling the beginning of the end of the reign of Latin and Greek.

Gone was one central church authority in Western Christianity. In its place there were several autonomous centers from which denominations of Christianity spoke their own truth and reached out for new membership. The resourcefulness, the liturgical creativity and the administrative autonomy that had its wellsprings from the reformation event was not abating by the nineteenth century. It merely found a new battle front, a new seemingly virgin arena for self-recreation, for self-glorification and for recruiting new membership into an epic battle for supremacy.

In the Catholic fold, the provisions of the Council of Trent, also called the Council of Counter-reformation was dominant and had by the nineteenth century begun to bear fruit in some of its more radical provisions such as the decree for the establishment of seminaries as formal places for the training and education of clergy and religious of the Catholic church; its endorsement of one liturgical language, namely, Latin and its development of catechisms as instruments for instructing the Catholic faithful.[14] By the nineteenth century the effects of the provisions of the Council of Trent had also largely restored the self-confidence of the Catholic Church, nearly traumatized by the devastating impact of the reformation and re-animated its missionary zeal.[15] The period when Catholics were so to say in hiding, its hierarchy afflicted by a siege mentality was effectively over.[16] It was ready again to reach out to the world and to seek converts. If anything Catholic triumphalism was abroad, the First Vatican Council, before its abrupt suspension following the disruptive effects of the Franco-Prussian war, even went ahead to restore and to underline the powers of the Pope, principally through the decree on papal infallibility.[17] The missionary enterprise was for Catholics a way of restoring their dignity, of reclaiming their pre-eminence in the scheme of things vis-à-vis the post-reformation churches.[18]

In sketching the theological background to the nineteenth century Christian missions in Africa, we must say that the theological and doctrinal voices were decidedly plural and the various missionary groups came into Africa with a strong feeling of intolerant rivalry and mutual suspicion carried over from the reformation event. The post-reformation churches were, in addition, considerably nationalized churches, sometimes merged intimately with the state.

While the Catholic missionaries cannot be said to be agents of a nationalized church, they were nevertheless implicated in the nationalistic fervor since the formation and organization of the Catholic religious and missionary congregations in the nineteenth century, were often along provincial, nationalistic and linguistic lines. Much later this picture would considerably change through the opening up of the various religious congregations to people of other languages and nations outside the original base or mother houses of the Catholic religious congregations. The decision taken by the Vatican in this century, instructing all religious congregations to move their administrative headquarters to Rome, is partly connected with this process of dismantling the provincial mental set that had begun to be encrusted among various religious congregations.

The rivalry between the Catholic Church and the post-reformation churches was also a struggle for "supremacy" of beliefs or doctrinal heritage as well as a struggle for power, especially when Rome was still seen by nations that had opted out of the Catholic Church as a foreign power exerting overarching influence and authority over their national affairs.

Beyond their own enduring internal rivalries, the Christian missions seemed to converge in their mutual fear, and even dread, of Islam as a rival religion. A number of missionary groups in both the Catholic and the Post-reformation camps were dedicated to rooting out Islam from Africa. The Sudan Interior Mission, (SIM), is a classic example. The mission to Africa was therefore in some ways a mission to halt the spread of Islam on the continent, and indeed a mission to penetrate the regions where Islam was already entrenched for the purposes of converting its faithful to Christianity. The enduring dogged rivalry between what could loosely be referred to as "Christian civilization" and "Islamic civilization" seems to have been also at stake.

Underneath the issues of worldview and values lay a struggle for power and control of territories between two rival civilizations and powers. Inter-religious dialogue and ecumenism were still ideas for the future.[19] Religious intolerance was the rule rather than the exception. The "no salvation outside the church" of the Catholics seemed to summarize the theological predisposition of the churches, for each did arrogate rightness and truth to itself and charged the others with being false and imperfect.

This triumphalistic theological predisposition of the various Christian missionary churches would not only fuel their mutual rivalry in the mission territories but also predisposed their relations with the Traditional religions of the vast majority of the people they met in Africa. There was hardly any serious dialogue initiated between Christian theology and the theology of the traditional religions, between the Christian liturgical and ritual practices and the modes of worship found in the traditional religions. There was a general assumption on the part of the Christian missionaries that the traditional religions were far inferior, had no theology worthy of the name,[20] and was in fact devilish. The missionary theologians invented numerous pejorative names to refer to the traditional religion and to their visible leaders, custodians and their chief priests.[21]

There was also a general disregard for the sacred objects, the sacred spaces, places and shrines, the sacred observances, rituals, totems and taboos of the traditional religions. Indeed flouting these observances and taboos, violating these sacred places and objects, were the rule rather than the exception among the Christian missionaries both Catholic and Protestant.[22] Such sacrilegious acts against the traditional religions were ways of demonstrating the supremacy of the Christian religion over them, of interiorizing them as publicly, as vocally and as scornfully as possible their visible representations, their main religious rival in most parts of Africa where the Islamic influence had not yet penetrated.[23]

IV. CULTURAL BACKGROUND

By the nineteenth century, the fruits of the enlightenment in Europe were beginning to be all the more tangible and visible. The age of discoveries was finally yielding its vast treasures and the nineteenth and twentieth centuries would showcase further this technological advancement. The industrial revolution was creating creative space for thinkers, for scientists, and opening wide the doors for path-breaking inventions, from electricity to the telephone, from the motorcar to the airplane.

These progressive epiphanies of the material culture of the western civilization translated into an unprecedented cultural pride and triumphalism among the citizens. The missionaries were no exception. The feeling of cultural superiority ran deep and high. In Great Britain, for example, the Victorian era was at the peak of its glorious achievements in the arts, in architecture and in technical progress. The expansion and consolidation of the British Empire could not have had a better period, after the down turn of the loss of its American colonies. In France the consolidation of the gains of the French Revolution, the triumph of the masses and the ethos of liberty, equality and freedom, was a source of deep pride for the vast majority of French citizens.

In general, Europe was in a buoyant mood and understandably excited by its cultural and material achievements. European missionaries generally participated in this buoyancy and cultural pride and went to the missions walking as on heels. It is therefore not surprising that the missionaries fully embraced the idea of a "civilizing mission", the idea of being heirs of a culturally superior people going out to share the riches and glories of their culture with people from cultures they generally assumed to be inferior to their own. Indeed some of the rivalry between the various missionary groups working in the same missionary territories in Africa were hinged on cultural battles, namely, who was the more superior as a distinct civilization: the French? Or the German? Or the English? Or the Irish?[24] The missionaries were therefore in general imbued with a spirit and attitude of cultural superiority as they embarked on the mission to Africa.

On the positive side, this predisposition fired the missionary zeal, for they saw themselves as pioneers and harbingers of a new and far superior civilization. They also saw themselves as ambassadors of their "glorious country". Carrying the flag both of their particular denominations and of their countries, the missionaries had a passion to etch their visions on the missions, to leave imprints of their culture and values, to reproduce the children in the missions after the mould of their distinct European civilizational heritage. The mission schools in particular gave them ample scope to embark on this self-imposed challenge in the civilizing mission.

On the other hand, this cultural predisposition created, under the vast majority of the missionaries, a negative attitude towards the cultures and values that they met. Again there was very little space for dialogue, for sifting through what they beheld and for comparing cultural notes with objectivity. Where cultural comparisons took place at all, these were lopsided and loaded in favor of the culture of the missionaries. Indeed the schools were centers of cultural immersion for the natives, immersion into European cultures and values. It was a centre where the children of the natives were weaned away from their own cultures, were consciously taught to despise their own language, their own cultural values and ethos.[25] European cultures were uncritically presumed to be *the* Christian culture and deliberate efforts were made by European missionaries in Africa to educate and socialize the children in the mission territories into it using the space and facilities richly offered by the mission schools.

V. SOCIAL AND PSYCHOLOGICAL BACKGROUND

Scholars are beginning to pay closer attention to the social class of missionaries *prior* to their going overseas for mission.[26] The work of the Comaroffs, for example, highlights the social background of missionaries in such a way as to enable us to gain an insight into the extra forces that motivated and fired their work in the mission, and affected their relations with the people they fondly called "natives".[27] In general, the vast majority of European missionaries came from the rural and lower classes of European society, with a smaller segment coming from the middle class. Understandably, the percentage of the presence of the nobility in the missionary class is negligible, partly because they already had careers cut out for them in their families and in the political arena of their society.[28]

This rural and poor social background of missionaries made them people not just on adventure, with very little at home to look back to, but indeed as a group of people in search for name and fame. Carving out a respectable identity for themselves was therefore a powerful motivation for embarking on missionary work in places like Africa. In such places, the poor missionary had the chance of a lifetime to make history, to etch his or her name in the sands of time. The mission provided the poor missionary with the space to shine and flourish, the space to be creative, the space to be in charge and in authority in a way that could possibly never have been available to him or her at home. In this way the mission land was for the missionary a virgin land, a land of personal hope, a land of promise, a unique space to prove themselves.[29] The mission land was not exactly Australia, for the missionaries were not on penal exile, but it was close to it as a frontier of self-re-invention.[30]

It might be far fetched to say that a great majority of the missionaries from such rural backgrounds, logged a heavy baggage of inferiority complex as they left for the missions, for they were also conscious of the rich cultural heritage into which they had been born and bred. However, that they did not belong fully to sharing the material riches of the Western cultural achievement, as the nobility did, provided an added incentive for making a success of the mission. The mission was, therefore, in many ways an opportunity for re-writing the missionary's place in the social body and many missionaries not only penetrated this vivifying insight but grasped the opportunity with both hands.[31]

The "mission fields" were also divided and scaled according to categories and classifications ranging from the most important and priced in the eyes of the particular missionary society to the least important and the ones considered dangerous. In this ranking, the Far East and India were top on the list of the most important missionary outposts, while Africa and central America were lower in that categorization. Even in Africa there were further breakdowns of the different parts, with a place like the West Coast of Africa being rather black-listed, because of the havoc the mosquito was causing and the high mortality of missionaries who were sent there. In sending forth missionaries to different parts of the world, the missionary societies took account of this categorization of the vast and differentiated mission fields, and were strategic in their deployment of the pool of missionaries at their disposal. Very often, therefore, the best of this pool, in terms of giftedness and promise, were sent to missionary fields that were strategically important for the people sending them, for a variety of reasons and the rest, in descending order of priority, were sent to regions considered less important and more dangerous. This calculation in the deployment of missionaries meant that certain regions received missionary personnel, who were not only poor and rural, but not as gifted as their counterparts sent to regions on which the missionary societies placed greater value and store. This kind of "investment" and "planting" of missionary personnel left its imprints on the administrative style and over all missionary strategy employed in different regions of the missionary field.

A further fall out from the social background of missionaries to Africa needs to be highlighted, namely, their zealous piety. The most telling manifestation of this zeal was the belief in heaven and hell. Whatever could be said of "the street wisdom" and ideological rootedness of the missionaries, it is difficult to down play the fact that these simple men and women sincerely believed in the Christian ethos, in the reality of the after life as described in the Christian narratives. In the face of the rivalry that existed between the various missionary groups, there is a danger to read too much intrigue in the rush to baptise new converts. That rush, that anxiety, that zeal to baptise as many people as possible into the faith, might very well point to the depth of faith the missionaries had in the sanctifying role of the sacrament of baptism to "wash away sins" and to bring the converts "into communion with God."[32] Among the Catholic missionaries the priority given to "sick calls", the seriousness attached to the sacrament of "confession" (now referred to as the "sacrament of reconciliation"), can further be flagged up as powerful indicators of this fundamental belief in the reality and efficacy of the sacraments they were professing.[33] There is hardly any other way to explain the rush, the anxiety and the sense of fulfillment that most missionaries derived from accomplishing these basic religious duties. Missionaries to Africa were, in general, men and women of simple faith. Certainly, the vast majority of them *were not* schoolmen, academic theologians or outstanding intellectuals. Missionaries were essentially *believers* who came to the mission to share their faith and religious values. They may have been intolerant and arrogant in the styles they employed to present their faith in the religious and cultural environment of their mission posts, they may have been jealous of the success of their colleagues in other Christian denominations or even over zealous and paternalistic, but it is hard to diminish the importance they attached personally to their Christian faith.

VI. MINISTERIAL FORMATION

In sketching the social background of the missionaries, some hints about the basic preparations that went into their training for the missions are imperative. Here, as elsewhere, there is no monolithic picture. Among the Catholic missionaries, for example, the recommendations of the Council of Trent, particularly its provision for a seminary, a noviciate as a formal place for training candidates for the priestly and religious life, considerably created institutions devoted specifically for training men and women called to either the priestly or the religious life in the Catholic Church.[34] Gone was the informality and apprenticeship model that dominated the career path of future priests and nuns in the period prior to the Council of Trent.

Missionary congregations, often dedicated to extending the faith to new contexts, to sharpening seemingly hidden or neglected dimensions of the Catholic faith and ethos, and to caring for borders outside the strict confines of sedentary dioceses in the church, benefited from this new formal educational structure in their recruitment of new candidates for the mission. There was, therefore, a more or less formalized and hierarchically graded approach to educating Catholic missionaries. Missionary congregations also extensively used the relatively uniform *theological manuals* from the mandate of the Council of Trent to standardize the curricula in the training of priests and the religious in the universal church and in its liturgical practice. This uniformity of formation curricula and ethos gave considerable consistency to the message of the Catholic missionaries in their missions.

In spite of these convergences, differences in emphasis and outlooks among different Catholic missionaries were evident. These differences are principally traceable to the unique thrust and "charism" of specific Catholic religious congregations, often referred to as "the spirit of their founder".[35] They are also partly accounted for by the organizational and devotional trappings and markers of "the national character" of various Catholic faith traditions, as when one says, "the *French* Catholic Church", "the *German* Catholic Church", "the *Irish* Catholic Church" and so on. Missionaries who came from these nations carried with them the unique traditions of their home countries and contexts, and brought them to bear on their style and work in the missionary context. Finally, the individual character, temperaments and creativity of the individual missionaries also accounted for certain differences, especially regarding the effects of the personalities of those individuals who held leadership positions, and therefore, to some extent, "policy-making" positions in the missions.

Varied experiences of missionaries were recycled into the formation process of future missionaries. For example, basic education in tropical medicine and hygiene came into sharp focus following the high mortality rate of missionaries who went to the tropical regions.[36] Pre-mission education of future missionaries in the language and culture of the people to whom they were destined to be sent increasingly became the rule rather than the exception as a way of smoothing the process of integration of the missionary into the new context. Institutions like the School of Oriental and African Studies (SOAS) London were set up primarily to attend to such needs by colonial administrators, and catered also for prospective missionaries departing from the United Kingdom for overseas mission.[37]

Beyond the strictly religious education of the missionaries, there is what could loosely be called their "secular socialization" and informal education. In this sense, missionaries, even those in "enclosed orders", *were not* quarantined from the realities of their culture, their society, their arts, their literature and the dominant media of the time.[38] They shared the same tastes, prejudices, social gossips and social vocabulary as the vast majority of their people. They were also subject to influence by both deep thinkers in their society and popular writers and authors. It seems rather banal to say this, but it deserves to be underlined that missionaries were no angels but were in a variety of ways children of their time, children of their context and children of their age by virtue of their birth, immersion and socialization in their given culture and context. The significance of this "cultural education" and socialization should not be diminished merely because of its informal nature. If anything, on account of its subtle power, its permeation and subtle determination of the cultural and social reflexes of the missionary, in much the same way as a background undercurrent force, it deserves to be flagged up as a critically important dimension of the education of the missionary. This underscoring saves one the huge disappointment in *failed expectations* that tends to come from simplistically assuming that the missionary is merely a product of the seminary, the noviciate or the missionary school. These formal centers were merely fragments of the numerous schools and influences to which the missionary is, in varying degrees, subject to and student of.

There is a paradoxical endowment unique to the missionaries. On the one hand, missionaries represented in many ways the "fundamentalist arms" of the church, understood in the sense of giving the basic faith education/the teachings of the fundamental elements of the faith to converts to the Christian faith. In this role, they had to be as faithful to the magisterium, the teaching authority of their church as possible, almost as core conservatives. In the case of Catholics, the missionaries were very often the "active carriers" of the triumphalism and pride of the faith of the church.

Yet the missionary represented the frontiersmen and women of the church, the growing tip of the church, the eyes and ears with which the church encountered new experiences, new cultural and religious frontiers, new ecclesial communities, new languages, new liturgical and ritual circumstances. They were therefore also the vanguard for appropriating changes in church life and practice. They were located in that criss-cross between the traditional and the new, between the taken-for-granted and the space of new, challenging, and sometimes disturbing, questions about "things taken for granted" by the "sedentary church." In this role that came to them as people on a journey, physically and mentally, as hybrids, as "amphibians", the missionaries also carried seeds of the newness, renewal, reformation and transformation of the church to which they belong. They played the role of "the look out," bearing both the "good news" and "warnings of danger", embedded in the unique experiences that came to them as people on the way. Perhaps more than the established church, seen incarnated in the dioceses, the missionary was the pilgrim church per excellence, the church on wheels as it were, the church in motion, the dynamic segment of the church.[39]

From a linguistic point of view, this meant that while the post-reformation churches were fast making capital of the many previously neglected vernaculars of various nations, the Catholic Church stuck to its guns with Latin as its official language and the official language for educating its priests and religious. This also meant that the celebration of the Mass/the Eucharist and the other sacraments in the Catholic Church were carried out in Latin. This was the situation right up to the Second Vatican Council (1962-1965) when the Council permitted an exceptional use of the vernacular in the church.[40] It is small wonder that in the missions, this basic training and orientation of the Catholic missionaries marked them out from their Protestant counterparts, and made the language issue a critically important one in the fortunes of the missionaries vis-à-vis the varying perceptions of the importance and role of languages among the people they worked with.[41] In general, while the Protestant missionaries made investment in the local language a prime aspect of their missionary work and achievement, their Catholic counterparts often lagged behind in mastering the language of the local people, for the simple reason that they had less incentive to do so due to their linguistic orientation and formation.[42] In terms of the diplomatic potentials of language in the missionary campaigns, the Catholic missionaries did make up for their general lack of interest in the vernacular by being the champions of the cultivation and learning of the colonial language, whether this was English or French or Portuguese, an issue that created recurring anxiety for their Protestant counterparts. Protestant missionaries quickly realized that in chasing their ideal of enabling the local people to appropriate their own linguistic and conceptual tool by investing their energy in developing their mother tongues, they were losing out to their Catholic counterparts! For paradoxically, the local people, at that early stage in their encounter with "the white man", saw acquisition and mastery of the colonial language as the way forward, anyone who was teaching them in their mother tongues was dragging them backwards![43]

VII. MISSIONARY METHODS AND TECHNIQUES FOR CONVERSION

Conversion of the people they met in the mission lands to the Christian faith was the main business of Christian missionaries in Africa. However, as we have labored to underline, after the reformation "the Christian Church" was no longer one but many and each denomination felt it was *the* home and *the* custodian of "the Christian Truth". In this enduring rivalry to capture and consolidate missionary territory the main battle line was drawn between Catholic missionaries and missionaries from the Protestant churches.[44] The struggle for territory was acute when it involved these two broad divisions. Elizabeth Isichei notes that there were no alliances made between the rival two, namely, the Catholic missionaries and their Protestant counterparts, in the mission field.[45] Unlike the colonial powers, missionaries lacked the brute force to arrogate specific and exclusive territories to themselves. Bereft of such powers of excising and controlling territories, missionaries of various denominations who found themselves struggling for the same territory, had to invoke other means to put down their trademark on the territories they desired.

Some of these means were far from holy. Elizabeth Isichei recounts that in Togo the church was referred to by the locals as "the house of battle," possibly echoing the truth they perceived about the intense struggle between the various denominations.[46] This struggle for self-assertion, in particular mission territories, took various forms. They included trading insults, casting aspersions on one another, defamation of one another, inferiorization of rival denominations through derogatory songs, dramas, tracts, leaflets and sermons, much as rival housewives in polygamous families.

Courting the attention and support of the incumbent colonial power in specific territories was also another important avenue used by missionary groups to consolidate and retain missionary territory. Each of the big two seemed to maximize its diplomatic advantages and leverages to edge out its rival or at least to reduce its influence in order to consolidate missionary territory.

However, within each big camp, there were indeed territorial alliances, more so, among the Catholics than among the Protestants. Fragmentation was the rule rather than the exception in the Protestant camp, with each church autonomous and often nationalized and therefore interested in relatively differentiated agendas. Among the Catholic missionaries, on the other hand, the common reference to the authority of Rome was a major source of stabilization of the inherent tendency to struggle for territory among the various Catholic religious congregations.[47] They therefore had something like "spheres of interest and control" in the mission territory. Thus Society of African Missions (SMA) Fathers, for example, could only be found in certain territories and not in others. The same was applicable to other congregations such as Society of Divine Word (SVD), The Holy Ghost Fathers (CSSP), and so on.[48] The same was applicable to the women religious, the nuns.

This division of territory or indeed division of labor made good administrative sense and created a stimulus for progress. Each religious congregation could therefore measure its progress and success. There was also greater chance of concentrated work and continuity in method, in programs and in ongoing appraisal of missionary activity. The division also reduced clashes of interest and created room for maximizing the potentials for evangelization in a given missionary territory. However, while enhancing the flourishing creativity of gifted missionaries, these divisions seemed to entrench weaknesses of particular missionary congregations, following the unspoken rule of "non-interference". Evidence suggests that there were occasional meetings and collaborations between missionaries of different religious congregations that shared geographical borders.[49] This kind of collaboration, however, did not extend to policy matters and other core administrative issues in the mission.

1. Doctrinal approaches to conversion

At the heart of the complex package embedded in conversion was indoctrination of new members. Through this process converts were inducted into the ethos, the doctrinal heritage, the way of life and core values of the new faith they were embracing. The missionaries were in this sense first and foremost preachers. They used several avenues to make the people they met in the missions turn around to the faith they brought. Initially, direct preaching was employed.

This ran into immediate problems because of difficulties of communication arising principally from the inability of the pioneer missionaries to speak the language of the local people. The need for and use of interpreters quite early in the missionary enterprise was therefore the rule rather than the exception. Indigenous converts in Sierra Leone, the home of many displaced resettled returnee slaves, provided a helpful reservoir of willing and capable interpreters of a number of indigenous languages such as Yoruba and Igbo. Among the more famous in this regard, includes Bishop Samuel Ajayi Crowther. These became the middlemen as it were, who not only functioned fully as pioneer missionaries in their own right, but also acted as powerful catalysts in the effort to reduce the indigenous languages to the written form, to develop dictionaries, grammars and primers for the study of various vernaculars. This active role is very often downplayed, and credit for such linguistic efforts given to their European missionary counterparts, whose names eventually appear as sole authors and translators.[50] Beyond the problems of communication posed by the language and cultural barrier, preaching by European missionaries, with the intention to persuade the people rationally to abandon the faith of their ancestors and embrace the Christian faith, was at best a stalemate, but in general failed to convince the adult population. The areas of convergence in beliefs, namely, the places where the Christian doctrines echoed the traditional values and beliefs merely re-enforced the conviction of the elders about what they already new and firmly believed in. The areas of "doctrinal differences", which should have influenced the persuasion effort, often seemed to produce jarring notes in the ears and religious sensibilities of the custodians of the traditional religious heritage. Some Christian doctrines were, in the eyes of the adult representatives of the traditional religion, simply illogical and even nonsensical.[51] From painful and frustrating experience, veteran missionaries realized that conversion by direct appeal to doctrinal logic and even to the threats of heaven and hell, just did not produce the kind of result they hoped for. On account of the failure of these earlier attempts at critical dialogue with the local people, the turn to other tools and techniques for enhanced "conversion" was invoked quite early in the missionary enterprise.

2. Deploying Extra-Doctrinal Techniques for Conversion

One of the most powerful extra-doctrinal techniques adopted in virtually every Christian mission, was the introduction of Western style education.[52] Nothing in the complex baggage of the missionaries appealed more to the dreams, aspirations, fears and reason of the people in the mission territories than did the introduction of Western style education. Western style education seemed to have a magical hold over the people in spite of their acute awareness of its inherent ambiguity and dangers.[53] The unspeakable humiliation brought upon them by the colonial enterprise, by the distressing fact of arrogant foreign domination, seemed to have rubbed in the importance of acquiring mastery over the ability *to read and write*. In the midst of their powerlessness before their oppressors, the elders perceived, even if vaguely, that perhaps their hope for eventual survival and triumph lay in the strange paradox of embracing, understudying and mastering the power and knowledge of their oppressors. Nothing seemed to separate the two, the oppressed and the oppressor, more than orality and literacy. There was a sharp perception that in the *"uli that never fades"*, in the ability to read and write, the key to unlocking the hidden knowledge and powers of the "white man" lay embedded.[54] It has to be noted that Western education became increasingly popular with the consolidation of the colonial enterprise at the turn of the century, when colonialism had acquired a raw visibility, with the interference of colonial administrators, district officers and so on, in increasingly disruptive ways, in the affairs of the local people. Between 1900 and the early 1930s, the so-called "pacification expeditions", carried out by the colonial military forces with decisive cruelty, were becoming increasingly successful in setting up colonial dictatorships even in the hinterlands.[55] Across the continent, challenges to colonial regimes were breeding and spreading with vigor, with the springing up of nationalist activities among the oppressed peoples of Africa. In the wake of the Second World War, this response would gain heightened consciousness and become more focused and strategic.

The introduction of Western style education as a tool for missionary evangelization radically changed the fortunes of the Christian missionaries in Africa. In the first place, the school created a creative framework for proselytizing work, for it was one space in the territory that the missionaries fully controlled. Prior to the construction of separate buildings for school and church activities, the school building doubled as church over the weekends. This practice was widespread. Secondly, the school enabled the missionaries to reach out to the children and considerably cut off the voice and influence of the adult populations.

By strategically reaching out to the children, the missionaries were making an investment in the future generations that would, with time, take over control of local affairs. Success in converting the children therefore meant success in converting future generations of the local people to the Christian faith. The school was therefore in many ways the *locus classicus* of missionary conversion efforts. The mission school was the nerve center of "the civilizing mission" of the Christian missionaries, the place to teach their new values, to re-produce young Africans in the mould of European civilization. "Mission education" was a loaded mix of religious, cultural and secular knowledge, principally aimed at comprehensive "*conversion*" of the pupils; religiously, culturally and socially.[56] It was in the mission schools that the inferiorization of the local culture was largely carried out in a structured and sustained manner. It was in the mission schools that Western Culture was advertised and marketed on all fours by the missionaries as the superior culture, with superior values and social mannerisms. It was through the schools that western tastes, dressing styles, language and accent were injected into the local minds of the younger generation of Africans.

As a principal recruiting ground for new converts, the school became another center of rivalry between the missionaries of various Christian denominations, and could be said to have been the principal avenue for passionately inducting impressionable young Africans into the lingering jealousies and battles of the reformation. The rivalry ingredient bore important positive fruits since it led to what has been called the "race for schools",[57] as the various missionary groups sought to establish and run as many schools as possible in a given mission territory. It also created a capillary for excellence in the schools so established, since the various rival missionary denominations sought to compete with one another, to raise the profiles of the schools they ran, and to push the frontiers of the academic excellence and popularity of these schools among the people.

During the colonial era, the introduction of western style Medicare in the mission territories belongs to one of the most attractive extra-doctrinal techniques developed by the missionaries. European missionaries to Africa were harbingers of the advances in medical science and technology already bearing fruits in Medicare in the West. Compared with the potency of the traditional Medicare, what the missionaries had in their clinics and maternities seemed to be working "miracles" and had great appeal among the local populations. In many missions the development of the medical arms of the missionary endeavor was an integral aspect of conversion. It "softened" the hearts of the people, created a sense of awe,[58] and therefore predisposed people for conversion. Nothing demonstrated the "compassionate hearts" of the missionaries more than their medical apostolate. It is perhaps important to underline that the medical apostolate appealed heavily to adults, particularly to women, for whose needs and roles as mothers, the maternities and other health care centers seemed to cater more than to the men.

Perhaps one of the most important avenues through which the missionaries enhanced their work of evangelization in the missions lay in the recruitment of local hands in the missionary project. We have already referred to the active involvement of the black missionaries as part of the vanguard of pioneer missionaries to various parts of Africa. The second movement in the active involvement of indigenous personnel in the mission was even more prodigious in its effect on the fortunes of the missionaries. These included interpreters, catechists, teachers and domestic hands. It is now being acknowledged that the success of the Christian mission to Africa depended heavily on the enormous work carried out by this extensive network of local participants.[59] They knew the terrain very well and therefore were in the best position to serve as guides and "compass" for the foreign missionaries. They knew the local language, culture, customs and traditional religious heritage, and therefore were better suited to know how best to convey the message of the Christian missionaries to their own people; they knew where the "dangers" lay, where the red lines in the two faiths, the two cultures, lay.

These advantages were put at the disposal of the missionary project sometimes with great success in terms of the response of the people. Local church leaders and animators vastly outnumbered the foreign missionaries and were located and deployed in the remotest parts of a given mission territory, where they did sustained and difficult spade work introducing their own people to the Christian faith, teaching catechisms, conducting Sunday schools, preparing converts for the reception of the various sacraments, leading worship "in season and out of season" and staying on to continue on-going Christian formation of their people.

However, the process and rate of creation of indigenous clergy in the missions differed from one missionary denominational group to another. In general, the Protestant missionaries were faster in incorporating local clergy into the band of missionaries than were their Catholic counterparts.[60] For decades, rather than work consciously towards the creation of indigenous clergy, the Catholic missionaries spent great energy campaigning for and recruiting vocations at home into the mission in Africa.[61] This trend would continue even though the official representatives of the Vatican, the papal nuncios stationed in Africa, ceaselessly urged the Catholic missionaries to invest in recruiting indigenous clergy.[62]

At the heart of these delays in raising indigenous clergy lay the vexed issue of the transfer of power from the European missionaries to the indigenous church leaders. Leadership of the Christian churches did not lie with the laity but with the clergy. Admittance to the clerical state did not merely create "more hands" in the cultic and sacramental work of the missionaries but indeed created potential leaders of the church from among the indigenous community. However gifted a catechist was as a preacher or teacher, however excellent he was in administration, in spite of his numerous advantages over the foreign missionary, he was still subordinate in hierarchy and in the administrative ladder of the church to the missionary who was a cleric,

Besides color, the clerical state was one of the principal things that separated the European missionary from the indigenous Christian leader. The clerical state put the European missionary squarely in the center of things, on account of a certain indispensability it carried with it in the legitimacy and validity of a whole range of cultic and sacramental activities. Admitting indigenous vocations into the clerical state were unavoidably granting them equality to European missionaries, and thereby endowing them with equal powers and privileges, which the missionaries hitherto monopolized. On account of this deeper core to admittance to the clerical state, missionaries, who felt comfortable in their positions and the many privileges that came with it, genuinely felt threatened by the quest of indigenous hands to be admitted to the clerical state.[63]

VIII. THE PADRE AND THE COMMISSAR IN AFRICA

The colonial and Christian missionary enterprises in Africa occurred side by side, and mutually impacted on one another's programs, orientation, and indeed survival in what was after all foreign territory for both groups. The concentration of our analysis here is on the impact of colonialism on the Christian missionary enterprise. We examine the structural, the administrative and the moral impact of colonialism on the Christian missionary enterprise in Africa.

Prior to the consolidation of colonialism in Africa from 1885 onwards, missionary enterprise was carried out with trepidation and largely in a spirit of adventure. The consolidation of the colonial enterprise provided enormous stability and territorial form to the missionary enterprise. Indeed, the gradual nationalization of the missionary enterprise began in full swing during the colonial enterprise, with missionaries following the trajectory of the routes traversed by their country's colonial flags, and, indeed, sometimes preceding the advance of their country's colonial flags, in much the same way as did traders and treasure hunters.

The Berlin conference divisions were unspoken boundaries and borders also for the various Christian missionaries who went to Africa. Among Catholic missionaries, for example, diplomatic efforts were made to ensure that religious congregations that were sent to particular mission territories were, to use a modern phrasing, "politically correct". The linguistic and national divisions of religious congregations seemed to be natural compartments for meeting this requirement of "political correctness". Consequently, missionaries from French Provinces of particular religious congregations were sent to French colonial territories. In the same way, missionaries from German Provinces of religious congregations were sent to German controlled colonial territories until after 1918, when they pulled out or were forced out, following Germany's loss of its colonial territories in the wake of their defeat by the League of Nations in the First Great European War. Belgian missionaries would, in similar fashion, be sent to the Belgian Congo and the outlying Rwanda. Togo and Cameroon in particular showcase the change of missionary hands in order to be in line with the changing incumbency of different colonial powers, from the German to the French and from the French to the English respectively.

The underlying logic of this matching of the colonial powers to "fitting" missionary groups lay in the need for a stable framework for the work of the missionaries. The colonial framework, therefore, created a powerful sense of security and protection and a psychological sense of at-homeness for the Christian missionaries. The very aura of power, which the colonial machine established through its ruthless campaigns in the *mission-colonial* territory, was capital for the missionaries. As they traversed the hinterlands, "in search of souls", missionaries could confidently be assured of the protective shield of the color of their skin, and its identification of them everywhere they went as brothers and sisters, if not exactly as allies and collaborators, of the colonial administrators. In order to appreciate the immense power of this association of the missionaries with the colonial administrators, and therefore the administration's role as a veritable protective shield, one has only to recall the incredible ruthlessness with which the British—but particularly the French and Belgian colonial forces—installed fear and terror into their colonial subjects. No one in his or her right minds dared challenge a group who exuded such cruel meanness in asserting their authority.[64] It is doubtful if the missionaries would have exhibited the level of confidence, sometimes bordering dangerously on arrogance, which they demonstrated in Africa, if they did not have the protective umbrella of the colonial forces behind them, at least tacitly, if not always explicitly.

The colonial enterprise provided a kind of "structural and moral legitimacy" to the missionary enterprise. Even though it is noteworthy that some of the missionaries opposed some of the policies of the colonial regimes in-charge, it is important not to lose sight of the fact that there were great convergences in both projects. One of the most outstanding of these convergences of expressed motives is the idea of the "civilizing mission". Colonial propaganda engaged recurrently in a rhetoric of the black man as the "white man's burden", and painted a rosy picture of themselves as "Samaritans" going to rescue Africans from their assumed "darkness" and "primitivity".[65] Missionaries shared deeply in this project of a "civilizing mission" and could therefore be said to have had all the makings of a charitable arm of the colonial mission. As the "legitimate" authority in the territories they controlled, colonial administrators were in a position to confer authority and legitimacy to the work of the missionaries in "their" territories. For example, in order for the acquisition of land for erection of churches, schools and hospitals to be legal, the endorsement of relevant colonial authorities had to be received.

The colonial structures also considerably aided the logistics of the work of the missionaries, especially regarding transportation and communication. As is well known, the colonial administration very often contributed financially to some aspects of the work of the missionaries, even if as token subsidies. This was the case with respect to the setting up and running of schools and sometimes hospitals, seen as social services in which the missionaries and the colonial administration collaborated considerably.

The self-erected authority of the colonial administration as final secular reference points in the colonial territory, especially in arbitration matters, served as a rudder stabilizing the relations between the various rival missionary groups, and therefore helped to cushion some of the negative effects of rivalry among the missionaries. In some cases, such as in northern Nigeria, colonial policy stood vehemently in the way of territorial advance of the Christian missionaries.[66]

Particularly with regard to social services such as schools and hospitals, the colonial administration in given territories enabled the creation of standards and controls for the setting up and actual operation of some of the extra-doctrinal ventures of the missionaries in the territories they controlled. By taking charge of approval and certification of schools, for example, colonial regimes raised the bars of excellence in terms of quality of staff and curricula. This stabilizing role meant that some schools set up in a hurry by over zealous missionaries were forced to close down until the conditions set were met.[67]

Sometimes there was rivalry between the missionaries and the colonial state, especially in their differing ideas, ideals, ambitions and interests in a given territory. For example, the French missionaries were perceived as a threat to the British interests in Nigeria at the turn of the century, not just religiously, but indeed culturally, economically, linguistically and politically! And the French missionaries therefore had to be negotiated out of the territory by the British traders and colonial administrators then working in Nigeria.[68]

The psychological boost which missionaries received from the colonial structures, tended in some cases to raise the temptations and real dangers of missionary nationalism—namely, of the missionaries gradually warming into and latching themselves to the colonial project. This was certainly very often the case with nationalized churches, such as the Church of England and churches that identified very closely with the state, as was largely the case with Belgian Catholic Church. In these instances it was difficult to mark rigid borders between the national loyalty and loyalty to the missionary ethos, strictly speaking. The French colonial administration displayed interesting relations with French missionaries in the colonial-mission field. While at home, the consolidation of the ethos of the French Revolution had driven the Catholic Church in France to the margins of the French society, while in the colonial-missionary outpost, the French missionaries formed a major plank in the implementation of the French colonial policy of assimilation.[69]

In some other cases, the sour relations that existed on the home front between the missionaries and the incumbent colonial powers, tended to replay itself in the mission-colonial territory. The case of the Irish missionaries and the British colonial administration is a classic example. At home, the Irish were under the British Crown until 1916, when Ireland gained Independence from the British colonial regime.[70] The gaining of independence did not wipe away over night the painful memory, both from personal experience and from family stories, the Irish—missionary or not—harbored. This memory contained many violent and violating dimensions of being under colonial bondage passed down the generational line.[71]

Under the British colonial regime, Catholics in Ireland, as indeed in other parts of the United Kingdom, including Scotland, Wales and even England, had a raw deal. The post-reformation ascendancy of Protestantism in England, the seat of power in Britain, to the status of state religion, systematically outlawed Catholicism, seen as lingering instrument of the imperial Roman Empire. Catholics in the United Kingdom effectively became second class citizens and were treated as rebels and saboteurs of the British Empire. They were dispossessed of their property, particularly land, which was in turn redistributed as incentives and rewards to faithful servants of the British Empire, who clearly professed the state religion. Catholics in the Kingdom were not allowed to fill certain political offices except if they renounced their Catholic faith and embraced Protestantism. On account of this sectarian persecution, Catholicism gradually became not just a religion but an identity marker for the vast majority of the Irish.[72] These charged memories and sour relations found varied expression in the relations between Irish Catholic missionaries, in particular, and the British colonial administrators.

Of particular note is the development of polarisation in the relations between the church and state in these instances. In general, Irish Catholic missionaries kept their distance from close ties with the British colonial regime in the African territories. This also meant discouraging their converts and members from active participation in the civil service of the colonial regime, and running what seems like a parallel, relatively self-sufficient "quasi-government" in the areas where they had control. Here they set up networks of functional schools and hospitals, run along the lines of the Irish grassroots model with parish priests as managers.

Their Protestant counterparts in the British mission-colonial territories had no such prominent complexes and indeed encouraged their promising and educated converts to take up positions in the colonial civil service. As long as the colonial regime was in power, it was difficult to see the cracks in the wisdom of the Irish Catholic missionaries in adopting this distance from the corridors of secular power in the territory. Indeed, in eastern Nigeria, there was among the Catholic missionaries a powerful, even if short-lived sense of being the stronger in the rivalry. But the advent of nationalism and the process of decolonization illuminated rather sharply the unconscious disadvantage into which the Catholic missionaries had thrown their vast indigenous membership, who then, at a rather late stage in the transfer of power from the colonial regime to the indigenous populations, had to start learning the political ropes. Their secure enclosure in the seemingly powerful and resourceful institutions set up by the Irish Catholic missionaries was found to be grossly inadequate in the re-configuration of power following the decolonization process.

In the first place, these institutions did not automatically guarantee political power for Catholics who had been weaned away from the corridors of secular power by their missionary mentors. Secondly, the survival and flourishing of those very institutions were themselves subject to and largely dependent on the whims and caprices of those who held political power. The seemingly ingrained political shyness, even naivety, of Catholics in certain regions of Africa derived in a large part from this polarisation practiced by missionary groups—like the Irish missionaries, who allowed their sour relations to affect their perception of the bigger picture of the political landscape of the *mission-colonial* territory.[73]

The creation of urban centers by the colonial regimes indirectly affected the location of the administrative centers of the various missionary churches. While the original centers from which the missionaries operated in a given territorial radius remain symbolically powerful, the actual current centers of church administration were moved to the urban centers and the centers of the political administration, with very few exceptions.

Finally, the close identification between some of the missionaries and the colonial regimes considerably secularized the missionary project and tended to compromise the high ethics and integrity expected of the missions by virtue of their professed gospel orientation. It is therefore not surprising that critics of the colonial affront have not spared the missionaries seen as allies and collaborators.[74]

IX. STOCK-TAKING: MISSIONARY ENTERPRISE IN COLONIAL AFRICA

Christian missionaries have made important contributions to the religious and cultural landscape of Africa. The primary legacy of course was the introduction of the Christian faith to parts previously untouched by the new faith. As is well known, North Africa and Ethiopia were active participants in the development of Christian theology and practice, right from the earliest days of the founding of the faith. However, other parts of the continent, such as West Africa and central Africa, had to wait until the fifteenth century for the first pioneer effort to introduce the Christian faith to their shores. The nineteenth and twentieth century missionaries vastly succeeded where other efforts failed in this mission.

In concrete terms, this meant advertising and recruiting membership to seemingly new ideas of God, new forms of worship, new and sometimes contrasting worldviews, especially new conceptions and images of the after-life, as well as new vocabularies to understand this new worldview—like the terms heaven and hell. It also meant the introduction of new religious ethos and practices, new religious calendars, new liturgical and ritual practices and costumes/vestments as well as the introduction of new sacraments, sacramentals and new devotional practices. It also meant the introduction of new hymns and music and new liturgical language/s.

Side by side with these were the many tools developed to share and transmit these faith creations, such as the Bible, the prime tool of the missionaries, and the catechism, through which the tenets of the churches were broken down for the consumption of the faithful. These material and immaterial paraphernalia of the Christian religion were of course intimately tied to the many cultures that had hitherto used and woven the core values of the Christian faith into the reality of their daily lives, their own cultural values and peculiar modes of expressing those values, their own linguistic and cultural genius as well as the cycle of the seasons in their own peculiar environment. Having dwelt in the Mediterranean and in Europe for close to 1,500 years before its introduction to certain parts of Africa, the Christianity that came to Africa was wrapped tightly in European and Mediterranean cultural garb and philosophical orientations.[75] All that baggage was tied together and parceled to the converts through the European missionaries.

The Christian missionaries were, more than the colonial administrators, the major agents for the introduction of Western style education and literacy style into the mission territories. Two problems seemed to hinder the colonial regimes from making greater input into the effort to introduce western style education into the territories they governed. First, colonial staff were spread quite thinly, and could hardly meet the demands that the vast populations clamoring for education made on their slender staff strength. Secondly, the colonial administrators saw education as strategic and key to changing the consciousness of the people. They projected that an educated class would be very problematic to govern, at the very least, and would have the capacity to jeopardize their continued stay in the territories. On account of this, colonial regimes, like slave masters of old, were very reluctant to introduce Western style education into the territories they governed. Indeed, using various techniques, they tried to discourage the missionaries from doing so, until this campaign against education became increasingly untenable and impractical on their part.

Various forms of writing were in existence in Africa. These were restricted in their use to cults and, possibly on account of the secrecy that surrounded them, they were poorly exercised and therefore poorly developed.[76] Through the mission schools, European missionaries were in the vanguard of the democratization of writing in Africa. In particular, through the mission schools the scripts and languages of the various colonial powers that dominated Africa during the period, namely, the English, the French and the Portuguese languages, were introduced into Africa.[77] The linguistic empowerment of the products of mission schools in this way gave them unprecedented access to the knowledge bank of the West stored in these scripts and languages. Armed with this key to the Western knowledge store, they could penetrate the logic of the texts, begin to have an illuminating window into the Western world, its philosophy, its theology, its artistic, cultural and technological heritage. Eventually this linguistic empowerment would translate into an ability to speak back, to dialogue, to re-visit and re-articulate their own hitherto denigrated cultural genius. Linguistic empowerment contained in its very womb the seeds of the recovery of self-identity and self-esteem of the mission school boys and girls consciously estranged from their own cultural roots. With it they would also begin the huge work of transcribing their own cultural and civilizational heritage previously locked in oral banks into the relative permanence of the written documentation.

The effort of the missionaries to translate the principal Christian literature, such as the Bible and the catechism, into the vernaculars triggered the reduction of the vernaculars into writing and the gradual development of standard orthographies. Of course the preferential choice of particular local languages and dialects over others for pastoral and translation uses by the missionaries, created its own problems for the traditional linguistic landscapes.[78]

The European missionaries as harbingers of Western cultural perspectives and values played a key role in the introduction of bits and pieces of the trappings of Western civilizational infrastructure into various parts of Africa, from the material cultural artifacts to the immaterial such as Western style music and musical instruments. Through the construction of their residences, their churches, the schools, and hospitals, new building architecture, new structural designs and concepts, new equipment and tools began to gain visibility in the environment. The same could be said of the introduction of Western culinary arts and cooking equipment.

Particularly through their social mission, the missionaries enabled the introduction of Western style Medicare. The institutions they set up, such as schools and hospitals, not only served to introduce western institutional models but also enabled the generation of new professionals such as teachers, medical doctors and nurses. The basic schools the missionaries set up prepared the products to enter firmly into other professions such as law and engineering and other forms of professional specialization. There is, therefore, very little doubt that the missionaries made lasting contributions to the religious and cultural landscape of Africa.

In examining the missionary enterprise in Africa in the colonial period, the picture that emerges is one of a complex phenomenon, imbued with criss-crossing and sometimes contradictory motives, passions and agendas. In its efforts at balanced self-understanding, this period deserves closer critical attention by African Christianity, bearing as it must, the marks left by that intensely active and charged period in its development.

Notes

1. This builds on the various histories of Christianity in Africa as mentioned in the preface.
2. The sheer volume of the courageous work of Bengt SUNDKLER and Christopher STEED, *A History of the Church in Africa* (Cambridge: Cambridge University Press, 2000), underlines the impossibility of cramming into a few pages the details of each moment of the missionary endeavor in the African continent. This chapter has a more modest goal, namely, to flag up key issues that deserve attention in the ongoing unveiling of the missionary factor in African Christianity.
3. Even though their eventual fortunes differed remarkably in various contexts, the Protestant missionaries were very often the ones who preceded the Catholic missionaries in the African mission. Bauer has in this respect noted, "For half a century (1792 –1842) Protestant missionaries were practically alone in the field, and until that great nineteenth century ended with World War I, Protestant evangelists were far more numerous than Catholic ones. The major reason for this is that in the previous century the Protestant Church in Europe had experienced a great revival movement, while the Catholic Church had suffered a serious decline from which she started recovering but quite slowly after the Napoleanic Wars (from 1815 onwards)." Cf. J. BAUER, *2000 Years of Christianity in Africa, An African History 62 – 1992* (Nairobi: Paulines, 1994), 105. See also A. HASTINGS, *A History of African Christianity 1950 –1975* (Cambridge: Cambridge University Press, 1979), 40 & 18-20.
4. For a helpful introduction to this scramble see, Thomas PAKENHAM, *The Scramble for Africa 1876-1912* (London: Abacus, 1991). For Historians like Uzoigwe the Berlin Conference was a morally bankrupt meeting and was nothing less than infamous. Cf. G.N. UZOIGWE, "Spheres of influence and the doctrine of the hinterland in the partition of Africa", in *Journal of African Studies,* 3, 2, 1976, 183-203, 184 & 186.
5. Numerous scholars have drawn attention to the flourishing of Christianity in contemporary Africa in such a way that they underline a critical shift in the epicenter of Christianity from the North to the South. See for example, David B. BARRETT, "AD2000: 350 million Christians in Africa", in *International Review of Mission,* 59, (1970), 39-54, 50; Kwame BEDIAKO, *Jesus in Africa. The Christian Gospel in African History and Experience* (Akropong-Akuapem, Regnum Africa, 2000),3-4.
6. For the importance of the discoveries in navigational technology, see for example, Daniel R. HEADRICK, *The Tools of Empire. Technology and European Imperialism in the Nineteenth Century* (Oxford: Oxford University Press, 1981), 17-42, 129-141.
7. The role of legends and eventual travel literature in the missionary enterprise deserves a separate treatment. However, it is important to underline that they played a crucial role in inspiring missionaries and in shaping their attitude to the peoples and the places they went to. See for example, David CHIDESTER, *Christianity: A Global History* (London: Penguin Books, 2000), 447, see also E.

OBIECHINA, *Culture, Tradition and Society in the West African Novel* (Cambridge: Cambridge University Press, 1975), 18-19. For a broader critical examination of travel literature in shaping the minds of subsequent European travelers see, Jas ELSNER & Joan-Pau RUBIES (eds), *Voyages & Visions. Towards a cultural history of travel* (London: Reaktion Books, 1999).

8. One of the most outstanding contributions to the campaigns of the abolitionists was *The Interesting Narrative,* authored by Oluadah Equiano, an Igbo ex-slave in 1789. Cf. Olaudah EQUIANO, *The Interesting Narrative of the life of Olaudah Equiano or Gustavus Vassa the African* (London, 1789); (reprinted in a facsimile edition by Paul EDWARDS, *The Life of Olaudah Equiano, or, Gustavus Vassa the African*, Colonial History Series (London: Dawson, 1969). This kind of work had enormous appeal and success, since it spoke from within the experience of an ex-slave. By appealing to the Christian sentiments of his primary audience, European slave owners, his autobiography carried a powerful moral authority. See in this regard, Elochukwu E. UZUKWU, *Resilient Diaspora – Keeping Faith with Destiny,* paper presented at the First *Muruako Lectures* (London: Whelan Research Academy, Owerri Nigeria, 20th December 2003); and Angelo COSTANZO, *Neither Saint, A Hero, Nor A Tyrant,* paper presented at first International conference on Olaudah Equiano, *Olaudah Equiano: Representation and Reality* (Surrey: Kingston University, Kingston-upon-Thames, 22 March 2003).
9. Equiano certainly pointed towards trade in Commodities rather than trade in human beings.
10. This obligation was often cast in zealous and self-righteous forms, as if they were obeying God's direct commands. See e.g., Sylvia JACOBS, *Black Americans and the Missionary Movement in Africa: Contributions in Afro-American and African Studies* (Westport: Greenwood Press, 1982), 5-6, F.K. EKECHI, *Missionary Enterprise and Rivalry in Igboland 1857–1914* (London: Frank Cass, 1971), 1. See also C.P. GROVES, *The Planting of Christianity in Africa* (London: Lutterworth Press, 1948), 197-205.
11. An outstanding example of this group of volunteers was Bishop Ajayi Crowther and the Sierra Leone Team of indigenous missionaries. See e.g., E.A. AYANDELE, *The Missionary Impact on Modern Nigeria 1842–1914, A Political Analysis,* London: Longmans, 1966, 205-230. For a helpful background to "the Sierra Leonean team" see Christopher FYFE, *A Short History of Sierra Leone* (London: Oxford University Press, 1962).
12. Cf. JACOBS, *Black Americans,* xi. See also S.M. JACOBS, "The Historical Role of Afro-Americans in American Missionary Efforts in Africa, in *Black Americans and the Missionary Movement in Africa,* in JACOBS, *Black Americans*, 5-29, 16ff; S.D. MARTIN, "Black Baptists, Foreign Missions, and African Colonization 1814-1882", in JACOBS, *Black Americans*, 63-76, 33, 64ff. See also E. ISICHEI, *A History of Christianity in Africa,* London: SPCK, 1995, 264; M.J. BANE, *The Popes and Western Africa, An Outline of Mission History 1460-1960s* (Staten Island NY: Alba House, 1968), xii, 143; and H.J. KOREN, *To the Ends of the Earth. A General History of the Congregation of the Holy Ghost* (Pittsburgh: Duquesne University Press, 1983), 177-180.
13. This motivation partly explains why they related in a spirit of collaboration rather than rivalry with other Christian groups who came to evangelize Africa. Witness for example, the fact that Bishop Ajayi Crowther, as Anglican Bishop on the Niger,

warmly welcomed the Catholic missionaries who came to Onitsha. He indeed was willing to share the Land he had been given by the Obi of Onitsha with a group that in the eyes of his European counterparts were their main rivals. Cf. EKECHI, *Missionary Enterprise*, 74.

14. See e.g., Michael A. MULLET, *The Catholic Reformation* (London: Routledge, 1999), 63-65. See also John C. OLIN, *Catholic Reform. From Cardinal Ximenes to the Council of Trent 1495–1563* (New York: Fordham University Press, 1990), 32.
15. Beyond the doctrinal disputes, the reformation event dealt heavy blows to the Catholic Church on several strategic fronts. There was the unprecedented continuous hemorrhage of its numbers as well as the erosion of its immense economic and political powers. From being the state religion in many European states, Catholicism was forced to take on the role of subordinate religion and was indeed suppressed for a long time in countries such as England. The radical change of its fortunes deeply affected the self-confidence of the Catholic Church. The Council of Trent was the first major concrete effort to redress the situation.
16. The publication of the *Syllabus of Errors* and the *Quanta Cura* of Pius IX in 1864 has been seen by some scholars as an important index of the siege mentality that enveloped the Catholic Church in the period following the reformation. See for example, G. BULL, *Vatican Politics at the Second Vatican Council, 1962–5* (London: Oxford University Press, 1966), 42.
17. See e.g. Norman TANNER (ed.), *Decrees of the Ecumenical Councils*, Vol. II (London: Sheed and Ward, 1990), 801; C. BUTLER, *The Vatican Council. The Story Told from Inside Bishop Ullathorne's Letters* Vol I (London: Longmans, 1930), 201-216; G. ALBERIGO, "The Christian Situation after Vatican II," in G. ALBERIGO, J.-P. JOSSUA & J.A. KOMONCHAK (eds), *The Reception of Vatican II* (Washington, DC: Catholic University of America Press, 1987), 1-24, 14; and BULL, *Vatican Politics* 94-95.
18. T. Okere has written, "A comparatively decisive moment in the church history came after the Protestant reformation. The church was already over 1,500 years old in Europe and had become not only Europeanized but also europocentric. Missionaries were then sent out to evangelize other areas of the globe, no doubt partially to make up for the loss to Protestants of a considerable portion of Christendom." Cf. Theophilus OKERE, *Culture and Religion* (Owerri, 1974), 43-44.
19. Even though the World Council of Churches was formed at the turn of the century to bring the various Christian churches together into one family, its outreach of solidarity did not extend to other religions, certainly to Islam. In its later transformations over the decades, the grounds have been softened. On the side of the Catholic Church, the opening to other churches and other religious had to await the convening of the Second Vatican Council (1962-1965) to receive the green light.
20. The dominant adoption of the oral techniques and forms of storage for the theology of the traditional religions was partly responsible for this reduced visibility of the theology of the traditional religions. Christian missionaries, belonging to the group of religions referred to as "religions of the book", because of their dependence on such sacred texts as the Bible and the Koran, were understandably fixated about their idea of "texts" as essentially *written* texts. The idea of *oral* texts as a veritable organ for storage and transmission of a clear body of knowledge was strange to

them and regarded as inadmissible and "hard" evidence. Elsewhere, I have examined the problems associated with this narrow misleading conception of texts in affecting the visibility of theologies of different religions. Cf. Chukwudi Anthony NJOKU, *On the Thresholds of Theological Conversations between the North and the South: Impediments and Hopes* (paper presented at the 3rd International Encounters in Systematic Theology, LEST III, *Theology and Conversation. Developing a Relational Theology,* Leuven, 6-9 November 2001).

21. Cf. Bolaji IDOWU, *African Traditional Religion. A Definition* (London: SPCK, 1974), 135.
22. For many missionaries, carting away these sacred objects from the shrines and households of the people and exhibiting them in their home countries in Europe was a sign of their success, their victory over "the evil heathen powers", and used them extensively in a variety of displays and exhibitions to campaign for extra moral and financial support at home for their work in the missions. Missionary museums in Europe still hold these objects as part of their treasures and trophies from Africa. Yet the market value of these sacred objects was quite high and was an important source of missionary funding both during the active days of the missionary enterprise, when they were often auctioned at public missionary fairs, and also much later when the artistic values of these objects began to be increasingly appreciated by Western curators. See for example Enid SCHILDKROUT & Curtis A. KEKIM (eds), *The Scramble for Art in Central Africa* (Cambridge: Cambridge University Press, 1998).
23. In two of his novels, Chinua Achebe has re-enacted some of these violations of the traditional religion. The incidents committed under Rev. Brown and Mr. Goodcountry, respectively, are vivid examples of this. Cf. Chinua ACHEBE, *Things Fall Apart* (London: Heinemann, 1958), 130-135; Chinua ACHEBE, Arrow *of God* (London: Heinemann, 1964, 1974), 46-54.
24. The ousting of the French Catholic Missionaries in Eastern Nigeria, the Holy Ghost Fathers, in 1905 from the territory by the British and their replacement by the Irish province of the Holy Ghost Fathers was occasioned as much by the fact that the French were perceived as political threats and by the fact that they were also perceived as a threat to the cultural hegemony of the British in the Nigerian colonial territory. See EKECHI, *Missionary Enterprise*, 73f & 98ff. See also J. MCGLADE, "The Missions: Africa and the Orient", in P.J. CORISH (ed.), *A History of Irish Catholicism,* VI (Dublin: Gill & Macmillan, 1967), 12f.
25. See e.g., C.C. AGU, *Secularization in Igboland* (Frankfurt: Verlag Peter Lang, 1989), 257.
26. We lay emphasis on the social class of the missionary before his or her entry into the "mission field", because the mission field often has a profound impact in changing the social class of the missionary. The mission field tends to *elevate* the missionary not only in the mission but even more so at home, where he or she often becomes a hero/heroine, and is enabled to climb up the ladder of his or her social class.
27. Jean COMAROFF & John COMAROFF, *Of Revelation and Revolution: Christianity, Colonialism and Consciousness in South Africa*, Vol. I. (Chicago & London: University of Chicago Press, 1991).
28. The mission, like vassal territory, was after all seen much as the periphery of the center, as outlying posts of the heart of the churches. Outposts are very often not

manned by the ruling class but by their delegated subjects. The former remain at home to call the shots and pull the strings of authority.

29. Njoku and Lamberigts have underscored that this fact, the positive role which the mission land played in the upgrading of the missionary, may have been largely responsible for the legendary intimate tie that often developed between missionaries and the people in the missions, making many missionaries survive some of the harsh realities of the mission territory and indeed sometimes opt to be interred among the people they have so labored and from whom they had gained so great a sense of fulfillment. Cf. Chukwudi Anthony NJOKU and Mathijs LAMBERIGTS, "Vatican II: The Vota of the Anglo-phone West African Bishops Concerning the Sacred Liturgy, in *Questiones Liturgiques* 81 (2000) 89-121, 119-120.
30. See e.g., Edward W. SAID, *Culture and Imperialism* (London: Chatto & Windus, 1993), xv –xviii.
31. David Livingstone is without doubt an outstanding example in this regard. From a rather obscure and unpromising background, Livingstone became in the course of his missionary engagement a cultural institution celebrated up till the present time in expanding tomes of literature. See e.g., The National Portrait Gallery, *David Livingstone and the Victorian Encounter with Africa* (London, 1996), 14-17. The bibliography on Livingstone at the end of this same publication (228-237) is quite telling in this regard. On the Catholic side, Bishop Shanahan of South-eastern Nigeria comes readily to mind. Sent away on mission by the Holy Ghost Fathers almost as a way of getting rid of a nuisance, he so rehabilitated himself in the Nigerian mission that he became a shining example and model of Catholic Irish Missionary endeavor, re-created in legendary proportions by a growing army of admirers and critics. See e.g., Desmond FORRISTAL, *The Second Burial of Bishop Shanahan* (Dublin: Veritas, 1990); John JORDAN, *Bishop Shanahan of Southern Nigeria* (Dublin: Dublin Echo Press Ltd, 1949); Sean FARRAGHER, *Bishop Joseph Shanahan CSSp. Selected Studies* (Dublin: Paraclete Press, 2002).
32. The official reports which missionaries sent back to their administrative centers in Europe very often contain statistics of the "growth of the church", sometimes detailing the number of converts who have received baptism, confirmation, or the sacrament of Matrimony. While the role of these statistics as an administrative and campaigning tool cannot be relegated, its echo of similar acts in the Acts of the Apostles, namely, "the counting of new members" to the faith and the attendant spiritual joy this event brings to the Christian community, cannot be side-stepped.
33. It is difficult to read some of the biographies and autobiographies of the veteran missionaries and miss the touching personal attachment to the accomplishment of these basic religious duties. See e.g., John JORDAN, *Autobiography of a Missionary* (Dublin: 1992), 49-51.
34. Cf. MULLET, *The Catholic Reformation*, 63-65.
35. For an examination of the influence of "the spirit of the Father Founder" in the case of the Holy Ghost Fathers Congregation, see KOREN, *To the Ends of the Earth*, 247-264.
36. The London School of Tropical Medicine started as a center for preparing colonial administrators and missionaries for mission to the Tropics. The same can be said of the School of Tropical Medicine in Antwerp, Belgium. University College Dublin offered six-week courses in Tropical Medicine for the same reasons. In

these institutions, the colonial projects shared facilities and concerns with the missionary projects. While in the first instance the training in tropical health was for the health and safety of the missionaries themselves, with time, this "tropical health knowledge" was transformed into a veritable instrument for mission work. See EKECHI, *Missionary Enterprise*, 74-78; and I.R.A. OZIGBO, "An Evaluation of Christian Pioneering techniques with particular reference to Nigeria," in *The Nigerian Journal of Theology,* 8, 1 (1994) 43-62, 50-51. These centers have undergone further qualitative transformations and become important centers for scientific research in tropical medicine.

37. Cf. Cyril PHILIPS, *A History of SOAS, 1917–67,* in David ARNOLD & Christopher SCHACKLE, (eds), *SOAS Since the Sixties* (London: SOAS, 2003), 21-43, 21-23.

38 In contemporary times, the radio, the television, and more recently the internet have come to stand out as the vocal and outstanding media for sharing and transmitting knowledge, almost threatening to jettison the relevance of the print medium. This recency should not make us forget that for centuries the print media was the dominant medium for sharing and conveying ideas in the West. Writers, especially gifted ones, therefore enjoyed a monopoly of audience, particularly in the area of the imaginative space, which even the new media, in spite of their profound presence and power of outreach, hardly can boast about. It is therefore easy to see that writers had such an incredible influence over people in their contexts, and for the same reason some of their critics have their finger right on target when they charge writers of the period before the advent and dominance of the new media with both credit and responsibility for shaping the minds, cultural, religious and political reflexes of their people. See in this connection, SAID, *Culture and Imperialism,* xi-xiii. Chinua Achebe's reasons for critically taking on Conrad hinges on similar reasons. Cf. Chinua ACHEBE, "An Image of Africa: Racism in Conrad's *Heart of Darkness*", in Chinua ACHEBE, *Hopes and Impediments: Selected Essays* (New York: Doubleday, 1990), 1-20, esp. 3. See also Chinua ACHEBE, *Home and Exile* (Oxford, Oxford University Press, 2000), 40-41.

39. In another work we have highlighted the creative role, which the missionary church, on account of its ceaseless youthfulness and footloose character can play in supplying theology with unusual insights, and challenge it to grow. Cf. Chukwudi Anthony NJOKU, *A Study of the Wishes of the Catholic Bishops of Anglophone West Africa (1959–1960) for the Second Vatican Ecumenical Council* (Licentiate Thesis, Faculty of Theology, Katholieke Universiteit Leuven, Belgium, 1998), 196-197.

40. Cf. *Sacrosanctum Concilium,* (The Constitution on the Sacred Liturgy), no. 36.2 & no. 63, 4th December, 1963, in Austin FLANNERY (ed), *Vatican Council II: The Conciliar and Post Conciliar Documents,* Revised Edition (Dublin: Dominican Publications, 1988), 13. It was an exception that, however, became the rule. Latin remains the official language of the Catholic Church but such was the popularity of the demand for the use of the vernacular that its use spread like wildfire, leaving Latin largely an impotent official language of the Catholic Church.

41. This linguistic dimension of the missionary encounter has received considerable attention in the work of Lamin Sanneh. Cf. Lamin SANNEH, *Translating the Message. The Missionary Impact on Culture* (Maryknoll, NY: Orbis, 1989).

42. Chukwudi Anthony NJOKU, *Vatican II and the Process of its Reception in the Igbo Speaking Church of Southeast Nigeria: 1959–1995* (Doctoral Dissertation, Katholieke Universiteit Leuven, Belgium, 2002), 68-71.

43. See e.g., Felix K. EKECHI, "The Missionary Career of the Venerable T.J. Dennis in West Africa, 1893 – 1917" in *Journal of Religion in Africa,* Vol. IX, fasc. 1, (1978) 1-26, esp. 20.
44. During the Colonial era, the Pentecostals and Charismatics were yet to make their presence felt in Africa, and therefore were not prominent in the rivalry scenario of the time.
45. ISICHEI, *A History of Christianity in Africa,* 266.
46. ISICHEI, *A History of Christianity in Africa*, 266.
47. Each religious congregation had ambitions to grow and expand! There was even an internal competition among the religious congregations.
48. See e.g., NJOKU & LAMBERIGTS, "Vatican II" 120-121.
49. Fr. John Jordan CSSP, member of the Holy Ghost Fathers stationed in Southeastern Nigeria, indicates that they received help from the German Catholic missionaries stationed in the Northern part of Nigeria, particularly with regard to technical matters, such as embarking on construction of churches or repairs of equipment, which arose now and again in the mission. Cf. JORDAN, *Autobiography of a Missionary,* 71-73.
50. There are a few liberating exceptions to this practice of giving sole credit to the European missionary counterparts in the linguistic endeavor of the missionaries. John Jordan, for example, makes it clear that even though he wrote the "English versions" of some catechetical texts, Joseph Nwanegbo, an indigenous priest from Igboland, did the actual translation of the text into Igbo Language. Cf. JORDAN, *Autobiography of a Missionary*, 76.
51. Some of these earlier attempts at critical dialogue with custodians of the traditional religion are re-constructed and re-presented in Chinua Achebe's *Things Fall Apart,* and *Arrow of God.*
52. See for example, OZIGBO, "An evaluation of Christian pioneering techniques", 43-62.
53. The Novelist Cheik Hamidou Kane captures these dangers in his Ambiguous *Adventure.* Cf. C.H. KANE, *Ambiguous Adventure* (René Juillard 1962, trans. from the French by Katherine WOODS, New York: Collier, 1963). In *Arrow of God* Chinua Achebe powerfully visits the anxiety of the elders as they struggled with the idea of allowing their children to go to the mission schools.
54 In Chinua Achebe's *Arrow of God,* when Ezeulu, the chief priest of the deity Ulu, returns from the great humiliation of detention and exile from Okperi, he set about passionately urging his son Oduche to go and learn the Whiteman's knowledge. Recounting his experience he says, "When I was in Okperi I saw a young white man who was able to write his book with the left hand. From his actions I could see that he had very little sense. But he had power; he could shout in my face; he could do what he liked. Why? Because he could write with his left hand. That is why I have called you. I want you to learn and master this man's knowledge so much that if you are suddenly woken up from sleep and asked what it is you will reply. You must learn it until you can write it with your left hand. That is all I want to tell you." Cf. ACHEBE, *Arrow of God,* 189-190.
55. See for example, Eyo O. EYO, *The Story of Old Calabar. A Guide to the National Museum at the Old Residency, Calabar* (Lagos, 1986). Se also, Adiele E. AFIGBO,

The Warrant Chiefs Indirect Rule in Southeastern Nigeria 1891-1929 (London: Humanities Atlantic Highlands, 1972).

56. See e.g., AGU, *Secularization in Igboland,* 257ff. See also, M.A. ONWUEJEOGWU, *Evolutionary trends in the history of the development of the Igbo civilization in the culture theatre of Igboland in Southern Nigeria, 1987 Ahiajoku Lecture* (Owerri: Ministry of Information, 1987), 57-69.

57 Cf. Anon., "The Race for Schools" in *Africa* 18 (1956) 1. See also Thomas KIGGINS, *Maynooth Mission to Africa. The Story of St. Patrick's Kiltegan* (Dublin: Gill & Macmillan, 1991), 217-218.

58. In Igboland, this sense of awe is encapsulated in the common saying "*Bekee wu agbara*" [The white man is a spirit].

59. Recognition of the vast contribution of catechists in particular is gaining currency. See e.g., A. SHORTER, "Developing Roles of the Catechists", in A. SHORTER & E. KATAZA, (eds), *Missionaries to Yourselves. African Catechists Today* (London: Geoffrey Chapman, 1972), 62. See also J. BALZER, "The Catechist," in *African Ecclesiastical Review,* 6 (1964), 1, 49-55, 49-51; J. BALZER, "The Role of the Catechist in the Missions," in HATTON (ed.), *Missiology in Africa Today. Thought Provoking Essays by Modern Missionaries* (Dublin, 1961), 76-84.

60. Already by the late 1930s, some of the indigenous Anglican clergy, sent to further their studies at Cambridge University, were returning home to contribute to the missionary effort. See e.g., Francis ANYIKA, "Church Missionary Society (C.M.S) Ministerial Formation on the Niger: Reverend V.N. Umunna as a pioneer", in *Nigeria Heritage: Journal of the National Commission for Museums and Monuments,* 4 (1995), 133-145, 140. The pioneer Catholic indigenous clergy from the same region, the late Bishops Anthony Nwedo and Mark Unegbu, would only be setting off for further studies in Dublin, for example, in the 1947.

61. In the case of Bishop Shanahan, see e.g., KIGGINS, *Maynooth Mission to Africa,* 7-18.

62. Archbishop Mathews, the papal nuncio to British West Africa, was particularly outstanding in his efforts to argue for incorporation of indigenous clergy, and indeed of handing over to them the reigns of leadership of the local church. See e.g., KIGGINS, *Maynooth Mission to Africa,* 221-222.

63. Njoku and Lamberigts have noted, "in spite of the many hardships which the missionaries faced in the mission lands, the level of reverence in which they were held by the indigenous populations is unspeakable. Their word was Law. And in the missions they had ample room for exercising their creativity and imagination and their pioneer status gave them manifold chance to chart new directions. Each step they took seems to have had clearly historic proportions." Cf. NJOKU & LAMBERIGTS, "Vatican II", 119.

64. See for example, M. CROWTHER, "The Administration of French West Africa", in *Tarikh, France in Africa,* 8, Vol. II, no. 4, Essex, 1969, 1981, 59-71, esp. 59-60; M. CROWTHER, "Indirect Rule – French and British Style," *Africa* 34 (1964) 3, 197-205, p. 197, 'Ladipo ADAMOLEKUN, "The Road to Independence in French Tropical Africa", in *Tarikh, France in Africa,* 8, Vol. 2, no. 4, Essex, 1969, 72-85, 84. In *Things Fall Apart,* the novelist Chinua Achebe underlines the effect of the terrible fate of the people of Abame in softening the grounds for the relatively smooth advent of the missionaries to Umuofia *Obodo dike.* Cf. ACHEBE, *Things Fall Apart,* 97-99. In *Arrow of God,* Achebe re-visits that painful memory to indicate its lin-

gering power in the fractured consciousness of subsequent generations. Through the recollections of the memory of Unachukwu, Achebe tells us, " In his youth he (Unachukwu) had been conscripted to carry the loads of the soldiers who were sent to destroy Abame as a reprisal for the killing of a white man. What Unachukwu saw during that punitive expedition taught him that the white man was not a thing of fun." Cf. ACHEBE, *Arrow of God*, 47.

65. Colonial anthropologists were powerfully recruited into this propaganda and used their skill, their "field researches" to expand creatively on this image of the colonial mission. See e.g., Chukwudi Anthony NJOKU, *Violent Research: Ethics and effects of Negative Representation of the other in Missionary and Anthropological Research* (paper presented at the International conference on *Reconciling Mission: Overcoming Violence,* British and Irish association for Mission Studies (BIAMS), Edinburgh, 23rd to 26th June 2003).
66. Concerning the issue of colonial policy in Northern Nigeria as hindrance for missionary advance in the territory, see, C.N. UBAH, "Problems of Christian Missionaries in the Muslim Emirates of Nigeria, 1900–1928", in *Journal of African Studies,* 3 (1976), 351-371; M.H. KUKAH, *Religion, Politics and Power in Northern Nigeria,* (Lagos: Spectrum, 1993), 4.; J.S. TRIMINGHAM, *The Christian Church and Islam in West Africa* (London: SCM Press, 1955), 25 and Emefie Ikenga METUH, "Muslim Resistance to Missionary Penetration of Northern Nigeria, 1857–1960: A Missiological Interpretation," in *Mission Studies,* Vol. III, 2 (1986) 28-39, 29.
67. On the moderating influence of colonial administration on the social services set up by missionaries, see e.g., N.I. OMENKA, *The School in the Service of Evangelization. The Catholic Educational Impact in Eastern Nigeria 1886–1950* (Leiden: Brill, 1989), 70-100, 218-230.
68. Cf. EKECHI, *Missionary Enterprise*, 73ff.
69. This perceived close identification between the French missionaries and the French colonial administration was partly responsible for the determination by the British colonial agents and traders to oust them from Southern Nigeria at the turn of the century. The Irish Catholic missionaries took their place by 1905. Cf. EKECHI, *Missionary Enterprise.*
70. Northern Ireland, however, remained attached to the United Kingdom and constituted in its own way a lingering source of sour relations between the British and the "Irish", a term which in Northern Ireland deserves to be nuanced and indeed further categorized into "Loyalists" or "Republicans", and "Protestants" and "Catholics", due to its charged connotations.
71. The memory of the Irish experience as colony of Britain lingered several decades after Irish independence in 1916. Bishop McGettrick, writing in 1988, recalls some of these events with a painful freshness. Cf. Thomas MCGETTRICK, *Memoirs of Bishop T. McGettrick* (Enugu, 1988), see esp. 9-45. See also M.N.G. PHADRAIG, "Ireland: The Exception that Proves Two Rules", in T.M. GANNON, (ed.), *World Catholicism in Transition* (New York: MacMillan, 1988), 205-217, esp. 206.
72. See e.g., PHADRAIG, "Ireland", 206-207. See also Sean FARRAGHER, *Dev and His Alma Mater. Eamon de Valera's Lifelong Association with Blackrock College 1898–1975* (Dublin & London: Paraclete Press 1984), 9-14 and JORDAN, *Autobiography of a Missionary,* 9-11.
73. For a closer exploration of this issue see, NJOKU, *Vatican II and the Process of its Reception*, 112-113, 404.

74. Cf. W. Buhlmann, *Missions on Trial,* Slough, 1978.
75. Cecil McGarry has in this regard written insightfully, "The union of Christianity with the Mediterranean culture was so successful, so complete and so long-lasting that we often forget that we have received Christianity in this cultural matrix. Too often we tend to identify this culturally conditioned expression of our faith in Jesus Christ simply with Christianity as such. We forget that "Christianity as such" does not exist. The faith is not a culture, but it can only find expression and live within cultures;" Cf. Cecil McGarry, "Preface", to John Walligo et al, *Inculturation: Its Meaning and Urgency* (Kampala: St. Pauls' Publications, 1986), 8.
76. See e.g., M.A. Onwuejeogwu, *Evolutionary Trends,* 57-69. See also O. Eluyemi, "African Systems of Contact and Communication", in *Nigeria Magazine,* Vol 55, no. 2, April–June 1987, 36-49.
77 The introduction of the German language, even though spirited while it lasted, was stillborn following the very early exit of the German missionaries from Africa in the wake of the loss of the German colonial territories in Africa at the end of the 1914-1917 Great War. While remnants of German church architecture survived, the language they tried to pass on to their converts was one of the first casualties once missionaries of other tongues took over control of these territories.
78. Hans Debrunner, *A History of Christianity in Ghana,* (Accra: Waterville Publishing House, 1967), 343. See also Isichei, *A History of Christianity in* Africa, 169ff, 268, 294; E.A. Dahunsi, "The Problem of Translating the Bible into African Languages", in E. Mveng & J.Z. Werblowsky (eds), *The Jerusalem Congress on Black Africa and the Bible* (Jerusalem, 1972), 117-120.

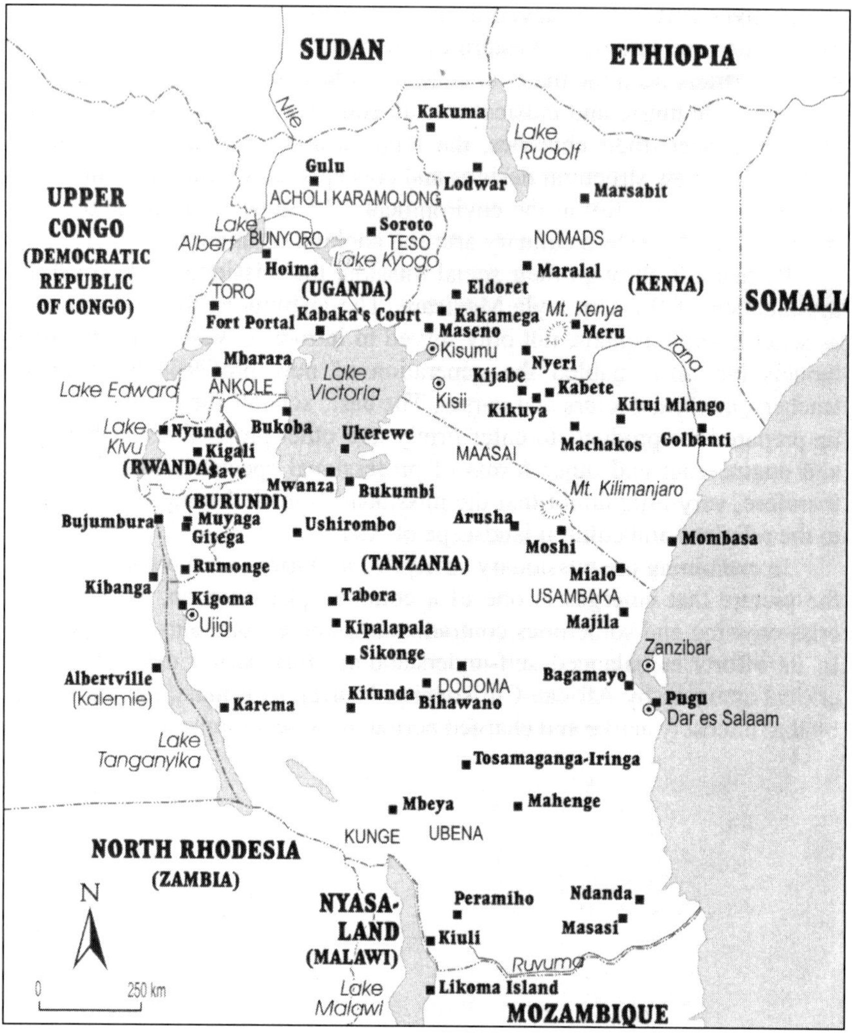

Map 7: Early missions in East Africa

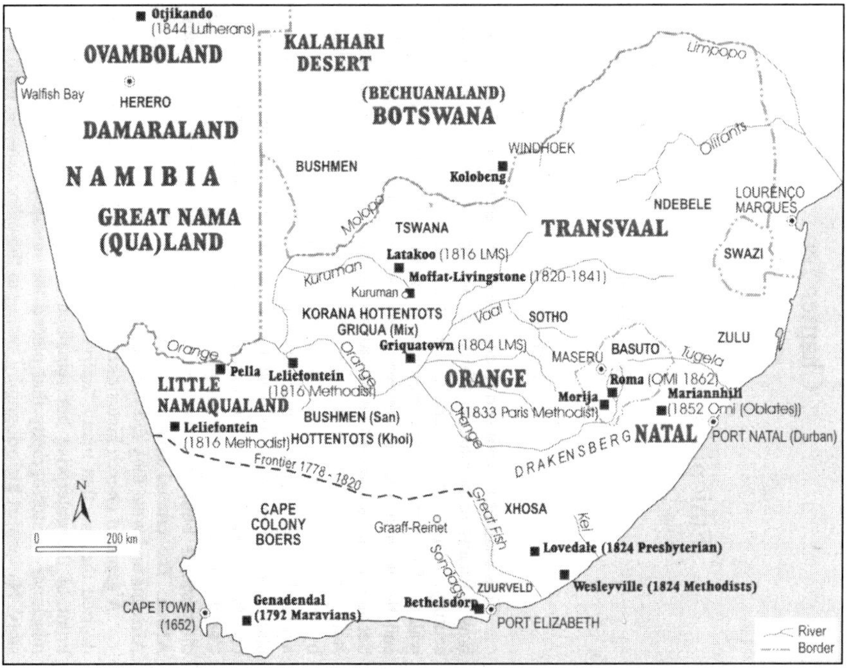

Map 8: Early missions in Southern Africa (1790's-1860's)

Chapter Ten

Ethiopianism in African Christianity

Ogbu U. Kalu

INTRODUCTION

This chapter is designed to achieve a number of things: first to explore how Africans responded to Christian presence as early as the nineteenth century, soon after missionary activities intensified in the continent in the wakes of two major movements, the abolition of slave trade and slavery and the second and largest wave of the evangelical revivals in Europe. Second, to demonstrate that all history is interpretation and, therefore, the story about the people who called themselves "Ethiopians", has been told by missionaries to portray them as people who were either cultural nationalists or people whose sinister goal was to secede from mission churches. Either profile is biased and less than the true image. What does this label mean during the period 1872-1922? Third, their story re-links Christianity in Africa homeland with Christianity among Africans in the diaspora. It buttresses the connection between African Americans and Africa. The crucial concern is about where the rain of the gospel met Africans and what they did with the showers of blessing.

A genre of church historiography during the early independence period decried the fact that many "native agents" or indigenous people bore the brunt of the enterprise but remained nameless, as unsung heroes, in a missionary historiography that placed the missionary at the center of the story. Nationalist historiography swung to the other extreme from two foci: one strand imaged missionary ideology as subversive of indigenous culture and leadership while another strand glorified the various types of local participation in the enterprise: chiefs who invited and patronized missionaries; communities who paid for the teachers and built the infrastructure, evangelists and interpreters; lay people who funded the enormous vertical expansion that occurred, especially in the inter-war years; and *émigrés* who returned from America and West Indies to prosecute mission. The native agency discourse became the staple diet of the 1970s.

One of the problems of the native agency discourse is that it operated within the missionary framework that privileged the insertion of the institutional church and gospel within the communities. Its concern was akin to the diatribe of a certain brand of feminism that queries the fact that in the gospel account two people took their needs to Jesus. One was a man and the other a woman. The writer named the man, Jairus and forgot the name of the woman who had an issue of blood. In the heat of political independence, the ecclesiastical brand of nationalism and indigenization project demanded that the African protagonists be named!

Years later, a different concern has appeared in a new historiography. It ceased to complain that missionary cultural policy demonized African culture and that even the neglect of African roles was an aspect of the racism that suffused the environment of the resurgent missionary enterprise of the nineteenth century. It boldly claimed that Christianity was a non-Western religion in the first place and the African version was an extension of African primal religion precisely because its expression of the gospel was forged in the heat of the gospel's challenge to the indigenous worldview. African Christianity, therefore, answered questions raised in the interior of the worldview.

This assertion was based on many unarticulated assumptions that could be easily unpacked. An aspect concerned the nature of church history and the place of theology in telling the story of gospel-people encounter. The assertion celebrates the contemporary growth of Christianity in the non-Western world that has challenged the perception of Christian expressions in those regions. Since people reconstruct from fragments of evidence what happened in the distant and contemporary past, the bias of either the missionary or the nationalist could be understood. But both operated from a predominantly institutional image of the church and its insertion into non-Western communities. When the gospel establishes a presence in another culture, it creates a culture and people encounters and the host community must perforce respond because the gospel affirms and challenges the presuppositions that prop the culture and life of the communities. The concern of this chapter is to show that those called "Ethiopians" were ahead of their times and had started a process of reflection that perceived Christianity as a non-Western religion, asserted African contribution in the Jesus movement and sought to fashion an authentic African response to the gospel's good news. Where is the black person in God's divine economy?

There are two things that must be emphasized: first, that early evangelical missionary enterprise in the nineteenth century was driven by a spiritual revival, a strong urge to share the gospel and a social activism that opposed the slave trade. But the situation or the exigencies of the mission fields compelled them to temper this hot spirituality for an institutional emphasis and character. Thus, the early indigenous response focused on the texture of this institutional presence. Missionary attitudes sometimes contested or colluded with colonial policies and ideology. In this particular case, colonial attitude to indigenous people changed dramatically after the Berlin Conference of 1885 and partition of Africa. Respect for indigenous rulers and acceptance of African capacity changed to jaundiced views.

Partition introduced virulent forms of European nationalism into the continent. The mission churches embellished this spirit with denominational stripes. The Berlin Conference's demand for physical presence rather than mere declarations of areas of influence opened the bowels of the African interior to missionary gaze. It was a moot point whether colonies were acquired in a fit of official absent-mindedness or by the machinations of the men-on-the-spot; the character of the cross-cultural process changed. European self-confidence, which replaced the initial respect for African chiefs as colonial weaponry, was now at the behest of gospel bearers. The scale of missionary activities was enormously enlarged making analysis complex; competition among missionaries became rife: broadly, Catholics squared off against Protestants but there were intramural competitions among the Catholic Orders and Protestant denominations because they came from different nations. Sometimes rivalry determined the pace, direction and nature of the Christian presence.

Missionary policy was forged amidst the competing claims of colonial ambitions, evangelical spirituality and obligations to the indigenous peoples. The allegation that missionaries colluded with the colonial governments must consider that these intimate enemies contested over cultural policy, educational curricula, and the moral temper of governance, and also the curious fact that colonialism benefited Islam more than several jihads could ever accomplish. The texture of colonial Christianity contained four strands that would challenge the indigenous peoples and evoke responses. First, *the character of the missionary presence* exhibited in such varied contexts as the mission centers of southern and central Africa, the protection of the settler communities in eastern Africa, and the increasing rejection of the large space that progressives, such as Henry Venn, advocated for African agency in West Africa. The second strand was a *cultural policy* that despised indigenous realities and embedded racism in mission practice. Third, the *institutionalization* of mission agencies that ignored the powerful resources of the Holy Spirit in the gospel, sapped the vigor of the original evangelical spirituality and encrusted the monopoly of decision-making processes and the practice of faith. Fourth, *translation* of the Scriptures exposed the underbelly of the missionary enterprise and produced unintended consequences.

The net effect of the first three strands loaded the cross of humiliation on African shoulders. Missionaries shared the Enlightenment worldview of the age and negative image of Africa. While they used education to create an elite that would mediate the new dispensation and carry the gospel to their people, education served as an instrument of rivalry and a means of evangelization; therefore, the range in the curricula was limited. Missionaries disdained the educated "black Englishman"; some stoutly resisted the belief in African capacity nurtured by Henry Venn. From the fate of the native pastorate in Sierra Leone, through the delimitation of the powers of Samuel Crowther's Niger bishopric, to his disgrace and the ousting of Africans from such high posts, the character of Christian presence in Africa was beclouded by racism. Missionaries showed more respect for South and East Asian cultures. In Africa this cultural policy created physical and psychological burdens and gave the enterprise a negative image embedded in a certain way of reading the Bible and in paternalistic principles that emphasized hierarchy, discipline and control. Race was particularly a major aspect of the Christian story in eastern and southern Africa. When Winston Churchill visited Kenya in 1906 as the Under-Secretary of State for the Colonies, he compared its racial issue to "*rhinoceros questions—awkward, thick-skinned, and horned, with a short sight, an evil temper, and a tendency to rush blindly upwind upon any alarm.*" That was a swipe at the settlers who reserved a sports cup named the *Kifaru (Rhinoceros)* for themselves.[1] Settlers implicated all whites by creating social and geographical boundaries between themselves and the indigenes. Ironies pervaded as white civilization, envisioned as the redemption of Africans, held them back, chafing for self-expression.

Control and the quest for a monopolistic interpretation of Christianity occupied the centre of much missionary ideology. This controlling attitude affected the pattern of African responses. For instance, the Africa Inland Mission among the Kikuyu from 1895 recruited only personnel who demonstrated strong piety, personal conversion, passion for evangelism, and could fund themselves. But their piety demonized local cultures and created tight-knit separate communities of believers (*athomi*). The tension between them and the rest of the community was so strong that the Kenyan novelist, Ngugi wa Thiong'o, has described this type of Christianity as a *River Between*. After 1914 such tensions would intensify, splintering the Kikuyu nation into competing Christianities. Nevertheless, the Kikuyu would reject, not Christianity itself but the mode of evangelization practiced by the missionaries. Much to the contrary, their nationalism contested the liberation offered by missionaries as being less than the translated Bible promised.[2]

Why did missionaries fail to disengage from the frontier mounted by the settlers? There appeared to be a strong evangelical reticence towards practical issues of social justice: for some it was the result of premillennial eschatology; for others it was the emphasis on the individual in their theology; for most, the openness that invited all people to be converted failed to dissolve the frontier of racial exclusion. The Anglicans and Scottish Presbyterians who were a part of the establishment were most inclined to accept the hegemony and justice of colonial rule. Most whites lived under fear of the African; the dark skin, large numbers, and cultures steeped in alien religiosity frightened outsiders. Control measures were adopted as a survival technique.

From this perspective, the wave of "Ethiopianism" in Africa from 1860 to the turn of the century may be viewed as an example of African response to colonial Christianity. According to a key figure, the Sierra-Leonean medical doctor, Africanus Beale Horton (1835-1883), it was a response to the European nationalism of the period that resulted in the partition of Africa and the change in white temperament that sought to restrain African initiative with European domination.[3]

I. THE LENS: MORAL ECONOMY AND AGENCY

It is useful to spell out how this re-interpretation of Ethiopianism will be done. The first is to borrow the notion of "moral economy", which may be helpful. The concept has been employed by the social historian E.P. Thompson to describe the failure by those in authority in early modern England to meet traditional and customary obligations towards the ruled. Thompson characterizes those expectations, embodied in values and roughly approximating to a consensus, as "moral economy". This concept could apply to the context of colonial Christianity, in which the original motives, included saving Africans from the evil caused by the nefarious slave trade, obeying the Great Commission, and bringing the resources of the kingdom of God to the continent. Within the colonial structure built on the tripod of civil administration, legitimate trade and judiciary, missionaries served as the civilizing agents, the conscience of a civilizing moral economy. They proceeded to build a structure that embodied certain values and the new indigenous members were compelled to respond to the structure. By structure is meant the ways social forces constrained, shaped and/or determined human behavior within such contexts.

A second way of looking at it is through the concept of "legibility"; that is, missionaries maintained the structure by making the new converts "readable". They read the "natives" by employing simple characterizations, stereotypes, simplifications, and prejudices. Nineteenth-century missionaries constructed physical and psychological tools for "reading" the new converts. The mission compound and its allocation of space, regimen in boarding schools and mission compounds, ethical boundaries, character formation strategies and dynamics of church polity were all designed to make the converts legible. The argument is Africans responded to missionary structures in three ways: some individuals and communities accepted them with *loyalty,* others *voiced* their dissent, and some took measures to *exit* from them.

Harris W. Mobley illustrates the pattern with an example from Ghana.[4] He draws a distinction between the literature of tutelage by courteous critics and the radical genre of critical literature by a second generation that avoided such deferential, tentative nuances. The new voices criticized the missionary's secluded habitation, social distance and vocational dominance. They explored the negative dimensions of missionary institutionalism or structure, harping on the imposition of ecclesiastical forms, the replacement of village community with church membership, marriage issues and the retarding effects of rivalry. They suspected the use of schools as a means of evangelization and faulted the missionary interpretation of Christianity, especially its failure to relate to indigenous beliefs. The ambiguity in the structure did not escape notice, recognizing what was dubbed as "coast conscience" that afflicted a minority of daring European "progressives" who cared for the welfare of Africans.

In contemporary social sciences, radicalism is profiled as "agency". Agency is used to refer to how individuals and groups self-consciously shape their behavior within such structures. It is the ability to make decisions, initiate redemptive actions and counter vulnerability or the inability to take decisions for oneself or one's community. Agency is a visioning gift that sees beyond simple tasks of survival and defines the importance of activism on behalf of self and community. As applied here, it refers to the dual processes by which black people confronted colonial social structures and institutions; they refused to accept the negative image of the black person. It must be stressed that colonialism was not just an administrative structure but also a psychological instrument that humiliated and wounded the soul and made the victim dependent on the master figure. In church historiography, agency is a tool for analyzing both the patterns of insertion of the gospel and the modes of appropriation; or, how Africans responded in the process of culture-encounter. Those described as "Ethiopians" were agents who "set to work" the missionary message, responded to the larger import of its moral values and gave voice to whispers from the ranges of infra-politics—that zone where the ruled talk freely about their rulers. Since missionary racial and cultural ideologies jarred most prominently against the biblical values that their translation of the gospel betrayed, and since the cultural hardware of the enterprise was intimidating, these two issues dominated the first African response to the missionary message.

II. ETHIOPIANISM: MYTH AND MEMORY

Ethiopianism was a movement with many strands. It was rooted in the Bible; specifically in the passage in Psalm 68:31 which prophesied that "*Princes shall come out of Egypt; Ethiopia shall soon stretch out her hands unto God.*" The prophetic reading of this passage is traced to African Americans who, in the golden age of black nationalism from 1870 to 1920, crafted an empowering exegesis around this passage. It has inspired generations who re-fashioned it freely. The Ethiopian tradition sprang from certain shared political and religious experiences and found expression in slave narratives, in the exhortations of conspiratorial slave preachers, folklore and songs of slaves. After 1872, it moved beyond the nostalgia of prideful heritage to communal assertion. The intellectual origin may include the impact of European ideals that were filtered through American revolutionary rhetoric to inspire African Americans who returned to the motherland. The Christianity of the returnees, argues Sanneh, was stamped with the values of anti-slavery and promoted as the cause of the oppressed and the stigmatized.[5] It called for freeing Africans from the religious and political tutelage of Europeans. The core concerns included a quest for a place of their own, for identity, self-respect, and an opportunity to nurse Africa back to its old glory. That glory was imaged with the achievements of ancient Egypt, Nubia and Ethiopia. There was a conflation of myth and history. Ethiopia was both a place and an ideological symbol and there is little doubt about the achievements of Egypt in science, architecture and government. The contributions of ancient Egypt were injected into western civilization through the Greeks and mistaken for Greek ingenuity. The contributions of this part of Africa to the consolidation of the theology and identity of early Christianity are equally immense. Ethiopianism, therefore, has three broad strands: in African American diasporic experience, western African manifestations, and southern African genre. In all incarnations, it fuelled black nationalism.

The first task is to explore the search for heroic roots, which often fails to underscore patches in the story. It is a puzzle why the Egyptians did not refer to themselves as *Kushites* but applied the term *Kush* to the region south of the first cataract of the Nile, and to the descendants of Ham, the son of Noah who witnessed his drunken father's nakedness. The notion of a curse was introduced into the story even though it was Canaan that was cursed. Did the ancient Egyptians perceive themselves as related to the Kush? Historically, the relationship between Egypt and the Kushite region was fraught with ambiguity. Egypt was attracted to the mineral wealth, commercial and cultural exchanges with the region that stood between it and central Africa, as well as the trade with Arabs from the Red Sea island of Dahlak and the sea port of Adulis. Nubians patronized the cultic temples at Philae (Aswan). Archaeological evidence of Egyptian cultural presence in the interior of the Nubian region abounds. Meanwhile, the Blemmyes, ancestors of the Beja of contemporary Sudan, constantly raided the southern Egyptian regions around Thebes and Philae. It is said that the rich Nubian kingdom of Meroe was once located around Napata; when the Nubians attacked Egyptian towns, the latter revenged, sacked its capital and forced its relocation down the Nile. The treasurer to the Queen Mother, Candace of Meroe, made it into the pages of the Bible as Philip met him returning from a pilgrimage to Jerusalem.[6] He was reading the Septuagint.

Matters darkened as the translators of the Septuagint Bible in 300BC mistakenly translated the Hebrew *Kush* into the Greek, *Aithiop*, a word that the Greeks used for any country south of their known world, and derived from their word for black face, *aithiops*. The entire region from Egypt to Ethiopia/Abyssinia thus became known as Ethiopia. This explains how "Ethiopianism" as a movement sought to re-create and moor itself onto the prideful, golden age of African civilization, the splendor of the kingdoms of Meroe and Aksum that survived the Islamic onslaught of the seventh century and retained the pristine traditions of early Christianity. In European imagination, this was the kingdom of Prester John, whose myth allured many crusaders into arduous sojourns and served as a key component of Iberian voyages of the fifteenth century. Ethiopia was an enchanted place, whose monarch claimed to be the Lion of Judah, a scion of Queen Sheba and King Solomon, whose land is said to hold the ark of the covenant, and who defeated the Italians at Adwa in March 1896 to prove that the whites were not invincible. Ethiopians maintained their independence into the modern times, though Nubia collapsed into Islamic embrace in the fifteenth century. "Ethiopia" passed into the nineteenth-century imagination as a generic term for blacks, the descendants of Ham and Cush. The Rastafarians of the West Indies equally celebrate this conflation of myth and historical memory because the movement was, like Ethiopianism, a form of cultural appreciation, a social and historical excavation, a recovery and re-contextualization of black traditions of emancipation hidden from consciousness of black peoples by colonial hegemony.

However, recent archaeological literature on the alluring Queen of Sheba, whose image rivals that of Delilah and Cleopatra, locates her in South Arabia rather than in Nubia or Ethiopia. Indeed, it was the dynasty of Tewodros of Ethiopia (1855-1868) that contrived the Solomonic succession into a messianic ideology of a king whose coming had long been prophesied. He would later add "*the son of David and of Solomon*" into his official titles. Ethiopia was imaged as the land from where Queen Sheba sojourned to consort with Solomon and produced the heritage of the monarchy. Tewodros superseded the story of the Falasha linkage with ancient Israel and conjured a myth. The Falasha or Beta-Israel trace a genuine religious heritage to Israel. Some Victorian observers claimed that there was a Semitic physiognomic resemblance; this is debatable.[7] The Falasha maintained a Mosaic tradition with a strong asceticism that borrowed elements of the indigenous culture. They inhabited a number of communities mostly in northern Ethiopia and were despised. The term *falasi* meant stranger.

Various Christian kings of Ethiopia sought to counter the Falasha claim to a more authentic heritage and tried to *Ambarize* them. They became generally poor, powerless artisans; some could not afford to retain the Mosaic rituals. The *zemana mesafent,* rule of princes (1769-1855), when the central authority virtually dissolved, was the worst period for the Falasha as the princes disenfranchised their lands. In the mid-nineteenth century, missionary efforts by Jewish organizations, such as the London Society for Promoting Christianity Amongst the Jews, attempted to consolidate their Jewish heritage and later to promote repatriation to Israel.

Thus, Ethiopian kings constructed the Hebraic linkage by disestablishing the direct line. The myth about Ethiopia, therefore, conflated different genres: the achievements of ancient Egypt that were staggering in their range, the achievements of the early Christian apologists in Alexandria and Carthage, the gilded kingdoms of Nubian Meroe, the exploits of Aksum, and the endeavors of various Abyssinian kings who sustained the Christian kingdom in the face of Islamic onslaught until Yohannes and Menelik modernized it. The defeat of the Italians crowned all these into a prideful past for Africans. Ethiopia became a symbol of African redemption, political and religious ideology that continued to inspire through generations.

III. "GOD IS A NEGRO": ETHIOPIANISM IN AFRICAN AMERICAN IMAGINATION

Henry McNeal Turner (1834-1915) was perhaps the greatest protagonist of the Ethiopian cause for the period. Confronted with a keen sense of the sovereignty of God and the cross of humiliation of the black people at home and abroad, he designed a providential theology hewn from the rock of the belief that God has the interest of Negroes so much at heart that he is a Negro. God providentially brought them as slaves to America to acquire the resources of the gospel for redeeming the fatherland. Black Manifest Destiny conferred a responsibility. Many others, such as Alexander Crummell (1819-1898), Martin Delany (1812-1885) and Henry Garnet (1815-1882), contributed to developing the idea.

Some understood the prophecy in Psalm 68:31 to mean that Africa would be saved from heathenism; others imagined it on a grand scale to say that Africa would one day rise to rule the world. For all, it explained the forced dispersion, countered the prevalent Hamitic theory, and imposed a sacred duty. African Americans were the instruments for achieving God's design. Each commentator prescribed how the task could be accomplished. Some urged the exercise of black religious genius and commitment already evident in Simon Cyrene's assistance to Jesus. Crummell imagined the black intellectuals as agents and leaders for redeeming the fatherland through religion. Delany, who was a Harvard trained medical doctor, harped on the cultivation of self-help ("elevation"), education and skills. Such trained manpower would return to Africa to develop it. Henry Turner labored to inspire and mobilize Africans in black churches.

All agreed on emigration and the imperative to appropriate the best of Anglo-Saxon civilization. Garnet buttressed the dream with an organizational structure. He scripted a constitution in 1858 for the American Colonization Society based on a voluntary and co-operative mobilization and re-direction of the energy of black people. For Turner, America held no hopes for the black person. Incidentally, the period coincided with white realization that the challenges of the climate in certain parts of Africa required black personnel. They toured institutions to recruit and founded others for training such personnel. Other blacks suspected white motives, arguing that those who did not care for the welfare of blacks in the United States could not possibly sympathize with Africans at home.

The American Colonization Society suffered challenges because of funding, the robust opposition of integrationists, and the American Civil War that distracted focus, but its ideal flowed into various Pan-African movements in latter years. In many ways, their activism buttressed the daring of the Nova Scotians and Maroons who had emigrated in 1792 to Sierra Leone and whose example inspired the foundation of Liberia in 1822. African Americans articulated some of the key themes that would be picked up on the continent precisely because some protagonists, such as Edward Wilmot Blyden (1832-1912), participated from both sides of the Atlantic Ocean.

IV. "WE ARE NO LONGER SLAVES": VOICE AND ANTI-STRUCTURE IN WEST AFRICA

Beyond myth and ideology, Ethiopianism was a daring voice of new confidence that was manifested in the Native Pastorate experiment by the CMS in Sierra Leone; it breathed with the hope that Africans would bear the responsibility to evangelize Africa, build an autonomous church devoid of denominations and shirk European cultural domination and control of decision-making in the church. It dreamt of developing a Negro state with a different type of education that included a tertiary facility; one that would mobilize Christian and Muslim resources in the larger African interest; preserve African culture, language, and racial distinctives. It would ironically do all these by absorbing the best in European culture. There was no rejection of European culture in the program. It wanted only a share in an envisioned new dispensation rooted in a prophecy of the destiny of the black race. The emphasis was on re-imagining the race in the face of denigration by the whites. This explains the strand in Ethiopianism that urged awareness and activist protest about the fate of oppressed Africans in the Congo, West Indies, South Africa, and Fernando Po.[8]

Jehu Hanciles has rooted the West African manifestation of Ethiopianism in Henry Venn's vision of the euthanasia of missionary control that promoted a counter-imagination built on confidence in African ability and created space for the indigenes to run their churches. Venn advised missionaries to build nuclei congregations, study and respect indigenous peculiarities, and avoid mistaking black nationalism for presumption or ingratitude. He predicted that the desire to supersede denominational distinctions was bound to grow.[9] James "Holy" Johnson of Freetown, and later of the CMS Yoruba mission, best expressed this view when he wrote in April 1873:

> The desire to have an independent church closely follows the knowledge that we are a distinct race, existing under peculiar circumstances and possessing peculiar characteristics, the desire to preserve this distinction uninjured, the conviction that it would materially contribute to give a purely native character and power to our religious profession, and that the arrangement of foreign churches made to suit their own local circumstances can hardly be expected to suit our own in all their details.[10]

Johnson anticipated the roots of the indigenization project of the future and could be seen as a forerunner of the moratorium debate of the 1970s. The Native Pastorate caused a vigorous debate over the availability of educated personnel, funding and the marginalized role of whites. While this was going on, an ideological fire from the African American emigration activists engulfed the West African educated elite who chafed under white control of decision-making processes in the churches and state.

Crucial to the nationalism of the period was the use of the Bible to legitimate racial ideology. It shared the diatribe by African-American protagonists such as Martin Delany who countered culture-based hermeneutics by declaring that "we are no longer slaves, believing any interpretation that our oppressors may give the word of God, for the purpose of deluding us to the more easy subjugation; but freemen."[11] Ethiopianism went beyond passive radicalism, that is, a coping mechanism against ideological and material disadvantage, to an active radicalism that sought to remove the source of the control system. African response would gradually move from voicing opposition to the moral economy of missionary structure to anti-structural agency. Some nationalists gave voice to dissent through their writings but remained within the structure; others sought to emasculate missionary structures.

By networking through Sierra Leone, Liberia, Gold Coast and Nigeria, Ethiopians in West Africa built a formidable following among the sector of the new elite who refused to be co-opted. It bonded the stars of West Africa. To name but a few: in the Gold Coast, J. E. Casely Hayford (Ekra-Agiman; 1868-1930), a brilliant lawyer and Methodist layman, wrote *Ethiopia Unbound* (1911) and initiated a critical tradition which rejected the literature of tutelage characteristic of missionary protégés. As an admirer of Wilmot Blyden, his activism centered on mobilizing the entire West African colonies in educational and political matters. Unlike Casely-Hayford, the educator Mensah Sarbah (b. 1864) avoided an open attack on missionaries but offered an insightful work on Fanti customary laws that would show the moral foundations of an African community. Attoh Ahuma (1863-1921) broke away and affiliated his Gold Coast African Methodist Church to the bastion of African American self-assertion, the American Methodist Episcopal Zion Church, in 1896.

In Nigeria, a leader in the Southern Baptist mission, David Brown Vincent (1860-1917), took to wearing only Yoruba clothes, founded a school with no foreign support, and in 1888 seceded from the Southern Baptists to form the Native Baptist Church in Lagos, the first indigenous church in West Africa. In 1894 he reverted to his original name, Mojola Agbebi. Similarly, another Yoruba, E.M. Lijadu (1862-1926), refused to be insulted by an Anglican agent, funded his "Self-Supporting Evangelist Band" (1900) through trade, and wrote two books in which he tried to articulate Christian theology with indigenous knowledge, arguing that the Yoruba deity, Orunmila, was a pre-figuration of Jesus. The educationist, Henry Car, asserted that education was a crucial tool for building African self-image. Car and the more famous Ghanaian, J.E.K. Aggrey (1875-1927) of the African Methodist Episcopal Zion Church, inspired a generation of educator. The ambiguity in the movement was encapsulated in the career of James "Holy" Johnson (c. 1836-1917), who led the movement before he was transferred from Sierra Leone to Lagos. He had a reputation for an unbending evangelicalism and as an agitator for African rights to education and ecclesiastical independence. He insisted on fighting the battle from inside the Anglican Church and would not be persuaded to secede. He did not even accept the platform of polygamy as the basis for Ethiopianism. The same pragmatism characterized the ideals of Julius Ojo-Cole, who was not averse to borrowing the best of other civilizations to improve Africa as long as it was affirmed that each race of people possessed its genius and must unite, co-operate to foster a spirit of national consciousness and radical pride. He was a founding member of the West African Students' Union; published the journal *West African Review* and sought to introduce a new type of education in West Africa.[12] Many of the Ethiopianists were inspired by Blyden, but did not share his optimism about the spread of Islam. From Liberia, Blyden traveled widely to promote the cause in Africa and America. His lecture in Lagos in 1891 entitled, *The Return of the*

Exiles, encapsulated the heart of the movement. Acknowledging the sacrifices of white missionaries, he argued nonetheless that the destiny of the Christianity lay in the hands of Africans or, as a weekly newspaper in Sierra Leone reported on a speech by Agbebi in 1892, "the sphinx must solve her own riddle. The genius of Africa must unravel its own enigma." Blyden braided cultural, religious and political strands of nationalism into a coherent prophetic logic of African response to the missionary structure and message. As he put it in a lecture to the Sixty-third Annual Meeting of the American Colonization Society in 1880:

> Africa may yet prove to be the spiritual conservatory of the world. Just as in past times, Egypt proved the stronghold of Christianity after Jerusalem fell, and just as the noblest and greatest of the Fathers of the Christian Church came out of Egypt, so it may be, when the civilized nations, in consequence of their wonderful material development, have had their spiritual perceptions darkened and their spiritual susceptibilities blunted through the agency of a capturing and absorbing materialism, it may be, that they may have to resort to Africa to recover some of the simple elements of faith; for the promise of that land is that she shall stretch forth her hands unto God.[13]

Blyden thus foresaw the coming shift in the centre of gravity of Christianity from the north to the south Atlantic and its import for African Christianity.

Perhaps, the significance of the movement can best be gleaned from the fact that African Christians choreographed all three movements of loyalty, voice and exit; as some loyally memorized the script written by the missionaries, others voiced their dissent through publications and media; gradually, a few, such as Mojola Agbebi, led a movement of exit to form Native African Churches which split from the mission-founded ones to experiment with interdenominational Christianity. In Nigeria, there were six main branches of the movement: three split from mainline churches and three sprouted thereafter on their own. By the 1921 census, these churches in aggregate constituted the third largest Christian form in southern Nigeria. The Ethiopian cultural register included the rejection of European baptismal names; the use of African clothes; praying for chiefs instead of the British monarch; and accepting polygamists as members of the church. They contested missionary polity, liturgy and ethics from an honest appropriation of biblical principles.[14] Indeed, by 1914 two of the Native Baptist churches had returned into fellowship with the Southern Baptist Convention. The image of a syncretistic endeavor is fictional.

This may explain the changing pattern of white responses to Ethiopianism. The conservative ones were often regarded as useful for controlling the natives, while those influenced by African Americans, such as the African Orthodox Church in Zimbabwe, were viewed as subversive, to be hounded out of the religious space. For the most part, Ethiopianism pursued the symbols of modernity such as education, but used anti-structural strategy to protest against the arrogance of power. Beyond cultural nationalism, Ethiopianism re-structured the ecclesiology and theology of the missionary churches and encapsulated the dilemmas of blending missionary endeavor, colonization and endogenous development in African societies. It confronted externality in African Christianity by asserting that all forms of Christianity were tribal and that a truly African Christianity was possible, even though its full character would emerge only with time: in the words of an Akamba proverb, "cattle are born with ears, they grow horns later." Ethiopians laid the foundations for modern forms of African nationalism whether in the political or ecclesiastical realm and initiated the current debates on inculturation and vernacularization in African theology. They voiced a new form of Christianity in Africa.

V. AGENCY AND EXIT: ETHIOPIANISM IN SOUTHERN AND CENTRAL AFRICA

In southern and central Africa, three interesting dimensions intrigue: first, the question of why Africans reacted with such confidence to the new face of missionary Christianity; second, the different faces of Ethiopianism in the region, where the movement occurred independently though rooted in the same principles as in West Africa; third, the role of African American black churches in catalyzing and sustaining African radicalism. Certain regional characteristics equally emerged: race was more prominent than culture in white settler communities; exit was sometimes forced and sometimes adopted out of frustration; the political dimension was buttressed by the religious as churches provided havens from the brutality and humiliations of the structure, and served as the forum for mobilizing dissent until the character of radicalism changed and the weight of frustration produced the violent genre of Ethiopianism.

Many forms of exit were led by people of chiefly pedigree, thus weaving religious movements into the communal quest for survival in the midst of the disruptions and internal stability caused by the expansions of whites. Missionary enterprise that started in earnest in the dawn of the nineteenth century, had by the third quarter of the century produced a bulge of educated people who had the confidence to seek the well-being of their people by confronting the exploiters and their moral subalterns/legitmizers. For instance, in 1892, Mangena M. Mokone (1851-c.1936), an ordained Wesleyan Methodist, rejected the racial segregation of the church and withdrew to found his Ethiopian Church in Pretoria. Four years later, he contacted the African Methodist Episcopal Church (AMEC) through the agency of his niece, Charlotte Manye. She was a member of a group of singers that had been stranded in the United States after a tour of America in 1893. The intervention of an African Methodist Episcopal minister helped her enter Wilberforce College in Ohio, where she graduated with honors. The two churches united. Mokone's agent, James M. Dwane (1848-1915), was made the General Superintendent of the AMEC, but in 1900 broke off and took his group into the Anglican Church, maintaining its quasi-independent identity as "the Order of Ethiopia".

A pattern of enclavement dominated the character of the missionary presence in the region; perhaps derived from the model of treating delinquents in

Europe. African responses varied from loyalty to exit, in rejection of the enclavement pattern. Nehemiah Tile (d. 1891), a member of a chiefly family, left the Wesleyans in Tembuland in 1884 in an effort to achieve political and religious freedom from whites; Pambani J. Mzimba abandoned the Presbyterians of Lovedale in 1890, just as Charles Domingo would exit from the Livingstonia Mission in Nyasaland in 1908. It should also be noted that the Second Anglo-Boer War (1899-1902) aided the spread of Christianity into the African camps; as many Africans dispersed from the mining centers, they took the radical Christian forms to their rural communities.

Moreover, African American influence was important, as the visit of Bishop Henry M. Turner of the AMEC to South Africa in 1898 did much to galvanize the Ethiopian movement of the period to the consternation of the settlers. His liaison with James Mata Dwane, son of a Ntinde ruler, catalyzed tremendous growth in the Cape Colony, Orange Free State and Transvaal. A cultural aside is that it was Mankayi Enoch Sontonga (c. 1873-1905), a product of the Lovedale Institution and member of Mzimba's African Presbyterian Church, who composed the famous song, "Nkosi Sikelel' Afrika" in 1897. This has become the theme song of African liberation, forms the national anthem of Zambia and Zimbabwe, and has been incorporated into the national anthem of South Africa.

Collectively, these men rejected the racism, insults, control, and European cultural and religious domination that frequently overshadowed the evangelical spirit in the missionary enterprise. They harped on the themes of a non-denominational African Christianity, self-expression, political and ecclesiastical freedom and inter-ethnic mobilization. Dwane's anti-white rhetoric may have been strident but there was something inexplicable that galled Africans in this period. This can be well illustrated by the case of John Chilembwe's exit from white tutelage in Nyasaland (modern Malawi). Like Mzimba and Domingo, Chilembwe (c.1871-1915) was nurtured by a loving missionary, who placed much hope on his loyalty. Joseph Booth of the Zambezi Industrial Mission reared him from the position of a cook to a status as a son and sent him to a black college in West Virginia. Chilembwe returned in 1900 to Nyasaland a changed person and founded the Providence Industrial Mission at Chiradzu, which was supervised by an African American Baptist missionary through its first six years. His preference for ebony kinship frightened the whites, even though they had no sympathy for Booth, who was later deported.

Chilembwe's resort to violence in 1915 was only one of seven cases that stoked white scares about Ethiopianism between 1906 (the last Zulu Bambata rebellion) and 1927. African American churches were blamed as the external agitators of African unrest until the Watch Tower challenge to civil polity (led in Nyasaland by Booth's former protégé, Elliot Kamwana) became the dread of white politics in southern Africa between 1909 and 1915. Indeed, white fears severely throttled the African American missionary impulse. The underlying reasons for the tense socio-political environment in the period were the political restructuring and creation of the Union in 1910, increased alienation of land from the indigenes, and the decline of the status of educated blacks, who responded by forming the South African Native National Congress in 1912 and sent a delegation to London to protest against the South Africa Native Land Act of 1913. Though some Ethiopians were involved, a political force took over control. Even in the United States, black nationalism took a political color as Garveyism and the United Negro Improvement Association captured the centre stage.

It could be argued that after 1915 Ethiopianism as a movement started to lose momentum, so that by 1930 it had become disengaged from the religious terrain and merged into a larger Pan Africanist political movement that had operated since 1896 as a component of a larger ideology.[15] Various reasons can be canvassed for this trend, some of which were discernible even before 1915. First is the diverse character of missionary ideologies; this means that no single person or group represented the whole. Within the same missionary movement some perceived the dangers of the missionary's cultural hardware and voiced African discomfort. Others went even further to wonder whether managerial mission did not overshadow the role of the Holy Spirit. The strength of the missionary enterprise lay in the capacity for internal criticism. Some aspects of missionary practices countered and chipped away the rough edges of its other manifestations, and hence weakened the appeal of the Ethiopian churches.

Second, Africans appropriated those resources in a variety of ways and differently in time perspective. The vision, sacrifice and range of social services by missionaries benefited Africans in their quest to adjust to new power realities. The effect of Bible translation, the power of the gospel working in spite of the bearers, thus appreciating and yet limiting human agency, ensured that Christianity began to answer the questions raised by the interior of the prevailing worldviews and the tensions encountered with colonialism. Soon African agents carried the burden of evangelization and grew more confident with the times. African Bible women, who visited kraals in the Transvaal enthused with a hot gospel, increasingly became adept. Xhosa evangelists worked in Malawi in the 1870s. South Africa was like a nodal point from which many migrant laborers, as black missionaries, fanned into the contiguous countries.

Third, by the turn of the century, the character of Christian presence and the mode of appropriating the gospel had changed; further shifts in geopolitics reshaped the character of Christian presence in Africa. For instance, political parties emerged in West Africa as cultural nationalism shifted to political nationalism. The reshaped character of Christian presence can be illustrated by the immense efforts made to consolidate the enterprise through ecumenical endeavor and to promote indigenization. The World Missionary Conference of 1910 depicts the character of this strand. After Edinburgh, many missionary groups shifted from comity or mere friendship among whites in foreign lands to more formal cooperation. They negotiated boundaries and delimited areas of operation to avoid rivalry and later, following Indian precedent, founded

National Councils of Churches. Examples include Nigeria, Zambia, Madagascar, Swaziland and Angola.

Fourth, the hopes of Edinburgh did not fully materialize because the whole missionary field soon became confused, insecure and vulnerable with the outbreak of the First World War in 1914. As it dragged on longer than anticipated, missionary logistics would become endangered: posts, supplies, transportation, and manpower. Nevertheless, the War would enlarge the space for African roles and initiative and thus reduce racial tensions. Moreover, mass movements of conversion to Christianity would enable a new era of consolidation for the mission churches after 1914.

CONCLUSION: THE ENDURING LEGACY OF ETHIOPIANISM

In 1964, the Nigerian Methodist theologian, E. B. Idowu, presented a series of radio talks, "Towards an Indigenous Church", which sounded like a close reading of earlier Ethiopian themes. The indigenization project that followed decolonization so mirrored the design of Ethiopianism that the movement could be said to have nurtured the roots of modern African Christianity. Ethiopianism deployed Christianity as an instrument to reconstruct the development of African cultural and political nationalism. Later African indigenous churches uncovered the Achilles' heel of missionary Christianity and also revealed the limits of the Ethiopian response. The legacies of the Ethiopian movement were, however, numerous: the quests to appropriate the gospel and modernity with dignity; to be both an African and a Christian; to express faith from an indigenous worldview and spirituality so that Africans could respond to their own realities and culture in the spheres of liturgy, polity and ethics; to tap the resources of indigenous knowledge in communicating the kerygma; and to practice local initiatives in evangelism, decision-making processes, ecclesial structures and funding. Some Ethiopians even advocated dialogue with other faiths by responding to Islam without confrontation. Dialogue was an African idea long before missionaries woke up to its import.

Notes

1. P. Lonsdale, "Mission Christianity & settler colonialism in eastern Africa", in H Hansen & M Twaddle (eds), *Christian Missionaries and the State in the Third World* (Oxford: Currey, 2002), 194-211, 196.
2. P. Lonsdale, "Kikuyu Christianities: A history of intimate diversity", in D. Maxwell & I. Lawrie (eds), *Christianity and the African Imagination* (Leiden: Brill, 2002), 157-97.
3. C. Fyfe, *Africanus Horton: 1835-1883: West African Scientist and Patriot*, Modern Revivals in African Studies (London: Ashgate, 1993).
4. H. Mobley, *The Ghanaian's Image of the Missionary: An Analysis of the Published Critiques of Christian Missionaries by Ghanaians 1897-1965* (Leiden: Brill, 1970).
5. L. Sanneh, *Abolitionists Abroad: American Blacks and the Making of the Modern West Africa* (Cambridge, MA: Harvard University Press, 2001).

6. Acts 8:27.
7. D. SEEMAN, "The Question of Kinship: Bodies and Narratives in the Beta Israel-European Encounter (1860-1920)", *Journal of Religion in Africa*, 30, 1 (2000) 86-120, 101-102.
8. E.A. AYANDELE, *The Missionary Impact on Modern Nigeria 1842–1914, A Political Analysis* (London: Longmans, 1966), 187.
9. J.J. HANCILES, *Euthanasia of a Mission: African Church Autonomy in a Colonial Context* (Connecticut, CT: Praeger Publishers, 2002).
10. E.A. AYANDELE, *'Holy' Johnson, Pioneer of African Nationalism, 1836-1917* (Southgate: Frank Cass, 1970), 42.
11. G. WILMORE, *Black Religion and Black Radicalism: An Interpretation of the Religious History of African Americans* (New York: Orbis Books, 1998 [1973]), 137.
12. G. OLUSANYA, "Julius Cole: a Neglected Nigerian Nationalist and Educationist", *Journal of the Historical Society of Nigeria*, 7,1 (December, 1973), 91-110.
13. E. HOLDEN, *Blyden of Liberia* (New York: Vantage Press, 1966); H.R. LYNCH, *Edward Wilmot Blyden: Pan-Negro Patriot, 1832-1912* (London: Oxford University Press, 1967), 147; E.W. BLYDEN, *Christianity, Islam and the Negro Race* (London: W.B. Whittingham, 1888), 143.
14. J.B. WEBSTER, *The African Churches among the Yoruba, 1888-1922* (Oxford: Clarendon Press, 1964), p. xvi.
15. P. O. ESEDEBE, *Pan-Africanism; The Idea and Movement 1776-1963* (Washington DC: Howard University Press 1994), ch. 2.

Chapter Eleven

Bakuzufu: Revival Movements and Indigenous Appropriation in African Christianity

Graham Duncan & Ogbu U. Kalu

I. ANATOMY OF REVIVALISM

Bakuzufu is the Luganda word for being re-awakened, or renewed or even resurrected; it is a very apt description for the English word "revival". Revivals are an endemic aspect of Christianity. At several points in time, a movement would flare up as certain elements in the gospel, either its charismatic/pneumatic resource or its ethical imperative, would be emphasized enough to compel a new expression of its spirituality and structure. There would be a great excitement and popular interest beyond what may have been witnessed in years. As Efraim Anderson said about *ngunza* movement or revivalism in the Congo, it was a different type of conversion from the normal reception of Christianity that was "quiet, almost passive, sometimes even routine-like confession to Christianity." In revivals, there could be "a violent expression of feelings with tears and cries, with shaking and convulsion, with a falling to the ground and even unconsciousness."[1] Some have drawn attention to the element of individuality in such conversion experience without ignoring the communal impact. A revival is not the mere appearance of a new version of Christianity but one that elicits massive attention and acceptance; it brings a new life to an old religion. A major characteristic is to accelerate the pace of expansion, determine the new direction of growth and reshape the religious landscape. Some last long and have long-term consequences, while others may be short-lived. Each brings new faces and styles of leadership to the fore and may aid or mar the quality of the Biblical roots of the Christian expression; thus, not all revivals could be positive. Some have caused schism for the worse. At all times, revivals are the responses to the character of Christian living and message at certain times, in certain contexts, and may reflect the impact of external secular forces as people seek answers from the religious sphere. A revival may, therefore, reflect the turmoil and dislocation in a community. For instance, Janet Hodgson set the careers of Nxele and Ntsikana within the disquiet among the Xhosa in the nineteenth century:[2]

> During the nineteenth century the Xhosa—Cape frontier was moved eastward step by step, following conquests by the British Imperial and Cape Colonial forces. By the 1880s after one hundred years of war, the Xhosa-speaking people from the Zuurveld in the East Cape to Pondoland, had been incorporated under the British sovereignty, suffering dispossession of their ancestral land, destruction of their polities, and displacement and domination by alien rulers. Every aspect of their daily lives, their customs, and their beliefs had come under sustained attack from missionaries. But while the Xhosa lost the struggle to retain their political and socio-economic independence, "the colonization of consciousness" itself was never complete, even among the Western educated black elite. The battle for sacred power between the intruding culture and the indigenous cultures continued unabated. Over the years, a number of Christian symbols and rituals were appropriated into the African worldview, providing a spiritually liberating potential with profound political implications.

In Africa, revivals occurred at different times right from the early insertion of the gospel into communities; people responded to the missionary message by deploying certain aspects of its doctrines to arouse communal interest in ways that the missionaries may not have wanted. Thus, the character of revivals, would include: (i) a response to a prevalent religious structure, message and their implications; (ii) a tendency to privilege a certain dimension of the message found most appropriate, especially the charismatic resources; (iii) an effort to re-shape the interior of a prevalent religious tradition; (iv) by re-directing the core message to deeply felt needs within the community; and (v) thereby provide an answer to socio-economic, political needs and restore moral order by appeal to supernatural intervention and anchor; (vi) A revival may act as a counter-culture by weaving a new identity with religious fabric to enable the community's survival in the face of new challenges; (vii) It throws up a new leadership able to deploy religion in the explanation, prediction and control of space-time events. Thus, in spite of operating in the religious zone, revivals tend to have political overtones and could be perceived as alternative power nodes, and thereby would elicit resentment from power-holders.

In Africa, many revivals appeared amidst African efforts to cope with colonialism, white settlers and missionaries. Later, the challenges of modernity and globalization would trigger widespread revivals in the quest for supernatural responses. However, there should be caution with predominantly functionalist interpretations. A religious explanation would emphasize that God has constantly renewed His people through the out-pouring of the Holy Spirit. This has occurred in many places at different times as an aspect of His love. For instance, it is said that Koreans enjoyed a massive revival just before the wars that traumatized generations; that the revival empowered their survival and recovery. It can also be claimed that a series of these charismatic revivals reshaped the face of African Christianity and catalyzed the massive growth that is a part of the shift of the center of gravity of Christianity to the south.

African Christianity experienced localized revivals in the nineteenth century but the frequency increased in the period, 1910-1947, when some revivals with a wide provenance (beyond country of origin) occurred. For instance, the *Balokole* (Luganda for *Saved Ones*) was a movement that flowed, like the waves of a river, from Rwanda through Uganda to Tanganyika and Sudan. The effects lasted through five decades. Similarly, the massive Pentecostal/charismatic revivals of the 1970s provide another example that has continued with great intensity through decades and covered the entire continent, including even those claiming either Moslem or communist ideologies.

II. TYPES OF REVIVALS IN AFRICAN CHRISTIANITY

In the course of this broad time frame, five types could be detected:

Type 1: A diviner or religious leader from the traditional context would shift base by appropriating some aspects of Christian symbols and message to create a new synthesis or emergent religious form that could respond to the felt-needs of the community. In seventeenth century Kongo, Kimpa Vita started as an *nganga*, traditional diviner, a member of the *Marinda* secret cult to claim possession by a Christian patron saint, St. Anthony. People perceived her as an *ngunza* or Christian prophetess; but her claims became too messianic for the authorities to suffer and she was executed as a witch. Nxele and Ntsikana achieved an identical status among the Xhosa in the nineteenth century in spite of their differences. Nxele wove a myth that included a God for the whites and another for the blacks, and redefined the massive European migration into the southern hemisphere as a punishment for killing their God's son. He delineated their potential threat to his people and turned his half-digested Christianity into a resistant religion. Ntsikana tried to persuade people to ignore Nxele's militant notions, but to drive in the line of the skid by deploying an evolutionary process that would utilize the Christianity to cure the moral challenges in the primal religion and weave an organized, united community, so as to preserve the race in the face of the incursions of land-grabbing Europeans. Ntsikana's spirituality could be detected in the rich language of his hymns, many of which have been retained in Protestant circles. The political dimensions of religious revivals are clear as both responded to the threat of new white immigrants after 1812. In far-away south-eastern Igboland, Dede Ekeke Lolo retained the tradition at the turn of the century among the riverine Akwete community. But his was more revelatory than political, because soon after his prophetic utterances, Christian missionaries came to the community.

Type 2: A prophet would emerge from the ranks of the Christian tradition, emphasizing the ethical and pneumatic components of the canon to intensify the evangelization of the community or contiguous communities. Sometimes, the tendency was to pose like an Old Testament prophet sporting a luxurious beard, staff, flowing gown and the mixed imagery of the cross. Some would go further by inculturating aspects of traditional religious symbols or ingredients of the culture; yet the diatribe against the indigenous worldview and acceptance of Christian solution would predominate. The examples include Wade Harris, whose ministry started in 1910; Garrick Braide, who operated between 1914 and 1918; Joseph Babalola, who left his employment as a driver in 1928 in West Africa; and Simon Kimbangu, whose ministry lasted through one year, 1921, in the Congo. Each was arrested by the colonial government and jailed: Harris remained under house arrest until his death; Braide died in prison in 1918; Kimbangu's death sentence was commuted to life imprisonment and exile at the intervention of two Baptist missionaries. He died at Elizabethville in 1951. Babalola was released through a plea by some Welsh Apostolic agents.

Type 3: A wave of African indigenous churches arose all over Africa at different times before the First World War, and especially during the influenza epidemic of 1918. Dubbed as *Aladura* in West Africa, *Zionists* in southern Africa and *Abaroho* in eastern Africa, some caused revivals, others did not; but they tended to emerge from mainline churches by recovering the pneumatic resources of the translated Bible. They equally deployed traditional symbols as in the category above. Soon differences appeared based on the dosage of traditional religion in the mix; indeed, some of the nativistic forms operated beyond the pales of Christianity. The sub-typology is as wide as the range and enduring contributions to African Christianity are immense. Equally, its character is complicated, as some are political while others are safe havens for brutalized Africans. It deserves a fuller treatment than is possible here.

Type 4: Sometimes a puritan and fundamentalist expression of Christianity would occur within the boundaries of mainline denominations challenging the regnant affirmations and seeking to enlarge the role of the Holy Spirit within their faith and practices. The hostile responses of the "rulers of the synagogue" would force an exit and foundation of new congregations; others would insist on reforming the denominations from the inside. Thus, some operate as churches or ministries while others remain as movements or sodalities within the main body. The degree of challenge may include doctrine, liturgy, polity and ethics or any permutations. Many attract enough mass support to become revival movements. In many ways, they resemble Type 2, but they reject the traditional cultural ingredients that some in this category utilize. Examples include the Ibibio Revival, which occurred within the Qua Iboe Church in eastern Nigeria in 1927; the Kaimosi revival, which occurred within the Friends Africa Mission/Quakers in western Kenya in 1927; the Balokole revival that swept through Anglican church from 1930 as mentioned earlier; and the Ngouedi revival, which occurred among the Swedish Orebro Mission in 1947 and resulted in the Evangelical Church of Congo (EEC).

Type 5: The contemporary face of Pentecostalism in Africa was catalyzed by charismatic movements, led by young people from mainline churches from the late 1960s in some parts of the continent, but more especially in the 1970s.

As Richard van Dijk puts the case of "Young Born Again Preachers in Post-Independence Malawi":[c]

> During the early 1970s the populace of some of the townships of Malawi's largest city, Blantyre, witnessed the emergence of a new religious phenomenon. Young boys and girls, referring to themselves as *aliki*, preachers, began to attract crowds by conducting large revival meetings. These young people, some of still in their teens, traveled from one place to another, and in fire and brimstone sermons strongly denounced the sinfulness and evils of everyday urban life.

The phenomenon became even more pronounced in the 1980s, in all denominations and most countries. Marshall-Fratani and Corten have collated the interesting case studies of the insurgence in Ghana, the Republic of Benin, Burkina Faso, Ivory Coast and Congo Brazzaville. In each case, it challenged the predominance of either voodoo or Islam, or changed the face of Roman Catholicism. Later, the movements from the different countries linked through the activities of the students' organization, FOCUS, and the migrations of students following foreign language programs. The reflection here would focus on the examples from the colonial period as the precursors of the larger theme of the origins of Pentecostalism in Africa.

In all the types, there is an intense religious experience, a vision, a dream that may issue in prophetic speaking and actions, healing and community building. Some operated as solo prophets whose charisma drew people to a new understanding of the power of the gospel; others formed new faith communities; still others operated as movements with inchoate leadership, but each affected the interior of Christianity just when colonial ideology colluded with missionary control and triumphalism. It is intriguing that most occurred during the period between 1914 and 1950 when missionary control reigned supreme, colonial power and white settlers consolidated, and labor problems and racial exploitation predominated. Did charismatic religiosity provide a survival technique for Africans in the midst of the disquiet of those years? Did the phenomena stamp African Christianity with an identity that gave it both an identifiable character and contested missionary control and its monopoly of Christian expression?

Matters are somewhat complex; precisely because the period was so alive with religious creativity, it is that many religious forms flourished. For instance, the mainline denominations engaged in strong institutional development with schools, hospitals and other charitable institutions; evangelized the hinterland areas, essayed to domesticate Christian values by confronting traditional cultures and in the Kikuyu case triggered off a rebellion that had enormous consequences. Education enabled many people to access newspapers and magazines and connected with Asia and Europe. A number of cultic and esoteric religious organizations advertised their wares in magazines and newspapers. It became the pastime of the literate few to search newspapers and magazines for advertisements and place mail orders for amulets, charms, rings and other cultic paraphernalia from these sources to ensure success in examinations, gain promotion and ensure security in the competitive and enlarged horizon of urbanity. Freemason and Rosicrucian lodges dotted the urban capitals of various countries just as the elite patronized the magazine, *Psychology*. As A.F Walls observes, Islam expanded more in the wake of improved transportation and commercial opportunities created by colonialism than many jihads would have accomplished.[4] Since most of the population still lived in the rural areas, traditional religion predominated in many countries. Thus, the revivalism of the period must be examined with a balanced perspective. The point is that the cumulative effect of these revivals intensified the process of Christianization, catalyzed vertical growth and increasingly stamped a charismatic character on African Christianity.

III. CASE STUDIES OF SOME PROPHETIC AND CHARISMATIC REVIVALS, 1910-1919

This section focuses on some key revival and charismatic movements that occurred between 1910 and 1950. To start with, illustrations from West Africa: Wade Harris and Garrick Braide have received the most scholarly attention, but there were many others such as Peter Anim and Sampson Oppong in the Gold Coast. Certain characteristics distinguished a prophet beyond the beard and emblem, either a cross, staff or a bowl with holy water: a prophet was a charismatic figure; stringently opposed to traditional religion and nominalism. They perceived that the pattern of Christianization merely replaced one culture for another and hardly attacked the core allegiances. It was as if Africans created a periphery where they dialogued with the missionary message, while preserving a core interior or epicenter where traditional allegiances predominated. The prophets focused their ministries on the interior of individual and communal allegiances. Prophets were sometimes precursors of Zionists, exhibiting the same features as praying and healing. But the prophet was imbued with a message, unwilling to found a church but anxious to save through word and miracles. Many were gifted with ability to compose choruses. Researchers have retrieved and translated 173 choruses by Garrick Braide, composed in his native Kalabari language.[5] A simple one that his followers used at the beginning of an outreach simply declared, "*Jesus has come and Satan has run away*." As it was repeated many times, the evangelists would pour holy water on shrines that would burst into flames to the consternation and conversion of votaries. Some were educated and others not; they attacked the symbols of traditional religion and nominal Christianity with the same hostility as missionaries, but demonstrated their engagement with signs and wonders. Their attitude to primal worldview declared a power-encounter scenario. Typically, people acclaimed that Braide was "Elijah II".

Before Braide came on the scene around 1914, Wade Harris itinerated on foot from Liberia into Ivory Coast and Gold Coast in the years between 1910 and 1914, preaching, performing miracles, and creating an enormous growth for both Roman Catholics and Methodists. He, too, composed many choruses.

Churches formed after their ministries. The colonial governments, both British and French hounded each of the prophets into prison, out of fear for an uncontrolled charisma. Braide was imprisoned on false charges in 1915 and died three years later. Strangely, his movement grew after his death. Similarly, Harris was confined to Cape Palmas where many came to visit and enlist his support. Churches grew in his name.

Wade Harris was particularly successful in Ivory Coast precisely because of the pattern of Christian presence in that region. The first mission arrived in the Ivory Coast in 1895. The area came under French authority in 1892. The French subsequently closed English-speaking congregations of the American Episcopal mission. Consequently, the area became predominantly Roman Catholic. The missions had little success despite being supported by the colonial government. The local populations were united in their stand against European imperialism. As the First World War approached the French colonists feared any uprising, including that which might arise within a Christian context. Liberia was under the control of Afro-Americans who had done little to enhance the lives of indigenous peoples. Power in Liberia rested on the tripod of church, Masonic Lodge and True Whig Party. Consequently, missionary zeal remained weak and the indigenous people underdeveloped. Throughout West Africa there was "a mysterious ripeness for conversion."[6] William Wade Harris appeared at this time. Economic factors may also have been a significant catalyst for the growth of prophetic movements as people tried to adjust to the new economic production system, changes in currency, the salary system and domestication of cash-nexus in exchange.

William Wade Harris (c.1865-1929) was a Grebo in Liberia. He became a Christian while he was a student at a Methodist school in Cape Palmas, Liberia. On leaving school he became a seaman before becoming a teacher for ten years in an American Protestant Episcopal Mission School. Harris married Rose Bodock Farr around 1885/1886. He received his call from God in 1910 while serving a prison sentence for participating in an anti-government demonstration. He had challenged Afro-American rule and led a revolt in the hope that British rule would be established. The revolt failed and Harris was imprisoned. During his incarceration, he experienced a vision of the Archangel Gabriel who identified him as a prophet to prepare the way for Christ, and instructed him to abandon his European ways. Following his release he began preaching to his fellow Grebo. He viewed himself in the role of an Old Testament prophet, in the mould of Elijah and John the Baptist, whose mission was to call people to repentance. He adopted a distinctive dress and carried a Bible, a cross, a gourd rattle and a bowl for baptism. In 1913, he moved to the Ivory Coast, and then to the Gold Coast to begin an extremely effective evangelical revival based on prophecy and healing. Christian communities were established and survived where no missionary had ever ventured. An important factor in Harris' success, in addition to his charismatic character, was the immediacy of the message he presented. Change was necessary now and it had to involve absolute commitment.

Throughout his mission among the Dida and Ebrie peoples, Harris challenged traditional religious practices and did not accommodate them to the Christian message. His message focused on the power of God and Christ to conquer traditional spirits and he insisted on the destruction of fetishes. Harris focused on the imminent *parousia* which required a radical life change/conversion. He urged his hearers to follow the Ten Commandments, observe the Lord's Day, avoid adultery, reject idols and accept the authority of the Bible. The baptized were encouraged to join the missionary churches in their area. Harris' authority in baptism caused offence to the missionaries who were the beneficiaries of his prophetism and its results! His forte was the use of songs, especially choruses that he created. Significantly, he did not condemn polygamy and appears to have had several wives. He appreciated the white man's insistence on education and hygiene.

On his return from the Gold Coast he was arrested at Kraffy, Ivory Coast, in 1914, the result of suspicion regarding his power over the people who might revolt during a time of war. He was brutally treated before he was extradited in 1915 and returned to Liberia, where he continued his ministry under house arrest until his death in 1929. He made numerous attempts to return to the Ivory Coast but was always refused entry. Assistants continued the actual ministry. One such was John Swatson, a Methodist, who himself made many converts; another was Helen Valentine. Though he never intended to establish churches, Harrist churches did emerge in a context where there were no established communities. In these situations, Harris appointed twelve apostles to lead each community and pursue his vision. This is true among the Dida people, who had no existing churches they could join and, consequently, the church developed rapidly. In these independent congregations, the gospel was preached, hymns were written and chapels were built—all based on the principles and beliefs Harris had enunciated, but with their own distinctive customs. Some were even integrated into denominational structures at a later time. The Methodist and Roman Catholic churches were beneficiaries of Harris' work. But a Harrist church survived in the Ivory Coast and the Church of the Twelve Apostles was established in the Gold Coast. Subsequently, many prophets emerged who originated from within the Harrist tradition as it spread inland to places where Harris himself never ventured. Although they claim Harris' authority for their practices, they have evolved their own distinctive forms through the "minor prophets" who followed Harris. Their ultimate purpose is clear: "we are here to heal."[7]

Harris, the most successful missionary in West Africa, demonstrates a movement from traditional religion to a form of New Testament Christianity, with himself as a personification of the prophet Elijah who is at the forefront of a messianic breakthrough in West African society. Yet, he remained fully African. Harris demonstrated clear leadership abilities; he lived a simple moderate lifestyle and observed the Lord's Day. Though he avoided forming a personality cult, he was the originator of a people's movement though not a church. His message did not deviate from that of the missionaries, yet he presented himself as an evangelist-catechist-prophet who "represented a new and populist level of African Christian initiative, quite removed from missionary control,"[8] and "an authentic Christian universality, yet one in which diversity—and Africanity in particular—was to be honored."[9]

Just as the vibrant ministry of Harris slowed down, Garrick Sokari Daketima Braide (c. 1885-1918) came on the scene in a different part of West Africa. He was born at Oponoma and grew up at Bakana in the north of the Niger Delta, south-eastern Nigeria. His mother was a Kalabari and his father an Igbo, possibly a slave. In early life he was a fisherman and a tradesman. He became a Christian and was baptized in 1910, becoming a member of St. Andrews Church in the New Calabar district of West Africa in 1912; he was also an evangelist. Gradually, he began to experience dreams and visions, healing powers and prophetic utterances. People flocked to his home and the church. Rev. M.A. Kemmer was quite excited at the increase in membership. Popular opinion pronounced him as the Second Elijah.

When an attempt to gain the due recognition of his ministry from the Niger Delta Pastorate Church (of the Anglican Communion) authorities failed, the majority of the congregation followed him out of the church in 1916. His strong ethical stance against immorality, liquor (especially the gin trade), and idolatry attracted many. He also acted as a judge in judicial cases.[10] So effective was his mission that a commentator observed that never was there "any instance where Garrick Braide consented to pray for any sick person in which prayers failed to be efficacious."[11] A strong belief also came to be held that Braide had power to protect people from malign divinities. While some local chiefs supported him, others colluded with the colonial authorities in signing petitions that alleged that he constituted a health hazard by inviting sick people into the community.

His success was due in large part to the dearth of local preachers in the vernacular. The vernacular Scripture in this region was the Union Ibo, which was hardly understood. His popularity attracted the suspicion of the colonial authorities, especially during the time of war; he was arrested because his followers destroyed some traditional shrines. This was a ruse, though the enthusiasm of his assistants cannot be denied. This cadre included a number of young men: Johannes Danilobo Ngiangia (called "son of the prophet"), Moses Hart (called "servant of the prophet") and Mark Ichie Uranta. Braide died in 1918. Ironically, his movement gained momentum after his death as it rolled into the contiguous Igboland. His followers formed the Christ Army Church that attracted some Ethiopianist leaders of African Native Church movement. J.G. Campbell from Lagos tried to take over the church and this created a split. Later, S.A. Coker was invited from Lagos to serve as the leader of the Christ Army, Garrick Braide Connexion. He brought together various strands that had originated in Braide's movement. This organization still continues to this day.

Robin Horton argues that Braide's movement is a natural development of traditional Kalabari religion and a response to political, cultural and social changes. E.A. Ayandele has suggested that the condemnation of the movement is an example of the collusion between the colonial government and the church; but it betrays the difference between the Ethiopian movement and the new charismatic spirituality that would shape the emergent African Christianity.[12]

IV. REVIVAL AND CHARISMATIC MOVEMENTS IN THE INTER-WAR YEARS

This factor could be further illustrated with a charismatic movement that arose within the missionary church and sought to transform its spirituality. Kevin Ward aptly dubs the ideal of the protagonists as "obedient rebels". Perhaps the most widespread with long-lasting effect was the *Balokole* revival. It started in a Rwandan mission of the Anglicans that was under the supervision of the Anglican mission in Uganda. The background is the socio-political development that occurred after 1893. Uganda entered a new political dispensation as a result of the secular imperial takeover by the British. This gave the ecclesiastical pre-eminence to the Anglicans over the Roman Catholics and Muslims. The church entered into an alliance with the tribal leaders. The Ganda regime identified with new Christian groups and developed into a Christian ruling class that controlled political developments in collaboration with the British administration. By the 1920s, the older chiefs were losing power and authority to the younger generation of emerging leaders, who were well educated and competent in English. It was also a time of a resurgence of traditional religion contesting the early successes of the missionary movement. Many chiefs had abandoned their early commitment and returned to polygamy. Modernity brought with it undesirable trends manifested in a substantial body of nominal Christians. In the Protestant churches, some urged a restoration of the faithfulness of the early church. Indeed, some revivals had occurred in Uganda and Nyasaland (Malawi) in the 1890s, notably under Pilkington who came from the background of the Keswick Conventions, which attacked worldliness and rationalism within the Anglican Church.

The *Balokole* (saved ones, spirit filled) movement originated in Rwanda in 1929 as a result of the mutual confession of the Muganda landowner Simeoni Ntsibambi and Dr. Joe Church, a missionary doctor of the Church Missionary Society (CMS) Ruanda Mission. Ntsibambi's brother, Blasio Kigozi, who was a teacher, brought the revival to Mbarara with the intention of introducing it through the Synod of the Anglican Church in Uganda.This single-minded personal yearning for holiness developed into "one of the most significant Christian movements in eastern Africa".[13] Africans felt that the church was suffering from the stagnation arising out of arid Anglican Church tradition, the patronage of traditional African values by some believers, and the liberal views of modernists among some white teachers. Ntsibambi and Dr. Church were responsible for drawing a large group of Baganda Christians to Gahini in Ruanda where a major manifestation of the Holy Spirit occurred in 1935. This had a positive effect in Uganda especially among the Buganda. Meanwhile, Kigozi, a deacon in the Anglican Church, died in 1936 on his way to the Synod. The movement quickly adopted him as a patron saint since he left a written call for repentance and renewal which so moved the synod that it unleashed a movement for revival that spread as far a field as Kenya, Sudan, and Tanganyika in the 1940s. The movement reached its zenith in the 1950s particularly in Kenya and Tanganyika and became integral to the life of the church. Kigozi was succeeded as leader of the *Balokole* by William Nagenda who although he underwent training for the priesthood became instead a lay evangelist.

This story resembled other traditional Protestant revivals in character, probably due to the influence of the Keswick Conventions and the "Oxford Group". But in an African context it displayed the characteristics of public confession and restitution, singing, dreams, visions, public witnessing, the close bonding of its community life, all night prayer vigils, and a strong missionary impetus which marked it out as a singularly African phenomenon. Its ethos was captured in its hymn *Tutukendereza Yesu, We praise you, Jesus, Jesus the Lamb. Your blood has cleansed me. I am grateful, Savior.* The blood of Christ was a key symbol of the *Balokole*. This movement was the source of growth in the Church Missionary Society. Its lay power contested the primacy of the clerical office; its fervency challenged the lukewarm faith of the members; it provided a corps of new enthusiastic leaders. Its gender ideology allowed women a significant role in itinerant evangelism. It represented a certain "piety which rejected social and economic action as irrelevant apart from conversion."[14] This spirituality supported the adherents during the turmoil of the Mau Mau resistance in Kenya. It was the bedrock of the modern phase of Pentecostal/charismatic movements. By the late 1940s, Kenyan evangelists such as Festos Kivengere spread it throughout central Tanzania.

While it was both a challenge to the symbiotic relationship between church and world, the *Balokole* revival was also a source of spiritual renewal, commitment, uncompromising truthfulness and moral integrity. Some of the church leadership perceived it as an elitist movement that indulged in self-righteousness and self-satisfaction and manifested exclusivist tendencies. They alleged that the young ardent men would hop and dance but despise those who had not been revived. They rejected certain cultural ingredients such as eating coffee-beans, groundnuts, using ornaments or spears. They soon started to have their own services and despised their former friends saying: "you have not yet been saved." In that way they refused to obey those missionaries and pastors who rejected the operation of the spirit; they listened only to their own elected leadership.[15] They organized massive revival conferences, with attendances ranging between 3,000 and 30,000. Largely unstructured in organization, informal and spontaneous in practice, there was the possibility of schism which was largely kept in check by its leader William Nagenda, Ntsibambi's brother in law, and the extremely tolerant Anglican bishop C.E. Stuart, as well as by the innate sense of authority of the Baganda. A threatened secession was averted in 1941 when twenty six *Balokole* ministerial students were expelled from Bishop Tucker Memorial College at Mukono, which was renowned for its "modernist" and "ritualistic" leanings.

The *Balokole* were labeled as "rebels" as a result of their fervent early morning prayer and preaching meetings. On their own part, they would retort that "the real issue is whether or not people will face the full preaching of the Cross and all it means in the life of full surrender."[16] The matter focused on whether or not the *Balokole* could find a place within the institution of the church, or whether they needed the freedom to operate beyond its confines. Most chose to work within the structures of the church though they did not proceed to ordination. Only eight out of twenty three "rebels" were ordained.

However, division did ensue when Ishmael Noo formed a small church in 1948 based on the principle of free love. In 1958, another schism occurred in the Kenyan church, leading to the establishment of the Church of Christ in Africa by Mathew Ajuoga, consisting of *Johera* (people of love). It does appear that the movement's ethics hardened as the leadership imposed a stricter discipline than that favored by the missionaries; it developed a tendency to marginalize those believers who could not identify with their experience, and taunted those who did not demonize traditional African values. Later, the more ardent members split to form the Holy Trinity Church in Africa. Sometimes the uncontrollable wind of the Spirit produced internal strife amongst the *Balokole*; some healed while others festered. For instance, in the 1960s some alleged that there was a growing spirit of conformity to the world, and a need for the emergence of a reawakening of the revival among the *Bazukufu*. By 1971 a split could no longer be avoided. Yet, through all of these, there remained an indomitable spirit of loyalty to the Church of Uganda, except in 1984 when some "trumpeters" initiated an attempt to form a new church, The Chosen Evangelical Revival. In Kenya, the story was slightly dissimilar because young students in the Scripture Union and Christian Union felt that the *Balokole* had become too rigid; they sought the breath of a more liberating spirit, and this soon occurred in the prayer retreat camps, and ushered the contemporary charismatic movement.

Under the rule of Idi Amin, the maintenance of an ethic of absolute truthfulness became nigh impossible and the movement went underground. The political situation put pressure on an individualistic ethic in a context that cried out for social engagement. By the time the situation normalized in the 1980s under President Museveni, other churches of a more Pentecostal disposition, as well as other traditions, had emerged which took over much of the impetus of the revival. It is interesting to note that new missionary groups must show a commitment to development as well as evangelism if they are to be allowed to work in Uganda. But the front of the movement had moved into Kenya where it continued to expand into rural communities.

The *Balokole* movement encouraged the principles of the three-self movement (to become self-propagating, self-supporting and self-governing) along with a strong sense of freedom and self-expression. Its lay emphasis facilitated the crossing of barriers—racial, tribal, gender and denominational—and evidenced an anti-hierarchical tendency. For the most part, it remained within the established churches although it displayed separatist tendencies. It was largely apolitical. It provided leadership within the Anglican Church for subsequent generations, including Archbishop Janani Luwum and Bishop Festos Kivengere.

The revival profoundly challenged the assumptions of European superiority in the Church and opened the way for a recovery of African responsibility and leadership. The miraculous element in this revolt against paternalism is the spirit of love and loyalty with which it was permeated and the fact that the issue on which the movement had taken a confessional stand, even to the point of martyrdom, has been the refusal to break fellowship with their white brethren.[17] Unlike the other case studies where "the prophetic witness loomed large in the midst of a people whose world was falling apart,"[18] or where the significant trend was not so much the trek of the prophets to the royal kraal as the pilgrimage of the chiefs to the prophet's temple,[19] this case study had less political import. Generally, prophets and prophetic movements emerged in a context of social, cultural economic and political upheaval. They often filled a vacuum and in periods of existential crisis formed the religious initiative of Africans in periods of transition and provided a vital role in the transitional phase. A significant part of their appeal was the immediacy of the prophets' message in such times promising relief and providing hope.

The prophets that emerged in times of social convulsion were marked by several features. For the most part they were marginalized characters, outsiders who experienced a call to challenge people and to adopt a new lifestyle. Nxele came from farm laboring stock; Ntsikana was marginalized through his exposure to mission influence; Shembe came from the borders of Zululand. All experienced prophetic visions prior to identifying their call to prophecy or their recognition prophetic ministry. Their careers were often of short duration though they often achieved a great deal by engaging in itinerant ministries, going to where the people are. Each prophet operated independently of white missionary control and achieved a greater response than the mission churches. Yet, it is true to say that in West Africa, at least, mass conversion depended on the prior existence of Christian communities. In each case there was a determined attempt to integrate Christian teaching in a traditional religious context to form a truly indigenous expression of Christianity, "an integration of African experience and biblical spirituality."[20] In this process they had the courage to challenge both African tradition and mission Christianity. The theology was down-to-earth in response to people's needs.

In varying degrees each manifested a form of messianic status, sometimes assumed by the prophet and sometimes attributed to him by others, and each displayed features of "iconic leadership" sometimes by the adoption of the role of tribal chief or a role similar to it. To a lesser extent this was also true of Nxele and Ntsikana and others. Their popularity confirmed the sense of inner calling. In each case, the prophet demonstrated a charisma and authority that could not be contained by missionary Christianity and was perceived as schismatic or anti-missionary. The concept of resurrection was taken over by prophets. It was believed that Shembe rose from the dead and Nxele predicted his rising again. Apart from Shembe, none formed a church possibly because they saw the dangers of formal organization that led to institutionalization. Shembe himself had functioned as a charismatic prophet before the routinization process. However, for the most part, the prophets rather encouraged their adherents, as did Harris and Braide, to identify with existing churches. Yet, churches and para-church movements did emerge perhaps resulting from the need to perpetuate the tradition established by the prophet. Where there was a degree of institutionalization, leadership had a tendency to be hereditary; always prone to schism.

Significant aspects of these movements included the development of holy places, new music, dance and distinctive forms of dress and the bearing of symbolic artifacts, such as staffs and gourds, as with Harris and Nxele. Worship focused on these and healing, visions and revelations were integral components of prophetic lifestyle. In all cases the Bible occupied an important role to a greater or lesser extent, implying that prophetic Christianity was "at least implicitly literate."[21] Holy places were important as venues for pilgrimage, healing and corporate worship, especially those focusing on healing. They are literally the centers of the movement and often the burial place of its founder. The prophetic and revival movements encouraged the development of lay leadership giving women equal status with men.

The prophetic and revival movements were catalysts of change in society and they altered the image of African response. Rather than produce black clones of white missionaries, they developed a distinctive and enthusiastic form of African Christianity. The effect of this was to completely reshape the religious scene. Often the beneficiaries were the established mission churches—the Roman Catholics and Methodists in West Africa and the Church Missionary Society (Anglican) in East Africa. Yet, the mission churches wanted to control the speed and nature of growth in an attempt to ensure the "purity" of the converts in terms of intellectual understanding of the faith, commitment and discipline. Consequently, they resisted the rapid expansion that the prophetic movements instigated.

The prophetic and revival movements in the African continent were a necessary and vital indigenous response to the incursion of white colonization and missionary enterprise. They made an impact on the social, political and economic contexts in which they functioned both in terms of the growing nationalism and ecumenism of the periods in which they emerged. They were responding to the Enlightenment missionary paradigm by introducing elements of their own particular world-views in a way that demonstrated a resonance and continuity with their traditional religious faith.

V. OTHER CHARISMATIC MOVEMENTS IN THE INTER-WAR YEARS

In a different stroke, many charismatic-type Christian groups in Africa linked with international evangelical or Pentecostal denominations because they needed the white support to survive in a hostile colonial terrain where the mission-churches deployed civil powers to persecute indigenous initiative. For instance, in West Africa, some indigenous Christians had contacted the Faith Tabernacle and used their literature, *Sword of the Spirit,* but since the latter did mission only through the Post Office, the Faith people turned to the Bradford Apostolic Church. After a reconnaissance trip in 1931 to the Gold Coast and Nigeria by a delegation comprising of Daniel Powell Williams, his brother, William Jones Williams and Andrew Turnbull, the church sent Pastor George Perfect and Idris Vaughan in 1932 to Nigeria and James McKeown to the Gold Coast in 1937. Later on a split occurred, because the Africans held firmly against using medicine while the white missionaries were driven by malaria to compromise. The Africans carved out Christ Apostolic Church while the whites moved into new areas and continued to spread the Apostolic brand. The Faith Tabernacle and Apostolic Church contacts flowed into early Pentecostalism by the late 1930s.

Christ Apostolic Church grew tremendously, because in 1928 a payload driver, Joseph Babalola, had a clear vision that he should preach and heal. He abandoned his employment in the Public Works Department in Nigeria and soon became a revivalist preacher. He set the western regions by the ears. Meanwhile, in eastern Nigeria, some Faith Tabernacle people spoke in tongues, were kicked out, founded Church of Jesus Christ in 1934, and invited the Assemblies of God, who quickly sent Rev. W.L. Shirer and his wife to take them over in 1939. The AOG had started a rural ministry in Sierra Leone in 1914, Burkina Faso in 1920, and entered the northern region of Dahomey (now the Republic of Benin) in 1947. It should be added that before denominational brands of Pentecostalism, a number of Pentecostal individual missionaries tried between 1906 and 1912 to establish in various parts of Africa especially western Kenya, Liberia and South Africa. Thus, Classical Pentecostals as well as indigenous ones emerged early in the religious landscape. A similar pattern occurred in many parts of the continent.[22] The intriguing aspect is that their presence did not cause a revival but supplied a tradition of charismatic spirituality in the African religious landscape.

Equally intriguing is a different cycle of charismatic revivals that occurred within mission churches that were open for the move of the spirit, between 1925 and 1947: in 1927, for instance, the Qua Iboe Mission among the Ibibio people of south-eastern Nigeria enjoyed an outbreak of spiritual outpouring during a weekend retreat of church workers. Samuel Bill started the QIM in the nineteenth century from Wales. His parents were adepts of the Welsh Revival. His ministry, therefore, continued a strong public, tent evangelism and church planting. By 1928, the mission felt that it was losing control and virtually instigated the District Officer to intervene and suppress the spiritual overflow among the indigenous believers.

Similarly, a revival occurred among the Quakers in Kaimosi in western Kenya in the same year, sporting public confessions, fasting, vigils and spiritual emotionalism. Western Province of Kenya was called North Karirondo in the nineteenth century when the British government staked its presence. It was an important link between the Kenyan coast and the new protectorate of Uganda. Missionaries surged into the area aided by the completion of the railroad between the coast and Kisumu in 1901. They delimited areas of operation. By 1920 at least six groups had consolidated: Mill Hill Mission (MHM), Church Missionary Society (CMS), South African Compounds and Interior Mission (SACIM), Church of God Mission (CGM), Apostolic Faith Mission of Iowa (AFM), and the Friends Africa Mission (FAM, Quakers). But during the inter war years, the Africans seethed with resentment and under pressure from taxation, forced labor and administrative restructuring that imposed chiefs on communities compelled to supply the labor for white plantations. Many former white soldiers were rewarded with large acreages of farm land. African discomfort could be gauged in the formation of North Karirondo Taxpayers' Association among the CMS in 1924, and in the North Karirondo Central Association organized among the Quakers in 1932. Yet missions thrived as the Africans wanted education.

Within this assortment of missions, two were outstanding in their charismatic religiosity: the AFM, which allied with Pentecostal Assemblies of Canada (PAOC), and the FAM (Quakers). The FAM had been deeply imbued by the wave of nineteenth century evangelical revivals and the Pentecostalism of the new century. However, they avoided ecstatic dimensions of charismatic spirituality. FAM was established in Kaimosi in 1902 and led by Willis Hotchkiss, Edgar T. Hole and Arthur Chilson. The choice of location was determined by availability of land, good climate and luxuriant forest for the sawmills. They engaged in industrial, medical, educational and evangelistic ministries. Progress was slow; so, they turned increasingly to indigenous personnel for assistance and thereby bred a cadre of capable evangelists who imbibed the puritan version of Quaker spirituality. Moreover, the Bible had been translated into the vernacular, *Oluluyia*, in 1925. FAM occasionally organized leadership training retreats for workers and this became the context for the 1927 Revival.

Arthur Chilson and his wife Edna came to Malava, another FAM station, in 1918. He was appreciated by the people as a very practical man who initiated road and bridge projects. He was also an electrifying preacher. In 1926, the couple moved to Kaimosi station to deputize for Ford, who was on furlough in America. The Chilsons usually prayed with the Otto Kellers, who took over the Pentecostal Nyag'ori mission station of the AFM from Clyde Miller. Chilson involved some indigenous people in praying and preparing for the 1927 annual conference. For that leadership conference, four other missionaries and some African teachers from adjacent centers converged on Kaimosi. Chilson shared from Acts 2:1-4 and Romans 10:9-13 and as he prayed, the Holy Spirit fell on the audience. Some cried, shook, fell down and spoke in tongues while others confessed their sins publicly. Participants spread the new spirituality with great effect throughout the surrounding regions.

In January 1928, Ford returned to find a new dispensation as the young people insisted upon tongues, public confession, prophecy, exorcism, night vigils with loud wailing prayers as mandatory components of the liturgy. They were nicknamed, *abandu wa rohi/abarohi (people of the spirit)* or simply as *abakambuli (people who publicly confessed their sins).* When the elders could not restrain them, they were forced out in 1932 and formed The African Church of the Holy Spirit, which has blossomed and successfully challenged the AFM in western Kenyan villages. In due course, they developed new ritual and liturgical practices. With their vigorous evangelism, they attracted the repressive attention of the colonial government until they registered as an independent body in 1957.[23] Coincidentally, it was the same period, 1930s, that witnessed the explosion of the *Balokole* and it resembled the Jamaa movement among the Catholics of the Congo. Noticeable is that a movement that started under the white missionaries was appropriated by African youth and reinvented into an enduring and new pattern. This became even more glaring in the Buana Kibongi's career and contribution to the *ngunza* movement in Brazzaville.

The Congo region was suffused with prophetic or *ngunza* movements. After Simon Kimbangu was deported to Elizabethville in 1921, where he died in 1952, other prophets claimed to be imbued by his spirit in very vibrant political rebellion against the colonial authorities. For instance, Andre Matswa formed the Association of Congolese in Paris and returned as a religious messiah before his arrest and deportation. But the revival that endured through the years in Congo Brazzaville was led by Raymond Buana Kibongi from 1947. It started among the Swedish Mission Covenant Church during a leadership retreat. The Swedish mission had two major centers at Kimpese in Belgian Congo and the Pastoral Seminary and Evangelical School at Ngouedi, situated 300 kilometers west of Brazzaville and just south of Loutete. In 1946, the Swedes engaged in soul searching because though the missionary work was progressing, there was a strong feeling that the horizontal impact on the moral lives of their people was low in the two Congolese states. As usual, the missionaries prayed for a revival. Then, on 19th January, 1947, during the celebration of the Bible Society day, something broke loose among the students of the school. Efraim Anderson, who witnessed the event, reports that John Magnusson, the Secretary of the mission, preached on John 3:16. After the sermon, there was an invitation for prayers and Raymond Buana Kibongi started to pray. Kibongi was a student and was the most affected when the spirit fell on the group. According to Carl Sundberg:[x]

> He prayed for the missionaries and for the seminary at Ngouedi, which is 'rotting in sin'. During the prayer, he became more and more excited and started shaking, as in ecstasy crying from his heart, 'Jesus, make me your servant, Jesus, Jesus, calm me down, calm me down', whereupon he sank on the bench exhausted.

The course of the revival took different forms: people confessed their "kintantu", envy or hatred and poor relationships across racial lines and changed dramatically. Others realized their Christian dullness and the level of church attendance and poor prayer lives in the school and warmed up. Still for others, a certain fire came on them. It was known as "the ecstasy of the cross". It gripped people as if they touched by the suffering of Christ. Some felt pains in their hands as if pierced by nails; others like Kibongi, would stretch out stiff on the ground. The movement spread as other ngunza adepts thronged to the site. Students spread it all over Belgian Congo and as it spread into the hinterlands east of Brazzaville, villages became reconciled under the power of God. As Buana would say, "just as hard iron can only melt in fire, so the black man's stone heart can only be melted in the all consuming fire of the ecstasy."[25]

He grew to leadership heights and turned the church into the Evangelical Church of the Congo. He succeeded because his vision was the unity of whites and blacks, an ecumenical vision for all churches in Brazzaville and because the Swedish were already open to pietistic tradition. He was such a peacemaker and proponent of reconciliation in a violent society that he took the initiative in 1970 that led to the formation of the Congo Conseil Oecumenic des Eglises Chretiennes au Congo. He was the first leader. His longevity till 1998 ensured that he provided long years of leadership and theological articulation. Unlike many others, Kibongi spoke in impeccable French and was rooted in the Scriptures, even though his church sports some ingredients like holy writing—when the spirit would move people's hands to write messages. He was a musical person. His influence remained so strong that contemporary Pentecostal churches in Brazzaville do not refer to themselves by that name but are called revival movements.

VI. YOUTHFUL CHARISMATIC MOVEMENTS IN THE 1970S

In the post-independece period, another cycle of revival swept through the continent, bringing with it a religious tradition whose face has changed drastically in every decade and whose full import is still in the making. This is illustrated with a brief sketch of the rise of charismatic movements in Nigeria between 1967 and 1975. It is argued that this form of pneumatic response to the gospel was a "setting to work" of missionary preaching, a recovery of the old Evangelical spirit which had catalyzed mission, a seepage to the surface of the type of Christianity which Africans wanted and their perception of the opportunities unleashed by decolonization. A Spiritual Revival swept through Nigeria from 1970 and created a phenomenon that is now known as the Pentecostal Movement. It has acquired various hues and become complex, but its origin was a wave of charismatic movements among the youth of various denominations that occurred in different parts of the country and eddied into churches, challenging the parent groups for power failure. The charismatic goals were both to re-evangelize the mainline churches as well as to win new souls for the kingdom. Evangelism and passion for the kingdom remained central to whatever followed.

To put matters in perspective, Nigeria witnessed a number of charismatic stirrings between 1914 and 1975: first, the scattered flares of 1914-1939, which were not part of the Aladura movement ending with the Christ Apostolic Church; second, the specifically Aladura movements; and third, the 1970 phenomenon. It is possible to weave connections between the three. In this book, an effort has been made to show the differences. Another key issue is the force of externality: to what extent were these indigenous? The cumulative effects of these movements changed the face of Christianity in Nigeria. More cogent is that they typify a phenomenon that occurred in most parts of Africa in the same time frame. This phenomenon became significant after political independence and during the long process of decolonizing African churches; yet it had little to do with the nationalist ideology that suffused the politics of independence. They derailed the path of decolonization of the churches by reshaping the religious landscape along charismatic lines and away from the indigenization strategies of the mission churches.

There were six components to this phenomenon: the Hour of Redemption ministry, which operated in Lagos before the Civil War broke out; the Benson Idahosa ministry, which was just gathering momentum in Benin when the Civil War started; the radicalization of the Scripture Union in eastern Nigeria, 1967-1975; the Hour of Freedom ministry, which started in the midst of the Civil War in 1969 and held sway in the East in the immediate aftermath; the charismatism of the Christian Union in the Universities of the south-western Nigeria; the phenomenon of "Corpers as Preachers" as the Christian University students invaded northern Nigeria while serving in the National Youth Service Corps (NYSC); and the special case of charismatism in the Roman Catholic Church. All these soon webbed together before divisions emerged—when many shifted from operating as fellowships to establish churches. Perhaps we can use the Scripture Union as the mascot or signifier to reconstruct the spiritual temper of the times and to demonstrate how the various groups co-operated in the heat of charismatism.

SU, as it is called, was introduced into Protestant Secondary Schools from Britain in the 1950s. It was one of those interdenominational groups that focused on Bible study, prayers, choruses and hospital visits and served as the character formation component of mission education. Occasionally, the senior friend, a missionary teacher would invite the young students for tea and biscuits. While he tried to make conversation, the students would be more concerned with drinking the tea "properly". It was an innocuous body until the Civil War broke out in 1967. Schools closed. A new Traveling Secretary, Bill Roberts, had just arrived from Britain. Instead of heading home, he decided to hold systematic Bible classes for the students around SU House in Umuahia. It soon turned into a prayer group, engaging in deep conversion, deliverance, evangelism and relief work. It spread like wild fire as young people formed prayer and evangelistic bands in their villages. By 1969, the character of the SU had changed tremendously as people gave their lives to Christ in large numbers, and healing occurred during many hospital visits. To illustrate the temper, Bill tells the story about young men in a village outside Umuahia who refused to participate in a communal oath-taking. Threats from parents, elders, traditional priests and even some church members failed. Instead they retreated to pray against the deity. On the day of the oath, a quarrel broke out among the elders and the ceremony could not be held. The gauntlet to the compromising ethics of the mission church was obvious as the village was enveloped by a new spirituality. A number of university students also participated in the charismatic activities.

The religious landscape during the civil war situation is an important backdrop. It took many forms: there was a cultural renaissance and with scarcity of money and native doctors, the old ways of resolving problems resurfaced. Occult groups also flourished because dire times needed quick solutions. The Aladura, which had not been very successful in certain parts of the country because of the strength of mission churches, now proliferated as prayer houses in the hinterland at the heels of fleeing refugees. The mission churches had quite a competition because their organized structures could not be maintained. Priests and nuns ran for safety having lost their congregations. British support for Nigeria surprised and angered many who thought that "Christian" England would know that the Easterners were the most Christianized in Nigeria. Many turned to the prayer houses to deal with the inner and physical needs of the war condition. So, the cutting edge of Christianity shifted to the prayer houses and young radicalized SU boys and girls, ranging in age from 17 to 25 years.

Just before Bill Roberts left Biafra, he came into contact with three lads who had been members of the Cherubim and Seraphim movement and later joined a more potent prayer house at Ufuma. They had risen to high offices variously as "visioner", "cross bearer" and "clairaudient"—who had ability to hear from the unseen world. They were groomed in the Book of Mars, Sixth and Seventh Books of Moses, Springfield Books and other mystic books. Through Bill Roberts, they became converted, renounced their dealings in candles and occult and went back to preach Christ to other votaries of prayer houses. Of course, the prophetess at Ufuma chased them out of town. Penniless, Stephen Okafor, Raphael Okafor and Arthur Orizu formed The Hour of Freedom Evangelistic Association (coined from the core message). The civil war ended in 1970. Based in Onitsha, they itinerated all over the East with a vibrant evangelical fervor. They built a support network of prayer groups as many young people flocked to the outreach programs. Some SU students joined them, others opposed them for preaching against prayer houses, because many SU young people patronized prayer houses for power and thought that they could combine both. During 1970-1971, it was as if a revival hit Igboland, the Freedom Hour became famous as healings and mass conversions occurred in town after town. Other groups formed in towns such as Enugu, Owerri, Aba and more. Many of these 17-18 year old boys and girls boldly took their mission to their own villages. Their ministry caused splits in many AICs over the use of means. For instance, the Christ Ascension Church splintered. Mike Okonkwo led a wing into a charismatic body, the True Redeemed Evangelical Mission. As schools re-opened, these young people returned to their Secondary Schools to form vibrant Scripture Union branches. Those who went to universities built evangelical Christian Union camps as formidable interdenominational evangelistic groups.

Just at this time, Benson Idahosa, who was converted in the early 1960s by an Assemblies of God leader in Benin, built up a vibrant ministry with the aid of his former pastor and a Welsh missionary, Pa G. Elton, who had come to Nigeria in 1954 under the Apostolic Church. He retired but stayed back to minister in the country. Elton put Idahosa in touch with Gordon and Freda Lindsay, who sponsored him to attend Christ For The Nations Bible Institute, Dallas. That was after the Gordons saw how the new ministry had grown and the intense energy of the young man who had "fire in his bones" for soul-winning. He later formed the Church of God Mission. By 1970 his theology was developing some of the themes from T.L. Osborn as he waxed strong with prosperity motifs which sounded like music in the ears of those who had just come out from the war and witnessed the growth of his huge Miracle Centre, Television ministry, All Nations for Christ Bible School and the effective musical group called "Redemption Voices". The leaders of Hour of Deliverance (Oye, Muyiwa, J.M.J. Emesin) from Lagos, Pa G. Elton of the Apostolic Church, Emma Harris, a Baptist missionary and a few other older charismatic leaders provided advice and encouragement as a youth-led religious revival enveloped Nigeria. These soon networked, with a different insurgence that occurred in western Nigeria among the students of the Universities of Ibadan and Ife—when members of the Christian Union started to speak in tongues during their Tuesday Prayer meetings and later organized National Conventions to arouse other Universities. The "CU" as they are known, broke away in 1962 from the Student Christian Movement (SCM) for being spiritually and ethically tepid. As this was happening, Pa Elton who lived at Ilesha turned his attention to foster charismatic spirituality in the universities and to cure the disunity among the SU boys who hurried to found their individual ministries. He urged them to lay down their signboards and partake in retreats. At one such retreat, they jointly formed the Grace of God Mission, saying that it was by the grace of God that they could detect the sinfulness of their rivalry.

These young people graduated just when the National Youth Service Corps was made compulsory. As they dispersed through the nation, they formed charismatic groups; those who traveled abroad for foreign language courses in neighboring French-speaking countries took their spirituality with them. Those who attended the Fellowship of Christian Union of Students (FOCUS) took the message to Kenya. In northern Nigeria they not only formed branches in Ahmadu Bello University and Kaduna Polytechnic, but took over the Traveling Secretary posts in such organizations as Fellowship of Christian Students, New Life for All, and Nigerian Fellowship of Evangelical Students. A central body, Christian Youth Corpers was constituted in 1973 to mobilize the dizzy evangelical enterprises. Some of the Southern youths, who had not gone through

Universities but drank their charismatic spirituality in secondary schools, surged through the North founding ministries just at the time when many southerners were returning to the North after the Civil War. About ten ministries blossomed in Jos, Kaduna, Kano and Zaria between 1973 and 1976. Northern indigenes have since joined the affray.

Raphael Okafor meticulously kept a diary of their activities and this section relies mainly on the entries. One entry is intriguing:

> 28th March 1971: Enu Onitsha campaign continues. Emmanuel Church authorities refused their church compound again. We moved to the Anglican Girls School, Inland town, Onitsha and began around 5.00pm. People still attended despite the disruptions. Michaelson gave his testimony. Brother Stephen preached while brother Arthur interpreted. Emmanuel Ekpunobi who said the opening prayers also prayed for the converts and later gave them additional instructions ... TO GOD BE THE GLORY.

Diary entries are often cryptic; so, certain aspects need comment: the impact on mission churches and their responses, the gender factor, the impact on the entire religious landscape including occult groups, the relationship of literacy, Bible and revival and the further radicalization of the SU as they worked in agreement with the Hour of Freedom. There are other ironies: mission schools that were created as means of evangelization now fulfilled the goal to the chagrin of proprietors; school children, on the fringes of mission power structures, created a challenge which was more radical than anything the missionaries anticipated. The youth, both in secondary and tertiary institutions, created a new situation where the leadership would be educated unlike in the earlier pneumatic challenges by the Zionists and Aladura.

First, the opposition of some mission churches: the responses of the missions varied. The Roman Catholic Church was initially hostile, defrocking two priests who succored the charismatic spirituality in the hurry to rebuild after the war. The gale of the wind proved irresistible and as they were already concerned about the impact of the prayer houses, which intensified during the war, Dr Arinze, the Archbishop of Onitsha appointed Fr. Ikeobi to start a charismatic service in Onitsha using Catholic liturgy which included healing and exorcism. Later on, Fr. Edeh returned from the USA to begin a Healing Centre at Elele near Port-Harcourt. Something else happened: in 1974, the Dominicans at Ibadan sponsored the visit of a charismatic team from USA led by Fr. Francis F. MacNutt to tour Nigeria. MacNutt claimed much success. Though Archbishop Arinze allowed them to operate in his domain and it was rumored that his mother was healed, the priests treated the team with much suspicion because of imbibed pattern of ministerial formation, but the lay people lapped up the opportunity and the import of the challenge was not lost on the rulers of the synagogue who had to ensure that their flock would not drift away. These are aspects of the origin of Catholic charismatic movement. The Anglicans were friendly while some churches were downright hostile. For instance, at Enugu, the Presbyterians rejected the application of the Scripture Union youth to use St. Andrew's Church hall. In Ohafia, a Presbyterian session drove the SU members away; they formed Evangel Church, which now competes successfully with the Presbyterian Church. By 1975, a new realism took over as mission churches embraced charismatic spirituality such as prayer vigils, fasting, tithing, the use of choruses, evangelistic tours and land deliverance. These have now become regular features of mission churches.

The second factor is the gender issue raised by the patronage of the School Principal, Madam Erinne. Many girls flocked to the SU and Hour of Freedom, and parents felt better that their girls were engaged in safe activities. Conflict occurred in cases where the parents' churches opposed the new spirituality. Older women patronized the youthful, healing ministries and served as "Mothers In Israel". Another diary entry by Okafor spells this out:

> 17th May 1971 Three of us, Arthur, Stephen and I, as well as Mrs. D. Erinne, met bishop L.M. Uzodike and we had a very good discussion for about one hour and later he prayed for us, Lawjua and others on 'Wisdom, Love and Power'.

This Anglican bishop remained a patron for many decades. The girl, Lawjua, was eighteen years old and in Secondary School. Her maternal grandfather brought Anglicanism to Obosi; she and her siblings were fully involved in radicalizing the church that their grandfather brought with the mother's support and resources. She is typical of the activism of girls who led in the music ministry and preaching. The enlarged role became increasingly significant. This cryptic account does little justice to what happened, but highlights how the youth posed as a subversive force to the mission churches within the era of decolonization. Around North-West Igboland alone, over fifty charismatic groups formed between 1974 and 1989. The young people evangelized Africa with a home-grown spirituality which was beyond mere adaptation.

The impact was to challenge the mission churches to either allow the young people more roles in the churches, permit charismatic activities, or risk the exodus of young people and women to Pentecostal fellowships. Initially the young evangelists stayed in their churches to share fellowship, but later, some founded churches variously specializing in evangelism, deliverance,healing camps, Child evangelism, Bible distribution, or intercession while a few functioned as ecumenical fellowships. Most secondary schools and all universities have charismatic fellowships comprising of young people in various denominations. [26]

Finally, this is another example of the cycles of charismatic revivals that became a part of African Christianity, right from the days of Vita Kimpa. Each cycle moved the church forward in a new direction, stamping it with a new character, betraying a certain sense of continuity with the traditional past, and embedding African Christianity into the deep structure of all African traditional religions in spite of varieties of names and symbols. Charismatism has been the strongest instrument of church growth in Africa since the 1970s. Outside the case study area, youths were most prominent in creating this form of challenge in Zambia, Malawi, Ghana, Tanzania, Liberia, Kenya, Ivory Coast, Uganda and more. This cameo also provides us with a glimpse into the birth of born-again people who are holding the cutting edge and have been catalysts in transforming the face of contemporary African Christianity.

In conclusion, the core argument in this chapter is that the prophetic movement, revivals and other forms of charismatic religiosity were appropriated by Africans to establish a charismatic spirituality that would define African response to the gospel: at once conservative, evangelical, with emphasis on the centrality of the Bible, interpreted without Western intellectual gymnastics, but with simplicity and immediacy. It is a Christianity with a vibrant liturgy with songs, music, and dance; its theology was embedded in orality thereby eschewing arid philosophy; it was under indigenous leadership, addressed problems raised within the interior of the primal worldviews, and emphasized miracles, vision, dreams and healing.

Notes

1. Efraim ANDERSON, *Messianic Popular Movements in the Lower Congo*, Studia Ethnographica Upsaliensa (Uppsala: Almqvist & Wiksell, 1958), 101; Carl SUNDBERG, "Conversion and Contextual Conceptions of Christ", in *Studia Missionalia Svecana*, LXXX, 1 (2000) 133.
2. In Richard ELPHICK & Rodney DAVENPORT (eds), *Christianity in South Africa* (Oxford: James Currey, 1997), 68.
3. In Paul GIFFORD (ed.), *New Dimensions in African Christianity* (Nairobi: AACC, 1992), 55; Andre CORTEN & Ruth MARSHALL-FRATANI (eds), *Between Babel and Pentecost: Transnational Pentecostalism in Africa and Latin America* (Bloomington: Indiana University Press, 2001).
4. Andrew F. WALLS, *The Cross-cultural Process in Christian History* (Maryknoll, NY: Orbis Books, 2002):135-154.
5. G.O.M. TASIE, *Thoughts and Voices of An African Church: Christ Army Church, Nigeria* (Jos: Connack Nigeria Ltd, 1997).
6. A. HASTINGS, *The Church in Africa, 1450-1950* (Oxford: Clarendon, 1994), 449.
7. C.G. BAETA, *Prophetism in Ghana* (London: SCM, 1962), 15.
8. HASTINGS, *The Church in Africa*, 489.
9. D. SHANK, "The Prophet Harris: A Historiographical and Bibliographical Survey", in *Journal of Religion in Africa,* 14,2 (1983) 147, n.1.
10. This caused him to clash with the colonial authorities because his approach struck at the heart of the economy as the result of declining revenue from taxes on liquor and unemployment in the courts resulting from his judicial activities.
11. M.A. KEMMER, *Niger Delta Chronicle* (1909) cit. in L. LUGWUANA, "Medicine, Spiritual Healing and African Response", in *Africa Theological Journal,* 23,1 (2000), 27.

12. See Frieder LUDWIG, "Radicalisation and Consolidation of the Garrick Braide Movement, 1915-1918", in *Journal of Religion in Africa*, 22, 4 (1993), 298, 315.
13. Kevin WARD, "'Obedient Rebels' – The Relationship Between the Early "balokole" and the Church of Uganda: The Mukono Crisis of 1941", in *Journal of Religion in Africa, 19*, 3, (1989), 194.
14. F.B. WELBOURN, *East African Rebels: A Study of Some Independent Churches* (London: SCM, 1961), 133.
15. Comment of old Kajero in Buhaya quoted in A. HASTINGS, *A History of African Christianity: 1950-1975* (London: Cambridge University Press, 1979), 53.
16. Dr Church in WARD, "Obedient Rebels", 209.
17. J.V. TAYLOR, "Process of growth in an African Church", IMC Research Pamphlets 6, SCM, 1958, 15ff., in WELBOURN, *East African Rebels*, 9.
18. L. SWITZER, *Power and Resistance in an African Society: the Ciskei Xhosa and the Making of South Africa* (Madison, Wis: University of Wisconsin Press, 1993), 67.
19. B.G.M. SUNDKLER, *Bantu Prophets in South Africa* (Oxford: Oxford University Press, 1961), 312.
20. A. HASTINGS, *A History of African Christianity*, 539.
21. A. HASTINGS, *The Church in Africa*, 533.
22. Ogbu U. KALU, "Doing mission through the Post Office: the Naked Faith People of Igboland,1920-1960", in *Neue Zeitschrift fur Missionwissenschaft*, 54,4 (2000), 263-280. See, John PEEL, *Aladura:* A *Religious Movement Among the Yoruba* (London: Oxford University Press, 1968).
23. This account has been based on the following: I) E. Musembe KASIERA, "The Foundation and Development of Nyang'ori Mission,1909-1924", (Seminar paper, Department of Philosophy and Religious Studies, University of Nairobi, 20 Feb 1980); see also his PhD diss., E.M. KASIERA, "Development of Pentecostal Christianity in Western Kenya" (Aberdeen, 1981); ii) Z.W. SAMITA, "The African Church of the Holy Spirit: Origins and Advent in Kabra Division, Kamenga District", in *TransAfrican Journal of History*, 25 (1996) 123-145; iii) J.M. LONSDALE, "European Attitudes and African Pressures: Missions and Government in Kenya between the Wars", in B.A OGOT (ed), *Hadith 2* (Nairobi: East Africa Publ. House, 1975), 229-242; iv) A.J. TEMU, *British Protestant Missions* (London: Longman, 1972).
24. C. SUNDBERG, "Conversion", 129.
25. C. SUNDBERG, "Conversion", 131.
26.. Okafor lives in Enugu and serves as a priest of the Anglican Church. Some of the entries in his diary can be found in a good account of those heady days by a participant, Frances BOLTON, *And We Beheld His Glory: A Personal Account of the Revival in Eastern Nigeria in 1970-71* (London: Christ the King Publishers, 1992). This section relies much on: i.) O.U. KALU, "Passive Revolution and Its Saboteurs: African Christian Initiative in the Era of Decolonization", (Currents in World Christianity, Faculty of Divinity, University of Cambridge, Position Paper no. 134, 2000); ii) O.U. KALU, *Embattled Gods: Christianization of Igboland, 1841-1991* (Trenton, NJ: Africa World Press, 2003).

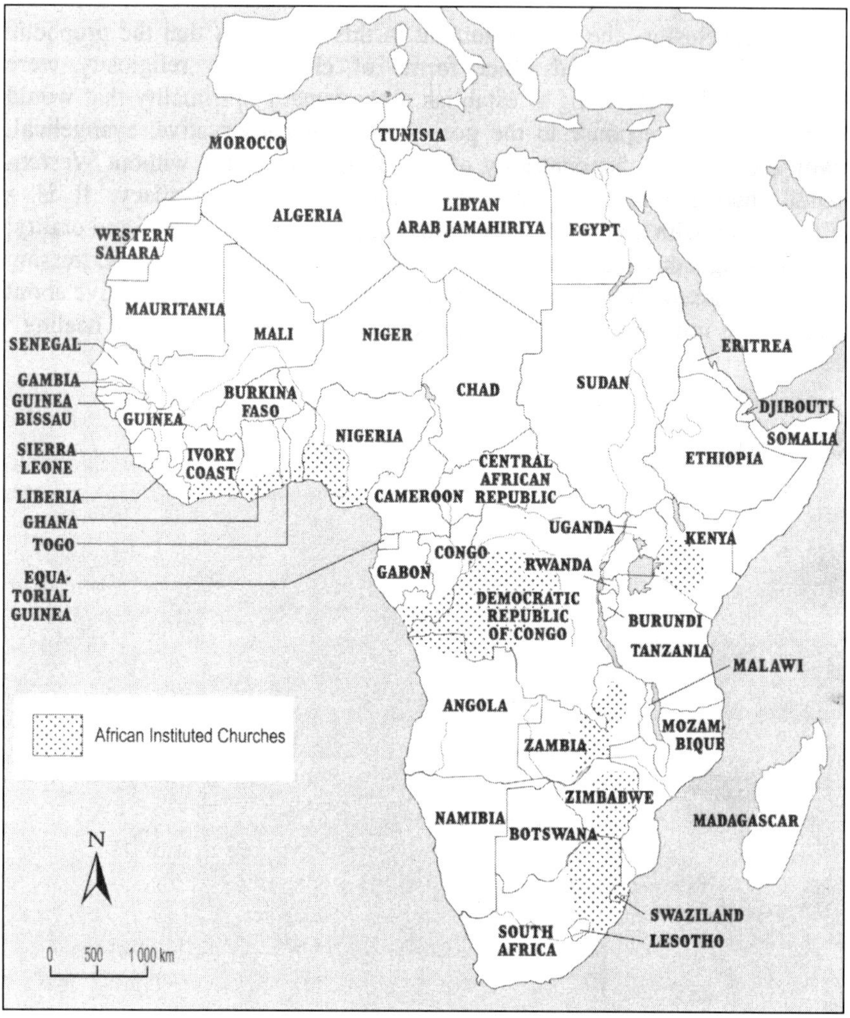

Map 9: Principal Locations of African Instituted Churches

Chapter Twelve

Zionists, Aladura and Roho: African Instituted Churches

Afe Adogame & Lazio Jafta

INTRODUCTION

The indigenous religious creativity crystallizing in the acronym, African Instituted Churches (AICs) represents one of the most profound developments in the transmission and transformation of both African Christianity and Christianity in Africa. Coming on the heels of mission Christianity and the earliest traces of indigenous appropriations in the form of Ethiopian churches and revival movements, AICs started to emerge in the African religious centre-stage from the 1920s and 1930s. The AICs now constitute a significant filament of African Christian demography. In an evidently contemporaneous feat, this religious manifestation came to limelight ostensibly under similar but also remarkably distinct historical, religious, cultural, socio-economic and political circumstances particularly in the western, southern and eastern fringes of the continent. Their unprecedented upsurge particularly in a colonial, pre-independent milieu evoked wide-ranging reactions and pretensions of a political and socio-religious nature, circumstances that undercut their bumpy rides into prominence both in public and private spheres. The AIC phenomenon in Africa has received considerable scholarly attention since the fourth decade of the last century. Available literature reveals the conspicuous dominance of theological, missiological, sociological perspectives and provides ample information regarding this complex but dynamic religious development. While the earliest historical developments, theologies and hierarchical structures of these churches have been largely documented; the contemporary religious vitality and growth process of most of these groups has been left largely under-investigated.

This chapter undertakes a comparative reconstruction of the AIC historical trajectory, situating it within the wider socio-cultural and religious milieu within which the movements were born and nurtured. One must refrain from assuming that all AICs are virtually identical. This tendency is rife in extant literature on the AICs, whereby the phenomenon is treated in such a way as if the wide, complex variety can simply be pigeonholed as a single whole. The uniqueness of this religious genre should be seen in terms of the affinity and differences that characterize their worldviews, ritual and organizational structures. They share many features in common—the reason for their common typology—yet it will be oversimplifying this comparison without highlighting the fact that each of the AICs has its own religious dynamic. While there are abounding affinities, they also reveal a significant, complex variety in terms of their foundation histories, the charismatic personality of the founders and leaders, their belief patterns and ritual structures, their organizational policies and geographical distribution. Three examples that will engage our comparative focus here are the Zionists in South Africa, the Aladura in West Africa and the Roho in East Africa. The rationale for isolating these case examples is no less evident in a very vast continent with cultural, linguistic variety as well as diverse historical experiences. Any claim to an exhaustive treatment of such a huge, expansive religious phenomenon, within this space limitation, is pretentious and bound to entail one's brushing in broad strokes. Although the religious geographies of these churches can no longer be confined to the respective local boundaries, yet these geo-cultural contexts have undoubtedly produced and experienced the most remarkable vitality of this religious phenomenon in a way that has attracted more scholarly attention than anywhere else on the shores of Africa. Therefore, a sufficient basis for analysis may already exist. One advantage of such a comparative endeavor is that it not only avails us of a succinct picture of what three particular African religious worlds look like, but also serves to illuminate our understanding of their religious systems. It allows us test the validity of some generalizations about the AICs, prevalent in extant literature, in the light of their overarching affinities and peculiarities.

I. TERMINOLOGY OF THE AICS: THE PROBLEM OF DEFINITION AND THE DEFINITION OF A PROBLEM

Bengt Sundkler was one of the pioneer scholars who engaged systematic exploration of what later partly became popularized as AICs. His pivotal study ended in a monograph, *Bantu Prophets in South Africa*, published in 1948. Sundkler took a terminological leap over a decade later by opting for Bantu Independent Churches as against the jaundiced official appellation of Native Separatist Churches.[1] Sundkler was ostensibly caught up in the web of ideological and political nuances from which he attempted to draw a distinction. The labels Native, Separatist and his own appropriation of Bantu were considered offensive and incongruous baggage, and thus they attracted a critical uppercut in the very tensile racial, political atmosphere that characterized apartheid South Africa. One of the less-polemical categories adopted to aggregate a large genre of independent churches in South Africa was Zionist.[2] Sundkler popularized his broad distinction between two types of South African Independent churches, which he described as Ethiopian and Zionist.[3] The latter gained some weight and credibility, not only because this indigenous religious creativity was seen to be heavily concentrated among the Zulu and Swazi peoples, but also as a result of the spiritual liberation and renaissance which the "Zion" biblical concept represents for its members in a highly segregated context.

With the limitations of "Bantu" as more of a linguistic rather than a racial category, "African" came and appeared as a suitable, more-embracing replacement that took cognizance not only of the partly racial sense it embraced but also of simultaneous religious manifestations elsewhere within the continent. The categorization of these indigenous religious initiatives as "independent", "separatist", "syncretistic", "protest", "nativistic", "tribal", "neo-pagan", "spiritist", "sectarian", "nationalist", "hebraic", "cultic", "messianic", "post-Christian", at different levels of their developmental histories amply reveal the ideological, political, religious orientations and climate which pervade scholarship as well as the public sphere at the time.[4] These perceptions cannot be claimed to have totally run under in the post-independence era, some scholars still continue to appropriate these loaded terms or their variations. In spite of the critical bashing it received, "African Independent Churches" received a fair nod and more popular acclamation as a working definition, as a provisional terminology that was perceived to be far less-nuanced and less-pejorative. In West Africa, Christian Baeta first captured this spiritual wave and dealt extensively with this phenomenon to be later popularized in Ghana as "Spirit" or "Spiritist" churches.[5] Harold Turner and John Peel both championed the course of popularizing African Independent Churches with their seminal works on the Aladura phenomenon in western Nigeria.[6] The scenario in pre-independent Kenya was not any different as Welbourn and Ogot undertook a study of independent churches in western Kenya.[7] Some early and latter significant works that dealt on the AICs in Kenya, in part or in whole, includes those of Jomo Kenyatta, Jocelyn Murray, David Sandgren, Francis Githieya and Cynthia Hoehler-Fatton.[8]

In order to bring definitional clarity to the expanding phenomenon, Turner adduced a provisional definition of AICs in the late 1960s as "churches founded in Africa, by Africans and for Africans." While this definition may appear to hold water especially when located within the specific milieu within which Turner first wrote, contemporary demographic profiles and the expanding religious geographies of these churches now renders his definitional gaze suspect, myopic and short-sighted. One backlash of the postcolonial reconstruction of African church historiography was the revisiting of the use of "Independent". Hitherto, these churches were largely mirrored as political protest groups, "pseudo-religious fanatics" and harbingers of nationalism, groups destined to sing their own obituaries in the aftermath of independence across Africa. The resilience and dynamism that characterized these churches in post-independent Africa, coupled with their rapid proliferation and splinter formations, reified the politics and inherent polemics that galvanize such a terminological construct. This opened the floodgate to a whole gamut of new, alternative terminologies such as "African Initiated Churches", "African Indigenous Churches", "African Instituted

Churches", "African International Churches". There is as yet no scholarly consensus as to which of these phrases is most appropriate and concise to delineate the phenomenon. The revolving abbreviation, "AIC", in all of them may lend credence to the fact that the designations do not necessarily suggest sharp, varied connotations beyond their semantic variations. However, they do convey powerful meanings of a critical nature, thus betraying other intellectual and ideological leanings, agendas and orientations. A revisiting of the dominant AIC typologies is expedient in order to reconstruct a new embracing typology in the light of overarching religious, political and socio-economic realities that characterize their histories. However, the existing classification in its narrowest sense refers to the movements which emerged from the dawn of the twentieth century either within or outside the institutional frameworks of the mission and mission-orientated churches such as the Ethiopian-type churches in South Africa, the African churches in West Africa, and the mainline churches in East Africa.

II. PATTERNS OF HISTORICAL EMERGENCE

The 1920s and 1930s marked the nascence of the Roho, Zionist, and Aladura churches. Two similar but distinctive patterns characterize their histories of emergence. They represent groups that started under the initiative of African leadership both within and outside the immediate purview of mission and mission-orientated churches. The first strand concerns groups that emerged from within already existing mainline churches. The nucleus of such movements had been mainly "prayer bands", "societies" or "bible study classes" prior to their expulsion, voluntary withdrawal, or separation from the parent body. Such separation may either have been occasioned by differences in understanding and interpretation of particular doctrines, accusations of practicing unorthodox or "strange" rituals, a revelation or vision claims to establish a new group, a result of personality clashes and leadership tussle. The second discernible pattern of emergence revolves around groups that neither existed within the mainline churches nor experienced any institutional friction and disengagement at their take-off stages. Explanations proffered by scholars for their emergence vary from religious to cultural, political to economic, ethnic to racial discrimination, and from social to psychological.

Scholars of AICs and African religions need to exercise caution in the terminologies appropriated, but also be conscious of the fact that such ideologically loaded categories may still be highly charged and misleading. In her typologization of AICs, Jules Rosette carries over a useful distinction between groups that have broken off from established churches (Separatist) and bodies "which have been started under the initiative of African leaders outside the immediate context of missions or historic religions (Indigenous).[9] Hoehler-Fatton aptly questions the usefulness of the dominant conceptual model of schism in understanding the emergence of independent churches in western Kenya. As she argues, "the schism model, as typically deployed in histories of East African independent churches, portrays mission churches as the repositories of normative Christianity. European missions are assumed to have set the standard, from which rebellions, innovative, African-led groups broke away."[10] For instance, Mango never made a declaration of secession himself. It was the Church Missionary Society (CMS) Archdeacon, Walter Edwin Owen who announced that Mango had seceded and who subsequently urged people to leave his congregations.[11] Many of Mango and Lawi`s followers continued to consider themselves part of the CMS for several more years. Rather than invoking a metaphor of abrupt, clear-cut rifts and splits (schisms) in a unified institutional setting, she opines, it is more appropriate to conceive of Christianity in Nyanza from 1900 through the 1940s as very fluid, with few firm links to institutional hierarchies of any kind, missionaries or otherwise.[12] This remark is very apt in considering both strands within which AICs emerged in other African socio-cultural settings. It is important to treat the peculiarities of each history of emergence in its own right rather than get caught in making blanket generalizations.

During the late 1920s and early 1930s, Luo and Kikuyu lands (Kenya) in East Africa witnessed a high proliferation of AICs. Welbourn and Ogot both recognize that the several independent churches that emerged in pre-independent Kenya provided Kenyans with "a place to feel at home", a sense of belonging that was absent in mission churches.[13] The independent churches that came into their purview falls under the two strands highlighted earlier. Examples of churches within the first strand are the Nomiya Luo Mission, which severed from the Anglican Church in 1914. There were other important Luo "schisms", such as the Church of Christ in Africa, which began as an Anglican revival movement called Johera or "People of Love" in 1952, though separated in 1957; and Mario Legio of Africa, a remarkable split from Roman Catholicism.

The emergence of the Roho movements among the Luo in western Kenya is traced to 1912, the year in which Roho (the Holy Spirit) was believed to have made its initial appearance in Ruwe sub location. The Roho or "Holy Spirit" churches emerged during the colonial era, a crucial time in Kenyan socio-political history characterized by scenes of serious conflicts over land, education and the controversy over clitoridectomy. One of the earliest charismatic figures was Ibrahim Osodo, who attracted and organized a small group of followers until his coercive conscription into colonial military service.[14] With their respective headquarters in Nyanza province, the Musanda Holy Ghost Church of East Africa, the Cross Church of East Africa, and the Ruwe Holy Ghost Church of East Africa share common historical traits. They view themselves as "custodians of the Spirit", tracing their origin to the ecstatic Roho movement. The latter, the Ruwe Church, crystallized under the leadership of Alfayo Odongo Mango of Masanda in the 1930s. The Wakorino is a collective name representing several other Kikuyu AICs, tracing their origin to the same period. A major indigenous movement that emerged in central Kenya during the religious and political upheavals of the 1920s was the Agikuyu spirit churches or the Arathi (prophets or seers). They were also variously dubbed Watu wa Mungu (People of God), Aroti (dreamers) or Akurinu (roaring prophets) because of their spiritual quest for possession of the Holy Spirit. The Arathi resulted from prophetic figures, such as Joseph Ng`ang`a and Musa Thuo, who claimed divine healing to their prophetic ministry.[15]

The earliest amaZioni (Zionist churches) surfaced in southern Africa during the first decade of the twentieth century. Among Zulu and Swazi, the name "Zion" invokes two different connotations. In a more specific sense, it refers to churches that lay claim to genealogical relationship to Zion City III, and to John Alexander Dowie, First Apostle, and founder of the Christian Catholic Apostolic Church on the city of Zion, Illinois, near Chicago. The wider and more all-embracing strand of the AIC historiography concerns churches which emphasize the guidance of uMoya, the Spirit, and healing as central concerns. Daniel Nkonyane and Elias Mahlangu, both hailing from the Afrikaner missionary Le Roux`s Zion Apostolic Church group at Wakkerstroom, led different amaZioni. The earliest definite separation from Le Roux took place in 1917 when Mahlungu founded the Zion Apostolic Church of South Africa. Between 1912 and 1920, Nkonyane founded the Christian Catholic Apostolic Church in Zion.

It was Nkonyane, who as a leader in the Christian Catholic Apostolic Church in Zion, had introduced certain elements in worship which have remained visible hallmarks of Zionism till the contemporary era. Such features include white robes, bare feet, holy sticks and Old Testament symbolism. In 1922, he changed its name to Christian Catholic Apostolic Holy Spirit Church in Zion. A remarkable number of older and more contemporary amaZioni have emerged to populate the South African religious landscape. Some of the largest groups include the Zion Christian Church, the Nazirite Baptist Church. Most of the amaZioni share a common denominator and ethos. The various titles, which the AICs variously adopt, indicate their ecclesiology and pedigree.

The 1918 influenza or bubonic plague is the backdrop of the earliest AICs in West Africa, particularly in Nigeria. The social despondency that characterizes this colonial era effaces a scenario where the local peoples came out in droves to embrace prayer as a proven alternative to the failure and impotence of western medicine. They derived their name due to their penchant and proclivity for prayer, healing, prophecy, vision and dreams. Aladura churches began to emerge among the Yoruba of western Nigeria from the mid-1920s onwards. The earliest group was the Cherubim and Seraphim (C&S) which for several years existed as an interdenominational society "preaching faith in prayers and a renunciation of the devil and all his works—including the worship of idols, the use of juju and charms and the fear of the power of the witches."[16] The formalization of the society as a church in 1925 was to a large extent a consequence of the intolerance of the mission churches. The Christ Apostolic Church (CAC) can be seen as a direct product of the fusion between the Precious Stone Society (PSS) or Diamond Society (prayer groups within the Anglican Church), the Nigerian Faith Tabernacle (NFT) and the Great Revival event of 1930 that served as an impetus towards unification. The nucleus church that became established under the triumvirate of Joseph Babalola, Isaac Akinyele and David Odubanjo commenced "unofficially" as a prayer group within the Anglican Church. Owing to a myriad of factors such as doctrinal conflicts—the question of faith or divine healing, infant baptism, personality clashes, administrative problems, persecution from the mainline churches, the movement metamorphosed through different names until 1943 when it was formally registered (No. 147) as the "Christ Apostolic Church" under the Lands Perpetual Succession Ordinance of 1924. The Church of the Lord-Aladura (CLA) also emerged from within the mission church tradition. Josiah Ositelu founded it in 1930 following his suspension from the Anglican Church—where he served as a catechist, primarily on doctrinal questions. The Celestial Church of Christ represents the second strand of Aladura emergence. It did not sever from any existing mainline church nor face any form of ejection but emerged rather independently through the visionary experience and charismatic initiative of Samuel Bilehou Oschoffa, a carpenter turned prophet, in 1947.[17]

One feature that characterizes the nascent histories of the earlier AICs is their encounter with colonial and mission authorities. Following their pragmatic approach to existential questions of life, their emphasis on visionary reinterpretations of the Bible and the backing of charismatic figures, the AICs quickly acquired local appeal, popular acclamation and drew clientele largely from the existing mission churches. This sudden popularity coupled with religious, political and socio-economic considerations put them on collision course with the respective colonial governments, and mission-church authorities often serving as collaborators in the politics of repression and demonization. At the inception of the Aladura churches in western Nigeria, a sudden drift of membership was witnessed from the mission churches. Peel has shown through his survey of the Aladura churches in the 1960s that 63 percent and 66 percent of converts into the CAC and C&S branches in Ibadan where from the Anglican Church alone.[18] It is therefore within these contexts that the apprehension by mission church authorities becomes understandable.

A process of mutual diabolization ensued with the Aladura churches accusing the mission churches of practising ambivalent Christianity, idolatry and a faith too dressed in foreign (western) garb in their polity and liturgical content, and the mission churches on the other hand, criticizing the Aladura of overshot rapport with Yoruba cultural matrix, syncretism, and of what they perceived as an indiscriminate use of charismatic gifts. With the religious, political and socio-cultural circumstances surrounding the emergence of the C&S in 1925, CLA and CAC in 1930 from within the Anglican mainstream, it is clear that the relationship between the Anglican Church and the severing groups in the pre-independence era was both genial and antipathetic. The colonial situation further made the relationship between the Aladura, during their formative years, and the mission churches far from being cordial. The somewhat intimate relationship between the colonial government and missionaries was in a way detrimental to the corporate existence of the emerging indigenous churches. The colonial administration often displayed a cold and spiteful posture on the Aladura churches. Omoyajowo highlighted the impression of a colonial officer—Captain Ross, the Resident at Oyo—about the indigenous churches when he wrote in 1930, "they are not recognized Christian missions and they should be regarded as enemies."[19] The colonial governments were also apprehensive of the danger that such groups may pose to constituted authority if they became "well established" and "strong". Babalola (CAC) and Oschoffa (CCC) were humiliated through incarceration on flimsy excuses.

The radicalization of the Arathi and Roho churches took place at their early historical phases. From as early as 1930, both groups had started facing increasing criticism from both the mission churches and the colonial government. Both groups laid emphasis on millennial deliverance and vehemently opposed the colonialists` occupation of lands. They preached and prayed that the interlopers would vacate the land, thus leaving the country to its rightful owners. They also opposed the missions` denunciation of polygyny and clitoridectomy. They rejected western money, amenities, clothing, food; and spoke against certain western and local beliefs and practices which they perceived were against the true tenets of the Christian faith.

The Arathi gave up western clothes and took to wearing *Kanzu* (a long white gown) and a white turban. Colonial government officials in collaboration with missionary authorities considered Mango and his Roho movement subversive and troubling, and thus carefully watched. His political activities heightened when he joined forces with other Kager in Buholo and Ugenya to campaign for the recovery of "lost lands". Due to his open opposition of the British colonial authorities and their partisanship in the land disputes, his involvement was perceived as politically motivated, and the Roho was seen as a last attempt to rally support through the vehicle of religious organizations. Owing to land disputes, Mango and others were arraigned before the Wanga Tribunal. They were fired for contempt of court and later exiled from their homes. They were granted pardon and returned to their homes in 1933. His further involvement in land disputes led to the Musanda massacres and his murder in 1934. Hoehler-Fatton aptly argues, "Roho religion should be understood as a matrix out of which Mango's political struggles arose, rather than depict the Roho church as a by-product of these disputes."[20] Ng`ang`a and his compatriots, like Mango, also suffered incarceration with hard labor under the colonial administration. Ng`ang`a was consequently assassinated in 1934, together with John Mungara and Samuel Muinami. Although, most of the AICs were often faced with harsh repression on two fronts, virtually all of them survived this subversion and gradually acquired legitimacy in the post-independence era.

III. PERSONALITY AND MYTHS OF FOUNDER

Virtually all the AICs trace their emergence to a charismatic, prophetic figure usually with claims of a traumatic religious experience. Such "turning point" visionary experiences are encounters from which special powers are vouchsafed. The centrality of the founding story is a feature that pervades the

AICs' spiritual and moral orientation. The re-enactment of these "sacred narratives" by members becomes a common feature during and after the demise of the charismatic figure. Isaiah Shembe (c. 1870-1935), the Zulu prophet who founded the amaNazaretha Church in South Africa, was variously known as a prophet, divine healer, as a messianic figure, a liberator and a messenger of God. Shembe hailed from a humble family background. He encountered a vision and dream experience in which he claimed to have been instructed by a voice to climb a mountain as well as go into a cave. This fundamental spiritual experience on the mountain led to a turn-around of his "immoral" life. This encounter story was vividly re-enacted by him and his later followers. Following this visionary experience, he started to preach, pray for the sick and engage in iconoclastic activities around the Orange Free State and later to environs. The Celestial Church of Christ emerged in Dahomey (Porto Novo) through the charismatic personality of Oschoffa, a "carpenter-turned-prophet", following a visionary experience that occurred while marooned in the forest in search for timber. He claimed to have received a divine injunction to establish a church, "the last ship of salvation" that will be charged with the task of "cleansing the world." After this experience in the bush where he was stuck for several days, he returned to his immediate community and to the astonishment of many, he started to exhibit his newly acquired spiritual gifts through healing and performance of miracles.

The historiography of the Joroho (People of the Spirit) is centered on the charismatic figure, Alfayo Odongo Mango. Mango was described as a strong-willed individual who emerged as a key religious and political personality in the Luo region. He was involved with the Anglican Church and was even appointed Deacon of a large, predominantly Luo area in 1927. Mango first had a vision in 1916 while he was visiting a congregation in Alego Nyadhi in his capacity as an authorized Anglican evangelist. He kept this unusual experience to himself and thought of the message he received while he and his small party left Alego. The journey back to Musanda took them through Uriya forest, where the Spirit suddenly knocked them down. Following this traumatic mystical experience in Alago, he began to preach to his people. Imbued with the Holy Spirit, he was able to heal people, foresee the future, and assert the need for an African-led church in the face of foreign domination. Roho members portray Mango today as both a temporal and spiritual liberator who introduced the first truly African church. Members claim that his death atoned for the sins of the Black people, giving them entry into heaven. He is not remembered by contemporary Roho Christians as a Luo nationalist, but as a charismatic religious figure. Mango's life and death became of central significance to Roho members and he is frequently mentioned during ritual services as they recount episodes in Roho ecclesial history. The account of his struggle against the colonialists has taken on a life of its own on a symbolic and theological level.

Even upon the demise of the charismatic leaders, founders of the AICs have continued to be venerated in annual celebrations of remembrance. At the

Sikukuu, which marks the anniversary of Mango's death, surviving members perform a dramatization of the fire in which he died, and sing hymns about the beginning of Roho religion. "Musanda (birthplace of Mango) constitutes the locus of an interlocking chain of ultimate consequences. On that sacred spot, the paradigmatic cycle of birth, death and renewal was enacted for Roho members by their own African prophet-savior."[21] This cycle is continually recapitulated in the rituals of the church and in members` individual lives. For them, the locus of this central story is Musanda, and they honor its auspiciousness in their annual pilgrimage. Lawi Obonyo is another central figure in Roho history, acknowledged as a "miracle worker". He was widely portrayed as Mango's jakony (helper). As a carpenter, he resided in Musanda with Mango, his uncle. He laid claims to a dream encounter in which he was instructed to "spread the word of God". Ng`ang`a, who became one of the most famous Arathi charismatic figures, had a dramatic experience in 1926 after his involvement in a bout of drunkenness from which he became incapacitated for several days. During his illness, he claimed that God revealed himself in a dream calling him to a new and active spiritual life. After this initial call experience in 1926, Ng`ang`a engaged in a spiritual preparation, a retreat which took him into seclusion for a period of three years. While in seclusion, he abstained from normal life and devoted himself to prayer, meditation, fasting, and intensive bible study. Emerging from this spiritual retreat, he began preaching in the villages near his home.

IV. RELIGIOUS WORLDVIEW OF THE AICS

The AICs hold tenaciously to the Bible as the source of all their knowledge. The centrality of God, Jesus Christ, the Holy Spirit and a myriad of angels are upheld in their belief systems. Many AICs attribute immense significance to the role of innumerable angels in their church life and worship. Angels occupy a conspicuous place as mediators and intermediaries between the human and the supersensible world. However, the number and significance of angels vary from one group to another. AICs' beliefs are of immense significance to members as they lie behind the praxis, rituals, worship, membership and decisions of the church. Each of them has a distinctive doctrinal trust, to them nothing is practiced which is not derived or cannot be located within Biblical locus.

The AICs demonstrate a pragmatic approach to Christian life through their prayer rituals. In fact, prayer forms the core of their spirituality. The AIC belief systems should also be understood in light of their respective socio-cultural contexts. Belief in spiritual agency remains a cornerstone of the AICs' worldview, a worldview that incorporates both this-worldly and other-worldly orientations. Special emphasis and attention is placed on spiritual healing, prophecy, visions and dreams, trance, exorcism. A feature germane to AIC worldview is in the acquisition, retention and manipulation of spiritual power to conquer the myriad of "evil" forces that populate the world around them. Members accept the traditional explanation for diseases, illnesses, and misfortunes but jettison the modus operandi of traditional healing. Through effectual prayers and elaborate ritual action, members attract the attention, power and action of the benevolent forces (God, Jesus Christ, Holy Spirit and the angelic forces) against the malicious, evil forces that parade the cosmos. This alternate methodology in dealing with existential problems explains why the AICs engaged in iconoclastic activities especially at their earlier stages of growth. The tenacity with which the Zionist, Aladura, Roho hold and engage these ritual activities, suggests why they are often accused of incorporating traditional Zulu, Yoruba and Kikuyu cosmological ideas into their Christian thought patterns.

The AICs draw from these cosmologies in such a way that they locate all features within the locus of the Bible and not as antithesis to it. In locating the Bible as the foundation of all their beliefs and mode of worship, the AICs vehemently refuse any connecting nexus with traditional religion. Their affinity and compatibility with indigenous ethereality is perhaps indicative of why they have remained very pervasive. Polygyny is tolerated but not encouraged by most AICs. Most founders and leaders have been known to marry more than one wife, and thus enjoin their followers as long as they have the material capability. Mango's marital history has it that he was married to four wives prior to his conversion experience. Consequently, Mango embraced the monogamous ideal, establishing a model that all subsequent Roho officials were expected to emulate. Dietary prescriptions and prohibitions are similar in most of the AICs. Pork meat, all kinds of alcoholic beverages, drugs, tobacco and cigarettes are strictly forbidden to its members.

V. RITUAL DIMENSION

The AICs offer a celebrative religion and engage a prodigious use of ritual symbols. Music, drumming, dancing characterize liturgical systems. The appropriation of spiritual songs, hymns and sacred language as a revelatory medium is central to the ethos and rhetoric of the AICs. Special esoteric and liturgical language is a feature common to the Roho, CCC, C&S, and CLA. For the Roho it is called Dhoroho (language of the Spirit). Spiritual hymns and songs are revealed to the church through the founder, prophets and prophetesses. While some of the AICs combine hymns from mission and other churches, the CCC, Roho and Zionist hymn repertoire is replete with revealed hymns. Although the C&S and CLA provide evidences of revealed songs, they have their hymn repertory developed directly within the structural guidelines and style of the western, mainline churches' hymnals.

All CCC hymns and songs contained in their hymnbook are believed to have been revealed to, or channeled through certain individuals such as the Pastor-Founder, prophets and prophetesses from a divine source, that is, under the influence of the "Holy Spirit". This represents the basic wellspring from which CCC hymn repertory developed. Such songs emerge especially when the prophets and prophetesses experience a state of vision or trance.

A feature prevalent in CCC hymnal repertory is the appropriation and rendering of words/phrases in esoteric "spiritual" language such as *Jerih mo ya mah;*

Yah rah Sarah Yah rah Samahtah; Yah rah man Hi Yah rah man; Yagol lolah Mariyanga rih yeh; Yah-Kirah-hihi-jah; Zevah Riyah, Zava Raye e.[22]

The use of concrete objects occupies a very fundamental place in their cosmology and praxis. Some of the ritual objects which are prominent in the ritual life of the AICs include consecrated water, candles, perfumes, incense, palm fronds, hand bells, staffs, spears and consecrated oil. Others are girdles, crosses, sacred numerology, invocation of psalms, and the appropriation of esoteric language in prayer and hymns repertoire. The amaZioni refer to their staff literally as isiKhali (a weapon). Sikhali (spear or staff) made of brass and wood are common symbols of power used by the jopolo (white-robe members of the AICs such as the amaZioni, Roho and Arathi) to ward off demons and evil forces. In Aladura churches, Ida (palm fronds) symbolizes the spiritual sword. The belief in the use and efficacy of sanctified water is very rife in the ritual life of the AICs. Sanctified water is significant for therapeutic and prophylactic functions, and it assumes a potent force and symbol for purification and for chasing away benevolent spirits. Symbolism of color and numbers plays a crucial part and varies from one AIC to another.

Most AICs are easily distinguished from other churches by the spiritual regalia worn by members during church services or other rituals, although the color of spiritual garments vary from one group to another. The collective identity of the amaZioni is partly expressed by the symbolism of their white garments. The CCC recommends and uses white garments (soutane or cloth of the spirit) for its members and prohibits any apparel made of black and red except on professional grounds. The use of white soutane symbolizes the outward purity of members as a projection of the inner purity and sanctity. The relationship between white and purity is derived from the fact that "white" in most traditional African cultures represents goodness, purity and life. When the soutane or white uniform is worn, members are required to go barefooted, both within and outside the church precincts. The Arathi (Wakorino) in Kenya are also noted for the long white robes and white turbans worn by their members. However, the CLA and C&S use white garments in addition to colored garments and the requirement to go barefoot may only apply within the church but not outside. Other colors are, however, also worn by some of the amaZioni. Sundkler mentions green, yellow and buff or sackcloth as being worn by Zionists.[23] In Soweto, yellow and green are worn but not black.[24] Green, blue, yellow, and occasionally red are worn by Shona Zionists.[25] There are also examples of newer Zionist churches that wear other colors than white. White is seldom worn as the main symbolic color by the emaJerikho (Church of Jericho) in Swaziland, also known as "red-dressed Zionists".[26] The red garment of the emaJerikho relates to their claim to possess a special power with which to fight malevolent forces. Red is however avoided by the older generation of Swazi Zionists. Color symbolism also applies to other concrete objects such as candles. The color and number of candles used for a specific ritual varies from one group to another. The CCC insists on white candles only while other colors of candles are used in the C&S, CLA and CAC. As ritual symbols help members to focalize prayer to and attention on the benevolent powers, they are frequently employed and given symbolic meanings in their ritual activities.

VI. CONSTRUCTION AND APPROPRIATION OF RITUAL SPACE

Sacred space among the AICs transcends the traditional church building of the mission churches. Mountains, rivers, and groves have been set aside and transformed into holy grounds where rituals are re-enacted. The phenomenon of a sacred city is a common feature of several AICs. Shembe established the Zion Centre on a holy mountain, the Ekuphakameni—near Durban, and another sacred village, the Inhlangakazi, both to which followers and non-adherents flock for festivals, healing and the rejuvenation of spiritual power. The earlier hosts the great July Festival, while the latter is where the January Feast of the Tabernacles usually takes place. Ogere, Oshitelu`s hometown was the divine choice for the CLA. Ogere, which provides the heavenly charter of the holy city, has become the centre for the commemoration of the annual Mount Taborah Festival. Imeko, the hometown of Oschoffa hosts the "Celestial City" or "New Jerusalem" on earth. His mausoleum at the Celestial City has been set aside as "holy ground" and a place of annual pilgrimages by members and non-members alike. The burial ground of late AIC founders usually transforms into a "sacred arena". The Wakkerstroom (Rapid Stream) remains the "Jordan" of Zulu Zionism to date, and represents the "source of the living waters". As shown above, soon after Mango's demise, Roho adherents began honoring Musanda as hallowed ground. The Joroho converge annually on Ruwe and Masanda for the Sikunuu mar Raper (Celebration of Remembrance) to worship and celebrate the bravery of their martyrs in the 1934 mach. These sacred sites also become their "New Jerusalem" and "new home". Roho members embrace Musanda as a place of earthly power but also as a place of familiarity, love and comfort. Phrases such as Musanda dalawa (Musanda our home) and dala maler, dala mar Lera (holy home, home of love), which frequently pepper the hymns, prayers, and testimonies offered during this festival, carry a poignant multivocal resonance.[27] The lyrics (songs) make plain the centrality of Musanda in Roho piety. The Joroho established rites that reinforce the sanctity of Musanda and constructed permanent graves for Roho pioneers in the vicinity.

AICs typify rituals of passage—birth, baptism, marriage, anointing, death and burial to create rigid and valid renewal in the life cycle. There are also rites associated with major festivals, seasonal changes, individual achievements, and sanctity in the case of women. The symbolism and re-enactment of these rituals resonates largely with respective traditional religious and cultural worldviews, although recourse is made to the Bible. Ritual space within the AICs is in flux and members have unlimited access as prophets/prophetesses are in attendance to diagnose and explain misfortunes, existential problems, while at the same time predicting, controlling and procuring spiritual remedies for members and other clients.

VII. ORGANIZATIONAL STRUCTURE

The AICs vary in their organizational systems depending on the extent of their local appeal and the demographic and cultural composition of their membership. The hierarchical structures are usually very complex with specific functions taken charge by prophets, prophetesses, visioners, dreamers, elders, teachers and other functionaries. CCC organization is structured around the centralized authority of the Pastor (Founder) or leader. As both the spiritual and administrative head of the church, the Pastor has unchallengeable authority on all matters, and legitimates this authority through his personal charisma. His position remains the constant reference point of the church as he occupies the apex of the church hierarchical structure. The titles "Reverend, Pastor, Prophet and Founder" were vested on the personality of Oschoffa from the incipience of the CCC, thus exhibiting the inter-mix of both charismatic authority and a bureaucratic priesthood. He exercised the dual rights of "chief priest" and "prophet" throughout his life.

The administrative and hierarchical structures, introduced during the lifetime of the Pastor-Founder, functioned side by side; though the Pastor-Founder is seen to have the ultimate and unchallengeable authority in all matters affecting the church. Most founders and leaders of the AICs, through their charisma, play these spiritual and administrative roles in addition to their father-figure status. As far as the Joroho are concerned, the sacrifices of the early Roho community at Musanda are salvific. In the person of Mango, "God fulfilled his promise to provide Africans with a saviour of their own". The internal organization of the AICs also provides a complex hierarchical structure that varies from group to group and according to the respective ranking systems. The different ranks within the hierarchy are clearly distinguished by their robes and regalia. The role of prophets, prophetesses, visioners, and dreamers is very central in AIC ritual systems as they "explain, predict and control" events. Their ability to prognosticate future events and provide a panacea for existential problems bears resonance to the functions of isangoma, ajuoke, babalawo (diviners and healers) in Zulu, Kikuyu and Yoruba cosmology. In both religious worldviews the prophet/prophetess/ healer and the traditional healer/diviner is a pivotal force for order and rapprochement between the human and the super sensible cosmos.

VIII. AICS IN GLOBAL CONTEXTS

The AICs emerged in specific geo-cultural milieus, with each context largely shaping its worldview. However, as each group started to witness vertical and horizontal growth, they also began to transcend the immediate geo-ethnic and cultural boundaries within which they were born and nurtured. The amaZioni spread beyond the Zulu to the Shona and the Swazi, as well as to other ethnic groups in southern Africa. The Roho and Arathi churches made footprints in Kikuyu and Luo regions and beyond to other parts of East Africa. The Aladura, which had its origin in western Nigeria, made inroads into other parts of Nigeria, the West and central African sub-regions. There has been a growing internationalization of some AICs as they use their strategies of evangelism to reach out beyond their local into global contexts. Since the 1960s, the Aladura churches have planted branches in Europe, America and other parts of the world. More than the Roho and Zionists, the membership structure of the Aladura churches is relatively mixed with the non-Yoruba membership forming a remarkable proportion.

The AICs have also been involved in local, regional, national and intercontinental ecumenical networks. The Aladura churches are affiliated to national ecumenical bodies such as the Christian Association of Nigeria (CAN), and the Christian Council of Nigeria (CCN) and have founded the Nigerian Association of Aladura Churches (NAAC). On the continental level, most AICs including the Aladura, Zionist and Roho are members of the Organization of African Independent Churches (OAIC). Through association with worldwide ecumenical movements such as the World Council of Churches (WCC), several well-established AICs have attempted to become international in outlook. The CLA was admitted into the WCC in 1975. In 1957, the Zionists came under a national umbrella, the Zion Combination Churches in South Africa.

In conclusion, this chapter used the examples of Zionists, Aladura, and Roho comparatively as variations of a theme, African Instituted Churches. It explores the affinities and differences that characterize their histories of emergence, worldviews, ritual cosmos, and organizational structures to underscore their unity in diversity. The chapter also highlights the tendency of AICs to move beyond their immediate local contexts, and how they are increasingly charting and inserting themselves into global maps of the universe.

Notes

1. See introduction to the second edition of B.G.M. SUNDKLER, *Bantu Prophets in South Africa* (Oxford: Oxford University Press, 1961), 18.
2. See B.G.M. SUNDKLER, *Zulu Zion and some Swazi Zionists* (Oxford: Oxford University Press, 1976). AICs in South Africa have received significant scholarly attention and the existing literature is quite extensive. These includes G.C. OOSTHUIZEN, *The Theology of a South African Messiah: An analysis of the hymnal of The Church of the Nazarites* (Leiden: Brill, 1967); M. WEST, *Bishops and Prophets in a Black City: African Independent Churches in Soweto, Johannesburg* (Cape Town: Dawid Philip, 1975); M.L. DANEEL, *Quest for Belonging: Introduction to a study of African Independent Churches* (Gweru: Mambo Press, 1987); G.C. OOSTHUIZEN & I. HEXHAM (eds), *Empirical Studies of African Independent / Indigenous Churches* (Lewiston, NY: The Edwin Mellen Press, 1992); J.P. KIERNAN, *The Production and Management of Therapeutic Power in Zionist Churches within a Zulu City* (Lewiston, NY: The Edwin Mellen Press, 1990); and G.C. OOSTHUIZEN, *The Healer-Prophet in Afro-Christian Churches* (Leiden: Brill, 1992) to mention a few.
3. See SUNDKLER, *Bantu Prophets*, 53, where he describes Ethiopian churches as AICs that broke from Protestant churches on political grounds, but have remained closely patterned on them. The Zionists, on the other hand, are "non-secession churches with a Pentecostal, healing emphasis," churches which also stress the pres-

ence and influence of the Holy Spirit in the church as well as in the life of the believer.

4. Cf. some early AIC typologies in SUNDKLER, *Bantu Prophets*; G.C. OOSTHUIZEN, *Post-Christianity in Africa: A Theological and Anthropological Study* (London: C. Hurst, 1968); D. BARRETT, *Schism and Renewal in Africa: An Analysis of Six Thousand Contemporary Religious Movements* (Nairobi: East African Publishing House, 1968); and H.W. TURNER, *Religious Innovation in Africa: Collected Essays on New Religious Movements* (Boston: G.K. Hall & Co., 1979).
5. C.G. BAETA, *Prophetism in Ghana* (London: SCM, 1962).
6. See H.W. TURNER, *African Independent Church, Vol. 1 - The Church of the Lord -Aladura; Vol. 2 - The Life and Faith of the Church of the Lord - Aladura* (Oxford: Clarendon Press, 1967); and J.D.Y. PEEL, *Aladura: A Religious Movement among the Yoruba* (London: Oxford University Press, 1968). For more recent works on the Aladura churches, see J.A. OMOYAJOWO, *Cherubim and Seraphim: The History of an African Independent Church* (New York: Nok Publishers, 1982); and A. ADOGAME, *Celestial Church of Christ: The Politics of Cultural Identity in a West African Prophetic-Charismatic Movement* (Frankfurt am Main: Peter Lang, 1999).
7. See F.B. WELBOURN, *East African Rebels: A Study of some Independent Churches* (London: SCM, 1961); F.B. WELBOURN & B.A. OGOT, *A Place to feel at Home: A Study of Independent Churches in Western Kenya* (London: Oxford University Press, 1966).
8. See J. KENYATTA, *Facing Mount Kenya* (London: Vintage, 1962 [1938]); J. MURRAY, "The Kikuyu Spirit churches", in *Journal of Religion in Africa*, 5, 3, (1974) 198-234; D.P. SANDGREN, *Christianity and the Kikuyu: Religious Divisions and Social Conflict* (New York: Peter Lang, 1989); C. HOEHLER-FATTON, *Women of Fire and Spirit: Faith and Gender in Roho Religion in Western Kenya* (Oxford: Oxford University Press, 1996); and F.K. GITHIEYA, *The Freedom of the Spirit: African Indigenous Churches in Kenya* (Atlanta: Scholars Press, 1997).
9. See Jules-Rosette, "African Religions: Modern Movements", in Mircea Eliade (ed.), *The Encyclopedia of Religion*, 1: 82-89, New York: Macmillan, 1987.
10. HOEHLER-FATTON, *Women of Fire and Spirit*, 206.
11. HOEHLER-FATTON, *Women of Fire and Spirit*, 68.
12. HOEHLER-FATTON, *Women of Fire and Spirit*, 77.
13. See WELBOURN & OGOT, *A Place to feel at Home.*
14. HOEHLER-FATTON, *Women of Fire and Spirit,* 12.
15. GITHIEYA, *The Freedom of the Spirit,* 123.
16. See, Omoyajowo, *Cherubim and Seraphim*, 9.
17. See ADOGAME, *Celestial Church of Christ,* 24.
18. PEEL, *Aladura*, 205.
19. OMOYAJOWO, *Cherubim and Seraphim*, 97.
20. HOEHLER-FATTON, *Women of Fire and Spirit*, 8.
21. HOEHLER-FATTON, *Women of Fire and Spirit*, 19.
22. See, *Orin Isipaya Mimo lati enu awon Woli Oluwa*, Yoruba and English Combined Edition (Ketu-Lagos: Celestial Church of Christ International Headquarters, n.d.).
23. SUNDKLER, *Bantu Prophets*, 213.

24. West, *Bishops and Prophets*, 177.
25. M.L. Daneel, *Old and New in Southern Shona Independent Churches*, vol. I (The Hague: Mouton, 1974), 164
26. See A. Fogelqvist, *The Red-Dressed Zionists: Symbols of Power in a Swazi Independent Church* (Uppsala: Uppsala Research Reports in Cultural Anthropology, 1986).
27. Hoehler-Fatton, *Women of Fire and Spirit*, 133.

Part Three

NEW DIMENSIONS OF AFRICAN CHRISTIAN INITIATIVES

Chapter Thirteen

African Christianity: From the World Wars to Decolonization

Ogbu U. Kalu

INTRODUCTION

An exciting event occurred in 1969 when the Pope visited Uganda. He told his hosts:[1]

> You must have an African Christianity. Indeed, you possess human values and characteristic forms of culture which can rise up to be capable of a richness of expression of its own, and genuinely African.

The audience was stunned as if he reversed the story of centuries of European relationship with Africa; as if he proclaimed release from a relationship that suffocated in favor of one which recognized the pluralistic context of mission. It was as if Europeans finally acknowledged, that after many years of missionary presence, that an African expression of Christianity had emerged. That speech turned attention from patterns of insertion to modes of appropriation and their consequences, especially as the numbers of Christians in Africa had grown enormously. Perhaps being a musical people, African responses to the pope's declaration could be traced in various liturgical initiatives and musical symbols. It meant that the story of African encounter with the gospel should privilege African initiatives and yet told in an ecumenical and irenic manner.

But this growth pattern was not so obvious in 1914 when the drums of war summoned Europeans to far-flung trenches. No African was invited to the Edinburgh Conference of 1910. Western missionary interest was in India, Japan and China. Within Africa, missionary presence was characterized by enclavement strategy, social distance and vocational dominance; and racial relationship was quite strained. Many Africans assumed that the war was a white man's war and wondered why they could not forgive themselves. They soon realized that the Anglo-French attacks on German colonies in Africa would implicate over half-million Africans as soldiers and many millions more as hapless porters and fodders. The First World War drastically reshaped the interior of African Christianity. But before the drums of war, the religious landscape was suffused with the din of Ethiopians who gave voice to African discontent and dared to exit from the white man's church to initiate gospel expressions that would be authentically African. By 1914 their relevance was increasingly ebbing, albeit with regional differences; indeed, the period 1914-1939 heard the swan song of Ethiopianism. A number of reasons have been adduced in the chapter dealing with Ethiopianism: among Africans in the diaspora, a broader Pan-African ideology gained prominence. In central Africa, Chilembwe's failed rebellion in 1915 yielded the premier place to Roman Catholics and scandalized the murderous and chiliastic turn of Ethiopian spirituality. In South Africa, the politics of the interwar years, characterized by an intense Afrikaans nationalism, land grabbing and political engineering, elicited an overtly political response from Africans beyond the ken of religious entrepreneurs. A similar shift from cultural to political nationalism occurred in West Africa as political parties emerged. In eastern Africa, the space may have widened for African agency in the church but white settlers garnered much economic and political dividends in the aftermath. The settlers benefited from the weakness at the home bases of missions. Untoward geopolitical forces such as rumors of war, wars, economic collapse, political instability and the rise of anti-Christian communist and totalitarian ideologies, were followed by another seven-year war. All these affected missionary presence and structures by 1945. Some contemplated massive restructuring and down-sizing in recognition of the new-fangled self confidence of the "younger churches".

Ironically, missionary structures showed a high degree of resilience in the inter-war years as "internationalism" became a new war cry that spurred young university students into the mission fields. Indeed, a process of domesticating the Christian values and hymns intensified between 1919 and 1950. The process was aided by two other factors, namely, an outbreak of an ecumenical spirit detectable in various assemblies of the International Missionary Council and in the formation of national councils of churches. But it was education and its mass appeal that rescued the missionary enterprise and ensured its recovery after the First World War.

Beyond the pursuit of "white power" or literacy, African Christian initiative could be traced through the choruses of spiritual churches, whether they were called *Zionists, Aladura* or *Roho*. As Ethiopianism lost its glow, Africans showed a stronger charismatic initiative from urban areas into rural enclaves. The literature has burgeoned as interpretations pile: that these constitute African Christian initiative and contribution to World Christianity; with immense creativity on the gospel-culture interface; a poignant reaction to colonial Christianity; a religion of the oppressed resembling cargo cults; the quest for belonging; safe havens amidst white racism; an emergent syncretistic spirituality; exploitation of the schismatic character of Protestantism; the religious stroke in nascent political nationalism and succor to displaced peoples amidst increased urbanization.

A few have profiled an indigenous brand of Pentecostalism and a theological response to missionary gospel, albeit one that privileged *Christus Victor*.

As a pneumatic response to the gospel, various forms of spiritual flares proliferated intensely in the immediate aftermath of the First World War. Was there a connection with the post-war environment? Obviously, the surge was aided by the translation of the message into indigenous languages to renew interest in those elements that missionary message ignored or muted. They mined the biblical resonance with indigenous worldviews. Their astounding popularity engendered persecution. It has been repeatedly emphasized that there were three different types of charismatic responses to the gospel message in these times. Individual prophets burst onto the scene and left; these were different from the spiritual churches that mushroomed as competitors to mission churches and early Pentecostalism could be traced with growing significance between 1906 and 1945. Admittedly, the spiritual wind in the 1970s gave it more prominence, but unknown tongues featured prominently in African Christian spirituality before the decolonization blues of the 1960s.

By the mid-1950s, a tired Europe was compelled by many negative forces to trim sails. Debates abound over the causes and nature of decolonization: whether it was a disheveled process, a creative enterprise or a passive revolution. Does the transfer of power or the change of rulers constitute *uhuru*? Missionary attitudes gyrated because the protagonists were products of mission schools: some opposed, arguing that the "children" had not sufficiently matured to govern themselves; others supported; still others devised a new strategy of ministerial formation to train indigenous priests, liaise with prominent laity and waltz with nationalists in the hope of securing the influence cultivated over the years. The music would later turn staccato as one-party states jettisoned colonial constitutions and disengaged from Christian roots. No prophecy in the heady politics of decolonization could have revealed the trend, because missionary bodies pretended to be different from colonial governments; thus, decolonization in the churches took much longer as indigenization cry turned into strident calls for moratorium. When the General Assembly of the World Council of Churches met in Nairobi in 1975, the choice of venue was as significant as the speech of the Pope in Kampala in 1969.

The burden of this chapter is to explore some of these themes that shaped the emergence of an African Christianity during the turbulent years of 1914-1975, with an cye on periodisation and regional coverage. It may perforce touch on matters that are dealt with in greater details in other parts of this book, but its goal is to provide a composite profile of African Christianity between 1914 and 1975. It is argued that from the drums of war in 1914, the swan songs of the Ethiopians gave place to the early morning calls of prophets, the gusty choruses of spiritual churches and the unknown tongues of early Pentecostals. Still, millions of Africans sang Western hymns and psalms of unity. The Second World War finally reconfigured the colonial landscape. Indigenisers boldly insisted on beating African drums in churches. Missionaries adjusted to the changing circumstances, ordained indigenous priests and waltzed with political nationalists before the tune turned staccato. A massive growth of Christianity in Africa ensued in this period that would escalate thereafter driven by a charismatic wind.

The explosion of Christianity in contemporary Africa occurred after the missionary period, but it is rooted in the charismatic agency that started in the inter-war years. Africans did not build a nationalist Christianity, because while the number of missionaries from some mainline churches declined in the decade between 1963 and 1973, the overall numbers of missionaries in Africa increased because new religious groups bathed in the overflowing rivers. This raises the crucial question: what might the breakthrough of African initiative in the religious sphere mean for the broader project of African realization? Some simply contend that the so-called African initiative is essentially a case of "extraversion". This borrows the concept from a political scientist who refers to an orientation of African states and rulers to rely on external sources of wealth and power, through cultivating relations with patrons, trading partners and multi-national establishments outside their domains. This dependence by the ruling elites on external support stultifies authenticity and causes failure. The problem is whether this concept could be transposed from one domain of life to another; from the political sphere to the Christian—especially given its combined indigenous and universal principles. Christianity has inbuilt universal and local characteristics. Its expression in any place must benefit from the forms of expression in other places without losing an indigenous quality. For instance, its evangelistic strategy must perforce borrow from the sophisticated media technology developed outside Africa and utilized in other spheres of living in the continent. What is essential is the ways that external forms are appropriated and utilized. Moreover, the organic nature of culture-contact compels deep contacts with other cultures as a means of growth. A dynamic culture must borrow from others to enhance its viability. Indeed, African Christian creativity may include the ability to borrow and integrate external cultural ingredients to create something better than they inherited from missionary groups. Their mission is to practice a Christianity that enables them to modify their environment and change themselves by acquiring spiritual power and cultivating holiness. After all, argues A.F. Walls, "the effectiveness of the Christian faith or any manifestation of it, is accordingly open to the test whether it gives access to power or prosperity, for protection against natural or spiritual enemies, purposes to which much traditional practice was directed and satisfactorily enforced familial and social unity."

I. DRUMS OF WAR: SWAN SONG OF ETHIOPIANISM, 1914-1939

To begin the reflection with the First World War, one dimension of the war environment was the role of rumors and the conflation of rumors with reality to heat the polity. When the war broke out, it was rumored among Africans that the rule of the whites was about to end. Colonial officials became quite apprehensive about security, control and the threat of rebellion. Provincial Commissioners urged the District Officers to keep files on intelligence reports about potential flash points and individuals. This increased the tension between the colonial governments and the communities. On the religious front, its exacerbated relationship with Ethiopianism was perceived as a form of black nationalism in a religious stroke. Its connections with African American missionary enterprise to Africa made it doubly suspicious, spurred by some confusion with Watch Tower's anti-authoritarian posture. As James Campbell argued for South Africa, "the concept of Black America retained an imaginative potency among Africans ... Moreover, the African Methodist Episcopal Church remained enmeshed within a system of racial domination in which the very essence of a black-run church could assume profound political significance."[2] In Malawi, it was rumored that an invading army of Black Americans had arrived at Karonga as messiahs who would make Africans be rich, educated and respected.[3] When one of Simon Kimbangu's songs referred to the change of baton and encouraged devotees to *"Be brave the kingdom is ours .We have it! They, the whites no longer have it. None of us shall be discouraged,"* the Belgians perceived treason rather than a theological affirmation.[4] In the interpretation of the connection between religious radicalism and the nationalist protest against colonialism, the Kimbangu movement provides an interesting case study for several reasons: first, Kimbangu himself made little political statement but posed as an undeclared opponent. Typical is a scene from his trial:

> Questioned as to why he thought he was a prophet, Kimbangu quoted a verse to the effect that 'thou hast hidden these things from the wise and prudent, and hast revealed them unto babes;' When the President of the court asked what 'these things' were, Kimbangu replied by repeating the ten commandments. When he started to repeat the seventh he was ordered to stop by the captain, whose native concubine was present in the court room.

Apparently he was an uncomfortable moral force that exposed the mighty. Second, a large dose of millennialism suffused the songs and ideology of his followers. They believed that the world was coming to an end and that the present order was bound to be destroyed; that some African Americans would come to relieve the Congolese from oppression. At other times they sang that Jesus had given them power and freedom: *Nous serons les vainqueurs envoyes par Toi/ Le Royaume est a nous/ Nous l'avons./Eux, les Blancs, ne l'ont plus.*" Third, Kimbangu catalyzed a tradition that inspired and generated a host of minor prophetic figures in the region.

In Zimbabwe, The African Orthodox Church, which had roots in Marcus Garvey's ideology, elicited negative responses as a subversive organization precisely because of its African American connection.[5] Beyond the pales of Christianity and millennial-driven anti-structure, some dug into primal religion for the empowerment to protest. A certain Onyango Dunde, a Luo from Alego founded a militant cult, named after the big snake, *mumbo,* which inhabits the depth of Lake Victoria. *Mumboism* proclaimed the demise of the whites, *wazungu*. An enthusiastic audience among the Gusii believed him. Some District Officers warned about a renaissance of secret societies as an anti-white bonding. Colonial governments dreaded the competition to rational administrative structures by religious power nodes as secret societies, cults and oracles. The political tendencies were clearer in southern and central Africa than in the western sector.

Beyond rumors, the war further heightened tension within African communities, because it required the services of recruits and porters and gave the local chiefs extraordinary powers to mobilize able-bodied men. In Kenya, some men escaped into the bush to avoid recruitment; others devised the subterfuge of conversion and moved into missionary enclaves/stations in large numbers and to the initial delight of missionaries. Soon all devices collapsed as missionaries themselves were compelled to engage in the affray.[6] The First World War severely disrupted the structure and moral economy of the missionary enterprise in Africa.

The location of the four centers of German colonies implicated all of Africa, and determined the size of recruits demanded from various regions: Kenya, Uganda and South Africa supplied over 40,000 soldiers for the Tanzanian front; Zambia, Malawi, Zaire yielded 18,000 for the Namibian, Rwanda and Burundi fronts; and West African countries provided several thousands to serve in Togo and Cameroon. Madagascar mobilized 45,000 men euphemistically termed "volunteers" to serve in Europe.[7] But it was the demand for millions of porters (*tenga-tenga*) that disrupted African communities and missionary work and caused so much suffering. The irony is that it betrayed a gap between missionary message and ethics, especially as it appeared to compromise missionaries who organized the cruel system and press-ganged potential converts, sometimes employing trickery. As Ian Linden put the matter:[8]

> As in England, recruiting officers passed through the villages with drums banging and trumpets blaring. If interest in joining the band failed to bring unsuspecting Africans from their huts, promises of huge financial rewards were made. Chiefs welcomed the opportunity to get rid of awkward villagers and would direct army officers to their huts. Africans were tricked and press-ganged into joining a war in which they had no stake or interest.

The Bishop of Zanzibar, Frank Weston, organized thousands in Tanzania; J.W. Arthur of the Church of Scotland Mission recruited 1750 Kikuyu members of the Mission Carrier Corps, who served nine months in southern Tanganyika.[9] Many died from poor feeding, arduous trekking and poor medical care. It was a war where more porters died than soldiers. Most troops on either side of the war in tropical Africa were in fact Africans recruited or pressed into service by colonial rulers. The Germans in eastern Africa gloried in their *askaris*, the Swahili word for "native soldiers". Since hundreds of thousands died, large sectors of the continent lost an average of three to seven percent of their populations.

Missionaries (priests and nuns) became soldiers in the transport, supplies and medical units and performed a number of mundane tasks for the governments leaving parishes without pastoral care. Indigenous people had the enviable opportunity to carry on the task. The lice they searched for in their hair just dropped on their feet. Meanwhile, Germans expelled priests from Allied countries and German missionaries were deported or incarcerated in many British and French colonies. The war disrupted supplies, mail, and funds of missions. At the end, the ecclesiastical map of Africa was re-drawn as German missionary societies lost their stations and had to face a harsh inter-war period that left them at the mercy of other European countries. Missionaries learnt to source locally for sustainability relying on indigenous resources for mission work more than before.

As has been argued, Ethiopians, as cultural and religious nationalists, were muzzled to express African discontent. Equally significant is the mood of the world war years, fraught as they were with physical conflict, insecurity, economic deprivation, epidemics, famine, labor and taxation burdens and unsettled psychological temper. The colonial government officials betrayed deep anxieties by repressive social policies that included religious matters. In southern Africa, George Shepphard computed seven cases of the dreaded African rebellions between 1906—when the last Zulu Bambata Rebellion occurred—and 1927.[10] But other Ethiopians pursued a different route and grew. Regional conditions mattered. In West Africa, Ethiopianism still grew in the midst of the strong racial antipathy that followed the war. More poignant, missionaries revamped their structures, the number of missionaries increased, and they employed education as a tool; Africans responded massively. Ethiopians had to intensify their educational programs in competition. But neither the Young Kikuyu nor the Harrists, Christ Army Church / Garrick Braidists and the Native African churches could mobilize enough resources for the cost intensive enterprise amidst the Great Depression whose effects reverberated into the colonies. Western missions defeated the Ethiopians on this front. But Africans initiated new spiritualities that took a charismatic character and challenged missionary Christianity. A number of these and the recurring cycles of revivals have been discussed in previous chapters.

II. CATECHISMS AND HYMNS: DOMESTICATION OF MISSIONARY CHRISTIANITY, 1919-1945

The end of the war was fraught with ambiguities: Africans tasted a dose of responsibility in the churches and in the survival of the colonial states. But in southern and eastern Africa, the British government felt more grateful to white settlers and rewarded them with enlarged political clout, land and labor. The Ex-Soldiers' Settlement Scheme settled many veterans in Kenya with huge acreages of land; everywhere in the eastern, central and southern regions, white settlement expanded during the interwar years. Plantations, farms and mines needed large supplies of labor because African agriculture became crucial during the war, cash crops and peasant production sustained metropolitan industries and exploitation of mines intensified. The owners of the means of production demanded that taxation should be used to pry Africans into the labor force, while low wages would keep them vulnerable. Only a few missionary voices, such as J.H. Oldham's, protested against forced labor and heavy taxation. The *kipande* or identity card system was imposed on the indigenous people in 1919 as a reward for being such helpful *tenga-tenga.* Missions turned attention to education so as to supply settlers "with trained boys, clerks, artisans and hospital dressers" as an honest Scot admitted.[11]

Soon after the war, missions re-organized, brought back some German-speaking priests and exploited the unsettled circumstances to steal bases and expand. Throughout this period, the "bush school" became the mascot of missionary presence. Schools were used as a means of evangelization, rivalry, civilizing project, legitimization of colonial industrial policy, vertical expansion into rural areas and domestication of Christian values. One had to be literate to read the catechism and sing the salvation hymns. School and church shared space and significance. Those who did not attend Sunday school were caned in the school on Mondays. Debates ranged on the curricula, level of education, use of indigenous personnel, governments' roles and the relationship between education and evangelism. Does an emphasis on education detract from the primary goal of leading the people to Christ? Some missionaries resisted the expansion of school apostolate while others saw it as the means to capture the future generation. Many perceived education as an good investment and objected to the notion of a consumer good concept, whereby Africans would study the classics and such like; they hated the pretensions of educated Africans; curricula should be confined to assisting them to cope within their cultural milieu, acculturate the values of the change agents, serve as intermediaries between western and traditional societies and mediate colonial civilizing policies and instruments. Industrial missions held much promise. The debate was fierce in the interwar years as the governments employed grants-in-aid to control the quality through an inspectorate unit. Mission churches colluded with government against the schools founded by Ethiopians who were denied accreditation and funding.

Ironies piled up as missions concentrated on teacher training and primary schools. There were only a few secondary and grammar schools until the 1940s. Africans instigated much of the expansion: those returning from the war or from mines and plantations urged the presence of schools as a sign of development, acquisition of white power, solving the riddle of the paper that talked, and coping mechanism for the new times. Communities would build the school and house for a teacher, carry the luggage, and even put a deposit towards the salary. Missionaries wrote home requesting for more personnel because of village delegations demand for schools. Either the war's experiences opened people's eyes to the power of white technology or the onslaught of the years on traditional mores finally took its toll or the new patterns of exploitation weakened primary resistance, but a mass movement to Christianity occurred. The presence of a school and church became an instrument of communal rivalry. Instead of sending their children to a school in a neighboring village, proud elders would contribute money for their own school. Competing missions exploited inter-communal rivalry while the District Officers delimited areas of operation. Rapid expansion compelled the use of half-baked teachers.

By the 1940s some indigenous entrepreneurs funded secondary education; sometimes, communities would provide the infrastructure while missions supplied the personnel. For the foundation of Dennis Memorial Grammar School, Onitsha in eastern Nigeria, the indigenous people raised most of the funds for the Anglicans in 1925. Government policy changed after the Phelps-Stokes Commission Report that showed off the capability of the brilliant Ghanaian, Dr J.K. Aggrey. But its reliance on Booker T. Washington's approach would meet with African criticism that it limited the ranges of African access to education. One effect of the First World War opened the space for some young Africans to go overseas for the "golden fleece". These would become the agitators of the post 1945 era. Already their strident tone could be heard in Nnmadi Azikiwe's brand of journalism in the Gold Coast from 1937. Agitation for university education after the Second World War induced government concern for secondary education.

Other crucial dimensions to the story of the interwar years include the increasing concern among missions about the employment goals for their pupils, many of whom deserted into government employ; urbanization grew with many moral implications; and education for girls became a key concern. The appeal of the gospel must be nuanced, because when the gospel spread to the villages and, like the roots of the mustard seed, changed the soil of the communities by contesting its cultures, the encounter of gospel and culture created disquiet. Thus, in spite of mass movement, a spectrum of responses appeared as the guardians of the ancestral calabash struck back in persecutions. Indeed, some of the patrons of church and school did not convert because it was education that they sought for their progenies. Novelists have captured this mood more accurately.

It has been surmised that the propaganda machinery for the Second World War was more sophisticated because it tried to show Africans the reasons for the war and their stake. Perhaps, Italian colonial attacks on Ethiopia, Libya and Egypt played into the Allied hands as many Africans volunteered to serve in North Africa. Still others were conscripted. But the aftermath was equally crucial as African eyes opened to possibilities for self-assertion. The French recognized the role of Africa in the cause of Free France. As Africans suffered in the trenches with whites, the aura that had clothed whites dimmed; they were mere mortals. In most countries, a corps of educated indigenes who were politically alert came to the fore, and African political agency reshaped itself. The interwar years were characterized by nascent trade unions, ad hoc industrial activities, mutual self aid associations and a host of primary forms of resistance. The post-

1945 period witnessed planned debates, political agitation, the popularity of Garvey's rhetoric—though he never visited Africa, industrial strikes and a shift from cultural to political nationalism. The career of Abdul Nasser of Egypt typifies the new activism that would later lead to political independence. The question is whether Christianity contributed to the temper of the political and social stirrings of these days. Did Christianity provide the impetus for African nationalism?

III. THE POLITICS OF THE NATIVE CHORUSES OF CHARISMATIC CHRISTIANS, 1914-1945

African Christianity in the public space has become an important means of examining the other side of history. The dominant voice in the story has been about the collusion and dialogues between colonial officers and missionaries. Perhaps, much of the African appropriation of the gospel message concentrated on the good news for individuals and communities without confronting the political presence of Europeans or even asking the missionaries to go home. In some places, the fact that nationalists were products of mission schools gave the impression that one of Christianity's unintended consequences was to tool nationalism. In other places, the disengagement from white churches could be regarded as a form of resistance. But there are examples where the politicization of religion was overt as influenza ravaged Africa from 1918 to add salt to the injury of coping with rapacious European presence. Some surmise that the epidemic triggered a radical reshaping of the Christian landscape.

The story of Zionists in Swaziland characterizes the new trends in the continent for the period. Many missionary bodies operated here from the arrival of the Methodists in 1845, followed by the Anglicans, 1880, and Lutherans in 1887. The country enjoyed a whiff of African American radical presence when the AMEC came in 1904, and by 1920 the number of organizations grew to fourteen. With a comity arrangement, the evangelicals shared the land as from 1911. Within three years, a new phenomenon appeared on the religious landscape when Joanna Nxumalo returned from South Africa where she had been working as a teacher and became converted as a Zionist. Others followed and founded their own versions as this fervent variety of evangelicalism grew rapidly. The League of African Churches bound them together. Apparently one of these healed the Queen Mother and Regent Labotibeni, of some eye ailment in 1914 and from this miracle, Zionism allied with the throne. The theology was gradually adjusted to make the monarch a type of "King Solomon" and the land, Zion. In this invented history, King Sobhuza II was imaged as the instrument for reclaiming the rights to the land from colonial settlers. By the 1930s the religious landscape was completely re-imagined; missionaries in Swaziland were perceived as the agents of settlers and colonial powers while the Independent churches posed as the instruments with which the Swazi people first expressed their desire for religious and political change. Independency combined religious innovation with protest and search for social justice and political freedom in evangelical language. The monarchy sealed this view by turning the Easter service into a program for celebrating the national heritage. The lion and the lamb lay together to produce a new version of African Zionist evangelicalism.

It needs to be underscored that the movement was not always at the center of the political system. Its varied colorations and increasing numbers have been traced in another chapter. For instance, Allan Anderson has argued, from official census data (fraught with bias in the Apartheid era), that the number of African Independent Church groups in South Africa proliferated from 30 at the turn of the century to 6,000 by the end of the millennium.[12]

Just as in Swaziland, some interpreters of this religious form have focused on the element of protest and schism. Surely, the issues of alienation of land, culture, political disenfranchisement under settler rule and colonialism, racial discrimination, economic deprivation bred psychological pressure that only a certain religious formation could help to assuage. Zion became a dream for recovery of alienated land, a place where there would be no more tears. The founder's home became a mecca, a powerful ritual Zion, a place of belonging. Some of the Ethiopian themes could be replayed but with a different type of exit. But the dominant character of this religion was in the prominence given to experience (revelation, dreams, visions, prophecy), orality, use of indigenous knowledge, symbols and ritual resources. The liturgical revolution was achieved by bringing traditional worship style into the church through song, dance, choruses and indigenous instruments. There was an intentional quest for resonance in biblical symbols and themes.[13] All over the continent, the nature, direction and pace of Christianity changed from the burst of the prophetic and spiritual revivals that succored people during the harsh days and the days during the period between 1919 and 1921 were harsh as South Africa witnessed about 66 strikes against those "getting them to work as hard as possible for the lowest possible wage, and keeping them from having any hand in the shaping of their own so far dolorous destiny."[14]

Equally intriguing in the story of radical Christianity in Africa is the emergence of Pentecostal spirituality from external sources in the period between 1906 and 1947. This excludes Keswick-type of evangelicalism. Most of the Pentecostal missions came from the United States, because evangelization was the heartbeat of the Pentecostal outpouring of the 1906/1907 period. People were so filled that they desired to take the experience abroad as quickly as possible. There were four types: first, the solo entrepreneur who imbibed speaking in tongues and forayed into Africa hoping to speak the indigenous language by the power of the Holy Spirit. They were disappointed. This type could be illustrated with the story of Clyde Miller who left Des Moines, Iowa, from a group that had much to do with Charles Parham's charismatic ministry in Topeka Kansas. Clyde founded the Nyang'ori mission in western Kenya, 1906-1920. Second, there were sponsored missionaries from Pentecostal groups such as Seymour's Azusa Street ministry, California, or the Swedish group who in 1904 sent Mary Johnson and Ida Andersson to Durban in South Africa. The Azusa Street group delegated Lucy Farrow and Henry M. Turney in 1908. Seven years later, they sent William F.P. Burton and James Salter to open the Congo Evangelistic Mission and Angel and Etta Post to Egypt. The case of J.G. Lake and Thomas Hezmalhalch connected with Zion City, Illinois has been mentioned.

Third, was an effort to co-ordinate Pentecostal groups to act in united missionary enterprises between 1909 and 1910, and Africa was one of the targeted mission fields. Indeed, in 1909, an effort was made to found the Pentecostal Missionary Union. It failed in the United States but motivated a missionary enterprise in Britain. The following year, the Bethel Pentecostal Assembly, Newark, New Jersey, organized the Pentecostal Mission in southern and central Africa and sent missionaries to Liberia, Swaziland, Mozambique and South Africa. In 1910, they sent George Bowie, a Scot who received the baptism of the Holy Spirit in America, to South Africa. He founded the Pretoria Pentecostal Mission. He was later joined by a Welsh, Eleazar Jenkins, and an English, Archibald Haig Cooper, who would take over the leadership in 1913. In 1921, it was renamed Full Gospel Church and in 1951, they merged with the Church of God (Cleveland Tennessee) to form the Full Gospel Church of God. Fourth, denominational brands of Pentecostalism established in various parts of Africa especially western Kenya, Burkina Faso, Republic of Benin and South Africa. These included the Assemblies of God, the Pentecostal Assemblies of Canada, Church of God in Christ, Pentecostal Assemblies of the World and International Pentecostal Holiness Church. Foursquare Gospel Church came later in the 1960s. Thus, classical Pentecostals as well as indigenous ones emerged early in the religious landscape. The crucial point is that none of these became important in the religious landscape until they benefited from the spiritual renewal of the 1970s. Many missionaries did not stay long in the field or cultivated any missions that outlasted them. As the force of the "faith movement" weakened, so did the activities of intrepid solo entrepreneurs. The world wars disrupted their enterprises. The denominational genre succeeded more than the others and, in many places individual missionaries sought the patronage of denominational bodies. From the outset, the white Pentecostals accepted racial segregation. Cumulatively, they added to the charismatic temper of the environment and certainly counter the impression that new crusaders recently forayed into Africa bearing the insignia of fundamentalism.

IV. AFRICAN DRUMS AND DECOLONIZATION BLUES, 1945-1960

The end of the Second World War was a momentous point in the story of African Christianity. It touched off the decolonization process that had a domino effect on the religious landscape. Besides the character of missionary presence in the colonial enterprise, the nature, process and consequences of decolonization also need to be considered. Was it planned or compelled and pursued hastily? Was it a transposition, passive revolution or a transformation? How did the missionaries respond? One impression is that they were uneasy about the prospects. For instance, in 1967, T.A. Beetham, Secretary of Conference of Missionaries Societies in Great Britain and Ireland, reflected on the anxieties of member churches in the face of decolonization. Uppermost were the resilience of primal religion in the midst of cultural revival and resurgent nationalism and the side-effects of years of missionary control. White control, he argued, bequeathed weak churches characterized by disunity, dependency syndrome and poor manpower development.[15] Commentators have pointed to the un-prophetic silence and passivity of post-Independence churches. As the Holy Ghost inspectors worried in 1939, the concentration on education apostolate diminished the imperative to preach the Word.[16]

Beetham's disquiet was partially because decolonization exposed the differing agendas of the colonial government and missionaries. Colonial rule, while it manifestly produced significant changes, both intended and unintended, was in many respects deeply suspicious and hostile towards anything other than highly instrumental and very tightly-controlled modernization. Its centralized, authoritarian administration and great concern for order were all designed to achieve this singular goal. Were missionaries bedfellows? Noll has pointed to the Evangelical roots of Enlightenment and modernity, but has also drawn attention to significant shifts.[17] A debate has ensued whether missions used education to plug into modernity. Beidelman and Strayer would argue that the missionaries met modernity halfway, opposing the full agenda to the chagrin of Africans and frustration of the colonial officers who threatened to withdraw their grants-in-aid. As Beidelman observes, the CMS missionaries at Kaguru bitterly regretted changes which secular education brought, "*replacing the bad old things with all the bad new things*." Adds Strayer, "the goal was not to create a highly educated elite."[18] This explains the virulent disdain for the "black Englishman" caricatured in Joyce Carey's *Mister Johnson* and Wole Soyinka's *Interpreters*. It explains the colonial French policy that cordoned off North Africa from missionary incursion and, as A.E. Barnes shows, the constraint on missionary presence and protection of Islam in northern Nigeria.[19]

Differences on the goals and curricula of education and cultural policies betrayed the ideological cleavages and competing visions between missions and colonial government. Meanwhile, as the missionaries pursued their goals with consummate passion, Africans became increasingly resistant and critical of the "intimate enemies": against the colonial enterprise for racism and for shutting the door to the decision-making echelon of white power. Similarly, they were reluctant to accept a mission demand for cultural transformation and demonstrated a desire for free access to a wider range of modern, cultural, educated and economic opportunities than missionaries were prepared to grant. Africans were sensitive to missionary unwillingness to afford them higher training, ordain an adequate number of indigenous priests, devolve power or overtly support nationalism. Among the Roman Catholics, priestly formation was riddled with humiliation, racism, abuse of privacy, rejection of African values and other forms of intolerance. For long, Irish seminaries refused to admit African candidates.[20] Meanwhile, virulent rivalry suffused the missionary enterprise as each denomination sought to imprint its own version of the shared agenda and thereby engendered immense social and political divides which would hinder the mobilization of the community in the modernity project. These factors fuelled the anti-missionary sentiments that underpinned African understanding of decolonization. Obviously, black Christians and white missionaries perceived the process differently.

Many signs warned that missionary power could not be exercised in the same way for much longer. For instance, at the heels of the anti-foreign movements in the Orient, the Jerusalem Conference of 1928 pressed the case for an indigenous church and a reappraisal of attitude towards other faiths. On the home front, attacks appeared from fundamentalists and academic circles in the next decade. Other alerts sapped missionary confidence as geopolitical events such as the Great Depression and the toll of rapid expansion combined as an onslaught on manpower and financial capabilities of the enterprise. Using a case study of British missionary responses to African colonial issues, 1945-1953, John Stuart has shown the increasing strain in the relationship, policies and power arrangements between missionaries and British government on the one hand, and Africans on the other. The latter tended to jettison the middleman role of the missionaries so as to deal directly with the secular authorities.[21] By the end of the Second World War, the Anglicans considered massive restructuring. But many missionaries were heedless; others talked about the situation, wrote wise memos on salient political ethics and reorganization of social services, but approached matters cautiously. Then, the nationalist challenge gradually picked up steam inspired by events in India and Ceylon and experiences in the Second World War. Stephen Neill, who participated in the first meeting of the International Missionary Council after the war in Whitby, Ontario, Canada, in 1947, pointed to the obvious change as many of the members of the younger churches spoke with great confidence and sure-footedness:

> And now, at Whitby, unmistakably they came as equals ... They showed in consequence a fuller understanding of the world-wide problems of the Church, a greater depth of Christian experience, a wider sympathy for the needs and cares of others.

He remained nonetheless skeptical about their readiness to assume leadership.

The missions were rudely awakened by the speed of decolonization. As Basil Davidson concluded, "it could accordingly be said that the colonial powers stumbled out of Africa as best they could, keeping their own interest always in view and at no time applying initiatives that were not, in one way or another imposed or provoked by African pressures for anti-colonial challenge."[22] The joke is that the British stumbled out of the colonies, the French and Belgians abandoned theirs, while the Portuguese had theirs snatched violently from them. Between 1952 and 1956, most of the Maghrib became politically independent, West Africa followed from 1957 through 1960, and the rest joined after protracted struggles. Four reasons have been adduced for decolonization: while some may query the concept of nationalism in the African context, many hold that the nationalism of the elite who chafed about their exclusion from power was core to igniting the process. Here, cultural nationalism was replaced by political nationalism. The geo-political scenario after the Second World War has been mentioned. The rise of the United States and its foreign policy goals loomed large. David Birmingham concludes that "African decolonization can be interpreted as a European retreat determined by weakness following a debilitating Second World War and the emergence of the two new tentacular empires of the United States and the Soviet Union." Along with this was the economic factor as Europe sought to rebuild. The role of the "official mind" leaves the impression of a deliberate calculation of British interests to be protected with constitutions and a conscious initiative to liquidate the empire. This perception has been vigorously challenged by the argument that in the politics of containment, decolonization was an opportunistic response in crisis management. In the course of it, the colonial governments abandoned their intimate enemy: "it is no longer Christianity, Civilization and Commerce but social engineering, technical assistance and capital investment which are expected to harmonize the interests of Africa and Europe."[23]

The inescapable conclusion is that decolonization did not imply a radical change of socio-economic structure. Gramsci explains the gap with the concept of *passive revolution,* describing the way that a dominant socio-political group may have to change its way of wielding power if it wants to maintain it.[24] The goal of decolonization was to return to informal empire where former rulers would retain sufficient economic and technological resources to exercise powerful influence upon future development, a limited transfer of power which bequeathed ossified state apparatus, institutions and extensions of colonial policies, which burdened the nations with artificial boundaries, incomprehensible constitutions and parasitic elites. Passive revolution has fuelled the modernization and dependency theories in political analysis of contemporary African pathology. It is the root of the divinity of the market and co-operation between a predatory elite and multi-national companies.

The perspective here is that missionaries shared a similar tactical response to decolonization, however, at a great cost, resilience and change of tack. For instance, they abandoned their opposition to modernity, embraced it, sought to channel it towards the hallmarks of liberal theology, reflecting the shift in European culture in the economic boom years, 1960-1970, and under the shivers of the cold war. However, the responses of the missionaries to nationalist insurgence at the twilight of colonialism, 1945-1959, differed in quality from the re-tooling strategies in the immediate aftermath, 1960-1975. Vast changes in the political climate of the decade 1966-1975 forced enormous changes in the religious landscape.

The story goes back to the late 1940s, when African nationalist activities rose in crescendo as political parties sprouted from country to country. One explanation is that a younger breed with sharper focus came to the fore sidelining both traditional rulers and moderates to bask in the fiery sun of mass adulation. Some appeasers such as Albert Luthuli abandoned the ideal of racial co-operation, disillusioned by the racism in the church. Undoubtedly, missionary responses to nationalism varied during the first decade, 1945-1954, according to individual whims, official or denominational/institutional policies and regional contexts. A certain shift followed as missionaries felt powerless to halt the process and betrayed by both government and protégés. Some, in the field, tried to use available facilities to stem the tide by posturing a dichotomy between Christianity and politics. Drama, public debates and lectures were pressed into the effort to warn Christians to eschew politics and seek first the kingdom of God; that colonialism, when properly reined, was for the good of Africans. The Moral Re-armament group networked through West Africa to inculcate salient political ethics. Some missionaries were indiscreetly hostile, such as William Carey, formerly Archbishop of Bloemfontein, while others such as the irrepressible Michael Scott, the voice of the Herero, represented those sympathetic to the African cause. Generally, institutional attitude varied: those at the home base espoused ideal positions which showed some sympathy for Africans, but were so cautious that these amounted to little.

In the field, some were alarmed at the prospects of Marxism or resurgence of paganism, angry about the ingratitude of the African elite and resolved to contain the damage. Nationalism was imaged as irreligious and the nationalists were portrayed as too immature to lead nations to a democratic vision. N.M. Bowman, writing in a Church of Scotland journal in 1947, put it succinctly. Entitled, "Democracy Without Religion", he argues:[25]

> A nation does not learn overnight to think of power as servant and not the master of justice. People do not acquire in a single generation that sense of responsibility, that sense of stewardship, that integrity without which corruption and greed will speedily threaten all attempts to run their own affairs.

The period of tutelage had been too short to produce the right moral environment for independence. The cautious mood could be traced in ecumenical political thought from the concern on the place of the state in God's design at Oxford in 1937 through Amsterdam's interest on "The Responsible Society" in 1948 to Willingen in 1952 when, for once, a strong social concern provided a shift.

Regional differences abound. West Africa had plenty of mosquitoes and no white settler community; therefore, indigenization policy predominated in the mid-1950s. It had three prongs: to waltz with nationalists, utilize the services of indigenous personnel and to seek to adapt Christianity to African culture in the belief that African need was to "baptize" ingredients of their culture. Many of the priests trained in the early 1950s were the vanguard. This limited perception of African Christian initiative in religion would be exposed later. Meanwhile, it formed a part of the arsenal for a passive revolution. The Belgians in central Africa sought to legitimize their rule with Catholicism. Salazar's Concordat of 1940 recognized and funded the Catholic Church as the official instrument to promote national colonial aims of the state in Angola and Mozambique. In the

Congo, the career of Bishop Jean de Hemptinne, Vicar Apostolic of Katanga, buttressed the loyalist support. Similarly, the church's manipulation of religion in Rwanda has become the subject of indictment.[26] In Ethiopia, the Emperor, Haile Selassie, used a revised constitution to rope the Orthodox Church into state structures as the *Abuna* sat in the Council of Regency and Crown Council. In eastern Africa, waltzing with nationalists in Uganda forced the church into the public space and, in the first elections, a Catholic Kiwanuka jostled with a Protestant Obote, celebrating the fruits of years of virulent rivalry and thereby dividing the society. Liberia offered an unenviable model where the state stood on the tripod of Christianity, Masonic Lodge and True Whig Party as the rulers bowed to the three power nodes.[27]

The impact of decolonization on church groups varied, based on certain indices: the size and ecclesiastical organization; the vertical spread and social quality of adherents; the inherited pattern of colonial relationship; and the theological emphasis and international relations. It also depended upon the manner of disengagement, the weave of neo-colonial fabric and the dosage of Marxism in the political mix. Any of these could aid weal or woe depending on the context. For instance, in the Congo, Mobutu perceived the Roman Catholics as a danger to be demolished as gods do not brook competition.

The core of godly passive revolution depended on the rear-guard actions to re-tool so as to maintain influence using indigenous personnel and resources. This was the main thrust of the missionary policy of indigenization. There were at least a dozen measures: manpower development; internal restructuring through church unity and ecumenism; balancing aid and selfhood in funding so as to cure dependency and nurture stewardship; revisiting cultural policy through adaptation and thereby catalyzing a controlled initiative in art and liturgy; re-aligning the church-state relationship by involving more Christians in politics; encouraging theological reflection; installing a new model of relationship which uses the idiom of partnership to camouflage paternalism and thus essaying to maintain social services along the old lines. These cumulatively would remedy the after-effects of the past excessive control, preserve the core of missionary structures, while broadening African participation to respond to the challenges created by the insurgent nationalism of the new African states. This counter-insurgence was aided by a paradigm shift in the ecumenical movement that occurred in Uppsala in 1968. Konrad Raiser terms it "*the expansion of the ecumenical perspective universally to all humanity*."[28] They raised a new understanding of mission, science and technology, the challenges of modernity, dialogue with other faiths and justice and race. The support for freedom fighters stirred an internal debate that only began to subside at the WCC General Assembly, Nairobi, in 1975.

Similarly, Vatican II, which had only 61 Africans out of 2,500 bishops, was a watershed in re-designing the church's policy in mission and social service. It released African energy in the church as a number of Papal pronouncements appeared to speak to Africans in a new voice.[29] Pope John Paul II's call for inculturation and enrichment released much hope before people realized that Curial control and liturgy within Roman rites shortened the ropes. Nonetheless, the renaissance of Christian art left an enduring mark as Father Kevin Carroll in Nigeria, Ethelbert Mveng in Cameroon, and John Groeber in southern Africa mentored a number of young artists.[30] Equally impressive was the depth of liturgical renewal in music, dance, use of native languages, radicalization of block rosary and formation of associations around new liturgical practices as vigils retreat centers and such like sprung up to the consternation of missionaries. Luis Luzbetak argued that the Roman Catholic Church witnessed major changes within the period of the world wars and that these seven forces determined the path for the future: the rise of social action, ecumenical initiatives, the biblical and liturgical movements, theological renewal, promotion of lay apostolate and missionary movement.[31]

The details of these strategies will not bear repetition. Suffice it to say that the level of ministerial formation galloped from the 1960s. Theological education had an enormous boost with the formation of regional and continental associations that encouraged theological reflection and revision of curricula in Bible Schools. Many experimented with Theological Education by Extension, while the genesis of Ecumenical Association of Third World Theologians (EATWOT), brought together many from those regions of the world where the pressing question would be, "*eat what*"? In the rainy season of 1973, the WCC met at Ibadan to explore how to readjust the funding of African churches so as to encourage them to learn the art of giving. When the Board of Faith and Order of the WCC met at Accra in August 1974, there were more Union talks going on in Africa than in other continents. The leaders of the Church of South India and those from Ceylon toured Africa to provide advice. Except in the case of Zambia, all others collapsed.

To use the case of Nigeria as an example, theological and non-theological reasons colluded to thwart the dream. The scions of the faith churches dismissed the Constitution of the Union as lacking adequate spirituality. Other minor doctrinal matters caused concern but the real weighty issues were personality clashes and rivalries, denominational hostilities that had not healed, competition for the bishoprics and ethnicity. Finally, some Methodist congregations took the Union Committee to court while the Civil War (1967-1970) scattered the litigants.[32] Studies from eastern Africa have confirmed how the same factors that destabilized African nation states wrecked havoc in Christian circles.[33] Admittedly, many of these could occur in any other context beyond Africa but the key difference was that it was felt that church unity was imposed from the outside.

Could the re-tooling strategies be interpreted as passive revolution? Stephen Neill's insider analysis of the various meetings on partnership from 1947 has been alluded to. Two other insiders who served the home base of missionary organizations testify so. T.A. Beetham queries the motives of the salvage operations:[34]

> Are the thinking and experiment and action ... merely a fumbling *attempt to retain influence*, to gain some new position of authority *to* compensate for privileges now being rapidly lost? Or has it a significant future?

In a similar vein, J.V. Taylor, who served as the General Secretary of the CMS in those heady 1960s gave a hardly garnished evaluation of the indigenization process. He observes that it has become fashionable for white men of his generation to join "*in the chorus of disparagement against the Gothic churches and pietistic hymn tunes that have everywhere stamped the church as a foreign import*" in Africa. Worse, indigenization has failed because the indigenous people believe that "*we are playing at it*" while holding to orthodoxy, fearing the dangers of syncretism, acting with "mixed motives" and unduly moralistic ethics:[35]

> Instead of waiting humbly to discover what kind of leadership the Lord is raising up for His church in Africa or Asia, missionaries have been busily engaged in grooming successors to themselves ... reproducing their stereotyped kind of leadership.

In a way, this was a truism having been the goal of missionary education and elite formation. The strategy was sharpened for new ends. But Taylor reveals that decolonization caused much soul-searching about the meaning and goal of mission. Attention turned briefly from the abilities of Africans to keep away from the warm embrace of witchdoctors. Lars Thurnberg calls it "the redemption for the wrongs of history", Lesslie Newbigin images a context where sending churches would become "bridge-builders" serving at "mission points". The Lutheran World Federation experimented with "reverse flow" in which African ministers were posted to German congregations where everybody treated them with cold civility.

V. WALTZING WITH THE NATIONALISTS, 1955-1975

The African story in the two decades between 1955 and 1975 worked out more clearly the issues raised in the period from the end of the Second World War in 1945. People increasingly found the missionary version of indigenization to be unsatisfactory and restrictive. Yet Christianity was attractive and grew tremendously as the charismatic spirituality, unleashed by the African Indigenous Churches and Pentecostal movements, was absorbed into the mission churches. Liturgical experimentation caused disquiet in many places as "traditionalism" impeded progress. Power conflicts followed the intensified process of laicization of the church. Many reasons are adduced: first, from the inside, the bible movement increased use of the Bible in the vernacular; the energy released by Vatican II and Uppsala released people from the restriction of yesteryears enabling the Africanization of the liturgy. Second, from the outside, government take-over of schools and hospitals jolted the ascendancy of the churches and compelled them to turn to their true calling. Third, from the fringes of the Christian body, the growing competition from the Christian left-wing or charismatic movements of various hues challenged polity, liturgy, ethics and in certain cases, doctrine. Fourth, the deliberate policy to encapsulate the elite combined with the impact of a new crop of trained clergy to create a ferment and a sense of being at the threshold of new beginnings and new theological reflections. The laicization of the church was particularly significant, because the churches wanted their people to use their powers and good offices to act as "*defensores fidei" (defenders of the faith).* Knighthood Orders were designed to attract the elite. These, in turn, found the church members as assured voters. Soon, their social and financial influence became more important in church affairs and decision-making than anticipated. From a different angle, African theology was loudly canvassed by the academics and the "nationalism" of the new theologians harped on the vestiges of missionary structures and the predicaments of an un-indigenized church. New terminologies were canvassed, such as *contextualization, traditionalization, incarnation* and *inculturation*, as Africans wanted a new type of church or renewed body of Christ and a new relationship with the West. While Roman Catholic priests challenged celibacy, their protestant counterparts wanted to celebrate the commensality of the Eucharist with palm wine and kola-nut. The Bible supplied precedents proffering the possibility that the spirituality of primal religion resonated and did not always conflict with the canon. There was much ferment in the churches and efforts to sabotage the limited indigenization project from the inside.

Outside the church, the growth of the state in Africa in this period was significant by causing political instability, human right abuse, environmental degradation and economic collapse. New states imaged their goals in Christian garbs in obvious attempt to bowdlerize: *national redemption, economic salvation, political justification, national regeneration, sanctity of the state.* Many became one-party states, others praetorian, while some took to Marxism. The churches became alarmed. The Catholics assigned the Jesuit veteran missionary, J.C. McKenna, to understudy the problem. Out of forty-four sub-Saharan nations fifteen leaned in this direction soon after Independence. On a closer look, none were Marxist purist, as the Cold War attracted a variety of leftist ideologies from USSR, China, Cuba, America and Europe. Africans responded with home-grown breeds as Conscientism, African Socialism, Humanism, and Centralized Democracy. In spite of Ratsiraka's Red Book in Madagascar, the churches thrived. The hostility in former Iberian enclaves soon diminished. Renamo flirted with the Pentecostals, FNLA with Baptists—even as peace in the Civil War was brokered by lay Catholics of the Communita di Sant-Egidio in Italy. In Angola and Zambia political rhetoric did not hurt the churches as much as the bad economic policies and disease.[36] On the whole, the power adventurism of the states forced major changes on the pattern of Christian presence in Africa.

All these chickens came to roost in the moratorium debate, 1971-1975. Moratorium was a more strident and different form of indigenization project. It reflected African impatience with the nature, pace and results of mission-initiated indigenization. Africans suspected a hidden agenda to embroil them in cosmetics while the same people retained real power. John Gatu, the Secretary-General of Presbyterian Church in Kenya, initiated the call during a visit to the USA in 1971. He embarrassed his hosts by declaring that he had not come to beg for money or personnel, but to request that missionary aid in money and personnel should cease for at least five years so that the short man could learn how to hang his knapsack within reach. Earlier, he led his church to produce a document stating what they believed. This raised the issue of doctrine. Burgess Carr, the Secretary of the AACC, Nairobi, was equally enamored to the idea, proposed it at Lusaka and invited African churches symbolically to Alexandria to draft an African Confession of Faith. By 1974, E.B. Idowu, the new leader of the Methodist Church in Nigeria, who for the last decade had spoken about the predicaments of an un-indigenized African church, moved the boundaries to matters of polity by proposing a patriarchal polity in consonance with the early church in North Africa. Were these romantic moves or sabotage?

Many Western mission bodies saw red and responded in a number of telling ways as a debate ensued in seminars, conferences and pages of journals. It was argued that *theologically*, moratorium was unacceptable because of the Pauline imagery of *soma*, that we are one body and one part cannot prevent the other from performing a mandatory task. Mission was the raison *d'etre* of the church, a command from the Lord. *Ecclesiastically*, it was dangerous to become a national church. This threatened catholicity; the pilgrim and the indigenous principles must be held in tension. *Logistically,* it would be impossible to dismantle the mission structures which had been built on for over a century. Then, there was the *gut* reaction of those who presumed that the Africans have proved ungrateful after years of sacrifices by missionaries. Eliot Kendall, who served the same constituency as Beetham, has documented the overt and subtle pressures mounted on African church leaders.[37] Dissent was punished with denial and low intensity operation to foment local rebellion as moratorium was perceived as sabotage. It did not take long for ranks to break: some leaders preferred aid rather than suffer as freedom fighters. Burgess Carr lost his job, while Idowu became embroiled in schism; the AACC languished until everyone forgot the spelling of moratorium.

Avoiding the cardinal sin of monocausality, there was more to the fates of these men, but the debate was crucial. Moratorium exposed the character of African relationship with the West: extraversion was in-built in the pattern of African relationship with the West as an essential ingredient to maintain "eternal juniority". Even the support among white liberals proved ambiguous as some Protestant missions took the opportunity to abandon missionary engagement. However, they have found that the collapse of their missionary involvement diminished both the volume of local funds and relevance in the public space; so, they are now forced to create new network patterns. Moratorium and African liberation struggles influenced the shifts in the strategy for decolonizing the African churches. When the WCC General Assembly met in Nairobi in 1975, the themes indicated a new mood that accepted African Christian maturity in ways hardly planned by the missionaries. The concept of the "Christendom" collapsed in this period as a new dispensation opened into the future in which African Christianity would be very important.

Notes

1. *Gaba Pastoral Letter*, 7 (1969) 50-51.
2. James CAMPBELL, "African American Missionaries and the Colonial State: the AME Church in South Africa", in H.B. HANSEN & M. TWADDLE (eds) *Christian Missionaries and the State in the Third World* (Oxford: James Currey, 2002), 234.
3. Ian LINDEN, *Catholics, Peasants, and Chewa Resistance in Nyasaland, 1889-1939* (Berkeley: University of California Press, 1974), 95.
4. Marie LOUISE, *Kimbangu* (London: Oxford University Press, 1957). See, Thomas HODGKIN, *Nationalism in Colonial Africa* (New York University Press, 1957), ch. 3. The trial is cited on p.98.
5. Michael O. WEST, "Ethiopianism and Colonialism: The African Orthodox Church in Zimbabwe, 1924-34", H.B. HANSEN & M. TWADDLE (eds), *Christian Missionaries and the State in the Third World* (Oxford: Currey, 2002), 237-254.
6. A.J. TEMU, *British Protestant Missions* (London: Longmans, 1972), 117.
7. Bengt SUNDKLER & Christopher STEED, *A History of the Church in Africa* (Cambridge: Cambridge University Press, 2000), 610-615.
8. LINDEN, *Catholics*, 109.
9. TEMU, *British Protestant Missions*, 118.
10. George SHEPPERSON, "Ethiopianism: Past and Present", in C.G. BAETA (ed.) Christianity in Tropical Africa (London: Oxford University Press, 1968), 253.
11. See TEMU, *British Protestant missions*, 117-139.
12. For an attempt to construct a coherent discourse on this form of spirituality, see, Allan ANDERSON, *African Reformation* (Trenton, NJ: Africa World Press, 2002).
13. Harold W. TURNER, "Pagan Features in West African Independent Churches", in *Practical Anthropology*, 12, 4 (1965) 145-151; H.W. TURNER, "A Typology for African Religious Movements", in *Journal of Religion in Africa*, 1, 1 (1967), 1-32.
14. See, James COCHRANE, *Servants of Power:* The Role of English-Speaking Churches in South Africa: 1903-1930 (Johannesburg: Ravan Press, 1987), 127.
15. T.A BEETHAM, *Christianity and the New Africa* (London: Pall Mall Press, 1967).
16. J.W. DE GRUCHY, *Christianity and Democracy* (Cambridge: Cambridge University Press, 1995), 183; A. HASTINGS, A *History of African Christianity, 1950-1975* (Cambridge: Cambridge University Press, 1979), 187ff; O.U. KALU, "Peter Pan Syndrome: Church Aid and Selfhood in Africa" in *Missiology*, 3, 1 (January, 1975) 15-29; D. FORRISTAL, *The Second Burial of Bishop Shanahan* (Dublin: Veritas Publishers, 1990).
17. M. NOLL, "Evangelical Identity, Power and Culture in the Great Nineteenth Century" (Currents in World Christianity Seminar, Oxford, 1997), 7; B. STANLEY, *The Bible and the Flag* (Leceister: Apollo-Varsity Press, 1990), 16.

18. R.W. Strayer, *The Making of Mission Communities in East Africa* (London: Heinemann, 1978); T.O. Beidelman, *Colonial Evangelism* (Bloomington: Indiana University Press, 1982).
19. A.E. Barnes, "Evangelization Where It Is not Wanted: Colonial Administrators and Missionaries in Northern Nigeria During the First Third of the Twentieth Century", in *Journal of Religion in Africa*, 25, 4 (1995) 412-441.
20. I.R.A. Ozigboh, *Igbo Catholicism* (Onitsha: Africana-FEP, 1985); A.N. Ekwunife, "Integration of African Values in Priestly Formation" in *AFER*, 39, 4 (1997) 194-213.
21. J. Stuart, "British Missionary Responses to African Colonial Issues, 1945-53" (XIXth Int. Congress of the Historical Sciences, Oslo, August 2000); C. Weber, "Christianity and West African Decolonisation" (Cambridge, NAMP Position Paper, 80, 1997); Stephen Neill, *Christian Partnership* (London, SCM Press, 1952), 14.
22. In P. Gifford & R.W Louis (eds), *Decolonisation and African Independence: The Transfer* of *Powers, 1960-1980* (New Haven: Yale Univeristy Press, 1988), 509; see, J.D. Hargreaves, *The End of Colonial Rule in West Africa* (London: McMillan, 1979).
23. Hargreaves, *The End of Colonial Rule*, xii; T.O. Ranger, "Connection between primary resistance and modern mass nationalism" *Journal of African History* 9, 3 (1968);T.O Ranger, "Religious Movements and politics in Sub-Saharan Africa" in *African Studies Review*, 29, 2 (1986), 1-69; R. Pearce, "The Colonial Office and Planned Decolonisation in Africa" in *African Affairs*, 83 (1984) 77-93; J.E. Flint, "The Failure of Planned Decolonisation in British Africa" in *African Affairs*, 82 (1983) 389-411; David Birmingham, *The Decolonisation of Africa* (Athens, Ohio: Ohio University Press, 1995), 89; see, Ajayi & Ekoko in Gifford & Louis, *Decolonisation and African Independence*, 245-270.
24. See, J. Haynes, *Religion and Politics in Africa* (London: Zed Books, 1996).
25. *Life and Work* (October 1947), 111.
26. Tim Longman, "Empowering the Weak and Protecting the Powerful" in *African Studies Review*, 41 (April, 1998), 49-72.
27. O.U. Kalu, "Tools of Hope: Stagnation and Political Theology in Africa, 1960-95", in M. Hutchinson & O.U. Kalu, *A Global Faith: Essays in Evangelicalism and Globalization* (Sydney: CSAC, 1998), 181-213.
28. Konrad Raiser, *Ecumenism in Transition: A Paradigm Shift in the Ecumenical Movement* (Geneva: WCC Publication, 1991), 54; Lesslie Newbegin, "Ecumenical Amnesia", in *International Bulletin of Mission Research*, 18, 1 (January, 1994) 1-5; Charles West, *The Power To Be Human* (New York: McMillan, 1971).
29. *Gaba Pastoral Letter*, 50-51; J. Mullen, *The Catholic Church in Modern Africa* (Dublin, 1965); E.E. Uzoukwu, *Liturgy: Truly Christian, Truly African* (Eldoret: Gaba Publications, 1982); F.K. Lumbala, *Celebrating Jesus in Africa: Liturgy and Inculturation* (Maryknoll: Orbis, 1998).
30. K. Carroll, *Yoruba Religious Art* (London: Geoffrey Chapman, 1967); R.I.J. Hackett, *Art and Religion in Africa* (London: Cassell, 1996).
31. Luis Luzbetak, *The Church and Cultures* (Maryknoll: Orbis, 1993), 103.
32. O.U. Kalu, *Divided People of God: Church Union Movement in Nigeria, 1867-1967* (New York: NOK Publishers, 1978); O.U. Kalu, "Church Unity and Religious

Change in Africa", in Edward FAKSHOLE-LUKE, Richard GRAY, Adrian HASTINGS, & Godwin TASIE (eds), *Christianity in Independent Africa* (Bloomington: Indiana University Press, 1978), 164-175.

33. J. MUGAMBI, J. MUTISO-MBINDA & J. VOLLBRECHT (eds), *Ecumenical Initiatives in Eastern Africa* (Nairobi: AACC/AMCEA Joint Research Project, 1992).
34. BEETHAM, *Christianity and the New Africa*, 151.
35. J.V. TAYLOR, "Selfhood: Presence or Personae?" in Bengt SUNDKLER, Peter BEYERHAUS & Carl F. HALLENCREUTZ (eds), *The Church Crossing Frontiers: Essays on the Nature of Mission. In Honour of Bengt Sundkler* (Studia Missionalia Uppsaliensia, XI, 1969), 171-176. See contributions by Thurnberg, pp 209-225, and Lesslie Newbegin, pp 245-265.
36. J.C. MCKENNA, *Finding a Social Voice: The Church and Marxism in Africa* (New York: Fordham University Press, 1997).
37. O.U. KALU, "Church, Mission and Moratorium" in O.U. KALU, *The History of Christianity in West Africa* (London: Longman, 1980), 365-374; O.U. KALU, "Not Just New Relationship But a Renewed Body", in *International Review of Missions,* 64 (April, 1975); Eliot KENDALL, *The End of An Era* (London, 1978), 85.

Chapter Fourteen

Mainline Churches in the Public Space, 1975-2000

J.W. Hofmeyr

INTRODUCTION

The wind of change that blew many African nations into political independence from the late 1950s to the 1960s turned into a gale after the independence anthems ended. The new nation states turned into predatory states: some became one-party states; others spawned leaders who used the states as private large farms; still others mistook their states as a military barracks. Coups and counter-coups followed amidst the ideological cant about socialism. By 1975, the political map of Africa was redesigned as the inherited democratic constitutions were shredded. The new states became virtually "theological states", seeking to control every aspect of the citizens' lives. Theorists initially praised the "politics of mobilization", arguing that it was necessary to "modernize" by curbing the inherited, divisive, politics of tribes and tongues that sported too many power nodes. Opponents yelled that it was *not yet uhuru* because the boils in the post-colonial period were worse than the yaws of colonialism.

Between 1975 and 1990, the effects of poor leadership and militarization of the society became daunting as economies collapsed, abuse of human rights and the ecology followed, civil society was decimated and corruption became rampant. European nations that had given huge loans to corrupt leaders moved in to collect on the debtor nations. The agent was the World Bank that used the structural adjustment program to rein in their victims and deployed NGOs to take the message into the hinterland bypassing the state apparati. Poverty hit Africa and civil wars ensued with incredible brutality as caged rats ate themselves. Something also snapped at the world scene as Soviet Russia collapsed. This gave the capitalist nations of the world, dominated by the United States of America, the leverage to intervene to the affairs of their corrupt satellites. Some thought that it was the end of history. The new powers read the riot act to the dictators and encouraged the indigenes to hold democratic assemblies for renegotiating the patterns of power. The end of the cold war ushered in the end of patronizing dictators. Admittedly, the results were mixed as many dictators either removed their military uniforms and donned civilian clothes, or permitted multi-party regimens as to return to power in new guises. Still, the "second liberation of Africa", as pundits dubbed the process changed the nature of African politics.

Among the major changes was the return of the churches into the public space. Though maimed, they appear to have been the only survivors within the civil society. Other components of civil society such as trade unions, academics and students, professional bodies, judiciary, traditional rulers and any other restraining social force had been compromised or destroyed. This backdrop gives poignancy to the story of African Christianity in the period 1975 to the end of the millennium. What was the role of the church in the recovery process? This is the burden of this chapter.

Some think that churches that colluded with the colonial enterprise and waltzed with nationalists had lost its relevance in the public space. Others think that the churches were in fact equipped to play such an important role; that, while the colonial powers hindered rather than helped prepare the way for democratic rule after independence, such preparation often did take place within Christian missionary institutions. These were not democratic in themselves, but they inculcated democracy as the ideal form of political organization. As De Gruchy so clearly states:[1]

> In much of sub-Saharan Africa, the principles of unity, democracy and self-government were developed in the church long before they were even dreamed of in the state.

Following on the heels of the Second World War came the collapse of the whole colonial system. In the 1940s and 1950s all of South and South-east Asia gained independence and in the Middle East the old League of Nations mandates were ended. A similar process of decolonization also occurred in the Caribbean and South Pacific islands. Between the years 1951 and 1968 all the North Africa Muslim states and most of the colonies south of the Sahara were liberated, beginning with Ghana in 1957. In 1974 and 1975 the Portuguese empire was dismantled. In 1980 Zimbabwe and in 1990 Namibia became independent. One-party states (e.g. Zaire, Kenya, Zambia) and socialist experiments (e.g. Congo, Tanzania) emerged to take their place. The only remaining factor in the liberation process was South Africa, which withdrew from the British Commonwealth in 1961 because of criticism against its apartheid policy, and only became a full democracy in 1994.

I. NEW DIMENSIONS IN MAINLINE CHRISTIANITY

Four new dimensions of African Christianity have characterized African Christianity in the twentieth century. In 1990, Richard Gray observed that two themes have dominated contemporary African church historiography: to tell the

African's own story of the encounter with the gospel, and to show Africa's contribution to world Christianity. For this second component, attention focused on the African Instituted Churches and the post-1970 growth of Charismatic and Pentecostal spirituality. He, therefore, warned against the neglect of the developments within the mainline churches. In most African countries, these mission founded churches with nineteenth century pedigrees have continued to grow. The Roman Catholic Church remains the single largest Christian group in Africa. The Anglican Communion in Nigeria has grown by over seven million in the last decade to about 17 million Anglicans out of 75 million worldwide. In 1979, the Nigerian church had sixteen dioceses, organized in a single province with a single archbishop; today it has nearly eighty dioceses, organized in ten provinces with ten archbishops. It would appear that various encapsulation strategies have ensured numerical growth and socio-political influence.

In 1998, Paul Gifford argued that the mainline churches, rather than the charismatic genres bore the brunt of social responsibility and played the most important roles in the public space from 1975 to the end of the millennium. The year 1975 is significant in African church history because the World Council of Churches held its General Assembly in Nairobi, Kenya. It signified that African Christianity had come of age and attracted world attention. In the meantime the process of decolonization was also succeeding and in all of this a measure of solidarity was reflected with Africans during the last throes of Western domination and the denial of justice to Africans in the central and southern regions of the continent.

First, the quarter century spanning from 1960 to 1985 was characterized by the implosion of the state, the attack on the dominant role of the church in the public space and the churches' various strategies for survival. The nationalism in the politics of independence turned against the church that had supported its path and trained its protagonists. Dictatorial one-party states, praetorian military juntas and the alliance with socialist ideologies reflected efforts to dislodge the vestiges of the colonial heritage. Recent scholarship argues that none of the African states were purist Marxist but the rhetoric impressed the masses to believe that an authentic African political culture and development would improve their lot. Christian churches were imaged as neo-imperialist symbols. Churches lost control of schools, hospitals and other charitable institutions. But by 1985, most economies had collapsed; poverty enveloped communities; abuse of human rights and legitimacy crises followed apace. Coups and counter coups symbolized that things had fallen apart. Aged rulers clung to power as if they were mafia godfathers. It was, however, eventually the change on the geopolitical front that catalyzed the rapid series of events that would bring Christianity to the center again. The collapse of the Berlin Wall, the collapse of Communist Russia and the end of the Cold War made democratic ideology popular again. Therefore, the question could be asked: What was the role of the churches in the democratization process during the last quarter of the twentieth century? A strange thing happened: churches had been accused of collusion in the colonial period and silent during the predatory army regimes but suddenly their relevance in the public space was recognized in one country after another. The leaders were the only trusted ones to chair or broker the democratic experiments. Was this an illusion? Many churches not only provided leadership during the overthrow of dictators but catalyzed the process. Some of the case studies below will provide more information in this respect.

The second factor, therefore, is the significant role, between 1986 and 1996 played by Christianity in combating racism and apartheid in Zimbabwe, Namibia and South Africa, and by intervening in the civil war in Mozambique. These interventions deserve attention because they moved beyond the cultural theology in many parts of Africa to the application of confession as a means of political engagement. *The Kairos Document* therefore, published in South Africa in 1986, was a major African contribution, especially as it diverged from a similar attempt by the German Christians in 1937. The support of the church for freedom fighters in Zimbabwe and Namibia paved the way for contributions in development.

Third, though ecumenism lost wind after the 1980s, African churches engaged in new co-operative ventures and used inculturation theology as a tool for evangelization. It is suggested that this fact engendered growth. African churches have in the decade of 1990-2000 developed new partnership relationships with overseas mentors and new forms of local cooperation. The All Africa Council of Churches (AACC) for instance, is regaining strength. The reasons include the decline of Christianity in the West; the withdrawal of long-term missionaries; the decline in funds for large-scale cross cultural missions; theological divisions over the ordination of gays that have weakened many metropolitan churches and the realization that the center of gravity of Christianity has shifted to the southern hemisphere.

Fourth, is the entry of churches into the zone of tertiary education that used to be the purview of the state. There is an increase in the number of church related universities. It reflects an attempt by churches to regain former command posts and to re-engage the public space in the wake of the failed economies and the confidence of the states. In the period 1980-2000, many Christian groups and churches created new colleges and universities in Nigeria, Cameroon, Kenya, Ghana and Zimbabwe. It could also be argued that this dimension has been compelled by competition with the rising challenge by Pentecostal and charismatic movements who first ventured into tertiary education. These processes will be picked up in greater detail in the next chapter.

It does appear that beyond these cultural matters, mainline churches have been compelled to adjust by enlarging the space for charismatic groups in polity, liturgy and ethics. Tithing, fasting, prayer bands, healing sessions, lively music, dancing and other forms of liturgical renewal are prevalent. Among Catholics, apparitions, monastic spirituality, black rosaries and the vernacularization of liturgy have released new devotional liturgies. This trend has two imports: at one level, it has catalyzed growth by renewing the old process of indigenization in a different key. But it has stamped African Christianity with a conservative character. The social policy on ordination of women in many churches, same-sex marriage and opposition to gays and lesbians are indications of a trend that has derailed the liberal attitudes of the Western metropoles of these churches.

However, it is often wondered whether this conservative character of African Christianity would hinder a creative response to the scourge of HIV/AIDS that is ravaging the continent. The question arises about the churches response in the face of the threat; to what extent has it served as a pressure group to ginger the governments? The importance of this question is heightened by the noticeable laicization of the Christianity in the twentieth century. Has this trend that has changed the power and leadership structure and brought women to the fore influenced the style of the churches' role in the public space?

II. SOME CASE STUDIES

Perhaps, it would best serve to illustrate these broad trends with case studies covering four regions of the continent: west, east, central and south. A different dimension of the mainline churches is highlighted in each case, such as growth at the expense of mainline churches in West Africa (Liberia); the clout of mainline churches in East Africa (Kenya); the mainline churches as a power broker in central Africa (Malawi); and the mainline churches' role in the transformation process in South Africa. The case studies rely on the works of contemporary scholars: Paul Gifford (1992), Ogbu Kalu (1998), Kenneth Ross (1999) and J.W. Hofmeyr (1994). In certain parts of Africa, mainline churches have lost their earlier monopoly, because of the growth of new Christian forms that have sprouted from within Protestant traditions. Years of monopoly created nominalism and the strategy proselytism made it impossible for the churches to evangelize and disciple the communities. Liberia sported two such cases before the Civil War that engulfed the country in the last decade. Bethel and Transcea were two different types that stole the center stage from the Methodists and Lutherans, who had dominated the religious power for years, often in collusion with Roman Catholics, Episcopalians and Presbyterians.

Paul Gifford provides a graphic account of Christianity in Doe's Liberia by contrasting the locations of the imposing Episcopal Cathedral, which occupies a commanding site on the hill on the main street of Monrovia, and the non-descript locations of the new churches. The Episcopal cathedral is probably the biggest church building in the country, elaborately furnished, with the organ donated by the Firestone family. In 1989, the cathedral attracted about 250 worshippers to its two Sunday morning services. Just 500 yards away, on a much less impressive site, the Transcontinental Evangelical Assembly Church (Transcea) met. This was founded in 1983; that is, 147 years after the Episcopal Church came to Liberia. Transcea had no buildings of its own, and rented schoolrooms every Sunday. Yet by 1989, 1600 people attended the four Sunday morning services, and the church was said to be growing at a rate of over 40 new members every week.

The Presbyterian Church was one of the first churches to come to Liberia, being established in 1833. The American missionaries later abandoned it, as they considered their foundation in Cameroon to be a far more viable proposition. Without missionary assistance, the Presbyterian Church remained very small. By 1989, it had only about 3000 members in the country. In 1977 a member of the Presbyterian Church went to the U.S.A to study. On his return in 1987, he did not return to the Presbyterian Church, but took over a young church founded the previous year, Bethel World Outreach. This church had about 120 members when he took over; by the end of 1987 the membership had increased to 250 and necessitated moving the Sunday services to the Monrovia City Hall. By late 1989, about 1200 people attended the two Sunday morning services. These examples illustrate an occurrence that was becoming more frequent in the 1980s throughout Africa. Mainline churches lost members and prominence to new churches that were growing and flourishing often at the expense of the mainline churches. This overview looks at Bethel and Transcea, Liberia's fastest-growing churches in the late 1980s, in an attempt to shed light on this development within African Christianity. Needless to add, all lost in the civil war and thereby created a new ecclesiastical situation.

1. The Context

Liberia is a small country situated at the south-western point of West Africa. Its 2.5 million inhabitants in 1989 were made up of sixteen principal tribes and a small group descended from repatriate American slaves or from slaves freed from slave-ships captured on the high seas. The first slaves were brought to Liberia in 1822. The number of these repatriate slaves was never large, but descendants of this small group of repatriates (about 3-5% of the population) monopolized all political power, and from 1870 ruled the country through their True Whig Party (TWP). Politics within this settler community were extremely corrupt. Incumbent presidents used every resource to stay in power. For example, in the 1927 elections, which returned President King, King was credited with 243,000 votes, and his opponent 9000, when the total electorate comprised no more than 15,000. In other words, the winner's majority was 17 times greater than the number of possible voters. This election won the title, in the Guinness Book of Records, as the "most bent" election of all time. Financial affairs were conducted in a similar fashion. There was a budget, but it was never adhered to. There was no system of accountability for public funds.

Firestone and other multinationals arrived after the 1920s. These multinationals contributed surprisingly little to the development of Liberia. They bought off Liberia's ruling elite, who in return for personal gain protected the companies' favorable terms, and made sure that government controls were kept to a minimum. Thus little was spent on planned expansion of the country's productive base, or on development of infrastructure. As late as the 1960s, the country had only ten miles of paved road. The government simply dispensed patronage to the increasing numbers of its own elite.

During the presidency of William Tubman (1944-1971), the patronage party state reached its limit. All government workers were required to contribute one month's salary to the TWP annually. The cult of the presidency also reached its peak in this period. Tubman subverted every institution of society to enhance it. Real opponents were victimized and destroyed, and at election time token opponents were produced to disguise the reality of a one-party state. He had a presidential yacht whose budget was greater than that for the country's justice system, and at one stage the appropriation for ceremonial bands surpassed the expenditure on public health.

After Tubman's death in 1971, his Vice-President William Tolbert took power. Tolbert was forced to make some changes, but the system remained fundamentally unaltered. In 1979, as chairman for that year, Tolbert was to host the annual conference of the OAU. He spent US$100 million in constructing a conference center, and not long afterwards announced that the price of rice would have to be raised. (It was not lost on the population that the Tolbert family, as the country's biggest rice producers, would derive most benefit from such an increase). This was the final straw, and on 14 April 1979 riots broke out, with widespread looting. Tolbert assumed emergency powers, put down the riots with great force, and postponed municipal elections. When a strike was called the following March, Tolbert had the leaders arrested on the grounds that they were plotting an armed insurrection. In the early hours of 12 April 1980, two days before the trial of the alleged plotters was to begin, a group of 17 enlisted men overthrew the government, killing Tolbert and 27 others.

Initially this coup was immensely popular. People danced in the streets and greeted the news with enthusiasm. But quite early, the event was perceived from ethnic lenses as the indigenous Liberians hailed the coup as their liberation after 158 years of domination by American-Liberians. The seventeen soldiers who carried out the coup declared Master Sergeant Samuel Doe as the Chairman of the People's Redemption Council that took over the reins of government. Doe announced that he had not assumed power to repeat the oppression of the past, and indicated that he would soon return the country to civilian rule. However, it was not long before the true nature of the regime became apparent. By 1984, Doe had lost all popular support. The general feeling was that the system was unchanged: "Same taxi, different driver", and, if anything, controlled by someone even more corrupt and inept than previous rulers.

In 1984, Doe set in motion the return to civilian rule. He immediately announced his own candidacy, and he obviously intended to win. For example, he immediately postdated a new decree of the defunct ruling council which made it a "felony of the first degree" to accuse any member of the assembly of any crime when one intended "to injure the official in his reputation, to create disharmony, spread rumors, lies and disinformation, to cause civil strife or confusions." By means of this infamous decree, "88A", he was making any criticism of him in the electoral campaign a criminal offence.

The ensuing election campaign was something of a charade. Doe simply banned the two leaders with the greatest following. Amos Sawyer and Bacchus Matthews were declared ineligible to take part in the election at all, because of "strange and foreign ideologies against our most tested and matured of life (sic)" and "espousal of and involvement in ideologies foreign to Liberia", respectively. Three parties besides Doe's National Democratic Party of Liberia were eventually permitted to contest the election. On the election day, 15 October 1985, there was a massive turnout. Voters queued for hours, and polling hours had to be extended from 6 pm till 11 pm. Observers soon announced that the Liberian Action Party was well in the lead, and would have a majority over all the other parties put together. So Doe's appointee as chairman of the elections' commission halted the count in the early morning of 16 October, and insisted that all votes be brought to Monrovia for counting. He established a new commission (packed with Doe's supporters) to count the votes. When the "official" results were announced on 29 October, Doe was credited with 50.9% in the four-way race for the presidency. The gloom that descended on Liberia that day was compared to the national gloom and stupefaction that enveloped the U.S.A. the day President Kennedy was assassinated.

The elections were barely over and the opposition parties were still protesting, when on 12 November 1985 there was a coup attempt. Initially it seemed to have succeeded, and there was unrestrained jubilation and dancing in the streets. The coup, however, lost momentum, and later in the day Doe came on the radio to announce that he was still in charge. Unfortunately, the dancing in the streets earlier had been recorded on video. Doe took revenge with indiscriminate repression, arrests, intimidation, torture and murder.

Doe was inaugurated as president of the second republic in January 1986. In reality, nothing had changed since the Tubman/Tolbert days, except that in many respects the regime was more blatant in its abuses and more inept. The new regime continued to make a mockery of the independence of the legislature and the judiciary. Freedom of speech was severely curtailed. Newspapers were threatened and closed at will. The community radio station ELCM was closed indefinitely in June 1989. And Doe continued to eliminate opponents, usually by discovering coup attempts, which would lead to the execution of alleged plotters, either with or without a form of trial. By 1988, only nine of the seventeen soldiers involved in the 1980 coup were still alive.

In all this greed, mismanagement, and single-minded pursuit of power, the economy disintegrated. Firms went bankrupt; unemployment soared. Liberia's GDP declined by an average of about 2.8% annually in 1980-1985, and continued to decline. Some revenues (for example, from logging) did not go into the national revenues at all; they went to Doe's private funds, to be dispensed as he saw fit. Misappropriation of funds was rife. Corruption crippled the system at every level. Immigration functionaries required a bribe before they would stamp a passport. School inspectors could threaten to close a school unless they were paid a bribe. Soldiers and police on duty at roadblocks required bribes to let passengers through. When corruption at the top was so shameless, there was no discouragement at lower levels.

Of course, the general deterioration affected everyone. Food and fuel shortages became common. The infrastructure crumbled. Roads in the interior became impassable during the rains, and even in Monrovia roads were often impassable. Public buildings fell into disrepair. (For example, the gaol in Greenville simply collapsed while prisoners were asleep; they escaped). Education regressed in all sorts of ways. A World Bank study in 1988 noted that Liberia had a literacy rate of 35%. Between 1982 and 1986 public primary school enrollment dropped 27%, from 109,681 to 80,048 students. The total percentage of expenditure on education in 1980 and 1983 was 24.3% and 13.2% respectively—a 45% decrease in the government's commitment to education. Teachers were not paid for months on end; books were scarce. The state of the health service became just as critical. In many regions there were no drugs at all between 1982 and 1985. Leprosy was on the increase—482 new cases were reported in 1988—and the TB program simply collapsed. Monrovia's teaching hospital became a national disgrace.

This was the situation when, on Christmas Eve 1989, Charles Taylor launched the invasion that led to the death of Doe on 10 September 1990, and the almost total destruction of Liberia that had always prided itself on being a Christian country. President Tubman had been a prominent Methodist. President Tolbert was president of the Liberian Baptist convention for the fifteen years prior to his death. (In fact he had been elected the 11th President of the Baptist World Alliance in 1965.) Doe also had joined the Baptist Church. Liberia is a case study where the church was at the helm of corrupt public role, because the mainline churches had always enjoyed a privileged position. However, as the socio-economic situation deteriorated, there occurred a veritable explosion of new churches. The most prominent among these churches were the two we will now consider.

Bethel was founded in January 1986 by a Liberian (a Kru), who had studied at the Moody Bible Institute in Chicago. As a fulltime employee of Liberia's Telecom, he had limited time to devote to the church. He needed someone with more training to serve as pastor. He thus approached a Liberian completing a DMin (in children's city ministry) at Oral Roberts University, Tulsa. This Liberian, a former Presbyterian, returned and effectively took over Bethel in July 1987, when the church numbered about 120 members and was meeting in a schoolroom. Under its new pastor (the original founder soon left for Oral Roberts University himself) the church grew rapidly; by November 1987 it numbered about 250 members and shifted to Monrovia's City Hall. By late 1989 it was attracting 1200 to its two services each Sunday morning. It had also started a daughter church across the St Paul River in Virginia County. Moreover, Bethel's influence extended beyond those who attended its services. The church attracted considerable publicity through its spectacular growth and high-profile activities. The pastor rapidly became one of the prominent churchmen in the city. He was one of those behind the establishment of the Liberia Fellowship of Full Gospel Ministers, and was made its first president. This body was established to promote Bethel's style of Christianity. The Bethel pastor's own status ensured that this body allowed him to exert a kind of hegemony over twenty or thirty similar churches.

Transcea, on the other hand, was founded in 1982 in Ghana by a 21 year old Ghanaian Presbyterian. He was then studying law through correspondence, and won a scholarship to study law at Oral Roberts University in Tulsa. In August 1983, on his way to the USA, he passed through Liberia; here he said the call became too strong, and he stayed and began Transcea. Initially, he started a very strong charismatic ministry that featured all signs such as healing of the dumb and deaf, and intensive prayer and Bible study. Later, in 1987, he moved back to his Calvinist roots, privileging holiness of life and asceticism. He spoke rather bitterly of the charismatic movement, calling it pure "salesmanship" which leads to no understanding or commitment on the part of its members, whose lives are normally no different from those of unbelievers. Privately he would talk of "all the rubbish I learned from that lot". At the time of this change of direction he abolished drums and dancing in the church as inconsistent with the Bible. He replaced them with an organ and intended introducing other biblical instruments (like flute and trumpet) as money allowed.

As another part of this change, he abolished praying in tongues in church; after 1987 members could pray in tongues in private at home, but not in public. Similarly, prayer for healing was restricted to after rather than during the service. Although the pastor expected God to meet the needs of his people, he said he ceased preaching the gospel of prosperity. At the same time he severed links with his original churches in Ghana, and a new one established in Sierra Leone. In Liberia he resisted all attempts to draw him into charismatic fellowships and maintained his isolation. In this, Transcea was unlike Bethel, which, as we have seen, worked to establish almost a hegemony over similar churches. Because the pastor was a Ghanaian and an English speaker, Transcea was not a tribal church, nor did it cater to Americo-Liberians.

Transcea grew enormously. By 1989 it had three small branches outside Monrovia, in Bong Mine, Firestone and Kakata, and a Sunday afternoon service at Monrovia's New Kru Town drew about 120, but its real strength was evident at its four services at Monrovia's Matilda Newport High School every Sunday. By September 1989 it had 1600 attending these services, and was growing by between 40 and 60 every Sunday. The pastor was expecting to have 2000 members by the end of 1989. Of these new members the pastor estimated that 50% were uncommitted members of other churches, 50% were new Christians. Other public services during the week included a Bible class, and a miracle service every Saturday afternoon, and from September 1989 a miracle revival each Wednesday evening in Monrovia's suburb of Paynesville.[2]

2. The Church as an Agent of Democracy in East Africa

There is a certain irony in the Liberian case study, namely, that the church did not challenge the government's social policies. Indeed, the mainline churches possess enormous clout due to their longevity, proselytism with social and charitable institutions, control of education and close contact with ruling groups. As Kalu states:[3]

> Her declarations can influence the national ethos, and her pulpits can be used to educate the members about particular issues. Church lobby or pressure group tactics can be quite effective. Civil disobedience and participation in revolution are exemplified in the careers of some churches in Africa.

Recent studies have focused on the role of The Church of the Province of Kenya (Anglican, CPK). It was the official church of British colonial power and enjoyed a relatively privileged position buttressed by a physical presence in people's every day life.

It acquired a powerful material base and tremendous organizational capacity. Even when Bishop Henry Okulu advocated a democratic power structure, the official theology still prescribed a constructive collaboration with the powers that ruled. Controversy surfaced more visibly under Arap Moi in 1982 after the coup attempt. A coercive centralizing process started. Repressive state surveillance and crackdowns followed apace. Varied forms of popular protest emerged among the *wanachi*, but Moi insisted on destroying all forms of opposition. He claimed to have played this role under Mzee Kenyatta. This is how, willy-nilly, by 1990 the onus of opposition was foisted upon the PCK.

Two issues were central: a critique of the structure of power advocating a shift from one-party to a multi-system polity; and the politics of transition, which brought to the fore the issue of pauperization. Sabar-Friedman's discourse and analysis traces the contours of public debate up to the formation of the multi-party structure.[4]The roles of the ruling elite, the press, the fact of ethnicity, all join to complicate the scene. There is data on the roles of other churches, such as the brutal odyssey of Timothy Njoya, a Presbyterian minister. The Roman Catholic bishops in July 1993 launched an attack on Moi. Equally noteworthy has been the career of Dr David Gitari, Bishop of Kirinyaga. His sermons have become a homiletic form of doing political theology. Graham King's study considers the use of Scripture in some of Gitari's sermons and in litanies and plays by students.

The twenty-four printed sermons of Bishop Gitari provide a good example of political theologizing in contemporary Africa—an area of scholarly inquiry for African Theology in the twenty-first century. In the end, however, ethnic conflicts within the churches and immaturity complicated the squabble among the opposition, giving Moi an opportunity to retain power in the changed circumstances.[5]

Another example of the mainline churches as power broker in the hub of restoration of democratic governance is from Malawi. "The victory of the multi-party advocates in the National Referendum of June 1993 led to the legalizing of opposition political parties and the promise of a General Election, which was finally held on 17 May 1994. In the struggle for legitimacy between government and opposition during this period the churches played an important role as power brokers. By virtue of the fact that they were not seeking political office for themselves, church leaders came to exercise a distinctive influence on the unfolding political drama. The Malawi Congress Party (MCP) government had long been aware of the ideological power of religion in the political realm. Systematically and successfully over many years it had pressed the churches into service to supply it with religious legitimization. Much was made in the party propaganda of the fact that Banda was an elder of the Church of Scotland. Indeed, the issue of the *Daily Times* that reviewed the year 1991, singled out as the highlight of the year the "triumphant moment" in which Dr Banda had been presented with a scroll to mark the 50th anniversary of this ordination to the eldership. It was a major blow, in the aftermath of the Pastoral Letter, when the Church of Scotland made it clear it no longer regarded Banda as an active elder. The extent to which the government was stung into serious over-reaction at that time, is a measure of how much it depended on the unquestioning support of the church.

This was further indicated, after almost all churches had rallied behind the work of the Public Affairs Committee (PAC), by the importance which the government attached to the continuing support of the Nkhoma synod—the Central Region section of the CCAP which had strong historical links with the MCP leadership. As it struggled to retain an air of legitimacy it turned to ministers of the Nkhoma Synod to officiate at government functions and to generally show solidarity with the MCP. This they were willing to do, especially during the early referendum period. Belatedly the Nkhoma Synod did seek to draw back from its unqualified support of the MCP government with a statement in April 1993 that "the Synod believes that genuine Christians can support either side of the referendum question without violating the genuine ideals and principles of Christianity." This attempt at "neutrality" did not convince the other churches, which saw it simply as an evasion of the demands of the gospel. It did, however, leave the government even more bereft of the church endorsement on which it had depended in the past. In desperation the MCP attempted to supply its own religious legitimization. When it launched its campaign newspaper, the *Guardian Today,* it was striking to note how many articles were devoted to portraying the MCP as having a divine mandate. This was epitomized by a cartoon series on the theme: "*MCP Points to God!; Multi-Party-Horns of the Devil!*"

Such desperate propaganda revealed how much the MCP government had depended on the legitimization that it had received from the churches in the preceding years. Once the churches had broken out of that ideological captivity, the MCP government faced a crisis of legitimacy that it was unable to surmount.

On the other hand, the emergent opposition was able constantly to appeal to the prophetic critique of the churches as justification for its political initiative. Indeed, the manifesto of the United Democratic Front, the first to be issued by an opposition party after the referendum, began with a quotation from the Lenten Pastoral Letter and stated that the movement for political reform had been initiated in response to the call from the Catholic Bishops. Occasions such as the Requiem Mass, held in May 1993 for four politicians who were widely believed to have been assassinated by government agents ten years earlier, were highly charged politically and very damaging to the credibility of the government.

It was no surprise that, when UDF leader Bakili Muluzi made his victory speech after the National Referendum, he went out of his way to thank the churches: "In particular, I would like to single out the seven Catholic Bishops and the [Presbyterian] Blantyre Synod." In a country where the Christian faith is highly esteemed by a large proportion of the population, the legitimacy which the churches bestowed on the opposition movement, in face of government attempts to brand its leaders "dissidents" and "confusionists", was a considerable factor in enabling the forces of change to succeed. At the popular level a significant factor was that many church songs were adapted to give expression to the movement for political liberation. Church choirs are very popular among young people and they took their church music as a medium for expressing a particular political message.

So *Ndiri ndi Bwenzi Langa Yesu* (I have my beloved friend Jesus) became *Ndiri ndi Bwenzi Langa Muluzi* (I have my beloved friend Muluzi—the leader of the UDF). In this way there occurred—on the popular level—a conflation of Christian belief with the call for political reform. Particularly influential were the songs of Paul Banda and the Alleluya Band, a well-known Malawian pop group. In a powerful song like *Tyamike Chauta* (Let us praise God) they played on the symbols of the opposing sides in the referendum—the hurricane lamp of the multi-party side and the black cock of the one-party side—to suggest an identification of multi-party with the light of Jesus Christ and of one-party with the darkness of Satan. A notable feature of the ideological struggle was that the opposition began to argue that Rev John Chilembwe, a Baptist pastor, not *Ngwazi* Kamuzu Banda, was the father of Malawian politics. There were good historical grounds for doing so, since Chilembwe led an armed rising against British colonial rule in 1915. A popular song during the campaign period, entitled *Kuno Kwathu ku Malawi*, suggested that just as Chilembwe fought against the oppression of the colonialists, so Muluzi would fight against the oppression of Dr Banda and the MCP. It was notable that when the new government announced the public holidays for the 1995 calendar, Kamuzu Day was missing and Chilembwe Day had been introduced!

For the churches there was a struggle involved in adapting to the new role as power-broker. On the one hand, some church leaders became so involved in the political arena that they eventually left the church ministry in order to devote themselves to politics. From Blantyre Synod, Rev Peter Kaleso became a Vice-President before later joining the UDF and becoming Ambassador to South Africa. From Livingstonia Synod, Aaron Longwe embarked on full-time human rights work with the newly established Foundation for Justice, Peace and the Integrity of Creation. From the Baptist Church, Emmanuel Chimkwita became first a shadow cabinet minister and parliamentary candidate then later Ambassador to Mozambique. In each case it has to be made clear that they were acting as politicians in their own right and no longer as representatives of their churches. On the other hand, there were those who believed that the churches became too detached from the political process, especially in the post-referendum period. When legislation was being passed in Parliament to establish the National Consultative Council and the National Executive Committee as the bodies that would oversee the transition to a multi-party political system, the Public Affairs Committee (PAC) declined to be represented and thus left the process of reform entirely in the hands of the political parties. This allowed the government later to claim that PAC was a body that had a role only in the pre-referendum period and affirming very clearly:

> PAC is a relevant body and there is need for its continuity now and after the General Elections. The church being the Conscience of Society shall continue to play his noble and prophetic role ... The formation of NCC and NEC does not mean the non-existence of PAC. PAC is here to stay for ever in Malawi.

In the run-up to the General Election, PAC was particularly active in working to avoid the "Kenyan scenario" of a divided opposition allowing the old regime to remain in power. In civic education and election monitoring, the churches remained by far the most effective organization and contributed significantly to the General Election being a very peaceful and highly efficient exercise.

On 17 May 1994, Bakili Muluzi, leader of the UDF, won Malawi's first democratic presidential election. In the new multi-party Parliament UDF won 85 seats, MCP 56 and AFORD 36 seats. Anastasia Msosa, the Chairperson of the Electoral Commission, commented:

> When you use the church, usually it is very effective. During the elections, if you appealed through the church it produced quick and effective results. The political change was positive in a short time because it came through the church.

To many Christians the peaceful transition to democracy was testimony to the power of prayer since, above all, the churches had engaged with the political process by turning to God and calling for divine help and guidance. In terms of the political process, the Public Affairs Committee made the church a significant force as a power broker. Integral to this development was the unity of the various groupings which allowed the PAC Secretary to sign himself in communications with government: "On behalf of the country's Religious Communities I beg to remain, Yours very sincerely, Misanjo E. Kansilanga."

A new kind of power would now be exercised in Malawi. It would be accountable—to the opposition in Parliament, to the free press, to the freedom of expression and freedom of association now enjoyed by the people at large. Would it also be accountable to God?

When Bakili Muluzi accepted the office of President he immediately invited the churches to offer correction to his government whenever it might stray from the path. This gave the churches the opportunity to subject the exercise of power in Malawi to the Gospel of Jesus Christ. How would they respond? History suggests that the church's social witness is strongest when there is some great evil to be confronted. Where the church often falters is when the great evil has been defeated and it is time for social and political reconstruction. What role would the churches play in shaping the exercise of power in the new Malawi? Answers to such questions may be sought by examining the prevailing understanding of power with the life of the churches and, especially, by attending to those who have been most excluded from power—the poor, the women, the young people, the prisoners, the Muslims, the Jehovah's Witnesses.[6]

3. Churches in the transformation process in South Africa

The Rustenburg Conference of Churches, which took place in November 1990, could justifiably be described as one of the most decisive events in recent South African church history, involving both mainline and other churches. About 230 church leaders from 80 denominations and 40 para-church organizations met in an attempt to work towards a united Christian witness in a changing South Africa. In many ways, the Rustenburg Conference was the response of a large body of South African churches to the political changes that began on 2 February 1990. This meeting was extraordinary in that it brought together a cross-section of all the traditions of churches in South Africa. It is estimated that the meeting was representative of more than 90% of the South African Christian community. This constitutes more than 70% of the total population of the country.

Rustenburg not only saw the Dutch Reformed Church publicly acknowledging its involvement in, and membership of a political system of discrimination, but it also took some important steps towards a change of mind-set and attitude. Also, the first steps in a process of forgiveness and restitution were taken. A new society could hardly be born if the pains and frustrations of the past are not attended to! All this not only creates hope, but also the possibility of again living in faith.

The Rustenburg Conference will go down in history as the "Conference of Confessions". In response to the prompting of the Holy Spirit, the greater part of the church in South Africa repented their past and thereby set a new course for the future. It appears that restitution was a far more difficult issue for the Rustenburg Conference than were confession and forgiveness. It should be remembered that the dominant view of reconciliation in South Africa was quite often the view of the dominant. The task the church now had to face was to rediscover and preach good news to all, this included the poor and the oppressed.

The Rustenburg conference fully realized that the churches in South Africa had a responsibility to combat the effects of apartheid. For decades to come, South Africa would have to battle to remove the effects of apartheid in many spheres of life. Some of the most important were national health and welfare, unemployment, education, and housing—where the effects of apartheid had been felt most by the oppressed.

In 1991 a representative group of church and business leaders came together to launch an important national peace initiative. On 14 September 1991, a National Peace Accord, signed by 23 organizations (including the ANC and the National Party) entrenched, for the first time, the principle of full accountability on the part of both the state and political parties for the actions of their servants or supporters. This provided an example of what could be done through sufficient compromise and goodwill.

In the spirit of the National Peace Accord, the South African Council of Churches arranged a training conference with the theme "Empowerment for Reconciliation with Justice" (ERJ). The ultimate aim of this conference was to build a national network of trainers, mediators, and negotiators to contribute to the work of the National Peace Accord. In the keynote opening address of this conference, which took place early in 1992, Bishop Stanley Mogoba, at that time the presiding bishop of the Methodist Church of southern Africa, stated that the convention for a Democratic South Africa (Codesa), the National Peace Accord, and the finest constitution devisable would remain mere words if there was no reconciliation. According to him, it was commonly believed that reconciliation was an easy way out. However, nothing was further from the truth; in fact, the path to reconciliation was the more difficult one. It required enabling a polarized people with deep feelings of hatred, fear, and distrust to find one another and to live together in the one country.

A wide range of churches were involved in the ERJ. Initially, with the encouragement of church leaders, such as Archbishop Desmond Tutu, Archbishop Denis Hurley, and Bishop Stanley Mogoba, the Anglican, Roman Catholic, and Methodist Churches, together with church-related organizations like Africa Enterprise, Diakonia, and Wilgespruit Fellowship Centre, met to explore the development of a consultative process. After consultation and deliberation, individuals from the Dutch Reformed Churches, the Pentecostal Churches, and the African Independent Churches were drawn into the ERJ initiative.

The ERJ was a Christian initiative that sought to enable South Africans to understand and address conflict and violence in the South African society. This was achieved by organizing consultations that seeked to equip participants in conflict analysis skills and consciousness raising, conflict handling, mediation, and negotiation. On the one hand there was a need at grassroots to teach people the skills needed to resolve their own conflicts in a peaceful, non-violent way.

On the other hand, an understanding of reconciliation that included justice for all was essential. The ERJ provided a vehicle to accomplish this.

In 1993, the churches were again challenged to become more concretely involved in the implementation of the National Peace Accord. The churches needed to press hard for the changes necessary for this venture: for a greater number of women and black leaders to be involved in the processes and structures of the National Peace Accord as well as to lobby government for a substantial increase of public money to support the process. Many different South African churches, men and women from different religious organizations, and international ecumenical monitors were indispensable to the national, regional, and local peace structures. There is little doubt that the ecumenical peace monitoring task force, EMPSA, established by the South African Council of Churches with the help of overseas ecumenical partners, had an important role to play as part of the wider monitoring task force.

In the difficult period of transition, 1990-1994, various areas in South Africa were especially badly affected by ongoing violence. One of the areas most affected was KwaZulu/Natal. Among the many ventures organized by different churches to counter the violence, both in this region and elsewhere, several could be mentioned. However, one of them, *Diakonia*, reflected the general attitude of these ventures. Apart from its on-going programs, Diakonia promoted the peace process in KwaZulu/Natal in a number of ways:

- participating in the Natal Church Leaders' Group that was established to help the church find a common response to the violence;
- promoting the National Peace Accord and encouraging the church to become involved in local and regional dispute-resolution committees;
- helping to monitor violence by participating in the Network of Independent Monitors (NIM) and by assisting the Ecumenical Monitoring Program in South Africa (EMPSA) which brought international church monitors to KwaZulu/Natal;
- training church people to play a role in peace making;
- helping to provide resources to victims of violence;
- informing members of the trends of violence;
- participating in the KwaZulu/Natal Hostel's Initiative which seeks to upgrade hostels and thus avoid a repetition of the violence in the Transvaal.

In the fields of justice, reconciliation, peacemaking, and countering violence, many church—and other—bodies were set up throughout South Africa, each with its own specific emphasis or geographical focus. They assisted local or regional justice or peace committees that were established; for instance, on the foundations of the National Peace Accord. There are far too many to mention, so four will be singled out as examples.

Vuleka Trust was established in 1974 as an ecumenical educational venture focusing on justice and reconciliation. It operated primarily in KwaZulu/Natal, which was under-resourced, poverty stricken, and conflict ridden. Vuleka offered programs and courses to empower people through the acquisition of interpersonal skills, to enable them to respond creatively to themselves, others, and their environment.

The National Initiative for Reconciliation (NIR) was founded in the 1980s. Its vision was to create new South Africans for a new South Africa in which the value of life was acknowledged. It sought to help Christians to recognize and confront alienation and to equip them with the skills needed to bring about true reconciliation. Christian involvement in the following four areas was crucial: violence and the peace process; the lost generation of (black) youth; economic justice for all; and democracy.

The Pietermaritzburg Agency for Christian Social Awareness (PACSA) was an independent Christian organization committed to involving the local Pietermaritzburg Christian community in the promotion of human rights and justice issues. It planned to involve the local church in sustainable and empowering development, while seeking to foster wholeness in church and society. This work for justice and peace was achieved through facilitating research, analysis, education publications, action, and spiritual reflection.

In October 1992; the Network of Independent Monitors (NIM) was launched in an attempt to address the problem of a lack of networking between violence monitors and monitoring organizations. Its major aim was to improve the effectiveness of independent monitoring by strengthening recognition, identity, and the status of monitoring. A code of conduct was drawn up to commit monitors to principles of the UN Declaration of Human Rights and the African Charter. A priority was set to train church volunteers in observation-type monitoring of political funerals, and rallies. This gave concerned individuals an opportunity to contribute to the peace process.

Historically the South African elections of 1994 will be viewed as South Africa's greatest watershed. A week before this event it seemed as though South Africa was heading for civil war and general decline; then in a staggering, almost breathless turnaround the people of South Africa collectively and democratically lurched in the direction of a relatively stable future. The Equal Opportunity Foundation, with trustees like Archbishop D Tutu, Dr A Boesak, Dean Colin Jones, and Archdeacon M Xundu, called on all South Africans to join them from Friday 22 April to Sunday 24 April (three days before the elections) for a time of reflection, contemplation, and forgiving so that the healing process could begin.

This Foundation was committed to assisting in the reconstruction of South Africa, and its members believed that the nation's covenanting and bonding together could not take place without first creating a climate in which all wounds, hurts, fears, and resentments could be given a chance to heal. Early in 1994, in a call for prayers during the period of transition, the Charismatic-Evangelical Dialogue for Justice and Transformation (CEDJT), together with the National Initiative for Reconciliation (NIR) and Concerned Evangelicals (CE), provided guidelines for an increased focus on and clarification of the prayer agenda. Apart from affirming God's sovereignty, thanksgiving, repentance, and commitment, a Christian's prophetic role was emphasized. The focus of prayers, issues, and attitudes needed for a peaceful, democratic, and just outcome, as well as those attitudes and issues that could lead to civil war, were identified. Issues that required prayer were hope, repentance, tolerance, righteousness, integrity, justice, and dignity. Prayers were also offered to negate selfishness, intolerance, apathy, injustice, fear, ignorance, hatred, anger, intimidation, insecurity, revenge, alienation, immorality, corruption and godlessness.[7]

To describe the first democratic and non-racial elections in South Africa's history as something of a miracle without becoming too euphoric is difficult. The elections had to do with past and future; with ending an era of oppression and beginning an era of possibilities and freedom. Tsele states, that on a theological level "the elections were an affirmation of the humanity of those whom apartheid had dehumanized." He adds that the elections were more than party political; in a sense no political party won, the country as a whole won. The elections were about more than party manifestos. "We have entered the dimension of a religious calling. These elections are more than mere justice."

The message at the presidential inauguration of the prisoner turned president, Nelson Mandela, was very clear:

> We enter into a covenant that we shall build a society in which all South Africans, both black and white, will be able to walk tall, without any fear in their hearts, assured of their inalienable right to human dignity—a rainbow nation at peace with itself and the world.

In an almost religiously inspired spirit of reconciliation he continued:

> The time for the healing of the wounds has come. The moment to bridge the chasms that divide us has come. The time to build is upon us.

During the four years, 1990-1994, both the black and white communities displayed an extraordinary tough-mindedness, amid terrible violence, in resisting appeals to bloodshed, and went faithfully about their business, while their leaders talked and talked and talked. This extraordinary display of courage, of tough moral fiber, held out hope for the future. It had, to a large extent, impressed and even awed the rest of the world.

In the course of their history, church and society have greatly influenced each other for better or for worse. The church has not existed in a vacuum, but has played a vital interactive role. Thus, in the period between 1990 and 1994, most commentators in South Africa perceive the interaction of church and society to be largely positive. Though South African society was strongly shaped in religious terms and had a strong religious base, the interaction was always positive.

Between 1990 and 1994 religious involvement was of such a nature that the churches kept a critical distance whilst remaining involved. The church history of these four years hold a relatively positive and strong message for the future, not only for South Africa, but also for the whole world. The level of moral leadership from both men and women, reached through the involvement of the churches in South Africa, is envied by many. This could also encourage Christians on a global scale in the decades to come.

The mainline churches played a major role in development strategies. Whilst the government had a duty to uplift the people, all communities, including the most underprivileged, could do something to improve their lives. The people of the post-apartheid South Africa should not only look to the government for all forms of development, but should realize their destiny is in their own hands. The church can provide enlightenment and moral support.

A massive effort to improve quality of life had to be made in the field of education. Although the churches in South Africa always played a major role in education, the rise of apartheid forced the churches' involvement in this regard to decline. The focus now should be broad and it should include the education of children, adults, and even communities to help them acquire skills to earn a living and promote confidence and dignity. The future can be built with great confidence on the foundations of the pre-apartheid Lovedale, Healdtown, Kilnerton and Rosettenville institutions for education and on a few of the recently established schools like St Mark's in Sekhukhuneland and St Gregory's in the Natal Midlands.

Another important area of interaction between church and society was to increase the social strength of the people and society. South African pastors and theologians were being challenged to complement the government's Reconstruction and Development Program with programs of moral reconstruction and spiritual development. Barney Pityana of the Cape Town Research Institute on Christianity refers to this in a thought-provoking article:[8]

> In order to live together in a community we must respect one another in our differences and our similarities. We need to recognize that we need one another, we are interdependent. Unless we work together and try to build up a new moral community together, we will soon have no community at all. The African moral principle of "*ubuntu*" will have to become something more than a mere catch-phrase.

Much hope was invested in the churches in South Africa. What they did and said was important to South African society. Many people were looking to the churches to provide the shared values on which to build a new South Africa. Hopefully all the churches in South Africa will continue preaching the full message of love, forgiveness, reconciliation, and hope.

In South Africa the stagnation of the mainline churches like the Dutch Reformed, Wesleyan Methodist, Congregational and Lutheran churches began already in the 1920s, about the same time that saw a rise in subscribers to the Catholic Church. On the other hand, the independent churches, as a group, were rising exponentially. A possible explanation could be that the independent churches created the mental space to experiment with the Christian message, at a time when the Bible was the only message that the apartheid state was prepared to allow to be freely disseminated. Therefore, Pentecostalism most probably became a spiritual space that assumed a political character, which the state did not bother to police very closely—because they assumed the majority of its members were illiterate and unschooled, which was not always the case. However late it may seem, a trend had been established in South Africa that shows that the influence of mainline churches on the black Christian community has also been diminishing since the 1970s. This trend according to J. Hendriks and M. Froise goes back to the end of the 1970s and the beginnings of the 1980s. This was when black activists were waging the struggle against apartheid, which was then at its peak.

CONCLUSION

In summary, some contexts are more salient because a church is more protected in the adoption of politically risky postures and more protected from the local subversion factor. These are advantages, according to Freston, stemming from social position and sociological type rather than theological factors. In Africa the actual performance of mainline churches does not always reflect these advantages. The Catholic Church is more heavily missionary-manned and foreign-funded, and this is crucial for its socio-political influence. Yet it and other mainline denominations have usually needed a threat to their institutional interests before opposing regimes.

Many mainline churches have supported far more years of authoritarian rule in independent Africa than other churches. A good example is, for instance, Liberia, where it was the mainline churches who supported a century of True Whig rule, who asked the United States to intervene militarily in 1990, who could not speak out against the regime in Monrovia because many of their members lived at the mercy of Charles Taylor, and whose generally fatalistic approach paved the way for catastrophe. According to Kalu, in West Africa, mainline churches have grown in numbers due to the resilience of their different strategies. They have been using new forms of charitable institutions to respond to the challenge of poverty. They have been developing internal structural changes in ministerial formation, liturgy and vernacularization of doctrine. Many of them have allowed charismatic ministries as a means of both theological reformation as well as encapsulation strategy. "New forms of ecumenism have mobilized resources and political clout above all, cultural policy has shifted significantly to root the message in the soil. Of course, traditional splits and virulent church politics have smeared the face of Christ in many places.

Civil war and coups in Liberia and Sierra-Leone, and military dictatorships in Nigeria are other adverse forces."[9] The increased evangelical thrust into Muslim states such as Guinea, Gambia, Ivory Coast and Senegal to mention just a few in Africa, merit further attention.[10]

Similarly, the growth pattern among mainline churches shows wide regional differentiation. In South Africa, for instance, support currently grows for African churches and the prosperity gospel, while mainline Protestant and Catholic and formerly segregated denominations are waning. Church attendance figures among whites are dropping while increasing among blacks. This is partly due to white society becoming more secular, following the trend in Europe and to what is seen as a growing cynicism of religion among whites. Pentecostal churches, on the other hand, have lately seen their number of young and affluent congregants rise, thanks to a large extent to their image of being trendy and fashionable. African Independent Churches like, for instance, the Zion Christian Church and the Shembe Nazareth Church, are gaining ground among the poor and ill because of their emphasis on God's healing power.

Pentecostal political practice has become more social activist in many parts of Africa and show four interlocking grooves: "(i) the rebuilding of the individual "the power to be truly human"; (ii) a "call to social activism", i.e. an attack on socio-political structures; (iii) "the rule of saints", i.e. politics of engagement; and (iv) "the new Israel", i.e. empowerment and foretaste of new order. It thus breaks the dichotomy of individual/society private/public, weaving a multifaceted and holistic response to the human predicament in the African ecosystem, using the resources of the gospel.[11]

In his fascinating and excellent book *Power, Poverty and Prayer*, Kalu focuses on the role Christianity, and therefore the mainline churches, and the more independent churches play in African political and socio-economic life. Colonialism is over, but the drums of liberation are still throbbing. Kalu argues that Christianity paved the way for colonialism, but also produced the new champions of independence. He attempts to provide answers to the question what role Christianity has played towards the second liberation of the African continent. Within the post second liberation society in Africa it becomes important to find out which groups or individuals still define themselves as Christian within the new society. We will have to determine what is making the universal church so popular among the working class. Perhaps it is a matter of religion being a thing that gives people a sense of relief from their everyday struggles with or against the powers of secular authority. It is, therefore, understandable that the church allows believers the space to organize themselves under the power of their beliefs.[12]

The question finally must be asked about the capacity of the churches amidst the malaise that afflicts so much of the African continent, and which has given it such a bad reputation. The problem is that Africa's hopelessness is some-
o widely perceived that it has become a self-fulfilling prophecy, deterring
rs from creating the new enterprises that might arrest its downslide and

causing a continuous brain drain with thousands of African professionals and other enterprising spirits abandoning the continent annually. Somehow, this vicious cycle must be turned around so that Africa's people can begin to regain their self-confidence through role models of achievement and success. This core idea that Africa should cease to look outside for help later found a new expression in Thabo Mbeki's concept of "an African Renaissance".

Notes

1. J.W. de GRUCHY, *Christianity and Democracy* (Cambridge: Cambridge University Press, 1995), 165 ff.
2. P. GIFFORD, *New dimensions in African Christianity* (Nairobi: All Africa Conference of Churches, 1992), 33-40.
3. O.U. KALU, "Tools of Hope: Stagnation and Political Theology in Africa, 1960-1995", in M. HUTCHINSON & O.U. KALU, *A Global Faith: Essays on Evangelicalism and Globalization* (Sydney: CSAC, 1998), 201.
4. KALU, "Tools of Hope", 198.
5. KALU, "Tools of Hope", 201.
6. K. ROSS, *God, People and Power in Malawi: Democratization in Theological Perspective* (Blantyre: CLAIM, 1999), 35-40.
7. J.W. HOFMEYR, "Christianity in the South African Context in a period of Democratisation", in *Studia Historiae Ecclesiasticae*, 20, 2 (1994) 110-129.
8. B. PITYANA, "The urgent need for moral reconstruction", in *Challenge*, (1994) 6-7.
9. O.U. KALU, "Jesus Christ, Where Are You? Themes in West African Church Historiography", in *Missionalia*, 3, 2 (2002) 254 ff.
10. KALU, "Jesus Christ", 255.
11. KALU, "Jesus Christ", 255. See also O.U. KALU, *Power, Poverty and Prayer: The Challenges of Poverty and Pluralism in African Christianity 1960-1996* (Frankfurt: P. Lang, 2000).
12. L. SANNEH, *Encountering the West* (Maryknoll: Orbis Books, 1993), 224ff.

Chapter Fifteen

"Born of Water and the Spirit": Pentecostal/Charismatic Christianity in Africa

J. Kwabena Asamoah-Gyadu

Pentecostalism is the fastest growing stream of Christianity in the world today, and in the verdict of Harvey Cox, the movement is reshaping religion in the twenty-first century.[1] This observation by Cox is very instructive for our purposes in this chapter, which deals with one of the most significant developments in African Christianity since the middle of the twentieth century—the rise, growth, and impact of Pentecostalism. Here we trace the major historical developments, identify the different types, and discuss some of the salient theological orientations of Pentecostal/Charismatic renewal movements in Africa. The experiential and versatile nature of Pentecostalism has allowed African Christians to take their spiritual destiny into their own hands by deploying within local contexts a religion with a global outlook. The observation by Cox is important because earlier in his book *The Secular City*, he had joined "death of God" theologians and sociologists of religion to predict the demise of Christianity under the weight of modernization. Cox's recent work, *Fire from Heaven,* is one among a number of recent publications that affirm the growing importance of Pentecostal churches and Charismatic renewal movements in world Christianity. Other publications on Pentecostal/Charismatic Christianity include: Poewe, *Charismatic Christianity as a Global Culture* (1994), Hollenweger, *Pentecostalism: Origins and Developments Worldwide* (1997); Dempster, *The Globalization of Pentecostalism* (1999), Anderson and Hollenweger, *Pentecostals after a Century* (1999), and Synan, *The Century of the Holy Spirit* (2001). Among publications that specifically address or devote significant space to African Pentecostal/Charismatic issues are: Anderson, *African Reformation* (2001), Gifford, *African Christianity: Its Public Role* (1998), Kalu, *Power, Poverty and Prayer* (2001), and Corten and Marshall-Fratani, *Between Babel and Pentecost* (2001).

Our focus in this chapter falls on specific African initiatives, appropriations, and contributions to the growth, significance, and impact of Pentecostalism on the continent. The differences in the nature of Pentecostal/Charismatic phenomena make the issue of definitions and nomenclature important for our study. "Pentecostalism" may be understood as that stream of Christianity that emphasizes personal salvation in Christ as a transformative experience wrought by the Holy Spirit; and in which such pneumatic phenomena as "speaking in tongues", prophecies, visions, healing, miracles, and signs and wonders in general, are sought, accepted, valued, and consciously encouraged among members as evidence of the active presence of God's Spirit. The coterminous designation "Charismatic" derives from St. Paul's expression *charismata pneumatika,* "Gifts of the Spirit" (I Corinthians 12-14), and which he uses to refer to those "extraordinary graces" attributable to the experience of the Holy Spirit. The key to our definition of Pentecostalism is Acts 2:38. In that passage, Peter explains the process of incorporation into Christ as requiring repentance from sin, and baptism in the name of the Lord Jesus Christ culminating in a forgiven life. Following this initial step, Peter assured the enquirers: "you will receive the gift of the Holy Spirit". Adult "baptism by immersion" is generally presumed to be what was being referred to here, and so is widely regarded by Pentecostals as the proper symbolic way of receiving the born again into the church. This process of incorporation into Christ is further justified from Jesus' statement to Nicodemus: "no one can see the kingdom of God unless he is born of water and the Spirit" (John 3:5). There are wide ranges of groups in Africa that give space to the presence of the Holy Spirit. Here we will follow conventional usage and retain "Pentecostal" for churches and denominations claiming the Biblical Pentecostal heritage as found in the Gospel of St. John and Acts of the Apostles cited above. The expression "Charismatic" is restricted to Pentecostal renewal movements that operate within historic mission denominations or mainline churches.

In *The Household of God,* Leslie Newbigin casts Pentecostalism in terms of a "third force" in Christianity, following the Protestant emphasis on the Word, and the Roman Catholic emphasis on the Sacraments.[2] In Africa, the precursors of Pentecostalism were indigenous prophet figures, many of whom were persecuted out of historic mission denominations for pursuing spiritualities sometimes scandalously perceived by church authority as belonging to the "occult". Prophets William Wadé Harris of the Gold Coast (Ghana), Garrick Sokari Braide of the Niger Delta, Simon Kimbangu of the Congo and others, challenged Africans to throw away their traditional resources of supernatural succor and turn towards the living God of the Bible. God alone, they taught, was able to rescue people from the fear of witchcraft, medicines, and principalities and powers before which inimical forces inherited mainline Western theologies just cringed. Many of these nineteenth and early twentieth century revivalistic prophetic campaigns only resulted in independent churches when the prophets had left the scene. The prophetic movements were thus followed by the emergence of the popular Spiritual, Aladura, or Zionist churches known collectively as "African Independent" or "African Initiated" churches (AICs). The AICs aimed at restoring to the African church the vitality of the presence of the Holy Spirit, which was seen as accounting for the "dry denominationalism" of the mission churches (see chapters 10 and 11 of this volume). Healing became their single most important activity, but many of them strayed into therapeutic methods that were not Christian. Subsequently, it has become contentious to regard these older AICs as Pentecostal. In any case most AICs belong to separate associations from those formed by mainstream Pentecostals. Except in southern Africa where Zionist churches are still doing well, AICs are no more paradigmatic of African Christianity. Nevertheless they are considered important for challenging the mission denominations into rethinking their resistance to Charismatic renewal. The emphasis of the AICs on healing, and their worldview of mystical causality in etiology and diagnosis are retained in the healing and deliverance sectors of African Pentecostal ministries and churches.

In terms of periodisation, it is pertinent to note from the outset that since the twilight years of the Aladura era in the 1970s, African Pentecostalism has blossomed in many directions. Classical Pentecostal denominations, some of which have roots in the 1901 Charles Parham and 1906 William Seymour Azusa Street revivals of North America, have gained much prominence in Africa. In South Africa, for example, the Assemblies of God, Apostolic Faith Mission, and the Full Gospel Church of God belong to this tradition. The bulk of classical Pentecostal churches operating in Africa, however, were initiated locally; foreign assistance often came later. Other Pentecostal collectivities found in Africa include: New [independent] Pentecostal Churches (NPCs), trans-denominational Pentecostal fellowships like the Full Gospel Businessmen's Fellowship International (FGBMFI), Women Aglow, and Intercessors for Africa; and Charismatic renewal groups of the mainline churches. These together with itinerant international Pentecostal preachers and prophets have taken over the religious landscape as the new faces of African Christianity. So in Africa today, we do not only have major Western mission-related Pentecostal denominations such as the Assemblies of God originating from the USA, but also African-initiated ones like William F. Kumuyi's Deeper Christian Life Ministry, which started in Nigeria in 1973. In addition, there are the multitudinous "mega" independent NPCs like Mensa Otabil's International Central Gospel Church in Ghana and Andrew Wutawanashe's Family of God in Zimbabwe, which were also born out of local initiatives.

As with the African initiated classical Pentecostal denominations, all these churches are now proliferating internationally. African Pentecostal churches have become a dominant force in Western Europe and North America providing participants the religious context to "sing the Lord's song in foreign lands". The fact that African religions have emerged in Europe not as primal forms but in terms of Christianity is itself evidence of the growing strength of the Christian faith in modern Africa. Current research indicates how African churches, particularly those from the Pentecostal stream, have re-crossed former mission boundaries forcing missionary countries to take note of the upbeat mode of African Christianity.[3] To this end, the largest single Christian congregation in Europe since Christianity began is Nigerian Pastor Matthew Ashimolowo's Kingsway International Christian Center (KICC) in London. Pastor Matthew Ashimolowo founded KICC in 1992, and has within ten years grown to become the biggest church in Europe. At the beginning of the year 2000, KICC, together with its satellite congregations in the UK, claimed a membership upwards of 6,000 adults. The Church had started to develop a 5000-seating capacity auditorium and office complex in East London where it is located. Into the twenty-first century, the fast trend of forming Pentecostal churches has not abated. NPCs split very often as pastors claiming "new visions" continue to establish "new altars". Charismatic renewal movements operate unofficially as ecumenical organizations and may on occasion grow bigger than the local churches within which they operate. The lay-orientation of Charismatic movements accounts for their success. Ordained clergy, who are not charismatic themselves, often feel their pastoral authority under threat leading to friction with lay charismatic leaders. The end results have always been secessions that increase the number of independent Pentecostals in the system.

Whichever of the groups listed here is being referred to, Pentecostal/Charismatic Christianity appeals for its legitimacy primarily to the biblical Pentecost predicted in Joel 28, and fulfilled in Acts 2. Pentecostal/Charismatic Christianity is a religion of the heart, so worship in these movements and churches is characterized in the main by spontaneity and pneumatic manifestations. Rijk van Dijk has written extensively on Pentecostalism in Malawi. His articulation of the spirituality of Malawi's "young born-again preachers" ties together the characteristic features of Pentecostal/Charismatic movements especially in African contexts. The Christianity of the "born-again preachers" is characterized by: a strict morality seen in their zero tolerance for the use of alcoholic beverages, cigarettes, and drugs. They fulminate against adultery, violence and theft. Frequenting bars, hotels and discos are castigated as "satanic habits". These negative injunctions are balanced with clear demands for a rejuvenated strict morality put forward in an atmosphere of "religious excitement and emotionalism". During evangelistic campaigns, repentant sinners are invited to surrender evil objects, which in African contexts include anything from stolen goods and offensive weapons to traditional amulets and charms. In this vein, traditional religious functionaries and Islamic "Malams" are constantly castigated in African Pentecostal discourses as purveyors of instruments that serve as conduits for demons. In Malawian Pentecostalism, van Dijk describes how worshippers seeking new birth are "urged to step forward at the Altar Call in order to receive the "infilling' of the Holy Spirit, which is stressed as the single most important way to become cleansed of worldly, defiling forces." Following this process of rupture with the past and encounter with the Spirit, the born-again is considered so empowered that "the forces of darkness, witchcraft, [and] evil spirits, can no longer hold sway over his or her life."[4] As one Pentecostal preacher averred, when you have the Spirit, you are like the traffic police officer in uniform: "when you raise your hand, the "traffic of evil" powers must stop. The Holy Spirit is like the police uniform, he gives you identity. Once you put him on, you have authority." Thus a familiar African Pentecostal chorus is rendered: "we conquer Satan, we conquer demons, we conquer principalities, we conquer powers; so sing hallelujah." Elsewhere it is said of Chisanpo's Pentecostal Christians that: they "long for secure employment and happy domestic life". "Security" is a recurrent notion in their Pentecostal discourse, "evoking the born-again condition as a refuge from witches who kill children and ruin successful business enterprises, tragedies all too familiar to the impoverished residents of Chisanpo township" in Malawi.[5]

It is important to acknowledge that although African Pentecostalism has resulted largely from local initiatives, indigenous founders and leaders in some cases worked in active collaboration with foreign Pentecostal missions. The Assemblies of God churches were for instance invited by local Pentecostals seeking protection from the religious hegemony perpetrated by historic mission denominations at the turn of the twentieth century. Classical Pentecostal churches did not become mass movements initially. They shot into prominence from the 1970s due to a combination of socio-religious factors, including opening up to younger university evangelical Christian leadership, rapid urbanization, and the collapse of African economies. The Zimbabwe Assemblies of God Africa (ZAOGA), led by Archbishop Ezekiel Guti with an estimated membership of over 600,000, is one of the largest in that region. Guti was originally part of South Africa Apostolic Faith Mission (AFM), founded in 1908, until 1959 when he was expelled together with a small band of followers after disagreements with white missionaries. The Assemblies of God Church in the West African state of Burkina Faso was established in 1921. From a registered membership of only 125,000 at their 50th anniversary in 1972, Assemblies of God churches in Burkina Faso now count nearly 400,000 members. In the case of Burkina Faso, it is instructive that this rapid growth has occurred in tandem with the country's political and economic difficulties, numerous cases of "madness" observed among redundant migrant workers returning from collapsing rural plantations, and the appearance of new incurable diseases; and all this in the face of the State's inability to intervene in the crises.[6] The theologies of the Pentecostals firmly address these issues.

African initiated classical Pentecostal denominations, such as the Christ Apostolic Church, the Church of Pentecost, and the Deeper Christian Life Ministry, are among the most popular in modern Africa. These Pentecostal denominations normally possess well-defined doctrinal orientation on issues such as the baptism of the Holy Spirit and "speaking in tongues". This may be illustrated with the West African examples of the Church of Pentecost and Christ Apostolic Church that as we will note below, started under the auspices of the Welsh Apostolic Church from Bradford. The Constitution of the CoP, for example, states among others: "all believers in Jesus Christ are entitled to receive, and should earnestly seek the Baptism of the Holy Ghost and Fire according to the command of our Lord." According to the CoP:[7]

> This is the normal experience of the early church. With this experience comes power to preach and bestowments of the gifts of the Spirit. When the believer is filled with the Holy Spirit, there is a physical sign of 'speaking in tongues' as the Spirit of God gives utterance. This is accompanied by a burning desire and supernatural power to witness to others about God's salvation and power.

The CoP, now an international organization with branches all over the world, is one of three "apostolic" churches to emerge from the initiative of a Ghanaian Pentecostal, Apostle Peter Anim (1890-1984), and his later collaboration with the Welsh Apostolic Church missionaries, James and Sophia McKeown in the 1930s. Anim's Pentecostal experience predated the contact with the McKeowns by more than a decade. In 1917, Apostle Anim triggered a revivalist type campaign around the eastern region of Ghana through the formation of a local prayer group with Pentecostal orientation. So Anim's experience, started as a personal quest for spiritual renaissance which he recounts as follows:

> I was faced with the necessity of contending for a deeper faith and greater spiritual power than what my primary religious experience was able to afford, and I began to seek with such trepidation to know more about the Holy Ghost.

Anim's Christian life had been affected by a Philadelphia based Faith Tabernacle movement and later in 1922 by another USA-based group, the Apostolic Faith, whose name they later adopted. In the midst of these developments Anim had come into contact with Pastor Odubanjo of Nigeria, who had himself seceded from the Faith Tabernacle movement and was seeking affiliation with the UK Apostolic Church. Odubanjo and Anim worked together and achieved the affiliation, and it was through that process that James McKeown was posted to Ghana as a missionary to help Apostle Anim. A faith-healing doctrine of Anim's group in which members were debarred from using medicine led to a series of intractable conflicts between Anim and McKeown; the collaboration eventually faltered under those strains. The two parted company with each leader being followed by some members; by 1953, the fallout in the relationships among Pastor McKeown, Apostle Anim, and the UK Apostolic Church, under whose auspices McKeown worked, had produced three main classical Pentecostal churches: Apostle Anim's Christ Apostolic Church, James McKeown's Church of Pentecost, and a UK affiliated Apostolic Church of Ghana. The Christ Apostolic Church (CAC) of Nigeria is another example of an indigenous classical Pentecostal church started by an African, Joseph Ayo Babalola. Babalola, a Yoruba, was originally Anglican who later became a pioneering Aladura prophet. In 1928, whilst operating a steamroller, Babalola claimed to have heard Jesus Christ call him to preach the gospel and heal the sick using holy water. He initially affiliated with the Faith Tabernacle movement. Babalola's prophetic ministry was to take off in 1930 when it is claimed he brought a dead person back to life. Aided by a hand-bell and a Bible, Babalola traveled through Yorubaland spreading his revelatory message of repentance, holiness, renunciation of idolatry and witchcraft, and healing the sick using water made holy through prayer. Faith Tabernacle later merged with the British Apostolic Church. Following a subsequent schism in the Apostolic Church, Babalola and others formed the Christ Apostolic Church (CAC) in 1941.

In *Theological Roots of Pentecostalism* (1987), Dayton identifies a common four-fold pattern in Pentecostal theology: Christ as Savior, Christ as Baptizer in the Spirit, Christ as Healer, and Christ as the soon coming King.[8] African classical Pentecostal theology falls within this four-fold pattern, so early members of Christ Apostolic Church, for example, drew parallels between their experiences of spiritual gifts and the biblical Pentecost. Sanneh explains that whereas in some of the independent Aladura churches, "the sense of Christ's unique life and work was only rather vaguely glimpsed behind all the color and sound of processions and testimonies, in the CAC, Christ occupied a central place." The CAC stressed the Bible as the written authority for its doctrines and although it did not abandon them completely, it placed less emphasis on visions and dreams stressing that spiritual gifts "should be brought in conformity with Scriptural teaching."[9] Indigenous classical Pentecostal churches therefore stress not just new birth, but also personal holiness, Bible Study, evangelism, and baptism in the Holy Spirit. Believers are expected to dress modestly and do away with semblances of flamboyance, materialism, and extravagance, in short worldliness in life. In the CoP and Deeper Life, for example, men and women neither sit nor dance together in church. In the case of Kumuyi's Deeper Life, Ojo shows how the Apostolic Church in which he served as a leader for a considerable while influenced a number of his holiness prescriptions.[10] It is from similar apostolic church backgrounds that a number of classical Pentecostal churches emerged in Africa. Women are also expected to cover their hair during worship, a situation that contrasts sharply with that of the NPCs, in which women may be tacitly encouraged through the example of the wife of the head pastor to makeup in order to reflect "God's glory", his goodness and favor. In the history of African Pentecostalism, the puritan or holiness ethic resurfaced strongly in the 1980s when local Christians felt scandalized by moral comprimises involving American televangelists. In the "controlled materialism" of the NPCs, Christians are required to take an upbeat approach to life.

Unlike the new Pentecostals, the use of excessive jewelry is not permitted in the indigenous classical Pentecostal churches and in almost all of them, including the Assemblies of God, women may serve in other capacities, but are not admitted into the ordained ministry. In recent years, however, classical Pentecostals have been forced to relax puritan ethics with regards to physical appearance in order to sustain the interests of young people. The forceful impact of Pentecostal movements in the 1970s, also renewed murmurings against the non-interventionist nature of mainline church theologies, and subsequently heightened the rate of drift of members into Pentecostal churches. These developments re-awakened the older mission churches to the need to tolerate renewal groups within their ranks. The principle underlying the formation of Charismatic renewal movements is captured very aptly in the title of Cephas Omenyo's book on renewal groups within mainline denominations: *Pentecost Outside Pentecostalism,* for that is what Charismatic renewal groups are.[11] Charismatic renewal movements in Africa, born entirely out of lay initiatives, simply aim at integrating renewal phenomena within existing mainline denominations in order to renew them from within. The formation of these movements constitute one way in which to understand how African Christians actually set to work in practical ways the Christian message as understood in their vernacular Scriptures in which God was encountered as Holy Spirit. An international example here is the Catholic Charismatic Renewal Movement, which having started in Duquesne, USA in 1967, now operates within Roman Catholic denominations worldwide with the African versions being among some of the most dynamic.

Rudolf Otto laments the inability of "orthodox Christianity" to recognize the value of the non-rational aspect of religion, thus giving the "idea of the holy" what he expresses as "a one-sidedly intellectualistic approach."[12] Pentecostalism is a response to such cerebral Christianity, and wherever it has appeared, the movement has defined itself in terms of the recovery of the experiential aspects of the faith by demonstrating the power of the Spirit to infuse life, and the ability of the living presence of Jesus Christ to save from sin and evil. This is even more so in Africa where religion is a survival strategy, and where spirit-possession with its emphasis on direct divine communication, intervention in crises, and religious mediation are central to religious experiences. The ministries of healing and deliverance have thus become some of the most important expressions of Christianity in African Pentecostalism. Charismatic movements practice "healing and deliverance" widely within their mission churches because it is in high demand. For example, before he was recalled to Rome in 1982, "healing and deliverance" was the specialty of Zambian Catholic exorcist, Archbishop Emmanuel Milingo. In most of Africa, Charismatic renewal movements, where they have been tolerated along with such ministries to the possessed and oppressed, have helped historic mission denominations to recover from the hemorrhage they used to suffer by the drift of their members into Pentecostal churches. The Charismatic Renewal Movement itself benefits tremendously from trans-denominational fellowships like the FGBMFI and Women Aglow. Members of Full Gospel and Aglow are expected to remain "responsible church members" serving as Bible study leaders and preachers, and in the process heightening what has since the 1980s, become known as the "pentecostalization" of historic mission Christianity. Thus, Pentecostalism has through its various streams, become such a forceful movement in Africa to the extent where churches refusing to integrate its spirituality in one form or another know they face atrophy.

The Intercessors for Africa have meanwhile also continued to function around the continent as trans-denominational groupings like the FGBMFI. Intercessors for Africa have set themselves the task of "redeeming the land" of Africa by doing warfare against powers inhabiting that space as a result of satanic African traditional rituals, and the activities of territorial spirits, that is, fallen angels who are hampering development on the continent. One of the major inspirers of this phenomenon is Fuller professor of missions, Peter Wagner. He has visited African countries, including Ghana in 1996, to talk about territorial spirits and how to combat their activities. In the hermeneutic of the Intercessors, even international financial institutions like the IMF, World Bank, and others operating from Islamic countries are demonized as agents of Satan perpetrating hardship in Africa. It is considered that the land must be redeemed, because "the earth is the Lord's and the fullness of it" (Psalm 24:1). Principalities and powers whether they exist in the heavens, on the earth, or inside the earth, must be dealt with for their pauperizing influence on African societies and governments. According to one of the leading exponents of the Intercessors for Africa movement:

> Satan expanded his hold over the earth by deploying his principalities and powers to cause and spread spiritual wickedness in this world. People have been deceived into worshipping idols, gods and Satan by building altars, offering sacrifices, creating groves and high places. Thus, Satan strengthened his hold over families, communities, cities, and nations.

So the land must be redeemed through intercession because as outlined in Colossians 1:19-22, God through Christ has reconciled all things unto himself: "whether they be things on earth or things in heaven." In short, "we need to pray and ask God to deliver us from slander against our land."[13] This worldview ties in with the redemptive and empowering thrust of African Pentecostal theologies. The phenomenon of interceding for nations is now being given further practical expression as African Pentecostals move into Muslim dominated countries on the continent as missionaries. Trans-denominational groups like Pioneers Africa are the main recruiting agencies.

The NPCs of Africa, clearly the most high profile of African Pentecostal groupings, have deep roots in the students' Evangelical movements of the 1950s and 1960s—Student Christian Movement, Scripture Union, and Campus Crusade for Christ. Most of the founding leaders of NPCs came from this evangelical background. Conservative Evangelical Christianity with its emphases on the authority of the Bible, the Cross of Christ, and personal holiness, existed in Africa's second cycle institutions through the Scripture Union (SU), and in the universities through the International Fellowship of Evangelical Students (IFES). Conservative Evangelicalism also encouraged "responsible church membership" in existing churches, but the evangelical view that the Holy Spirit must not be sought as a subsequent experience following new birth proved counterpoint to grassroots experiences. With time, however, precisely by the late 1970s, generations of young people passing through the post primary educational system had acquired new pneumatic spiritualities that did not fit into the mainline churches in which they were supposed to worship. The evangelical movement in Africa's second cycle and tertiary institutions simply became charismatic at the grassroots. Having been exposed to Holy Spirit experiences, the new generation of African Christians started to form independent churches to avoid the encumbrances associated with existing denominations with their stereotypical Christian traditions. The movement started in the late 1970s, but the Rheinhard Bonnke Harare Fire Conference for pastors of 1986 served as a launching pad for many young men and women seeking to establish their own churches. The Flaming Fire of God Ministries in Zambia formed by Billy Lubansa from the DR Congo resulted from the founder's participation in Harare 1986. His influence since then has extended much further to Cameroon where he is credited with hosting several international crusades and in the process spawning many other new Pentecostal ministries.[14]

The major African inspirer behind the formation of NPCs, and the penchant of its leaders for a prosperity gospel, was the late Nigerian Charismatic, Archbishop Benson Idahosa. One of the cardinal worldviews of the new Pentecostals is, contrary to official evangelical opinion at the time, that it was possible to be born again and be fashionable. Idahosa was a protégé of several American televangelists, and his Church of God Mission International founded in 1972 was one of the first among such new Pentecostal movements in Africa. Idahosa's influence on modern African Christianity has been phenomenal. A number of leading Charismatic pastors in West Africa, including almost all the pioneers, were either trained at Idahosa's Christ for All Nations (CfAN) Bible School, or have drawn their inspiration from his success story. He traveled widely around Africa and beyond speaking at crusades and on the African continent in particular; he challenged young people to form their own Pentecostal ministries. Today NPCs may be found all over Africa's major cities meeting in converted cinema halls, refurbished abandoned factories and warehouses, or newly constructed large chapels with modern architectural designs that members appropriately designate, auditoriums. In Uganda, not only has the new Pentecostal phenomenon overshadowed that country's version of older AICs, the *balokole* movement, but we are also told that the new Pentecostal communions are "mushrooming in luxuriant fashion."[15] The NPCs, like the classical Pentecostal denominations before them, are very critical of the traditional rituals and religious symbolism that the older AICs keenly infused with Christian significance. In places like Kenya and Ghana, older AICs are feeling the heat from the new Pentecostal waves and are transforming themselves to survive.[16] The new churches preach a Faith Gospel that focuses on this-worldly blessings, and that is balanced with a "healing and deliverance" theology built on an amalgamation of African traditional worldviews and biblical thought.

NPCs also have a special attraction for Africa's upwardly mobile youth, a lay-oriented leadership, ecclesiastical office based on a person's charismatic gifting, innovative use of modern media technologies, particular concern with congregational enlargements, and a relaxed and fashion-conscious dress code for members. In the prosperity discourse, there is continuity between coming to Christ and experiencing a redemptive uplift that is evidenced partly through the possession of material goods. NPCs do not encourage the use of religious symbols like the crucifixes and mounted portraits of Jesus in places of worship. The preferred decorations are potted plants and colors of various countries to underscore their international leanings. English is often the principal mode of communication where the church is an urban one, and there is an ardent desire to appear successful, reflecting a modern outlook and portraying an international image. Many of its leaders come from professional backgrounds and some have earned PhDs in their fields. To give practical expression to their new images as leaders of the born again however, independent Pentecostal pastors are now frequently "Dr", "Bishop", or both. The Prosperity Gospel espoused by NPCs hold that God wills spiritual and material prosperity for all believers and so every Christian must appropriate the victory that Christ has won over sin, sickness, curses, poverty and setbacks in life. Christians may appropriate these blessings through positive confessions of faith as found in "the prayer of Jabez" (I Chronicles 4:9-10), and also the faithful payment of tithes and offerings. Such giving is reciprocal, so the Faith Gospel teaches that "sowing" gifts of money and other valuables in the lives of "God's anointed", as the pastors are called, is one principal means of attracting God's prosperity. Tithes and offerings, in keeping with this reciprocal giving, bring in millions in cash that enable NPCs to undertake gigantic and grandiose projects from internal resources. The theological outlook of the NPCs therefore tends to be more immediate, and this is reflected in everything they do. For instance, the words of the born again have performative effect, so debts, unemployment, unhappy marriages, and spiritual torments, may all be cursed in prayer whilst blessings of money, children, promotions at work and happiness, are claimed. The Kingdom is seen in earthly terms, and is established through the power of prayer, positive thinking, and adherence to the principles of success and prosperity such as giving.

NPCS belong to transnational networks and is reflected in their names, which invariably include the words, "world", "international" or "global": "Kingsway International Christian Center", "Living Faith World Outreach", "Christian Action Faith Ministries International", "Global Revival Ministries", and "International Central Gospel Church". The favored church logo is the globe embellished with other Pentecostal symbols such as the dove, a lamp, Bible, or burning flame. The internationalism of the new Pentecostals has generated accusations that these African Pentecostal movements and their leaders are clones of USA-based televangelists. Contrary to this view, the international links must be understood in terms of visits abroad, visits of foreign evangelists to Africa, and to some extent the adaptation of the American Pentecostal Bible School culture. Ray MaCauley, founder of Rhema Bible Church of South Africa, for instance, regularly ministers in several countries including Germany, Australia, the United States, Zimbabwe and the DR Congo, and his bookstores stock the books, video and audiotapes of influential foreign evangelists notably Kenneth Hagin and Rheinhard Bonnke.[17] Much inspiration has also been drawn from foreign, mainly North American televangelists, in the formation of these new churches. Oral Roberts, T.L. Osborn, Morris Cerullo, Benny Hinn, and Rheinhard Bonnke are a few of the international evangelists who have influenced the formation and development of new Pentecostal churches in Africa. Of these foreigners, one of those with the most enduring effect on Africa is Evangelist Morris Cerullo, whose establishment of the "Morris Cerullo School of Ministry" has benefited many new Pentecostal leaders.

The foreign influences, as noted, have come from personal visits, and access to the media ministries of international evangelists: book publications, and audio and videocassette tape recordings. The global view and international character that the NPCs take of their movement are what has led to submissions that Africa's new Pentecostals are North American creations. Together Brouwer, Gifford and Rose deny that the Christianity evolving through NPCs "is a genuinely African construct, arising from African experience and meeting African needs."[18] Liberia is an exceptional case in which large numbers of pastors acted as agents for North American churches and Bible Schools operating in that country. The internationalism of the new Pentecostals has simply resulted from "a multi-source diffusion of parallel developments encompassing Europe, America, Africa, and Asia." These parallel developments, as Hexham and Poewe note, "are grounded in core ideas and elementary religious experiences that are told to a pattern within the discourse of Christian testimonies."[19] Pastors, evangelists, and prophets, travel widely promoting North-South and South-South co-operations as speakers at Pentecostal meetings, which are now dubbed conferences and summits.

African Pentecostal churches differ from the older AICs in several respects. The concentration of charismatic power in the personality of the prophet has been replaced among Pentecostals with a new theology of empowerment based on the accessibility of the Holy Spirit to each individual. There is thus an anti-hierarchical tendency within the African Pentecostal movements; so although the prestige or anointing of an extraordinary gifted charismatic person makes for differentiation, the leader is only a first among equals. Thus, one of the most distinguishing theological features of modern African Pentecostalism is its radicalization of the biblical idea of the priesthood of all believers. The Pentecostals emphasize that God is directly accessible in the experience of the Spirit, thus in principle destroying the necessity of every kind of external priestly mediation. The special anointing of the leadership still makes for differentiation and their personal psychology and religious orientation is crucial in shaping the lives of the churches they lead. In spite of the belief in the "priesthood of all believers", Simeon Kayiwa founder of the Namirembe Christian Fellowship of Uganda, is for his large following, "a mighty man of God with overflowing anointing." Like all the others who lead such churches, it is his spiritual gifts that "brought the church into being, and preserve it."[20] The ecclesiology of the new churches follows the New Testament principle particularly evident in Pauline thought that participating in Christ is like functioning as a member of the human body. Each part has by definition, a function within the body, hence the reference to the believing community as the "body of Christ" (I Corinthians 12:12-31). The *charismata* or "gifts of grace", as exercised by an individual or groups of believers, constitute their "ministry". The different ministries are coordinated within the local church, to make it charismatically functional. Within a single local new Pentecostal church, one may find diverse team ministries, such as praise and worship, healing and deliverance, counseling, welcome and ushering, video and tape recording, prayer force, youth and children, and publications. These ministries are built around the collective belief in spiritual gifts and the fact that even natural talents are conferred by God and should be employed in his service through Christian ministry.

In the hands of its African agents, Pentecostalism also addresses itself to the structures of oppression that consign Africa to backwardness, mediocrity, and non-achievement. In *Beyond the Rivers of Ethiopia*, for example, Mensa Otabil argues forcefully that God did not curse black people; rather they are very much a part of his agenda. This is a message that Otabil has carried to many African countries. Through such motivational messages, African Pentecostalism has initiated a move from Afro-pessimism to Afro-optimism and hope. In the areas of education, health, and general infrastructure, Africa has become a laughing stock among the nations. Pentecostalism has blossomed in this context of precipitous decline and the leadership is challenging the continent to rise up and be counted. As part of the journey towards the restoration of black pride, Pentecostalism rejects not only socio-cultural practices that are considered inimical to African well being, but also encourages believers to work their way into public offices and influence the agenda of the state. In the recent past, Pentecostals showing interest in political office have been encouraged to go for it, because it is when Joseph became governor that the lot of the children of God began to change from being in bondage to inheriting the Promised Land. The New Testament paradigm is the "prodigal son". Once the prodigal returns home as "born again", God refurbishes his image, and despite a shameful past, he is now able to take his rightful place in the Father's house. Blacks may have a shameful past located in slavery and colonialism, but Christ now empowers the black man to sit at table with the powerful of the world. The media ministries of the various Pentecostal leaders provide the platform for these messages of black pride and empowerment to be shared across denominational, ethnic, gender, and socio-political divides. These are messages for the whole continent. The thought here is that African Pentecostal theology is not merely this-worldly; Jesus has bequeathed enough power to his church with which to change the circumstances of whole generations.

The involvement of Pentecostal/Charismatic Christianity in Africa has been felt at all levels of African civil life, including economics, education, and politics. Though by no means popular throughout African Pentecostal thought, Christian Zionism is being touted in some quarters. Pentecostal leaders now proudly preach about pilgrimages to Israel and this, together with hostility towards Islam, appears as covert affirmations of divine favors for those who wish Israel well. In the political arena, the independent Pentecostal/Charismatic churches in particular, have played both functional and dysfunctional roles. Pastors of Pentecostal churches in innumerable instances, have served as providers of supernatural protection for politicians seeking to consolidate power by entrenching themselves in office. Many of such politicians were perceived as corrupt individuals who relied on medicines from shrines to keep themselves in office, so by providing "Christian alternatives" of such shrine services, the reputation of such Christian "prophets" has suffered tremendously. In African countries like Ghana and Zambia, politicians have courted the friendship of popular Charismatic leaders in order to take advantage of a movement with massive youthful following to achieve political ends. In Ghana, Bishop Duncan-Williams virtually served as the chaplain to the Rawlings government. The former president of Zambia, Frederick Chiluba, not only declared Zambia a Christian nation when he took office in 1991, but he also constantly put in appearances at Pentecostal crusades and conventions. In the 1980s, when leading churchmen from the historic mission churches joined the opposition in challenging Moi's dictatorial regime, leaders of some Pentecostal churches, notably the Gospel Redeemed Church, publicly upheld Moi as a God appointed leader who had brought freedom of worship to Kenya.

In recent years, Pentecostal/Charismatic churches have started playing key roles in nation building by following the lead of the mission churches to establish Christian educational institutions of higher learning. A good example here is the Central University College of Otabil's International Central Gospel Church that graduated its first batch of students in Theology and Business Studies in May 2003. That the guest speaker at the Congregation was the president of Ghana, John A. Kufour, was testimony to the credibility that the newer independent Pentecostals have gained since their beginnings almost three decades ago. The efforts of Otabil's Central Gospel are being replicated among several such movements in various African countries and these endeavors have gradually moved the movement from the periphery to the center of African church life. A number of African Pentecostals—agents and pastors alike—are now pursuing higher degrees in theology, subjecting their own movements to critical academic study as insiders. Such an approach, if it is maintained in the future will help bridge the gap between the academy and experiential faith that exposed the deficiencies in the training of historic mission pastors in the face of African religio-cultural realities.

In his seminal work, *Bantu Prophets in South Africa*, Sundkler wrote of African initiated churches that in these movements, one has an idea of what Africans, when left to themselves, considered important in Christian faith and in the Christian church.[21] What people consider important in theology are the things that address their religious needs. Encounters with the spiritual world, either as malevolent powers seeking to destroy people, marine spirits negating efforts at public morality, or as the performance of ritual in order to solicit help from the powers of beneficence, are important elements in African religiosity. In continuity with the African religious paradigm, Pentecostal/Charismatic Christianity has proven successful in Africa because of its openness to the supernatural, through its interventionist and oral theological forms that resonate with traditional African piety. The intention of the practitioners, though, has always been to be biblical, and this theology as we have seen, is expressed in several ways.

First, we find that there is in African Pentecostal theology a keen emphasis on transformation. The constitutive act of the Pentecostal movement is the offer of a direct and particularly intense encounter with God that introduces profound changes in the life and circumstances of the person who experiences it. The Holy Spirit, God's empowering presence, is the one who facilitates the direct character of the encounter. A sense of transformation takes place at the personal and communal levels including a new dynamism in worship inspired by the Holy Spirit. The foremost theological emphasis of Pentecostal/Charismatic Christianity is therefore the transformative encounter with God who is "holy" and who is "spirit". In the African context, participants in Pentecostalism keenly testify not only about their new life, but also the transition often made from resorts to traditional religious resources in order to be sincere Christians believing in God alone. In this vein, Kalu takes issue with those who explain the explosion of African Pentecostalism in terms of modernization theories by refocusing attention on the core factor of religious experience:[22]

> The ordinary Pentecostal in Africa is less concerned with modernization and globalization and more about a renewed relationship with God, intimacy with the transcendental, empowerment by the Holy Spirit, and protection by the power in the blood of Jesus as the person struggles to eke out a viable life in a hostile environment.

For those African founders and members encountered in the Pentecostal and Charismatic churches and movements, their being there constitute a popular reaction against former churches, which in their process of institutionalization had become overly cerebral and theologically distant from the people.

Second, African Pentecostal theology is a theology of empowerment. In other words, there is an emphasis on the empowering effect of the gospel of Jesus Christ. There is a relationship between transformation and empowerment. The African Pentecostal insistence that it is possible to be a Christian and be dominated by desires of the flesh and demonic influences has led to the provision of ritual contexts in which people could renounce such stumbling blocks through healing and deliverance in order that they may be empowered to victory in life.[23]

> The core of the new experience is that it re-defines personality and reinvents identity as the born again person develops a new vision, life goals and ethics which constitute a rupture from a sinful past.

Such empowerment may be conceived of in terms of anointing, often symbolically applied in the form of oil. Empowerment is needed not just for ministry, but also for survival in a precarious African environment. Empowerment occurs first through the infilling and manifestations of the Holy Spirit, second, the ministries of healing and deliverance, and third, general prosperity and well-being.

African religion is expected to deal with the effects of evil caused by demonic spirits and witchcraft. Evil powers represented by those with evil eyes, demons, witchcraft, and curses, in the African context, result in all sorts of misfortunes—sickness, failure, childlessness, and other setbacks in life. The worldview underpinning the practice of healing and deliverance in African Pentecostalism is based primarily on Jesus' encounters with the powers of affliction and Pauline notions of the wrestle with principalities and powers (Ephesians 6). The basic theological orientation of the healing and deliverance phenomenon is the belief that demons may either possess a person and take over his or her executive faculties or simply oppress people through various influences. Whether the human crisis has resulted from possession or oppression, African Pentecostal churches and movements including the classical Pentecostal churches provide the ritual contexts for prayer and exorcism to deliver the afflicted. The African worldview of mystical causation looms large in the practice of healing and deliverance. It has become popular because mainline denominations with their over cerebral theologies proved inadequate in the face of the fears and insecurities of African Christians attributed to the work of devils. As it often requires the gifting of the specially anointed of God to deal with the demonic, African Pentecostal pastors are in the popular imagination upheld as more powerful and more spiritually alert than their mainline counterparts. The belief of having been called to proclaim the power of Jesus to liberate individuals from the power of the devil is what has given rise to healing and deliverance ministries and centers within all sectors of African Pentecostalism.

Thirdly, a successful implementation of a healing and deliverance ministry, paves the way for good health, success and prosperity in life, and makes possible the realization of God-given abilities. Thus it is possible to view the deliverance theology as a response to or the mutation in the face of the shortfall of faith preaching. When things are not going well, the appeal to the work of demons and witches come in handy as explanations. African Pentecostal prosperity theology may have some ground to recover in respect of its weak theology of suffering. Be that as it may, the Cross of Christ is not just a symbol of weakness, but also one of victory over sin, the world, and death. Pentecostals draw attention to the fact that the gospel is about restoration, so it is expected that the transformation of the personality would be manifest in personal health, well-being, and care, in short salvation is holistic and includes spiritual as well as physical abundance. The process of restoration is not individualistic as people are encouraged to disengage from generational curses and through fasting, prayer, and personal ministration also release family members from any such bondage. In African Pentecostalism generally, prayer for well-being and success has become one of the critical concerns. Some may view this as an obsession with this-worldly concerns but this could hardly be otherwise in a precarious context in which, besides the divine, people may virtually have no other means of survival. Undoubtedly, there are excesses both in the operations of healing and deliverance ministries, and the materialistic orientation taken to the gospel by some Pentecostals. However, by taking the African worldview seriously, Pentecostal/Charismatic Christianity has proved a more credible alternative to existing mission churches whose theology has proved a bit too distant from the aspirations of people.

As one who is in high demand as an international speaker on Pentecostal conferences in Africa and beyond, I asked Pastor Mensa Otabil of Ghana to sum up what he considers accounts for the huge success and impact that Pentecostalism is making in Africa. He aptly articulated his answer in one word: "relevance".

African Pentecostalism has proven relevant in responding to the challenging religious quest in the African heart. The Pentecostal emphasis on direct access to God through the Holy Spirit means for many of its African adherents, the ability to live the Christian life without recourse to the traditional ritual symbols that the older AICs incorporated into Christianity, and to which people continued to resort to in the face of the staid, silent and cerebral Christianity of the mission churches. Pentecostal spirituality is one in which Jesus Christ saves people from sin, heals sicknesses, and delivers them from the power of Satan. Salvation is here given a holistic meaning that includes "a sense of well-being evidenced in freedom from sickness, poverty and misfortune as well as in deliverance from sin and evil".[24] That the presence of Pentecostalism has forced former mission churches into emulative action in order to survive is enough evidence of how seriously the phenomenon of Pentecostal growth should be taken in modern African Christianity. Pentecostal/Charismatic movements and churches, as we have seen, are not in any way unified in their doctrines, practices and outlook, the popularity of its different streams against the backdrop of the previous hegemony of mainline churches only signals that "theology is more than an intellectual exercise but is as well a commitment and life-style, in short praxis".[25] Reliable statistics are lacking to enable us put exact numbers to the following of these churches, but the fact that they have changed the face of African Christianity and are likely to continue to do so in their ever-changing forms, underscores the viability of Pentecostal/Charismatic Christianity in a context where religion and life constitute inseparable entities.

Notes

1. Harvey G. Cox, *Fire from Heaven: The Rise of Pentecostal Spirituality and the Reshaping of Religion in the Twenty-First Century* (Reading, MA: Addison-Wesley, 1996); H.G. Cox, "The Myth of the Twentieth Century: The Rise and Fall of Secularization", in *Harvard Divinity Bulletin,* 28, 2/3 (1999) 6-8.
2. Leslie Newbigin, *The Household of God* (London: SCM, 1953). The expression "third force" is owed to Henry P. van Dusen.
3. See for instance, Gerrie ter Haar, *Halfway to Paradise: African Christians in Europe* (Cardiff: Cardiff Academic Press, 1998); Rijk van Dijk, "Time and Transcultural Technologies in the Self in the Ghanaian Pentecostal Diaspora", in André Corten & Ruth Marshall-Fratani, *Between Babel and Pentecost: Transnational Pentecostalism in Africa and Latin America* (Bloomington & Indianapolis: Indiana University Press, 2001), 216-234.
4. Richard van Dijk, "Young Born-Again Preachers in Post-Independence Malawi: The Significance of an Extraneous Identity", in Paul Gifford (ed.), *New Dimensions in African Christianity* (Nairobi: AACC, 1992), 55-56.
5. Harri Englund, "The Quest for Missionaries: Transnationalism and Township Pentecostalism in Malawi", in Corten & Marshall-Fratani *Between Babel and Pentecost,* 241-242.
6. Pierre-Joseph Laurent, "Transnationalization and Local Transformations: The Example of the Church of Assemblies of God in Burkina Faso," in André Corten and Ruth Marshall-Fratani (eds), *Between Babel and Pentecost: Transnational Pentecostalism in Africa and Latin America* (Bloomington and Indiananapolis: Indiana University Press, 2001), 256-273.
7. Emmanuel Kingsley Larbi, *Pentecostalism: the Eddies of Ghanaian Christianity* (Accra: Center for Pentecostal and Charismatic Studies, 2001), 278.
8. Donald W. Dayton, *Theological Roots of Pentecostalism* (Metuchen, NJ: Scarecrow Press, 1987), 21ff.
9. Lamin Sanneh, *West African Christianity: The Religious Impact* (Maryknoll, NY: Orbis Books, 1983), 195-196.
10. Matthews A. Ojo, "Deeper Christian Life Ministry: A Case Study of the Charismatic Movements in Western Nigeria", in *Journal of Religion in Africa,* 28, 2 (1988) 141-162. Ojo discusses how some of the rigid prescriptions are being relaxed to accommodate present trends.
11. Cephas N. Omenyo, *Pentecost Outside Pentecostalism: A Study of the Development of Charismatic Renewal in the Mainline Churches in Ghana* (Amsterdam: Boekencentrum, 2002).
12. Rudolf Otto, *The Idea of the Holy: An Inquiry into the Non-Rational Factor in the Idea of the Divine and Its Relation to the Rational* (London: Oxford University Press, 1950 [1923]), 3.
13. Emeka Nwankpa, *Redeeming the Land: Interceding for the Nations* (Accra: ACP, 1998), 7-19.
14. Paul Gifford (ed.), *New Dimensions in African Christianity* (Nairobi: AACC, 1992), 295-296.
15. Gifford, *New Dimensions,* 157.
16. Paul Gifford, "Some Recent Developments in African Christianity", in *African Affairs,* 93 (1994) 525.

17. Irving HEXHAM & Karla POEWE, "Charismatic Churches in South Africa: A Critique of Criticisms and Problems of Bias", in Karla POEWE (ed.), *Charismatic Christianity as a Global Culture* (Columbia, S.C.: University of South Carolina Press, 1994), 61.
18. S. BROUWER, P. GIFFORD & S.D. ROSE, *Exporting the American Gospel: Global Christian Fundamentalism* (New York: Routeledge, 1996).
19. HEXHAM & POEWE, "Charismatic Churches", 61.
20. GIFFORD, *New Dimensions*, 159.
21. Bengt SUNDKLER, *Bantu Prophets in South Africa* (London: SCM, 1961 [1948]).
22. Ogbu KALU, "Pentecostal and Charismatic Reshaping of the African Religious Landscape in the 1990s", in *Mission Studies,* 20, 1-39 (2003) 88.
23. KALU, "Pentecostal and Charismatic Reshaping", 92.
24. Allan ANDERSON, "Global Pentecostalism in the New Millennium", in Allan ANDERSON & Walter HOLLENWEGER (eds), *Pentecostals after a Century: Global Perspectives on a Movement in Transition* (Sheffield: Sheffield Academic Press, 1999), 215.
25. John S. POBEE, "Moving Towards a Pentecost Experience in Ministerial Formation", in *Ministerial Formation* 68 (January 1995) 17.

Chapter Sixteen

Gender and Power in African Christianity: African Instituted Churches and Pentecostal Churches

Philomena Njeri Mwaura

INTRODUCTION

Scholars of African Christianity have acknowledged the tremendous growth of the church in Africa in the twentieth century. Elizabeth Isichei observes that despite Christian presence in Africa in the first five centuries A.D. and again in the fifteenth and sixteenth centuries through Catholic Portuguese traders, it was not until the end of the nineteenth century and the beginning of the twentieth century that any sizeable conversions were made.[1] Even then in the nineteenth century, it is only in places like Buganda and the Creole community in Sierra Leone, that a handful of people became converts. This was the work of pioneer Christian missionaries from Europe representing various churches and missionary organizations.

Male and female missionaries prosecuted the modern missionary movement in Africa. Female evangelists took the initiative to open up outstations and indigenous bible women took the gospel into many kraals. While this has been acknowledged, more attention has been placed on the role of men in the propagation of the gospel and spread of Christianity despite the fact that women were the most ardent adherents.[2]

Many scholars have noted the preponderance of women in African churches. Questions have been asked regarding women's propensity to conversion at the pioneering stage of the missionary endeavor and today. Adrian Hastings proposes some factors. First, the essential message of Christianity that advocates equality for all; "that sense of freedom, of a co-operative effort in which men and women were both strenuously engaged, was communicated to the converts."[3] Women were taught that they were equal, free and capable of independent responsibility. Second, missionary Christian morality tended to impinge particularly upon various specific aspects of female existence. African women experienced Christianity as empowering. It gave them a place on which to stand;

from which they could challenge the male dominated sacred world and traditions. Such traditions were the killing of twins, the pursuit of alleged witches and polygamy. The missionary interest in the vulnerable women attracted the attention of the victims. Third, missionaries exaggerated the marginalization of women in indigenous patriarchal communities.

The attraction of African women to Christianity was not confined to the pioneer period. Today, women still dominate the pews in mainline churches, African Instituted Churches, Charismatic movements and Pentecostal churches. They are, however, absent from the power structures of the churches, which are male dominated. Their contribution to the growth of the church in Africa cannot be gainsaid. Elizabeth Isichei[4] and Bengt Sundkler emphasize that women were often the first converts and the most enthusiastic local evangelists. They even sacrificed their resources in propagating the gospel. Sundkler and Steed note that though women appear invisible, they have been the pillars of the parish and take care of the local church and its worship. The church has provided them with support systems and solidarity.[5] Women are animators of the church and society not only during times of crisis, even in times of stability. Whether women are educated or not, they continue to be devoted to the church.

A dominant male ideology has ensured that women continue being clients in the churches just as they were in shrines of traditional society. Patriarchal ideology that props up the structure of African societies, whether matrilineal or patrilineal, has influenced the perception of gender roles in society. Patriarchy has defined women as inferior, thus perpetuating marginalization and oppression of women. The resultant unequal gender relations have translated into male dominance and female subservience in church and society.

Sundkler and Steed observe the ambivalent role the church has played in being a catalyst for women's liberation and her complicity in their subordination.[6] The church, they note, had opened up new opportunities for women through education for girls and through roles of leadership. On the other hand "there operated in and through the churches, discriminating practices upheld by divine authority."[7] They attribute this to the fact that "the missions whether Catholic or Protestant originating in the nineteenth century, were largely expressions of a patriarchal society and these attitudes seemed to fit with an African society in its patriarchal and matriarchal form."[8]

The question too arises, apart from the explicit status and roles of women in church and society, how have they been represented in the academy? Ursula King observes that although the study of religion has undergone many changes in the last ten years, it is still deeply rooted in an androcentric framework, which women scholars continue to question and challenge.[9] She further notes that this androcentricism is particularly apparent in the historiography, methodology and conceptual tools of the discipline which express the marginality and invisibility of women as both subjects and objects in the study of religion. Writing about the study of religion in Africa, Isabel Phiri decries the same invisibility of women. She argues:[10]

> Studies on religion in Africa have predominantly centered on the role of men, both expatriate and local and have generally been silent on women's involvement. Yet it has long been recognized that the majority of church members are women.

She provides two reasons for this, firstly there have been more male scholars than female, and secondly, scholars have privileged male experience relative to women. The result has been an absence of theological writings on African women by African women. A glance at the study of church history displays similar oversights.

Feminist church historians have, for example, decried the invisibility of women missionaries in mission histories. In African Christian historiography, there is minimal documentation by African male and female scholars of the roles women have played, not only in presenting themselves for conversion, but also conducting evangelistic work among their own people. Jocelyn Murray rightly observes that "it is increasingly recognized that women were of fundamental importance in defining, developing and shaping the course of the modern missionary movement."[11] However, older missionary accounts did not take into account the role women played. Classical texts on mission history have also failed to record anything substantial on women even though there were chapters relating mission to social service, education and creating a bourgeoisie which were areas in which the role of women was central.

Currently there are few studies by women scholars, both African and non-African, on the impact of Christianity on African women and their role in evangelism. The work of Dana Roberts,[12] Fiona Bowie,[13] Nyambura Njoroge[14] and the Circle of Concerned African Women Theologians[15] have contributed in the reassessment of women's roles, not only in the modern missionary movement, but also the agency of indigenous African women in challenging patriarchal power structures and being catalysts in the evolvement of their own scale of values, identity and culture. Gender has been a factor in missionary work and hence it is imperative that a gender analysis of missionary activities be done at all levels.

Although there is plenty of literature on women in the New Religious Movements like the African Instituted Churches, Charismatic and Pentecostal churches, it has been mostly by Africanist scholars. It has also focused on an analysis of gender roles, significance of women in ritual as participants, healers and charismatic leaders. Not much has been done on their contribution to the growth of the church in Africa through outreach. Daneel avers that there is need to do a "thorough analysis of AIC women missionaries—their mission strategies, theologies, interpretation and propagation of the Good News in the African context."[16]

African Christian history has also been written from a male perspective that depicts women as helpers or totally absent in shaping African Christianity. Writings have been locked into an entirely androcentric perspective in treating the theme, and no attention is given to gender differences. A balanced historiography must integrate women's perspectives and experiences. Contemporary women scholars, as we have seen, are critiquing and reshaping the concepts inherited from male scholars, but as long as their thoughts and findings are not integrated into existing scholarly discourse, women scholars will remain muted as a group. Perhaps women need to evolve their own agencies for the production of knowledge and avoid marginalization. In historical and theoretical work, there is need to employ a "hermeneutic of suspicion" concerning data so far found and recorded as their perspective usually remains one sided and androcentric.

Rosalind Hackett also argues that women's "attitudes, behavior and so on are too frequently studied or ignored as peripheral invisible and non-interactional in the face of universal male dominance."[17] Gender is an important organizing category in the religious movements in Africa. It is integral to any informed understanding and analysis of African's New Religious Movements and their way of structuring the world.

This chapter explores how the planting and growth of Christianity in Africa has been facilitated by female agency. It attempts to portray women as protagonists and key actors in the evolution, development and growth of Christianity in Africa in various ways. It adopts a historical perspective focusing mainly on African Instituted Churches (AICs), particularly those of the spirit type and the more recent Neo-Pentecostal or Charismatic churches. It is argued in this chapter that, despite its apparent contradictions, the church in Africa has created an enlarged space for women and contributed to their emancipation from oppressive cultural practices and their culturally ascribed gender roles. The chapter begins by defining the phenomenon of African Instituted Churches, Charismatic and Neo-Pentecostal churches; followed by a mapping out of their prevalence in Africa before discussing their spectrum of operations and participation available to women there in.

I. AFRICAN INSTITUTED CHURCHES: A SURVEY

Ever since Christianity became established in the African soil there has been a variety of indigenous responses ranging from the development of prophetic movements in the eighteenth and nineteenth centuries, to the recent emergence of Neo-Pentecostal Christianity towards the end of the twentieth century. The variety of responses is viewed by scholars as a manifestation of religious independency and innovation in Africa. It is an attempt by Africans to forge new identities for themselves experimenting with and breaking down traditions. They provide an "interface for the encounter of African and Western ideas and a forum for social and religious change."[18] In theological terms they are regarded as processes of inculturation of Christianity in the African context. They have retained an African ethos and their theology has a distinctive African flavor.

These African responses to Christianity have been described variously as African Initiatives in Christianity, African Indigenous / Initiated / Instituted and Independent Churches. They can simply be defined as autonomous church groups with an all African leadership and an all African membership.[19] Some of them arose initially as breakaways from former mission churches. Others have arisen spontaneously around a charismatic or prophetic personality, who often draws upon the beliefs and practices of a number of Christian groups. They are what Dickinson describes as manifestations of:[20]

> ... a Christianity consistent with their own unique historical experience, rooted more self-consciously in their own culture and contributing to a richer world-wide interpretation of the Gospel.

These movements/churches as we shall see, have been labeled variously depending on their origin, historical period and theology as; prophetic, Ethiopian / Spiritual / Zionist / Aladura / Prophet healing / Charismatic and Neo-Pentecostal. Some churches, for example Ethiopian, are not found in some countries such as Ghana. At the outset, it is necessary to emphasize the sheer complexity of the subject under discussion. The topic under discussion is complex, not just in terms of regional, ethnic and cultural differences, but also in terms of numbers and the varieties of Christian expressions. Indeed, some scholars like Aylward Shorter[21] prefer to use the term "new religious movements" to describe the varieties of Christian religious expressions in Africa. For the purpose of this study it is imperative to attempt from a historical perspective a typology of the different Christian expressions in Africa before we assess the roles and place of women in them.

These matters have been dealt with in various parts of this book, and a chapter is devoted to the AICs because of their significance in the African religious landscape. As argued earlier, by the end of the First World War and the middle 1920s, Ethiopianism yielded to prophet-founded religious movements in several parts of Africa. They also emerged as a response to the lethargy of western mission Christianity, revivalism and particularly over African experience of the Holy Spirit. Others trace their origin to a charismatic figure, prophet-healer or prophetess-healer who underwent a resurrection experience coming back with a new message of repentance, of renunciation of witchcraft, and belief in the God of the Bible. Ogbu Kalu describes these churches and movements as "increasingly creative in their pneumatic emphasis, in the use of the Bible, innovative gender ideology, African religion and culture."[22] These churches changed the face of Christianity in Africa by their enlarging of religious space for women. To use an example from Zimbabwe, Mai Chaza, a former Methodist, started the Guta La Jehova in 1955. It was a prophet-healing church emphasizing divine healing and witchcraft eradication. Its significance included the fact that it was started by a woman. These churches reclaimed the pneumatic and charismatic experience that was suppressed by mainline Christianity and which resonated well with African spirituality. They emphasized healing, use of African symbolism, music, musical instruments and leadership patterns.

Since this chapter will use much data from the East African region, it should be useful to provide a backdrop on the emergence and vertical expansion of the Roho. In East Africa, AICs are more numerous in Kenya than in Tanzania. Spirit churches emerged in the 1930s. They were influenced by various revival movements at the turn of the twentieth century, particularly around the time of the First World War. In about 1912, the Roho (Spirit) movement emerged among adherents of the Anglican Church. It started as a popular charismatic movement among young people. Its most known founders are Alfayo Odongo Mango (1884-1934) and his nephew Lawi Obonyo (1911-1934). Mango had undergone ecstatic experiences characterized by seeing visions and speaking in tongues. He and others were murdered in 1934 over his revivalist activities and disputes over land with the neighboring ethnic group of Wanga. The revival that had started in Nyanza province of western Kenya continued, and several Roho churches among the Luo trace their origin to the revival spearheaded by Alfayo Odongo Manyo.

In 1927, another wave of revival emerged among the Abaluhyia also of western Kenya, but this time among the adherents of Friends African Mission in Kaimosi, and later in 1942 among the Pentecostal Assemblies of Canada in Nyangori Mission. This resulted in the formation of spiritual AICs, when those who experienced revival were expelled from the mission churches and schools. In central Kenya the "Arathi" (prophets) among the Gikuyu experienced the Holy Spirit in 1926 and this culminated in the formation of a host of "Akorino" (people who roar) churches emphasizing, prophetic experiences, healing, speaking in tongues and confessions of sin and preservation of certain traditional cultural practices like polygamy, ritual uncleanness observance and female circumcision. Examples of the Abaluhyia churches are the Africa Israel Church Nineveh of Zakayo Paul Kivuli (1942); Holy Spirit Church of East Africa; and Africa Church of the Holy Spirit. These churches have undergone further splintering since then. Other similar churches have been founded by charismatic personalities since the 1950s. Such churches include Jerusalem Church of Christ, founded in 1985 by Mary Sinaida; Dorcas Akatsa, in Kawangware Nairobi; and Nabii Christian Church of Kenya, started by Petro Mavia in 1981 in Kibera. In Kenya AICs—both the Africa/nationalist (Ethiopian) and Spiritual (Roho) types—form about 25% of the Christian population. There are over 800 AICs in Kenya most of them unregistered by the government. The spirit churches in Uganda and Tanzania are mainly Kenyan ones.

All these churches and movements tried to make Christianity more African and relevant to the people. They represent religious innovation that has produced a Christianity consonant with people's spiritual social and other needs. Men and women are protagonists in the creation of this type of Christianity. It has been suggested by recent scholars that spiritual/Zionist/Aladura/Prophet-healing churches have been losing members to the newer type of Charismatic and Neo-Pentecostal churches mushrooming all over Africa. They have also been demonized by the latter churches due to their rootedness in Africa religion and culture.[23] However, it should be noted that the spiritual AICs appeal to an older generation clientele and are therefore still relevant. Others have charismatized in order to sustain the appeal to the youth and be sensitive to the changes in the religious landscape in Africa. More information on these churches and their theology is provided in the relevant chapters of this book.

Since the 1970s there have been new developments in African Christianity. Charismatic revivals from within the mainline churches soon fed into Pentecostal forms as young Christians emerged from the mainline churches and formed current day charismatic ministries and churches. These churches all over Africa have their roots in the para-church evangelical associations. These are "non-denominational prayer groups, fellowships, gospel musical teams and individuals whose evangelistic aim is to shore up the mission of existing churches in gospel witness and Christian nurture."[24] These churches gained prominence in the 1990s. Their emergence and proliferation is attributed to a reaction to the bureaucratization of the mainline churches and their subsequent lethargy. They are also linked to the legitimacy, economic and social-political crisis in Africa since the 1980s.

The churches are Pentecostal in character and have been influenced by developments in international Pentecostalism, particularly from North America. These churches, which are known differently in Africa (for instance, African Pentecostals, Charismatic, Pentecostal and Neo-Pentecostal Churches [NPCs]), exhibit varieties of emphasis. The older ones espouse a holiness ethic while the younger ones emphasize prosperity. They adopt a faith-gospel focused on this worldly blessings and a deliverance theology which though built on "African traditional conceptions is expressed strongly in terms of modern western charismatic thinking."[25]

Like other Pentecostal churches, NPCs identify with the central act of conversion in which the individual consecrates his or her life to Christ, atones for past sins and becomes "born again" or "saved".[26] Like older AICs, they are for most part initiated by Africans for Africans. They share a similar worldview with the spiritual AICs in their concern for a theology of deliverance, and according to Kalu, "both lie on the same side of the typology of Christian forms"[27] and both draw from the same issues raised in primal religion.

Since the 1990s, the NPCs have become the fastest growing churches in Africa. Writing about Ghanaian Christianity, Asamoah-Gyadu observes that in terms of religious and theological influence Neo-Pentecostalism at the moment represents the most poignant, powerful and viable evidence of renewal and influence.[28] They have challenged the historic churches and older AICs to reinvent themselves to become more relevant and in tune with the spiritual needs of their flocks. The growth of NPCs is most dramatic in Ghana and Nigeria, where new churches abound in every neighborhood and are planted everyday. Many of them have acquired an international profile and have established branches all over Africa, Europe and North America.

In western, eastern, southern and central Africa, a similar phenomenon has been observed. Such churches in Nigeria and Ghana include: Deeper Life Bible Church, 1982; Redeemed Christian Church of God; Church of God

Mission International, 1972; Winners Chapel International, 1981; Central Gospel Church International. Lighthouse Church International, Liberia, too, has its share, for example: Transcontinental Evangelical Association Church, in 1989; and Bethel World Outreach, 1986. In Kenya, the most prominent church is Jesus Is Alive Ministries, founded by Bishop Margaret Wanjiru, 1993; Maximum Miracle Center of pastor Pius Muiru, 1994; and Chrisco Fellowship Church, 1985. In Zimbabwe one of the largest denominations is the Zimbabwe Assemblies of God (ZAOGA), 1980, which has its roots in South African Pentecostalism. In South Africa, Neo-Pentecostal Churches exist, but are not as prominent as in West and East Africa. Charismatic churches are numerous too in Malawi and Zambia, and many of them have been founded by women and young people.[29]

Regardless of where they are found in Africa, these churches have certain distinguishing characteristics, for example, prominent roles for women and youth, appropriation of American prosperity Gospel in the 1990s, and riveting to holiness and intercessory traditions in the 1990s. They are also noted for their aggressive use of media technologies. More details on these churches are found in the relevant chapters of this book. We shall now turn to the place and role of women in these churches.

II. SPIRIT-FILLED WOMEN AS AGENTS OF RELIGIOUS INNOVATION

We have already noted that women are proportionately more highly represented in all types of churches compared to men. This has been attributed to various reasons, including opportunities for leadership, entrance into a caring support network outside formal structures of society and the possibility for personal advancement. AICs are said particularly to provide women with the chance to recover their traditional status and positions that had been undermined by the teachings of mission churches. In traditional religions, women functioned as mediums, diviners, prophetesses, medicine persons, herbalists and priestesses. In West Africa, they even owned deities, cults and shrines.[30] Deities were even classified as males and females. These traditional roles thus became a resource for women founders of churches to draw from.

Western Christianity, whose tradition, mainline Christianity in African adopted, provided women with no leadership roles in their church structures. African Christians were able to find legitimacy for their inclusion in leadership in the mission churches from the Bible, which depicts women like Deborah, Miriam, Prisca and Lydia playing prominent roles. Missionaries often overlooked these sections of the Bible, and possibly considered them irrelevant to their missionary situations. These passages were, however, meaningful to the African converts—for missionaries had often criticized and condemned the African forms of religious expression in which women had a part to play. Scholars suggest that many women started and others were attracted to the AICs, because here they were able to reclaim the functions of customary institutions that were weakened by cultural change. Barrett remarks:[31]

> The missionary assault on the family complex caused women to act, for they felt the issues at state for more keenly than men. With more to lose, they vehemently defended their traditional institutions and way of life. Then, as the influence of the scriptures spread the emphasis changed to the contrast between the mission's rigidity and the New Testament's vision of freedom of women in Christ. Through the religious influence they exercised in the home, women spread the growing disaffection they felt concerning this discrepancy.

Women within Christian churches also found out that they were not permitted to hold positions in the ministry, nor in the executive structures of the churches. Women in polygamous unions experienced rejection when their husbands accepted mission baptism. Women thus joined AICs to seek religious legitimization for their rejection.

AICs are also regarded as sites for women's liberation. They have provided women with a forum where they find liberation from the ever present fears of witchcraft and other forces that undermine their well being. Writing about the Legio Maria of Kenya, Marie Perin-Jassay asserts that women find liberation from:[32]

> The duties and tensions of the home, from the domination of men over women, from the burdens of traditional customs and innumerable taboos, from the threat of death and disease of their children. Liberation in faith from everything that oppressed them, until a source of power stronger than the traditional sources, ancestors, spirits and magicians, was offered them: Christianity, in which all human beings regardless of age or sex could reach God.

Women in these churches find relief for their physiological and psychological symptoms which are often linked with dissatisfaction at home. Elsewhere in Africa, AICs, have healing homes and even hospitals that deal with women's specific problems like infertility, maternity care and their roles as wives and mothers.

Women thus give each other material and spiritual support, which could be interpreted as liberation. This applies to charismatic and Neo-Pentecostal churches as well. As earlier observed, spiritual AICs, Charismatic and Neo-Pentecostal churches are Pentecostal in character. This characteristic, when reinforced by the pneumatic traditional context, provides women with opportunities in worship, and leadership. In the Pentecostal tradition, all Christians have the possibility of receiving the same experience and gifts of the Holy Spirit as described in the New Testament.[33] Women, just like men, therefore experience the Holy Spirit and are endowed with the ability to dream, see visions, prophesy, preach, teach, exorcise and even heal. There are consequently many women in older AICs, Charismatic and Neo-Pentecostal churches working as pastors, evangelists, prophetesses and healers. Let us now examine some of these roles.

III. WOMEN AS FOUNDERS OF AFRICAN INSTITUTED CHURCHES

The founding of churches by women in Africa is the ultimate act of religious independency and self-determination. Since the establishment of Christianity in Africa there has always been an upsurge of female religious leadership particularly in the prophetic, revival movements, African Instituted Churches and Neo-Pentecostal Christianity. In these churches, women have been experiencing a measure of Christian ministerial freedom and equality hitherto denied them in the mainline churches. Not only are they visible in ecclesial leadership as founders of churches, bishops, pastors and evangelists, but they also function as prophetesses, prayer leaders, healers and heads of church organizations and departments. They are promoting the inculturation of Christianity by interpreting the Gospel message in a new perception that is both liberating and empowering especially to their female colleagues and followers.

Not only have they managed to break cultural barriers engendered in the patriarchal culture, but they are also agents of change, for they have contributed to the evolution of a new concept of church which is more inclusive and recognizes the varied talents and insights of both men and women. The road to this process has not been smooth, but women have been able to surmount various odds in their attempt to shape new communities and new personal and collective values. It is important to point out from the outset that this preponderance of women is not found in equal measure in all Christian new religious movements in Africa. Women's involvement in the churches is prominent in churches with a pneumatic emphasis. Hence, their leadership and participation is mainly evident in the Spiritual/Zionist/Apostolic/Aladura AICs, the Charismatic/Neo-Pentecostal churches and the revival movements.

Their involvement in the Ethiopian/Nationalist/African churches seems relatively muted. As was noted earlier, these churches adopted the theology and polity of the churches they seceded from. In the nineteenth and most part of the twentieth centuries, former mission churches had no women in the ordained ministries. However, even after the mainline churches started ordaining women, some of the former Ethiopian/African churches did not modify their stand. The African Independent Pentecostal Church of Africa, for example, adopted the organizational structure and some practices of the Eastern Orthodox Churches. Hence ordination of women is out of the question. Their women's organization, mother's union has adopted the pattern and objectives of similar women's associations in the mainline churches like, the Woman's Guilds, Catholic Women Association and Dorcas Society of the Seventh day Adventists. Women's power in these associations can, however, not be underestimated. Through them, women are deeply involved in evangelism, providing social and spiritual support to each other as well as organizing family life and fund raising for the church. Women's need for status and opportunities for initiatives are provided in these associations. This chapter will therefore confine itself to the spiritual AICs and Charismatic/Neo-Pentecostal churches.

It is not possible to give exact figures on the number of AICs and Charismatic churches in Africa founded by women. Barrett, in his 1968 study, *Schism and Renewal in Africa*[34] suggests several hundred out of six thousand Christian movements. In a geographically focused study in the town of Calabar, southeastern Nigeria, Rosalind Hackett identifies six AICs founded by women out of 248 known religious institutions. All over Africa even the recent Neo-Pentecostal churches and ministries count among them hundreds of women founders not to mention adherents. A few examples will suffice to demonstrate women's agency in the development of Christianity in Africa.

Women founders of religious movements are not a recent phenomenon in Africa. One of the most famous among African founders and prophetesses was Kimpa Vita, later baptized Dona Beatrice, who in 1704 founded the Antonian movement in the Kongo. She was reportedly a woman of noble birth and a leader of a traditional ritual society known as Marinda before she emerged as a Christian prophetess. Like many African prophetesses after her, she had ecstatic experiences. She claimed to have died and resurrected and also alleged that she was the reincarnation of St. Anthony.

Kimpa Vita claimed to have been commissioned to preach, teach and proclaim the coming judgment. She proclaimed an anti-colonial contextualized Gospel and held that a messiah would come to restore the Kongo kingdom to its former glory. Her "attempt to organize an African church with black saints and an indigenous hierarchy presented a challenge to the hegemony of the Portuguese Roman Catholic Church."[35] She is considered an innovator, for she called for cultural nationalism, political unity and self-determination at a crucial time of political and social unrest. She challenged the ideology of white supremacy that was a crucial tool for colonization by calling for removal of white portraits. Kimpa Vita's message appealed to the people because of her synthesis and reinterpretation of Kongo and Catholic beliefs and practices. Her attack against Portuguese hegemony led to her being accused of propagating heresy, and she was burnt at the stake in 1706. She became a national heroine and martyr. Kimpa Vita is today regarded as a prototype of the widespread African modern phenomenon of prophecy.

Grace Tani and Marie Lalou are well known founders of churches in West Africa. They were both prominent prophetesses, healers and leaders in the Harrist movement. Tani founded the Church of the Twelve Apostles in 1918, together with Kwesi John Nackabah, who became the administrative and public leader. This dual arrangement was a convenient method used by several AICs to overcome traditional male resistance to women's leadership. Tani was a traditional priestess before she had an extraordinary encounter with Harris in Ghana. Her church emphasized healing through faith in God and through the use of sanctified water.[36]

Mary Lalou, on the other hand, founded the Deima Church. She too experienced dreams before her conversion and was instructed to preach a message of peace and healing. She performed healings using holy water and urged people to abandon witchcraft. She had also been instructed to abandon conjugal relations and the persistence of her husband led to his death and that of his brother who inherited her. She was accused of witchcraft and had to flee to her natal home. Mary Lalou was childless. Her successor, princess Geniss, whom she had nominated, was succeeded by an unapproved spiritual successor, Ble Nahi, also a childless woman.

Both Marie Lalou and Ble Nahi shared similar characteristics. They were social misfits of a type, since both were childless and were accused of harming or killing their husbands. Both women transformed and legitimized their socially unacceptable circumstances through spiritual means. They claimed status and were valued as ideal spiritual mothers who had renounced their roles as traditional mothers for the good of the community. This was unprecedented in traditional context. Mary Lalou and Grace Tani imbibed Harris' message of radical social transformation particularly in terms of existing gender ideology. Some of the changes that he instituted concerned societal attitudes towards menstruating women. Harris urged the abandoning of practices of secluding women and even discouraged expensive and elaborate funeral practices. The mourning period for widows was also shortened and women were no longer expected to shave their heads or mourn for a whole year.[37] This address of cultural practices that oppressed women was also evident in the Lumpa church of Alice Leshina.

Alice Lenshina Mulenga Lubusha, popularly known as "Prophetess Leshina", was born in the early 1920s in Chinsali District of Zambia.[38] In 1954 she founded the Lumpa Church during politically turbulent times and it grew to be one of the most successful churches in Zambia. Like Dona Beatrice and other prophetesses before her, she underwent a death and resurrection experience after a period of illness, and came back with a message of repentance, destruction of witchcraft and healing. She is renowned for her witchcraft eradication activities and evolving an indigenous theology especially in worship and liturgy. Her church was attractive to women due to its enforcement of monogamy, denouncement of widow inheritance and other practices that were inimical to women's well being. Lenshina governed the church like a Bemba chief, and this elicited hostility from the local traditional chiefs who felt their positions threatened by her overwhelming authority.

In Alice Lenshina, as Hackett observes, "we have once again the example of a woman revitalizing and reforming both indigenous and exogamous traditions and establishing a new community which provided new values and new security in the midst of social, political and religious upheavals."[39] It is unfortunate that she was not able to establish an authority structure inclusive of women or exclusively for women. After her imprisonment by the Kaunda government in 1964 and subsequent death in 1978, the church splintered and none of the factions are led by women.[40]

Mai Chaza, a Shona prophetess who founded the Guta la Jehova movement (City of Jehova), had similar death and resurrection experiences like Dona Beatrice and Alice Lenshina. Like Marie Lalou and Ble Nahi she left her husband, claiming to have had revelations to lead a celibate life, and preached healing, especially for barren women the blind and the infirm. Her fame as a healer spread and people from Zimbabwe and all over southern Africa came to her for healing. Her movement initially operated within the Methodist Church, where she was a member. However, due to the challenges it created to official authority, it became a separate organization, the Mai Chaza Church in 1955. Like Grace Tani and Dona Beatrice, she conducted herself as a traditional woman ritualist, drawing upon the methods of spirit medium and traditional healer among the Shona. She died in 1960 and was accorded messianic honors. She too did not bequeath leadership to a woman and the church split eventually falling into the hands of a Malawian man, Mapaulos, later known as Vamatenga (someone from heaven). Mai Chaza's spirit is alleged to have possessed him and the subsequently revitalized and reorganized the church.

In Nigeria, the Aladura churches give women room to express their leadership abilities. This is especially so in the Cherubim and Seraphim churches which have produced remarkable women leaders. As in all spiritual/Zionist AICs, leadership patterns follow closely those in African traditional religion where women were ritual leaders and agents of spirits. As we noted earlier, the Sacred Eternal Order of the Cherubim and Seraphim was founded by Christianah Abiodun Akinsowon and Moses Orimolade. At the age of 15 in June 1925, Christianah is said to have fallen into a trance for several days after attending a Corpus Christ Day procession in a Roman Catholic Church. While in this state, she was taken to heaven by an angel and subjected to spiritual tests. She was taught prayers for healing and commanded to abandon traditional medicine. When she woke up from the trance she found her family had called Moses Orimolade, a renowned prayer healer, to pray for her. She had been shown this man in her trance. Captain Abiodun, as she was later known, differed with Orimolade and organized her own independent faction of the movement. She is considered as the "most prominent and energetic evangelist in the movement. She was instrumental in establishing the society throughout Yorubaland."[41] She married in 1942. Despite major challenges to her authority and various legal battles, she is still regarded as the founder of the movements. In 1986 she finally won the headship of the entire Cherubim and Seraphim movement."[42]

In Kenya, several women have founded AICs. Gaudencia Aoko started the Legio Maria Church of Africa in 1963, together with Holy Father Melkio, Lodivicus, Simeon Ondeto. They were both Catholics. Gaudencia received a prophetic call to denounce witchcraft and sorcery after both her children had died through witchcraft. As a result of this incident, she began a religious crusade and established her own anti-witchcraft movement that ultimately broke away from the Legio. She sought assistance of Marcellinus Orongo, a prophet and preacher in Tanzania, who baptized her. She returned to Kenya, crucifix and rosary in hand, healed the sick, burnt amulets and battled against evil spirits.[43]

Her example inspired Luo women by introducing the possibility of freedom from the domination of their husbands and in-laws—a continued source of tension and frustration in Luo society. In encouraging these reforms, Aoko's movement reacted to the political structure of the Catholic Church and developed a lay clergy with married priests and priestesses. Unfortunately, Aoko was not able to establish a stable church community. Her influence waned in both Kenya and Tanzania. As Jules-Rosette argues, here we see a problem of female leadership, the inability to transform ceremonial influences into an official position of full-time leadership and to transfer that leadership to other women in subsequent generations.[44]

Besides these prominent women founders of AICs in Africa, there are several others who are lesser known and they too have had a remarkable influence in the development of Christianity in their regions. Mother Christinah Mokotundi Nku, a Ndebele woman from South Africa and reared in the Dutch Reformed Church, experienced visions in 1906. She eventually founded the St. John's Apostolic Faith Mission in 1933. This is one of the largest and most prominent AICs in the northern province of South Africa. She became renowned for her efficacious prayers for healing and use of holy water. She was known as the "Founder and Life President" of the church. Unfortunately, as she grew older, her grip on the church began to wane and Peter John Masango was elected Archbishop in 1970. However, while Masango retained the administrative position, Ma Nku continued to be the "spirit" of the church. Though the church had a large membership by the time Mesango and ma Nku died in 1984 and 1988 respectively, it subsequently splintered. Dr. Lydia August, Ma Nku's daughter, continued her mother's work of healing until she died in 1997. There have been at least six secessions from the church led by women.[45]

In Kenya, Mary Senaida Dorcas Akatsa has been drawing thousands of people to her church, Jerusalem Church of Christ in the sprawling Kawangware slums, in the outskirts of Nairobi city since 1985. She is renowned as a faith healer and her denunciation of witchcraft. Like Lenshina, Ma Nku and others before her, she too experienced visions and received gifts of prophecy and healing since she was 12 years old. She is married with two children. Her healing ideology is derived from her indigenous Luhyia background. Mary retains the spiritual authority and is the patron of the church, while men have occupied legal authority.[46]

In the town of Calabar, in the Cross-river State, Nigeria, Rosalind Hackett identified six AICs founded and ran by women. Examples of these churches are: the Church of Christ the Good Shepherd, founded by Mrs Lucy Harret Harrison in 1946; Holy Chapel of Miracles of Mrs Theresa Effiong, 1946; The Church of God Lamentation of Jehova, of prophetess Theresa Sunday U. Inyang 1976; and Mount Olive Church of Christ 1978 of Mrs Maddie Raymond.[47] Like Akatsa's church, these are all spiritual AICs whose main attraction is faith-healing, which accounts for the vast majority of converts and casual associates. A characteristic feature of all of them (including the earlier ones mentioned) is their dealing with women's gender specific problems of infertility, sickness and family problems. Men also generally exercise the executive power of the churches while women retain the more spiritual roles and are often addressed as "spiritual mothers".

It is an interesting fact that these women prophetesses and healers often begin their ministry at a very young age. Dona Beatrice began at the age of 22, Lenshina at the age of 29, Aoko was 20 years old, Captain Abiodun was 15, Akatsa was 12 and Mrs Maddie Raymond of Mount Olive Church of God was barely 20 when she began having religious experiences. Some of these women married early and the arduous task of raising a family can be regarded as consistent with and even the norm of prophetic office. Others, like Mai Chaza and Marie La Lou, who operated totally within the framework of indigenous African religion, had to separate themselves from traditional conceptions of women in order to access ritual power. They therefore had to renounce all sexual relations and marriage.

IV. WOMEN IN CHARISMATIC/PENTECOSTAL MINISTRIES

In the more recent Charismatic and Neo-Pentecostal churches, women play even greater leadership roles. This is due to the Pentecostal theology that provides avenues for Charismatic gifting regardless of gender. To some extent the attitudes towards women's leadership has been positive. An examination of structures of authority in these churches reveals an egalitarian structure influenced by a democratic spirit. Women have therefore been able to experience ministerial freedom not possible even in the spiritual AICs. They are not just "spiritual mothers" but have executive administrative positions as well. We agree with Asamoah-Gyadu that the emerging role of women in these charismatic ministries is indicative of their theological position, where God's call to them is not passive but a compelling call to participate fully in Christian missions at all levels.[48]

Since the 1970s, ministries and churches founded by women have multiplied all over Africa. In Kenya Margaret Wangare started having religious experiences when she was in high school in Banana Hill, Kiambu District in 1974. She was a member of the student revival movement at the time. She operated as an itinerant revival evangelist before she founded her own church. Her ministry involved faith healing and the preaching of salvation and revivalism. Initially she operated in her parent's compound but later traveled all over the country from the 1980s till today. She is now the presiding bishop of the Church of the Lord. In 1980, Wangare underwent theological education in the All Nations Bible School in Benin City, Nigeria, under the tutelage and guidance of the late Archbishop Benson Idahosa, founder of Church of God Mission International. Other recent founders of Charismatic churches and interdenominational ministries in Kenya are Margaret Wanjiru, founder, Bishop of Jesus Is Alive Ministries (1993), and Teresia Wairimu of Faith Evangelists Ministries respectively (1989). These women leaders have managed to empower fellow women that have established churches elsewhere.

Asamoah-Gyadu notes the influence and authority of Pastor Christy Doe Tetteh, founder and leader of the Solid Rock Chapel based at North Kaneshie in Accra, Ghana. She is famous for her pioneering role as the first female founder of a Charismatic church. Like Margaret Wangare of Church of the Lord, she was trained in Benson Idahosa's All Nations Bible School in 1982. Hers is a ministry of deliverance which she interprets as part of Divine plan. Her ministry, like that of others, is legitimized by encounter with God through a conversion experience and subsequent endowment with divine power that manifests itself in the ability to heal and deliver from demonic powers.

In Nigeria, Bolaji Olayinka has commented on the increase in women-founded Charismatic/Pentecostal churches, particularly in Yorubaland since the 1970s. Dorcas Olaniyi founded the Agbala Daniel Church in 1979, after several religious experiences interpreted as signs of her call to ministry. She is the archbishop of her church, which has opened several branches in Nigeria and New Jersey, USA. Sḥe has a master's degree in Divinity. Another woman church founder is Stella Ajisebutu, founder/minister in charge of Water from the Rock Church (Faith Covenant Church). Though her religious experiences and activities as leader of a prayer group started while she was a university student, it was not until 1999 that she established her church under God's command.[49]

Analyzing the role of women leaders in the new generation churches, Olaniyi poignantly states that these women have become effective role models in the promotion of equality between men and women in church and society. They have given credence to the view that "failure to make use of women's potential represents a serious under utilization of human resources and abilities for the development of human society."[50] The women leaders are renowned just like those of an earlier generation for faith-healing, pastoral care that is gender specific, motherly concern for their adherents and capacity to inspire and support other women in the ministry. Many of these churches have established Bible schools for training pastors, and college enrollment comprises a sizeable number of women trainees. Their promotion of theological education is a radical departure from leadership in the spiritual AICs, which are purely based on charisma, and end up being ceremonial. In spiritual AICs like the Church of the Twelve Apostles, until the 1980s only men would acquire theological training and hence become evangelists, while women would be confined to the roles of healers and prophetesses. AICs still limit the role of women by sourcing their gender ideology from traditional society. Charismatic and Pentecostal groups have provided a larger space, though some groups still debate women sanctuary roles. Explanations for the enlarged space include the fact that many of the women are educated and operated in universities with their male counterparts. Some even acquired proficiency through Full Gospel Businessmen's Fellowship International that admits female membership unlike the situation in America. Sodalities like Women Aglow have also equipped many. Some women trained along with their husbands and minister with them. Indeed, it is quite fashionable for couples to found and minister together. As in the case of Benson Idahosa, his wife inherited the mantle of leadership at his death.

In Malawi, Bishop Mercy Yami is another example of a founder and leader of a charismatic ministry. Born in 1950, she had her spiritual formation in the Keswick movement, which was introduced to Malawi through revival meetings, organized by the Evangelical Christian Association. She became "born again" in 1976 and was discipled at the Assemblies of God until 1978 when she started working part time for "New Life For All," a fellowship established to nurture new converts in the faith in Blantyre.[51] In 1978, during an Easter Fellowship, she rededicated her life to God and was called to become an evangelist to preach whenever she found people, on the streets, in prisons and particularly among the blind and destitute. She had to choose between evangelism and marriage and consequently left her marriage.

In 1994 she started Zodabwitsa (Miracles) ministry at Chilomoni in Blantyre, and later teamed up with pastor Lumwira to establish Blessed Hope Church. Bishop Mercy (now Yami, meaning "Jesus in me"), became the office director while pastor Lumwira was the field director. Her work involved overseeing training of pastors managing the finances and grounding new converts in the word. She differed with Pastor Lumwira, who was not comfortable with women leadership. He claimed that female leadership was contrary to biblical teaching. They parted ways in 1995 and she founded another church, "The Love of God Church". This leadership dispute is reminiscent of that between Moses Orimolade and Captain Abiodun of Sacred Order of the Cherubim and Seraphim. Although leadership disputes in churches are not purely gender based, when they involve men and women, the Bible is used to justify women's exclusion or relegation to the periphery.

Other churches like Vine Branch Church and Christ Life Church in Nigeria have numerous female priests.[52] Churches like Redeemed Christian Church of God, Winners Chapel International and Lighthouse Church have prominent roles for women as wives of pastors, evangelists, pastors and even heads of departments. Before we analyze the nature of women's leadership roles in the AICs, we shall discuss other opportunities for participation available for women in these churches.

V. WOMEN AS HEALERS

The healing function is significant in AICs, Charismatic and Neo-Pentecostal Churches and is usually the basis for their appeal. Most usually join after experiencing healing, and in fact, some Spiritual AICs function as hospitals. Culturally perceived illnesses, usually related to women's problems of infertility and childbirth, are dealt with by male and female healers. As Jules-Rosette argues, women can easily identify with AICs by using a maternal healing metaphor, for they join sometimes due to reasons associated with their nurturing roles as wives and mothers.[53] Among the Maranke Apostles of Zimbabwe there are several types of women healers, healer-prophets, ordained healers and midwives. As healers, they diagnose illness and even develop a reputation for their profound cures. Similarly the activities of midwives, who are charismatic healers, involve hearing mother's confessions and delivery of babies.

Paul Breidenbach notes the prominence of women as healers and patients in the Church of the Twelve Apostles. He observes:[54]

> The Sofo (prophetess) is the primary healing adept within the movement. They (women) seem to command both affection and respectful obedience not just because they are confirmed with the 'a spirit to work with', but also because of the wide range of their specialized knowledge and activity. They act as diviners of illness, in many instances they interpret the participants' or their own dreams to effect healing; particularly all of them are expert midwives; they bear no major burden of directing the healing rituals and during the rest of the week they minister to the physical wants of the patients; throughout all this activity, they are continuously involved in giving counsel and advice.

In most countries in Africa, due to the prevailing economic hardships and poverty, most people cannot afford the expensive medical care. Besides the prohibitive costs of drugs, most clinics are often crowded, understaffed and inefficient. These factors make life unbearable, particularly for the poor. Modern medicine has also not been able to respond to culturally perceived illnesses and this has led to many people turning to traditional or charismatic healers in AICs and Neo-Pentecostal churches. These healers provide alternative medical care, spiritual healing and services equivalent to psychotherapy and group therapy; to those unable to afford the high cost of professional services.

Furthermore, the healing is mediated in a loving communal context with ecstatic dancing, singing and spiritual experiences. The healers are people who share a similar worldview with the patients and they diagnose illness and treat it in a manner understandable to the people. The churches thus serve as a refuge to those who feel the need for this form of ministry. Healers like Mary Akatsa of Jerusalem Church of Christ and others in Spiritual AICs employ healing methods that take into account indigenous African causal explanations, and sometimes, remedies.

The healing metaphor in these churches, not only enables women to ascend the social ladder and gain status and recognition, but it also empowers them to fight forces of oppression. Such forces are unemployment, breakdown of family relationships, poverty, lack of resources and witchcraft. Through their claim that God's Spirit empowers them to heal, these women join God in a constant struggle against personal and communal oppression. Healing is therefore a metaphor for a spirituality of survival and a search for well being. Daneel also argues that it is in their "healing colonies that a balance between male patriarchy and female emancipation is struck. These centers are in a sense the symbols of women's liberation where reputed prophetesses are free to pay full attention to the afflictions and a wide range of domestic concerns of women."[55] The prophetesses' healing ministry may sometimes stride other sectors for example church leadership and management or even local political matters. He cites the example of the late Bishop Mutendi's wife, a prominent prophetess-healer in the Zimbabwe ZCC, who acted as a pastoral consultant and gave advice to ZCC chiefs and elders on local disputes. Another woman prophetess, Mai Febi was highly regarded for her fairness and dignified autonomy in relation to church leaders.[56] Women in the Neo-Pentecostal churches like Margaret Wanjiru and Christy Doe attain status and recognition due to their successful deliverance ministries, which also deal with among other things women's gender specific problems.

VI. WOMEN AS EVANGELISTS

AICs, Charismatic and Pentecostal churches have organizations within them that are involved in evangelistic outreach, and this facilitates the numerical growth of the church in Africa. In southern Africa, the women's associations known as Rwadzano can rightly be described as missionary or evangelistic task forces.[57] Evangelism is engaged in through organized seminars, retreats and conferences. Neo-Pentecostal churches like Jesus Is Alive Ministries, Winners Chapel International and Lighthouse Church hold monthly ladies conferences that focus on issues concerning women and how to empower them in their spiritual lives and in their gender roles. They also have women organizations that are responsible, not only for organizing evangelistic campaigns, but also the general welfare of the churches. Like in the mainline churches, these associations are the pillars and lifelines of the AICs and Neo-Pentecostal churches.

The women do evangelism in a variety of ways including, personal witnessing to their faith in their daily activities, house to house evangelism and distribution of tracts in market places and other centers within their respective communities. Olubanke observes that the women in the Good Women Association of the Christ Apostolic Church evangelize through their gift of prophecy. Like in many other spiritual AICs, the prophetic office is dominated by women who use their prophecies to challenge male authority and give guidance to the church. Through their prophecies, new church branches have been established in zones that had not been evangelized by the Christ Apostolic Church (CAC).[58] Women in the CAC also engage in prison ministries.

We have already seen how Bishop Yami of Malawi established ministries to poor rural women, the blind, destitute and even prisons. Daneel also notes how in the Ruwadzano in the ZCC in Zimbabwe women actively participate in missionary campaigns which are launched thrice a year. The women act as hosts. They "accommodate the Zionist messengers, cook their food, wash their clothes and guide them into the surrounding villages for house visitations, healing ceremonies and housing evangelistic open air services."[59] The evangelizing teams also build on what the women have done throughout the year through door to door evangelism and living exemplary lives. Women evangelism in these churches features in the form of compassionate ministry of service, but also through actual preaching and Bible study. Through their persistent word and deed ministry, the women in the ZCC Ruwadzano and other AICs and Neo-Pentecostal churches have gained for themselves the reputation of being dedicated evangelizers due to their zeal. Unfortunately like both Daneel and Olubanke observe, women do not always receive the credit for contributing in expanding the church. In societies that are predominantly patrilineal and patriarchal, the general progress and success of the church is possibly attributed to male players, even where women's contribution is internally recognized. Where women are ordained as pastors and evangelists, like in the Neo-Pentecostal churches, their roles as evangelists are more evident. However, they too surmount various difficulties despite their Charismatic endowment.

VII. GENDER AND CLIENTELE: WOMEN AS PARTICIPANTS

We have already noted that AICs, Charismatic and Neo-Pentecostal churches provide a caring support network to women and opportunities for personal development. Women, who because of their poverty and personal circumstances find themselves excluded from other self-help groups, find a place in these churches.[60] Not only do women receive social, spiritual, psychological and material benefits in these churches, but they also feel affirmed and their dignity upheld. Commenting on this, Hackett avers:[61]

> Within the intimacy of the compound church, women may become 'known and accepted as persons' and become 'full citizens of the Kingdom of God', in which they can take initiatives and responsibilities.

This source of personal validation is especially important for women who are sick, childless, divorced or accused of witchcraft. Whereas single mothers, divorced and separated women are rarely given positions of responsibility in mainline churches, the AICs and Neo-Pentecostal churches ordain such women and give them other church responsibilities.

Here it is acknowledged that spiritual power is Charismatic and both men and women are equally channels of God's power. In spiritual AICs, for example, mobility within the church hierarchies is rarely determined by formal education but by spiritual gifts, seniority and experience. A woman may therefore have little formal education, limited economic means and low social status, and yet within the ritual context her role may be heightened or reversed.[62] However, in progressive AICs, where there may be women with professional skills and higher education, they could be considered in assignment to responsible positions. Churches like the Christ Apostolic Church, Celestial Church of Christ and Church of the Lord (Aladura) have highly qualified men and women in their ranks. They may not be regarded as churches of the poor like most older AICs in eastern Africa. Neo-Pentecostal and Charismatic churches may, as already noted, provide leadership opportunities to women, but here mobility is determined by both charisma and educational achievement. Their pattern of ministry requires arduous theological training for their clientele may comprise a majority of the middle class in urban and rural areas.

Worship also provides women an opportunity for spiritual rejuvenation and escape from the drudgery of life. Here worship is participatory, and every person's needs—men, women and children—are mediated in the context of prayer, singing and dancing. This creates a sense of belonging and community. In these churches, which are like families, women are able to express themselves freely through prayer, sharing testimonies, leading the singing, ecstatic experiences like falling into a trance, prophesying, speaking in tongues and dancing. They feel that their spirituality is not repressed or devalued. Women are also able to show initiative in the area of music as composers, choir leaders and conductors. Barrett notes how women gained fame as hymn composers in the Wanga AICs in Kenya.[63] Mai Chaza too composed a number of hymns that were used in her church, as did Alice Lenshina.

Scholars have noted the important role AICs and Neo-Pentecostal churches play in providing entertainment and relaxation for women. Since women do not have the same social outlets like men, the church and church women associations become centers for socialization and welfare. The churches not only provide fellowship, but solidarity in terms of need. Women here, not only exchange ideas on how to run their families, but they also share and access empowering information like legal counsel, how to conduct business and even to lead a prayerful life. This is, for example, evident in Jesus Is Alive Ministries, Winners Chapel International and Africa Independent, Pentecostal Church of Africa. Hoehler-Fatton notes the liberation experienced by women in the Roho Movement in Kenya. Women are able to "from time to time reject the self-effacing posture that dominant ideology prescribes for (them). Women experience peace, reconstruct their identity as a result of the "gradual spiritual personal development grounded in a new worldview and faith."[64]

The sharing of language and cultural background, particularly in the rural areas, provides a common bond and understanding. In the urban areas where so many things seem to be beyond the control of the individual, the sense of belonging created in the churches is important. In their participation, women benefit from being a part of a community, whose worship they can enjoy. This enjoyment and entertainment AICs and Pentecostal churches provide, is an important aspect in the attraction of women. In Nairobi, Accra, Lagos, Harare, Johannesburg and other areas in Africa, these churches provide services and mediate for those in the fringes of society. With regard to women, it is the prostitutes, unmarried mothers, the widowed and divorced for whom these churches in particular provide services.

VIII. CONCLUDING EVALUATION: WOMEN'S ROLES AND STATUS

We have noted that several scholars hail the opportunities availed for leadership and participation availed to women in AICs, Charismatic and Neo-Pentecostal churches. These churches have created structures within which women may acquire power and responsibility. But how empowering are these roles and opportunities? Have they led to women's equality with men in the management and life of the churches? Jules-Rosette argues that in the Vapostori, which is a highly patriarchal church, women do not hold administrative positions. Their roles are confined to nurturing functions and hence women attain little more than "ceremonial leadership and symbolic" roles. She further observes that ceremonial leadership may imply political subordination.[65]

It has also been noted that women founders of churches are not able to bequeath leadership to other women. This happened in the Mai Chaza Church, Lumpa Church of Alice Lenshina and the Legio Maria Africa of Gaudencia Aoko. These attitudes should be seen in the light of wider social-cultural norms. Though women may have religious authority, inherit and acquire ascribed status in some societies in Africa, they may not become clan heads or be eligible for kingship. However, as Hackett observes having a woman founder has led in some churches to the emergence of other women in the same movement. In the Church of the Twelve Apostles, Grace Tani and John Kwasi Nackabah had a "ritual parallelism" with distinct roles for men and women. This church has two distinct services: the Friday healing service conducted by the prophetesses in the garden and the Sunday "Chapel" service, conducted by young educated men. The healing service is the central event of the week.[66] This church, therefore, has provided women opportunities for service.

In the Cherubim and Seraphim churches women are found in the hierarchy, like Lya Alakoso (Superintendent mother). Many of them have played major roles in the expansion of the movement by establishing several branches. For example, Madam Christianah Olatunrinle from Ondo was a great evangelist and became Lya Alokoso of the Western Conference of the Cherubim and Seraphim. Another woman was "Alanke Igbalaolu, founder and leader of the Ija-Igbo No 1 (Ibadan). More generally within the organization women may attain such high offices as mother Cherub, mother Seraph, Captain and mother-in-Israel ranks equivalent to Apostles and Senior apostles."[67] These titles are, however, Charismatic titles rather than administrative.

In the Celestial Church of Christ, Crumbley observes that there are dual roles and responsibilities for men and women. Women's roles are confined to the Charismatic domain while administrative functions are restricted to men. However, women may preach and have administrative roles among women and within women's organizations. Space in the sanctuary is also gendered and boundaries are strictly adhered to.[68] This is true also in the Arathi churches in central Kenya, Maranke Apostles and the Johana Mosowe Apostles of Zimbabwe. Olubanke observes the same in the Christ Apostolic Church. In the Church of the Lord (Aladura), however, there are parallel positions for women right up to the top of the hierarchy. "Women can found and head churches and can theoretically become primate."[69] This situation is not obtained in many Aladura churches. Hackett attributes this progressive attitude to the fact that the church is more exposed due to its membership in international bodies.

Although women's spiritual powers are recognized in these churches, they nevertheless experience restriction and have to contend with negative attitudes. This is the paradoxical attitude to women particularly in Spiritual AICs. Their full participation and exercise of leadership is hampered and restricted by taboos surrounding menstruation and childbirth. In the Celestial Church of Christ, Arathi, Nomiya Luo Church and Jerusalem Church of Christ, women occupy subordinate roles because ritual impurity is attributed to them. This fear of defilement of the sacred by women is demonstrated by the fact that the altar sanctuary is a male only preserve. Congregational segregation is common with separate doors for each sex.[70] Much attention is also paid to the way women dress in church—so that they do not distract male attention. In some churches, men may pray for both male and female supplicants, whereas women may only pray for women.

Many women leaders also face resistance from male authority. As already noted, Captain Abiodun, co-founder of the Cherubim and Seraphim faced opposition in her attempt to be recognized as the supreme head of the church. Throughout her life she had to consistently fight against male prejudice.[71] The Cherubim and Seraphim, just like many spiritual AICs, have fewer openings for women leaders in the hierarchy (five as opposed to nine for men).[72] Olubanke also observes how Mrs Pearce, an acting principal of a CAC theological college, despite her serving with dedication, was ungraciously removed from office and died shortly afterwards, dejected and frustrated. Bishop Yami of the Love of God Church had also to part ways with Pastor Lumwira due to gender based differences.

In South African Zionist churches, a distinction is also made between legal and Charismatic authority. Charismatic positions of healers and prophets are outside the hierarchy, which is administrative. This authority runs parallel to legal authority and both are usually in tension. Women mostly occupy the Charismatic authority as prophetesses and healers and do not necessarily pose a threat to male authority. Nevertheless, they have influence and power since they are regarded as channels of God's will though the Holy Spirit. They give guidance to the church on important matters.

In the Spiritual AICs, leadership for women is also facilitated through the principle of co-dependency. Women may therefore hold positions of authority because of their husbands' positions as bishops. Where a woman may be the permanent head, a male may exist as a nominal head. This was the case in the St. John's Apostolic Faith Mission when Masango was Archbishop and Ma Nku "spiritual mother". Wives and even daughters of bishops may be ordained pastors due to positions of their husbands or fathers. Such women may exert tremendous influence, for they may have a free hand in the formation of organizations and setting up projects that benefit women. For example, the wife of Adejobi the late primate of the Church of the Lord, Aladura, was able to initiate women's prayer unions, and women's local unions and appointed the new members.[73]

Despite these restrictions, AICs provide women with structures within which they may acquire and exercise responsibility. Though they may be barred from accessing the higher echelons of the churches' hierarchy, they exercise power and influence through their prophetic gifts, through which they command respect and influence the church. Men may have legal authority, but women have spiritual authority that is sometimes not disputed. Nevertheless indirect authority, no matter how influential it is, cannot be equated with legal authority. There is need to bring women into the mainstream of church leadership. Very often women's prophecies have been ignored as happened with prophecies of women in the Good Women Association of CAC. Their prophecies that pastor Olutimehim should succeed Pa Latunde and not Pa Orogun went unheeded. The revelations were treated with contempt by a section of the hierarchy. The choice that was made has, since 1982, created rancor, bitterness and division.[74]

In the Charismatic and Neo-Pentecostal Churches women are provided with a wider range of opportunities, and without overt restrictions like in the AICs. The unstructured nature and unrestricted orientation of many of these churches and ministries allow women to take initiative. These churches and ministries, as we have seen, are prevalent in Kenya, Nigeria, Ghana, Democratic Republic of Congo, Zambia, Zimbabwe, Malawi and South Africa. In Kenya hundreds of women have since the 1980s emerged as founders of Charismatic churches, ministries and prayer fellowships. Lunch time revivals may be held on the streets and many cinema halls, social halls and bars are used for the same purpose.

Women are involved in leading intercessory gatherings, Bible study, praise and worship, prayer and even preaching. Several have been ordained as pastors and evangelists by their international partners, mostly based in America. In these churches, women just like in the AICs, may be vehicles of the spirit and receive spiritual gifts in the same way as men. Unlike in Spiritual AICs, they are not bound by any traditional restrictions. As Asamoah-Gyadu observes:[75]

> The Charismatic ministries do not impose any levitical or traditional taboos on women. They regard this as being inconsistent with New Testament teaching particularly with the missionary experience that followed the outpouring of the Holy Spirit in Acts.

The churches have even set up Bible Schools where, among those being trained, there are women. According to Bishop Margaret Wanjiru of Jesus Is Alive Ministries, God calls both men and women to serve Him at all levels. God' s power through the Holy Spirit and Christ's death and resurrection have dismantled the hold of negative cultural traditions. These women are free to participate in ministry. These churches also apply a liberating hermeneutic in their readings of scripture in this respect. Hence Pauline injunctions directed to women are critiqued within their cultural and historical context. However as Hackett observes, with regard to Nigeria Charismatic Churches:[76]

> [... there still exists] ambivalent attitudes towards women. At one level they may enjoy greater participation and leadership opportunities in God's army, at another level, they are frequently stigmatized and demonized (notably those of the unmarried and 'liberated' vanity).

Charismatic views of women also show fundamentalist tendencies. Though women, as we have noted, may have freedom to exercise their spirituality and may experience relative stability within marriage due to emphasis on a holiness ethic, churches that adopt a literalist interpretation of scriptures can be oppressive to women. For some, their conception of the female and marriage is patriarchal and sexist. Although they may recognize the need and value of women's occupation outside the home out of economic necessity, the sign of true womanhood to them is a woman devoting her life sacrificially to the demands of husband and children. Her primary function is as wife and mother and being subject to the authority of her husband in all spheres of life.

Those propagating a male-centered theology prescribe and encourage women's silence and subordination in church and society. Such a theology is considered normative and a basis of shaping attitudes and behavior within the churches. These churches embrace the household codes in the New Testament, which prescribe silence of women and apply them literary in practice. Matthew Ojo, writing about perceptions of marital relationships among some Nigerian Charismatic and specifically Deeper Life Bible Church, says:[77]

> Charismatics teach that a couple should have a joint account which they call a common purse to which all incomes go and expenses are deducted. However, the financial responsibilities of the home are those of the husband. The *wife should be obedient and submit completely to the husband* ... A sure and unmistakable mark of a woman's spirituality is her meek, humble, obedient and whole hearted submission to the husband in everything unto the Lord.

Though this teaching is biblical, and mutual respect and obedience are virtues within human relationships, an uncritical acceptance of it can be detrimental to a woman's well being. It perceives women as lacking in moral agency which is unbiblical. All the same, the Charismatic churches just like the AICs offer women greater avenues of participation as leaders and members.

CONCLUSION

Africa, since the nineteenth century, has exhibited varieties of responses to the Gospel depending on the historical, geographical, social, religious and cultural contexts. These responses have produced different types of Christianities that have been labeled as Ethiopian / African / Nationalist / Zionist / Spiritual / Aladura and Pentecostal / Charismatic / Neo-Pentecostal. They have also had gender dimensions. Men and women experienced Christianity differently. Its teaching on the equality of men and women before God—and that they are both equally mediators of God's grace and the Holy Spirit— was empowering to people who experienced the brunt of the negative aspects of African culture. On the other hand, where missionary control and colonial hegemony interlocked to deny women their traditional social, economic, political and religious space, women founded and joined African indigenous churches, where they could utilize their resources and exercise their spiritual power.

In the churches women seem to access power and religious space more easily through the exercise of spirituality in healing, evangelism and leadership. Kalu argues that women have always been healers as is evident among ancient temple priestesses.[78] This too is evident in the African indigenous context and this is the resource that women in the African Instituted Churches, old and new draw from. The potency of female spirituality is acknowledged in these churches and its manifestation explains the attraction, impact and strength of these churches. The Neo-Pentecostal Churches may deny this link, but feminist scholars on spirituality have linked the ascendancy of female roles in churches to their inherent spirituality. In these churches, women's spiritual power is recognized although it is more evident in ritual than in affirmation.

Through the AICs and Neo-Pentecostal Churches, women have displayed innovations in religious ethic and practice through their challenge of cultural practices like widow inheritance, prolonged periods of mourning and other funeral and burial rites affecting them, and witchcraft. Through their experiences as prophets, speaking in tongues and spirit possession, women are also able to challenge male authority and hence acquire a voice in Neo-Pentecostal churches. Where ecclesiastical and cultural prohibitions do not obtain, they are able to empower other women and create positive change. Women have contributed to the humanization of the church by utilizing their talents.

The AICs and Neo-Pentecostal churches have facilitated enlarged female participation and leadership. Nevertheless, their participation is circumscribed, depending on the church, by cultural and ecclesiastical/biblical controls. In some churches, women's "roles are defined in function of male authority and male conceptions of the female."[79] The challenge therefore continues for Africans to evolve theologies that will challenge cultural elements that do not promote women's well being and that create a holistic community where men, women and children experience God's kingdom. This is the subject of the next chapter. There is no doubt however, that women have contributed to the growth of Christianity in Africa through their evangelistic zeal, leadership, gift of healing, prophecy and committed service.

Notes

1. Elizabeth Isichei: *A History of Christianity in Africa from Antiquity to the Present* (London: SPCK, 1995), 31.
2. Isichei, *A History of Christianity*, 190; see also Adrian Hastings, "Were Women a Special Case?" in *African Catholicism: Essays in Discovery* (London: SCM 1989).

3. HASTINGS, *African Catholicism*, 38.
4. ISICHEI, *A History of Christianity in Africa*, 190.
5. Bengt SUNDKLER & Christopher STEED, *A History of the Church in Africa* (Cambridge: Cambridge University Press 2000), 681.
6. SUNDKLER & STEED, *A History of the Church*, 681.
7. SUNDKLER & STEED, *A History of the Church*, 679.
8. SUNDKLER & STEED, *A History of the Church*, 680.
9. Ursula KING, "A Question of Identity: Women Scholars and the Study of Religion", in U. KING (ed.), *Religion and Gender* (Oxford: Blackwell, 1995), 199.
10. Isabel A. PHIRI, "Doing Theology as African Women", in John PARATT (ed.), *A Reader in African Christian Theology* (London: SPCK, 1997), 45.
11. Jocelyn MURRAY, "The Role of Women in the Church Missionary Society, 1799-1917," in Ward, Kevin and Brian Stanley (eds.) *The Church Mission Sociaty and World Christianity* (Grand Rapids: Eerdmans, 1996) 66.
12. Dana L. ROBERTS (ed.), *Gospel Bearers, Gender Barriers: Missionary Women in the Twentieth Century* (Maryknoll: Orbis Books, 2002).
13. Fiona BOWKIE, Deborah KIRKWOOD & Shirley ARDENER (eds), *Women and Missions: Past and Present: Anthropological and Historical Perceptions* (Providence: Berghan, 1993).
14. Nyambura J. NJOROGE, *Kiama Kia Ngo: An African Christian Feminist Ethic of Resistance and Transformation*, Ecclesiastical Studies 2, Legon, Theological Series (Accra: Asempa Publishers, 2000).
15. Members of the Circle of Concerned African Women Theologians have written several books on African Women's Theology. One of them is a collection of papers on biographies of women founders of churches, histories of women founded churches and women organizations in a variety of churches, both mainline and African Instituted Churches. See Isabel A. PHIRI, D.B. GOVINDEN & S. NADAR (eds), *Her Stories, Hidden Histories of Women of Faith in Africa* (Pietermaritzburg: Cluster Publications, 2002).
16. M.L. DANEEL, "AIC Women as Bearers of the Good News", in *Missionalia*, 28, 213 (November 2000) 312.
17. Rosalind I.J. HACKETT, "Women and New Religious Movements in Africa", in KING, *Religion and Gender*, 260.
18. Rosalind J. HACKETT (ed.), *New Religious Movements in Nigeria* (Lewiston: The Edwin Mellen Press, 1987), 1.
19. Martin E. WEST, "People of the Spirit: Charismatic Movements among African Independent Churches", in *Journal of Theology of Southern Africa* (7 June 1974).
20. R.D.N. DICKINSON, *To set at Liberty the Oppressed* (Geneva: WCC 1975), 50.
21. Aylward SHORTER, *New Religious Movements in Africa* (Nairobi: Paulines 2001).
22. Ogbu U. KALU, *Power, Poverty and Prayer: The Challenges of Poverty and Pluralism in African Christianity, 1960-1996* (Frankfurt: Peter Lang, 2000), 105.
23. See Gerrie TER HAAR, "Standing up for Jesus: A Survey of New Developments in Christianity in Ghana", in *Exchange*, 23 (1994) 221-240, 223; Ogbu U. KALU, "Estranged Bedfellows: The Demonization of the Aladura in African Pentecostal Rhetoric" in *Missionalia* 28 (2000) 121.

24. Kwabena ASAMOAH-GYADU, "Renewal within Christianity: A Historical and Theological Study of some current developments within Ghanaian Pentecostalism", (PhD Thesis, University of Birmingham, 2000), 33.
25. Paul GIFFORD, *African Christianity: In Public Role* (London: Hurst & Co., 1998), 320.
26. Ruth MARSHALL, "'God is not a Democrat': Pentecostalism and Democratization in Nigeria", in P. GIFFORD (ed.), *The Christian Churches and the Democratization Process in Africa* (Leiden: Brill, 1995) 244.
27. KALU, *Power, Poverty and Prayer*, 105.
28. Kwabena ASAMOAH-GYADU, "'Fireballs in our Midst': West Africa's Burgeoning Charismatic Churches and the Pastoral Role of Women", in *Mission Studies,* XV,1 (1998) 19-20.
29. Isabel A. PHIRI, "African Women in Mission: Two case studies from Malawi", in *Missionalia,* 28 (2000) 267; 293.
30. Protus KEMDIRIM, "Towards Inclusiveness for Women in the African Churches", in *Mission Studies,* XII, 1, 2, 3 (1995) 1-8.
31. David B. BARETT, *Schism and Renewal in Africa: An Analysis of Six Thousand Contemporary Religious Movements* (Nairobi: Oxford University Press, 1968), 147.
32. Marie-Perrin JASSY, *Women in African Independent Churches* (Geneva: Risk Books, 1971), 3.
33. Acts of the Apostles 2:1-4; cf. 1 Corinthians 12.
34. BARETT, *Schism and Renewal*, 148.
35. A. ANDERSON, *African Reformation* (Trenton, NJ: Africa World Press, 2002), 48.
36. Inus DANEEL, *The Quest for Belonging: Introduction to a Study of African Independent Churches* (Gweru: Mambo Press, 1987), 46. See also James AMANZA, *African Christianity in Botswana* (Gweru: Mambo Press, 1998), 62-65.
37. Sheila S. WALKER, "Women in the Harrist Movement", in Benetta JULES-RESETTE (ed.), *The New Religions of Africa* (Norwood, NJ: Ablex, 1979), 87-115, 96.
38. Kampamba MULENGA, *Blood in Their Hands* (Lusaka: Zambia Educational Publishing House, 1998).
39. HACKETT, "Women and New Religious Movements", 263.
40. MULENGA, *Blood in their Hands*, 90.
41. HACKETT, "Women and New Religious Movements", 265.
42. Mercy Amba ODUYOYE, *Daughters of Anowa: African Women and Patriarchy* (New York: Orbis Books, 1995), 126.
43. Peter J. DIRVEN, *The Maria Legio: "The Dynamics of a Breakaway Church among the Luo in East Africa"*, (Unpublished PhD Thesis, Pontifica Universitas Gregorians, Rome, 1970), 139-156.
44. Bennetta JULES-ROSETTE, "Cultural Ambivalence and Ceremonial Leadership: The Role of Woman in Africa's New Religious Movements," in John C.B. WEBSTER & Ellen L. WEBSTER (eds), *The Church and Women in the Third World* (Philadelphia: Westminster Press, 1985), 95.
45. HACKETT, "Women and New Religious Movements", 266.
46. Philomena N. MWAURA, *A Theological and Cultural Analysis of Healing in Jerusalem Church of Christ and Nabii Christian Church of Kenya* (Unpublished PhD Thesis, Kenyatta University, 2001).

47. R. HACKETT, "Women as Leaders and Participants in the Spiritual Churches", in *Journal of Religion in Africa*, XXI, 2 (1991) 191-208.
48. ASAMOAH-GYADU, "Fireballs in our Midst", 21.
49. Bolaji Olukemi OLAYINKA, *Female Leaders of New Generation Churches as Change Agents in Yorubaland* (Unpublished PhD Thesis, Obafemi Awolowo University, 2000), 137-166.
50. OLAYINKA, *Female Leadership*, 128.
51. PHIRI, "African Women in Mission", 280.
52. Dorcas A. OLUBANKE, "The History of Good Women: Association of the Christ Apostolic Church", (Unpublished Paper, January 2002), 8.
53. JULES-ROSETTE, "Cultural Ambivalence", 93.
54. Paul BREIDENBACH, "The Woman on the Beach and the Man in the Bush: Leadership and Adepthood in the Twelve Apostles Movement in Ghana", in Bennetta JULES-ROSETTE (ed.), *The New Religions of Africa* (Norwood, NJ: Ablex, 1979), 109.
55. DANEEL, "AIC Women", 313.
56. DANEEL, "AIC Women", 313.
57. DANEEL, "AIC Women",319.
58. OLUBANKE, "The History of the Good Women", 4-5.
59. DANEEL, "AIC Women as Bearers", 320.
60. Janet SEALEY, *"We have the Healing Power": Independent Churches and Women in Urban Kenya* (Cambridge: Anthropology, 1984), 2.
61. HACKETT, "Women as Leaders", 203-204.
62. HACKETT, "Women and New Religious Movements", 279.
63. D.B. BARRETT, *Schism and Renewal in Africa: An Analysis of Six Thousand Contemporary Religious Movements* (Nairobi: East African Publishing House, 1968), 150.
64. C. HOEHLER-FATTON, *Women of Spirit and Fire: History Faith and Gender in Roho Religion in Western Kenya* (New York: Oxford University Press, 1996), 183.
65. JULES-ROSETTE, "Cultural Ambivalence".
66. BREIDENBACH, "The Woman on the Beach", 107-113.
67. HACKETT, "Women and New Religious Movements", 269.
68. Deidre Helen CRUMBLEY, "Even a Woman: Sex Roles and Mobility in an Aladura Hierarchy", in *West African Journal of Archeology* (1985) 133-150.
69. OLUBANKE, "The History of Good Women", 5.
70. CRUMBLEY, "Even a Woman".
71. HACKETT, "Women and New Religious Movements", 27; See also J.Y.D. PEEL, *Aladura: A Religious Movement among the Yoruba* (London: Oxford University Press, 1968), 183.
72. J.A. OMOYAJOWO, "The Role of Women in Traditional African Religions and Independent Church Movements", in *Dialogue and Alliance*, 2, 3, (1988) 201.
73. Harold TURNER, *The Life and Faith of the Church of the Lord (Aladura)* (London: Oxford University Press, 1967), 169.
74. OLUBANKE, "The History of the Good Women", 4.
75. ASAMOAH-GYADU, "Fireballs in our Midst", 27.

76. R.I.J. HACKETT, "Charismatic/Pentecostal Appropriation of Media Technologies in Nigeria and Ghana", in *Journal of Religion in Africa*, XXVIII, 3 (1998) 259-277, 261.
77. Mathew OJO, "Marriage and Piety among Charismatic in Nigeria", in James COX, *Rites of Passage in Contemporary Africa* (Cardiff: Cardiff Academic Press, 1998), 180-197; 199.
78. KALU; *Power, Poverty and Prayer,* 189.
79. HACKETT, "Women as Leaders", 201.

Chapter Seventeen

A New Way of Facilitating Leadership: Lessons from African Women Theologians

Nyambura J. Njoroge

INTRODUCTION

This chapter is about the historical events and the strong and collaborative leadership of Mercy Amba Oduyoye of Ghana that led to the launch and creation of the Circle of Concerned African Women Theologians in 1989. The Circle, as it is commonly referred to in Africa, is an interfaith association that aims at producing theological literature by encouraging and mentoring women to research, write and publish in the wide scope of religion and culture. Some key areas of concern are highlighted: theological education for women; gender and theology; biblical and cultural hermeneutics; imperialism and globalization; gender-based violence; theology of lamentation; and theology on HIV and AIDS pandemic. Indeed, this is a very timely topic if not already overdue given the many death-dealing challenges confronting us in the world today and in particular in Africa.

My intention in this chapter is to uplift the example of how African women theologians have collaborated in discovering our theological voices and creating a powerful theological platform from which to operate and to reclaim our true identity as people created in the image and sound of God.[2] In 1989, we named this theological platform the Circle of Concerned African Women Theologians,[3] hereafter the Circle, even though not all African women theologians use this space to research, write, and publish theological literature and mentor one another according to our mission statement. The Circle is organized according to three European languages, English, French and Portuguese, which obviously tells of our colonial past and reality. The Circle has mainly flourished in Africa south of Sahara or tropical Africa and most of the writings are from Anglophone countries.

Certainly, a number of us have written about the Circle and doctoral theses are increasing by the number. In this chapter, however, I will try and trace the nature of leadership that has emerged over the years and the collaborative pattern among the women as well as a few men. I will also highlight key areas that were otherwise overlooked and silenced by western scholars and African male theologians as we seek to create authentic and life-giving Christianity, church and theologies in Africa. From the outset let me declare that I will take the liberty to cite some of the writings at length to do justice to the ideas expressed by individuals or even communally. I am writing as one who has been involved in the making of the Circle long before it was launched and because of my current job I am also involved in the empowerment of women in theological education and ministry.

I. A LEADER AND A LEGACY WORTH EMULATING

As I have demonstrated elsewhere, the World Council of Churches (WCC) and the ecumenical movement in general have played a significant role in providing opportunities and resources for African Christian women to discover one another and to grow in many diverse ways.[4] For our purposes and as an example, I would like to highlight the Consultation of Women Theological Students, July 24-30, 1978, hosted by the women's department in the WCC[5] as one occasion that laid the ground work for the creation of the Circle. This consultation is also significant for my own theological and ecumenical journey because I happened to be among the eight African women present out of 53 women who gathered at Cartigny, Switzerland.[6] Among the other African participants was Mercy Amba Oduyoye, a Ghanaian university lecturer teaching at the University of Ibadan in the religious department, Ibadan, Nigeria, and the most seasoned among us. Like in many consultations, we had the opportunity to meet according to our continents to deliberate on issues of common concern and report to the plenary with resolutions and plans of action. This is part of what African women participants said:[7]

> 'Is our theological education culturally relevant?' Many of the women in the group felt that the emphasis in their education was on the academic rather than the practical. And that the practical skills they will need to minister to the people in their communities are neglected in their education. *Affirming that the true Christian is involved in the world, the women felt that theological education relevant to their culture would enable them to work within the community from a basis of sound biblical and theological principles: not that they neglect academic and biblical part of their training but that they be shown how to use it in their daily lives and work.*
>
> Recognizing the tension that often exists between the church and the culture, the women agreed that this tension should not be ignored but explored throughout their theological education. An honest understanding of the tensions in which they must live will provide them with a theological basis for criticism and creativity within the culture ... *Looking specifically at theological education for women, the group felt that many theological institutions are still unresponsive to*

> *the needs of women. Realizing that male students, as well as female, need a broader understanding if they are to minister to both women and men, we should work for a larger number of women on theological faculties as well as attempting to influence how male professors think and teach.* Finally, we must encourage other women to study theology and seriously consider ordained ministry as a vocation.

Having identified what was most important and challenging, African participants made the following resolution:[8]

> Pleased to discover one another, they determined that, once back in Africa they would look for the other women in Africa studying theology and bring as many as possible together in a consultation of African Women in Theology. The African Consultation would be a way to share the experience of Cartigny, to find out just what women theologians are doing in Africa, to question the meaning of ministry and women's part in it, to look critically at theological education in Africa, to encourage women to become more active in the emerging theologies and to discover how the church can be more responsive to the issues and needs of women.

Mercy Amba Oduyoye owned this collective resolution and left Cartigny determined to fulfill it whether others present joined her or not. She started collecting new names of any women enrolled as students and/or teachers in theological institutions and religious departments of secular and Christian universities. Clothed with passion for justice and great courage, Oduyoye did not allow any difficulties on the way to deter her from her commitment and motivation from Cartigny. She made good use of any space she found to recruit new women and in particular through the Ecumenical Association of Third World Theologians (EATWOT) and the WCC Community of Women and Men Study (1978-1981). In 1980, Oduyoye helped to organize the first conference of African Women Theologians in Ibadan, Nigeria, with Daisy Obi, then director of Institute of Church and Society of the Christian Council of Nigeria, and Isabel Johnson, then secretary of women's department of All Africa Conference of Churches (AACC).[9] She spent the rest of the 1980s reaching out, recruiting and sharing her vision and commitment. In 1987, she moved to Geneva, Switzerland, to become the deputy general secretary of the World Council of Churches. The following year she convened the first planning committee for the official inauguration of the Circle which took place in Accra, Ghana, September 1989 with 69 women present.

In addition to reaching out, recruiting and mentoring other women to share in her dream and vision, Oduyoye brought with her great open-mindedness and deep Christian commitment that is tolerant of other religions. She writes, "The women of the Circle are practitioners of African Traditional Religion, Christianity, Islam and Judaism may be others too. We do not ask for religious affiliations in the Circle, only that one should consciously live by a belief in God."[10] In other words, the Circle is both an ecumenical and multi-faith movement, even though the membership is largely Christian. Hardly does one get to know Oduyoye's denominational affiliation, because what matters to her is that one is interested in reflecting, exploring and analyzing the impact of our faith, religion and culture in the life of African women in their religious communities and society to create sound theological literature. Tirelessly, she provided empowering leadership and helped to nurture collaborative model of working together that is captured by Musimbi Kanyoro.[11]

It was agreed that the Circle should not become an organization with a structure and headquarters. While it was obvious that the Circle would need some funds for its work, it was resolved that it must be driven by commitment of African women to write and publish and not by external factors such as money. The Circle was to be a space for women to mentor each other by doing communal theology. Thus the Circle was to remain an open-ended forum, always hospitable to new people. Hierarchical structures of leadership, such as with a president or a chairperson, or general secretary, were not seen as essential. It was envisaged that members would take up any task that needed to be done and apply themselves to it. The Circle members were free to write and publish in forums other than the Circle. The important fact was for African women to nurture and support one another as writers. The Circle women would engage in debate and dialogue with all other theologians, women and men, in Africa and beyond.[12]

Despite being multi-faith the Circle has a strong and sound biblical and theological basis that is embodied in the choice of the gospel story of Jairus' girl-child presumed dead who was called to get up or arise—*Talitha cum*!—by Jesus. It is also important for women in the Circle that this story is intertwined with the story of the bleeding woman who touched Jesus for healing.[13] This pioneering small group of women who planned the launching of the Circle, felt called to arise and to seek for healing from deep wounds of being submerged, silenced, overlooked and devalued. The titles of the published proceedings of the launching of the Circle *Talitha Qumi* and the first publication *The Will to Arise* and another book *Talitha Cum! Theologies of African Women* attest to Circle's biblical commitment and to ensure that posterity will not miss its *raison d'etre*. For the launching of the Circle, Teresa Okure, Nigerian religious sister and New Testament theological educator and scholar, wrote the bible study on these two women and connected them to the African women theologians.[14]

The daughter of Jairus and the woman with the flow of blood: two women who met Jesus at critical points in their lives, when all hope of cure and restoration was gone, one at the age of twelve, the other after twelve years of illness, one through the intervention of the father, the other by the sheer will to live. Women who were as good as dead, physically and socially, but who were personally touched by Jesus and empowered thereby to arise and live; women who, by living, proclaimed God's marvels and God's reign. These two women have much to teach us. Let us lend supportive hands to one another and help one another to arise. For Africa will not arise unless its womenfolk, the mothers and bearers of life, arise. What an awesome thought! What a heavy responsibility on our part! May God give us the will to arise and the desire genuinely to help one another and the whole continent to arise.[15]

Heavy is the responsibility in that even when Oduyoye retired from the World Council of Churches and after passing the coordination of the Circle to Musimbi Kanyoro during the second Pan-African Conference of the Circle in 1996, she decided to deepen the vision of "the will to arise" by building *Talitha Cumi* Centre, the home for the Institute of African Women in Religion and Culture, at Trinity Theological Seminary, Accra, Ghana. The Centre hosts seminars on gender and theology on a variety of issues for people in Ghana, and once every two years, it hosts an international seminar for Circle members and their partners. Through the leadership of this great daughter of Africa, who is always up and about spreading the mission and vision of the Circle, African women theologians have a solid legacy worthy emulating, if we care to listen and to be engaged. Oduyoye is regularly invited to lecture in theological institutions in this country (USA) and elsewhere and is still active in the ecumenical movement.

II. COLLABORATIVE MODEL: THE STRENGTH OF THE CIRCLE

Still strongly committed and living up to the concerns highlighted at the Cartigny consultation on the nature of theological education in Africa, Oduyoye and Kanyoro collaborated with John Pobee, a Ghanaian Anglican priest, theological educator and scholar responsible for global coordination of Ecumenical Theological Education (ETE) Program in WCC.[16] This collaboration increased the possibilities for more African women to receive scholarship grants to undertake masters and doctoral studies. These women were also encouraged to becoming theological educators and participate in the Circle and ecumenical conferences and activities. As luck would have it, the Circle was born during the Ecumenical Decade of Churches in Solidarity with Women (1988-1998), hereafter Ecumenical Decade, launched by WCC.

The Ecumenical Decade helped to create critical awareness for women's theological concerns in the churches and theological institutions. It also increased forums where African women theologians, pastors and leaders of churchwomen's organizations could develop their theological knowledge and voices. This again increased the level and depth of collaboration of the Circle members with a number of staff in WCC, LWF, WARC and AACC, which gave the Circle international recognition even among funding agencies.[17] In addition to undertaking masters and doctoral (PhD) studies, some Circle members have benefited from the program on International Feminist Doctoral of Ministry (DMin) degree, which is a product of the Ecumenical Decade and ETE Program in WCC.[18] This degree is coordinated by Letty Russell and Shannon Clarkson (white American theological educators and scholars), who are assisted by a team of women theologians from different parts of the world, including Circle members. The degree has been awarded by San Francisco Theological Seminary, California, USA, since 1995.[19]

One more illustration of global and ecumenical collaboration in God's mission will suffice. By the end of the twentieth century, it had become clear that the global HIV &AIDS pandemic had affected more Africans than in any other continent and that women and children are more vulnerable. In 2001, a small group of women theological educators at Yale Divinity School, New Haven, Connecticut, USA, extended an invitation to Circle members to attend a conference on "Gender, Faith and Responses to HIV & AIDS in Africa", held during February, 2002.[20] This collaboration led to the invitation of four women from Yale to the third Pan-African Circle Conference held in Addis Ababa, Ethiopia, in August 2002.[21] The Conference theme was "Sex, Stigma and HIV/AIDS: African Women Challenging Religion, Culture and Social Practices".[22]

I will return to this theme, however, for now it is important to note that this collaborative model with women theological educators at Yale Divinity School further opened another door for Circle women. In January 2003, the Center for Interdisciplinary Studies at Yale (CIRA) in collaboration with Yale Divinity School (YDS) and the Yale School of Epidemiology and Public Health (EPH), and with support from the Fogarty International Center, began a program to provide research fellowship training grants to African women, members of the Circle. In the spring of 2003 (January-April), three women attended the first training program, and in 2004 the training was extended to eight months, with two women attending. In addition to the training, the women who benefit from this program are supposed to design a research project for their community to put into practice what they have learned.[23]

More examples of collaboration with African men will be cited as we discuss other issues. Thus far, I can say with confidence that even though still in its infancy, the success of the Circle has been born and nurtured by a small group of wise, determined and courageous women. These women believe in reaching out, recruiting, mentoring and opening doors for others to come in and share their dreams, vision, skills and potentials in the creation of theological literature that takes seriously women's experiences, perspectives and God-given gifts. These doors have been opened to women and men beyond Africa. No doubt, we can claim that reaching out, recruiting, mentoring and opening doors for others are the hallmarks of the collaborative model of facilitating empowering, effective and responsible leadership. On the other hand, effective, empowering and responsible leadership demonstrates deep passion for justice, yearning for healing and quest for true identity and power with the divine as we participate fully in God's mission. Aware of our vulnerability and powerlessness, we chose to focus on "Transforming Power: Women in the household of God", during the second Pan African Conference of the Circle held in Nairobi, Kenya, in 1996.

III. NAMING THE MISSING LINK IN GOD'S MISSION

By retelling the story why and how the Circle came into being, I have alluded to what a few African Christian women named as the missing link in God's mission: lack of affirmation of women's full humanity and denial of women's full participation in God's mission in the church and society as our voices and contributions are overlooked, silenced, devalued and not recognized as fully authentic and credible. In other words, African women have named the "evil" and "injustices" that hinder half of humanity's full participation in God's mission in the church and in society. It is no secret that even in the USA, theologizing and theological education and leadership in the church and participation in decision-making organs of ecclesial institutions has been the preserve of men over the centuries. Even today there are people who cannot comprehend that women are equally endowed with theological mind and leadership qualities, especially if they happen to be black women.

Furthermore, it is not that women do not theologize and articulate their faith and struggle to comprehend the divine in their lives, but it is that our voices are not heard, heeded to or taken seriously. Even when women are present, sometimes men act as if women are invisible. Being heard, seen, valued and acknowledged as full human beings created in the divine image and sound cannot be disputed as key to the success of African women's theologies. Unfortunately, the Bible has been misinterpreted and misused to deny women (and people of African descent) our God-given identity and the power with the divine (our likeness with the divine) despite the biblical affirmation that human beings, female and male, are created equal in God's image. In theology, Mercy Amba Oduyoye brilliantly named this missing link by reminding us that "a bird does not fly with one wing" at her inaugural speech at the launching of the Circle.

In a recent article, "Gender and Theology in Africa today", hosted in the Circle website, Oduyoye has perceptively elaborated the crux of the matter.

Gender in current parlance signifies the power relation between masculine and feminine. The gender ideology presupposes that the masculine encompasses the female, or takes priority in relation to the female and is entitled to expect subordination and submissiveness and self-abasement of the female. The gender ideology is not limited to biology. It is also social and appears in relations among men as among women and among nations. It functions, as a pecking order where colonies were females in relation to the colonizing nations. Men slaves are females in relation to women in the master's household. White women are gendered males in relation to black women, a realization that was among the reasons for a specific women's theology in the USA named womanist by black women of the USA. Though gender refers to hierarchy associated with roles based on biological sex, it transcends it. In this chapter however it is gender as male superiority, patriarchy, androcentrism and kyriocentrism. This offering is about the hegemony of men and androcentrism in African theology. Gender relates to the patriarchal phenomenon that structures relationships in hierarchies and pyramids. When women's voices were heard on how women experienced life, words like sexism, sexist, patriarchy, androcentric, misogyny, feminist, feminism, androcracy on the tongues of women begun to jar men's ears and to make "the good women nervous". As women began to narrate and to substantiate how language, tradition, culture, religion, legal codes, household arrangements stifle their humanity, the word began to go round "women are their own worst enemies."[24]

In this article Oduyoye gives us a glimpse of the issues and concerns that have preoccupied the Circle members as we struggle to create a "two-winged theology" in Africa. This article is worth reading in its totality because Oduyoye illustrates power dynamics between women and among men and "among nations". I single out "among nations" because as people who have been subjected to slave trade and colonization by foreign powers, critical analysis of racism, apartheid and imperialism are critical in our writings. Oduyoye has powerfully demonstrated by telling the story of how a British woman imposed herself on the Circle during the second Pan-African Conference held in Nairobi, Kenya, in 1996. She also helps the reader to see some of the old-age gender stereotypes in theology, religion and culture and how they impact on African women's lives and relationships. It also profiles some of the key Circle publications that demonstrate our commitment to collaborative model of doing theology in what has been called "communal theology". Church theology, leadership and our understanding of God's mission in Africa has been largely articulated by foreigners and African men and the Circle wants to bring this long legacy to an end. This may explain the fact that the most recent activity by the Circle is the project on "Engendering Theological Education in Africa" in which we seek to transform the theological curriculum in Africa by mainstreaming gender.[25] Oduyoye writes, "Recognizing and becoming sensitive to gender in theology leads to a theology that is liberative, one that does not remain theoretical but demands ethical choices that will empower the transformation of relationships that have been damaged by sexism and misogynist attitudes."[26]

IV. KEY ISSUES OF CONCERN IN THEOLOGY IN AFRICA: BIBLICAL AND CULTURAL HERMENEUTICS

In this section I will attempt to give a summary of the key issues that have been left out in doing theology and God's mission in Africa from women's experiences and perspectives bearing in mind that the list is far from being complete.

From the beginning the Circle acknowledged that religion and culture are the basis of our theologizing, and as Christian women, the Bible has a central place in this discourse. Hence contextual bible studies have been critical in our writings, and as already mentioned, the stories of Jairus's daughter and the bleeding woman have motivated and challenged us to rise to the occasion. In this area of biblical hermeneutics we have particularly benefited from the work of Teresa Okure, Musa Dube, Madipoane Masenya, Hebrew Bible scholar from South Africa, and Musimbi Kanyoro, a biblical theologian from Kenya. Each of these women have contributed in "communal theology" as well as individually published books. Together with a few others, they have demonstrated "other ways of reading the Bible", which is actually the title of one of the Circle books.

However, in addition to biblical hermeneutics, the Circle has identified cultural hermeneutics as a necessary step for in-depth understanding of the Bible as Kanyoro has rightly argued:[27]

> All questions regarding the welfare and status of women in Africa are explained within the framework of culture. Women cannot inherit land or own property because it is not culturally 'right'. Women may not participate in the leadership because it is culturally the domain of men ... However, it is not enough simply to analyze culture without reference to the people who maintain the culture and on whom the culture impacts. Here is where the need arises for a gender-sensitive cultural hermeneutics because it doubles in addressing issues of culture while being critical of that culture from a gender perspective. As a project done within the framework of theological education, this work must also show how the church is a part and parcel of the subject of analysis. It is in the church that the dilemma of how Africans should live as Christians and cultural people thrives. Since the Bible forms the base and informs the African Christian on what they can validate or not validate in their culture, I will start from the framework of reading the Bible with cultural eyes. I present in this study (on book of Ruth) some of the clues to understanding cultural hermeneutics. I suggest that a cultural hermeneutics is a first step towards a biblical hermeneutics. I argue that the culture of the reader in Africa has more influence on the way the biblical text is understood and used in communities that the historical culture of the text ... Cultural hermeneutics is a necessary tool for those teaching homiletics and pastoral work in seminaries and other clergy institutions, and it is prerequisite to African women's liberation theology. I have discovered this by reading the Bible with communities of African rural women.

Like Kanyoro, Oduyoye has also creatively expounded women's experiences and perspectives on culture in *Daughters of Anowa: African Women & Patriarchy*, which articulates the West African context including matriarchal societies.

1. Imperialism and Globalization

We are also writing in a highly globalized and changing world, which demonstrates Africa's interdependence with the rest of the world and its impact on our lives as women and as Africans. Musa Dube has focused on this area of globalization in her creative ways of retelling and contextualizing the gospel and by articulating the postcolonial theories. In her writings, Dube always attempts to put Africa within the context of imperialism and globalization processes. Her thought provoking *Postcolonial Feminist Interpretation of the Bible* is particularly critical for missiologists and biblical scholars. However, for a quick glance at Dube's analysis of globalization, especially in a context where others argue that globalization has redeemed Africans from the African village to the joys of global village, I highly recommend her article, "Talitha Cum! Calling the Girl-Child and Women to Life in the HIV/AIDS and Globalization".[28] Decolonizing our mind, theology, church and literature is key to our success in creating life-giving theologies and Christianity in Africa.

With this comes the urgent need for the Circle to contend with the social injustices and death-dealing challenges that have condemned millions of Africans to a life of extreme poverty and culture of silence, violence and senseless death, including social and ecclesiastical death. Reflecting on the Lord's Prayer in her social location in the context of globalization, Dube asserts:[29]

> As a black African woman of Botswana—who is a survivor of colonialism and the subsequent neo-colonialism of globalization—I live in the deep shadow of death. To live with the intensification of poverty in African countries, to live with wars and coups, to live with corruption and exploitation, to watch helplessly as beloved friends, neighbors, and relatives slowly shrivel as HIV/AIDS gnaws at them, is to live where death and life have become identical twins ... This context of death-dealing challenges me to reflect on what it means to profess Christian faith and to pray the Lord's Prayer in the global economic era. I am confronted with a crisis that necessitates a re-examination of the Lord's Prayer. What, in other words, is God's vision for God's creation? What are the roles of Christian men and women, individually and corporately, in bringing God's kingdom on earth? Is there any vision that is pledged to God and to each other when Christians recite the Lord's Prayer? If so, is this a vision we can implement? And, how? These questions shall be the subject of my reading of the Lord's Prayer, through a close reading of the prayer.

2. Social Injustices and Gender-Based Violence

By taking our social location seriously since "African woman" is not a monolithic entity, the Circle has attempted to unpack the plight of African women in different contexts and their contributions in the church and society. In this regard we have attempted to demonstrate churchwomen (including women from African Instituted Churches) as moral agents and their capacity to resist social injustices and gender-biased harmful rituals and to become agents of transformation and bearers of hope. Many of the articles in our "communal theology" have focused on this area but also some individually written books have emerged by Isabel Phiri, Malawi, Christina Landman, South Africa, Helene Yinda, French-speaking Cameroon, Bernadette Mbuy-Beya, Democratic Republic of Congo and Nyambura Njoroge, Kenya.

From the beginning gender-based violence and injustices as sources of misery, suffering and death have taken centre stage. Silence surrounding the area of human sexuality and violence against children and women has been a major concern from the beginning. Breaking the conspiracy of silence and stopping gender-based violence have become even more urgent in the global HIV & AIDS pandemic era which has claimed millions of people in Africa alone and millions of children have been orphaned. This explains why the third Pan-African Conference of the Circle held in Addis Ababa, Ethiopia, August 2002, focused on global HIV & AIDS pandemic. The first book from this Conference has been published; *African Women, HIV/AIDS and Faith Communities,* and three manuscripts are with the publishers.

It is significant to note that when the World Council of Churches (WCC) focused its attention on HIV & AIDS pandemic in Africa, since 1999, Musa Dube was instrumental in creating the HIV & AIDS theological curriculum for theological institutions in Africa as a theological consultant.[30] Through training of trainers workshops in theological institutions, Dube has trained more than 400 theological educators and 100 church leaders on how to use the curriculum and to create liturgies that speak to our context of death-dealing challenges. As I write, Dube is busy training more theological educators and church leaders. In addition to resource material produced through WCC, Dube was instrumental in soliciting articles on HIV & AIDS pandemic in Africa for *Missionalia* (August 2001), a refereed journal in southern Africa. Other members of the Circle, like Musimbi Kanyoro and Helene Yinda, have been very involved in the battle against HIV & AIDS pandemic in their respective responsibilities at the World Young Women Christian Association (YWCA).

In this regard, creative works of collaboration with male theologians has begun to take shape. On gender-based violence Tinyiko S. Maluleke, South African theologian and one of the few African men who cite Circle writings, worked with Sarojini Nadar, South Africa Hebrew Bible scholar, to solicit and edit papers on "Overcoming Violence against Women and Children" for the refereed *Journal of Theology for Southern Africa,* November 2002. He also worked with Musa Dube to solicit and edit articles on HIV/AIDS for *Missionalia* (August 2001) mentioned earlier. However the most creative and constructive collaborative work that is gaining global recognition is the contribution of the Institute of the Study of the Bible at the University of KwaZulu Natal, School of Theology, South Africa, which is the current host of the Circle. Through the leadership of Gerald West, professor of Biblical Studies, the Institute of the Study of the Bible and Worker Ministry Project mostly working with women but not exclusively members of the Circle, is focusing on contextual Bible Studies. For instance, the Project has Solidarity Program which journeys with people living with HIV/AIDS from diagnosis until death, but with a predominant emphasis on living positively and with dignity.[31] Another Program focuses on Women and Gender with a bias on stopping violence against children and women, which has given birth to Tamar Campaign. This methodology of doing contextual bible studies with women (some who are living with HIV & AIDS) produces biblical and theological resources that restore dignity, healing and wholeness to people. Since 1996, West has worked with women on the Tamar rape story. Recently, I asked West to write an article for *Ministerial Formation,* July 2004,[32] on how Tamar Campaign came into being and in summary West and Phumzile Zondi-Mabizela write:[33]

> This campaign has changed many people's lives; Tamar's protest has given many women a voice. Young women have been infuriated by

> the actions of the many men in the story who are accomplices in the rape of Tamar. This has encouraged them to promote a different culture of respect and protecting their loved ones. Church leaders have used this text as a tool to encourage a spirit of openness with churches. These issues were for a long time seen as taboo and had no place within the church. Just like during the apartheid years, it took a long time for the church to exercise its prophetic authority. The increase in the number of children and women who are raped has forced the church to recover its prophetic voice and Tamar's story has provided important resources and has built a capacity for doing this. Aluta continua, the struggle does indeed continue, but we can win the battle against gender violence and the spread of HIV and AIDS, if we work together.

Because of the impact this Campaign has had on many people's lives, West has accepted to work with WCC-ETE program so that we can introduce the Campaign to other theological institutions in Africa (and even beyond) through workshops and seminars for women and theological educators. West has also collaborated with Musa Dube in soliciting and editing *Bible in Africa,* a volume that has attempted to document the nature and profile of biblical scholarship that has emerged in Africa over the years. Slowly, African male theologians are beginning to appreciate the work of the Circle, but we have a long way to go to be heard and taken seriously.

No doubt speaking out on issues of human sexuality, HIV & AIDS status, gender-biased rituals and gender-based violence, and especially rape and incest require a lot of courage, spiritual stamina, creative and constructive solidarity. Circle women and others have written on such topics as widowhood, wife inheritance, childlessness, single parenting, female genital mutilation; but so far, great courage has been epitomized by Thandeki Umlilo, a religious sister from South Africa who in *Little Girl, Arise!* relates her experience of incest and sexual abuse by her father, brothers, uncle and other men from her fourth age. At the age of 50, Umlilo writes:[34]

> For too many years have I lived in the valley of dead bones. Incest and abuse violated the essence of me and held me bound in deadly shame, guilt and self-rejection—a human being that housed a withdrawn, timid and vulnerable child. Today, however, I experience myself as alive, able to take risks, eager to LIVE life to the fullest, knowing the joy of freedom, deeply appreciating the woman that I am, the person whose very Source is the Giver of all life.
>
> This transformation is the hope I hold out to all people who have been abused or victimized in any way. My story in its very frankness is to tell all victims of abuse that we are not sure our experience. Within us is the power to transcend any trauma and to rise victoriously in the glory and splendor of New Life. The second purpose is to make as many people as possible, especially the perpetrators, aware of the devastating effect of abuse. My hope is that this aware-

> ness raising will enable perpetrators to treat themselves and all persons with respect and dignity that is rightfully theirs.

Even though not a member of the Circle, as far as I know, Umlilo chose *Talitha Cum!* to tell her story that speaks for many African women who have suffered incest, sexual abuse and rape, but who unlike her are not so fortunate as to go through the process of counseling, spiritual guidance and healing. Among friends, African women continuously share personal encounters with gender-based violence, including incest and rape, if not their own, those of their daughters, sisters, nieces, cousins, aunts, mothers and friends. Some of these women suffer social death because of deep psychological trauma while others commit suicide. Social death has become such a reality among people living with HIV & AIDS because of stigma, discrimination and silence surrounding the pandemic. The survivors of rape and incest are also deeply traumatized and usually suffer from shame and guilt throughout their lives.

Unfortunately, sufferers and survivors of rape have increased (including girl-children) because of the many war-torn and conflict-infested countries in Africa—where rape is used as a weapon of war (as it has been elsewhere)—and the lack of privacy in refugee camps. African women are also subjected to sex slavery among warring rebel groups and soldiers as well as the trafficking of sex workers outside the continent. In a recent research through the sponsorship of United Nations Development Fund for Women (UNIFEM), Elisabeth Rehn and Ellen Johnson Sirleaf report:[35]

> Violence against women in conflict is one of history's great silences. We were completely unprepared for the searing magnitude of what we saw and heard in the conflict and post-conflict areas we visited. We knew the data. We knew that 94 percent of displaced households surveyed in Sierra Leone have experienced sexual assaults, including rape, torture and sexual slavery. That at least 250,000—perhaps as many as 500,000—women were raped during the 1994 genocide in Rwanda. We read reports of sexual violence in the ongoing hostilities in Algeria, Myanmar, southern Sudan and Uganda. We learned of the dramatic increase in domestic violence in war zones, and the growing numbers on women trafficked out of war zones to become forced labors and forced workers. But knowing all this did not prepare us for the horrors women described. Wombs punctured with guns. Women raped and tortured in front of their husbands and children. Rifles forced into vaginas. Pregnant women beaten to induce miscarriages. Fetuses ripped from wombs ... We heard accounts of gang rapes, rape camps and mutilation. Of murder and sexual slavery. We saw scars of brutality so extreme that survival seemed for some a worse fate than death.

Much is at stake in the battle against gender-based violence in Africa. Rape, incest and sex slavery and trafficking have contributed to the rapid rate of HIV infection among women and girl-children. Nevertheless, it is no secret that unhealed wounds of incest, rape and sexual abuse affect the sexual lives of the survivors and some of it has been the cause of dysfunctional marriage relationships. Certainly, this is an area that demands in-depth research and creative pastoral theology, care and counseling that addresses their pain and suffering. This is why Tamar Campaign has become very important for many women in southern Africa and the reason some Circle members would like to see it spending in other countries.

3. Theology of Lamentation

Not surprisingly our death-dealing context and senseless suffering has forced some of us in the Circle to turn to theology of lamentation, as has been the case in most of my writings. It is not enough to argue like John Mbiti, a pioneering African theologian from Kenya, that "one would hope that theology arises out of spontaneous joy in being a Christian, responding to life and ideas as one redeemed."[36] I can attest to the fact that when I am deeply depressed, disillusioned and angry and lack words because of the deafening silence of the church on social injustices and evil, such as the ones named above, the only language I understand is lamentation and that is when I have written most of my articles. Similar views about lamentation have been expressed by another Circle member, Denise Ackermann, a South African theologian, who writes:[37]

> Stigma is nourished by silence. Internalized trauma, fear or rejection, cultural restraints and wrong understandings of sin and punishment, all rob people of the ability to speak out and to name their reality. I suggest that our scriptures have given us a language that can deal with suffering. In the ancient language of lament we have a way of naming the unnamable and of crying out to God in situations that are unbearable. What is lament? It is a form of mourning but it is more purposeful. It signals that relationships have gone terribly wrong and it reminds God that God must act as partner in the covenant. It is both individual and communal. It is a primal cry that comes out of the human soul and beats against the heart of God. It calls God to account for our human suffering. Lament is risky and dangerous speech; it is restless; it pushes the boundaries of our relationships, particularly with God; it refuses to settle for things the way they are.

I contend that African Christians need to recognize and acknowledge the deep valleys of death that Tamar (raped daughter of king David), Musa Dube, Thandeki Umlilo and many others have so eloquently named, have been a missing link in African theology and mission. We must hold ourselves accountable, our churches, governments, religious and political leaders and even God by using every possible language including art to name our suffering and culture of violence and death as we seek for ways of addressing the misery, loss and grief they brings in our lives.

4. Empowering Women in Theological Education

We have come a full cycle from the Cartigny consultation, where a few of us made the commitment to look for one another and to address issues of women, theological education and ministry. We in the Circle must hammer the fact that we cannot be effective, empowering and responsible leaders without the right skills, tools and resources. In addition to writing theological literature, still a lot of work needs to be done in uplifting and empowering our sisters through theological education, especially in the Lusophone (Portuguese speaking) countries where we hardly have women with advanced theological training and who find it difficult to contribute theological literature. Equally important, we need to increase the number of women as theological educators and administrators in theological institutions, as well as in leadership positions in the churches.

Lack of scholarship grants remain the largest hindrance in empowering women through theological education. On the other hand, theological institutions must be willing to change to meet the practical needs of women, their experiences and perspectives that shape their theologies, teaching and research methodologies and ways of doing ministry. These concerns will continue to be part of our struggle in our writings because we cannot bring change unless we are empowered and endowed with the right skills, tools and resources. However, our greatest hope and encouragement is to see the slowly but steadily growing body of theological literature being listed in required readings in theological institutions and the new project on mainstreaming gender in theology. And on this note, I would like to recall the words of our pioneering leader Mercy Amba Oduyoye:[38]

> The power of definition of what is theology has to be exercised by community of women and men in theology. The academic world remains uncertain as to assess the alternative epistemologies and methodologies that women claim mainstreaming gender in theology demands. But like it or not the concern for gender has opened up a new academic field, and this has to be acknowledged and appropriated to make the academy responsible and responsive to the world out there. The presumed right of church and bishops to determine what is to be believed, stands in the ways of mainstreaming gender in theology as long as leadership in the ecclesia remains male.

CONCLUSION: CALLED TO BE BEARERS OF HOPE AND LIFE

A chapter like this one cannot do justice to the creative and collaborative work of the Circle in facilitating new leadership in Africa in the area of producing theological literature. My task was to try and provide a glimpse of what the labor of love in Christ Jesus can achieve in a continent where sometimes we feel as if "the angels have left us", the title of a book by Hugh McCullum after the 1994 Rwanda genocide. Or from a continent others have called "the dark continent" as in the days of missionary enterprise and colonialism and more recently "the forgotten continent" in the globalization era. In our small and delicate ways, the Circle, still in its infancy, has demonstrated great potential of recruiting, mentoring and nurturing a generation of bearers of hope and life against many odds. Our courage to speak out, to tell the truth and write about our joys and sorrows in the family, church (and other religious communities) and society have become a threat to some who would rather we remain silenced and submerged or "in our place".

But we have chosen to touch the cloak of Jesus and to hear his voice calling us to arise! We have chosen to participate fully in God's mission and to name the missing links in African theology, mission and life, for we too like the men, the Lord says, "See, I have inscribed you on the palms of my hands; your walls are continually before me."[39] This is the true identity and power with the divine that we yearn for as we seek to be moral agents and bearers of hope, empowerment, liberation, justice, peace, healing and fullness of life. The Circle women are determined to learn from others and to make a difference in our death-dealing context. May God bless our yearning for freedom and fullness of life promised by Christ Jesus.

Notes

1. This chapter was presented as a paper at the American Society of Missiology 2004, and offers a collaborative model of facilitating leadership in God's mission in Africa today.
2. For more insight on being created in the sound of God see Mary Donovan TURNER & Mary Lin HUDSON, *Saved from Silence: Finding Women's Voice in Preaching* (St. Louis, MO: Chalice Press, 1999), 19-33.
3. http://www.thecirclecawt.org.
4. See, Nyambura J. NJOROGE, "Reclaiming our Heritage of Power: Discovering our Theological Voices", in Isabel Apawo PHIRI, Betty GOVINDEN & Sarojini NADAR (eds), *Her-stories: Hidden Histories of Women of Faith in Africa* (Pietermaritzburg: Cluster Publications, 2002), 39-57.
5. Jean SCOTT & Bertrice Y. WOOD (eds), *"We listened long, before we spoke"* (A Report of the Consultation of Women Theological Students, Cartigny, Switzerland, July 1978), Geneva: WCC Publications, 1979.
6. This was the first consultation I attended outside my church and country. Whenever I look back at my theological and ecumenical journey, I recognize how significant these days were, which has taught me to value any gathering that brings people together, ASM 2004 included.
7. SCOTT & WOOD, *"We listened long"*, 36—italics my emphasis.
8. SCOTT & WOOD, *"We listened long"*, 45.
9. See, Mercy Amba ODUYOYE, "The Search for a Two-winged Theology: Women's Participation in the Development of Theology in Africa—The Inaugural Address", in M.A. ODUYOYE & M.R.A. KANYORO, (eds), *Talitha Qumi! Proceedings of the Convocation of African Women Theologians 1989*, Ibadan: Daystar Press, 1990, 31-56. In her address, Oduyoye narrates the story of this conference and the *raison d'etre* for the Circle of Concerned African Women Theologians.
10. Mercy Amba ODUYOYE, "Gender and Theology in Africa Today", in http://www.thecirclecawt.org, 2003, 1.
11. Musimbi Kanyoro, a Kenyan biblical theologian, moved to Geneva, Switzerland, in January 1988 to work at the Women in Church and Society Desk of Lutheran World Federation (LWF). She worked at the Desk until 1998 when she became

General Secretary of the World Young Women Christian Association (World YWCA), the first African women to hold this position. She was the Circle coordinator from 1996-2002.

12. Phiri, Govinden & Nadar, *Her-stories*, 19.
13. Mark 5:21-43 & Luke 8:40-56.
14. Kanyoro facilitated the first bible study at the convocation of the Circle, on Jairus' daughter and the bleeding women. Later, Musa Dube from Botswana, another New Testament theological educator and scholar, wrote a number of articles on the same text. See Musa W. Dube (ed.), *Other Ways of Reading: African Women and the Bible* (Geneva: WCC Publications & Atlanta: SBL, 2001, 50-60); Nyambura J. Njoroge & Musa W. Dube (eds), *Talitha Cum! Theologies of African Women* (Pietermaritzburg: Cluster Publications, 2001), 3-24; Phiri, Govinden & Nadar, *Her-stories*, 71-93.
15. Mercy Amba Oduyoye & Musimbi R.A. Kanyoro (eds), *The Will to Arise: Women, and the Church in Africa* (Maryknoll: Orbis Books, 1992), 230.
16. In 1992 I moved to Geneva to work with the World Alliance of Reformed Churches (WARC) to establish the department of Women and Men in Partnership, and was welcomed by Oduyoye and Kanyoro to collaborate with them on Circle matters. In 1999 I moved to the World Council of Churches to replace John Pobee, and continued to create more opportunities for African women to further their theological studies.
17. In addition to the financial support from WCC & LWF, the Circle has been supported by EMW (*Evangelisches Missionwerk in Deutschland*—Association of Protestant Churches and Missions in Germany) and Protestant Churches in Netherlands.
18. Rev. Ofelia Ortega, a Presbyterian minister from Cuba, was the member of staff of ETE responsible for the Caribbean and Latin America region, who in 1993 suggested that ETE as a program should seek ways of being in solidarity with women in theological education during the Decade. John Pobee, the ETE global coordinator, supported this idea, and this is how this program was born. It involved women staff from WCC, LWF, WARC and Conference of European Churches (CEC), also with offices in the Ecumenical Centre of WCC.
19. This program is based on seminars over a period of 10 weeks, thereafter candidates spend time conducting research and writing their project theses under the supervision of a theologian (female or male). Two weeks in January are spent at the Ecumenical Institute Bossey, Celigny, Switzerland, another two weeks the following January are spent in any part of the world where a small group of women theologians are willing to host and teach together with Letty Russell and Shannon Clarkson, and a further six weeks are spent at San Francisco Seminary, where the candidates join other students following a doctor of ministry degree. The Circle members have hosted the seminars twice, in Nairobi, Kenya (1998) and in Accra, Ghana (2002), and a few of them have supervised theses. While the two coordinators assist in fundraising in the USA for women from the South, most of the funds are raised and administered by the ETE program in WCC, of which I am responsible.
20. The women at Yale who planned the conference are Letty Russell, Shannon Clarkson, Margaret Farley and Kristen Leslie.

21. These are Letty Russell, Shannon Clarkson, Margaret Farley and Yolanda Smith. In addition, Karen Bloomquist, director of theology studies at LWF, and Martha Fredricks, theological educator at Utrecht University, Netherlands, were also invited guests of the Circle.
22. As far as I know, this was the first time the Circle received financial support from outside church-related institutions. The Conference at Yale was supported by United States Agency for International Development (USAID), as well as a large portion of the budget in Addis Ababa.
23. In *The Circle Newsletter,* No 2-3, November 2003 & April 2004, the first three women who benefited from the training, Fulata Moyo, Malawi, Vuadi Vibila, DR Congo and Sylvia Kadenyi Amisi, Kenya tell about their experiences at Yale and their future plans.
24. ODUYOYE, "Gender and Theology, 2.
25. Since September 2003, a few Circle members have been discussing how to mainstream gender into theological curriculum in Africa. Each in their own discipline, ten women drafted an engendered theological curriculum and then held a workshop in Johannesburg, South Africa (16-21 May, 2004), to thoroughly scrutinize and revise the drafts. More workshops would then be held to test the curriculum and to introduce it to other Circle members and male colleagues. I happened to be part of this process, and my role has been to encourage the women to give the curriculum a strong ecumenical perspective from the beginning. This initiative by Esther Mombo (Kenya) and Musa Dube (Botswana) was yet another follow-up on a plan of action from the Conference on Theological Education and Ecumenical Formation with the theme "Journey of Hope in Africa" sponsored by WCC and held in Johannesburg, September 2002. I was responsible for organizing the Conference together with my colleagues who work on Education and Ecumenical Formation.
26. ODUYOYE, "Gender and Theology, 2.
27. Musimbi R.A. KANYORO, *Introducing Feminist Cultural Hermeneutics: An African Perspective* (Sheffield Academic Press, 2002), 18-19.
28. PHIRI, GOVINDEN & NADAR, *Her-stories*, 71-93.
29. Gerald O. WEST & Musa W. DUBE (eds), *The Bible in Africa: Transactions, Trajectories and Trends* (Leiden: Brill, 2000), 617.
30. CD-Rom exists on resource material for churches and communities by WCC Ecumenical HIV/AIDS Initiative in Africa (EHAIA).
31. Gerald O. WEST, "Reading the Bible in the Light of HIV/AIDS in South Africa" in *Ecumenical Review* (WCC Publications), 55, 4, October 2003, 335-344.
32. Published by WCC-ETE Program.
33. Gerald O. WEST & Phumzile ZONDI-MABIZELA, "The Bible Story that became a Campaign: the Tamar Campaign in South Africa (and beyond)" in *Ministerial Formation* (Geneva: WCC Publications), July 2004, 4-12, 12.
34. Thandeki UMLILO, *Little Girl, Arise! New Life after Incest and Abuse* (Pietermaritzburg: Cluster Publications, 2002), book cover.
35. UMLILO, *Little Girl, Arise*, book cover.
36. Quoted in Josiah U. YOUNG, *Black and African Theologies: Siblings or Distant Cousins?* (Maryknoll: Orbis Books, 1986), 92.

37. Denise ACKERMANN, "Implications of HIV and AIDS for the Theological Agenda" (Unpublished paper delivered at the UNAIDS Theologians' Workshop on Stigma and Discrimination, Namibia, December 2003), 4.
38. ODUYOYE, "Gender and Theology, 1.
39. Isaiah 49:16, NRSV.

Chapter Eighteen

Half a Century of African Christian Theologies: Elements of the Emerging Agenda for the Twenty-First Century

Tinyiko Sam Maluleke

The topic of this essay is an ambitious one; I cannot and do not mean to satisfy it. Proceeding topically rather than chronologically, I wish to highlight certain themes and sub-themes with which African theology has been occupied in the twentieth century. From these, I hope to sketch an outline of the emerging face of African Christian theologies in the next century.

I. DYNAMISM AND INNOVATION

From the early 1980s, calls for African theologies and African churches to either recognize the "paradigm shifts"[1]—which are occurring before their own eyes—or to effect some "paradigm shifts" themselves, have increased.[2]

More significantly, major works on African theology during the 1990s indicate that African Christian Theology will not be allowed to degenerate into an immutable museum ornament. It is a dynamic, growing, multifaceted and dialectic movement built diachronically and synchronically upon contextualization and constant introspection. Rightfully, the All Africa Conference of Churches (AACC) has taken a leading role in providing direction to the burgeoning suggestions for new forms of African theology and Christianity.[3]

One of my operating assumptions is that, in order for African theology to grow and effect meaningful paradigm shifts, a careful note of the ground already captured must be made. This may prevent an unbridled manufacturing of an infinite number of supposedly "new" and "projective" African theologies that are not thoroughly informed by what has been done before. Kwesi Dickson[4] makes the same point:

> ... the present stagnation may be accounted for by reference to the fact that recent discussants often seem to be unaware of past discussions on the subject. Again and again contributions made at confer-

> ences have not been such as to build upon the insights which have already been gained into the subject....

Construction, innovation and contextualization in African theology/Christianity should not be left entirely in the hands of each generation of African theologians as if African theology was a frivolous and merely cerebral activity that is unconnected either to African Christian life or previous African theologies.[5]

For nearly half a century, Africans have attempted to articulate their own brands of Christian theologies consciously and deliberately. Generally this production has been ecumenical in nature, consultative, and in written form. Before the 1950s, African Christian theologies (henceforth referred to only as African theologies) had existed largely in less deliberate, consultative, ecumenical, organized, and written forms. Without discounting or doubting the value of unwritten forms of African Christian expressions prior to the 1950s, we shall focus on those articulations of African theologies since the 1950s.[6] Most of these have either been expressed as self-conscious theologies, or at least been documented as ecclesiastical, ecumenical or theological events. Yet even this apparently well-delimited focus on consciously constructed and written forms of African theology has become a vast and dynamic field that defies easy classification and simplistic analysis.

II. "AFRICA", "AFRICA CHRISTIANITY" AND "AFRICAN THEOLOGY"

I assume that the phenomena of African Christianity and African theology are so closely related that the two terms may be used interchangeably. African theologies exist because of African Christianities, and without African theologies we would not have any sustainable African Christianities. African Christianities are therefore expressions of African theology.

However, while these terms have become common today, their meaning (or even the fact that they have meaning) has not always been taken for granted. Oduyoye speaks of those who still question whether there ever can be "such an animal as African Christianity".[7] During our own times, African philosophers such as Anthony Appiah and Mudimbe also appear to be questioning the usefulness of the concept "Africa" beyond a reductionist conceptual level. Appiah seems to argue that while Africa is a physical and geographical reality with some shared experiences (such as slavery and colonialism), it is still precarious to believe that expressions such as "African Christianity", "African philosophy", "African literature", or even simply "African", have intrinsic meaning. He also points out the irony of the fact that African intellectuals need the languages of their former colonial masters in order to construct "African literature", "African philosophy"—and, we may add, "African theology". However, as Oduyoye says, while African intellectuals debate whether "African Christianity" or "African theology" either exist or make sense at all, Africans everywhere are fashioning theologies and Christian forms with which they can identify.

It is important to be conscious of the vastness, divisions, affinities, and diversities of Africa. To that extent, there is some truth in the suggestion that "Africa" does not exist as such, but rather to the extent that people articulate a shape and form for the Africa they desire.[8] There are several other possible reasons why it took so long for the phrases "African Christianity" and "African theology" to be accepted as valid expressions. The most basic is simply the strong grip of the West's tutelage of African Christianities in the twentieth century. Neither westerners nor Africans risked a hasty qualification of the term "Christian" with "African". This was part of the reason why Africa was at one time full of "missions" as opposed to churches. The adjective "African" would only gradually and with care be placed alongside terms such as "church", "Christian", "Christian", or "theology".

"From 1854 onwards", we may confidently say, "West African Christian leaders, lay and clerical had felt and indeed initiated schemes to indigenize the Christian faith."[9] However, among many African theologians, the idea of African theology or an African Indigenous Theology[10] started rather tentatively.[11]

Less tentative was Bolaji Idowu's call for an indigenous African church with its own theology.[12] John Mbiti expresses concern over the use of the term "African theology" as a big banner under which could be placed "all sorts of articles and references ... the substance [of which] often turns out to be advice on how African theology should be done...."[13] For himself, however, Mbiti[14] confidently declares that "I will use the term 'African theology' ... without apology or embarrassment, to mean theological reflection and expression by African Christians."[15] According to Mbiti, the chief yardstick for determining the validity of any Christian theology purporting to be African is its "Biblical basis".[16] For him "nothing can substitute for the Bible". For this reason, Mbiti has tended to be suspicious (to say the least) of what he sees as "theological debates.... propagated without full or clear grounding". Such theologies would include "theologies of liberation", the moratorium debate of the 1970s, and South African Black theology—which he sees as "primarily [a] ready-made European theology turned into a consumption commodity for Africans."[17]

We can thus see that even after the term "African theology" and/or "African Christianity" had found general acceptance, the debate on the sources and criteria for truly African and truly Christian theology has continued to our times. Henry Okullu attempts to cut through the arduous process of debate about the criteria and sources of African theology:[18]

> .... when we are looking for African theology we should go first to the fields, to the village church, to the village church, to Christian homes to listen to those spontaneously uttered prayers before people go to bed. We should go to the schools, to the frontiers where traditional religions meet with Christianity. We must listen to the throbbing drumbeats and the clapping of hands accompanying the impromptu singing in the independent churches ... Everywhere in Africa things are happening. Christians are talking, singing, preach-

ing, writing, arguing, praying, discussing. Can it be that all this is an empty show? It is impossible. This then is African theology.

III. THE WIDE-RANGING AGENDA AND TASKS OF AFRICAN THEOLOGY: ENABLING THE CHURCH, ARTICULATING AFRICAN CHRISTIANITY

The more basic issue that caused differences in degrees of acceptance of the term "African theology" was and still is the use for which African theology is constructed. That African Christian theology ought to be at the service of the church in Africa is seldom in doubt. In other words, its chief task is that of enabling the church to develop her own theologies so that she may cease depending on "prefabricated theology, liturgies and traditions,"[19] to be "not an exotic but a plant become indigenous to the soil."[20] Thus from the earliest times, written African theology was inspired by the conviction that "the opportunity for evangelism has never been greater ... but it will take a church which is alive and vigorous"[21] to muse of such an opportunity. While this basic church-enabling task of African theology has never been seriously disputed, other voices within African theology, at least in recent times, have called for theologies that are more critical of both received traditions within the church and of the church itself—enabling the church to be both prophetic and self-critical. One of the early criticisms leveled against the then emerging African theology was that it threatened the catholicity of both the global church and Christian theology. The response of Kwesi Dickson[22] to this criticism is one of the most lucid offered by an African theologian in defense of African theology.[23] Yet, as indicated above, African theology has from the 1950s on always been connected to the (African) church. To that extent, we could say that it has largely been church theology done by church people for the sake of the church and its missionary task. It was by no accident, therefore, that issues of selfhood and the moratorium have loomed large in the African theological agenda. Incidentally, the questions of (in)dependence and ownership inherent in the moratorium debates do connect to issues of negritude, "African identity", and inculturation.

In connection with African theology's church-enabling task, we can and should inquire about the form and shape of the African church or African Christianities which African theology was meant to enable and bring about. Was it (and is it) the whole Christian church in Africa? What visions of the church should and do inspire African theology? The church is not the sole and primary subject of God's mission. It is itself a product of God's mission and that mission encompasses more than the churches we see and dream about. African theology may therefore need to explore ways in which to speak not only to, about, and for the church, but for the larger African society. After all, the church, in some parts of Africa at least, has grown to be one of the important players in society—sometimes too important a player. The Christian theology of Africa does, therefore, almost by definition, have a public function beyond its magisterial one. This means that it may have to do and articulate things that are not always comforting or acceptable to (sections of) the African church. South African Black theology has certainly fulfilled this particular task, because, according to Mosala:[24]

> .... it [Black theology] has never been co-opted by the Establishment. No church has ever officially affirmed black theology as a legitimate and correct way of doing theology in South Africa. Not even the South African Council of Churches has given official recognition to black theology.

What cannot be denied, however, is that by and large, church and theology have been related in Africa. Even South African Black theology originated and flourished in church caucuses, movements, and organizations.[25] Indeed, the bulk of Africa's ecumenical and theological consultations have been initiated by churches or church organizations and Christian councils.[26] However, all is not well in the "African church" itself. It faces challenges such as "denominationalism and religious competitiveness,[27] the reduction of Africa into a "dumping ground" for curious forms of North-American Charismatic and Pentecostal groups, the rise of church independentism and the concomitant decline in "historic mission church membership",[28] growing urbanization,[29] as well the cultural, political, economic, sexual, and ecclesiastical oppression of African women.[30]

IV. INCULTURATION ISSUES

African culture and African Traditional Religions (ATRs) have long been acknowledged as the womb out of which African Christian theology must be born. From various fronts, African Christians insisted that the church of Africa and its theology must bear an African stamp. This insistence went beyond theological and ecclesiastical matters as other African thinkers also attempted to construct "African philosophy", "African literature", "African art", and "African architecture". The question we asked earlier about Africa, African Christianity, and African theology can and has indeed been asked of African culture and ATRs, namely: "are there such animals?" Given the vastness and diversity of the continent's peoples, this is justifiable. However, African church leaders and theologians have not allowed this question to dampen their spirits. Unlike European imperial historians, explorers, and missionaries of the previous centuries, African theologians have generally been wary of generalizations about "Africa" and African culture. Special efforts have been made to speak in contextualized and specified terms, such as "the Akan Doctrine of God", "the image of God among the Sotho-Tswana", "Oludumare", and "West African Christianity". In her book on African women and patriarchy, Oduyoye[31] is at pains to demonstrate that the primary context of her reflections is the Akan of Ghana and the Yoruba of Nigeria. Even Mbiti, who has been accused of making generalizations and reductions about "Africa", is careful to contextualize his research and findings in terms of tribes—at least in his work *Concepts of God in Africa*. Generalizations are still made, but mostly on the basis of well-focused contexts of research. In that way, therefore, serious attempts have been made to ensure that the terms ATRs have not been allowed to degenerate into meaningless generalizations and clichés.

However, references to both African Traditional Religions and to African culture remained a hazardous exercise in African theological construction. It has been the source of much tension, both within and without African theology. The central bone of contention may be summarized this way: African Christian theology needs to decide not only how to refer to African culture and ATRs but to carefully weigh the objectives of such references. Various proposals have been made. Those who advocate the position that both African culture and ATRs are part of the *praeparatio evangelica* have been highly critical of the two. Many missionary councils have wholly condemned ATRs as something to be converted from.[32]

Scholars like Bediako and Turner actually argue that the "phenomenal growth" of Christianity in Africa cannot be understood without reference to ATRs as an excellent preparation for the gospel. However, the granting of *praeparatio evangelica* status to ATRs and African culture may be a veiled refusal to accept the latter on its own terms.[33] This is the theological practice which Okot p'Bitek characterized in 1970 as "intellectual smuggling". Thus, other African theologians, such as Setiloane, Christian Gaba, Bolaji Idowu, and Samuel Kibicho, have called for the suspension of any evangelical or "missionary" motives when African theology refers to ATRs. In any case, it is probably bad research methodology to mix what purports to be objective research with a hidden proselytizing agenda. If ATRs are such a fertile ground waiting to be "fulfilled" by Christianity, other African theologians have asked, why are ATRs so resilient? Indeed, some African thinkers, both Christian and non-Christian, have argued that, not only has Christianity brought nothing "new", but that ATRs are "superior" to Christianity. These types of assertions have greatly troubled some African Christian theologians—especially Evangelicals, who tend to feel that if the theology being constructed intends to be Christian theology, ATRs should not be viewed as equal to Christianity, let alone "superior".[34]

What this debate demonstrates rather clearly, however, is that theological reference to ATRs and African culture comes at a price—as with other religions, ATRs must be taken seriously in their own right, beyond the *praeparatio evangelica* framework. Some among the first generation of African theological writers made admirable attempts to take ATRs seriously, in their own terms, without relinquishing their own belief in the "superiority" of Christianity. These are examples worthy of being followed. In fact, it is possible to argue that the increasingly pluralistic context in Africa demands that we "listen" to other religions more carefully and more respectfully, without ceasing to be committed Christians ourselves and yet without a hidden evangelistic motive. We should, in the words of the late David Bosch:[35]

> ... Regard our involvement in dialogue and mission as an adventure [and be] prepared to take risks ... Anticipating surprises as the Spirit guides us into fuller understanding. This is not opting for agnosti-

> cism, but for humility. It is, however, a bold humility—or a humble boldness. We know only in part, but we do know. And we believe that the faith we profess is both true and just, and should be proclaimed. We do this, however, not as judges or lawyers, but as witnesses; not as soldiers, but as envoys of peace; not as high-pressure salespersons, but as ambassadors of the Servant Lord.

1. Christianisation or Africanisation?

Kwame Bediako has identified as a distinct but no longer crucial emphasis in African theology what he calls "the Christianisation of the African past". This task, he argues, served its valuable purpose of providing Africans with "cultural continuity", which in turn helps to clarify African Christian identity. But it is now a task whose time has passed. Therefore, Bediako is concerned when African theologians appear unable to transcend their África past, so that it continues to dictate an agenda for the present. Bediako (1992) almost blames African theologians' pre-occupation with identity issues on eighteenth and nineteenth century European perceptions of Africans, based on the slave-trade. It is to this legacy that African theologians are supposed to be reacting when they harp on past traditions and religions. My feeling is that this may be a simplistic view of African theology's reference to African traditions and the African past. To view it as a "tendency" from which African theology is supposed to graduate may be shortsighted.

What is needed now, Bediako argues, is the Africanization of Africa's Christian present.[36] Without unquestioningly accepting Bediako's reduction of decades of African theologies into a "quest for Christianizing the African past", he puts his finger on an element that provides a fruitful angle into the wide-ranging agenda of African theology during the past forty years. But, "Christianizing the African past" is only one perspective on the agenda of African theology, and it is therefore reductionistic to analyze, evaluate, and classify African theologians mainly and only on this criteria—which is virtually what Bediako does.[37] Juxtaposing Christianization and Africanization appears to rest on too rigid a separation between that which is Christian and that which is African. Besides, many African theologians understood and still understand themselves to be "Africanizing" Christianity when they appear to be "Christianizing" their past and vice versa! To posit the Africanization of Christianity as the new task facing African theology may not, in reality, be as groundbreaking as it appears. For African Christian theologians, the two processes—Christianization and Africanization—have not and cannot be artificially separated.

2. Beyond Christian Theology

There is a deep sense in which African theology has never been just Christian theology. From its earliest times, written African theology has always sought, not merely to dialogue with ATRs and African culture, but also to make sense of the complex world of ATRs.[38] Strictly speaking, therefore, there has been, up to now, no such thing as a purely "African Christian theology". Therefore, the majority of African theologians have not been highly concerned with a specifically "African Christian identity" either for themselves or for the church. Is this a weakness? Bediako and probably other evangelical theologians seem to think so. Therefore, a significant concern in his theology is the quest for a truly Christian African identity. However, it is possible to see the non-Christian concern as a sign of realism and maturity. African theology has always been inter-religious, seeking to be more than a proselytizing theology without denigrating Christianity. In other words, it is with good reason that African Christian theologians have had to ask themselves and to be asked by others "why do we continue to seek to convert to Christianity the devotees of African traditional religion?"[39] This is a crucial question for all African theologies as we move into the twenty-first century. It seems to me that we will have to redefine the role of our theologies beyond seeking either to "convert" unreached Africans or support those who carry out such a task. For himself, Setiloane answers this question thus:[40]

> I am like someone who has been bewitched, and I find it difficult to shake off the Christian witchcraft with which I have been captivated. I cannot say I necessarily like where I am. Second, I rationalize my position by taking the view that to be Christian I do not have to endorse every detail of western theology.

There may be some leads for African theology to follow in our times from this. Will it be possible to do exclusively Christian African theology—anymore than it was possible for the first generation of African theologians? I doubt it. If anything, the growing plural situation in Africa demands an even broader and more rigorous inter-religious approach. African Christian theologians and their churches have to learn new ways of speaking to and relating to other religious people. We have to listen anew to the critiques that have been leveled against African Christian theology by (apparently) non-Christian Africans such as P'Bitek and others.[41] This listening and dialogue must not be done on a basis of a rigid separation between "African Christian" theologians/ intellectuals as opposed to "non-Christian African" intellectuals—as Bediako sometimes seems to imply.[42] In reality, such a distinction is, strictly speaking, very difficult to sustain. There is, therefore, a sense in which African theology, even African Christian theology can only be truly African if it abandons artificial identity boundaries—including the tag "Christian" when and where it is used merely as a boundary marker.

3. The Bible

As with ATRs and other aspects of African culture, the Bible has enjoyed a respected status and place in African theology. "Any viable theology must and should have a biblical basis,"[43] Mbiti declares. Similarly, Fashole-Luke declares that "the Bible is the basic and a primary source for the development of African Christian Theology."[44] To underscore the significance of the Bible in the construction of African theology, Mbiti also says:[45]

> Nothing can substitute for the Bible. However much African cultural-religious background may be close to the biblical world, we have to guard against references like "the hitherto unwritten African Old Testament" or sentiments that see final revelation of God in the African religious heritage.

We have already mentioned that Mbiti's basic criticism of Black and Latin American liberation theologies has been that these "theological debates have been propagated without full Biblical grounding." However, even those who, according to Mbiti, made exaggerated connections between the Bible and African heritage still underscore the significance of the Bible in African theology. The very fact that theologians felt the need to make such outrageous connections between the world of the Bible and the African world is proof of the esteem with which the Bible was held. The emerging African Feminist or Womanist theology has also underscored the importance of the Bible. The very titles of some of the books on African Feminism emphasize this reality: *Talitha, qumi*, *Who Will Roll Away the Stone* and *The will to Arise*.

What has, in my opinion, been lacking is a vigorous debate on biblical hermeneutics akin to the vigorous debate that African (and non-African) theologians have held on culture, politics, and ATRs. In fact, for a long time the very notion of "biblical hermeneutics" would not be mentioned even by trained biblical scholars such as Mbiti. Instead, it is the authority of the vernacular Bibles that seems to be emphasized.[46] It was almost as if some of these theologians were afraid to alert African Christians to the fact that the Bible can and needs to be interpreted. Those who attempted to interpret the Bible creatively and boldly would be accused of extravagance, as we have illustrated above. Indeed, "fidelity to the Bible" or "biblical grounding" have remained the chief control mechanisms with which to regulate the pace and scope of African theology particularly in its reference to socio-political liberation and to ATRs.

Unfortunately, this has led to a situation in which, throughout Africa, the Bible has been and continues to be absolutized: it is one of the oracles that we consult for instant solutions and responses.[47] What makes the situation worse is that any unconventional reading of the Bible quickly earns one the charge of not being respectful of the authority of scripture. There are other socio-religious reasons for the almost fanatical attachment to the Bible—especially in Protestant Africa. Bereft of the rituals and symbols of ATRs, Roman Catholicism, and African Independentism, African Protestants have nothing but the Bible—*sola scriptura*. Once their attachment to "the big black book" is attacked they have nothing else to hold onto. However, on the whole, and in actual practice, African Christians are far more innovative and subversive in their appropriation of the Bible that they appear. Developments within South African Black theology, Latin American-type liberation theologies and African theology in the area of Biblical hermeneutics since the early eighties give us hope.[48] Here attempts are being made not only to develop creative Biblical hermeneutic methods, but also to observe and analyze the manner in which African Christians "read" and view the Bible.

In an illuminating article, Nthamburi and Waruta propose a set of common themes that would characterize the Biblical hermeneutics of African Christians:[49] a quest for salvation/healing and wholeness, a keen awareness of human alienation, an appreciation of God's promise to "put things right", a desire to know how to deal with the spirit world, attaching importance to initiation rites, an awareness of God's advocacy for the down-trodden, a sense of belonging in and to a visible community, commitment to social morality, and an intense concern for death and life beyond it. The biblical hermeneutical "principles" of South African Black theology could be summarized in this way: a "suspicious" and critical view of the status, contents, and use of the Bible, a commitment to a materialist reading of the Bible ("behind the text"), a commitment to the cultural struggles of black workers and women, and finally a view of the Bible as (or a need for it to become) a "weapon of struggle" in the hands of blacks, workers, and women.

4. Rethinking Distinctions within African Theologies

As with the Bible and African Culture, socio-economic and political issues have been on the agenda of African theology, especially what has been termed the African theology of liberation and South African Black theology. However, as we shall see in the next section, the conventional distinctions of "Black" from "African" theologies as "siblings", "distant cousins", "old guard", or "new guard",[50] "soul mates or antagonists",[51] theologies of "inculturation and liberation"[52] are no longer adequate. They do not sufficiently account for either the supposed similarities, or differences between the various, dynamic, and emerging strands of African theologies. With the changing ideological map of the world and the sweeping changes on the African continent itself, the agendas of what has been termed "African theologies of inculturation" as opposed to "African theologies of liberation" plus South African Black theology are moving closer together.[53] Having been cautious to speak about "African culture"—due probably to the apartheid state's manipulation of African culture into the Bantustan system—South African Black theologians are now beginning to speak more freely about culture.[54] This is illustrated by the increasing references being made to the concept of ubuntu (African personhood) in numerous South African intellectual debates.

The coming together of agendas of African theologies does not, and should not, be interpreted to mean that some forms of these theologies are becoming redundant and are about to be phase out. This is a common, hasty judgment often made in the zeal to construct ever and more definitive African theologies or theological paradigms. First generation African theologians responded to the charge that African theology—and calls for the selfhood of the African Church—were a threat to Christian catholicity, by debunking the myth of a uniform and universal theology. In like manner, we must respond to those who are either trying to exaggerate similarities between various African theologies, or to replace all previous African theologies with one all-encompassing theological paradigm, by indicating that African Christianity need not have "one" Christian theology in order to be valid and authentic.

What the coming together of different agendas does mean is that we can no longer rigidly separate the various African theologies from one another. The established "cleavages" of African theologies are, furthermore, no longer an adequate indication of the variety and lively ferment that is taking place within African Christianity and between African Christian theologies. So we have to begin to "speak" and "do" African theology differently; in more dialogical, consultative, and open-ended ways. I now sketch a few emerging models of African theology. These merely illustrate some new currents, and are by no means comprehensive. I regard these new currents as indicators of the possible directions into which African theologies will move in future.

V. EMERGING THEOLOGIES

1. Theologies of the AICs

A few scholars deserve special mention for their pioneering role in the irruption of AIC studies and the subsequent exposure of the significance of these churches for African Christianity and African theology: Bengt Sundkler, who wrote one of the earliest in-depth studies of AICs,[55] Christian Baeta,[56] David Barrett,[57] Martinus Daneel,[58] and Harold Turner.[59] Following the work of these scholars, a flood of theses and books on AICs has occurred.[60] The basic proposal of many AIC "theologians" is that the praxis of these churches must now be regarded not only as the best illustration of African Christianity, but also as "enacted", "oral", or "narrative" African theology—a type of theology that is no less valid than written African theologies, they would add. In this way, AICs are adding to and becoming a facet of African theology at one and the same time. Furthermore, the numerical growth of these churches[61] means that they have, in many parts of Africa, become, the mainline churches.

These churches, together with similar Christian movements among other primal societies may indeed be seen as the fifth major Christian church type, after the Eastern Orthodox Churches, the Roman Catholic Church, the Protestant Reformation, and the Pentecostal Churches.[62]

African theologies will no longer be able to ignore or dismiss the theological significance of the AICs in African Christianity. However, these churches must neither be romanticized nor studied in isolation from other African churches—including the so-called "mainline churches". In the same way that an African theology based only on a reference to mainline churches is inadequate, so too will any African theology based exclusively on African independent churches.

The tendency to regard AICs as the most authentic, if not as the only authentic African churches, has often created some unhealthy theological rivalry—notably between theologians rather than African Christians—wherein AIC praxis is supposed to be more African, more grassroots-based, more local, and more genuine than so-called written African theologies. I have found such distinctions and theological rivalries to be generally unreliable and artificial—at least in the South African context.[63] The issues are further complicated by the fact that, by and large, authoritative AIC scholars in the twentieth century have been overwhelmingly white (missionaries), with Africans themselves taking a back seat. But African silence on AICs may be a loaded and eloquent one, needing to be decoded and reflected upon. The white missionary domination of AIC studies may be attributable to the fact that the emergence of AICs, almost without exception, was initially viewed as a "problem", "reflection", or "failure" of missionary work. In many colonial African countries, AICs were supposed to either be political movements (Ethiopianism) or ecclesiastical movements with a political agenda. The call for a distinction between African Christianity, on the one hand, and literature on African Christianity on the other,[64] may help clarify here. Reflection and research on AICs, however excellent and authoritative, must never be equated with the actual praxis of AICs. Yet at the end of the day no serious African theology can ignore either the studies mentioned or the African Christianities displayed in AICs—for research and reality always mirror one another, albeit imperfectly.

2. African Charismatic/Evangelical Theology

Not only is African Christianity generally evangelical, if not Pentecostalist in orientation, but there is a sizable body of literature and events that could be said to be representative of a theological strand of African theology. We remember, without necessarily discussing it, the debate between Byang Kato's evangelical and "biblical" theology and John Mbiti's alleged "universalist" theology in the 1970s.[65]

Without joining this debate we need to recognize that it demonstrated the existence of a different theological orientation from that which we normally assume when we speak of African theology. All over Africa, evangelicals exist in organized and confessional communities. They are, of course, no less heterogeneous in theological outlook than "ecumenical" African Christians. Within South Africa, one may think of Ray McCauley's Rhema Church and its affiliates, Michael Cassidy's Africa Enterprise, and a grouping which has until recently been called "the Concerned Evangelicals". We must take note of a movement such as the Pan African Leadership Assembly (PACLA).[66] Indeed, there have been tensions and probably justifiable suspicions between PACLA and the AACC,[67] and tensions remain between many sectors of evangelicalism and ecumenism all over Africa. But the twenty-first century will not allow us to either ignore or smooth these over. One of the challenges we face, is to seek out all expressions of African theology and Christianity, however inadequate and suspicious, so that we may expose them to serious and dialogical theological reflection. I am not calling for superficial confessional and theological unities. We are better off without those, even if we suffer the terrible situation of denominationalism. My feeling is that in as much as we have seen tensions between evangelicals and ecumenicals in Africa, there are also cases of solidarity in action and theological dialogue between these groups in many African countries. These may serve as a framework for further theological dialogue and partnership. At the end of the day, African theology may be the richer for it.

3. Translation Theologies

Elsewhere,[68] I have linked translation theologies to the names of Lamin Sanneh[69] and Kwame Bediako.[70] This, however, must not be taken to mean that Sanneh and Bediako present us with exactly the same agenda. Both of them are important, innovative voices whose thinking bear significant implications for African theology. In a series of works spanning a decade and culminating in his *Translating the Message*, Lamin Sanneh has mounted a passionate argument in defense of both African Christianity and the twentieth century missionary enterprise.[71] The gist of his argument is that the clue to the tremendous growth of African Christianity during this century was the logic of the translatability of the Christian message or gospel into African vernacular languages. This is signified most potently in the historic necessity of translating the Bible into vernacular languages. It is this translatability of the Gospel rather than the agency of missionaries that accounts for African Christianity. Therefore, focus must shift from a preoccupation with missionary omissions and the supposed link between Christianity and colonialism to the "heart of the matter", namely gospel translatability.

Bediako shares with Sanneh the conviction that it is the translatability of the gospel more than anything else that made large parts of Africa so vastly Christian. He therefore argues that African Christians and theologians alike must let the gospel speak to the African situation, "in its own right". For this reason Bediako is highly critical of a section of African theologians who insist on assuming that Christianity is foreign to Africa almost as a fundamental datum. Since the gospel is essentially translatable, it no longer makes sense to speak of Christianity as "foreign"; hence he confidently calls African Christianity a "non-western" religion. Bediako admits that the task of African theology is not finished simply because the gospel is translatable. But its essential task is to assist African Christians, theologians, and non-Christian intellectuals alike to exorcise the phantom foreignness of Christianity. While understanding it, Bediako sees African theology's decades-long preoccupation with both the foreignness of Christianity and the African past as ultimately no longer necessary.

The boldness and projectiveness of Bediako and Sanneh's proposals are indisputable. But their reliance on dubious distinctions (e.g. gospel versus Christianity) and equations (e.g. Bible equals Word of God) are a serious drawback.[72] Also, the translatability of the gospel does not eliminate the significance of the role of the missionary enterprise or colonialism. While the gospel may indeed be eminently translatable, human intervention can affect the pace and quality of such translation—even arresting it into all sorts of orthodoxies.

4. African Feminist/Womanist Theologies

We have seen an explosion of African women's theological events, organizations and publications since the mid-eighties. In reality, women's issues have been on the agenda of such organizations as the Ecumenical Association of Third World Theologians (EATWOT), the AACC, local Christian councils, and in para-church organizations since the early 1980s. However, it is a serious indictment of African male theologies that women's issues have not received immediate and unreserved acceptance.

Within South Africa, the first feminist conference that was predominantly black, was held at Hammanskraal in 1984; immediately followed by a predominantly white feminist conference at the University of South Africa. The Hammanskraal conference noted that, "whereas women form the majority of the oppressed, we note with regret that Black theology has not taken women seriously, but has seen theology as a male domain."[73] Participants in a Black theology conference held in Cape Town that same year concurred, albeit cautiously, in their final statement: "There are evidently structures oppressive of women inherent in both the Black community and the Church."[74] From these tentative beginnings African Feminist/Womanist theology has grown in South Africa.[75] Continentally and internationally one of the significant catalysts for African Feminist/Womanist theology was EATWOT. From its inception, EATWOT has always had a strong contingent of women in its ranks. But the women felt that "our voices were not being heard, although we were visible enough ... We demanded to be heard." The result was the creation within EATWOT of a Women's Commission.[76] Within the World Council of Churches (WCC), Oduyoye[77] notes that "it took seven years from its founding for the WCC to establish a department to deal with the issue of cooperation of women and men in church and society"—in the establishment of a Department of Cooperation of Men and Women in Church and Society. Special note must be taken of the WCC's "Decade of Churches in Solidarity with Women", which officially ended in August 1998. Some of the "target areas agreed upon [for the Decade] in 1987 were church teachings about women, women and poverty, women and racism, and violence against women."[78] These ecumenical conferences and events have resulted in chains of local consultations, events, and publications all over the world. A significant consultation of Third World Women took place under the auspices of EATWOT in 1986 at Oaxtepec, Mexico. One of the results of this event was the publication of *With Passion and Compassion*. On the African continent, the Circle of Concerned Women in Theology, as well as its Biennial Institute of African Women in Religion and Culture, was established in 1989 in Accra, Ghana.[79] Some of the papers read at the Accra meeting were published in the book *The Will to Arise*. Since then several regional circles have been formed. One specific objective of the circles has been the production of African feminist literature. More recently, the circle has produced the book *Groaning in Faith*.[80] However, it would be a mistake to limit the influence of the Circles, EATWOT, the WCC, or local Christian councils to publications linked directly to their consultations. What these organizations have managed to do is to create space for Feminist/Womanist theology to grow and blossom, not only in Africa but in the wider Third World.

One of the most peculiarly African publications on Feminist theology is Mercy Oduyoye's recent work *Daughters of Anowa*. Whereas Black and African theologies have for the past half-century argued for the validity of African Christianities and the legitimacy of African culture, African Feminist/Womanist theology is charting a new way. This theology is mounting a critique of both African culture and African Christianity in ways that previous African theologies have not been able to do. From these theologies, we may learn how to be truly African and yet critical of aspects of African culture. African womanist theologians are teaching us how to criticize African culture without denigrating it, showing us that the one does and should not necessarily lead to the other. My prediction is that the twenty-first century is going to produce an even more gendered African theology. All theologians and African churches will be well advised to begin to take heed.

5. Theologies of Reconstruction

Leading the pack in the theologies of reconstruction are Kenya's Jesse Mugambi[81] and South Africa's Charles Villa-Vicencio.[82] Although Villa-Vicencio's work was published first,[83] Mugambi had already been propagating the idea of a Theology of Reconstruction in 1990 in the context of AACC consultations.[84] It was, of course, Gorbachev's "*perestroika*" (reconstruction), which led to the break-up of the old USSR, which helped to popularize the notion of "reconstruction". For Mugambi, both the inculturation and liberation paradigms within which African theologies had been undertaken were no longer adequate frameworks for doing African theology after the cold war. Both inculturation and liberation responded to a situation of ecclesiastical and colonial bondage. In the place of the inculturation-liberation paradigm, which was, according to Mugambi, mainly "reactive", we should install a "pro-active" theology of reconstruction. Mugambi's originality lies in that, instead of calling for the ascendancy of liberation over inculturation or vice-versa (a "game" well-rehearsed in African theologies), he calls for an innovative transcendence of both. For this part, Villa-Vicencio appeals for a post cold-war (African) theology to engage in serious dialogue with democracy, human rights, law-making, nation-building, and economics in order to ensure that these do indeed improve the quality of human life.

My main critique of both Mugambi and Villa-Vicencio is in their assumption that the end of the "cold war" has immediate significance for ordinary Africans and that the so-called "New World Order" is truly "new" and truly "orderly" for Africans. Yet, as Mugambi himself rightly points out, Africa's problems of poverty, war, dictatorships, and American bully-boy tactics are unlikely to decrease. In fact, the New World Order is not only likely to relegate Africa into a "fourth world" but it will also impose its own prescriptions on African countries. One such prescription is "democracy" or its semblance. I am also critical of the fact that both Mugambi and Villa-Vicencio appear to minimize the value of previous African theologies of inculturation and liberation. Formations such as EATWOT and l'Association oecuménique des théologiens africains (AOTA) in Francophone Africa have done a tremendous amount of theological reflection and construction. Weaknesses notwithstanding, twenty-first century African theologies cannot afford to simply abandon them. We must look for ways in which to move on without despising what has already been achieved. Otherwise we might think we have progressed forward when in reality we have moved backwards.

CONCLUDING REMARKS

Firstly, I want to restate my basic thesis, the contours of the emerging face of the twenty-first century African theologies must be sought in a thorough grasp of the ground captured so far, plus a keen awareness of new and emerging currents. African theologies are already reassessing their objectives and redefining their agendas. I have tried to indicate some of the ways in which the "traditional agendas" of African theologies may need to be altered. I have also indicated how many of the tags and categories used to describe and differentiate African theologies have become dated. Finally, new African theologies, capable of dealing with the New World Order can only be fashioned out of a vigorous interrogation of such emerging theologies as I have sketched above. What about previous theologies? Am I suggesting that their usefulness consist only in terms of "the ground that they have captured" so that they are of no direct relevance now? No. The issues that were being addressed by these theologies are far from finished. South African Black theology needs to continue its anti-racist critique of African Christianity. It must also develop its tremendous strides in biblical hermeneutics further. Nor have issues of Africanization, enculturation, and identity expired. African theology needs to continue addressing these issues. What I am saying is that in addressing these established and still relevant agendas, Black and African theologies will need to do so in consultation with insights from such emerging theologies as I have sketched above.

Notes

1. David J. Bosch, *Transforming Mission: Paradigm Shifts in Mission Theology* (Maryknoll: Orbis Books, 1991) uses the idea of paradigm shifts to explain the manner in which theologies of mission have changed over the centuries. It is an idea borrowed from the scientist Thomas Kuhn.
2. Cf. e.g. David B. Barrett et al, *World Christian Encyclopedia: A Comparative Survey of Churches and Religions in the Modern World AD 1900-2000* (New York: Oxford University Press, 1982); John S Mbiti, *The Bible in African Christianity* (Nairobi: Oxford University Press, 1986); Charles Villa-Vicencio, *A Theology of Reconstruction: Nation-Building and Human Rights* (Cape Town, Cambridge: David Philip, Cambridge University Press, 1992); Lamin Sanneh, *Translating*

the Message: The Missionary Impact on Culture (Maryknoll: Orbis Books, 1989); J.N.K. MUGAMBI, *From Liberation to Reconstruction: African Christian Theology After the Cold War* (Nairobi: East African Educational Publishers, 1995); Kwame BEDIAKO, *Christianity in Africa: The Renewal of a Non-Western Religion* (Maryknoll: Orbis Books, 1995); A. KARAMAGA, *Problems and Promises of Africa: Towards and Beyond the Year 2000* (Nairobi: All Africa Conference of Churches, 1991); Mercy Amba ODUYOYE, *Daughters of Anowa: African Women and Patriarchy* (Marynoll: Orbis Books, 1995); M.A. ODUYOYE "Christianity and African Culture", in *International Review of Mission*, 84, 332/333 (January/April 1995) 77-90; Allan ANDERSON & Samuel OTWANG, *Tumelo: The Faith of African Pentecostals in South Africa* (Pretoria: University of South Africa Press, 1993).

3. KARAMAGA, *Problems and Promises*; José CHIPENDA, "The Church of the Future in Africa", in Douglas WARUTA (ed.) *African Church in the 21St Century: Challenges and Promises* (Nairobi: AACC, 1995), 16-36.
4. Kwesi A. DICKSON, *Theology in Africa* (Maryknoll: Orbis Books, 1984), 8.
5. Cf. Tinyiko Sam MALULEKE, "Black and African Theologies in the New World Order: A Time to Drink From Our Own Wells", in *Journal of Theology for Southern Africa*, 96 (November 1996) 3-19; T.S. MALULEKE, "Recent Developments in the Christian Theologies of Africa: Towards the 21st Century", in *Journal of Constructive Theology*, 2, 2 (December 1996) 33-60.
6. In this recent work on African theology, Josiah U. YOUNG, *African Theology: A Critical Analysis and Annotated Bibliography* (Westport: Greenwood Press, 1993), 6f., identifies those whom he calls "the ancestors of African Theology" such as Clement of Alexandria, Origen, Athanasius, Tertullian, Cyprian, Augustine of Hippo and Kimpa Vita or Dona Beatrice. See also John PARRATT, *Reinventing Christianity: African Theology Today* (Grand Rapids: Eerdmans, 1995); Marie-Louise MARTIN, *Kimbangu, an African Prophet and His Church* (Oxford: Oxford University Press, 1975); David J. Bosch, "Currents and Crosscurrents in South African Black Theology", in Gayraud S. WILMORE & James H. CONE (eds), *Black Theology: A Documentary History, 1966-1979* (Maryknoll: Orbis Books, 1979); Kwame BEDIAKO, *Theology and Identity: The Impact of Culture Upon Christian Thought in the Second Century and Modern Africa* (Oxford: Regnum Books, 1992).
7. ODUYOYE, "Christianity and African Culture", 8.
8. The same could be said of places like Jerusalem or Israel.
9. Harry SAWYERR, *The Practice of Presence: Shorter Writings of Harry Sawyerr*, John PARRATT (ed.) (Grand Rapids: Eerdmans, 1996), 87.
10. Edward W Fashole-Luke, *An African Indigenous Theology: Fact or Fiction?* (Aberdeen: University of Aberdeen Press).
11. Both Sawyerr (SAWYERR, *The Practice of Presence*, 93-99) and Fashole-Luke—in heavily qualified terms. Indeed they use it almost reluctantly. See, Edward W. FASHOLÉ-LUKE, "An African Indigenous Theology: Fact or Fiction?", in *Sierra Leone Bulletin of Religion* 11 (1971).
12. Bolaji IDOWU, *Towards an Indigenous Church* (London: Oxford University Press, 1965).
13. John S. MBITI. "The Biblical Basis for Present Trends in African Theology", in Kofi APPIAH-KUBI & Sergio TORRES, *African Theology en Route: Papers from the*

Pan-African Conference of Third World Theologians. Accra. December 17-23, 1977 (Maryknoll: Orbis Books, 1977), 90.

14. MBITI, "The Biblical Basis", 83.
15. The approach of Kwesi A. DICKSON, "The African Theological Task", in Sergio TORRES & Virginia M.M. FABELLA (eds), *The Emergent Gospel: Theology from the Underside of History: Papers from the Ecumenical Dialogue of Third World Theologians, Dar es Salam, August 5-12* (Maryknoll: Orbis Books, 1978), 46, is similar if not slightly more radical in that he rejects the notion of universal theology and thus argues for the validity of African Theology. For a fuller discussion of the merits of an 'African Theology' see one of his other works: DICKSON, *Theology in Africa,* 1-10.
16. MBITI, "The Biblical Basis", 90. Cf. MBITI, *The Bible in African Christianity.*
17. MBITI, "The Biblical Basis", 90.
18. Henry OKULU, *Church and Politics in East Africa* (Nairobi: Uzima Press, 1974), 54.
19. Idowu quoted by SAWYERR, *The Practice of Presence*, 85.
20. James Johnson quoted by SAWYERR, *The Practice of Presence*, 86.
21. SAWYERR, *The Practice of Presence, 85.*
22. DICKSON, *Theology in Africa,* 1-10.
23. See also Ngidi MUSHETE, "Unity of Faith and Pluralism in Theology", in TORRES & FABELLA, *The Emergent Gospel, 50-75.*
24. Itumeleng J. MOSALA, "Spirituality and Struggle: African and Black Theologies", in TORRES & FABELLA, *The Emergent Gospel.*
25. Tinyiko Sam MALULEKE, *"A Morula Tree Between Two Fields": The Commentary of Selected Tsonga Writers on Missionary Christianity* (DTh dissertation, University of South Africa, 1995).
26. Cf. J.N.K. MUGAMBI, "The Ecumenical Movement and the Future of the Church in Africa", in J.N.K. MUGAMBI & Laurenti MAGESA, *The Church in African Christianity: Innovative Essays in Ecclesiology* (Nairobi: Initiatives, 1990), 14-20; Margaret S. LAROM (ed.), *Claiming the Promise: African Churches Speak* (New York: Friendship Press, 1994).
27. D.W. WARUTA, "Towards an African Church: A Critical Assessment of Alternative Forms and Structures", in MUGAMBI & Laurenti MAGESA, *The Church in African Christianity*, 33.
28. BARRETT, *World Christian Encyclopedia*; ANDERSON & OTWANG, *Tumelo.*
29. Aylward Shorter, *The Church in the African City* (London: Geoffrey Chapman, 1991).
30. Cf. Virginia M.M. FABELLA & Mercy Amba ODUYOYE (eds), *With Passion and Compassion: Third World Women Doing Theology* (Maryknoll: Orbis Books, 1988); Mercy Amba ODUYOYE & Musimbi R.A. KANYORO (eds), *Talitha, Qumi!: Proceedings of the Convocation of African Women Theologians 1989* (Ibadan: Daystar Press, 1990); Mercy Amba ODUYOYE & Musimbi R.A. KANYORO (eds), *The Will to Arise: Women, Tradition and the Church in Africa* (Maryknoll: Orbis Books, 1992); ODUYOYE, "Christianity and African Culture", 77-90; Aruna GNANADASON, Musimbi R.A. KANYORO & Lucia Ann MCSPADDEN (eds), *Daughters of Anowa: African Women and Patriarchy: Women, Violence and Non-Violent Change* (Geneva: World Council of Churches Publications, 1996); Denise ACKERMANN,

Jonathan A. DRAPER & Emma MASHININI (eds), *Women Hold up Half the Sky: Women in the Church in Southern Africa* (Pietermaritzburg: Cluster Publications, 1991).

31. ODUYOYE, "Christianity and African Culture", 77-90; ODUYOYE, *Daughters of Anowa.*
32. Cf. BEDIAKO, *Theology and Identity.* For a contrary view, see J.S. FRIESEN, *Missionary Responses to Tribal Religions at Edinburgh, 1910* (Frankfurt: Peter Lang, 1996).
33. MALULEKE, "Black and African Theologies".
34. K. BEDIAKO, "Understanding African Theology in the 20th Century", in *Themelios,* 20, 1 (October 1994) 14-20; K. BEDIAKO, "Five Theses on the Significance of Modern African Christianity: A Manefesto", in *Transformation*, 13 (1996) 21-29.
35. Quoted on the title page: Willem SAAYMAN & Klippies (J.J.) KRITZINGER (eds), *Mission in Bold Humility: David Bosch's Work Considered* (Maryknoll: Orbis Books, 1996).
36. Cf. BEDIAKO, *Theology and Identity.*
37. BEDIAKO, *Theology and Identity.*
38. Bolaji IDOWU, *African Traditional Religion: A Definition* (London: SCM Press, 1973); SAWYERR, *The Practice of Presence.*
39. Gabriel SETILOANE, "Where Are We in African Theology?", in K. APPIAH-KUBI & S. TORRES, *African Theology en Route: Papers from the Pan-African Conference of Third World Theologians. Accra. December 17-23, 1977* (Maryknoll: Orbis Books, 1977), 64.
40. Cf. J.N.K. MUGAMBI, *Critiques of Christianity in African Literature* (Nairobi: East African Educational Publishers, 1992).
41. Cf. MUGAMBI. *Critiques of Christianity.*
42. BEDIAKO, *Theology and Identity.*
43. John S. MBITI, *Concepts of God in Africa* (London: SPCK, 1979), 90
44. Edward W. FAHOLE-LUKE, "The Quest for African Christian Theologies", in G.H. ANDERSON & T.F. STRANSKY (eds), *Mission Trends No 3: Third World Theologies* (Grand Rapids: Eerdmans, 1976), 141.
45. MBITI, *Concepts of God in Africa,* 90.
46. Cf. SANNEH, *Translating the Message*; MBITI, *The Bible in African Christianity.*
47. ODUYOYE, *Daughters of Anowa,* 174
48. Here attempts are being made not only to develop creative biblical hermeneutic methods, but also to observe and analyze the manner in which African Christians "read" and view the Bible.
49. Zablon NTHAMBURI & Douglas WARUTA, "Biblical Hermeneutics in African Instituted Churches", in J.S. MBITI (ed.), *The Bible in African Christianity* (Nairobi: Oxford University Press, 1986), 40.
50. Josiah U. YOUNG, *Black and African Theologies: Siblings or Distant Cousins?* (Maryknoll: Orbis Books, 1986); YOUNG, *African Theology.*
51. Desmond TUTU, "Black Theology and African Theology: Soulmates or Antagonists?", in Dean William FERM (ed.), *Third World Liberation Theologies: A Reader* (Maryknoll: Orbis Books, 1986), 256-264.

52. Emmanuel MARTEY, *African Theology: Inculturation and Liberation* (Maryknoll: Orbis Books, 1993).
53. Mokgethi G MOTLHABI, "Black or African Theology? Toward and Integral African Theology", in *Journal of Black Theology in South Africa*, 8, 2 (November 1994) 113-141.
54. Tinyiko Sam MALULEKE, "African Culture, African Intellectuals and the White Academy in South Africa", in *Religion and Theology*, 3, 1 (1996) 19-42.
55. Bengt G.M. SUNDKLER, M., *Bantu Prophets in South Africa* (Oxford: Oxford University Press, 1948); B.G.M. SUNDKLER, *The Christian Ministry in Africa* (Liverpool: Charles Birchal, 1962); B.G.M. SUNDKLER, *Zulu Zion and Some Swazi Zionists* (Oxford: Oxford University Press, 1976).
56. C.G. BAÉTA, *Prophetism in Ghana* (London: SCM Press, 1962).
57. David B. BARRETT, *Schism and Renewal in Africa: An Analysis of Six Thousand Contemporary Religious Movements* (Nairobi: Oxford University Press, 1968); BARRETT, *World Christian Encyclopedia.*
58. M.L. DANEEL, *Old and New in Southern Shona Independent Churches* (New York: Mouton Publishers, 1971); M.L. DANEEL, *Quest for Belonging: Introduction to a Study of African Independent Churches*, (Gweru: Mambo Press, 1987).
59. H.W. TURNER, *History of an African Independent Church* (Oxford: Clarendon Press, 1967).
60. Cf. Tinyiko Sam MALULEKE, "Theological Interest in African Independent Churches and Other Grass-Root Communities in South Africa: A Review of Methodologies", in *Journal of Black Theology in South Africa*, 10, 1 (May 1996) 18-48.
61. Cf. BARRETT, *World Christian Encyclopedia;* ANDERSON & OTWANG, *Tumelo.*
62. Bosch in DANEEL, *Quest for Belonging*, 9.
63. MALULEKE, "Theological Interest", 18-48.
64. Bediako, "Five Thesis", 264.
65. Cf. Byang KATO, *Theological Pitfalls in Africa* (Kisimu: Kenya Evangelical Publishing House, 1975); MBITI, *The Bible in African Christianity,* 48f; BEDIAKO, *Theology and Identity*, 386f.
66. Michael CASSIDY & Gottfried OSEI-MENSAH, *Together in One Place: The Story of PACLA, December 9-19, 1976* (Nairobi: Evangel Publishing House, 1978).
67. CASSIDY & OSEI-MENSAH, *Together in One Place*, 31.
68. MALULEKE, "Black and African Theologies", 3-19; Tinyiko Sam Maluleke, "Recent Developments", 33-60.
69. SANNEH, *Translating the Message.*
70. BEDIAKO, *Theology and Identity*; BEDIAKO, *Christianity in Africa.*
71. Cf. MALULEKE, "Black and African Theologies", 3-19.
72. See MALULEKE, "Black and African Theologies", 3-19.
73. D. RAMODIBE, "Women and Men Building Together the Church in Africa", in FABELLA & ODUYOYE, *With Passion and Compassion.*
74. RAMODIBE, "Women and Men", 20.
75. A recent issue of the *Bulletin for Contextual Theology in Southern Africa & Africa,* 4, 2 (July 1997) has been devoted to Feminist/Womanist theology in South Africa. It also contains an annotated bibliography on South African Feminist/Woman-

ist works. Cf. also Christina LANDMAN, *The Piety of Afrikaans Women: Diaries of Guilt* (Pretoria: University of South Africa Press, 1994); ACKERMANN et al, *Women Hold Up Half the Sky.*

76. FABELLA & ODUYOYE, *With Passion and Compassion*, x.
77. Mercy Amba ODUYOYE, *Who Will Roll the Stone Away? The Ecumenical Decade of the Churches in Solidarity with Women* (Geneva: World Council of Churches Publications, 1988), 3.
78. ODUYOYE, *Daughters of Anowa,* 187.
79. Cf. Mercy Amba Oduyoye, "The Circle", in ODUYOYE & KANYORO, *Talitha.*
80. Musimbi R.A. KANYORO & Nyambura J. NJOROGE (eds), *Groaning in Faith: African Women in the Household of God* (Nairobi: Acton Publishers, 1996).
81. MUGAMBI, *From Liberation to Reconstruction.*
82. MALULEKE, "Recent Developments"; T.S. MALULEKE, "Review Mugambi, J N K 1995. From Liberation to Reconstruction: African Christian Theology After the Cold War. Nairobi: East African Educational Publishers", in *Missionalia*, 24, 3 (November 1996) 472-473; "African Culture, African Intellectuals and the White Academy in South Africa". MALULEKE, "Recent Developments".
83. VILLA-VICENCIO, *A Theology of Reconstruction.*
84. Cf. KARAMAGA, *Problems and Promises*; J.N.K. MUGAMBI, "The Future of the Church and the Church of the Future Africa", in J. CHIPENDA, A. KARAMAGA, J.N.K. MUGAMBI & C.K. OMARI (eds), *The Church of Africa: Toward a Theology of Reconstruction* (Nairobi: AACC, 1991); Tinyiko Sam MALULEKE, "The Proposal For a Theology of Reconstruction: A Critical Appraisal", in *Missionalia*, 22, 3 (November 1994) 245-258.

Chapter Nineteen

African Christian Communities in Diaspora

Afe Adogame

INTRODUCTION

Migration and diaspora discourses have engaged scholarly focus and analysis in various fields, and literature on the phenomena is steadily burgeoning. In an increasingly globalizing age where these discourses are assuming centre-stage in both academic and public domains, the public tone and flavor on immigration issues often take on a controversial posture especially with the growing politicization of migration. Although scholarly debates on transmigration and diaspora are no longer new, the privileging of political and socio-economic considerations have largely hijacked such discourses in a way that often glosses over religious and other factors that stimulate and impact on such processes. In the prevailing circumstances of "space-time compression", demographic influxes and shifts have far-reaching implications on the interconnectedness of local-global spaces. In fact, migration is both an ingredient and consequence of globalization. On the template of religion, such demographic considerations help to reconfigure the interdependence between religious praxis in the communities of the migrants' homelands and in the diaspora. Population mobility serves as a viable instrument of religious and cultural expansion, transmission and renegotiation. People's religious belonging is not merely part of their cultural heritage retained at the high point of emigration. Religious conviction can, on the one hand, be a central motive for migration or a support for organizing refuge in exile. Religious identity can be a crucial resource for decision-making processes in the home countries; for vitalizing culture of origin; and of action within the integration processes in a host context. Religious institutions provide migrants with opportunities of vital import for mixing with people from different cultural backgrounds under the umbrella of a common religion.

The trans-cultural encounter and exchange between Africa, Europe, the Americas and the Arab world has a long history that predates the fifteenth century and the era of the obnoxious human trafficking. Contacts between Europe and Africa in particular were constant throughout Europe's Antiquity, Middle Ages and the so-called Modern Age.[1] European presence and interest in Africa through these periods have been largely mixed and split along the contours of commerce, politics and religion. The imperial expansionist agenda generated new situations, circumstances and posed as a catalyst towards diaspora formation. One of the inherent consequences of these exploits and distension was that it later created several situations that brought Africans at varied times to other continental shores such as of Europe and the New World, thus also resulting in the formation of enclaves and communities. African diaspora is one theoretical construct to describe this global dispersal of indigenous African populations at different phases of world history. By employing "Black Atlantic" Gilroy contextualizes the voluntary and involuntary migration of Africans to Europe, Latin America and North America since the Age of Discovery.[2] The breadth of African diaspora even transcends the popular geographical fixation to Europe and the New World, and includes the Mediterranean and Arab worlds as well as the cross-migration within the African shore itself. Zeleza notes:[3]

> The flow of people at the global level has lagged behind the flows of capital and commodities ... African migrations are as much a part of the complex mosaic of transnational cultural flows as they are of labor and other economic flows ... Between 1965 and 1990 Africa's migrant population grew at a faster rate than any other region in the world. The continent increased its share of international migrants from 10.6 percent to 13.1 percent ... By 1995 African countries were second only to European countries in the numbers of economically active migrants they hosted, excluding refugees and asylum seekers ... Clearly, many Africans who migrate go to other African countries.

Exploration, slave trade, colonialism, poverty, cultural exchange and ecological disasters all contributed to an African diaspora that has scattered Africans to Europe, the Americas and elsewhere. The emergence of enclaves and communities can be pinned down to the different waves of emigration. The earliest strata aggregated young, virile, able-bodied Africans, mopped up in the obnoxious web of human trafficking, and catapulted them involuntarily to various metropolises in Europe, the Americas, and the Mediterranean and Arab geo-spaces. The fortunate survivors of this excruciating ordeal, their descendants, and slave remnants in the post-nineteenth century abolition scheme constituted the first African diaspora enclaves.

Physical contact between Africa and the West increased in frequency in the nineteenth century. Decades-long agitation for overseas colonies as settlement areas, sources of raw materials, and markets for the manufactured goods preceded the colonial politics of the 1880s and the subsequent bisecting of Africa. Thus, a second coterie of African diaspora communities may be located in the wave of migrants that swelled as a consequence of the Berlin-Congo 1884/5 Conference's official partition of the African continent into spheres of artificial geographical zones of European influence, exploitation and expropriation. The inter-war years (1914-1945) and its aftermath also experienced a reasonable degree of demographic shifts within and beyond Africa. Some uprooted Africans, commissioned as pawns in the European war game, either stayed back or charted for themselves new destinies, pathways and family relationships in the desolate battle fields. Debrunner notes that Africans present in Europe before 1918 were always numerically few, but their very presence and the prestige they enjoyed or suffered makes an interesting tale, often a story of adaptation and survival of individuals trying to find their own identity between Africa and Europe.[4]

An unprecedented upsurge, especially in the last decades, in the number of African migrants into Western Europe, North America and elsewhere heralds a new phase in the history of African diaspora.[5] Remarkable changes are evident in the composition and direction of international migration, features that make contemporary migration different from the historical African diaspora in several respects. In 1990 there was estimated to be 30 million voluntary international migrants in sub-Saharan Africa, about three and a half percent of the total population.[6] Hitherto, African migration to Europe had followed the historical and linguistic trails of colonialism with Great Britain[7] and France[8] as preferred destinations of migrants. In more recent times, African migration assumed a more diffused dimension with noticeable numbers of immigrants from several African countries flocking to countries with which they had no colonial ties, mainly in Western Europe, North America, and the Arab world. African immigration was thus marked by increasing diversification, in both the number of countries sending and receiving the immigrants. The emigrants increasingly included both highly and less-educated labor migrants, thus resulting in a loss of scarce manpower in their home countries. This demographic mobility forms an integral part of the global phenomenon of international migration. The upsurge in migration is due to rapid processes of economic, demographic, social, political, cultural and environmental change, which arise from decolonization, modernization and uneven development.[9] Incessant crises and upheavals in some parts of Africa have exacerbated immigration and exodus, thus generating the economic pool of mostly able-bodied youths particularly to Western Europe and North America.[10] The 1990s witnessed a major increase in involuntary or forced migration and, by the middle of the decade, refugees and internally displaced persons in some countries outnumbered voluntary international migrants by a ratio of more than two to one. By 1997, there were almost 17 million forced migrants, inclusive of nearly 4 million refugees.[11]

Many Africans who undergo these complex forms of migration have largely carried traits of their religious and cultural identity with them. As a matter of fact, their sojourn in new geo-cultural contexts has enlivened these migrants to identify, organize, and reconstruct "their religion" both for themselves and their host societies. The last three decades has witnessed a rapid proliferation of African Christian communities in diaspora, thus resulting in the remapping of old religious landscapes. This migratory trend and development bring to the fore the crucial role, functions and import of religious symbolic systems in new geo-cultural contexts. While religion has remained a constant identity variable in African diaspora communities, the historiography of African diaspora and migration has often largely neglected this religious ferment. The African American community has been integral to the shaping of the American religious mosaic. The obvious dehumanization process and the racial discrimination witnessed by the historical African diaspora in late eighteenth and early nineteenth century America gave birth to a number of African-American denominations from the Methodist, Baptist and Presbyterian backgrounds.[12] The Pentecostal Movement is by far the largest and most widespread religious movement to originate in the United States. Although the Wesleyan-Holiness tradition fuelled the quest of the Pentecostal movement prior to 1901, its origins are mostly traced to the Topeka-Kansas religious revival.[13] Some of the earliest groups included the predominantly African-American Church of God in Christ (1897), the Pentecostal Holiness Church (1898), the Church of God with headquarters in Cleveland, Tennessee (1906), and other smaller groups. The modern Pentecostal movement in the US began in 1906 with William J. Seymour, a black holiness preacher.[14] This chapter will, however, limit its scope and focus on the "new" African migrants and their religious communities. Why has and is religion so important for the African diaspora? From a historical perspective, the chapter shall examine the place of religion as a "motor" of African diaspora formation using the incipience and proliferation of new African Churches as a case example. It demonstrates how and to what extent religious, social, cultural, political and economic realities of specific host contexts impact and shape the *raison d'être, modus operandi* and worldviews of African churches in diaspora.

I. TYPOLOGY OF AFRICAN CHURCHES IN DIASPORA

African churches in the new diaspora reveal a complex variety in terms of their historical origins and development, social composition, geographical distribution, polity, ethics, and liturgical orientations. This religious repertoire can be distinguished under two broad categories, that is, religious communities that exist solely as branches, parishes or mission posts of their mother churches headquartered in Africa; and those which were established independently by Africans living in diaspora. Through their headquarters and branches in Europe and North America, the latter category is expanding to Africa and other parts of the world. In terms of their histories of emergence, belief systems and ritual traditions, a working typology that aggregates the characteristic features of these genres can be outlined as: Mission churches (Methodist, Catholic, Coptic, Orthodox); African Instituted Churches (AIC type such as the Aladura, Kimbanguism); Charismatic/Pentecostal (Classical and Neo-Pentecostals), groups existing within foreign-led churches (such as the African Christian Church, Hamburg under the *Nordelbian Kirche* in Germany). There is also an increasing number of African clergy within or outside mainstream churches ministering solely to African groups. Supportive ministries, fellowship groups and house cells (inter-denominational) is a common feature of the new African religious diaspora. For illustrative purposes, this section presents a sketchy historical trajectory of new African religious communities in diaspora.

II. THE AFRICAN CHURCHES MISSION IN LIVERPOOL, 1931-1964

One of the earliest African churches that took root in Europe in the early twentieth century was the African Churches Mission (ACM), founded in 1931 by the Nigerian-born Daniels Ekarte in Toxteth, one of the slums in Liverpool (UK).[15] The socio-political and economic milieu of Liverpool is important in order to understand the circumstances under which the ACM was born, and how the environment impacted on its growth and development. Liverpool's prosperity in the mid-nineteenth century depended largely on slave economy. The black (African) resident population in Liverpool increased considerably during and after the First European War. One of the fall-outs of this war on Liverpool was the rapid upsurge of unemployment and the abysmal, squalid conditions in which the poor and unemployed lived, coupled with an escalation of racial tensions. Another highly volatile issue with which the Liverpool society had to contend during the war interregnum was that of bi-racial marriages between Africans, African-American seamen, soldiers with English women and the "resultant population of half-caste children." Such a development heightened the already existing racial hostility by the public. This was the socio-cultural, economic and political scenery into and within which the ACM emerged.

Following a spiritual experience in 1922, Ekarte (raised originally under the Scottish Mission in Nigeria) commenced services in private rooms, open-air services with mixed audiences of different cultural persuasions. This practice often brought him into the harsh gaze of local authorities (police). Ekarte also undertook frequent visits to Africans on ships, in lodging houses and hospitals. After switching between several temporary religious spaces, he became concerned with establishing a permanent mission home for his steadily growing group. Through local financial support, a permanent space was acquired through a three-year lease agreement, and Ekarte officially assumed the office of Pastor of the ACM in July 1931. In the 1930s and 1940s, Ekarte became a popular and well-respected figure within both black and white communities, and the ACM grew larger and rapidly assumed a social centre catering to the multifarious needs of many in the immediate community.[16] His activities went beyond the Mission house as he also visited the poor and the needy in their homes, in hospital and in police cells.[17] In defense of the course of Africans living in Liverpool, he often engaged in spirited correspondence with many anonymous, racial letter-writers who expressed ill-feeling about the growing influx of "Negro men, women and children" and inter-marriages. Ekarte took on both religious and extra-religious roles as he became involved in social, philanthropic, humanitarian as well as overtly political activities in both local and international circles.

His engagement in the brawl for equal wages and better working conditions for African seamen in Liverpool put him ostensibly on a collision course with the local authorities and the city's shipping companies, and visited dire consequences on Ekarte and the ACM. The ACM and its activities under Ekarte came to further limelight in the post-Second European War as it struggled to deal with one of its attendant consequences, that is, the "illegitimate" children resulting from the presence of thousands of allied troops in the United Kingdom and their illicit relationships with English women. His interest in transforming the Mission into a Children's Home as well as rehabilitating women with colored illegitimate babies was largely hampered by financial constraints. The distrust and suspicion by the local authorities of an African who believed fervently in "racial equality, self-help and who openly castigated those responsible for the rape of Africa," led to a dismal failure in his long-term objectives of providing better educational facilities for Black youngsters, a permanent home and a better equipped social centre for abandoned children and the down-trodden in British society. On June 3, 1949, the Mission house was ordered closed, the children forcefully transferred to the city's children home and Ekarte barred from any further contacts with them. Ekarte became and remained a hero in the eyes of many Africans and a suspect in the eyes of many others. The life of the Mission continued as a struggle for survival, until the building housing it was demolished on the order of the local authorities in 1964. Even though Ekarte was moved to a new home, this devastation was too much for him to bear. He survived only a few weeks, and he met his death on 12 July 1964. The Mission did not die with Ekarte, services continued to be held under new leadership until the late 1970s when it gradually fizzled out.

III. AFRICAN CHURCHES IN THE 1960S AND BEYOND

The 1960s was the period when many African countries attained selfhood and political independence from European colonial hegemony. During this time, a new crop of African migrants charted new routes into the diaspora. These were no longer enslaved Africans, seamen, domestic workers or soldiers as experienced in the inter-wars era or during the immediate aftermath of the war. This new stream of migrants largely comprised African students sent or commissioned to pursue further studies abroad, civil servants, businessmen, and diplomats deployed to newly-established African embassies and consulates in foreign countries. As they settled in the new contexts, many became involved in religious activities that either led to the establishment of new branches of their home churches back in Africa or even the founding of new ones. The most popular of the churches established in Europe in the 1960s and 1970s was what has been popularly referred to as African Instituted Churches (AICs). AICs, such as the Aladura, have come to represent a very significant factor in the contemporary life situation of the African diaspora. The planting overseas of this brand of Christianity, influenced by African culture, could be said to have emerged only from the 1960s, first in Great Britain (UK),[18] and afterwards in continental Europe. They have increasingly made their footprints more visible on the European religious landscape since the establishment in London of the first branches of the Church of the Lord-Aladura (1964), Cherubim & Seraphim (1965), and the Celestial Church of Christ (1967). It was from here that other branches, as well as their new splinter formations, spread to other parts of Europe and North America. Another Aladura category in diaspora is those that have emerged in Europe, either by severing from an already existing one, or that which emanates from the charismatic quality of a leader. An example of the latter is the Aladura International Church founded in London by Olu Abiola.

Another variant of African Christianity which had its foothold in diaspora was the Coptic Orthodox Church planted by migrants from Egypt.[19] A tenth of the over 10 million Copts migrated from the mid-1950s and 1970s to North America, Europe, Canada, Australia and the Arab world as an escape from religious discrimination and persecution in Egypt during the last half of the twentieth century. They established churches, cultural centers that became places of worship, retreat and social gatherings. The earliest Coptic churches established in the North American diaspora were in Toronto (1964), Los Angeles (1969) and in Jersey City (1970). The monasteries built by the Copts in the USA, Germany and Australia are also serving as pilgrimage sites in the diaspora. Coptic Orthodox theological seminaries have been established in the USA and Australia. Bishops and priests were consecrated by Pope Shenouda III in Cairo for specific religious services in the diaspora. About 60 Coptic Bishops have been assigned to govern dioceses within and outside Egypt such as in Israel, Sudan, western Africa, Europe and the United States.

The religious geography of African churches in diaspora is most spectacular in the 1980s and 1990s. The increasing emigration of Africans has occasioned a concomitant proliferation of new religious communities in diaspora. The religious landscape is increasingly undergoing transformation and diversification with the most recent entry of African-led Pentecostal/Charismatic movements. What started with a few groups in the late 1970s is now characterized by a complex plurality. It is with the Pentecostal/Charismatic variety that African churches have witnessed the most remarkable geographical spread and multiplication in diaspora. This includes large groups with headquarters in Africa, such as the Redeemed Christian Church of God (RCCG), the Deeper Christian Life Ministry (DCLM), both with their headquarters in Nigeria, and the Church of Pentecost International (CPI) with headquarters in Ghana. There are also several African-led churches that started in various parts of Europe, such as the Christian Church Outreach Mission International (CCOMI) led by Bishop Dr. Abraham Bediako (Hamburg), the Kingsway International Christian Centre (KICC) led by Matthew Ashimolowo (London). In recent times, African churches have extended their domains into Eastern Europe (former USSR). An example is the Embassy of the Blessed Kingdom of God for All Nations (formerly known as the Word of Faith Bible Church), founded by Sunday Odulaja in Kiev, Ukraine.[20]

This religious mosaic of the African diaspora is further characterized by African groups, clergy and laity existing within foreign churches. Examples include the African Christian Church, Hamburg under the *Nordelbian Kirche* in Germany, African groups within the American and European mainstream churches such as the Episcopal, Anglican, Methodist, Lutheran and Catholic. There are growing numbers of Nigerian Roman Catholic and Anglican priests in the USA, Tanzanian Lutheran and Ghanaian Methodist priests in Germany. African priests and ministers in these churches are sometimes employed by the host churches, but have the African congregations as their primary constituency. This exportation of clergy and missionaries on "reverse-mission" from Africa to the diaspora demonstrates the stature of Africa as an emerging global theatre of Christianity. Another growing feature within the African religious diaspora is the proliferation of para-churches, supportive or inter-denominational ministries. Freelance evangelists and short-term missionaries from Africa embark on frequent visits to a network of churches overseas. Such Ministries associated with Abubakar Bako, Omo Okpai are characterized by somewhat loose, flexible and non-formalized organizational hierarchies and administrative structures. Such freelancing is carried out within and between African and other Pentecostal/Charismatic church circles under the rubric of evangelism and intra-religious networks. The conscious missionary strategy by mother churches in Africa of evangelizing the diaspora is a relatively recent one. Diaspora has been a key aspect to their response to European mission. The "reverse flow" initiative which entails sending African missionaries abroad came as a backdrop of the moratorium by the Lutheran World Foundation. The moratorium call was designed, among other things, to awaken the Third World peoples to their responsibility, creating new goals and of formulating a viable evangelical strategy towards Europe.[21] In the early 1980s, Tanzanian Lutheran pastors were sponsored to serve in various parishes in Germany. The reverse-mission agenda is becoming a very popular feature among African churches, with pastors and missionaries commissioned to head already existing branches or establish new ones in diaspora.

IV. SOCIAL-ETHNIC CONFIGURATION

Most African churches that came to be established in diaspora from the 1960s were the initiative of a few individual students, or people on business and official assignments who had no intention of residing permanently abroad. This group, made up of few members met and worshiped together in "house cells or fellowships" and later transformed into full-fledged branches with acquired or leased properties as religious buildings. In some cases, a new branch sought official recognition or affiliation with headquarters in Africa. The demographic change of the migrant communities has slightly altered this original composition in the last two decades. The arrival of migrant families and the birth of children (first and second generation) has led to a major shift to long-term migrants or settlers. This no doubt has far-reaching implications on the status and growth of some African religious communities.

African churches have demonstrated determination to make global links and make non-Africans targets in their membership drives. A majority of the migrant churches lack a cross-cultural appeal, thus leaving their membership predominantly African. The socialization process of African migrants, whereby they mix and interact mainly with fellow Africans, is another barrier towards the realization of a multi-racial group. In fact, some of them are simply labeled as ethnic or national churches. However, there are a few others that have transcended racial-ethnic precincts to include non-Africans in their membership. The existing non-African element is largely owing to bi-racial couples, friendship and sometimes as a dividend of personal/impersonal evangelism. This membership structure is likely to be transformed and altered in the future if the churches continue to gain inroads more and more into the new religious landscape. The social anatomy of the churches is complex and variegated. The majority of these are not illiterates, but elites of their countries, or those who have ventured out in search for the "golden fleece". In most recent times, the membership of these churches has been characterized by skilled and unskilled factory workers, the unemployed, asylum seekers and refugees. With such a socio-ethnic structure, African churches in diaspora largely remain the locus of identity, community and security primarily for African immigrants.

V. PARADIGMS OF PROLIFERATION

The expansion of African churches in diaspora can be attributed to both remote and immediate factors. The implications of the globalization process, prevailing political and socio-economic conditions of home countries and the economic push in search of "greener pastures", transformations in the technology of communication and transportation, liberalization of immigration laws, immigrants' development of networks and activities have stimulated demographic shifts to Europe and North America. The perceived affluence that magnetizes people from poorer settings, the quest for global connections and representations, the acute need for soul care of immigrant communities in the face of escalating xenophobic tensions and discrimination, migrants' quest for identity, security and spiritual satisfaction in a hostile environment, the niche for material enhancement are explanations for this growing trend. Owing to the ongoing secularization and decline of Christianity, African churches are now targeting what they call the "Dark Europe" to re-evangelize and annex it "for Christ". Some of these groups have also burgeoned owing to the insensitivity of host foreign churches. Many African migrants had assumed that Europeans and Americans would perceive them in the first place as Christians. Upon arrival, they identify with mainstream churches or denominations similar or related to their home churches. The disaffection with drab liturgies, the disappointment and "pastoral" neglect faced in the mainstream churches, resulted in churches with African initiatives and under African leadership. As Olu Abiola, the founder of the Aladura International Church describes his experience:[22]

> As an ordained minister of the Church Missionary Society of Nigeria (Anglican), I attended and worshipped at one of the Church of England near my home the very first Sunday after my arrival in London. But to my surprise, I was told at the end of the service by the officiating minister that I will be much at home with my own kind and he directed me to a Black Pentecostal Church.

John Adegoke, the Spiritual Leader of the Cherubim and Seraphim in Birmingham, had been a member of the Anglican Church back home in Nigeria and even when he came to London in 1964. He had attended the services of the Church of England for about a year. When the first meetings of the Cherubim and Seraphim Church were held, he experienced this as a break-through. Contrasting his experience with his expectation, he remarks:[23]

> Any Nigerian will find the church here different from what he expected. The missionaries came to Nigeria, faking people to live like Christians. But here in England people do not live like Christians, many things are contrary to Christian principles. Sunday is not literally taken as the Christian Sabbath. Nobody has time for the Sunday service, whereas in Nigeria the services are long. You begin to wonder. After suffering for one year, I found people who were interested. I found myself there.

One consequence of such experiences was a greater identity of the African Christians with churches that were more likely to express their interests and sentiments. African churches in diaspora have come to fill a spiritual vacuum and offer "a home away from home" for many disenchanted Africans. The churches also became avenues where people could go and feel important, feel valued. Irrespective of members' cultural backgrounds, a sense of belonging and community was rekindled in the church and a kind of religious and ethnic identity was also engendered through the process.

VI. SOCIAL RELEVANCE AND EXTRA-RELIGIOUS PRISMS

With the proliferation of African churches in virtually all parts of the world, Africa has become fully part of a global cosmos in religious terms. The salience of Christianity has been assisted by African migrant churches in Western societies, particularly Europe, where the insignificance of religion is prevalent. The relevance of African churches is not only located in the unique expression of African Christianity they exhibit, they also constitute international ministries and groups that have implications on a global scale. The impact and import of the "exportation" of African churches, driven by a vision of winning converts, is that it offers a unique opportunity to analyze its impact at local levels such as in diaspora. African churches are yet to make remarkable incursions into the white populations. This lack of a cross-cultural appeal and wherewithal, coupled with a myriad of contextual factors such as accommodation problems, language barriers, hostility of neighbors, poor economic base, fluid membership, status of churches in host contexts, immigration regulations, are largely responsible for this trend. The changing face and character of contemporary migration has occasioned new problems and challenges for African churches in diaspora. However, African churches in diaspora have gained some inroads into the religious life of local mainstream churches. The influence exerted has resulted in joint worship services and programs as well as the "exchange of pulpits". The liturgical revolution of the African churches and their display of charismatic propensities draw some attraction from the local publics.

Many African churches are increasingly taking up extra-religious functions, such as social welfare programs within the diaspora context. Thus, their focus is not only the spiritual wealth of members but their social, material and psychological well-being as well. Beyond their church vicinity, they have taken up functions, such as the regeneration and rehabilitation of drug-ridden youths in the society, the socially displaced, under-privileged, refugees, asylum seekers. African churches in diaspora today display a significant model of African Christianity in the way they organize themselves, with features emanating from both their new contexts as well as their African heritage. Their character and maturity are evident as they have grown to acquire immense properties and real estate. For instance, the Embassy of God Church acquired between 15 and 51 hectares of land (total area: 140,000 square meters) in Kiev to erect a magnificent edifice for multi-religious purposes.[24] The Redeemed Christian Church of God, North America, recently acquired a multimillion dollar property of over 250 hectares of land in Dallas, Texas, for the construction of a Redemption Camp in the US similar to the Nigerian camp located on the Lagos-Ibadan Expressway.[25] The KICC plans "to build a 5,000-seater church building and a four floor office—a state-of-the-art facility to provide: 5,000 seats for worship, 1,000 place children's church, 600 place teenage church, a counseling and prayer centre, class rooms for Bible School, 100 place nursery, 400 seater restaurant, a fully equipped gym, a place for the total healing of the total man and the total nation."[26] In many large cities, such as London, New York, Hamburg, Paris, Köln, Amsterdam, Berlin, erstwhile warehouses,[27] abandoned church buildings, cinemas, disco halls and pub houses have been acquired at huge financial costs. Some were procured outrightly, while others were leased or rented for several years.

There is a growing acquisition and renegotiation of space, whereby "desecrated space" is acquired and resacralized for ritual ends. There are further examples of African churches that have erected buildings[28] of their own or those who currently lease and use hotel premises as temporary ritual space pending the acquisition of a permanent place. Some churches have also acquired fleets of cars and buses, which are either used by members for church official purposes, or for commercial purposes as hire/rentals. Business centers, lodging and accommodation, religious book centers, guidance and counseling units, recreation and rehabilitation centers, cyber cafes and computer training centers, musical halls, video and audio cassette shops, and shopping malls are also owned by these churches. The KICC and the Embassy of God are examples of African churches that have even proposed religious banks to "empower God's people economically, and promote the Kingdom of God."[29] Such extra-religious activities no doubt have immense religious, social and economic import for the churches as well as for the immediate environment and communities in which they are located. This development suggests that some of these churches have come of age in this new cultural environment.

VII. NEW MEDIA, CORPORATE PROFILING AND RECRUITMENT STRATEGY

African churches in diaspora are increasingly appropriating new communication technologies[30] in the transmission of their religious messages. Although the use of media is not at all a novel feature, what is new is their deliberate effort towards making their presence known and felt on the World Wide Web. While the church web sites act as a new and relatively effective means of outreach to the larger community, most of these groups who appropriate it do so in order to also draw potential clientele. Such intentions are clearly portrayed in their introductory statements. The Celestial Church of Christ (CCC)[31] seeks to create a global network through the use of Internet websites and electronic mail.[32] In a "web release" in 1997, announcing its (Riverdale, USA site) presence on the Internet, it stated *inter alia*,

> Halleluiah!!! ... Celestial Church of Christ now has a dominant presence on the World Wide Web. The main focus of this page is to present a unified and cohesive communication vehicle for Celestial Church as a whole, world-wide ... As the web site evolves, we hope to use it as a vehicle to communicate news about Celestial Church of Christ on a global basis, both information geared toward Celestians and non-Celestians alike.

The UK site complements this objective through its mission statement which partly states:

> To introduce CCC to the whole world ... to bring all the parishes together by obtaining free e-mail addresses for interested parishes and contribute to the free flow of information in the church ... to use the medium of the Internet as a vehicle to recruit new members....

In the Redeemed Christian Church of God (RCCG)[33] Internet Outreach, the introductory statement on the Parish directory states *inter alia*:

> Over the years The Redeemed Christian Church of God has experienced an explosive growth with branches being planted all over the world. It has become pertinent to create a directory and online data base for all The Redeemed Christian Church of God parishes worldwide ... This will enable us to do a complete, relational online database that will be useful for the Body of Christ. Furthermore online database will help us in our evangelism, fellowship and interaction among member parishes. It will also serve to assist travelers in their efforts to find a place of worship wherever they find themselves.

Members' visions and goals, as expressed in the RCCG "Mission Statement", includes:

> It is our goal to make heaven. It is our goal to take as many people as possible with us. In order to accomplish our goals, holiness will be our lifestyle. In order to take as many people with us as possible, *we will plant churches within five minutes walking distance in every city and town of developing countries; and within five minutes driving distance in every city and town of developed countries.* We will pursue these objectives until every nation in the world is reached for JESUS CHRIST OUR LORD.

Although, these goals may appear somewhat ambitious, idealistic and utopian to attain, yet one point of significance here is the fact that the church has demonstrated optimism and enthusiasm towards the realization of its global vision. The church is not only concerned with the local setting but what transpires beyond it, within so-called "developing" and "developed" countries. The recourse by African churches in diaspora to new, alternative evangelistic strategies is intricately tied to new, global socio-cultural realities. The somewhat individualistic nature of Western societies for instance has largely rendered some of the known conventional modes inept and far-less productive. Thus, the "personal" modes of communication (i.e. door to door, street to street, market-place and bus evangelism) is giving way systematically to more "impersonal", "neutral" modes (i.e. computer web sites, electronic mail, fax). The relevance and urgency which these alternative modes of communication demand in the western context, lends credence to why virtually all the web sites of these churches have been established, developed and maintained in Europe, USA or elsewhere outside Africa.

VIII. LOCAL-GLOBAL NETWORKS

The import of local and global networks among these churches in Africa and in diaspora cannot be over-emphasized. The trans-national linkages between them, in the "home" (African) and the "host" societies are assuming increasing importance for African migrants. The range and nature of these ties include intra-religious networks and new ecumenical affiliations, such as the Council of Christian Communities of an African Approach in Europe (CCCAAE).[34] The scope of these trans-relations and networks also include "pastoral exchanges"[35] between Africa and the diaspora, or through special religious events and conferences, prayer networks, Internet sites, International ministries, publications, video, tele-evangelism. African churches in diaspora frequently organize religious events that are local in nature but which have a global focus that links the local church with other churches globally. The increasing vigor geared towards charting and maintaining intra-religious networks is linked to religious, social, political as well as economic concerns. The motivations for joining or engaging in intra-religious networks are complex and vary. Most African churches often locate this tendency as a vital strategy for global mission and evangelism. Others undertake such processes as a necessary way of acquiring status improvement within the host society.

IX. NEGOTIATING IDENTITY

Demographic variables indicate that the Africans, who make up the majority membership of African churches in diaspora, often come from different socio-ethnic backgrounds and varied religious affiliations. Within the new religious space, they operate on new levels of organization where doctrinal differences and ethnic exigencies do not seem to serve as the most vital reference point. Rather, what is important for the Africans in this case is simply a place to share similar sentiments, "a place to feel at home" or "a home away from home", thereby establishing a frame of reference for the preservation, transformation and transmission of their specific local religious traditions. As religious and ethnic identities are intricately intertwined, they may sometimes defy any clear-cut demarcation. The complex cultural diversities and historical specificities of the African continent renders the notions of "African identity" and "religious identity" too simplistic to be taken unilaterally. A collective identity "African" is undoubtedly not a fundamental issue among most Africans within their continental shores. However, beyond the continent, the urge for collective representation comes to assume immense meaning and relevance thus coalescing the several, multiple identities (ethnic, religious, class, gender) into what may seem a complex whole—African identity.

Similar to the issue of African identity is the corollary of religious identity. The membership structure of most African churches in diaspora evinces an interpretation of varied levels of religious identity. Members emerge from wide-ranging religious backgrounds and orientations to form a new religious diaspora identity. One level of interpretation is that, while not undermining the factor of individual choice and preferences, the specific religious, political, socio-cultural circumstances and climatic factors in the host contexts are quintessential factors, which dictate and impact on the nature of identity—single or multiple—forged and desired by African migrants. Religious identities are not necessarily static and fixed, but susceptible to change and transformation depending on a legion of factors. People often engage in switching religious affiliation or (re)negotiating religious identities. Three levels of African diaspora Christians can be distinguished: those who became Christians for the first time while residing in diaspora; members who swap religious denominational affiliations; and those who consciously maintain dual or multiple religious affiliations and identities. In the last category, for instance, a member remains a bona fide Catholic in the home context, but takes up membership of a Pentecostal or an Aladura-type church while residing temporarily or indefinitely in the diaspora. Such a member sees no problem with combining these two traditions, although occurring in different socio-cultural contexts. These various levels of religious action are largely occasioned by a multiplicity of factors, ranging from specific spiritual/visionary experiences, unavailability of their home church in the new context, and the spiritual quest for panacea to existential problems. Other explanations include exigent factors, insensitivity of host historical churches, xenophobia and other prevailing socio-economic, cultural and political circumstances.

CONCLUSION

This chapter describes the incipience and consolidation of African brand of Christianity in diaspora by locating it within different historical epochs. The incursion of African churches is significant as a major constituent of the religious mosaic of diaspora communities. African migrant churches have helped in the resuscitation and reconfiguration of Christianity, and contribute to the increasing religious diversification witnessed in the host Western societies. It demonstrates how African churches, through their developmental processes, have become more and more variegated in their social composition, membership structure, as well as in their modes of operation. The host socio-cultural, economic and political milieu largely impacts on and shapes the nature, course, and scope of African churches in diaspora. Thus, within the locus of changing, more complex migration trends and policies, these collective religious representations will continue to assume immense meaning and relevance particularly for African immigrants as the churches serve both as loci for identity, security, as well as avenues for adapting into the host socio-cultural and religious society.

Notes

1. Hans W. Debrunner, *Presence and Prestige: Africans in Europe. A History of Africans in Europe before 1918* (Basel: Basler Afrika Bibliographien, 1997).
2. Paul Gilroy, *The Black Atlantic: Modernity and Double Consciousness* (Boston: Harvard University Press, 1993).
3. Paul Tiyambe Zeleza, "Contemporary African Migrations in a Global Context", in *African Issues*, XXX, 1 (2002) 9.
4. Debrunner, *Presence and Prestige*, 7.
5. See Zeleza, "Contemporary African Migrations", 9-14. He cautions that although the number of international migrants has grown significantly in absolute numbers since the 1960s, the percentage of people who have left and remained outside their countries of origin has been remarkably steady and small.
6. Stephen Castles & Mark Miller, *The Age of Migration: International Population Movements in the Modern World* (New York: The Guilford Press, 2003[3rd Ed.]), 139.
7. Despite Britain's massive export of migrants, its immigrant population has historically been lower than that of France. Foreigners made up 3.2 % of its total population between 1986 and 1990, and 3.4 % between 1994 and 1996. Immigrants from Western and Eastern Africa increased from 79,000 in 1984 to 127,000 in 1995; 69,000 were women. In the 1990s migrants from Africa and the Indian subcontinent accounted for the largest group undertaking naturalization. Between 1993 and 1996, 32,400 Africans were granted citizenship in the United Kingdom, out of a total of 173,400 citizenship grants. As for the labor force, in 1996 African immigrants composed 10 % of the total foreign labor force, estimated at a little

over 2 million, as compared with 23 % for those from Asia and 40 % for migrants from the European Union (ZELEZA 2002: 11); *OECD, Trends in International Migration - Annual Report*. 1998 Edition (Paris: OECD 1998), p. 175.

8. In the 1990s more than half of the immigrants into France from non-European Economic Area (EEA) countries came from Africa. Similarly, in 1996, a quarter of the 109,800 foreigners who acquired French citizenship were African nationals and another quarter were Europeans (See Zeleza, "Contemporary African Migrations", 11) and also *OECD, Trends in International Migration - Annual Report*. 1998 Edition (Paris: OECD 1998), 101-107.
9. CASTLES & MILLER, *The Age of Migration*, 152.
10. Zeleza aptly argues that the complex maelstrom of rapidly changing international migration that African migrants, including the intellectual elites (Brain drain syndrome) found themselves has led to what he calls "the racialization of immigrants" in the North. Immigrants become an alibi for national failings; their presence serves as both threads that tie together and threats that tear asunder the cherished but increasingly troubled marriage between nation and state. See ZELEZA, "Contemporary African Migrations", 10. See also the special issue of *African Issues*, XXX, 1 (2002) devoted to the highly contentious—*brain drain-brain gain* discourse—under the theme "The African 'Brain Drain' to the North: Pitfalls and Possibilities".
11. S. FINDLAY, "Compelled to Move: the Rise of Forced Migration in Sub-Saharan Africa", in M. SIDDIQUE (ed.), *International Migration into the 21st Century* (Cheltenham/Northampton, MA: Edward Elgar, 2001), 275-278.
12. Some of the earliest initiatives by people of African descent and heritage include the African Methodist Episcopal Church, the African Methodist Episcopal Zion Church, the National Baptist Convention of America, and the Presbyterian Church of USA. One of the few remarkable efforts at documenting the histories of these churches was by Carter WOODSON, *The History of the Negro Church* (Washington D.C: The Associated Publishers, 1921 [2nd ed.]).
13. See Eric C. LINCOLN & Lawrence H. MAMIYA, *The Black Church in the African American Experience* (Durham: Duke University Press, 1990); Cheryl J. SANDERS, *Saints in Exile: The Holiness-Pentecostal Experience in African American Religion and Culture* (New York: Oxford University Press, 1996); Anne H. PINN & Anthony B. PINN, *Fortress Introduction to Black Church History* (Minneapolis: Fortress Press, 2003).
14. See Larry MARTIN, *The Life and Ministry of William J. Seymour and a History of the Azusa Street Revival* (Joplin: Christian Life Books, 1999).
15. Marika SHERWOOD, *Pastor Daniels Ekarte and the African Churches Mission* (London: The Savannah Press, 1994).
16. In 1934, 380 men and women were "registered" with the Mission and 148 children were on the Sunday School list. By 1936 membership had risen to 558 (see, SHERWOOD, *Pastor Daniels Ekarte*, 32ff.). Apart from the Sunday morning and evening services, the Mission embarked on other activities such as Scouting, music and secondary school classes for the black children. Free meals and temporary accommodation was provided for the poor and homeless (both Black and White) at the expense of the Mission. The Mission became the local centre for the needy.

17. Sherwood notes that one of the Mission's report for 1936 lists 427 hospital visits and 4,213 house calls as well as 430 visits to ships. See, SHERWOOD, *Pastor Daniels Ekarte*, 40.
18. As Nigerians represent one of the largest African immigrants into the UK, the most visible indigenous religious initiative that characterizes their community was the Aladura movement.
19. See El MASRI & Iris HABIB, *The Story of the Copts, The True Story of Christianity in Egypt*, 3 Volumes (End-Time Handmaiden, 1982); B. IBRAHIM & F.N. IBRAHIM, "Zuwanderer nach Deutschland: Das Beispiel der ägyptischen Kopten", in H. KOSCHYK & R. STOLZ, R. (eds), *30 Jahre Zuwanderung. Eine kritische Bilanz* (Landsberg am Lech: Olzog Verlag, 1998), 129-161.
20. See http://www.godembassy.org. This is one of the exceptional African churches in Europe which has a majority non-African membership. More than half of the membership is Ukrainians and Russians.
21. See Ogbu KALU, "Church, Mission and Moratorium", in O. KALU (ed.) *The History of Christianity in West Africa* (London & New York: Longman, 1980), 365-374.
22. See O.U. ABIOLA, "The History of the Aladura International Church", in O.U. ABIOLA, *An Introduction to Aladuraism* (London: n.d), cited in Frieder LUDWIG, "Die Entdeckung der schwarzen Kirchen. Afrikanische und Afro-karibische Gemeinden in England während der Nachkriegszeit", in *Archiv für Sozialgeschichte*, 32 (1992) 136.
23. Interview with John Adegoke (18.10.1991) quoted in LUDWIG, "Die Entdeckung der schwarzen Kirchen", 136.
24. See full details at the church website: www.godembassy.org/eng/projnewbuild_e.shtm
25. See RCCG North America web site at http://www.rccgna.org/news.htm
26. See church website at: http://www.kicc.org.uk/
27. The huge building hosting the International headquarters of the Christian Church Outreach Mission located in the Bergedorf Industrial area in Hamburg is a former abandoned warehouse which the church procured at the cost of 1.5 million Deutsche marks in 1991.
28. The Kingsway International Christian Centre was established in September 1992, and it describes itself as the fastest growing church in the UK and Europe. In August 1998 they relocated to 57 Waterden Road, now called the Miracle Centre, an eight acre-facility that has a 4,000-seater auditorium and parking for more than 1,000 cars. The church is about "to embark upon building a 10,000-seater arena that is to be the first of its kind in Europe."
29. Cf. Christian Bank Project of the Embassy of God, www.godembassy.org/eng/projsbank_e.shtm and KICC' Vision at http://www.kicc.org.uk/.
30. Matthew Ashimolowo, Pastor of the Kingsway International Christian Centre, and his Winning Ways Program is aired daily on Premier Radio (London) and Spirit FM (Amsterdam) and viewed on television by a potential audience of over 200 million in Nigeria, Ghana, Zimbabwe, TV Africa and Europe on the Christian Channel and Inspirational Network.
31. For details on the use of media by the CCC, see A. ADOGAME, *Celestial Church of Christ: The Politics of Cultural Identity in a West African Prophetic-Charismatic Movement* (Frankfurt am Main: Peter Lang, 1999), 82-89.

32. See for instance the website addresses: http://www.celestialchurch.com (operated by a parish in Riverdale, USA); http://www.celestialchurch.mcmail.com (administered from the United Kingdom), and http://mageos.ifrance.com or http://www.ChristianismCelest.com (administered from France). Their electronic mail addresses are webmaster@celestialchurch.com, celestialchurchofchrist@mcmail, and jl_degnide@hotmail.com respectively.
33. See the official website of the RCCG in http://www.rccg.org created and maintained by the RCCG Internet Project, Houston Texas, USA. See also UK parish web sites http://www.jesus-house.org.uk/ and http://www.rccgarea4.org.uk/.
34. See details on the "Council of Christian Communities of an African Approach in Europe" at their website: http://membres.lycos.fr/ccceae/.
35. The RCCG consciously send missionary pastors to Germany and other parts of Europe. A missionary is sent to head an already existing branch without a leader or to establish a new branch. In either case, the missionaries are given full financial backing (salary, honorarium and other related expenses) by the Directorate of Missions at the International headquarters or by any sponsoring parish of the RCCG.

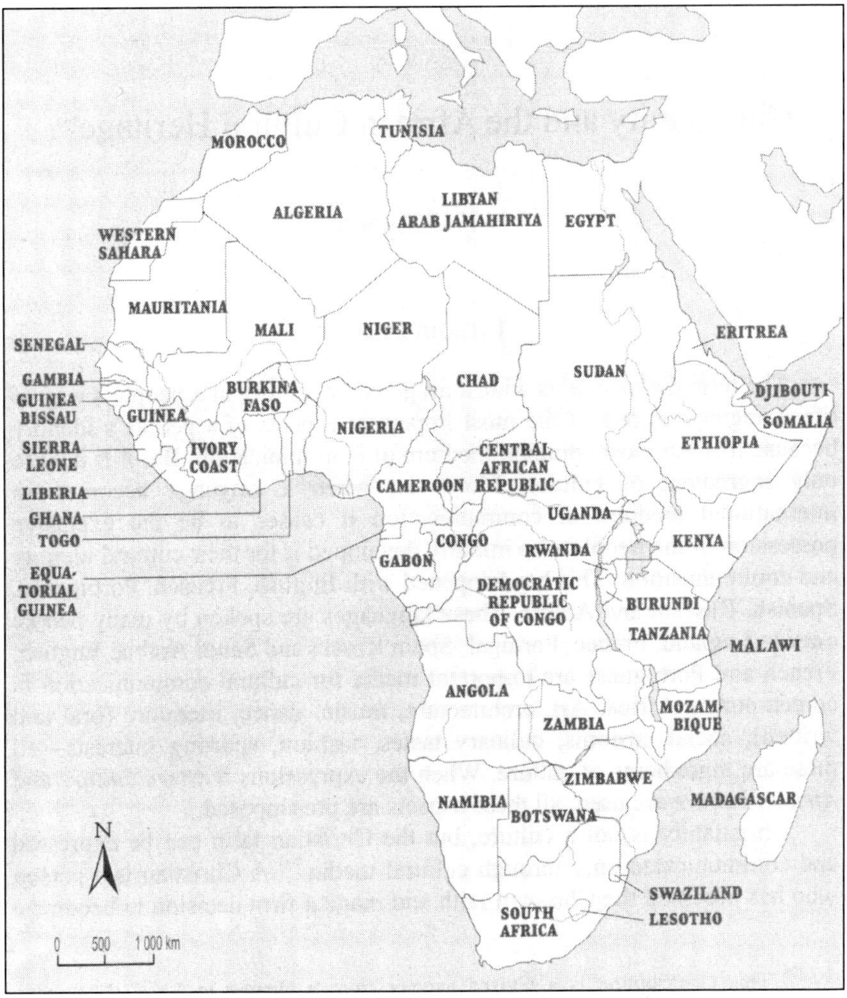

Map 10: Contemporary Africa

Chapter Twenty

Christianity and the African Cultural Heritage

J.N.K. Mugambi

INTRODUCTION

The term *Culture* in its widest usage is the totality of a people's way of life. Language is one of the most important aspects of a people's identity because it is the most common medium of communication. But it is not the only ingredient of culture. Moreover, when a language becomes an international medium of communication it ceases to be the exclusive possession of the people who initially developed it for their cultural identity and communication. This has happened with English, French, Portuguese, Spanish, Russian and Arabic. These languages are spoken by many people outside England, France, Portugal, Spain Russia and Saudi Arabia. English, French and Portuguese are important media for cultural communication in contemporary Africa. Art, architecture, music, dance, literature (oral and written), social customs, culinary tastes, fashion, sporting interests—all these are ingredients of culture. When the expressions *Western culture* and *African culture* are used, all these aspects are presupposed.

Christianity is not a culture, but the Christian faith can be expressed and communicated only through cultural media.[2] A Christian is a person who has accepted the Christian faith and made a firm decision to become a follower of Jesus Christ. To become a Christian is to accept Jesus Christ and His teachings as preserved in the Christian scriptures and maintained by the Church of one's choice. The question as to what constitutes authentic Christian tradition is complicated by the existence of numerous Christian denominations. But there is no doubt that the need for cultural freedom and cultural identity has been an important factor in the establishment of Independent African Churches during the colonial period.[3]

The term *Church* can be loosely defined as the community of people who have accepted the Christian faith and are consciously bound together as a community by the commitment to implement the teaching of Jesus Christ in the world. Christianity affirms that Jesus of Nazareth is Christ the "Son of God", but each church lives this faith according to its understanding of the demands of the Gospel. Each individual adult must decide for himself whether or not to become a Christian. Christians normally desire that their children grow up to become Christians, and each church has developed a system of nurturing children towards adult membership in the church. However, when the children of Christian parents grow up, they have to make up their minds whether or not to remain Christians. Their decision depends very much, on the impact which the Christian faith will have on them during childhood. No person can be forced to remain Christian against one's will. This is one of the remarkable differences between commitment to Christianity and commitment to the African religious heritage. Just as an African cannot choose the ethnic community into which one is born, so it is almost impossible for one to dissociate one's religious heritage from one's total cultural background.

I. CULTURE AS THE MEDIUM OF CHRISTIAN IDENTITIES

Christianity cannot be expressed or communicated without a cultural medium. Any culture can be a medium for the expression and communication of the Christian faith. One missionary scholar likened the Christian faith to a jockey who rides a racing horse as long as the horse is a faster runner. When the horse loses its racing ability, the jockey chooses another horse, and by so doing he remains on the racecourse.[4] Christianity began within the Jewish culture. That culture became incapable of sustaining the Christian faith because the leaders of Judaism believed that the new faith was a threat to the Jewish culture. They tried to contain it within Judaism, but Christianity broke off from Judaism and Jewish culture to become one of the most dynamic religions of the world. Then it was greatly influenced by Greek philosophy, without being swallowed by it. In the fourth century Christianity became the popular religion of the Roman Empire, after the conversion of Emperor Constantine. His edict of Milan in A.D. 313 made Christianity a tolerated religion all over the empire. Christian leaders took advantage of this toleration and began to persecute those who were critical of the Church.

The first great schism in Christianity occurred when Christians from the eastern part of the empire refused to be subjected to the cultural, intellectual, political and theological domination of leaders in the western part of the empire. The Orthodox Churches, which grew independently after this schism, have remained with their own cultural and liturgical identity. The Catholic Church acquired a distinctly Roman character during the Dark Ages and in the Medieval Period. Roman culture was imposed on the peoples of Europe in the name of a Church. During the Reformation the authority of the Pope was challenged, and many national churches mushroomed in Europe. These in turn spread to North America with the immigrants who sailed across the Atlantic in search of freedom and fortune. The modern missionary movement has introduced Christianity to Africa, Asia and the oceanic islands. During the modern missionary enterprise Christianity was riding on western culture. Scholars are now predicting that in the twenty-first century Christianity will be riding on the cultures of Africa and Asia.

Each church portrays the culture in which it has developed. There is no church not culturally bound in this way. The modern missionary enterprise overlooked this fact when it introduced Christianity to Africa. There are no "Christian Cultures". But Christians in a culture can greatly influence that culture. This happened in Europe and in North America. But in both those continents there were, and still are, many people who are not Christians. Lamentably, the modern missionary movement imposed western culture on the peoples who were being evangelized on the assumption that western culture was "Christian", while other cultures were dismissed as "pagan" and "heathen". This was a theological error. The Ecumenical Movement in the twentieth century has greatly contributed towards the correction of that error.[5]

The Christian faith can be effectively expressed and communicated only in "culturally designed" media. If a missionary's work in a culture other than his own is to be effective, he must learn to appreciate the culture of the people whom he wishes to evangelize. He must learn their language and appreciate their art, music, dance, architecture, ritual and all other aspects of that culture. He must identify himself with the community of those whom he is introducing to Jesus Christ. Then he must go further and translate his understanding of the Christian faith into the cultural terms familiar and traditional to his prospective converts. He must be willing to be changed. This is a very difficult task, but effective Christian mission demands nothing less. Saint Paul, one of the greatest missionaries in the history of Christianity, appreciated this demand, and lived up to it. To the Corinthians he said:[6]

> ... For though I am free from all men, I have made myself a slave to all, that I might win the more. To the Jews I became a Jew, in order to win Jews; to those under the law I became as one under the law—though not being myself under the law—that I might win those under the law. To those outside the law I became one outside the law—not being without the law toward God but under the law of Christ—that I might win those outside the law. To the weak I became weak, that I might win the weak. I have become all things to all men, that I might by all means save some. I do it all for the sake of the Gospel, that I may share in its blessing.

It is regrettable that these profound insights from Paul were not heeded in the modern missionary enterprise. The effect of this theological error was that many African converts to the Christian faith were taught to accept the view that becoming a Christian meant adopting the cultural norms of foreign missionaries. Conversion was determined through behavioral norms, in terms of abandoning traditional African customs and adopting western ones. This resulted in a life of double standards among African converts. On the one hand, they accepted the norms introduced by the missionaries who saw nothing valuable in African culture. On the other hand, the converts could not deny their own cultural identity. They could not substitute their denominational belonging for their cultural and religious heritage. Yet they could not become Europeans or Americans merely by adopting some aspects of the missionaries' outward norms of conduct.[7]

II. THE ATTRACTIVENESS OF MISSIONARY TEACHING AMONG AFRICAN CONVERTS

There is no doubt that the appeal of the Christian faith among many African converts was genuine and profound. In Jesus Christ they found new hope and clung to that hope in the face of great challenges which would otherwise have broken their lives, especially in situations of extreme oppression, exploitation and dehumanization during the colonial period.[8] But the affirmation that Jesus identifies himself with their suffering was one thing, and the practical demand of that faith was another. The genuineness of their faith cannot be doubted: only God knows the genuineness of a person's faith. Nor should they be held fully responsible for thinking that their commitment to the Christian faith implied adopting western cultural norms. This was the teaching they had received from the missionary masters. Moreover, their Christian theological awareness was minimal; it was as much as they had received from catechetical classes and from sermons.

Academic schooling for most African converts did not go beyond the acquisition of basic literacy skills, only in their local languages. They could not, therefore, read theological works by theologians of the west, except the few which might have been translated into African languages. Critical theological reflection was not encouraged because the teaching of the missionaries was expected to be accepted without question, as "the whole truth, and nothing but the truth". Missionaries in general ought to have been more modest and followed St. Paul's example.

What should be the proper relationship between Christian identity and a Christian's cultural identity? The dominant missionary opinion in the past has been that Christian identity is identical with western cultural and religious heritage. We have seen that this is a mistaken view. Can an African accept the Christian faith and still retain African cultural identity without leading a life of double standards as was the case in the earlier part of the modern missionary enterprise? This is a question many African Christians ask today. If it is true that the Christian faith changes *all* cultures, then the answer to that question must be positive. Becoming a Christian has nothing to do with adopting the western or any other culture. *Conversion* is not *acculturation.* Conversion to the Christian faith demands that the convert identifies oneself with Jesus Christ and all that He stood for, and that this identification leads the convert to a fundamental change in attitude towards God, oneself and others. Conversion should help the convert to launch a *critical* examination of one's own cultural background. It should lead the convert to review one's personal life, towards a future guided by Jesus Christ. But conversion does not demand a wholesale denunciation or rejection of one's cultural and religious heritage.

III. THE SUNDAY CULT

It has been argued above that Christianity is not a culture, although it was introduced in tropical Africa as if it were an integral part of western culture. In a situation of cultural and religious plurality such as that prevalent in Africa today, Christianity can easily become a *cult,* and this would be a distortion of the Gospel for which the Christian faith stands. Cults integrate the norm of conduct and belief to which all members of those cults must adhere irrespective of the general *culture* in which they live. Within one *culture* there can be many *cults.* Such was the situation in the Graeco-Roman Empire during the first three centuries of the Christian era. The Roman Empire officially regarded Christians as members of one cult among many. It was not until the conversion of Emperor Constantine that it became fashionable in the Roman Empire to become a nominal Christian.

A *church* becomes a *cult* when Christians isolate and insulate themselves from the challenges of the society in which their church has to make a practical impact in order to be faithful to the demands of the Christian mission. During the modern missionary enterprise, this often happened. The *mission station* became the centre of the new cult, with the resident missionary as *its cult leader.* The Christian faith among the African converts then became a Sunday affair. For six days they would live according to their traditional customs, and on Sunday they would wear the new garb they had been given. Dressed in these they would go to the mission station where they would sing new hymns and become involved in a strange ritual. To many an African, the Christian faith appeared irrelevant. If it were concerned with what the convert did on Sunday, would it make any serious difference whether or not a person became a committed Christian? *Classroom Religion* and *Sunday Religion* are labels which fit this kind of Christian expression. But cultic expressions of the Christian faith are a distortion of the "Kingdom of God" which Jesus dramatically inaugurated. Jesus spent His public ministry interacting with the ordinary people, especially in the rural areas, rather than in the Temple at Jerusalem—as the leading rabbis did.

Today the same temptation of *cultic detachment* remains an approach Christians would do well to avoid. If Christians choose to detach themselves from the challenges of the society in which they live, the church to which they belong will appear to be a cultic club with exclusive membership, irrelevant to the needs of contemporary society. It is a matter of regret that this happens too often. Jesus mixed with the society of His earthly time, and by so doing He made a profound impact on its members and its culture. If the Church refuses to be soiled by the world in which it lives, then it will be like salt which has lost its taste (Mattew 5:13). Pietistic isolation is a disservice to Christian mission, because it encourages the impression, both within and outside the Church, that Christians are qualitatively "better" human beings than all other people. But

Jesus teaches that no one is good except God alone. The fear of "syncretism" is not a convincing excuse for failing to be concerned and involved in solving the problems confronting contemporary society. The public ministry of Jesus is instructive on this point.

Christianity is a religion, which from its beginning sought to transcend particular cultures, in the sense that the Gospel (related to the Old Testament background) was not tied to the Hebrew cultural heritage. Jesus called for a new way of life in which all social barriers would be transcended, so that all people would regard each other as brothers and sisters and treat each other as such (e.g. Mark 3:31-35; Luke 8:19-21; Mattew, 25:31-46). This teaching was, and is, universally relevant.[9] At the same time, however, Christianity throughout its history has become accepted and expressed within the cultural heritage of its followers in various parts of the world. As early as the Medieval Period, Christianity became so integrated in the European cultural heritage that the concept of "Christendom" developed. The modern missionary movement of the nineteenth and twentieth century, which introduced Christianity to the interior of East Africa, grew within the background in which the Christian religion and western culture were incorporated to form a "Christian civilization".[10] Thus when Christianity reached East Africa the distinction was not obvious, both to missionaries and to their converts, between the Gospel as a message with a universal challenge, and the particularly European cultural response to the challenge.

In the establishment of Christianity there have been at least three significant aspects worth noting. The first is the Gospel message whose core is the teaching of Jesus Christ as recorded in the gospels and passed on in the tradition of the Church. The second is the western culture, in which the Gospel was expressed for a long time before the rise of the modern missionary movement and the spreading of European and North American denominations—which formed a part of missionary activity in tropical Africa. The third aspect is the African heritage in the totality of which the African converts lived before their encounter with Christianity. This third aspect includes the African religious beliefs that embodied the African traditional understanding of physical and metaphysical reality.

The term *culture*, used in the broadest sense, refers to "that part of the total repertoire of human action and its products, which is socially, as opposed to genetically, transmitted".[11] Only some aspects of culture are considered below. Christianity is a spiritual religion. The Bible is central as the basis of Christian doctrine. Reading it and interpreting its message are central aspects of Christian worship. In the introduction of the faith to Africa, it became necessary to teach the converts to read and write so that they might be able to read the Bible for themselves. The liturgies were also written, and the converts needed to be able to follow them in worship. Hence literary schooling became a very important aspect of missionary activity in Africa.[12] Schools were built, in which prospective converts were taught to read and write, and having acquired these skills they would be introduced to the Bible. From these schools the first generation of catechists, teachers, pastors and evangelists were trained. In these schools also basic skills were taught, which would enable the converts to become carpenters, masons, better farmers, dressers and so on.[13]

This form of schooling was characteristically different from traditional African education.[14] The school became an institution to which the interested Africans went in order to acquire literacy and the new skills which had become necessary in the new situation. At first, the schools did not attract much interest because it was seen as a distraction from the traditional way of life. As it became clearer that the traditional life could not go on unchanged, the school became more and more popular.[15] Traditionally there had been no institution equivalent to the school. Children would receive their basic instruction and training at home from their parents, grandparents and other relatives. At puberty they would be given further social education in the process of the ceremonies which they would undergo in connection with initiation. After marriage, the councils of elders would provide means by which men and women would increase their wisdom and experience, while participating in the decision-making process for the welfare of their community.[16]

Often the mission schools preceded the church building. Classrooms would be used as initial meeting places for worship, until the congregation was large enough to necessitate the construction of a large and more special place of worship. Hence the school became a very important institution for the recruitment of converts during the early part of missionary activity.[17] This development led to the impression, among Africans, that becoming a Christian was synonymous with acquiring the skills of literacy.[18] This was the case to begin with. Later on, however, the need for literacy grew beyond the urge for conversion to Christianity. It was soon realized that the new employment opportunities needed basic literacy skills. These would be required in the school, and most of the schools were provided and managed by societies in their programs of evangelization.

The interests of the denominational schools and those of the pupils and parents were not necessarily congruent. For example, as far as the missionary societies were concerned, the school was an institution for both Christian instruction and the preparation of African pupils for new employment opportunities under colonial rule. The main interest of the pupils, and their parents, was to obtain the latter. This point is illustrated, for example, by the fact that as the demand for schooling grew, Africans did not mind which denominational schools they or their children attended, provided they would receive effective instruction to enable them to pass examinations which would qualify them for better-paid jobs. Hence it was not unusual for Protestant parents to take their children to Catholic schools if they were convinced that better instruction was available there. On the other hand, every pupil was expected to follow, at least outwardly, the denominational traditions of the school attended, irrespective of one's previous denominational background. With the passing of examinations and employment as priorities, pupils would have to follow these denominational traditions and give a good impression to the missionary managers, even though one might not be religiously committed to them. The African catechists and evangelists, who occupied a central role in the early development of instruction in denominational schools, served the respective missionary societies that owned these schools. If a catechist or evangelist were dismissed from their services of one denomination, one could transfer allegiance and services to another missionary society, taking advantage of the competitive attitude that was the main feature of early missionary activity.

These two points illustrate that the view of African converts was that denominational allegiance was not of paramount importance as far as schooling was concerned. What mattered most was good training as the means to a job. For the missionaries, what mattered beyond general schooling and training was "good" Christian instruction to increase the number of converts to their respective denominations. Reading and writing were not part of the cultural heritage of the peoples in the interior of East Africa. The introduction of Christianity was accompanied by the introduction of literacy. The African cultural and religious heritage was passed on orally from generation to generation, and the wisdom of the ancestors was conserved not in written books but in songs and oral traditions.[19] Hence the coming of Christianity as a "Religion of the Book" was a new religious experience as well as a new cultural innovation.

The skills of reading and writing which were learned at the mission stations and mission schools became useful not only for the new religious purposes, but also for the general adaptation to the new cultural situation which had developed. Although not everyone could read and write, the literate Africans were able to learn from books other than the Bible, especially when they became proficient in languages such as English, French and Latin. Their acquired knowledge, in addition to that which they had received in their traditional up-bringing, enabled them to become leaders in the cultural changes that were already taking place.[20] Literacy has continued to be an important felt need in Africa as one of the basic tools necessary for development. In view of this fact, literacy, though it came with Christianity and was at first provided mainly by missionary societies as a means of evangelization, became a distinct factor worthy to be considered on its own with regard to cultural change in Africa. Those who could read the Bible and the Catechism could also read other books. Those who could write sermons could also write other things, and those who could count the number of converts they had made, could also utilize their arithmetical knowledge in other spheres of life.

IV. CHURCH AND FAMILY

Christianity came with the teaching that the Church is to be understood as a new family whose head and centre is Jesus Christ. This new family is not based on kinship, clans or ethnic identity. Neither is it based on racial origins or social status. Primarily, it is founded upon faith in Jesus Christ, and its cohesion is maintained with the Church whose individual members are expected to live according to the new relationships as proclaimed by the gospel.[21] The early missionaries first recruited to the mission station young unmarried individuals and instructed them according to the missionary emphasis on the individual salvation of *souls.* A problem arose when these unmarried converts felt a need to get married. If they could not find Christian spouses, what were they to do? The most feasible solution was for the missionaries to develop the concept of the "Christian Home" and urge converts to encourage their spouses to become Christians if they were not already converts.[22]

Marriage was and continues to be regarded as a very important aspect in the development of the Church, in the sense that the socialization of children in the life of the Church would begin at home.[23] Hence the concept of a "Christian home" became a new idea in African cultural life.[24] Christian homes were to become the nuclei of the new wider family, the Church. This did not always work, because the children of the converts would have to choose when they grew up whether or not to follow the faith of their parents. Marriage and Christianity came to be understood as neo-local, so that the wedded couple would set up a new home, leaving the household of their parents.[25] The basic family unit became the husband, his one wife, and their children if any were born.

In the African cultural heritage, the marriage between two individuals was understood as a means of initiation or cementing the union of the households and clan from which the couple belonged. Hence, the individual man and woman intending to marry needed the approval of their respective parents and relatives. The established family sanctions regarding marriage had to be observed if a marriage was to be allowed to take place. For example, no man or woman belonging to an exogamous clan would be allowed to marry within his own clan, no matter how distant the blood-relationship, and no matter how strong the affection might be.[26] The transactions of marriage were carried out at two levels, first between the couple, and then between the households. Relatives and age-mates wanted to feel like they were participating at the second level of the marriage transactions. Moreover, marriage was understood as a process taking many years to complete. The relationship between the man's household and that of his wife or wives was expected to continue without end in normal circumstances—which included the birth of children.[27]

Among African Christians, the two concepts of "family" are maintained. At one level they belong to the ecclesial family which cuts across kinship ties and unites peoples of varied backgrounds in one faith and common ecclesial life. At another level and at the same time, they belong to their kinship groups, although the social links in the extended family may not be as strong as they used to be. Kinship ties, if they are known, are acknowledged irrespective of whether the relatives are Christians or not. Thus it is recognized that kinship relations are a social fact which a person cannot choose, whereas one becomes a member of the ecclesial family through his option to become a Christian.[28]

The concept of monogamous Christian homes as the nuclei of the ecclesial family presented significant challenges for African churches. Although not all marriages were polygamous, the churches had to decide whether or not the men and women living in polygamous union would be allowed to become members of the church. The common rule was that the husband should abandon all wives except the first one. This would mean the future welfare of the wives and children that might be abandoned would be shaken. There was no easy solution to this problem. This issue has continued to be discussed in the churches as an important pastoral challenge.[29] It should be noted, however, that the question of admitting into church membership converts living in polygamous families is a distinct issue from the suggestion that polygamy be an acceptable general principle.

V. RITES OF PASSAGE

The rites of passage are the communal ceremonies performed as an individual passes from one stage to another: at birth, adolescence, adulthood and death. They are expressions of the understanding and expectations of communities regarding the role of the individual in society.

a) Birth

In the African heritage there were rituals of thanksgiving and welcoming the new-born child. The child would be named according to the established customs of the community. For example, a child might be named after an important event that had taken place around the time of birth, after the season or time of day in which birth took place. Also, a child might be named after a relative in the family of its father or mother. Among the communities in which the latter custom was followed, there were some guidelines to indicate which of the relatives would be named, and which order the children would be given the names of such relatives.[30] The birth of a child was a great joy to the whole family and the whole clan. Relatives and friends would come to visit the mother and the child for many months after delivery, and there would be much feasting to express that joy, congratulate the mother and help restore her health by bringing food and drinks, and temporarily relieving her of the work at home.[31]

The traditional rituals concerning the birth of a child were eventually different from those which came with Christianity. Prayers of thanksgiving, for example, would include reference to the deity, spirits and ancestors. The ancestors would be beseeched to keep the child healthy and remove any curses which might negatively affect his life. They would be requested to bless the child and guide him to grow in wisdom, courage, generosity and in any other values which were cherished by the community.

Christianity introduced new rituals concerning the growth of the individual in the context of the Church, from birth to death. With regard to birth, Christian parents would be expected to take their new-born child to the Church for thanksgiving.[32] The ceremony of thanksgiving was an expression of appreciation to God for the gift of the child, for its safe delivery and health condition of the mother. In the ceremony the child and its parents would be committed to God's care and guidance. Prayers would be made that the child might grow up to be a faithful Christian who would become an active member of the Church. Unlike the traditional thanksgiving—which was spontaneous and impromptu, the Christian liturgy would normally be written, and the parents would be guided through it by the priest. Their responses through the service would be indicated in the liturgy. This ceremony continues to be an aspect of the life of the Church, and in some denominations it is linked with the practice of infant baptism.

Infant baptism is practiced as the wish of the parents that the child will grow up within the setting of the Church. A "god-parent" is chosen to become the sponsor of the child at the ceremony, and takes the vows of initiation into the Church on the child's behalf. The "god-parent" is expected to ensure that the child whom he has sponsored for baptism will be brought up in Christian instruction and that when the child grows up he will learn the catechism of the Church and be confirmed as a full member. Baptism as a Christian sacrament is more than what has been stated above. According to the Anglican catechism, for example, "god-parents" make three promises to God on behalf of the infant being baptized:[33]

i) that while growing up the child will renounce the devil and fight against evil;
ii) that he will believe and hold fast the Christian faith and put his trust on Christ as Lord and Savior; and
iii) that he will obediently keep God's commandments and serve Him faithfully, all the days of his life. At confirmation, the child is expected to express that same ready acceptance publicly before the Church.

This ceremony of infant baptism is also associated with the giving of new names. In the beginning, the names given at baptism were normally those of biblical characters and saints such as Moses, Joshua, Elijah, Peter, Paul, Augustine, Anthony, Anselm. The idea behind this practice was that those who were baptized would be frequently reminded to order their lives in a Christian way, following the example of the characters whose names they had been given. Later on, however, this principle of choosing such names was not rigidly followed, and normally European names were allowed. The popular consequence of this practice has been that baptism is often understood more as a re-naming ceremony than as a central sacrament of the Church. The concept of "Christian names" seems to have overshadowed the sacramental significance of baptism in the sense that the acquisition of a noticeably new name came to be popularly understood as a mark of becoming a Christian.[34] Some of the customs concerning birth have continued as part of the life of African Christians. The naming of children as discussed above is an illustrative example of such continuation. A child born of Christian parents may have two names, one of which will have been chosen according to the traditional customs, and the second given at baptism.

b) Initiation

Adolescence, marked outwardly by the physical changes of puberty, was another stage at which a rite of passage would be performed. The community would prepare the adolescent socially, psychologically and religiously for the next stage of growth in the life of the community—adulthood. In the initiation into adulthood, the adolescents (both boys and girls) would be guided through a series of experiences contrived for that purpose, to learn the implication of the puberty changes. One was expected by the community to conduct oneself responsibly, without degrading oneself and one's family. The rite would include a physical ordeal which the adolescent was expected to go through courageously as proof of readiness to leave childhood behind and enter adulthood with maturity. In some communities, for example, circumcision was practiced as part of the initiation rite.[35]

The fundamental significance of initiation for the total African cultural life was not fully realized by most missionaries. For some of them, the practices were considered to be unnecessary ordeals, causing great suffering to the adolescents. In African traditional life, however, the education and training which was given during initiation was vital for the community's maintenance of its self-understanding, and for providing every individual with the opportunity to learn what the community expected of him.[36] Initiation was understood differently in Christianity, in the sense that the admission into full membership of the Church did not involve any physical ordeals, although there were catechetical procedures for preparation of converts towards maturity in the Christian faith. The test for readiness for confirmation in the Church was the extent to which the converts understood the doctrines outlined in the catechism, and their willingness to conduct themselves according to the expectations of the Church. Thus, whereas initiation in the African cultural heritage was an inevitable stage in the social development of the individual, in Christianity it would be undergone only by those who in the opinion of the catechist and the priest were doctrinally prepared. The preparation in Christianity mainly involved the recitation of the doctrines stated in the catechism.

Adult baptism and confirmation came to be the Christian rituals through which the converts would be progressively initiated into full membership in the Church.[37] In the main Protestant denominations, only after confirmation would the convert be welcome to participate in the Holy Communion. The principle behind this was that only after going through the catechetical instruction of baptism and confirmation could the converts be able to comprehend the meaning of the Eucharist—the mystery of the suffering of Jesus Christ for the salvation of mankind and the benefits accruing from it.

In traditional life, initiation was a long process involving the whole community and lasting at least several weeks. It was the integral part of the life of the community. The youth of a particular age group would be initiated into adulthood together. Although the traditional process of initiation was not adopted into the life of African churches, African Christians have continued to appreciate the importance of preparing their children for responsible and mature adulthood. However, social change and development of modern education—in which parents can be with their school children for only a quarter of a year during the school holidays—are factors that make the counseling of adolescence, both in school and at home, a great challenge.[38]

c) Marriage

In the African cultural heritage, marriage was one of the most important marks of social adulthood. A man or woman would not be socially recognized as a grown-up without being married, no matter how old he or she might be chronologically.[39] As mentioned above, marriage was a social concern in which the kin of the two bonding families were fully involved. The process of marriage was characterized by rites of transactions through which the marrying individuals were welcomed into social adulthood. Tokens in kind (dowry) were exchanged as part of these transactions, to cement the social relationships and seal the union. Such goods were at first mistakenly considered by some missionaries and anthropologists to be "bride-price" implying that African marriage involved the "buying" of individuals. Marriage in African tradition was very different from slavery. The importance of marriage as a rite of passage supports this statement.[40]

Procreation was very important in the African concept of marriage. A marriage in which children were not born was considered to be problematic, and sometimes a bride might be returned to her parents for such a reason. Polygamy was potentially allowed by custom, especially if an earlier marriage did not produce children, or if the children born in an earlier marriage were only girls. The birth of boys was considered to be very important, both for inheritance and for the defense of the community. It was also important as the means to perpetuate and expand family or clan.[41] Sometimes polygamy was practiced simply because a man could afford it.

Christianity came with a new understanding of marriage. There were three main purposes of marriage according to the Christian teaching. Procreation was one of them. Secondly, marriage was understood as the accepted means of establishing basic companionship among adults of the two sexes. Basing this teaching on the account of creation in the book of Genesis (Chapters 1 & 2), Christianity emphasized that in the beginning God created man and woman to be companion and helpers to one another, and to avoid loneliness. Thirdly, marriage was understood in Christianity as a means of avoiding sin. Adultery was forbidden in Christian teaching, and to make provision for the avoidance of this sin, monogamous marriage was instituted.[42]

Procreation was considered as the subsidiary to the other two purposes of marriage according to Christian teaching. Thus, childlessness was not considered grounds for dissolving a marriage, nor was polygamy allowed because an earlier marriage was childless. In contrast, the African cultural heritage placed great importance on children, and this was an important factor on which the success of a marriage would depend.

The Christian wedding was introduced as a new experience in African cultural and religious life. It was performed in the church, following a liturgy that was new to African religious practice. In the Catholic Church, matrimony was understood as one of the seven sacraments.[43]

African Christians accepted the Christian teaching about marriage and celebrated Christian weddings as the climax of the social marriage rite. At the same time, however, they did not entirely abandon the traditional understanding of marriage. There were several reasons for this. A Christian convert who wanted to get married to a woman or man belonging to a non-Christian family, would be expected to go through all the traditional marriage transactions. For example, a man would be expected to contribute goods in kind (dowry), such as honey and livestock to seal the marriage. If he was determined to marry, he would have no option but to comply with the customs, although his Christian instruction might have taught him that such customs were heathen.[44] Furthermore, African Christians, though recognizing themselves as members of the Church, did not and could not entirely sever their ties with their kin.

Considering that not all the kith and kin of African Christians embraced Christianity, a Christian wanting to get married peacefully needed to gain the approval of his relatives as well as that of the Church. Consequently, the Christian wedding came to be only one aspect of the African marriage rite. The second aspect was the traditional one, in which the kith and kin of the marrying couple would celebrate the inaugurated relationship—irrespective whether Christian or not, would participate in this aspect of the wedding. The dual celebration of the marriage rite is an illustrative instance of the African Christians' adaptation of their understanding of the Gospel to their cultural heritage. In this way they realize their double faithfulness—to their kith and kin, and to the unity of mankind as embodied in Christianity—in the Church centered on Jesus Christ.

Consummation after the Christian wedding was considered to be the completion of the marriage contract. A marriage that had not been consummated could be nullified, but once consummation had taken place, divorce was not possible, since such allowance, according to the Christian teaching, would reduce the couple to fornicators, or to adulterers if either of them chose to marry again.[45] Moreover, the Christian wedding came as a new cultural experience in which the bridal party wore new clothes indicative of the new culture; new foods and drinks were served at the celebration, such as wedding cakes (and baked bread), rice and tea.

From the basic observations made above regarding the marriage rite, it follows that even without the contemporary emphasis on the indigenization of Christianity,[46] African Christians have already initiated ways of dealing with the problem of accepting the new religion in the context of their culture. Christian doctrines and worship are accepted, but at the same time some aspects of African culture, which African Christians consider necessary, are maintained in their way of life.

d) Death

Both in Christianity and African cultural heritage, the death of an individual causes great concern to the community of which he has been a member and in which he has been living. This is especially so if the deceased had favorable relations with the members of the community. Rituals are organized for the expression of this concern. In African tradition, the death of an elderly popular individual was felt to be a great loss to the community. Funeral rituals expressed this feeling of sorrow and loss and emphasized that the physical death was not the end of the person's existence. It was believed that the dead person would continue to influence the lives of the living relatives. In accordance with this belief, it was considered essential that those who were physically alive should continue to conduct themselves in such a way as to maintain peaceful and healthy relations with one another and with the departed ones. The latter relationship would be maintained by observing strict and established customs of the community, pouring libation in remembrance of the departed, singing praises to them and naming children after them. The departed would be consulted occasionally through the elders and the diviners to find out their will for the living community. It was feared that any offence to the departed would bring suffering and misfortune to the relatives and to the community as a whole.[47]

If a deceased person had many children and had been living according to the established customs of the community, there was also an expression of joy because he had not departed without leaving some descendants. The continuation of the family lineage was felt to be obligatory; hence, marriage and procreation were primary responsibilities that must be fulfilled before a person reached old age. The death of an unmarried person was not regarded to be as great a loss as that of one who had fulfilled this obligation. Thus, the rituals concerned with the death of accepted members of the community were a mixture of sorrow and joy—sorrow that the community would miss physically one of its members, and joy that the deceased had fulfilled his obligations to the community according to custom.[48]

Christianity came with new rituals for the burial of Christians. The liturgy for burial reflected the Christian beliefs in eternal life, resurrection and the communion of saints, as stated in the Apostles' Creed. The Christian funeral was a new cultural experience in Africa in which texts from the Bible were read and new hymns sung. A new theological understanding of the destiny of man was articulated, expressing the conviction that after physical death a faithful Christian would enter the Kingdom of God to live with Him eternally while the unfaithful would be condemned to eternal suffering in hell.

In contemporary African Christian life there is an overlap of African cultural heritage and Christian teaching. The death of a Christian is felt to be a loss to the Church, and the congregation expresses this feeling at the Christian funeral. There is also the affirmation of the Christian belief, that physical death is not the end of human existence—God in Jesus Christ has promised eternal life to humankind. At the same time, the relatives of the deceased and the community of which one has been a member feel the loss caused by the death. They feel it both as Christians and as members of his family and community. Although some African Christians may not conduct the traditional death rituals, such as ritual of cleansing, all continue to feel the presence of the deceased long after physical death.

VI. CHRISTIAN AND AFRICAN SYMBOLISM

Christianity came with new symbols[49] that embodied its basic doctrines and theology. In this section several of these are considered in the light of their theological significance in Christianity and according to what they may mean in the context of the Church in Africa.

a) The Cross

This is one of the most significant Christian symbols in the life of the Church, being a visible sign to remind Christians and other people of the suffering, death and resurrection of Jesus Christ for the salvation of humanity.[50] The symbol embodies the Christian belief that God became incarnate in Jesus Christ, so that through Him the estranged relationship between God and man might be restored. God took the initiative to re-establish the relationship which man, through the sin of disobedience, had broken. The cross is also a constant reminder that Jesus conquered death, and in the resurrection mankind became assured of eternal life for all those who believe the Gospel and became followers of this way, as exemplified by Jesus Christ.

The cross also embodies the Christian belief in God's gracious forgiveness, which is freely extended to all those who repent and believe the Gospel. The Kingdom of God, as a present experience and an eternal promise, is open to all those who choose to follow the way of the cross. Since the Apostolic Period, Christians have been called people of the "Way of the Cross" (Mark 8:34, 38, Acts 9:2, 19:9, 24:14). Thus the cross is a very loaded theological symbol in the life of the Church. It embodies the Christian belief in the triune of God, whose presence is experienced by the believer through the inspiration of the Holy Spirit. For many centuries, it has been a Christian tradition to place a cross on Church buildings, at the altar, at the pulpit and at other conspicuous places. In many denominations it is part of the clerical dress. Hence it is one of the most common symbols in all the various strands of Christianity.

Before the coming of Christianity the cross was not a religiously significant symbol among African communities.[51] Hence, the widespread use of it in the Church made the cross one of the most visible distinguishing characteristics of the presence of Christianity in Africa. Wherever the Church has been established, one can notice the presence without necessarily being told about it, by observing the use of this symbol on church buildings, clerical dress and on Christian graves. The cross has continued to be the mark of identity for Christian churches all over the world. Although its cultural origin was not in Africa, it has come to be accepted by African Christians for the deep theological meaning that it signifies.

b) Bread and Wine

The Eucharist is one of the central sacraments of the Church.[52] In it the Christian community enacts the Last Supper which Jesus Christ had with His disciples just before His crucifixion. During that occasion Jesus, pointing to His death and resurrection, offered Himself as the Bread of Life. The Bread in that meal signified His body tortured and broken for the salvation of mankind. The wine signified His blood, shed for the same purpose. He commended His disciples to enact that event as the central ritual of the Christian community.[53] Hence the Eucharist came to signify and embody the new Covenant which inaugurated a new era of faith and life, unified in Jesus Christ. Thus bread and wine, which were elements basic to the staple food for the people of Palestine in the time of Jesus, acquired symbolic significance for the early Christian community, and for the Church throughout its history to the present time. This sacrament—sometimes called "The Lord's Supper", "The Last Supper", "Eucharist" or "Holy Communion"—also reminds Christians that animal sacrifices, or any other offerings to God, are no longer necessary for restoration of the estranged relations between God and humankind. Jesus Christ offered Himself for that purpose, once and for all. Through His crucifixion and resurrection, humanity had freely received the gift of salvation and became reunited with God.[54] For the Churches that give prominence to apostolic tradition, the Eucharist is the centre of Christian worship, expressing the experienced reality of the Incarnation, and constantly reminding Christians of God's presence among His people. It is the climax of the Church's corporate life.

The use of bread and wine in the Eucharist came as a new cultural and religious experience for African peoples. In their traditional life, Africans made animal sacrifices and other offerings to the deity, spirits and ancestors. There was no teaching about a personal savior, nor was there a belief in personal salvation such as taught in Christianity.[55] African Christians in the churches that grew directly out of the modern missionary movement accepted the teaching about the Eucharist, and adopted bread and wine as the elements with which to enact the central sacrament of the Church. Whereas in the Apostolic Period bread and wine were a common diet, in African Christianity these elements came as a new cultural experience so that some Christians would taste bread and wine only at Holy Communion.

c) Water

The ritual of baptism was another new cultural and religious experience in Africa. Baptism as conducted by John the Baptist and by the Apostles in the Early Church was by total immersion. It was a very significant ritual, symbolizing publicly the ceremonial washing of the penitent sinner in the clean water of the river Jordan which, rising in the lofty mountains of Lebanon, drained into the Dead Sea. As the river flowed to the sea without outlet, its waters would symbolically wash the old life out of those being baptized, and then they would continue to live according to the new teaching.[56] Jesus was baptized by John in that river, and from that example His followers continued the practice of baptism. He advised Nicodemus that unless a person was "born again" with water and the spirit he could not enter the Kingdom of God.[57]

As the Church continued to mould its theology, baptism became the central sacrament and the ritual by which converts would be initiated into life and membership of the Church. Some churches today practice baptism by total immersion as in the Early Church, while others sprinkle water over the head of the convert and then declare him baptized in the name of God the Father, the Son and the Holy Spirit. Whatever procedure of baptism is followed, water is the important symbol.

In traditional African life, there was ritual washing in which water was accorded symbolic meaning. For example, a person who touched a corpse would have to be ritually cleansed before he could rejoin the normal life of the community.[58] Water was considered to be a very important element, essential to the life of the individual and the community, and also for the life of the livestock. It was against custom to deny a thirsty person some water to drink.[59] African Christians, especially during the early period of missionary activity, understood baptism to be very significant in their lives. They were prepared to go through several years of catechetical instruction in order to be baptized and become members of the Church.[60] The ritual was also linked to the giving of new names, especially those of biblical characters and of saints. The water was accorded new symbolic significance when Christianity was introduced in Africa. In the ritual of baptism, the baptized convert was considered to have been "washed" of all aspects of the old existence, and was therefore expected to abandon the traditional customs of his community. It has been noted, however, that this missionary expectation was not fully realized because African Christians continued to hold some of the traditional ideas although they would not publicly participate in traditional ritual.[61]

d) Blood

According to the teaching of Christianity, the blood of Jesus Christ was shed in the final sacrifice for the salvation of all sinners. The coming of Christianity to East Africa thus brought a new way of re-establishing the relationship between God and man. An illustrative example of the acceptance of this new teaching by African Christians is a chorus, which is very popular within the East

African Revival Movement. The chorus expresses the joy of a Christian after being cleansed by the blood of Jesus Christ.[62] In the New Testament, Jesus was referred to as the "Lamb who takes away the sin of the world" (John 1:29-30). His blood became the "Blood of the new covenant" (Matt. 26:28, Mark 14:24, Luke 22:20). In the Old Testament, the blood of the sacrificial lamb symbolized the Old Covenant between God and His people, and this understanding remained central to the Old Testament religion since the exodus from Egypt. The incarnation became the New Covenant in which animal, human or any other form of sacrifice was no longer necessary. To Africans, the practice of offering sacrifices was not new, what was new was the teaching that Jesus had shed His own blood, making the last and only necessary sacrifice for man's salvation.

CONCLUSION

In view of the observations made in this chapter, the establishment of Christianity in tropical Africa can be considered to have been a double-sided process. On the other hand, there was *conversion* in which some individuals, having encountered Christianity, chose to follow its new teaching and adopt a new way of life. Catechetical instruction was the main means through which the converts were prepared for initiation into the fellowship of the new faith. They were taught new doctrines, and after being tested, to ensure that they could at least recite them, the converts would be admitted into the full membership of the Church. In this sense they were converted from their African religious heritage to Christianity. On the other hand, the acceptance of the new doctrines in conversion implied the adoption of a new way of life, which would correspond to these beliefs. The translation of Christian teaching into practical living could not be done without cultural reference and cultural interaction—*acculturation.*

It has been observed above that while African Christians accepted the basic Christian teachings almost without debate,[63] they did not necessarily abandon their traditional values and ideas. Although they may have publicly detached themselves from traditional rituals and practices, the positive values and ideas embodied in those expressions remained part of the African Christian experience. The establishment of Christianity in tropical Africa was also a process of both conversion and *acculturation*.[64] African Christians, through encounter and interaction with the new religion already expressed in terms of another culture, acquired and developed a new way of life which was distinct from, but also related to, both the old (local) and the new (foreign) cultural backgrounds.

Notes

1. This Contribution is a revised excerpt from a chapter in J.N.K. MUGAMBI, "Christianity and African Cultural Heritage", in *Christianity and African Culture* (Nairobi: Acton, 2002), ch. 8.
2. For a discussion on the relationship between Christianity and Culture, see H. Richard NIEBUHR, *Christ and Culture* (New York: Harper and Row, 1951). See

also Eugene A. NIDA, *Customs and Cultures: Anthropology for Christian Missions* (New York: Harper and Brothers, 1954).

3. D.B. BARRETT, *Schism and the Renewal in Africa: An Analysis of Six Thousand Contemporary Religious Movements* (London: Oxford University Press, 1968).
4. The present author is indebted to Dr. Donald Jacobs, a Mennonite Missionary who delivered a public lecture on this analogy at Kenyatta College, Nairobi, in 1968.
5. The interested reader may consult publications of the World Council of Churches, especially those by the Commission of World Mission and Evangelism (CWME) and the Unit on Dialogue with People of Living Faiths and Ideologies. The catalogue is available from the WCC Publications Office, P.O. Box 66, 1211 Geneva 20, Switzerland.
6. Cor. 9:19-23.
7. In the East African Context, this problem has been raised by such writers as: F.B. WELBOURN, *East African Christian* (London: Oxford University Press, 1965); J.V. TAYLOR, *Christian Presence amid African Religion* (Nairobi: Acton, 2001 *[Primal Vision,* London: SCM Press, 1963, 2nd ed. 2001]).
8. This continued to be true for African Christians under the yoke of *apartheid* in South Africa and Namibia. See, e.g., Desmond TUTU, *Crying in The Wilderness* (Grand Rapids, MI: Eerdmans, 1982); Allan BOESAK, *Farewell to Innocence* (New York: Orbis Books, 1977).
9. This point has been discussed by Charles W. FORMAN, *A Faith for the Nations* (London: The Carey Kingstgate Press, 1965). Also Louis EVELY, *In the Christian Spirit* (London: Burns & Oates, Herder & Herder, 1969), 95-108.
10. Herbert Muller, *op. cit.* pp. 235-249: S.C. Neill, *op. cit.,* pp61-139; NIDA, *Customs and Cultures*.
11. H.D. MUNRO, "Culture", in G.D. MITCHELL (ed.), *A Dictionary of Sociology* (London: Routledge & Kegan Paul, 1968).
12. OLIVER, *The Missionary Factor*, 184-185; Allan J. GOTTNEID (ed.), *Church and Education in Tanzania* (Nairobi: East African Publishing House, 1975).
13. E. MUGA, *African Response to the Western Christian Religion* (Nairobi: East African Literature Bureau, 1974), 88.
14. GOTTNEID, *Church and Education*, 5-26.
15. R.W. MUTUA, *Development of Education in Kenya: Some Administrative Aspects* (Nairobi: East African Literature Bureau, 1975), 8f.
16. For a study of education in traditional Africa, J.P. OCITTI, *African Indigenous Education* (Nairobi: East African Literature Bureau, 1973); W.R. MWONDELA. *Traditional Education in North-western Zambia* (Lusaka: National Educational Co. of Zambia, 1970).
17. The missionary societies were concerned that the pupils admitted to the mission schools should belong to the sponsoring denominations. This situation has changed since Independence. See WELBOURN, *East African Christian*, 84.
18. For a discussion of this point, see e.g. J.V. TAYLOR, *The Growth of the Church in Buganda* (London: S.C.M. Press, 1958), 155-168; W.B. ANDERSON, *The Church in East Africa, 1840-1974* (Dodoma: Central Tanganyika Press, 1977), 11-117.
19. On the importance of oral tradition in African history, see Jan VANSINA, "The Use of Oral Tradition in African Culture History", in Creighton GABEL & Norman R. BENNETT, (eds), *Reconstructing African Culture History* (Boston University Press, 1967).

20. Leadership especially in the Church activities is discussed by MUGA, *African Response,* ch.4; Paul M. MILLER, *Equipping for Ministry in East Africa* (Dodoma: Central Tanganyika Press, 1969).
21. WELBOURN, *East African Christian*, 9; Dietrich BONHOEFFER, "The Visible Community", in Dietrich BONHOEFFER, *The Cost of Discipleship* (New York: MacMillan, 1963), 129-134.
22. Eph. 5:23-4, 1 Cor. 11:1-3. Interview with Rev. Johana Muturi and Paulo Gatema, 9th March 1975. These were pioneer evangelists in Embu, Kenya, see also, M. LIKIMANI, *They Shall be Chastised* (Nairobi: Noni's Publicity, 1974), 55-68, 166-172; OLIVER, *The Missionary Factor*, 63-65.
23. For example, counselling about marriage and the socialisation of the children was one of the primary concerns of the Family Life Education Programme of the National Christian Council of Kenya during the 1970s and 1980s. See also, R.S. Ndingi Mwana a' NZEKI, "The Church and Family Life" in *Target*, 236 (21st May, 1977).
24. Edwin WEAVER & Irene WEAVER, *The Uyo Story* (Elkhart, Indiana: Mennonite Board of Missions, 1970), 66; OLIVER. *The Missionary Factor.*
25. Genesis 2:24, Matthew 19:5, Mark 10:7. This passage is often quoted on wedding invitation cards. Also A. HASTINGS, *Christian Marriage In Africa* (London: S.P.C.K, 1973), 63; Margaret PEIL, *Consensus and Conflict in African Societies* (London: Longman, 1977), 139-140.
26. A.R. RADCLIFFE-BROWN & Daryll FORDE, (eds), *African Systems of Kinship and Marriage* (London: Oxford University Press, 1950), 60.
27. RADCLIFFE-BROWN & FORDE, *African Systems,* 46; for a study of the interaction between traditional African marriage customs and marriage practices among Christian revivalists, see, Derrick STENNING, "Salvation in Ankole", in M. FORTES and G. DIETERLEN, *African Systems of Thought* (London: Oxford University Press, 1965), 273.
28. For a discussion on "social fact", see MITCHELL, *A Dictionary of Sociology*, 76.
29. E.g., HASTINGS, *Christian Marriage*. See also, MUGA, *African Response,* 102, LIKIMANI, *They Shall be Chastised*, 155-162. G. Mdimi MHOGOLO, "God the Father and Family Life in Contemporary Africa", in D.M. GITARI & G.P. BENSON (eds), *Witnessing to the Living God in Contemporary Africa* (Kabare, Kenya: Africa Theological Fraternity, 1986), 180-195.
30. RADCLIFFE-BROWN & FORDE, *African Systems,* 266; also J.S. MBITI, *African Religions and Philosophy* (London: Heinemann, 1969), 118-20; T.A. BEETHAM, *Christianity and the New Africa* (London: Pall Mall, 1967), 156-59.
31. Birth as a rite of passage is discussed in MBITI, *African Religions and Philosophy*, 112-118.
32. In the Anglican *Book of Common Prayer* the ceremony is called *Churching*.
33. The god-parent serves an educative role similar to that of a sponsor in the initiation rite, guiding the child to maturity of faith in the new Christian community. For detailed discussion on this point see H.G.G. HERKLOTS, *The Call of God: An Explanation of the Revised Catechism* (London: Hodder & Stoughton, 1962), 91-100.
34. The situation may be attributed to the lack of adequate theological education among the laity. For further discussion, J.S. MBITI, *New Testament Eschatology in an African Background* (Oxford: Oxford University Press, 1971), 108-13. The correct

theological balance has been restored in the Ecumenical Consensus on *Baptism, Eucharist and Ministry,* approved at the WCC Faith and Order Conference in January 1982, Lima, Peru. Faith and Order Paper No. 111, WCC, Geneva.

35. The importance of such practices is continually diminishing with social change in African communities. The cultural conflict resulting from the disregard by missionaries of African initiation rites is portrayed by NGUGI WA THIONG'O (James NGUGI) in *The River Between* (London: Heinemann, 1966). See also, J. KENYATTA, *Facing Mount Kenya* (London: Secker & Warburg, 1938); PEIL, *Consensus and Conflict.*
36. J.S. MBITI, "Some African Concepts of Christology", in Georg F. VICEDOM, *Christ and the Younger Churches* (London: S.P.C.K., 1972), 56.
37. A. SHORTER, *African Culture and the Christian Church* (London: Geoffrey Chapman, 1973), 177; HERKLOTS, *The Call of God,* 91-100.
38. E.g., this problem was one of the primary concerns of the School and Community Conference held at Limuru Conference Centre, November 1976. Various aspects of the problem are discussed in PEIL, *Consensus and Conflict.*
39. MBITI, *African Religious Philosophy,* 148.
40. The issue is discussed by SHORTER, *African Culture,* 167-72. See also, RADCLIFFE-BROWN & FORDE, *African Systems.*
41. MBITI, *African Religious Philosophy,* 142-143; David MAILLU, *Our Kind of Polygamy* (Nairobi: Heinemann, 1987).
42. HASTINGS, *Christian Marriage,* 63-65. See also Aylward SHORTER & B. KISEMBO (eds), *African Christian Marriage* (London: Chapman, 1977); Eugene HILLMAN, *Polygamy Reconsidered* (New York: Orbis Books, 1975).
43. HASTINGS, *Christian Marriage,* 83-86.
44. For further discussion, WELBOURN, *East African Christian,* 116-29; SHORTER, *African Culture,* 156-95.
45. HASTINGS, *Christian Marriage,* 86.
46. For studies of selected aspects of indigenisation see, David B. BARRETT (ed.), *African Initiatives in Religion* (Nairobi: E.A. Publishing House, 1971).
47. For further discussion see, J.S. MBITI, *African Religious Philosophy,* 75-91, 162.
48. J.S. MBITI, *African Religious Philosophy,* 84.
49. For literature on symbolism, see, e.g., I.T. RAMSAY, *Religious Language: An Empirical Placing of Theological Phrases* (London: S.C.M. 1957); F.W. DILLISTONE (ed.), *Myth and Symbol* (London: S.P.C.K., 1966); Raymond FIRTH, *Symbols Public and Private* (London: George Allen & Urwin, 1973); V.W. TURNER, *The Forest of Rituals: Aspects of Ndembu Ritual* (Cornell University Press, 1967); Peter L. BERGER & Thomas LUCKMANN, *The Social Construction of Reality* (Harmondsworth: Penguin University Books, 1971).
50. Louis EVELY, *In the Christian Spirit,* 45; also, Gustaf AULEN, *The Drama and the Symbols* (London: S.P.C.K., 1970), 167-184; Jurgen MOLTMANN, *The Crucified God: The Cross of Christ as the Foundation of and Criticism of Christian Theology* (London: SCM Press, 1974).
51. MBITI *African Religious Philosophy,* 90, has noted that the Gikuyu shaved children in the form of a cross during rituals designed to keep off malicious spirits. (This symbolism was not connected with Christianity). Among the Embu, the emphasis in this custom fell on the incompleteness of the shaving, rather than on the design

made on the scalp. Mbiti's suggestion to link this custom with Christianity has been criticised by Prof. Ali MAZRUI, "Epilogue", in Okot P'BITEK, *African Religions in Western Scholarship* (Kampala: East African Literature Bureau, 1970), 126.

52. R.P. MARTIN, "The Lord's Supper", in J.D. DOUGLAS (ed.), *The New Bible Dictionary* (London: Inter-Varsity Press, 1962); World Council of Churches, *Baptism, Eucharist and Ministry*, Faith and Order Paper No. 111, Geneva, 1982, 10-17.
53. Luke 22:20; HERKLOTS, *The Call of God*, 98-100.
54. For fuller discussion, see MBITI, *New Testament Eschatology*, 101-105; Moltmann, *The Crucified God*; Paul TILLICH, "Existence and the Christ", in *Systematic Theology*, vol. II (Chicago: Chicago University Press, 1957), 150-165.
55. MBITI, "Some African Concepts of Christology", 60.
56. For the symbolic significance of water in the Bible, see, for example, J.A. MOTYER, "Baptism" in J.D. DOUGLAS, *The New Bible Dictionary*; and J.B. TAYLOR, "Water", in J.D. DOUGLAS, *The New Bible Dictionary*.
57. John 3:1-13. It should be remembered that the challenge of Jesus to Nicodemus was *not* that he should go through a ritual or experience a charismatic trance. Rather, the challenge was for him to repent of the old life and enter the new Christian community founded on love rather than pharisaic legalism.
58. For example, among the Bugusu, G. WAGNER, *The Bantu in Western Kenya, with special reference to the Bugusu and Logoli*, vol. I (London/New York: Oxford University Press, 1949, 1970), 485. Among the Gikuyu, Lydia WAKANYI-KAHINDI, *The Agikuyu Concept of* Thahu *and its bearing on the Christian Concept of Sin* (M.A. Thesis, Kenyatta University, Nairobi, 1988).
59. This custom prevailed in many cultures, even non-African ones. E.g., Jesus referred to it in His teaching, Matt. 25:35.
60. E.g., the Akamba Christians, in MBITI, "Some African Concepts of Christology", 108-113.
61. TAYLOR, *Christian Presence*, 24 (*The Primal Vision*, 24); WELBOURN, *East African Christian*, 104-115.
62. One version of that chorus in English has the following words: "Glory Alleluyia, Glory, Glory to the Lamb; Oh! the cleansing blood of Jesus; Glory, Glory to the Lamb". This is sung in many East African Languages.
63. Contrasting the modern missionary movement's activity in Africa with the spreading of Christianity in the Graeco-Roman world, the establishment of the church in the nineteenth century was characterised by *cultural*, rather than theological and philosophical controversies in East Africa. Theological critique of the modern missionary enterprise is only just beginning, and this volume is a contribution to the discussion.
64. *Acculturation* is used in this section as the process whereby an individual or group acquired the cultural characteristics of another through direct contract and interaction". A.H. RICHMOND, "Acculturation" in MITCHELL, *A Dictionary of Sociology*. The problem of conversion and acculturation in the context of East African cultural and religious heritage, is satirically portrayed by Okot P'BITEK, in *Song of Lawino* and *Song Of Ocol* (Nairobi: East African Publishing House, 1966 & 1967).

Select Reading List

ABIOLA, O.U. n.d., "The History of the Aladura International Church", in O.U. ABIOLA, *An Introduction to Aladuraism*, London.

ACHEBE, C. 1958, *Things Fall Apart*, London: Heinemann.

ACHEBE, C. 1974, [1964], *Arrow of God*, London: Heinemann.

ACHEBE, C. 1990, "An Image of Africa: Racism in Conrad's *Heart of Darkness*", in C. ACHEBE, *Hopes and Impediments: Selected Essays*, New York: Doubleday, 1-20.

ACHEBE, C. 2000, *Home and Exile*, Oxford: Oxford University Press.

ACKERMANN, D. 2003, "Implications of HIV and AIDS for the Theological Agenda" (Unpublished paper delivered at the UNAIDS Theologians' Workshop on Stigma and Discrimination, Namibia, December 2003).

ACKERMANN, D. DRAPER, J.A. & MASHININI, E. (eds.) 1991, *Women Hold up Half the Sky: Women in the Church in Southern Africa*, Pietermaritzburg: Cluster Publications.

ADAMOLEKUN, L. "The Road to Independence in French Tropical Africa", in *Tarikh, France in Africa,* 8, Vol. 2, no. 4, Essex, (1969), 72-85.

ADAMS, W. 1977, *Nubia, Corridor to Africa*, Princeton: Princeton University Press.

ADOGAME, A. 1999, *Celestial Church of Christ: The Politics of Cultural Identity in a West African Prophetic-Charismatic Movement*, Frankfurt am Main: Peter Lang.

AFIGBO, A.E. 1972, *The Warrant Chiefs Indirect Rule in Southeastern Nigeria 1891-1929*, London: Humanities Atlantic Highlands.

AFIGBO, A.E. 1981, *Ropes of Sand*, Lagos: Oxford University Press.

AFIGBO, A.E. 1986, K.O. *Dike and the African Historical Renaissance*, Owerri: RADA Publ. Co.

AGU, C.C. 1989, *Secularization in Igboland*, Frankfurt: Verlag Peter Lang.

AJAYI, J.F.A. 1969, *Christian Missions in Nigeria, 1841-1891: The Making of a New Elite*, Evanston: Northwestern University Press.

ALBERIGO, G. 1987, "The Christian Situation after Vatican II," in G. ALBERIGO, J.-P. JOSSUA & J.A. KOMONCHAK (eds.), *The Reception of Vatican II*, Washington, DC: Catholic University of America Press, 1-24.

AMANZA, J. 1998, *African Christianity in Botswana*, Gweru: Mambo Press.

ANDERSON, A. 1999, "Global Pentecostalism in the New Millennium", in A. ANDERSON & W. HOLLENWEGER (eds.), *Pentecostals after a Century: Global Perspectives on a Movement in Transition*, Sheffield: Sheffield Academic Press.

ANDERSON, A. 2002, *African Reformation*, Trenton, NJ: Africa World Press.

ANDERSON, A. & OTWANG, S. 1993, *Tumelo: The Faith of African Pentecostals in South Africa*, Pretoria: University of South Africa Press.

ANDERSON, E. 1958, *Messianic Popular Movements in the Lower Congo*, Studia Ethnographica Upsaliensa, Uppsala: Almqvist & Wiksell.

ANDERSON, W.B. 1977, *The Church in East Africa, 1840-1974*, Dodoma: Central Tanganyika Press.

AN-NA'IM, A.A. 1997, "Islam and Human Rights in Sahelian Africa", in D. WESTERLUND and E.E. ROSANDER (eds.), *African Islam and Islam in Africa: Encounters between Sufis and Islamists*, London: Hurst.

ANSTEY, R. 1975, *The Atlantic Slave Trade and British Abolition 1760-1810*, London: Macmillan Press.

ANYIKA, F. 1995, "Church Missionary Society (C.M.S) Ministerial Formation on the Niger: Reverend V.N. Umunna as a pioneer", in *Nigeria Heritage: Journal of the National Commission for Museums and Monuments,* 4 (1995), 133-145.

ASAMOAH-GYADU, K. 1998, "'Fireballs in our Midst': West Africa's Burgeoning Charismatic Churches and the Pastoral Role of Women", in *Mission Studies,* XV, 1 (1998).

ASAMOAH-GYADU, K. 2000, *Renewal within Christianity: A Historical and Theological Study of some current developments within Ghanaian Pentecostalism* (PhD Thesis, University of Birmingham).

AULEN, G. 1970, *The Drama and the Symbols*, London: S.P.C.K.

AXELSON, S. 1970, *Culture Confrontation in the Lower Congo. From the Old Congo Kingdom to the Congo Independent State With Special Reference to the Swedish Missionaries in the 1880's and 1890's*, Uppsala: Gunmessons.

AYANDELE, E.A. 1966, *The Missionary Impact on Modern Nigeria 1842–1914, A Political Analysis*, London: Longmans.

AYANDELE, E.A. 1970, *'Holy' Johnson, Pioneer of African Nationalism, 1836-1917*, Southgate: Frank Cass.

AZUMAH, J.A. 2001, *The Legacy of Arab-Islam in Africa: A Quest for Inter-Religious Dialogue*, Oxford: One World.

BAÉTA, C.G. 1962, *Prophetism in Ghana*, London: SCM.

BALOGUN, S.U. 1985, "Arabic Intellectualism in West Africa: The Role of the Sokoto Caliphate", in *Journal Institute of Muslim Minority Affairs*, (1985), 6, 2, 394-411.

BALZER, J. 1961, "The Role of the Catechist in the Missions," in HATTON (ed.), *Missiology in Africa Today. Thought Provoking Essays by Modern Missionaries*, Dublin, 76-84.

BALZER, J. 1964, "The Catechist," in *African Ecclesiastical Review,* 6 (1964), 1, 49-55.

BANE, M.J. 1968, *The Popes and Western Africa, An Outline of Mission History 1460-1960s*, Staten Island NY: Alba House.

BARNES, A.E. 1995, "Evangelization Where It Is not Wanted: Colonial Administrators and Missionaries in Northern Nigeria During the First Third of the Twentieth Century", in *Journal of Religion in Africa*, 25, 4 (1995), 412-441.

BARRETT, D.B. 1968, *Schism and Renewal in Africa: An Analysis of Six Thousand Contemporary Religious Movements*, Nairobi: East African Publishing House.

BARRETT, D.B. 1970, "AD2000: 350 million Christians in Africa", in *International Review of Mission,* 59 (1970) 39-54.

BARRETT D.B. (ed.) 1971, *African Initiatives in Religion*, Nairobi: E.A. Publishing House.

BARRETT, D.B., KURIAN, G.T. & JOHNSON, T.M. (eds.) 2000 (1982), *World Christian Encyclopedia: A Comparative Survey of Churches and Religions in the Modern World*, New York: Oxford University Press.

BARTELS, F.L. 1965, *The Roots of Ghana Methodism*, Cambridge: Cambridge University Press.

BAUER, J. 1994, *2000 Years of Christianity in Africa, An African History 62 – 1992*, Nairobi: Paulines.

BAUER, W. 1971 (1934), *Orthodoxy and Heresy in Earliest Christianity* (R. KRAFT & G. KRODEL eds), Philadelphia: Fortress Press.

BEBBINGTON, D. 2000 (1989), *Evangelicalism in Modern Britain: A History from the 1730s to the 1980s*, New York: Routledge.

BEETHAM, T.A. 1967, *Christianity and the New Africa*, London: Pall Mall Press.

BEDIAKO, K. 1994, "Understanding African Theology in the 20th Century", in *Themelios*, 20, 1 (October 1994) 14-20.

BEDIAKO, K. 1995, *Christianity in Africa: The Renewal of a Non-Western Religion*, Maryknoll: Orbis Books.

BEDIAKO, K. 1995, *Theology and Identity: The Impact of Culture Upon Christian Thought in the Second Century and Modern Africa*, Oxford: Regnum Press.

BEDIAKO, K. 1996, "Five Theses on the Significance of Modern African Christianity: A Manifesto", in *Transformation*, 13 (1996) 21-29.

BEDIAKO, K. 2000, *Jesus in Africa. The Christian Gospel in African History and Experience*, Akropong-Akuapem: Regnum Africa.

BEIDELMAN, T.O. 1982, *Colonial Evangelism*, Bloomington: Indiana University Press.

BEIER, U. 1979, *Modern Poetry from Africa,* London: Penguin Books.

BERGER, P.L. & LUCKMANN, T. 1971, *The Social Construction of Reality*, Harmondsworth: Penguin University Books.

BIRMINGHAM, D. 1995, *The Decolonisation of Africa*, Athens, Ohio: Ohio University Press.

BLYDEN, E.W., 1888, *Christianity, Islam and the Negro Race*, London: W.B. Whittingham.

BLYDEN, E.W. 1891, *The Return of Exiles*, London.

BOESAK, A. 1977, *Farewell to Innocence*, New York: Orbis Books.

BOLTON, F. 1992, *And We Beheld His Glory: A Personal Account of the Revival in Eastern Nigeria in 1970-71*, London: Christ the King Publishers.

BONHOEFFER, D. 1963, *The Cost of Discipleship*, New York: MacMillan.

Bosch, D.J. 1979, "Currents and Crosscurrents in South African Black Theology", in G.S. WILMORE & J.H. CONE (eds.), *Black Theology: A Documentary History, 1966-1979*, Maryknoll: Orbis Books.

BOSCH, D.J. 1991, *Transforming Mission: Paradigm Shifts in Mission Theology*, Maryknoll: Orbis Books.

BOWKIE, F. KIRKWOOD, D. & ARDENER, S. (eds.) 1993, *Women and Missions: Past and Present: Anthropological and Historical Perceptions*, Providence: Berghan.

BOXER, C.R. 1978, *The Church Militant and Iberian Expansion: 1440-1770*, Baltimore: Johns Hopkins University Press.

BREIDENBACH, P. 1979, "The Woman on the Beach and the Man in the Bush: Leadership and Adepthood in the Twelve Apostles Movement in Ghana", in B. JULES-ROSETTE (ed.), *The New Religions of Africa*, Norwood, NJ: Ablex.

BROWN, P. 1967, *Augustine of Hippo*, Berkeley: University of California Press.

BROWN, P. 1978, *The Making of Late Antiquity*, Cambridge, Massachusetts: Harvard University Press.

BROUWER, S. GIFFORD, P. & ROSE, S.D. 1996, *Exporting the American Gospel: Global Christian Fundamentalism*, New York: Routeledge.

BULL, G. 1966, *Vatican Politics at the Second Vatican Council, 1962–5*, London: Oxford University Press.

BUTLER, C. 1930, *The Vatican Council. The Story Told from Inside Bishop Ullathorne's Letters*, vol I, London: Longmans.

BUXTON, T.F. 1968 (1839), *The African Slave Trade and Its Remedy*, London: Dawsons of Pall Mall.

CAMPBELL, C. 1993, *Back to Africa, George Ross & the Maroons: From Nova Scotia to Sierra Leone*, Trenton, NJ: Africa World Press.

CAMPBELL, J. 2002, "African American Missionaries and the Colonial State: the AME Church in South Africa", in H.B. HANSEN & M. TWADDLE (eds.), *Christian Missionaries and the State in the Third World*, Oxford: James Currey.

CAREY, W. 1792, *An Enquiry into the Obligation of Christians to use Means for the Conversion of the Heathen*, London.

CARR, E.H. 1964, *What is History?*, London: Penguin Books.

CARROLL, K. 1967, *Yoruba Religious Art*, London: Geoffrey Chapman.

CASLEY-HAYFORD, J.E., 1911, *Ethiopia Unbound: Studies in Race Emancipation*, London.

CASSIDY, M. & OSEI-MENSAH, G. 1978, *Together in One Place: The Story of PACLA, December 9-19, 1976*, Nairobi: Evangel Publishing House.

CASTLES, S. & MILLER, M. 2003 (3rd ed.), *The Age of Migration: International Population Movements in the Modern World*, New York: The Guilford Press.

CHIDESTER, D. 2000, *Christianity: A Global History*, London: Penguin Books.

CHIOVARO, F. 1981, "History as Lived by the Christian People" in L. VISCHER (ed.), *Church History in an Ecumenical Perspective,* Papers and Reports of an International Ecumenical Consultation, Basle, 12-17 October 1981.

CHIPENDA, J. 1995, "The Church of the Future in Africa", in D. WARUTA (ed.), *African Church in the 21st Century: Challenges and Promises*, Nairobi: AACC, 16-36.

CHIRENJE, J.M. 1987, *Ethiopianism and Afro-Americans in South Africa, 1883-1916*, London: Louisiana State University Press.

CHUTA, S.C. 1986, *Africans in the Christianization of Southern Igboland, 1875-1952* (Unpublished PhD dissertation, University of Nigeria, Nsukka).

CISSOKO, S.I. 1984, "The Songhay from the 12th to the 16th Century", in D.T. NIANE (ed.), *Africa from the Twelfth to the Sixteenth Century*, London: Heinemann.

CLARKE, P.B. 1982, *West African and Islam*, London: Edward Arnold Publishers.

CLARKE, P.B. 1986, *West Africa and Christianity,* London: Edward Arnold.

CLARKE, P.B. 1988, "Islamic Reform in Contemporary Nigeria: Methods and Aims", in *Third World Quarterly*, 10, 2 (1988), 535.

COAN, J.R. 1974, "Redemption of Africa: The Vital Impulse of Black American Overseas Missionaries", in *The Journal of the Interdenominational Theological Center*, I, 2 (Spring, 1974), 27-37.

COCHRANE, J. 1987, *Servants of Power: The Role of English-Speaking Churches in South Africa: 1903-1930*, Johannesburg: Ravan Press.

COMAROFF, J & COMAROFF, J, 1991, *Of Revelation and Revolution: Christianity, Colonialism and Consciousness in South Africa*, Vol. I., Chicago & London: University of Chicago Press.

CORTEN, A. & MARSHALL-FRATANI, R. (eds.) 2001, *Between Babel and Pentecost: Transnational Pentecostalism in Africa and Latin America*, Bloomington: Indiana University Press.

COSTANZO, A. 2003, "*Neither Saint, A Hero, Nor A Tyrant,*" (paper presented at first International conference on Olaudah Equiano, *Olaudah Equiano: Representation and Reality*, Surrey: Kingston University, Kingston-upon-Thames, 22 March 2003).

COUPLAND, R. 1964, *The British Anti-Slavery Movement*, London: Frank Cass.

COX, H.G. 1996, *Fire from Heaven: The Rise of Pentecostal Spirituality and the Reshaping of Religion in the Twenty-First Century*, Reading, MA: Addison-Wesley.

COX, H.G. 1999, "The Myth of the Twentieth Century: The Rise and Fall of Secularization", in *Harvard Divinity Bulletin*, 28, 2/3 (1999), 6-8.

CROWTHER, M. 1964, "Indirect Rule – French and British Style", in *Africa* 34 (1964), 3, 197-205.

CROWTHER, M. 1969, "The Administration of French West Africa", in *Tarikh, France in Africa,* 8, vol. II, 4, Essex, 1969, 1981, 59-71.

CRUMBLEY, D.H. 1985, "Even a Woman: Sex Roles and Mobility in an Aladura Hierarchy", in *West African Journal of Archeology* (1985), 133-150.

CURTIN, P.D. 1969, "Scientific Racism and British Theory of Empire", in *Journal of the Historical Society of Nigeria*, (*JHSN*), 2, 1 (1969) 40-51.

DAHUNSI, E.A. 1972, "The Problem of Translating the Bible into African Languages", in E. MVENG & J.Z. Werblowsky (eds.), *The Jerusalem Congress on Black Africa and the Bible*, Jerusalem.

DANEEL, M.L. 1971, *Old and New in Southern Shona Independent Churches*, New York: Mouton.

DANEEL, M.L. 1974, *Old and New in Southern Shona Independent Churches*, vol. I, The Hague: Mouton.

DANEEL, M.L. 1987, *Quest for Belonging: Introduction to a Study of African Independent Churches*, Gweru: Mambo Press.

DANEEL, M.L. 1990, "Exorcism as a Means of Combating Wizardry", in *Missionalia*, 18, 1 (1990), 220-247.

DANEEL, M.L. 2000, "AIC Women as Bearers of the Good News", in *Missionalia*, 28, 213 (November 2000).

DAVIDSON, B. 1961, *The African Slave Trade: Precolonial History, 1450-1850*, Boston: Little Brown.

DAVIDSON, B. 1980 (1961), *The African Slave Trade*, New York: Back Bay Books.

DAVIDSON, B. 1991, *Africa in History: Themes and Outlines*, London, Weidenfeld & Nicolson.

DAYTON, D.W. 1987, *Theological Roots of Pentecostalism*, Metuchen, NJ: Scarecrow Press.

DEBRUNNER, H.W. 1956, *Notable Danish Chaplains on the Gold Coast.*

DEBRUNNER, H.W. 1967, *A History of Christianity in Ghana*, Accra: Waterville Publishing House.

DEBRUNNER, H.W. 1997, *Presence and Prestige: Africans in Europe. A History of Africans in Europe before 1918*, Basel: Basler Afrika Bibliographien.

DE GRUCHY, J.W. 1995, *Christianity and Democracy*, Cambridge: Cambridge University Press.

DENIS, P. 1998, *The Dominican Friars in Southern Africa A Social History (1577-1990)*, Leiden; Boston, MA: Brill Academic Publishers.

DICKINSON, R.D.N. 1975, *To Set at Liberty the Oppressed*, Geneva: WCC.

DICKSON, K.A. 1978, "The African Theological Task", in S. TORRES & V.M.M. FABELLA (eds.), *The Emergent Gospel: Theology from the Underside of History: Papers from the Ecumenical Dialogue of Third World Theologians, Dar es Salam, August 5-12*, Maryknoll: Orbis Books.

DICKSON, K.A. 1984, *Theology in Africa*, Maryknoll: Orbis Books.

DILLISTONE, F.W. (ed.) 1966, *Myth and Symbol*, London: S.P.C.K.

DIRVEN, P.J. 1970, *The Maria Legio: "The Dynamics of a Breakaway Church among the Luo in East Africa"* (Unpublished PhD Thesis, Pontifica Universitas Gregorians, Rome).

DOUGLAS, J.D. (ed.), 1967, *The New Bible Dictionary*, London: Inter-Varsity Press.

DRESCHER, S. 1977, *Econocide: British Slavery in the Era of Abolition*, Pittsburg, PA: University of Pittsburg Press.

DUBE, M.W. (ed.), 2002, *Other Ways of Reading: African Women and the Bible*, Geneva: WCC Publications & Atlanta: SBL.

DUFFY, J. *Portuguese Africa* Cambridge MA: Harvard University Press, 1959.

DUNCAN, G.A. 2003, *Lovedale – Agency: Power & Resistance in Mission Education*, Pietermaritzburg: Cluster Publication.

EDWARDS, P. 1969, *The Life of Olaudah Equiano, or, Gustavus Vassa the African*, Colonial History Series, London: Dawson.

EKECHI, F.K. 1971, *Missionary Enterprise and Rivalry in Igboland 1857–1914*, London: Frank Cass.

EKECHI, F.K. 1978, "The Missionary Career of the Venerable T.J. Dennis in West Africa, 1893–1917", in *Journal of Religion in Africa*, Vol. IX, fasc. 1 (1978), 1-26.

EKWUNIFE, A.N. 1997, "Integration of African Values in Priestly Formation" in *AFER*, 39, 4 (1997) 194-213.

ELLIOT-BINNS, L.E. 1953, *The Early Evangelicals: A Religious and Social Study*, London: Lutherworth Press.

ELSNER, J. & RUBIES, J.-P. (eds.) 1999, *Voyages & Visions. Towards a Cultural History of Travel*, London: Reaktion Books.

ELPHICK, R. & DAVENPORT, R. (eds.) 1997, *Christianity in South Africa*, Oxford: James Currey.

ELUYEMI, O. "African Systems of Contact and Communication", in *Nigeria Magazine*, Vol 55, no. 2, April–June 1987, 36-49.

ENGEL, J.F. & DYERNESS, W.A. 2000, *Changing the Mind of Missions*, Downers Grove, IL: InterVarsity Press.

ENGLUND, H. 2001, "The Quest for Missionaries: Transnationalism and Township Pentecostalism in Malawi", in in A. CORTEN & R. MARSHALL-FRATANI, *Between Babel and Pentecost: Transnational Pentecostalism in Africa and Latin America*, Bloomington & Indianapolis: Indiana University Press.

EQUIANO, O, 1789, *The Interesting Narrative of the Life of Olaudah Equiano, or Gustavus Vassa, the African*, vol. I & II, London.

EQUIANO, O. 1999, *The Life of Olaudah Equiano, or Gustavus Vassa, the African*, New York: Dove Publications.

ESEDEBE, P.O. 1994, *Pan-Africanism; The Idea and Movement 1776-1963*, Washington DC: Howard University Press.

ESPOSITO, J. 1992, *The Islamic Threat: Myth or Reality?*, New York & Oxford: Oxford University Press.

EPHSON, I.S. 1969, *Gallery of Gold Coast Celebrities 1632-1958*, Accra: Ilen Publications Ltd.

EVANS, R.J. 1999, *In Defense of History*, New York: N.W. Norton & Company.

EVELY, L. 1969, *In the Christian Spirit*, London: Burns & Oates/ Herder & Herder.

EYO, E.O. 1986, *The Story of Old Calabar. A Guide to the National Museum at the Old Residency*, Calabar, Lagos.

FABELLA, V.M.M. & ODUYOYE, M.A. (eds.) 1988, *With Passion and Compassion*, Maryknoll: Orbis Books.

FAHOLE-LUKE, E.W. 1976, "The Quest for African Christian Theologies", in G.H. ANDERSON & T.F. STRANSKY (eds.), *Mission Trends No 3: Third World Theologies*, Grand Rapids: Eerdmans.

FALOLA, T. 1998, *Violence in Nigeria: The Crisis of Religious Politics and Secular Ideologies*, Rochester, NY: University of Rochester Press.

FARRAGHER, S. 1984, *Dev and His Alma Mater. Eamon de Valera's Lifelong Association with Blackrock College 1898–1975*, Dublin & London: Paraclete Press.

FARRAGHER, S. 2002, *Bishop Joseph Shanahan CSSp. Selected Studies*, Dublin: Paraclete Press.

FASHOLÉ-LUKE, W. 1971, "An African Indigenous Theology: Fact or Fiction?", in *Sierra Leone Bulletin of Religion* 11 (1971).

FINDLAY, S. 2001, "Compelled to Move: the Rise of Forced Migration in Sub-Saharan Africa", in M. SIDDIQUE (ed.), *International Migration into the 21st Century*, Cheltenham/Northampton, MA: Edward Elgar.

FIRTH, R. 1973, *Symbols Public and Private*, London: George Allen & Urwin.

FISHER, H.J. 1973, "Conversion Reconsidered: Some Historical Aspects of Religious Conversion in Black Africa", in *Africa*, (1973), 43, 2, 27-40.

FISHER, H.J. 1985, "The Juggernaut's Apologia: Conversion to Islam in Black Africa", in *Africa*, (1985), 55,2, 153-70.

FISHER, M.P. 1999, *Living Religions*, Upper Saddle River, NJ: Prentice Hall.

FLANNERY, A. (ed.) 1988, *Vatican Council II: The Conciliar and Post Conciliar Documents,* Revised Edition, Dublin: Dominican Publications.

FLINT, J.E. 1983, "The Failure of Planned Decolonisation in British Africa" in *African Affairs*, 82 (1983) 389-411.

FOGELQVIST, A. 1986, *The Red-Dressed Zionists: Symbols of Power in a Swazi Independent Church*, Uppsala: Uppsala Research Reports in Cultural Anthropology.

FORMAN, C.W. 1965, *A Faith for the Nations*, London: The Carey Kingsgate Press.

FORRISTAL, D. 1990, *The Second Burial of Bishop Shanahan*, Dublin: Veritas.

FOSTER, P. 1986, "Missionaries and Anthropology: the case of the Scots of Northern Malawi", in *Journal of Religion in Africa*, 16,2, (1986), 101-120.

FREND, W.H.C 1952, *The Donatist Church*, Oxford: Clarendon Press.

FREND, W.H.C. 1965, *Martyrdom and Persecution in the Early Church: a Study of a Conflict from the Maccabees to Donatus*, Oxford: Blackwell.

FRENKEL, M.Y. 1978, *Edward Blyden and African Nationalism*, Moscow: Institute of Academy and Science.

FRIESEN, J.S. 1996, *Missionary Responses to Tribal Religions at Edinburgh, 1910*, Frankfurt: Peter Lang.

FYFE, C. 1962, *A Short History of Sierra Leone*, London: Oxford University Press.

FYFE, C. 1993. *Africanus Horton: 1835-1883: West African Scientist and Patriot*, (Modern Revivals in African Studies), London: Ashgate.

GANNON, T.M. (ed.) 1988, *World Catholicism in Transition,* New York: MacMillan.

GIFFORD, P. (ed.) 1992, *New Dimensions in African Christianity*, Nairobi: All Africa Conference of Churches.

GIFFORD, P. 1994, "Some Recent Developments in African Christianity", in *African Affairs,* 93 (1994).

GIFFORD, P. 1998, *African Christianity: In Public Role*, London: Hurst & Co.

GIFFORD, P. & LOUIS, R.W (eds.) 1988, *Decolonisation and African Independence: The Transfer* of *Powers, 1960-1980*, New Haven: Yale Univeristy Press.

GILROY, P. 1993, *The Black Atlantic: Modernity and Double Consciousness*, Boston: Harvard University Press.

GITHIEYA, F.K. 1997, *The Freedom of the Spirit: African Indigenous Churches in Kenya*, Atlanta: Scholars Press.

GNANADASON, A. KANYORO, M.R.A. & MCSPADDEN, L.A. (eds.) 1996, *Daughters of Anowa: African Women and Patriarchy: Women, Violence and Non-Violent Change*, Geneva: World Council of Churches Publications.

GOEHRING, J. 1999, *Ascetics, Society, and the Desert: Studies in Early Egyptian Monasticism*, Harrisburg, Pennsylvania: Trinity Press International.

GOTTNEID, A.J. (ed.) 1975, *Church and Education in Tanzania*, Nairobi: East African Publishing House.

GRIGGS, C.W. 1990, *Early Egyptian Christianity from its Origins to 451 CE*, New York: E.J. Brill.

GROVES. C.P. 1948-1958, *The Planting of Christianity in Africa*, 4 vols, London: Lutterworth Press.

HAAFKENS, J. 1992, *Islam and Christianity in Africa*, Nairobi: Procmura.

HAAFKENS, J. 1994, "PROCUMURA and the Churches in Africa," *Project for Christian-Muslim Relations in Africa,* 3, 3 (May/ June, 1994).

HAAFKENS, J. 1995, "The Direction of Christian-Muslim Relations in Sub-Saharan Africa", in Y.Y. HADDAD & W.Z. HADDAD (eds.), *Christian-Muslim Encounters*, Gainesville: University of Florida Press.

HACKETT, R.I.J. (ed.) 1987, *New Religious Movements in Nigeria*, Lewiston: The Edwin Mellen Press.

HACKETT, R.I.J. 1991, "Women as Leaders and Participants in the Spiritual Churches", in *Journal of Religion in Africa*, XXI, 2 (1991) 191-208.

HACKETT, R.I.J. 1995, "Women and New Religious Movements in Africa", in U. KING (ed.), *Religion and Gender*, Oxford: Blackwell.

HACKETT, R.I.J. 1996, *Art and Religion in Africa*, London: Cassell.

HACKETT, R.I.J. 1998, "Charismatic/Pentecostal Appropriation of Media Technologies in Nigeria and Ghana", in *Journal of Religion in Africa*, XXVIII, 3 (1998) 259-277.

HAIR, P.E.H. 1964, "Freetown Christianity and Africa", in *Sierra Leone Bulletin of Religion*, 6 (December 1964), 13-21.

HAIR, P.E.H. 1967, "Africanism: the Freetown Contribution", in *The Journal of African Studies*, 5 (December, 1967), 521-539.

HANCILES, J.J. 2002, *Euthanasia of a Mission: African Church Autonomy in a Colonial Context*, Connecticut, CT: Praeger Publishers.

HANCILES, J.J. 2002, "Bishop and Archdeacon Crowther: Inter-Generational Challenge and Opportunity in the Building of an African Church", in *Studia Historiae Ecclesiasticae* 28, 2 (December 2002) 170-196.

HANSEN, H.B. 1984, *Mission, Church and State in a Colonial Setting: Uganda, 1890-1925*, London: Heinemann, 1984.

HARGREAVES, J.D. 1979, *The End of Colonial Rule in West Africa*, London: McMillan.

HARRIS, J.E. (ed.) 1981, *William Leo Hansberry: African History Notes, vol. II: Africa and Africans as Seen by the Classical Writers*, Washington: Howard University Press.

HART, T.A. 1968, *Clergy and Society, 1600-1800*, London.

HASTINGS, A. 1973, *Christian Marriage In Africa*, London: S.P.C.K.

HASTINGS, A. 1979, *A History of African Christianity 1950–1975*, Cambridge: Cambridge University Press.

HASTINGS, A. 1989, *African Catholicism: Essays in Discovery*, London: SCM Press.

HASTINGS, A. 1994, *The Church in Africa: 1450-1950*, Oxford: Clarendon Press.

HAYNES, J. 1996, *Religion and Politics in Africa*, London: Zed Books.

HAYS, R.B. 1996, *The Moral Vision of the New Testament*, Harper: San Francisco.

HEADRICK, D.R, 1981, *The Tools of Empire. Technology and European Imperialism in the Nineteenth Century*, Oxford: Oxford University Press.

HERKLOTS, H.G.G. 1962, *The Call of God: An Explanation of the Revised Catechism*, London: Hodder & Stoughton.

HEXHAM I. & POEWE, K. 1994, "Charismatic Churches in South Africa: A Critique of Criticisms and Problems of Bias", in K. POEWE (ed.), *Charismatic Christianity as a Global Culture*, Columbia, S.C.: University of South Carolina Press.

HILLMAN, E. 1975, *Polygamy Reconsidered*, New York: Orbis Books.

HOARE, P. 1820, *Memoirs of Granville Sharp*, London: Henry Colburn & Co.

HOEHLER-FATTON, C. 1996, *Women of Fire and Spirit: Faith and Gender in Roho Religion in Western Kenya*, Oxford: Oxford University Press.

HODGKIN, T. 1957, *Nationalism in Colonial Africa*, New York University Press.

HODGKIN, T. 1975, *Nigerian Perspectives: An Historical Anthology*, London: Oxford University Press.

HOFMEYR, J.W. & PILLAY, G.J. (eds.) 1994, *A History of Christianity in South Africa*, Pretoria: HAUM Tertiary.

HOFMEYR, J.W. 1994, "Christianity in the South African Context in a period of Democratisation", in *Studia Historiae Ecclesiasticae*, 20, 2 (1994) 110-129.

HOLDEN, E. 1966, *Blyden of Liberia*, New York: Vantage Press.

HOORNAERT, E. 1989, *The Memory of the Christian People*, Maryknoll, NY: Orbis Books.

HORTON, R. 1971, "African Conversion", in *Africa*, 41, 2 (1971), 87-108.

HOWE, S. 1998, *Afrocentrism: Mythical Pasts and Imagined Homes*, New York: Verso.

HOWSE, E.M. 1971 (1953), *Saints in Politics: The 'Clapham Sect' and the Growth of Freedom*, London: George Allen & Unwin Ltd.

IBRAHIM, B. & IBRAHIM, F.N. 1998, "Zuwanderer nach Deutschland: Das Beispiel der ägyptischen Kopten", in H. KOSCHYK & R. STOLZ, R. (eds.), *30 Jahre Zuwanderung. Eine kritische Bilanz*, Landsberg am Lech: Olzog Verlag, 129-161.

IDOWU, E.B. 1965, *Towards an Indigenous Church*, London: Oxford University Press.

IDOWU, E.B. 1973, *African Traditional Religion: A Definition*, London: SPCK.

ISAAC, E. 1967, *The Ethiopian Church*, Boston: Henry N. Sawyer Co.

ISICHEI, E. 1995, *A History of Christianity in Africa: From Antiquity to the Present*, London: SPCK.

JACOBS, S.M. 1982, Black Americans and the Missionary Movement in Africa: Contributions in Afro-American and African Studies, Westport: Greenwood Press.

JACOBS, S.M. 1982, "The Historical Role of Afro-Americans in American Missionary Efforts in Africa, in Black Americans and the Missionary Movement in Africa, in S.M. JACOBS (ed.), *Black Americans and the Missionary Movement in Africa: Contributions in Afro-American and African Studies*, Westport: Greenwood Press, 5-29.

JASSY, M.-P. 1971, *Women in African Independent Churches*, Geneva: Risk Books.

JENKINS, P. 2000, *The Next Christendom*, New York: Oxford University Press.

JENKINS, P. 2002, "A New Christendom" in *The Chronicle Review*, Section 2.

JORDAN, J. 1949, *Bishop Shanahan of Southern Nigeria*, Dublin: Dublin Echo Press Ltd.

JORDAN, J. 1992, *Autobiography of a Missionary*, Dublin.

JULES-ROSETTE, B. 1985, "Cultural Ambivalence and Ceremonial Leadership: The Role of Woman in Africa's New Religious Movements," in J.C.B. WEBSTER & E.L. WEBSTER (eds.), *The Church and Women in the Third World*, Philadelphia: Westminster Press.

KAEGI, W.E. 1998, "Egypt on the eve of the Muslim conquest," in Carl F. PETRY (ed.), *The Cambridge History of Egypt*, vol. I, New York: Cambridge University Press.

KALU, O.U. 1975, "Peter Pan Syndrome: Church Aid and Selfhood in Africa" in *Missiology*, 3, 1 (January, 1975), 15-29.

KALU, O.U. 1975, "Not Just New Relationship But a Renewed Body", in *International Review of Missions*, 64 (April, 1975).

KALU, O.U. 1977, "Gods in Retreat: Models of Religious Change in Africa", in *Nigerian Journal of Humanities*, 1,1, (1977), 42-53.

KALU, O.U. 1978, *Divided People of God: Church Union Movement in Nigeria, 1867-1967*, New York: NOK Publishers.

KALU, O.U. 1978, "Church Unity and Religious Change in Africa", in E. FAKSHOLE-LUKE, R. GRAY, A. HASTINGS, & G. TASIE (eds.), *Christianity in Independent Africa*, Bloomington: Indiana University Press, 164-175.

KALU, O.U. 1979, "Over a Century of Christian Presence in Africa: A Historical Perspective", in *Bulletin de Theologie Africaine,* 1, 1 (January-June, 1979), 112-126.

KALU, O.U. 1980, "Church, Mission and Moratorium", in O.U. KALU, *The History of Christianity in West Africa*, London: Longman, 365-374.

KALU, O.U. 1980, *The History of Christianity in West Africa*, London: Longman.

KALU, O.U. 1995, "The Dilemma of Grassroots Inculturation of the Gospel, in *Journal of Religion in Africa*, 25 (1995) 48-72.

KALU, O.U. 1998, "Gospel, Culture and Mission: Revisiting an Enduring Problem", in *Skrif en Kerk*, 19, 2 (1998) 283-300.

KALU, O.U. 1998, "Tools of Hope: Stagnation and Political Theology in Africa,1960-95", in M. HUTCHINSON and O.U. KALU, *A Global Faith: Essays in Evangelicalism and Globalization*, Sydney: CSAC, 181-213

KALU, O.U. 2000, "Doing Mission Through the Post Office: the Naked Faith People of Igboland,1920-1960", in *Neue Zeitschrift fur Missionwissenschaft*, 54, 4 (2000) 263-280.

KALU, O.U. 2000, "Passive Revolution and Its Saboteurs: African Christian Initiative in the Era of Decolonization", (Currents in World Christianity, Faculty of Divinity, University of Cambridge, Position Paper no. 134).

KALU, O.U. 2000, *Power, Poverty and Prayer: The Challenges of Poverty and Pluralism in African Christianity, 1960-1996*, Frankfurt: Peter Lang.

KALU, O.U. 2000, "Estranged Bedfellows: The Demonization of the Aladura in African Pentecostal Rhetoric" in *Missionalia* 28 (2000).

KALU, O.U. 2002, "Jesus Christ, Where Are You? Themes in West African Church Historiography", in *Missionalia*, 3, 2 (2002).

KALU, O.U. 2003, "Black Missionaries and White Abolitionists: The Careers of Joseph and Mary Gomer in the Good Hope Mission, Sherbro, Sierra Leone, 1871-1894", in *Neue Zitschrift Für Missionwifsenschaft* (June, 2003), 161-174.

KALU, O.U. 2003 (1996), *Embattled Gods: Christianization of Igboland, 1841-1991*, Trenton, NJ: Africa World Press.

KALU, O.U. 2003, "Pentecostal and Charismatic Reshaping of the African Religious Landscape in the 1990s", in *Mission Studies,* 20, 1-39 (2003).

KALU, O.U. 2006, "Ethiopianism and the Roots of Modern African Christianity", in B. STANLEY, et. al. (eds.), *Cambridge History of Christianity,* vol. 8, London: Cambridge University Press.

KANE, C.H. 1962, *Ambiguous Adventure, René Juillard* (trans. from the French by Katherine WOODS, New York: Collier, 1963).

KANYORO, M.RA. 2002, *Introducing Feminist Cultural Hermeneutics: An African Perspective*, Sheffield Academic Press.

KANYORO, M.R.A. & NJOROGE N.J. (eds.), 1996, *Groaning in Faith: African Women in the Household of God*, Nairobi: Acton Publishers.

KARAMAGA, A. 1991, *Problems and Promises of Africa: Towards and Beyond the Year 2000*, Nairobi: All Africa Conference of Churches.

KASIERA, E.M. 1980, "The Foundation and Development of Nyang'ori Mission, 1909-1924" (Seminar paper, Department of Philosophy and Religious Studies, University of Nairobi, 20 February 1980).

KASIERA, E.M. 1981, *Development of Pentecostal Christianity in Western Kenya* (Unpublished PhD dissertation, Aberdeen).

KATO, B. 1975, *Theological Pitfalls in Africa*, Kisimu: Kenya Evangelical Publishing House.

KELSAY J. & J.J. TURNER, 1991, *Just War and Jihad: Historical and Theoretical Perspectives on War and Peace in Western and Islamic Traditions*, New York: Greenwood Press.

KEMDIRIM, P. 1995, "Towards Inclusiveness for Women in the African Churches", in *Mission Studies*, XII, 1, 2, 3 (1995), 1-8.

KEMP, D. 1898, *Nine Years at the Gold Coast*, London: Macmillan & Co. Ltd.

KENNY, J. 1996, "Sharia and Christianity in Nigeria: Islam and a 'Secular' State", in *Journal of Religion in Africa*, 26, 4 (1996).

KENDALL, E. 1978, *The End of An Era*, London.

KENYATTA, J. 1962 (1938), *Facing Mount Kenya*, London: Vintage.

KIERNAN, J.P. 1990, *The Production and Management of Therapeutic Power in Zionist Churches within a Zulu City*, Lewiston, NY: The Edwin Mellen Press.

KIGGINS, T. 1991, *Maynooth Mission to Africa. The Story of St. Patrick's Kiltegan*, Dublin: Gill & Macmillan.

KILLINGRAY, D. "The Black Atlantic Missionary Movement and Africa, 1780s-1920s", in *Journal of Religion in Africa*, 33, 1 (February 2003), 3-31.

KING, K. 2003, *What is Gnosticism?*, Cambridge, Massachusetts: Belknap Press of Harvard University.

KING, N.Q. 1971, *Christian and Muslim in Africa*, New York: Harper & Row Publishers.

KING, U. 1995, "A Question of Identity: Women Scholars and the Study of Religion", in U. KING (ed.), *Religion and Gender*, Oxford: Blackwell.

KNUTSFORD, L. 1900, *The Life and Letters of Zachary Macaulay*, London: Edward Arnold.

KOPYTOFF, J.H. 1965, *A Preface to Modern Nigeria: The Sierra Leoneans in the Yoruba, 1830-1890*, Madison: University of Wisconsin Press.

KOREN, H.J. 1983, *To the Ends of the Earth. A General History of the Congregation of the Holy Ghost*, Pittsburgh: Duquesne University Press.

KPOBI, D.N.A. 1993, *Mission in Chains*, Zoetermeer: Boekencentrum.

KUKAH, M.H. 1993, *Religion, Politics and Power in Northern Nigeria*, Lagos: Spectrum.

LAITIN, D. 1986, *Hegemony and Culture: Politics and Religious Change Among the Yoruba*, Chicago: University of Chicago Press.

LANDMAN, C. 1994, *The Piety of Afrikaans Women: Diaries of Guilt*, Pretoria: University of South Africa Press.

LARBI, E.K. 2001, *Pentecostalism: the Eddies of Ghanaian Christianity*, Accra: Center for Pentecostal and Charismatic Studies.

LAURENT, P.-J. 2001, "Transnationalization and Local Transformations: The Example of the Church of Assemblies of God in Burkina Faso", in A. CORTEN and R. MARSHALL-FRATANI (eds.), *Between Babel and Pentecost: Transnational Pentecostalism in Africa and Latin* America, Bloomington and Indianapolis: Indiana University Press, 256-273.

LEVTZION N. (ed.), 1979, *Conversion to Islam*, New York and London: Holmes & Meier.

LEVTZION, N. & VOLL J.O. (eds.), 1987, *Eighteenth-Century Renewal and Reform in Islam*, New York: Syracuse University.

LAROM M.S. (ed.), 1994, *Claiming the Promise: African Churches Speak*, New York: Friendship Press.

LATOURETTE, K.S. 1939, *A History of the Expansion of Christianity, Vol. III, Three Centuries of Advance A.D. 1500 – A.D. 1800*, New York: Harper & Brothers.

LIKIMANI, M. 1974, *They Shall be Chastised*, Nairobi: Noni's Publicity.

LINCOLN, E.C. & MAMIYA, L.H. 1990, *The Black Church in the African American Experience*, Durham: Duke University Press.

LINDEN, I. 1974, *Catholics, Peasants, and Chewa Resistance in Nyasaland, 1889-1939*, Berkeley: University of California Press.

LONGMAN, T. 1988, "Empowering the Weak and Protecting the Powerful" in *African Studies Review*, 41 (April, 1998), 49-72.

LONSDALE, J.M. 1975, "European Attitudes and African Pressures: Missions and Government in Kenya between the Wars", in B.A OGOT (ed.), *Hadith 2*, Nairobi: East Africa Publ. House, 229-242.

LONSDALE, P. 2002, "Mission Christianity & Settler Colonialism in Eastern Africa", in H. HANSEN & M. TWADDLE (eds.), *Christian Missionaries and the State in the Third World*, Oxford: Currey, 194-211.

LOUISE, M. 1957, *Kimbangu*, London: Oxford University Press.

LUDWIG, F. 1992, "Die Entdeckung der schwarzen Kirchen. Afrikanische und Afrokaribische Gemeinden in England während der Nachkriegszeit", in *Archiv für Sozialgeschichte*, 32 (1992).

LUDWIG, F. 1993, "Radicalisation and Consolidation of the Garrick Braide Movement, 1915-1918", in *Journal of Religion in Africa*, 22, 4 (1993).

LUGWUANA, L. 2000, "Medicine, Spiritual Healing and African Response", in *Africa Theological Journal*, 23, 1 (2000).

LUMBALA, F.K. 1988, *Celebrating Jesus in Africa: Liturgy and Inculturation*, Maryknoll: Orbis.

LUZBETAK, L. 1993, *The Church and Cultures*, Maryknoll: Orbis.

LYNCH, H.R. 1967, *Edward Wilmot Blyden: Pan-Negro Patriot, 1832-1912*, London: Oxford University Press.

MAGESA, L. 1997, *African Religion: The Moral Foundations of Abundant Life*, Maryknoll: Orbis Books.

MAILLU, D. 1987, *Our Kind of Polygamy*, Nairobi: Heinemann.

MALULEKE, T.S. 1994, "The Proposal For a Theology of Reconstruction: A Critical Appraisal", in *Missionalia*, 22, 3 (November 1994), 245-258.

MALULEKE, T.S. 1995, *"A Morula Tree Between Two Fields": The Commentary of Selected Tsonga Writers on Missionary Christianity* (DTh dissertation, University of South Africa).

MALULEKE, T.S. 1996, "African Culture, African Intellectuals and the White Academy in South Africa", in *Religion and Theology*, 3, 1 (1996), 19-42.

MALULEKE, T.S. 1996, "Black and African Theologies in the New World Order: A Time to Drink From Our Own Wells", in *Journal of Theology for Southern Africa*, 96 (November 1996), 3-19.

MALULEKE, T.S. 1996, "Recent Developments in the Christian Theologies of Africa: Towards the 21st Century", in *Journal of Constructive Theology*, 2, 2 (December 1996), 33-60.

MALULEKE, T.S. 1996, "Theological Interest in African Independent Churches and Other Grass-Root Communities in South Africa: A Review of Methodologies", in *Journal of Black Theology in South Africa*, 10, 1 (May 1996), 18-48.

MALULEKE, T.S. 1986, "Review Mugambi, J N K 1995. From Liberation to Reconstruction: African Christian Theology After the Cold War. Nairobi: East African Educational Publishers", in *Missionalia*, 24, 3 (November 1996), 472-473.

MARSHALL, R. 1995, "'God is not a Democrat': Pentecostalism and Democratization in Nigeria", in P. GIFFORD (ed.), *The Christian Churches and the Democratization Process in Africa*, Leiden: Brill.

MARTIN, L. 1999, *The Life and Ministry of William J. Seymour and a History of the Azusa Street Revival*, Joplin: Christian Life Books.

MARTIN, M.-L. 1975, *Kimbangu, an African Prophet and His Church*, Oxford: Oxford University Press.

MARTIN, S.D. "Black Baptists, Foreign Missions, and African Colonization 1814-1882", in JACOBS, *Black Americans and the Missionary Movement in Africa: Contributions in Afro-American and African Studies,* Westport: Greenwood Press, 63-76.

MARTEY, E. 1993, *African Theology: Inculturation and Liberation*, Maryknoll: Orbis Books.

MASRI, E. & HABIB, I. 1982, *The Story of the Copts, The True Story of Christianity in Egypt*, 3 Volumes, End-Time Handmaiden.

MAZRUI, A. 1970, "Epilogue", in O. P'BITEK, *African Religions in Western Scholarship*, Kampala: East African Literature Bureau.

MBITI, J.S. 1969, *African Religions and Philosophy*, London: Heinemann.

MBITI, J.S. 1970, "Christianity and Traditional Religions in Africa", in *International Review of Missions*, 59, 236, 1970: 430-441.

MBITI, J.S. 1971, *New Testament Eschatology in an African Background*, Oxford: Oxford University Press.

MBITI, J.S. 1972, "Some African Concepts of Christology", in G.F. VICEDOM, *Christ and the Younger Churches*, London: S.P.C.K.

MBITI. J.S. 1977, "The Biblical Basis for Present Trends in African Theology", in K. APPIAH-KUBI & S. TORRES, *African Theology en Route: Papers from the Pan-African Conference of Third World Theologians. Accra. December 17-23, 1977*, Maryknoll: Orbis Books.

MBITI, J.S. 1979, *Concepts of God in Africa*, London: SPCK.

MBITI, J.S. (ed.), 1986, *The Bible in African Christianity*, Nairobi: Oxford University Press.

MCCALL, E.L. 1977, "Black Christianity in America", in R.P. BEAVER (ed.), *American Missions in Bicentennial Perspective*, Pasadena, CA: William Carey Library, 249-274.

MCGARRY, C. 1986, "Preface", to John WALLIGO et al, *Inculturation: Its Meaning and Urgency*, Kampala: St. Pauls' Publications.

MCGETTRICK, T. 1988, Memoirs of Bishop T. McGettrick, Enugu.

MCGLADE, J. 1967, "The Missions: Africa and the Orient", in P.J. CORISH (ed.), *A History of Irish Catholicism,* VI, 8, Dublin: Gill & Macmillan.

MCINTIRE, C.T. 1974, *The Ongoing Task of Christian Historiography*, Toronto: Institute of Christian Studies.

MCKENNA, J.C. 1997, *Finding a Social Voice: The Church and Marxism in Africa*, New York: Fordham University Press.

MCKENZIE, P. 1976, *Inter-religious Encounters in West Africa: Samuel Ajayi Crowther's Attitude to African Traditional Religions and Islam*, Leicester: Leicester University Bookshop.

METUH, E.I. 1986, "Muslim Resistance to Missionary Penetration of Northern Nigeria, 1857–1960: A Missiological Interpretation," in *Mission Studies,* Vol. III, 2 (1986), 28-39.

MHOGOLO, G.M. 1986, "God the Father and Family Life in Contemporary Africa", in D.M. GITARI & G.P. BENSON (eds.), *Witnessing to the Living God in Contemporary Africa,* Kabare, Kenya: Africa Theological Fraternity.

MILLER, P. 1983, *Biography in Late Antiquity: A Quest for the Holy Man*, Berkeley: University of California Press.

MILLER, P.M. 1969, *Equipping for Ministry in East Africa*, Dodoma: Central Tanganyika Press.

MITCHELL, G.D. (ed.), 1968, *A Dictionary of Sociology*, London: Routledge & Kegan Paul.

MOBLEY, H. 1970, *The Ghanaian's Image of the Missionary: An Analysis of the Published Critiques of Christian Missionaries by Ghanaians 1897-1965*, Leiden: Brill.

MOLTMANN, J. 1974, *The Crucified God: The Cross of Christ as the Foundation of and Criticism of Christian Theology*, London: SCM Press.

MONTGOMERY, J.W. 1970, *Where is History Going? A Christian Response to Secular Philosophies of History*, Minneapolis: Bethany Fellowship Inc.

MOSALA, I.J. 1978, "Spirituality and Struggle: African and Black Theologies", in S. TORRES & V.M.M. FABELLA (eds.), *The Emergent Gospel: Theology from the Underside of History: Papers from the Ecumenical Dialogue of Third World Theologians, Dar es Salam, August 5-12*, Maryknoll: Orbis Books.

MOTLHABI, M.G. 1994, "Black or African Theology? Toward and Integral African Theology", in *Journal of Black Theology in South Africa*, 8, 2 (November 1994), 113-141.

MOTYER, J.A. 1967, "Baptism", in J.D. DOUGLAS (ed.), *The New Bible Dictionary*, London: Inter-Varsity Press.

MUDENGE, S.I.G. 1988, *A Political History of Munhumutapa c1400-1902*, Harare: Zimbabwe Publishing House.

MUGA, E. 1974, *African Response to the Western Christian Religion*, Nairobi: East African Literature Bureau.

MUGAMBI, J.N.K. 1990, "The Ecumenical Movement and the Future of the Church in Africa", in J.N.K. MUGAMBI & L. MAGESA (eds.), *The Church in African Christianity: Innovative Essays in Ecclesiology*, Nairobi: Initiatives.

MUGAMBI, J.N.K. 1991, "The Future of the Church and the Church of the Future Africa", in J. CHIPENDA, A. KARAMAGA, J.N.K. MUGAMBI & C.K. OMARI (eds.), *The Church of Africa: Toward a Theology of Reconstruction*, Nairobi: AACC.

MUGAMBI, J.N.K 1992, *Critiques of Christianity in African Literature*, Nairobi: East African Educational Publishers.

MUGAMBI, J.N.K. 1995, *From Liberation to Reconstruction: African Christian Theology After the Cold War*, Nairobi: East African Educational Publishers.

MUGAMBI, J.N.K. 2002, *Christianity and African Culture*, Nairobi: Acton.

MUGAMBI, J.N.K. & MAGESA, L. (eds.), 1990, *The Church in African Christianity: Innovative Essays in Ecclesiology*, Nairobi: Initiatives.

MUGAMBI, J.N.K., MUTISO-MBINDA, J. & VOLLBRECHT, J. (eds.), 1992, *Ecumenical Initiatives in Eastern Africa*, Nairobi: AACC/AMCEA Joint Research Project.

MUGYENZI, S. 2000, "Seeking Understanding in Uganda" in *Transformation* (2000), 17, 1, 42.

MULENGA, K. 1998, *Blood in their Hands*, Lusaka: Zambia Educational Publishing House.

MULLET, M.A. 1999, *The Catholic Reformation*, London: Routledge.

MUNRO, H.D. 1968, "Culture", in G.D. MITCHELL (ed.), *A Dictionary of Sociology*, London: Routledge & Kegan Paul.

MURRAY, J. 1974, "The Kikuyu Spirit Churches", in *Journal of Religion in Africa*, 5, 3, (1974), 198-234.

MUSHETE, N. 1978, "Unity of Faith and Pluralism in Theology", in S. TORRES & V.M.M. FABELLA (eds.), *The Emergent Gospel: Theology from the Underside of History: Papers from the Ecumenical Dialogue of Third World Theologians, Dar es Salam, August 5-12*, Maryknoll: Orbis Books.

MUTUA, R.W. 1975, *Development of Education in Kenya: Some Administrative Aspects*, Nairobi: East African Literature Bureau.

MWAURA, P.N. *A Theological and Cultural Analysis of Healing in Jerusalem Church of Christ and Nabii Christian Church of Kenya* (Unpublished PhD Thesis, Kenyatta University, 2001).

MWONDELA. W.R. 1970, *Traditional Education in North-western Zambia*, Lusaka: National Educational Co. of Zambia.

NEILL, S. 1952, *Christian Partnership*, London: SCM Press.

NEILL, S. 1986, *A History of Christian Missions*, 2nd Edition, New York: Penguin, 1986.

NEWBIGIN, L. 1953, *The Household of God*, London: SCM.

NEWBIGIN, L. 1994, "Ecumenical Amnesia", in *International Bulletin of Mission Research*, 18, 1 (January, 1994), 1-5.

NGUGI WA THIONG'O (James NGUGI), 1966, *The River Between*, London: Heinemann.

NIDA, E.A. 1954, *Customs and Cultures: Anthropology for Christian Missions*, New York: Harper and Brothers.

NIEBHUR, H.R. 1937, *The Kingdom of God in America*, New York: 1937.

NIEBHUR H.R. 1951, *Christ and Culture*, New York: Harper & Bros.

NJOKU, C.A. 1998, *A Study of the Wishes of the Catholic Bishops of Anglophone West Africa (1959–1960), for the Second Vatican Ecumenical Council* (Licentiate Thesis, Faculty of Theology, Katholieke Universiteit Leuven, Belgium).

NJOKU, C.A. 2001, "On the Thresholds of Theological Conversations between the North and the South: Impediments and Hopes" (paper presented at the 3rd International Encounters in Systematic Theology, LEST III, *Theology and Conversation. Developing a Relational Theology,* Leuven, 6-9 November 2001).

NJOKU, C.A. 2002, *Vatican II and the Process of its Reception in the Igbo Speaking Church of Southeast Nigeria: 1959–1995* (PhD Dissertation, Katholieke Universiteit Leuven, Belgium).

NJOKU, C.A. 2003 "Violent Research: Ethics and effects of Negative Representation of the other in Missionary and Anthropological Research" (paper presented at the International conference on Reconciling Mission: Overcoming Violence, British and Irish association for Mission Studies (BIAMS), Edinburgh, 23rd to 26th June 2003).

NJOKU, C.A. & LAMBERIGTS, M. 2000, "Vatican II: The Vota of the Anglo-phone West African Bishops Concerning the Sacred Liturgy, in *Questiones Liturgiques* 81 (2000), 89-121.

NJOROGE, N.J. 2000, *Kiama Kia Ngo: An African Christian Feminist Ethic of Resistance and Transformation*, Ecclesiastical Studies 2, Legon, Theological Series, Accra: Asempa Publishers.

NJOROGE, N.J. 2002, "Reclaiming our Heritage of Power: Discovering our Theological Voices", in I.A. PHIRI, B. GOVINDEN & S. NADAR (eds.), *Her-stories: Hidden Histories of Women of Faith in Africa*, Pietermaritzburg: Cluster Publications, 39-57.

NJOROGE, N.J. & DUBE, M.W. (eds.), 2001, *Talitha Cum! Theologies of African Women*, Pietermaritzburg: Cluster Publications.

NKRUMAH, K. 1964, *Conscientism*, London: Heinemann.

NOLL, M. 1992, *A History of Christianity in the United States and Canada*, Grand Rapids, MI: Wm. B. Eerdmans.

NOLL, M. 1997, "Evangelical Identity, Power and Culture in the Great Nineteenth Century" (Currents in World Christianity Seminar, Oxford, 1997).

NTHAMBURI, Z. & WARUTA, D. 1986, "Biblical Hermeneutics in African Instituted Churches", in J.S. MBITI (ed.), *The Bible in African Christianity*, Nairobi: Oxford University Press.

NWANKPA, E. 1998, *Redeeming the Land: Interceding for the Nations*, Accra: ACP.

NWOGA, D.I. 1984, *The Supreme God As Stranger in Igbo Religious Thought*. Ekwereazu in Imo State, Nigeria: Hawk Press.

NYANG, S.S. 1984, *Islam, Christianity, and African Identity*, Vermont: Amana.

NZEKI, R.S.N.M. 1977, "The Church and Family Life" in *Target*, 236 (21st May, 1977).

O'TOOLE, T. 1977, "The Persistence of Colonial Thinking in African Historiography" in *UFAHAMU* (California), 7,2, 1977, 43-52.

OBIECHINA, E. 1975, *Culture, Tradition and Society in the West African Novel*, Cambridge: Cambridge University Press.

OBINKARAM, E.T. 1976, *The Land's Lord*, New York: Laurence Hill & Co.

OCITTI, J.P. 1973, *African Indigenous Education*, Nairobi: East African Literature Bureau.

ODUYOYE, M.A. 1988, *Who Will Roll the Stone Away? The Ecumenical Decade of the Churches in Solidarity with Women*, Geneva: World Council of Churches Publications.

ODUYOYE, M.A. 1995, *Daughters of Anowa: African Women and Patriarchy*, New York: Orbis Books.

ODUYOYE, M.A. 1995, "Christianity and African Culture", in *International Review of Mission*, 84, 332/333 (January/April 1995), 77-90.

ODUYOYE, M.A. & KANYORO, M.R.A. (eds.), 1990, *Talitha, Qumi!: Proceedings of the Convocation of African Women Theologians 1989*, Ibadan: Daystar Press.

ODUYOYE, M.A. & KANYORO, M.R.A. (eds.), 1992, *The Will to Arise: Women, Tradition and the Church in Africa*, Maryknoll: Orbis Books.

OJO, M.A. 1988, "Deeper Christian Life Ministry: A Case Study of the Charismatic Movements in Western Nigeria", in *Journal of Religion in Africa*, 28, 2 (1988), 141-162.

OJO, M.A. 1998, "Marriage and Piety among Charismatic in Nigeria", in J. COX, *Rites of Passage in Contemporary Africa*, Cardiff: Cardiff Academic Press.

OKERE, T. 1974, *Culture and Religion*, Owerri.

OKAFOR, R. 2002, *Crisis and Renewal: Civil War Revival and the New Pentecostal Churches in Nigeria's Igboland*, Leiden: Brill.

OKULU, H. 1974, *Church and Politics in East Africa*, Nairobi: Uzima Press.

OLAYINKA, B.O. 2000, *Female Leaders of New Generation Churches as Change Agents in Yorubaland* (Unpublished PhD Thesis, Obafemi Awolowo University).

OLIN, J.C. 1990, *Catholic Reform. From Cardinal Ximenes to the Council of Trent 1495-1563*, New York: Fordham University Press.

OLIVER, R. 1965, *The Missionary Factor in East Africa*, London: Longman.

OLORUNTIMEHIN, B.O. 1976, "History and Society", in *Inaugural Lecture Series*, 18, Ile-Ife: University of Ife.

OLUBANKE, D.A. 2002, "The History of Good Women: Association of the Christ Apostolic Church", (Unpublished Paper, January 2002).

OLUSANYA, G. 1973, "Julius Cole: a Neglected Nigerian Nationalist and Educationist", in *Journal of the Historical Society of Nigeria*, 7,1 (December, 1973), 91-110.

OMENKA, N.I. 1989, *The School in the Service of Evangelization. The Catholic Educational Impact in Eastern Nigeria 1886-1950*, Leiden: Brill.

OMENYO, C.N. 2002, *Pentecost Outside Pentecostalism: A Study of the Development of Charismatic Renewal in the Mainline Churches in Ghana*, Amsterdam: Boekencentrum.

OMOYAJOWO, J.A. 1982, *Cherubim and Seraphim: The History of an African Independent Church*, New York: Nok Publishers.

OMOYAJOWO, J.A. 1988, "The Role of Women in Traditional African Religions and Independent Church Movements", in *Dialogue and Alliance*, 2, 3, (1988).

ONWUEJEOGWU, M.A. 1987, *Evolutionary Trends in the History of the Development of the Igbo Civilization in the Culture Theatre of Igboland in Southern Nigeria, 1987 Ahiajoku Lecture*, Owerri: Ministry of Information.

OOSTHUIZEN, G.C. 1967, *The Theology of a South African Messiah: An Analysis of the Hymnal of The Church of the Nazarites*, Leiden: Brill.

OOSTHUIZEN, G.C. 1968, *Post-Christianity in Africa: A Theological and Anthropological Study*, London: C. Hurst.

OOSTHUIZEN, G.C. 1992, *The Healer-Prophet in Afro-Christian Churches*, Leiden: Brill.

OOSTHUIZEN G.C. & HEXHAM I. (eds.), 1992, *Empirical Studies of African Independent / Indigenous Churches,* Lewiston, NY: The Edwin Mellen Press.

OTTO, R. 1950 (1923), *The Idea of the Holy: An Inquiry into the Non-Rational Factor in the Idea of the Divine and Its Relation to the Rational,* London: Oxford University Press.

OZIGBOH, I.R.A. 1985, *Igbo Catholicism*, Onitsha: Africana-FEP.

OZIGBO, I.R.A. 1994, "An Evaluation of Christian Pioneering techniques with particular reference to Nigeria," in *The Nigerian Journal of Theology,* 8, 1 (1994), 43-62.

PAKENHAM, T. 1991, *The Scramble for Africa 1876-1912*, London: Abacus.

P'BITEK, O. 1966, *Song of Lawino*, Nairobi: East African Publishing House.

P'BITEK, O. 1967, *Song Of Ocol*, Nairobi: East African Publishing House.

PARRATT, J. 1995, *Reinventing Christianity: African Theology Today*, Grand Rapids: Eerdmans.

PEARCE, R. 1984, "The Colonial Office and Planned Decolonisation in Africa" in *African Affairs*, 83 (1984), 77-93.

PEARSON, B.A. 1990, *Gnosticism, Judaism, and Egyptian Christianity*, Minneapolis: Fortress.

PEARSON, B.A. & GOEHRING, J.E. (eds.), 1986, *The Roots of Egyptian Christianity*, Philadelphia: Fortress Press.

PEEL, J.D.Y 1968, *Aladura:* A *Religious Movement Among the Yoruba*, London: Oxford University Press.

PEEL, J.D.Y. 2003, *Religious Encounter and the Making of the Yoruba*, Indiana: Indiana University Press.

PEIL, M. 1997, *Consensus and Conflict in African Societies*, London: Longman.

PHILIPS, C. 2003, *A History of SOAS, 1917–67,* in D. ARNOLD & C. SCHACKLE, (eds.), *SOAS Since the Sixties*, London: SOAS, 21-43.

PHIPPS, W.E. 2002, *William Sheppard: Congo's African American Livingstone*, Louisville, KY: Presbyterian Publishing.

PHIRI, I.A. 1997, "Doing Theology as African Women", in J. PARATT (ed.), *A Reader in African Christian Theology*, London: SPCK.

PHIRI, I.A. 2000, "African Women in Mission: Two Case Studies From Malawi", in *Missionalia,* 28 (2000).

PHIRI, I.A., GOVINDEN, D.B. & NADAR, S. (eds.), 2003, *Her Stories, Hidden Histories of Women of Faith in Africa*, Pietermaritzburg, Cluster Publications.

PINN, A.H. & PINN, A.B. 2003, *Fortress Introduction to Black Church History*, Minneapolis: Fortress Press.

PITYANA, B. 1994, "The Urgent Need for Moral Reconstruction", in *Challenge* (1994), 6-7.

POBEE, J.S. 1995, "Moving Towards a Pentecost Experience in Ministerial Formation", in *Ministerial Formation* 68 (January 1995).

POBEE, J.S. 1996, *West Africa: Christ Would Be an African Too*, Geneva: WCC Pamphlet, No. IX.

POPE-HENNESSY, J. 1967, *Sins of the Fathers: A Study of the Atlantic Slave Traders 1441-1807*, London: Weiden & Nicholson.

POSTMA, J.M. 1990, *The Dutch in the Atlantic Slave Trade 1600-1815*, Cambridge: Cambridge University Press.

RABOTEAU, A.J. 1983, "'Ethiopian shall soon Stretch out her Hands': Black Destiny in Nineteenth Century America", lecture at Arizona State University (January 27, 1983).

RADCLIFFE-BROWN, A.R. & FORDE, D. (eds.), 1950, *African Systems of Kinship and Marriage*, London: Oxford University Press.

RAMODIBE, D. 1988, "Women and Men Building Together the Church in Africa", in V.M.M. FABELLA & M.A. ODUYOYE (eds.), *With Passion and Compassion*, Maryknoll: Orbis Books.

RAMSAY, I.T. 1957, *Religious Language: An Empirical Placing of Theological Phrases*, London: S.C.M.

RAISER, K. 1991, *Ecumenism in Transition: A Paradigm Shift in the Ecumenical Movement*, Geneva: WCC Publication.

RANGER, T.O. 1968, "Connection Between Primary Resistance and Modern Mass Nationalism" *Journal of African History* 9, 3 (1968).

RANGER, T.O. 1986, "Religious Movements and politics in Sub-Saharan Africa" *African Studies Review*, 29, 2 (1986), 1-69.

RANGER, T.O. & Ogot, B. (eds.), 1972, *The Historical Study of African Religion*, London: Heinemann.

RANGER, T.O. & WELLER J. (eds.), 1975, *Themes in the Christian History of Central Africa*, London: Heinemann.

RASMUSSEN, R. 1993, *Christian-Muslim Relations in Africa: The Cases of Northern Nigeria and Tanzania Compared*, London & New York: British Academic Press.

REYNOLDS, J.T. 2001, "Nigeria and Shari'a: Religion and Politics in a West African Nation", in M.A. O'MEARA (ed.), *History Behind the Headlines: The Origins of Conflicts Worldwide* Vol. 2, Farmington Hill, MI: Gale Group.

RICHMOND, A.H. "Acculturation" in in G.D. MITCHELL (ed.), *A Dictionary of Sociology*, London: Routledge & Kegan Paul.

ROBERTS, D.L. (ed.), 2002, *Gospel Bearers, Gender Barriers: Missionary Women in the Twentieth Century*, Maryknoll: Orbis Books.

ROSS, K. 1999, *God, People and Power in Malawi: Democratization in Theological Perspective*, Blantyre: CLAIM.

SAAYMAN, W. & KRITZINGER, J.J. (eds.), 1996, *Mission in Bold Humility: David Bosch's Work Considered*, Maryknoll: Orbis Books.

SAID, E.W. 1993, *Culture and Imperialism*, London: Chatto & Windus.

SAMITA, Z.W. 1996, "The African Church of the Holy Spirit: Origins and Advent in Kabra Division, Kamenga District", in *TransAfrican Journal of History*, 25 (1996), 123-145.

SANDERS, C.J. 1996, *Saints in Exile: The Holiness-Pentecostal Experience in African American Religion and Culture*, New York: Oxford University Press.

SANDGREN, D.P. 1989, *Christianity and the Kikuyu: Religious Divisions and Social Conflict*, New York: Peter Lang.

SANNEH, L. 1983, *West African Christianity: The Religious Impact*, Maryknoll: Orbis Books.

SANNEH, L. 1989, *Translating the Message: The Missionary Impact on Culture*, Maryknoll: Orbis Books.

SANNEH, L. *Encountering the West*, Maryknoll: Orbis Books, 1993.

SANNEH, L. 1994, "Translatability in Islam and in Christianity in Africa: A Thematic Approach", in T.D. BLAKELY, W.E.A. VAN BECK & D.L. THOMSON (eds.), *Religion in Africa*, London: John Curry Ltd.

SANNEH, L. 1996, *Piety and Power: Muslims and Christians in West Africa*, Maryknoll, NY: Orbis Books.

SANNEH, L. 2001, *Abolitionists Abroad: American Blacks and the Making of the Modern West Africa*, Cambridge, MA: Harvard University Press.

SAWYERR, H. 1996, *The Practice of Presence: Shorter Writings of Harry Sawyerr*, J. PARRATT (ed.), Grand Rapids: Eerdmans.

SCHILDKROUT, E. & KEKIM, C.A. (eds.), 1988, *The Scramble for Art in Central Africa*, Cambridge: Cambridge University Press.

SCHÖN J.F. & CROWTHER, S. 1970 (1842), *Journals of the Rev. James Frederick Schön and Mr. Samuel Crowther: Who, with the Sanction of Her Majesty's Government, Accompanied the Expedition up the Niger in 1841 on Behalf of the Church Missionary Society*, London: Frank Cass & Co. Ltd.

SCHREITER, R. 1994, "Inculturation of the Faith With Culture", in N. GREINACHER & N. METTE (eds.), *Christianity and Cultures*, Maryknoll, Orbis Books, 15-24.

SCHUSSLER-FIORENZA, E. 1983, *In Memory of Her*, Boston: Beacon Press.

SCOTT, J. & WOOD, B.Y. (eds.), 1979, "*We listened long, before we spoke*" (A Report of the Consultation of Women Theological Students, Cartigny, Switzerland, July 1978), Geneva: WCC Publications.

SEALEY, J. 1984, *"We have the Healing Power": Independent Churches and Women in Urban Kenya*, Cambridge: Anthropology.

SEEMAN, D. 2000, "The Question of Kinship: Bodies and Narratives in the Beta Israel-European Encounter (1860-1920)", in *Journal of Religion in Africa*, 30, 1 (2000), 86-120.

SELASSIE, B. 2003, *Towards a Fuller Vision*, Leicestershire: Upfront Publishing.

SERNETT, M. 1991, "Black Religion and the Question of Evangelical Identity", in D.W. DAYTON & R.K. JOHNSTON (eds.), *The Variety of American Evangelicalism*, Downers Grove, IL: InterVarsity Press, 1991, 135-147.

SETILOANE, G. 1977, "Where Are We in African Theology?", in K. APPIAH-KUBI & S. TORRES, *African Theology en Route: Papers from the Pan-African Conference of Third World Theologians. Accra. December 17-23, 1977*, Maryknoll: Orbis Books.

SHANK, D. 1983, "The Prophet Harris: A Historiographical and Bibliographical Survey", in *Journal of Religion in Africa,* 14,2 (1983).

SHEPPERSON, G. 1968, "Ethiopianism: Past and Present", in C.G. BAËTA (ed.), *Christianity in Tropical Africa*, London: Oxford University Press, 249-264.

SHERWOOD, M. 1994, *Pastor Daniels Ekarte and the African Churches Mission*, London: The Savannah Press.

SHORTER, A. 1972, "Developing Roles of the Catechists", in A. SHORTER & E. KATAZA, (eds.), *Missionaries to Yourselves. African Catechists Today*, London: Geoffrey Chapman.

SHORTER, A. 1973, *African Culture and the Christian Church*, London: Geoffrey Chapman.

SHORTER, A. 1988, *Toward a Theology of Inculturation*, Maryknoll: Orbis Books.

SHORTER, A. 1995, *Jesus and the Witch Doctor,* Maryknoll: Orbis Books.

SHORTER, A. 2001, *New Religious Movements in Africa*, Nairobi: Paulines.

SHORTER, A. & KISEMBO, B. (eds.), 1977, *African Christian Marriage*, London: Chapman.

SIMENSEN, J. 1986, "Religious Change as Transaction: The Norwegian Mission to Zululand, South Africa, 1850-1906", in *Journal of Religion in Africa,* 16,2, 1986, 82-100.

SMITH, S. 1850, *Letters of Sydney Smith,* vol. I, London: Longmans.

STANLEY, B. 1990, *The Bible and the Flag*, Leceister: Apollo-Varsity Press.

STENNING, D. 1965, "Salvation in Ankole", in M. FORTES and G. DIETERLEN, *African Systems of Thought*, London: Oxford University Press.

STARK, R. 1996, *The Rise of Christianity*, Princeton: Princeton University Press.

STRAYER, R.W. 1978, *The Making of Mission Communities in East Africa*, London: Heinemann.

STUART, J. 2000, "British Missionary Responses to African Colonial Issues, 1945-53" (XIXth Int. Congress of the Historical Sciences, Oslo, August 2000).

SUNDBERG, C. 2000, "Conversion and Contextual Conceptions of Christ", in *Studia Missionalia Svecana*, LXXX, 1 (2000), 133.

SUNDKLER, B.G.M. 1961, *Bantu Prophets in South Africa*, Oxford: Oxford University Press.

SUNDKLER, B.G.M. 1962, *The Christian Ministry in Africa*, Liverpool: Charles Birchal.

SUNDKLER, B.G.M. 1976, *Zulu Zion and Some Swazi Zionists*, Oxford: Oxford University Press.

SUNDKLER, B.G.M. & STEED, C. 2000, *A History of the Church in Africa*, Cambridge, Cambridge University Press.

SWITZER, L. 1993, *Power and Resistance in an African Society: the Ciskei Xhosa and the Making of South Africa*, Madison, Wis: University of Wisconsin Press.

TANNER, N. (ed.), 1990, *Decrees of the Ecumenical Councils,* Vol. II, London: Sheed and Ward.

TAMRAT, T. 1972, *Church and State in Ethiopia, 1270-1527*, Oxford: Clarendon.

TASIE, G.O.M. 1997, *Thoughts and Voices of An African Church: Christ Army Church*, Nigeria: Connack Nigeria Ltd.

TAYLOR, J.B. 1967, "Water", in J.D. DOUGLAS, J.D. DOUGLAS (ed.), *The New Bible Dictionary*, London: Inter-Varsity Press.

TAYLOR, J.V. 1958, "Process of growth in an African Church", IMC Research Pamphlets 6, SCM.

TAYLOR, J.V. 1958, *The Growth of the Church in Buganda*, London: S.C.M. Press.

TAYLOR, J.V. 1969, "Selfhood: Presence or Personae?" in B. SUNDKLER, P. BEYERHAUS & C.F. HALLENCREUTZ (eds.), *The Church Crossing Frontiers: Essays on the Nature of Mission. In Honour of Bengt Sundkler* (Studia Missionalia Uppsaliensia, XI, 1969), 171-176.

TAYLOR, J.V. 2001, *Christian Presence amid African Religion* (Nairobi: Acton).

TEMPERLEY, H. 1980, "Anti-Slavery as a Form of Cultural Imperialism", in C. BOLT & S. DRESCHER (eds.), *Anti-Slavery, Religion, and Reform: Essays in Memory of Roger Anstey*, London: Wm. Dawson & Sons, 335-350.

TEMU, A.J. 1972, *British Protestant Missions*, London: Longmans.

TEMU, A.J. & SWAI, B. 1981, *Historians and Africanist History: A Critique*, London: Zed Press.

TER HAAR, G. 1994, "Standing up for Jesus: A Survey of New Developments in Christianity in Ghana", in *Exchange*, 23 (1994), 221-240.

TER HAAR, G. 1998, *Halfway to Paradise: African Christians in Europe*, Cardiff: Cardiff Academic Press.

THOMPSON, T. 1758, *An Account of Two Missionary Voyages*, London: SPG.

THORNTON, J. 1992, *Africa and Africans in the Making of the Atlantic World, 1400-1680*, New York: Cambridge University Press.

TILLEY, M.A. 1997, *The Bible in Christian North Africa: The Donatist World*, Minneapolis: Fortress.

TILLICH, P. 1957, "Existence and the Christ", in *Systematic Theology*, vol. II, Chicago: Chicago University Press.

TORK, L. 1997, *The Kingdom of Kush*, Leiden: E.J. Brill.

TORRES S. & FABELLA, V.M.M (eds.), 1978, *The Emergent Gospel: Theology from the Underside of History: Papers from the Ecumenical Dialogue of Third World Theologians, Dar es Salam, August 5-12*, Maryknoll: Orbis Books.

TRIGG, J.W. 1983, *Origen*, Atlanta: John Knox Press.

TRIMINGHAM, J.S. 1955, *The Christian Church and Islam in West Africa*, London: SCM Press.

TURNER, H.W. 1965, "Pagan Features in West African Independent Churches", in *Practical Anthropology*, 12, 4 (1965), 145-151.

TURNER, H.W. 1967, *African Independent Church, Vol. 1 - The Church of the Lord - Aladura; Vol. 2 - The Life and Faith of the Church of the Lord – Aladura*, Oxford: Clarendon Press.

TURNER, H.W. 1967, "A Typology for African Religious Movements", in *Journal of Religion in Africa*, 1, 1 (1967), 1-32.

TURNER, H.W. 1967, *The Life and Faith of the Church of the Lord (Aladura)*, London: Oxford University Press.

TURNER, H.W. 1967, *History of an African Independent Church*, Oxford: Clarendon Press.

TURNER, H.W. 1979, *Religious Innovation in Africa: Collected Essays on New Religious Movements*, Boston: G.K. Hall & Co.

TURNER, M.D. & HUDSON, M.L. 1999, *Saved from Silence: Finding Women's Voice in Preaching*, St. Louis, MO: Chalice Press.

TURNER, P. 1971, "The Wisdom of the Fathers and the Gospel of Christ", in *JRA,* 4, 1, 1971, 45-68.

TURNER, V.W. 1967, *The Forest of Rituals: Aspects of Ndembu Ritual*, Cornell University Press.

TUTU, D. 1982, *Crying in The Wilderness*, Grand Rapids, MI: Eerdmans.

TUTU, D. 1986, "Black Theology and African Theology: Soulmates or Antagonists?", in D.W. FERM (ed.), *Third World Liberation Theologies: A Reader*, Maryknoll: Orbis Books, 256-264.

UBAH, C.N. 1976, "Problems of Christian Missionaries in the Muslim Emirates of Nigeria, 1900–1928", in *Journal of African Studies,* 3 (1976), 351-371.

UMLILO, T. 2002, *Little Girl, Arise! New Life after Incest and Abuse*, Pietermaritzburg: Cluster Publications.

UZOIGWE, G.N. 1976, "Spheres of influence and the doctrine of the hinterland in the partition of Africa", in *Journal of African Studies,* 3, 2, 1976, 183-203.

UZOUKWU, E.E. 1982, *Liturgy: Truly Christian, Truly African*, Eldoret: Gaba Publications.

UZUKWU, E.E. 2003, "*Resilient Diaspora – Keeping Faith with Destiny,*" paper presented at the First *Muruako Lectures*, London: Whelan Research Academy, Owerri Nigeria, 20th December 2003.

VAN DANTZIG, A. 1980, *Forts and Castles of Ghana*, Accra: Sedco Publishing Ltd.

VAN DIJK, 1992, "Young Born-Again Preachers in Post-Independence Malawi: The Significance of an Extraneous Identity", in P. GIFFORD (ed.), *New Dimensions in African Christianity*, Nairobi: AACC.

VAN DIJK, R. 2001, "Time and Transcultural Technologies in the Self in the Ghanaian Pentecostal Diaspora", in A. CORTEN & R. MARSHALL-FRATANI, *Between Babel and Pentecost: Transnational Pentecostalism in Africa and Latin America*, Bloomington & Indianapolis: Indiana University Press, 216-234.

VANSINA, J. 1967, "The Use of Oral Tradition in African Culture History", in C. GABEL & N.R. BENNETT, (eds.), *Reconstructing African Culture History*, Boston University Press.

VANTINI, V. 1981, *Christianity in the Sudan*, Bologna: EMI Publishers.

VILLA-VICENCIO, C. 1992, *A Theology of Reconstruction: Nation-Building and Human Rights*, Cape Town, Cambridge: David Philip, Cambridge University Press.

WAGNER, G. 1970 [1949], *The Bantu in Western Kenya, with special reference to the Bugusu and Logoli*, vol. I, London/New York: Oxford University Press.

WAKANYI-KAHINDI, L. 1988, *The Agikuyu Concept of* Thahu *and its bearing on the Christian Concept of Sin* (M.A. Thesis, Kenyatta University, Nairobi).

WALKER, S.S. 1979, "Women in the Harrist Movement", in B. JULES-RESETTE (ed.), *The New Religions of Africa*, Norwood, NJ: Ablex, 87-115.

WALLS, A.F. 1970, "A Christian Experiment: The Early Sierra Leone Colony", in C.J. COMING, *The Mission of the Church and the Propagation of the Faith*, Studies in Church History 6, London: Cambridge University Press, 107-129.

Walls, A.F. 1996, *The Missionary Movement in Christian History*, Maryknoll: Orbis Books.

Walls, A.F. 1992, "The Legacy of Samuel Ajayi Crowther", in *International Bulletin of Missionary Research* (January 1992), 15-21.

Walls, A.F. 1999, "African as the Theatre of Christian Engagement with Islam in the Nineteenth Century", in *Journal of Religion in Africa,* 1999, 29,2, 155-74.

Walls, A.F. 2002, *The Cross-Cultural Process in Christian History*, New York: Orbis Books.

Walls, A.F. & Fyfe, C. 1996, *Christianity in Africa in the 1990s,* Edinburgh: Centre for African Studies, University of Edinburgh, 1996.

Walsh, J. 1994, "'Methodism' and the Origins of English-Speaking Evangelicalism", in M. Noll, D.W. Bebbington & G.A. Rawlyk (eds.), *Evangelicalism: Comparative Studies of Popular Protestantism in North America, the British Isles, and Beyond, 1700-1990,* New York: Oxford University Press, 19-37.

Walvin, J. 1980, "The Rise of British Popular Sentiment for Abolition, 1787-1832", in C. Bolt & S. Drescher (eds.), *Anti-Slavery, Religion, and Reform: Essays in Memory of Roger Anstey*, London: Wm. Dawson & Sons, 149-162.

Ward, B. 1975, *The Sayings of the Desert Fathers*, London: A.R. Mowbray: Kalamazoo, Michigan: Cistercian Publications.

Ward, K. 1989, "'Obedient Rebels' – The Relationship Between the Early "balokole" and the Church of Uganda: The Mukono Crisis of 1941", in *Journal of Religion in Africa*, 19, 3, (1989).

Warneck, G. 1906, *A History of Protestant Missions*, tr. George Robson, New York: Revell.

Waruta, D.W. 1990, "Towards an African Church: A Critical Assessment of Alternative Forms and Structures", in J.N.K. Mugambi & L. Magesa (eds.), *The Church in African Christianity: Innovative Essays in Ecclesiology*, Nairobi: Initiatives.

Weaver, E. & Weaver, I, 1970, *The Uyo Story*, Elkhart, Indiana: Mennonite Board of Missions.

Weber, C. 1997, "Christianity and West African Decolonisation" Cambridge, NAMP Position Paper, 80, 1997.

Webster, J.B. 1964, *The African Churches among the Yoruba, 1888-1922,* Oxford: Clarendon Press.

Welbourn, F.B. 1961, *East African Rebels: A Study of Some Independent Churches*, London: SCM.

Welbourn, F.B. 1965, *East African Christian*, London: Oxford University Press.

Welbourn, F.B. & Ogot, B.A. 1966, *A Place to Feel at Home: A Study of Independent Churches in Western Kenya*, London: Oxford University Press.

Wells, R. 1989, *History Through the Eyes of Faith*, San Francisco: Harper & Row.

Werner, R., Anderson W. & Wheeler, A. 2000, *Day of Devastation, Day of Contentment: The History of the Sudanese Church Across 2000 Years*, Nairobi: Paulines Publications Africa.

West, C. 1971, *The Power To Be Human*, New York: McMillan.

West, G.O. 2003, "Reading the Bible in the Light of HIV/AIDS in South Africa" in *Ecumenical Review* (WCC Publications), 55, 4, October 2003, 335-344.

West, G.O. & Dube, M.W. (eds.), 2000, *The Bible in Africa: Transactions, Trajectories and Trends*, Leiden: Brill.

West, G.O. & Zondi-Mabizela, P. 2004, "The Bible Story that became a Campaign: the Tamar Campaign in South Africa (and beyond)" in *Ministerial Formation*, Geneva: WCC Publications, 4-12.

West, M.E. 1974, "People of the Spirit: Charismatic Movements among African Independent Churches", in *Journal of Theology of Southern Africa* (June 1974).

West, M.E. 1975, *Bishops and Prophets in a Black City: African Independent Churches in Soweto*, Johannesburg, Cape Town: Philip.

West, M.O. 2002, "Ethiopianism and Colonialism: The African Orthodox Church in Zimbabwe, 1924-34", H.B. Hansen & M. Twaddle (eds.), *Christian Missionaries and the State in the Third World*, Oxford: Currey.

Wilberforce, W. 1797, *A Practical View of The Prevailing Religious System of Professed Christians in the Higher and Middle Classes in this Country Contrasted with Real Christianity*, London.

Williams, E. 1964, *Capitalism and Slavery*, London: Andre Deutsch.

Williams, W.L. 1982, *Black Americans and the Evangelization of Africa 1877-1900*, Madison: University of Wisconsin Press.

Wilmore, G. 1986, "Black Americans in Mission: Setting the Record Straight", in *International Bulletin of Missionary Research*, (July 1986), 98-102.

Wilmore, G. 1998 (1973), *Black Religion and Black Radicalism: An Interpretation of the Religious History of African Americans*, New York: Orbis Books.

Wiltgen, R.M. 1956, *Gold Coast Mission History 1471-1880*, Techny: Divine Word Publication.

Wink, W. 1992, *Engaging the Powers*, Philadelphia: Fortress Press.

Woodson, C. 1921 (2nd ed.), *The History of the Negro Church*, Washington D.C: The Associated Publishers.

Yoder, J. 1972, *The Politics of Jesus*, Philadelphia: Fortress Press.

Young, F. 1983, *From Nicaea to Chalcedon*, Philadelphia: Fortress Press.

Young, J.U. 1986, *Black and African Theologies: Siblings or Distant Cousins?*, Maryknoll: Orbis Books.

Young, J.U. 1993, *African Theology: A Critical Analysis and Annotated Bibliography*, Westport: Greenwood Press.

Zeleza, P.T. 2002, "Contemporary African Migrations in a Global Context", in *African Issues*, XXX, 1 (2002).

Index

Abolition 169-173, 176, 178, 179, 183, 227, 432
Abolitionist 31, 171-173
Abyssinia 27, 89, 93, 97, 233
Accra 130, 139, 308, 374, 379, 391, 393, 422
Adegoke, John 440
Adogame, Afe 34, 38, 271, 431
Africa
  Architecture 25, 29, 35, 93, 96, 196, 213, 232, 451, 453
  Art 25, 26, 29, 59, 80, 96, 173, 307, 308, 402, 441, 451, 453
  Church History 4, 5, 8-14, 16-19, 35, 59, 228, 317, 329, 361
  Clergy 36, 50, 53, 93, 94, 97, 151-161, 168-170, 176, 194, 206, 207, 310, 342, 372, 397, 434, 437, 438
  Demography 271
Africa Church of the Holy Spirit 364
Africa Inland Mission 230
Africa Israel Church Nineveh 364
Africa, Central 15, 27, 30, 211, 229, 233, 239, 292, 319, 365
Africa, East 33, 34, 106, 224, 258, 272, 274, 275, 284, 319, 325, 364, 366, 456, 458, 468
Africa, Horn of Africa 36, 95
Africa, North 23, 25, 41, 43, 45, 47, 49, 51, 53, 55, 57, 59, 61, 63, 64, 104, 106, 115, 124, 211, 299, 303, 311, 316
Africa, South Saharan 31
Africa, Southern 33, 34, 37, 151-155, 157, 159, 161, 225, 230, 240, 276, 284, 297, 308, 330, 341, 371, 377, 399, 402
Africa, Sub-Saharan 107, 117, 123, 124, 182, 316, 433
Africa, West 13, 31, 34, 106, 108, 110, 111, 116, 123, 125-129, 131, 133, 135, 137, 139, 141, 143, 145, 149, 151, 153, 177, 181, 229, 235, 237, 239, 241, 248, 250-253, 257-259, 272-274, 276, 292, 297, 306, 319, 320, 335, 348, 366
African American 31, 177, 233, 234, 236, 237, 239, 240, 295, 300, 434, 435
African Americans 15, 31, 32, 183, 227, 232, 235, 238, 295
African Churches Mission (ACM) 435, 436
African Colonization 24, 32, 179-181, 235, 238, 239, 246, 258, 369, 396
African Confession of Faith 311
African culture 7, 106, 128, 182, 228, 236, 306, 384, 413-416, 418, 423, 436, 451, 454, 465
African Initiated Churches, African Independent Churches, African Indigenous Churches, African Instituted Churches (AIC) 34, 114, 248, 270, 271-277, 279- 285, 317, 330, 336, 352, 359-362, 368, 384, 398, 419, 420, 434, 436
African Instituted Churches 270, 271, 273, 275, 277, 279, 281, 283, 285, 317, 359-362, 368, 384, 398, 434, 436
African Methodist Episcopal Church (AME) 34, 178, 181, 239, 295

African Methodist Episcopal Zion Church (AMEZ) 237
African nationalism 183, 239
African Orthodox Church 295
African Orthodox Church in Zimbabwe 238
African Presbyterian Church 240
African theology, theologies, theologians 6, 239, 310, 325, 395, 402, 404, 409, 410, 411, 413-416, 418, 419, 421, 423, 424
African traditional religion 8, 105, 108, 115, 371, 391, 416
Africanization 309, 415, 424
Aithiopia 28
Ajayi 15, 203
Ala-Amida, King 91
Aladura 34, 248, 263, 264, 266, 271-279, 281-285, 292, 340, 341, 344, 345, 363, 364, 368, 371, 378, 380, 381, 383, 434, 436, 437, 439, 444
Alexandria 24-26, 28, 43-52, 54-59, 61-63, 69-71, 73-75, 77, 78, 80, 82, 83, 86, 90, 91, 104, 234, 311
Alexandrian Christianity 49
Algeria 63, 104, 115, 124, 401
All Africa Council of Churches (AACC) 311, 318, 391, 393, 409, 420, 422, 423
Alwa 68, 69, 71, 77, 86, 87
Ambuila 156
American Colonization Society 235, 238
Anglican Church 133, 138, 237, 239, 248, 254, 257, 275-277, 279, 364, 440
Angola 33, 151-153, 160, 161, 242, 306, 310
Apostolic Church of Ghana 344
Apostolic Faith Mission of Iowa (AFM) 260, 261, 343
Arab 30, 62-64, 73-76, 83-88, 103, 104, 106, 109, 131, 152, 159, 431-433, 437
Asceticism 48, 52, 53, 57, 61, 145, 234, 324
Askiya Mohammed 109
Assemblies of God 265, 302, 341, 343, 345, 375
Axum 90-92, 104
Ayandele, E. A. 5, 11, 15, 253

Babalola, Joseph Ayo 248, 259, 276, 278, 344, 345
Baganda Christians 254
Bakuzufu 245, 247, 249, 251, 253, 255, 257, 259, 261, 263, 265, 267
Balokole 36, 247, 248, 254-256, 261, 348
Bantu 159, 272, 352
Bantu Independent Churches 252
Barshambo, Abdallah 85, 86
Bediako, Kwame 4, 7, 414-416, 421, 437
Belgium 33
Benin 30, 117, 126, 127, 249, 259, 263, 265, 302, 373
Berlin Conference 33, 192, 208, 228
Biennial Institute of African Women in Religion and Culture 422
Blantyre, Blantyre Synod 249, 327, 375
Blyden, Edward W. (Wilmot) 34, 41, 107, 180, 182, 235, 237, 238
Bohairic 55
Britain, British 31, 32, 88, 96, 97, 116, 133, 167-174, 179, 180, 196, 209, 210, 238, 246, 251, 254, 260, 263, 278, 297, 302-305, 316, 325, 327, 345, 396, 436
British and Foreign Bible Society 170
Byzantium 28, 62

Caliph, Caliphate 27, 62, 75, 76, 83, 110, 111
Cameroon 117, 127, 208, 296, 308, 318, 320, 348, 398
Candace, Treasurer of Candace 23, 68, 75, 233
Cape Verde 30, 33, 126, 127
Capuchins 127, 156
Carthage 50, 53, 59, 60, 63, 234
Catholic Christians 50

Catholic Church 8, 58, 126, 129, 156, 194, 195, 199, 201, 210, 263, 266, 306, 308, 317, 335, 369, 371, 372, 419, 464
Catholic Women Association 368
Celestial Church of Christ (CCC) 277-279, 281, 282, 284, 378, 380, 437, 442
Charismatic 6, 15, 24, 28, 34-38, 90, 245-251, 254-256, 258-260, 262-268, 272, 275, 277-280, 284, 292-294, 297, 300-302, 309, 317, 318, 324, 332, 335, 339-343, 345-353, 355, 360-369, 373-383, 413, 420, 434, 437, 438, 441
Charismatic-Evangelical Dialogue for Justice and Transformation (CEDJT) 333
Christ Apostolic Church (CAC) 259, 276-278, 283, 343-345, 377, 380- 382
Christ for All Nations (CFAN) 348
Christian Action Faith Ministries International 349
Christian Association of Nigeria (CAN) 37, 112, 114, 285
Christian Catholic Apostolic Church 276
Christian Church Outreach Mission International (CCOMI) 437
Christian Council of Nigeria 117, 285, 391
Christian orthodoxy 56
Christian Union 256, 263, 265
Christian Youth Corpers 265
Christian Zionism 352
Christianization 8, 15, 97, 176, 178, 179, 250, 415
Christians 8, 9, 12, 19, 24, 25, 33, 48, 50, 52-57, 60, 63, 64, 69, 71-74, 77, 78, 80-86, 88, 89, 94, 103, 104, 112-118, 124, 126, 140, 144, 175-177, 179, 180, 182, 238, 254, 259, 279, 291, 300, 304, 306, 307, 318, 324, 326, 328, 332, 334, 339, 343, 345, 346, 348, 349, 353, 354, 365-367, 397, 398, 402, 411, 413, 414, 417, 418, 420, 421, 439, 440, 444, 452-455, 459, 461, 463-469
Church Missionary Society 260, 275, 440
Church of God Mission (CGM) 260
Church of the Lord 277, 374, 378, 380, 381, 437
Church of the Lord-Aladura (CLA) 276, 277, 281-283, 285, 437
Church of the Province of Kenya (CPK) 325
Church of the Twelve Apostles 252, 369, 376, 380
Circle of Concerned African Women Theologians 389
Classical Pentecostals 259, 302
Clement 45, 50-52, 91
Cleopatra 43, 234
Cleopatra VII 43
CMS 33, 176, 235, 236, 254, 260, 275, 303, 309
Congo 33, 36, 126, 151, 181, 208, 236, 245, 248, 249, 261, 262, 302, 307, 316, 340, 348, 350, 382, 398, 432
Congo Evangelistic Mission 302
Constantine 23, 28, 56, 61, 74, 91, 452, 455
Consultation of Women Theological Students 390
Coptic, Copts 23-26, 29, 48, 51, 53, 55, 57-59, 61-64, 69, 72-75, 78, 80, 87, 96, 97, 104, 434, 437
Crowther, Samuel Adjai 32, 176, 203
Crummel, Alexander 15
Cush 233
Cyprian 51, 53, 60
Cyrene 44, 45, 59

Da Presentacao 157, 158
Demotic 43, 72
Diaspora 31, 45, 227, 292, 431-445
Diaspora Christians 444
Didymus 57, 91
Donatism 61
Dongola 28, 63, 71, 74, 75, 77, 78, 81, 83, 85

Doro mission 89

Ecumenical Association of Third World Theologians (EATWOT) 308, 391, 422, 424
Ecumenical Decade of Churches in Solidarity with Women 393
Ecumenical Theological Education Program (ETE) 393, 400
Edinburgh 4, 24, 192, 241, 242, 291
Egypt 25-29, 41-49, 52, 53, 56-59, 61, 62, 64, 66-78, 80, 82, 84-88, 90-95, 104, 114, 115, 124, 179, 232-234, 238, 299, 300, 302, 437, 469
Egyptian 25, 27, 28, 41-49, 51, 53-56, 58, 59, 70, 72, 74-76, 78, 82, 84, 85, 87-89, 92, 94, 96, 104, 115, 116, 233
Egyptian Orthodox Church 94
Elmina 126-130, 135-137, 139-141
Emma Harris 265
Emperor Amde Zion 94
Episcopal Church in Sudan 89
Equiano, Olandah 31, 172
Ethiopia, Ethiopian 24, 27-29, 34, 58, 61, 62, 64, 67, 69, 71, 73, 75, 77-79, 81-87, 89-97, 104, 106, 117, 179, 182, 211, 232-234, 237- 242, 254, 271, 272, 274, 292, 299, 301, 307, 351, 363, 364, 368, 383, 394, 398
Ethiopianism 179, 182, 183, 227, 229, 231-242, 292, 294, 295, 297, 363, 420
Ethiopians 86, 89, 90, 92, 94, 95, 233, 237, 239, 241, 242, 292, 293, 297, 298
European 14, 24, 29, 30, 33, 34, 84, 107, 121, 123-126, 129-132, 136, 138, 144, 151, 152, 156, 160, 167, 173, 176, 178, 183, 191-193, 196, 197, 204-208, 212, 213, 229-233, 235, 236, 238, 240, 247, 251, 257, 275, 291, 297, 300, 305, 315, 389, 411, 413, 415, 432, 433, 435, 436, 438, 456, 461
Eusebius 12, 45
Evangelicalism 31, 32, 169, 170, 237, 300, 301, 347, 420

Falasha 97, 234
Feminist, Feminism, Womanist 26, 38, 228, 361, 384, 393, 395, 397, 417, 422, 423
France, French 73, 74, 96, 97, 128, 130, 133, 170, 173, 196, 197, 200, 202, 208-210, 213, 251, 262, 265, 291, 297, 299, 303, 304, 389, 398, 451, 458
Friends African Mission (FAM) 248, 260, 364
Frumentius 29, 90, 91
Full Gospel Business Men's Fellowship International (FGBMFI) 341, 346, 347
Full Gospel Church of God 302, 341

Garnet, Henry 235
Garveyism 241
Ge'ez 72, 91, 96, 97
Gender 255, 256, 266, 267, 351, 359-363, 365, 367, 369-375, 377-379, 381, 383, 389, 393, 395-401, 403, 444
German 10, 13, 177, 197, 200, 208, 291, 296, 297, 309, 318
German colonies 291, 296
German Provinces 208
Germany 143, 145, 349, 434, 437, 438
Ghana 6, 14, 15, 106, 117, 177, 231, 249, 268, 273, 316, 318, 324, 340, 341, 344, 347, 348, 352, 355, 363, 365, 369, 374, 382, 389, 391, 393, 413, 422, 437
Goa 153, 157-159, 161
Gold Coast 30, 31, 34, 36, 127, 128, 133-136, 139-144, 237, 250, 252, 259, 299, 340
Grace of God Mission 265
Greek 6, 8, 12, 18, 28, 42, 43, 45-47, 49, 52, 55, 57, 58, 63, 67, 72-74, 80, 91, 135, 194, 233, 452

Hagin, Kenneth 350
Harris, William Wadé 36, 231, 248, 250-253, 258, 265, 340, 369, 370
Hausa society 110

Hausaland 110, 111
Hauseas 107
Historiography 3-9, 11-19, 151, 158, 227, 228, 232, 273, 276, 279, 316, 360, 361, 434
HIV/AIDS 397-399
Hofmeyr, J. W. 36, 315, 319
Holy Ghost Fathers (CSSP) 33, 203

Iberian 29, 30, 124, 126, 128, 129, 131, 151, 152, 161, 233, 310
Ibo 14, 172, 253
Igbo 3, 203, 253, 380
Independent African Churches 451
International Fellowship of Evangelical Students (IFES) 347
International Missionary Council 292
Islam 24, 27, 29, 30, 35, 62, 63, 73-75, 77, 78, 84, 86-88, 93, 95, 103-118, 125, 127, 195, 229, 237, 242, 249, 250, 303, 352, 391
Islamic Brotherhood 115
Italy, Italians 24, 26, 61, 233, 234, 310
Ivory Coast 36, 134, 249-252, 268, 336

Jehovah's Witnesses 329
Jesus Is Alive Ministries 366, 373, 377, 379
Jewish tradition 4, 80
Jews 18, 25, 42, 43, 45-47, 51, 234, 453
Jihad 73, 74, 108-112
Judaism 25, 41, 44, 46-48, 92, 391, 452

Kaimosi 248, 259, 260, 364
Kairos Document 318
Kapararidze, Nayambo Domingos 157, 159, 160
Kenya 15, 36, 117, 230, 248, 255, 256, 259, 260, 265, 268, 273-275, 282, 296, 297, 301, 302, 311, 316-319, 325, 348, 352, 364, 366, 367, 371-373, 379, 380, 382, 394, 396, 398, 402
Kenyatta, Jomo 273, 325
Keswick Conventions 254, 255
Khartoum 68, 71, 86, 88
Kikuyu 230, 249, 275, 281, 284, 296, 297
Kimbangu, Simon 36, 248, 261, 295, 340
Kimbanguism 434
King Ezana 28
Kingsway International Christian Center (KICC) 342, 437, 441
Kongo 30, 151-156, 160, 247, 369
Kongo-Soyo 30
Koran 107, 117
Kush, Kushites 27, 28, 42, 67, 73, 89, 97, 233

Lali-bella, Emperor 93
League of African Churches 300
Liberia 15, 32, 34, 36, 180-182, 235, 237, 250-252, 259, 268, 302, 307, 319, 320, 322-324, 335, 336, 350, 366
Libya 45, 63, 299
Lighthouse Church International 366
Livingstone 14, 181
Longinus 28, 71-73, 88
Lusophone 403
Lutheran World Federation (LWF) 309, 393
Lutheran, Lutherans 300, 309, 319, 335, 438

Maghrib 23, 27, 31, 38, 41, 42, 51, 61, 63, 64, 104, 304
Malawi 117, 240, 241, 254, 268, 295, 296, 319, 326-329, 342, 343, 366, 375, 377, 382, 398
Mamluke 85, 87
Mandela, Nelson 116, 333
Mavhura 157, 159, 160
Mbiti, John 6, 402, 411, 413, 416, 417
Mbuy-Beya 398
Mecca 29, 104, 301
Melitius, Melitians 55, 56

Melkites 75
Menelik 29, 90, 97, 234
Meroe, Meroitic 23, 27, 28, 68, 72, 73, 75, 89, 90, 233, 234
Methodist, Methodism 6, 14, 15, 32, 34, 140, 169, 178, 179, 237, 239, 242, 251, 252, 295, 308, 311, 323, 330, 335, 363, 371, 434, 438
Migrants, migration 42, 64, 104, 181, 247, 431-434, 436-439, 441, 443-445
Miguel da Presentacao 157, 158
Mission, missions 4, 6, 7, 9, 13, 14-19, 26, 31-33, 36, 69-71, 88, 89, 94-96, 123, 124, 126-129, 131-136, 138, 140-145, 149, 151, 152, 156, 159, 176, 180-182, 192, 193, 195-213, 224, 225, 227-231, 236-238, 240-242, 248, 251-254, 257-267, 271, 274-278, 281, 283, 291-294, 296-304, 307, 309-311, 317, 318, 340, 341, 343, 346-348, 352, 355, 360, 361, 363-368, 372, 373, 381, 389, 393-396, 402, 404, 412-414, 434-438, 442, 443, 453, 455, 457-459
African 181, 203, 364
congregations 15, 17, 179, 195, 199, 200, 203, 208, 236, 248, 251, 252, 264, 275, 308, 309, 342, 438
enterprise 5, 6, 17, 32, 176, 180, 182, 191-194, 203, 204, 207, 208, 211, 213, 228, 229, 240, 241, 258, 292, 296, 303, 403, 421, 453, 455
European 275
historiography 3-9, 11-19, 151, 158, 227, 228, 232, 273, 276, 279, 316, 360, 361, 434
ideology 14, 227, 230
schools 197, 205, 213, 293, 300, 457, 458
Nigeria 11, 14, 15, 24, 35, 37, 110-115, 117, 127, 172, 209, 211, 237, 238, 242, 248, 253, 259, 262-266, 273, 276, 277, 284, 285, 299, 303, 308, 311, 317, 318, 336, 341, 344, 365, 369, 371-375, 382, 390, 391, 413, 435, 437, 440
south-eastern Nigeria 253, 259
Mohammed 29, 109, 111
Monophysite 28, 29, 57-59, 75, 76, 91, 104
Montanism 61
Moslems 35, 63, 64, 125, 126
Mozambique 33, 151, 153, 157, 159, 160, 302, 306, 318, 328
Muhammad 88, 104, 108, 109, 115
Muslim 24, 27, 35, 59, 62, 64, 74, 76-78, 84-86, 88, 93, 95, 103, 104, 106, 108-118, 236, 316, 336, 347
Muslim Brotherhood 115
Muslim Students Association 116

Nabii Christian Church of Kenya 364
Namirembe Christian Fellowship of Uganda 350
Nazaretha Church in South Africa 279
Neo-Pentecostal churches 350
New [independent] Pentecostal Churches 362, 364-368, 373, 375-379, 382, 384
New Religious Movements 362
New Testament 11, 44, 47, 55, 80, 91, 252, 351, 367, 383, 392, 469
Nigerian Association of Aladura Churches (NAAC) 285
Nile 26, 28, 42, 49, 53, 54, 58, 61, 64, 67, 68, 86-89, 93, 233
Nkrumah, Kwame 105
Nubia, Nubians 24, 27, 28, 63, 64, 67-70, 72-88, 90, 93, 94, 96, 101, 232-234

Oduyoye, Mercy Amba 389-391, 393, 395-397, 403, 410
Old Testament 6, 51, 67, 80, 90, 247, 251, 276, 456, 469
Oman 30
Organization of African Independent Churches 285
Orunmila 35, 237

Pan African Leadership Assembly 420
Pan-African Conference 393, 394, 396
Parham, Charles 341
Pentecost 25, 38, 45, 339, 342-346, 437
Pentecostal 17, 34, 35, 37, 38, 247, 255, 256, 258-260, 262, 267, 301, 302, 309, 317, 318, 330, 336, 339-355, 359-369, 373-379, 382-384, 413, 419, 434, 437, 438, 440, 444
  Denominations 258, 341, 343, 348
  fellowships 267, 341
  groups 301, 302
  spirituality 35, 301, 317, 355
  theology 345, 351, 353, 373
Pentecostal Assemblies of Canada 260, 302, 364
Pentecostal Assemblies of the World 302
Pentecostal Church 38, 344, 351, 368, 379, 440
Pentecostal Churches 262, 330, 336, 339, 341-346, 350, 352, 354, 359, 360, 362, 364-368, 373-379, 382, 384, 419
Pentecostal Missionary Union 302
Pentecostal Movement 262, 353, 434
Pentecostal/Charismatic Christianity 339, 341-343, 345, 347, 349, 351, 353, 355, 362, 368
Pentecostal/Charismatic phenomena 348, 354
Pentecostal/Charismatic renewal movements 339, 340, 342, 346
Pentecostalism 37, 248, 249, 259, 260, 293, 302, 335, 339-343, 345, 346, 350, 351, 353-355, 365, 366
  missions 343
Pentecostals 24, 259, 293, 302, 310, 339-343, 345, 347-352, 354, 355, 365, 434
Perpetua 59
Philae 27, 28, 69, 70, 72, 233
Population 24, 25, 46, 49, 59, 61, 76, 85, 86, 92, 112, 115, 123, 128, 133-135, 144, 159, 167, 174, 178, 204, 250, 320, 321, 327, 329, 364, 431-433, 435
Portugal, Portuguese 30, 33, 86, 87, 93, 95, 124-132, 151-161, 173, 202, 213, 304, 316, 359, 369, 389, 403, 451
Post-Independence churches 303
Presbyterian Church 240, 267, 311, 320
Prester John 29, 30, 124, 233
Prophet Muhammad 104, 109, 115
Protestantism, Protestants 33, 114, 203, 210, 229, 292, 417

Qur'an 107, 109, 115
Qutb, Sayyid 114, 116

Redeemed Christian Church of God (RCCG) 38, 365, 437, 441, 442, 443
Rhema Bible Church 349
Roho 34, 271-275, 277-285, 292, 364, 379
Ruwe Holy Ghost Church of East Africa 275
Rwanda 36, 208, 247, 254, 296, 307, 401, 403

Sacred Congregation for the Propagation of the Faith 128
Sacred Eternal Order of the Cherubim and Seraphim 371
Sahara 24, 35, 67, 108, 124, 125, 151, 316, 389
Saharan 30, 31, 106, 107, 117, 123, 124, 182, 310, 316, 433
Sanneh, Lamin 15-17, 105, 107, 128, 232, 345, 421
Sao Thome 30
School of Oriental and African Studies 200
Selassie, Haile, Emperor 29, 92, 95, 307
Senegambia 109, 133
Seymour, William J. 341, 434
Shaikh Muhammad 108
Sharia 111-113
Sheba, Queen 90, 233, 234
Sheppard, William 181

Sierra Leone 15, 32, 117, 126, 170, 174-177, 179-182, 203, 229, 235, 237, 238, 259, 324, 336, 359, 401
Slave Trade 13, 24, 31, 32, 94, 123, 131, 132, 134, 136, 142, 145, 168, 170-173, 175, 183, 191, 193, 194, 227, 228, 231, 396, 415, 432
Slaves, slavery 31, 32, 67, 72, 74, 88, 108, 125, 131-133, 135, 136, 144, 157, 168, 170-179, 181-183, 193, 227, 203, 232, 235, 236, 320, 351, 395, 401, 410, 463
Society for the Propagation of the Gospel (SPG) 133, 138, 140
Society of African Mission Fathers (SMA) 203
Society of Divine Word (SVD) 203
Society of Oriental and Asia Studies (SOAS) 200
South Africa 17, 37, 116, 181, 236, 240, 241, 259, 272, 274, 276, 279, 285, 292, 296, 300-302, 316, 318, 319, 328-336, 341, 343, 349, 352, 366, 372, 382, 396, 398-400, 413, 420, 422
South Africa Apostolic Faith Mission 343
South African 116, 117, 241, 260, 272, 276, 329-334, 366, 381, 402, 411, 413, 417, 418, 420, 424
South African Black theology 413, 417, 418, 424
South African Council of Churches 413
South African Zionist churches 381
Spain 55, 126, 129-131, 451
Spirituality 6, 7, 26, 29, 32, 35, 53, 55, 90, 92, 93, 95, 96, 106, 145, 178, 179, 228, 229, 242, 245, 247, 254, 255, 257, 259, 260, 264-268, 280, 292, 293, 301, 308-310, 317, 318, 342, 346, 355, 363, 376, 379, 383, 384
Student Christian Movement (SCM) 37, 265
Sudan 27, 29, 30, 36, 67-69, 71, 73, 75, 77, 79, 81, 83, 85, 87-89, 91, 93, 95, 97, 103, 106, 108, 109, 111, 115, 116, 195, 233, 247, 255, 401, 437
Sudan Interior Mission 195
Sufism 104
Sunni Islam 77
Sunni tradition 109

Tanganyika 36, 247, 255, 296
Tanzania 255, 268, 296, 316, 364, 371, 372
Tertullian 24, 50, 51, 59, 60
Theologians, theology 4, 6, 8, 12, 24, 27, 29, 36, 38, 49, 50, 55, 56, 58, 59, 133, 135, 138, 142, 155, 158, 196, 199, 211, 213, 228, 230, 233, 234, 237-239, 257, 265, 268, 300, 305, 308, 310, 318, 325, 334, 339, 345, 348, 350-355, 362, 363, 365, 368, 370, 373, 383, 389-393, 395-404, 409-424, 454, 466, 468
Third World 308, 391, 422, 423, 438
Tunisia 63, 104, 115, 124
Tutu, Desmond 330, 332

Uganda 15, 36, 87, 115, 116, 247, 254, 256, 260, 268, 291, 296, 307, 348, 350, 364, 401

Vatican II 307, 309
Venn, Henry 176, 177, 229, 236

Walls, Andrew F. 4, 5, 7, 250, 294
Welsh Revival 259
Womanist 395, 417, 422, 423
Womanist theology 417, 422, 423
Women 19, 25, 27, 32, 34, 37, 38, 48, 54, 55, 142, 173, 199, 201, 203, 206, 241, 255, 258, 267, 283, 319, 329, 331, 334, 341, 345, 346, 348, 359-364, 366-384, 389-404, 413, 418, 422, 435, 436, 457, 460
Women Aglow 341, 346, 374
Women's Islamic Movement 116

World Alliance of Reformed Churches (WARC) 393
World Council of Churches (WCC) 285, 293, 307, 308, 311, 390, 391, 393, 399, 400, 422
Worldview 4, 5, 9, 19, 20, 25, 35, 105, 106, 108, 191, 195, 228, 229, 242, 246, 248, 250, 280, 284, 341, 347, 354, 355, 365, 376, 379

Xhosa 241, 246, 247

Yoruba 11, 32, 107, 176, 203, 236, 237, 276, 277, 281, 284, 285, 344, 413
Yoruba Mission 176, 236
Young Women's Christian Association (YWCA) 399

Zacharia 76, 78, 83
Zagwe 92
Zambia 8, 240, 242, 268, 296, 308, 310, 316, 348, 352, 366, 370, 382
Zanzibar 33, 296
Zimbabwe 37, 151, 159, 238, 240, 295, 316, 318, 341, 343, 350, 363, 366, 371, 375, 377, 380, 382
Zimbabwe Assemblies of God Africa (ZAOGA) 343, 366
Zion 34, 89, 91, 92, 94, 97, 179, 237, 276, 283, 285, 300-302, 336
Zion Apostolic Church of South Africa 276
Zion Christian Church 276, 336
Zion Christian Church, Ruwadzano (ZCC) 377, 378
Zion City, Illinois 34, 276, 302
Zion Combination Churches in South Africa 285
Zionist 35, 272, 274, 276, 281, 282, 285, 300, 301, 340, 341, 363, 364, 368, 371, 377, 381, 383
Zionist churches 276, 282, 340, 341, 381
Zulu 240, 273, 276, 279, 281, 283, 284, 297
Zululand 17, 257